"In this highly readable book, Alan Riding presents a thorough, balanced account of the ways French artists and writers responded to Nazi occupation, ranging from active resistance to enthusiastic collaboration. . . . Riding marshals details with the verve and care of a great reporter." —Susan Suleiman, C. Douglas Dillon Professor of the Civilization of France and Professor of Comparative Literature, Harvard University

"Riveting. . . . This fine book reminds the reader of the many shades of collaboration in an occupied country." —*The Washington Times*

"A tale of betrayal and resistance, patriotism, and bold opportunism— and in the end, vengeance and forgetfulness."
—*The Jewish Exponent*

"A superb account of intellectuals under pressure. . . . Alan Riding, deeply versed in French politics and culture, is the ideal guide to Parisian life under the Nazis. He has written a wonderful book."
—Ward Just, author of *An Unfinished Season* and *Echo House*

"A remarkable cultural history of the City of Lights at its darkest hour. . . . A work of intellectual history in its purest form."
—*Jewish Journal*

"This book raises many questions about degrees of guilt, unjust accusations, and changing sides. It successfully shows that, for many, the occupation was rarely black and white."
—*Sacramento Book Review*

"Only someone as deeply versed in French culture as is Alan Riding, and as completely in command of his subject, could have written this magisterial account. . . . It is star-studded and makes fascinating reading." —David Fromkin, author of *A Peace to End All Peace*

ALAN RIDING

AND THE SHOW WENT ON

For twelve years, Alan Riding was the European cultural correspondent for *The New York Times*. He was previously bureau chief for the *Times* in Paris, Madrid, Rio de Janeiro, and Mexico City. Riding is the author of *Distant Neighbors: A Portrait of the Mexicans*. He continues to live in Paris with his wife, Marlise Simons, a writer for the *Times*.

www.alanriding.com

ALSO BY ALAN RIDING

Distant Neighbors: A Portrait of the Mexicans

AND THE SHOW WENT ON

Cultural Life in Nazi-Occupied Paris

ALAN RIDING

VINTAGE BOOKS
A DIVISION OF RANDOM HOUSE, INC.
NEW YORK

FIRST VINTAGE BOOKS EDITION, OCTOBER 2011

The Library of Congress has cataloged the Knopf edition as follows:
Riding, Alan.
And the show went on : cultural life in Nazi-occupied Paris /
by Alan Riding. — 1st ed.
p. cm.
Includes bibliographical references and index.
1. World War, 1939–1945 — France — Paris.
2. Paris (France) — Social life and customs — 20th century.
3. Popular culture — France — Paris — History — 20th century.
4. Paris (France) — Intellectual life — 20th century.
5. Paris (France) — History — 1940–1944. I. Title.
D802.F82P3772 2010
944'.3610816 — dc22
2010016841

Vintage ISBN: 978-0-307-38905-3

Author photograph © Naka Nathaniel
Book design by Maggie Hinders

www.vintagebooks.com

146122990

To Alexander

CONTENTS

Map · ix

Preface · xi

1. Everyone on Stage · 3

2. Not So Droll · 28

3. Shall We Dance? · 50

4. *L'Américain* · 73

5. Paris by Night · 90

6. Resistance as an Idea · 108

7. *Maréchal, Nous Voilà!* · 117

8. *Vivace Ma Non Troppo* · 141

9. A Ripped Canvas · 163

10. Distraction on Screen · 187

11. Mirroring the Past · 206

12. Writing for the Enemy · 227

13. Chez Florence · 255

14. "On the Side of Life" · 269

15. The Pendulum Swings · 297

16. Vengeance and Amnesia · 315

17. Surviving at a Price · 338

Acknowledgments · 351

Bibliography and Notes · 353

Index · 379

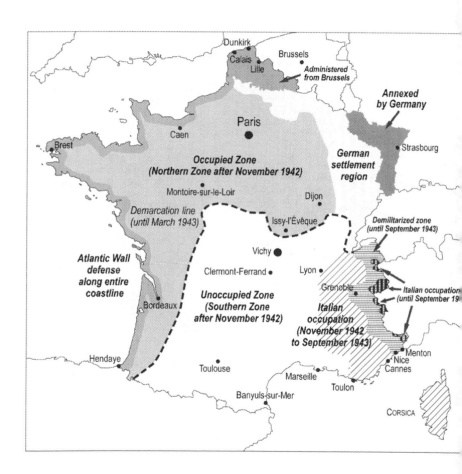

Dunkirk

Brussels

Calais

Lille

Administered from Brussels

Annexed by Germany

Paris

Caen

Brest

German settlement region

Strasbourg

Occupied Zone (Northern Zone after November 1942)

Montoire-sur-le-Loir

Dijon

Demarcation line (until March 1943)

Issy-l'Évêque

Demilitarized zone (until September 1943)

Vichy

Atlantic Wall defense along entire coastline

Clermont-Ferrand

Lyon

Grenoble

Italian occupation (until September 19

Unoccupied Zone (Southern Zone after November 1942)

Italian occupation (November 1942 to September 1943)

Bordeaux

Hendaye

Toulouse

Menton

Nice

Cannes

Marseille

Toulon

Banyuls-sur-Mer

CORSICA

PREFACE

HOW ARTISTS AND WRITERS respond to politics and society has intrigued me since I was a reporter covering the harsh military regimes of Latin America in the 1970s and 1980s. There, cultural elites variously kept a low profile, supported armed resistance or protested from abroad, but few sold out to the dictatorships. When I moved to Paris in 1989, the subject came into sharper focus: now I found myself in the birthplace of the *intellectuel engagé,* of the legendary Left Bank intellectual always ready to take on the political establishment. But the question that interested me most—how artists and writers react to oppression—belonged, I realized, to an earlier era, not of the Paris of today but of Paris under Nazi occupation. How, I wondered, had artists and intellectuals addressed the city's worst political moment of the twentieth century? Did talent and status impose a greater moral responsibility? Was it possible for culture to flourish without political freedom?

Such questions were, of course, examined—and with passion—immediately after the liberation of Paris. At the time, the imperative was to punish those artists and writers who had supported the occupying power or the puppet regime in Vichy, those deemed to have failed both their nation and their peers. But then, as now, the judgments were not clear-cut. Did working during the occupation automatically mean collaboration? Should any writer be sanctioned for the "crime" of an opinion? Do gifted painters, musicians or actors have a duty to provide ethical leadership? The search for answers became the starting point for this book.

Many French people believe that the occupation is still a taboo subject; French friends warned me that my inquiries would be met by suspicion, embarrassment, even silence. I did not find this to be true. Since the early 1970s, when Robert O. Paxton published his book *Vichy France: Old Guard and New Order, 1940–1944,* the myth of *la France résistante* has crumbled. Books have been written on every aspect of the occupation. Through movies like Marcel Ophüls's *The Sorrow and the Pity* and Louis Malle's *Lacombe Lucien,* the French public also learned that collaboration and self-preservation were stronger instincts than resistance.

In my case, I sought out artists, writers and others who had witnessed the "dark years." Well into their eighties or even older, they all agreed to see me and, I believe, responded openly and frankly. Their testimony was crucial in demonstrating that life during the occupation was not a still photograph in which one moment represents all others; it was a constantly evolving drama, a teeming stage where loyalty and betrayal, food and hunger, love and death found room to coexist, where even the line separating good and bad, *résistants* and *collaborateurs,* seemed to move with events. This was no less true in the world of culture. Its leading players behaved much like the rest of the population, except that, with them, more was at stake: their artistic calling made them role models and, as such, they were held to higher standards of propriety.

The main actors have now gone, yet all around me the décor stands largely unchanged. The very streets and buildings of Paris still carry the memory of those who peopled the stage seven decades ago. Often, while preparing this book, I felt that the past was my companion. Just a short bus ride separates the desk where I did my writing from the places I describe. It is both easy and hard to imagine the Wehrmacht marching down the Champs-Élysées, the swastika flying in the place de la Concorde, the Louvre desolate and stripped of its paintings, German uniforms filling the boxes at the Paris Opera. The Hôtel Lutetia, on the Left Bank, bears a double scar: from 1940 to 1944, it was the Abwehr's Paris headquarters; then, in 1945, it became the reception center for returning prisoners of war and deportees. In a few cases, the décor has changed. Across from the Lutetia, the old Prison du Cherche-Midi, so convenient for the Gestapo and so feared by its enemies, has been demolished and replaced by the kind of glass-and-steel anonymity that has no history.

Around my office in the 6th arrondissement, the memories are even fresher. On my own street, rue Monsieur-le-Prince, the early resistance group known as the Musée de l'Homme network held meetings at No. 30. One block away, a German-language bookstore catering to the Wehrmacht once stood on the place de la Sorbonne.

That square was also home to Jean Galtier-Boissière, a satirist who kept the sharpest and wittiest journal of the occupation. To the north, on the rue du Sommerard, a plaque outside a primary school remembers those pupils who were "deported from 1942 to 1944 because they were born as Jews, innocent victims of Nazi barbarity with the active complicity of the government of Vichy." Running past the square is the boulevard Saint-Michel, still pockmarked from intense fighting during the insurrection of Paris. Nearby, the French Senate was the Luftwaffe headquarters and, behind it, the last tank battle in the city was fought in the Luxembourg Gardens. On many a wall, plaques record where young fighters died. And every year on August 25, the anniversary of the liberation, these fallen are remembered with bouquets of flowers. I often stop to look at the unfamilar names on these plaques, and I sometimes ask myself if France's renowned artists and intellectuals served the country as loyally. But I also try not to forget the words of Anthony Eden, Britain's wartime foreign secretary: "If one hasn't been through the horrors of an occupation by a foreign power, you have no right to pronounce upon what a country does which has been through all that."

AND THE
SHOW
WENT ON

CHAPTER I

Everyone on Stage

ON JUNE 14, 1940, the German army drove into Paris unopposed. Within weeks, the remnants of French democracy were quietly buried and the Third Reich settled in for an indefinite occupation of France. Who was to blame? With the country on its knees, many in France now saw this as a defeat foretold, a debacle that had been in the making since France emerged from World War I, victorious in name but shattered in spirit. In the bloody and muddy trenches of the Western Front, 1.4 million Frenchmen died, representing 3.5 percent of the population and almost 10 percent of working-age men. Further, the 1 million Frenchmen who were left badly maimed, those ever-present *mutilés de guerre,* made it impossible to forget the past. With France already alarmed by its low prewar birthrate, this slaughter of men and future fathers meant that it was not until 1931 that the country exceeded its 1911 population of 41.4 million—and, even then, this was in large part thanks to immigration.

At the same time, the country was being let down by its political class. The Third Republic, founded in 1870 after France's defeat in the Franco-Prussian War, was plagued by instability and consumed by political bickering. Although the economy fared relatively well in the 1920s, postwar reconstruction lagged far behind. Then, in the 1930s, confronted by the twin threats of the Great Depression and the spread of extremist ideologies across Europe, France's rulers chose to ignore both. In a country that had long boasted the originality of its political ideas, a string of dysfunctional governments eroded public faith in democracy and boosted the appeal of the Nazi, Fascist and Communist alternatives. Most critically, with the Great War spawning a nation of pacifists, the French preferred to ignore mounting evidence that the country would soon again be at war with Germany. And when war became inevitable, they chose to believe official propaganda boasting that their army was invincible. This monumental self-delusion only compounded the shock at what followed. When Hitler's army swept across western Europe in the spring of 1940, French defenses crumbled in a matter of weeks. Neither 1870 nor 1914 had been this bad.

Yet even in the deepening gloom of the interwar years, as artistic and intellectual freedoms were being extinguished across Europe, Paris continued to shine as a cultural beacon. The majority of Parisians were poor, but they had long since been evicted from the elegant heart of Paris by Baron Haussmann's drastic urban redesign a half century earlier. This "new" Paris was the favored arena of elitist divertimento, drawing minor royalty, aristocrats and millionaires to buy art, to race their horses in the Bois de Boulogne, to hear Richard Strauss conduct *Der Rosenkavalier* at the Paris Opera, to party in the latest Chanel and Schiaparelli designs.

Painters, writers, musicians and dancers also flocked there from across Europe and the Americas, in some cases seeking sexual freedom, in others fleeing dictatorships, in many hoping for inspiration and recognition. Embracing everything from the literary solemnity of the Académie Française through the avant-garde of Surrealism to the high kicks of the Moulin Rouge, Paris offered both enlightenment and entertainment. And wandering across its pages and stages like eloquent courtesans were intellectuals, artists and performers. Whether admired for their ideas, their imagination or simply their Bohemian lifestyle, they enjoyed the trappings of a privileged caste. "The prestige of the writer was something peculiarly French, I believe," the astute essayist Jean Guéhenno later wrote. "In no other country of the world was the writer treated with such reverence by the people. Each bourgeois family might fear that its son would become an artist, but the French bourgeoisie as a group was in agreement in giving the artist and the writer an almost sacred pre-eminence."[1] Put differently, culture had become inseparable from France's very image of itself. And the rest of Europe recognized this. But with the swastika now flying over Paris, how would French culture—its artists, writers and intellectuals, as well as its great institutions—respond? Again, the answer lay in the turmoil of the interwar years.

Nowhere was French cultural leadership greater than in the visual arts. Between the Franco-Prussian War and World War I alone, art movements born in France—Impressionism, Post-Impressionism, Les Nabis, Fauvism and Cubism—succeeded one another in what came to resemble a permanent revolution. The 1914–18 conflict did little to disrupt this. While German artists like Otto Dix, George Grosz and Max Beckmann addressed the nightmare of trench war-fare, artists in France paid little heed to a war being fought barely a hundred miles north of Paris. When it was over, those nineteenth-century giants Renoir, Monet and Rodin were still alive, while the influence of Pablo Picasso, Marcel Duchamp and Henri Matisse continued to grow. Many artists with prewar reputations, men like Georges Braque, André Derain, Maurice de Vlaminck, Kees van Dongen, Pierre Bonnard and Aristide Maillol, also remained faithful to their prewar styles. Fernand Léger was a rare exception. After he spent two years on the front, his art was transformed, with his sketches of artillery and planes anticipating his tubular "mechanical" paintings of the 1920s. Bonnard avoided the trenches, serving briefly as a war artist and painting just one scene of desolation, *Un Village en ruines près du Ham.* But he quickly returned to his cherished themes of nudes and interior scenes.

For European artists, Paris was the place to meet great artists and to aspire to become great oneself. And it helped that the city was an important art market. From the late 1890s, the legendary dealer Ambroise Vollard carried the names of Cézanne, Gauguin and Van Gogh abroad and, in 1901, he gave Picasso his first exhibition in Paris. In the interwar years, it was the turn of other dealers, notably Daniel-Henry Kahnweiler and the Rosenberg brothers, Léonce and Paul, to keep European and American collectors supplied with the new art from Paris. For foreign artists, the city's energy, bubbling away in the studios and cafés of the Left Bank, was as appealing as any specific art movement. True, Salvador Dalí, Max Ernst, Man Ray and Joan Miró embraced Surrealism, but other foreigners went their own ways, among them Constantin Brancusi, Chaïm Soutine, Piet Mondrian, Amedeo Modigliani and Alberto Giacometti. The list of prominent French artists in Paris at that time was even longer. And to these could be added the architects and designers who created Art Deco as a style that would define the 1930s. Probably at no time since the Italian Renaissance had one city boasted such a remarkable concentration of artistic brilliance.

In the performing arts, change came from abroad, with Sergei Diaghilev's Ballets Russes leading a revolution in dance that would influence ballet for much of the twentieth century. In 1912, the troupe's star dancer, Vaslav Nijinsky, shocked Paris with his erotic interpretation of Claude Debussy's *Prélude à l'après-midi d'un faune.* The following year, the dancer was at the center of a riot in the Théâtre des Champs-Élysées during the premiere of Igor Stravinsky's *Rite of Spring,* when some spectators mutinied against Nijinsky's unorthodox choreography and the music's disturbingly primitive rhythm.

Diaghilev's role as a promoter and organizer of talent was still more important. Among choreographers, he recruited Michel Fokine, already a major figure in Russian dance, and he made the names of Léonide Massine, Bronislava Nijinska (the dancer's sister) and George Balanchine. Among dancers, along with the inimitable Nijinsky, he turned the English-born Alicia Markova and the Russians Tamara Karsavina and Serge Lifar into international stars (Lifar later also ran the Paris Opera Ballet). A strong believer in the "total art" that Wagner had called *Gesamtkunstwerk,* Diaghilev also pulled different art forms together as never before. He invited Derain, Rouault and Picasso, as well as the Russian artists Léon Bakst and Alexandre Benois, to design his stage sets. And while his favorite composer was Stravinsky, who also wrote *The Firebird, Petrouchka, Les Noces* and *Apollo* for the company, Diaghilev commissioned ballets from Sergei Prokofiev, Maurice Ravel, Darius Milhaud, Francis Poulenc and Strauss. One memorable example of "total art" was *Parade,* a ballet that was conceived by the artist-poet Jean Cocteau and combined music by Erik Satie, choreography by Massine, scenario by Cocteau himself, set, curtain and costumes by Picasso and program notes by Guillaume Apollinaire. First performed at the Théâtre du Châtelet in Paris on May 18, 1917, it, too, caused a scandal.

Diaghilev never returned to Russia. By the time of his death, in 1929, other Russian artists and writers—among them the painters Marc Chagall and Natalia Goncharova—had fled the Bolshevik Revolution for the safety of Paris. After Hitler took power in 1933, it was the turn of more artists and intellectuals, many of them Jews, to seek refuge in France; these included the abstract painter Wassily Kandinsky and the composer Arnold Schönberg, as well as the writers Joseph Roth, Hannah Arendt and Walter Benjamin.

Other foreigners found a different kind of liberty in Paris. When the novelist Edith Wharton settled in France shortly before World War I, the experimental writer Gertrude Stein was already receiving the likes of Picasso and Matisse in her Left Bank apartment at 27 rue de Fleurus, where she lived with her lesbian partner, Alice B. Toklas. In the 1920s and 1930s, Stein became a kind of eccentric matron to the "lost generation" of American writers, notably Ernest Hemingway, Thornton Wilder, John Dos Passos, Ezra Pound and F. Scott Fitzgerald. Henry Miller moved in a different—and more impecunious—circle, but he, too, enjoyed a freedom that, he later noted, "I never knew in America."[2] Little wonder, since three of his 1930s novels, *Tropic of Cancer, Black Spring* and *Tropic of Capricorn,* were banned in the United States as obscene. One gathering point for both American and French writers was Shakespeare & Company, the Left Bank bookstore that Sylvia Beach had opened at 12 rue de l'Odéon, across the street from La Maison des Amis des Livres, run by her friend and lover, Adrienne Monnier. Beach also came to the rescue of James Joyce, who had moved to Paris in 1920; with American and British publishers shying away from Joyce, fearing charges of obscenity, she dared to publish his monumental *Ulysses* in 1922. In the late 1930s, Samuel Beckett followed Joyce to Paris, equally determined to escape the suffocating strictures of deeply Catholic Ireland. Their relationship became strained only when Joyce's troubled daughter, Lucia, fell for Beckett—and Beckett did not reciprocate.

Josephine Baker, the black American dancer and singer, was another who flourished in the artistic melting pot of interwar Paris. Happy to escape racial discrimination in the United States, she arrived in Paris in 1925 to perform *La Revue nègre* at the Théâtre des Champs-Élysées with a black American dance troupe; almost immediately, she was hired away by Les Folies Bergère. There, she became a star, winning over Parisians with her erotic and funny cabaret shows, which included her love song to Paris, "J'ai deux amours,

mon pays et Paris," and her trademark "Danse sauvage" performed
bare breasted and wearing just a skirt of artificial bananas. Soon she
was also exploiting her exotic image in French movies like *Zou-Zou*
and *Princesse Tam Tam,* where she played a Tunisian shepherdess–
turned–Parisian princess in true Pygmalion style. In 1934, she even
sang the title role in Offenbach's operetta *La Créole.* It helped that,
at a time when the French were becoming increasingly xenophobic,
black American culture was all the rage in Paris. Above all, jazz and
swing brought by black Americans was enthusiastically adopted by
French musicians, none more brilliant than the Gypsy guitarist
Django Reinhardt and his Hot Club de France. La Baker, as she was
known, was not the only cabaret diva. Music halls and cabarets were
by far the most popular entertainment in Paris and, by the time Édith
Piaf joined Josephine on the scene in 1935, Léo Marjane and particularly Mistinguett—La Miss—had long been queens of the night.
Press speculation that La Miss and La Baker were feuding only
helped to pull in the crowds. Male crooners like Maurice Chevalier
and Tino Rossi and bandleaders like Ray Ventura were no less
admired.

The French movie industry, in contrast, was in crisis. Although the
new talkies were popular in the 1930s, the French industry felt threatened; it had placed a quota on Hollywood movies in 1928, and some
in the business resented the growing power of Jewish producers, who
had immigrated to Paris from central Europe. Struggling to raise
money in France, many French directors and producers sought German backing, first with Tobis, a production company that set up a studio in Paris in 1930, then with Universum Film AG, or UFA, a
Nazi-controlled production company in Berlin. As a result, not only
were dozens of French films made in Berlin, with the same story then
reshot with German actors, but UFA, Tobis and other German companies also began distributing films in France. Such was German
involvement that the French secret service warned that the Nazis
were using cinema as a weapon against France. But the abundant talent of French cinema, both behind and before the camera, was also
envied by Germany. From the mid-1930s, when a gritty genre known
as *réalisme poétique* made its mark, two directors stood out: Jean
Renoir for *La Grande illusion, La Bête humaine* and *La Règle du jeu;*
and Marcel Carné for *Le Quai des brumes, Hôtel du Nord* and *Le Jour
se lève.* France could also boast star power. To character actors like

Fernandel, Michel Simon and Pierre Fresnay and the rugged leading man Jean Gabin, it added the trump cards of glamorous actresses like Arletty, Edwige Feuillère, Viviane Romance and Danielle Darrieux.

In theater, Paris had writers for all tastes. France's national theater, the Comédie Française, offered a steady fare of classics by Corneille, Racine, Molière and Shakespeare, but it also presented the work of living authors. The most popular playwrights, though, were Sacha Guitry, Marcel Pagnol and Henri Bernstein, who were writing sentimental tragedies, comedies of manners and tales of provincial life for the *théâtre de boulevard*. Among weightier dramatists, Jean Giraudoux stood out. A World War I veteran, former diplomat and novelist, he was forty-six when his first play, *Siegfried,* was staged, in 1928. Others followed, but his most apposite commentary on the times came in 1935 with *La Guerre de Troie n'aura pas lieu* (The Trojan War Will Not Happen), a witty play that slyly suggested that France, like Troy, was blind to what lay ahead. The veteran playwright Paul Claudel clearly did not see Giraudoux's irony because he termed "this apology of cowardice and peace at any price repugnant."[3] No one, though, provoked more scandal than the multitalented Cocteau, whose 1938 play *Les Parents terribles* (The Awful Parents) was closed down after a week of protests. Examining these plays with a sharp eye for both writing and staging was Colette, doubling up as prolific novelist and drama critic for *Le Journal.*

Two veteran directors were particularly influential in shaping modern French theater. André Antoine challenged convention in 1887 when he created the Théâtre Libre—"free" in the sense that it was unconstrained by traditional rules. Using a permanent ensemble of actors, he presented both banned and foreign plays. And as a stage director, he emphasized realism and naturalism, rejecting the stylized acting of the Comédie Française. In 1916, Antoine gave up directing for theater and film criticism, but he remained an influential voice until his death in 1943. To this day, the Théâtre Libre stands as a reference point in French drama; the Théâtre Antoine, on the boulevard de Strasbourg in Paris, carries his name. His successor was Jacques Copeau. While Antoine began his career as an actor, Copeau's initial approach was more theoretical, reacting against the commercialism of the *théâtre de boulevard* and stressing the supremacy of the text. From 1913 through the interwar years, he implemented his ideas as a director and teacher, forming a generation of actor-directors, notably

Louis Jouvet and Charles Dullin, who would dominate postwar theater in Paris. At the time Paris fell, Copeau himself was running the
Comédie Française.

The world of letters was also bubbling, cheerfully keeping alive
the tradition that writers hold forth on politics, too. The Académie
Française, for all its self-importance, was the least interesting forum.
It offered prestige to its forty *immortels* but, since its new members
were often elected more for their political clout than their literary talent, it remained a very conservative body. Far more dynamic was the
Nouvelle Revue Française. Founded in 1909, the monthly featured
both new and established writers and set the agenda of intellectual
debate. Acting as a kind of referee was André Gide, a playwright,
novelist, essayist and diarist who was unchallenged as the dominant
French intellectual—despite the storm that erupted when he proclaimed his homosexuality in print in *Corydon* in 1924. The poet
Paul Valéry and the Roman Catholic writer François Mauriac were
also treated with reverence, while novelists with a large following
included Antoine de Saint-Exupéry, Paul Morand, André Maurois
and Colette, whose indiscreet memoir of her first tumultuous marriage, *Mes apprentissages,* sold particularly well in 1936.

Among younger authors, André Malraux won the Goncourt Prize
for *La Condition humaine* (published in English as *Man's Fate*) in
1933 and Roger Vercel for *Capitaine Conan* (Captain Conan) in
1934. Jean-Paul Sartre's first attempt at fiction, his existentialist novel
La Nausée (Nausea), appeared in 1938 and was followed in 1939 by
Le Mur (The Wall), a collection of five stories and a novella. It was
also a time when books by leading French authors sold well across
Europe. And this brought international recognition: Nobel Prizes in
literature were awarded to the political man of letters Anatole France
in 1921, the philosopher Henri Bergson in 1927 and the novelist
Roger Martin du Gard in 1937.

The period would be best remembered, however, for three
remarkably original works. In early 1923, Raymond Radiguet published his World War I novel *Le Diable au corps* (The Devil in the
Flesh), which tells of an affair between a teenage boy and a woman
whose husband is fighting in the trenches. A high school dropout,
Radiguet became the toast of the Left Bank, with Cocteau as his
champion, but he died of typhoid in December 1923, just months
after his twentieth birthday. Meanwhile, Marcel Proust's fin de siècle
masterpiece, *À la recherche du temps perdu* (In Search of Lost Time),

was finally published in its entirety in 1927, five years after his death. For many critics, both French and foreign, it remains France's greatest literary work of the twentieth century. At the time, however, a still greater sensation was *Voyage au bout de la nuit* (Journey to the End of the Night) by the irascible doctor Louis-Ferdinand Destouches, better known as Céline. Published in 1932, this raging and misanthropic novel defied the conventions of French writing, much as Joyce's *Ulysses* had those of English literature ten years earlier, testing readers' comprehension with ellipsis, vernacular, street slang and vulgarities in a revolt against French literary style and bourgeois society. The novel was favored—but failed—to win the Goncourt, angering Céline, who took little solace when it won the Renaudot Prize.

While *Voyage* was a literary tour de force, however, it was also semiautobiographical and, in that sense, a mirror on the period. Like many men of his age, Céline had been deeply scarred by World War I, although he had spent only a few months in the trenches before he was wounded and demobilized. After the war, he traveled widely, then became a doctor, working for the League of Nations in the mid-1920s before setting up a private practice among the poor of Montmartre. Having previously written only two unpublished plays, he was totally unknown in literary circles when *Voyage* came out. In the novel, it is Céline's alter ego Bardamu who recovers from war wounds before setting out on travels, first to Africa, then to the United States, where he works in a Ford factory, and finally back to Paris, where he becomes a doctor. Everything he has witnessed, from colonialism and industrial capitalism to urban squalor, disgusts him.

In this dyspeptic view of humanity, Céline was not alone. The disastrous political and psychological legacy of the Great War was felt by other artists and writers, many of them veterans, whose initial response to the threat of a new war was to become outspoken pacifists. For instance, just as Céline's novel was anti-war, so was Vercel's *Capitaine Conan*, which dwelled on the psychological damage caused by the recent war. In 1937, the writer Jean Giono even announced that, in the event of a new Franco-German conflict, he would rather be a living German than a dead Frenchman.

But if pacifism was at times hard to distinguish from defeatism, artists and writers were also being buffeted by the ideological winds blowing from Moscow and Berlin. By the end of the 1930s, many writers and intellectuals, as well as some artists and musicians, felt called on to choose sides and take their places in the warring camps. The path that led some of them there had begun two decades earlier with the belief that, after the war to end all wars, art could produce something different.

The first proposal came from Dada, a semianarchic anti-war movement that was founded in neutral Switzerland by the Romanian poet Tristan Tzara, who was just twenty at the time. Launched in 1916 in Zurich's Cabaret Voltaire with a performance defined as "anti-art," Dada sought to mobilize painting, design, theater and poetry as weapons against "capitalist war." The idea spread quickly to Berlin, Amsterdam and New York, where in 1917 Duchamp famously presented an upturned urinal as a work of art—or, rather, "anti-art"—called *Fountain* and, in the process, gave birth to conceptual art. Dada also awakened interest in Paris, where André Breton, a young poet with big ideas, founded a Dadaist journal, *Littérature.* In 1919, Tzara himself moved to Paris and continued to issue manifestos and organize "anti-art" performances. But Breton was not a natural follower. In 1923, when he was twenty-seven, he broke with Tzara and, with the publication of the *Surrealist Manifesto* the following year, gave birth to a new movement, which he would lead, in France and in exile, for the next four decades.

Over time, Surrealism would be best known for its paintings, for the dreamlike or phantasmagorical images created by Dalí, Ernst, Miró, René Magritte, André Masson and Yves Tanguy. But Breton saw the movement as an all-encompassing way of life, one that involved connecting to an inner world—what he called "pure psychic automatism"—as well as transforming the outer world. Breton had studied medicine and neurology and, in treating victims of shell shock in World War I, he used some of Freud's psychoanalytical techniques. Among the Surrealists, he promoted exploration of the unconscious through interpretation of dreams and through "automatic writing," in which the unconscious guides the hand in a form of free association. Breton's own writing included an experimental novel, *Nadja,* which revolved around madness, another subject of great interest to him. Also drawn to the movement were some of the leading poets of the day—Louis Aragon, Paul Éluard, Robert Desnos and Benjamin Péret—who saw Surrealism as a liberation from the French classical order. Satie, the avant-garde composer who died in 1925, was soon part of the circle, demonstrating that all art—indeed, all life—could be surreal.

The Spanish director Luis Buñuel and Dalí illustrated this in two bizarre and provocative movies, *Un Chien andalou* (An Andalusian Dog) and *L'Âge d'or* (The Golden Age). In the case of *L'Âge d'or*, which was promptly banned by the Paris police chief after violent protests in some theaters, the movie was financed by Charles and Marie-Laure de Noailles, aristocratic art patrons who delighted in shocking *la bourgeoisie*. The couple also backed Cocteau's *Le Sang d'un poète* (The Blood of a Poet), a Surrealist movie that, typically, Cocteau denied was Surrealist. Indeed, there were other artists, among them the Mexican painter Frida Kahlo and Magritte, who, while using the language of Surrealism, rejected Breton's authoritarian leadership and refused to join his movement.

Breton himself was more interested in poetry than politics, but he also defined Surrealism as revolutionary in the broadest sense. Hoping to reach beyond his tight Left Bank circle, he led his followers into the French Communist Party in 1926. If their aim was to liberate society, however, their timing was poor. Following Lenin's death in 1924, Stalin installed the one-man rule that began by smothering artistic freedom in the name of Socialist Realism and would soon terrorize millions. Abroad, Stalin's agents increasingly forced foreign Communist parties to follow Moscow's orders to the letter—and this included holding up the Soviet cultural model as an example for all. By 1933, Breton had had enough and began criticizing party positions. He and Éluard were promptly drummed out of the party as heretics. When Aragon chose not to follow them, he was in turn expelled from the Surrealist movement by Breton. In the escalating drama of French politics, this was merely a sideshow. But it presaged how culture—and, notably, the world of letters—would soon be sucked into the ideological maelstrom.

What mattered to most of the people of France was who governed the country—or, rather, whether France was actually governable. About this, there were serious doubts, particularly under the Third Republic. Its constitution, a reaction against Napoleon III's imperial centralism, created a weak presidency and spawned endlessly squabbling coalition governments. Power lay with the Chamber of Deputies, which elected every prime minister and which, in the eyes of many French citizens, existed largely to make deals.

Leading the non-Communist left was a charming Jewish intellectual and former theater critic, Léon Blum. Floating somewhere in the middle were the Radicals, who usually joined conservative-led coalitions but were themselves divided between old-school leaders like Camille Chautemps and Édouard Herriot and a younger group led by Édouard Daladier; between them, these three alone served as prime minister on ten different occasions. On the right, Raymond Poincaré and André Tardieu also frequently passed through the revolving doors: each was prime minister three times. So also was Pierre Laval, who began his political career as a socialist and ended up as prime minister of France's collaborationist government during the German occupation.* Providing a rare voice of sanity was Paul Reynaud, who alone campaigned for rearmament, although he took over the government only in March 1940, too late to make any difference.

These, then, were the men leading France as it drifted toward calamity. "Why is France governed by seventy-five-year-old men?" the satirical weekly *Le Canard Enchaîné* famously asked. It answered, "Because the eighty-year-olds are dead."[4] While the Soviet Union produced Stalin, Italy Mussolini and Germany Hitler, France had no fewer than thirty-four governments between November 1918 and June 1940.

How these governments handled the Depression only added to the paralysis. The French economy—though not necessarily the population—had fared well in the 1920s, spawning a stubborn faith in the importance of a strong franc and a balanced budget. And when the French economy appeared to survive the immediate aftershocks of the 1929 Wall Street crash, this faith was reinforced. But in 1931, the Depression reached France, and it was quickly aggravated by devaluation of the British pound and, later, of the American dollar. With the franc suddenly overvalued, French exports fell sharply and domestic unemployment began to grow. With the exception of Reynaud, France's political leaders remained firmly opposed both to devaluing the franc and to fighting deflation with deficit spending; instead, to preserve a balanced budget, they cut back government expenditures, including military spending.

The consequences of this policy were disastrous: the Depression

---

*Laval's name reads the same from right to left as from left to right, prompting quips that he was at home on either extreme.

lasted longer in France than in many other countries; social unrest fed political extremes; and the country fell behind in the accelerating European arms race. Finally, in September 1936, the franc was devalued, but by then the slump in industrial production was bringing inflation. In contrast, by the mid-1930s, Hitler was priming the German economy and financing his massive rearmament program almost entirely through huge deficits.

The weakness of successive French governments became an invitation for extremes to fill the vacuum. It could be argued that France had long been a nation at war with itself, with its history since the 1789 revolution punctuated by oft-violent confrontations like the 1848 workers' revolt, the 1871 Paris commune and the 1905 separation of church and state. No less polarizing in intellectual circles was the Dreyfus affair. And, like other major political crises, it shaped the future. In 1894, Captain Alfred Dreyfus, a Jewish officer in the French army, was falsely accused of treason and sentenced to life imprisonment for spying for Germany. The case set off a wave of anti-Semitic hysteria, but also a response from a small group of intellectuals led by the novelist Émile Zola, who on January 13, 1898, published an open letter in *L'Aurore* under the headline *"J'accuse . . . !"* In it, he charged the French army of falsifying evidence against Dreyfus. The army's outraged response forced Zola into exile in London for a year, but in 1906 Dreyfus was exonerated. If Dreyfus himself was now officially an innocent man, however, the end of the "affair" did not end anti-Semitism. In fact, anti-Semitism had even acquired a degree of respectability.

Among leading anti-Dreyfusards were two writers, Maurice Barrès and Charles Maurras, who would have enormous influence on intellectuals through the 1930s. Barrès began on the left, but he ended up promoting what became known as "ethnic nationalism," a form of xenophobia in which anti-Semitism played a large role. Barrès died in 1923, leaving the intellectual extreme right in the hands of Maurras, a poet and critic who in 1898 had founded a nationalist, monarchist and anti-Semitic movement called L'Action Française. Maurras was also deeply anti-German, persuaded after World War I that the Germans would seek to avenge the 1919 Treaty of Versailles. And it was Maurras who in the early 1930s became the mentor of a generation of young writers, notably Abel Bonnard, Lucien Rebatet and Robert Brasillach, who all became outspoken advocates of anti-Semitism. Yet even Maurras was not extreme enough for many of them. By the end of the decade, these and other "graduates" of L'Action Française had distanced themselves from Maurras's Germanophobia and embraced the new Nazi model.

What upset many conservatives was the large influx of foreigners into France, a human wave unmatched in any other European country and comparable to migration to the United States over the same period. Put differently, the loss of lives in World War I and the low fertility among French couples after the war had been compensated by the arrival of large numbers of Poles, Italians, Spaniards, Belgians, Russians, Greeks and Armenians. As a result, the proportion of people living in France who had been born abroad rose from 2.6 percent to 8 percent of the population between 1900 and 1931. The Jewish population in France also more than tripled in four decades, from 90,000 in 1900 to 300,000 in 1940, with a good number of these immigrants living in the crowded neighborhoods of eastern Paris. This reinforced the view among French xenophobes that all Jews were somehow foreign and that wealthy and influential French Jews had infiltrated and taken over parts of society on behalf of some ill-defined alien interest. The reaction of many long-established French Jewish families, on the other hand, was to distance themselves from those impoverished foreign Jews who had just arrived from the shtetls of eastern Europe, who spoke no French and who, if given the chance, would leave for the United States. All this made France fertile ground for Fascism.

Some extreme rightist groups took the battle onto the streets of Paris. The Camelots du Roi, a thuggish group linked to L'Action Française, fought leftist students, attacked Jewish targets and in 1936 dragged Blum from his car and beat him severely. Jeunesses Patriotes, the Francistes and Solidarité Française were openly pro-Fascist, while the Croix-de-Feu, founded by World War I veterans and led by Lieutenant Colonel François de La Rocque, favored Mussolini's Italy over Hitler's Germany as a role model. In the mid-1930s, the Comité Secret d'Action Revolutionnaire, better known as La Cagoule, also opted for terrorist actions. One of the most striking features of the extreme right was how many of its key figures came from the Communist Party and still considered themselves socialists of sorts. Among these was Jacques Doriot; elected mayor of Saint-Denis on a Communist ticket in 1930, he was expelled from the party in 1934 and, two years later, founded the extreme rightist Parti Populaire Français, with financial support from Mussolini's Fascist regime. And even though Doriot himself was a former metalworker, he attracted many intellectuals to his new party, including the writers Pierre Drieu La Rochelle, Ramon Fernandez, Alfred Fabre-Luce and Bertrand de Jouvenel, Colette's former stepson and lover. Unknowingly contributing to this ideological confusion was still another intellectual, Charles Péguy, a poet and essayist who was killed on the Marne in 1914 at the age of forty-one. He variously promoted socialism, nationalism and Catholicism and, while as a Dreyfusard he was not anti-Semitic, his thoughts came to influence left, right and center. In 1927, the philosopher Julien Benda published *La Trahison des clercs* (The Betrayal of the Learned), admonishing intellectuals for bowing to inane nationalism, but the predictable response of the right was abuse, not least because Benda was Jewish.

By the mid-1930s, the extreme right was clearly on the rise. Several groups—they were known as *ligues,* or leagues—targeted university students, with student elections often turning the Latin Quarter in Paris into a battleground. At the Sorbonne, the lines were drawn, with pro-Fascists in a majority. Controlled by the hard right, students at the Faculty of Law and the Faculty of Medicine were openly anti-Semitic and were always ready to join anti-government demonstrations. The Faculty of Letters was still being fought over, while the Faculty of Sciences was run by various Communist front organizations, which came together as the Union Fédérale des Étudiants in 1939. Students attending other leading academic institutions, like the elitist École Normale Supérieure, whose recent graduates included Sartre and Brasillach, were also confronted with the choice of Communism or Fascism. The pressure to take sides was enormous. François Mitterrand, France's socialist president from 1981 to 1995, demonstrated alongside the Croix-de-Feu while studying at the École Libre des Sciences Politiques in the mid-1930s. Jean-Louis Crémieux-Brilhac, who joined the Gaullists in London during the war and later became a renowned historian, recalled being a member of a leftist group at the Sorbonne without realizing that it was controlled by the Communist Party. But, himself of Jewish extraction, he was all too aware of the extreme right. He recalled that one fellow student, Philippe Ariès, who was close to L'Action Française and would also become a noted historian, once said to him: "A Jew, I can smell one!"[5] Democracy, it seemed, was the one option that held little appeal for the educated young.

Fueling this polarization were the country's newspapers, which also served as forums for well-known writers. The Communist Party published *L'Humanité* as well as the afternoon paper, *Ce Soir,* which from 1937 was edited by Aragon, by then the dominant Communist intellectual. The editorial line of both papers was defined by the party's leader, Maurice Thorez, and was unswervingly loyal to Moscow. *Le Populaire* spoke for the socialists, with Blum himself writing many editorials. The socialists could also count on support from *Marianne* and *L'Oeuvre,* while two satirical weeklies, *Le Canard Enchaîné* and *Le Crapouillot,* were unpredictable. General information dailies like *Le Matin, Paris-Soir* and *Le Petit Parisien* had enormous circulations, while *Le Temps* usually backed the government of the day. In 1922, François Coty, a perfume magnate with Fascist sympathies, bought *Le Figaro,* the country's oldest paper, and maintained its conservative line, but he also founded an extreme rightist paper, *L'Ami du Peuple,* and financed Fascist groups. On the far right were Maurras's daily, *L'Action Française,* as well as *Je suis partout,* a weekly that from 1934 drew many intellectuals away from Maurras's movement and, starting in 1937, was edited by Brasillach. The popular literary and political weeklies *Candide* and *Gringoire,* both with circulations of around a half million, also campaigned steadily against the Third Republic and parliamentary rule.

A defining moment for both the left and the right occurred on February 6, 1934, when L'Action Française, the Croix-de-Feu, the Camelots du Roi and other extreme rightist groups marched on the Chamber of Deputies in the apparent hope of occupying the building and overthrowing the government. What provoked the uprising was outrage at the so-called Stavisky affair, a crisis prompted by the mysterious death of the infamous embezzler Serge Alexandre Stavisky one month earlier. The involvement of some ministers in protecting Stavisky highlighted the corruption endemic in successive governments and led to right-wing demonstrations that resulted in Daladier succeeding Chautemps as prime minister on January 27. When Daladier fired the right-wing Paris police chief, Jean Chiappe, the extreme right was still more outraged and summoned its followers to the place de la Concorde. Daladier was ready to call in the army, but in the end mounted police of the Garde Nationale Mobile managed to block the pont de la Concorde, which leads to the Chamber of Deputies. A prolonged battle ensued, with buses set alight, shots fired, at least fifteen people killed and hundreds more wounded. The repercussions of this confrontation were felt for years. It radicalized the right, pushing many nationalist and monarchist followers of L'Action Française toward outright Fascism. It also provoked a backlash against the extreme right, with Moscow ordering the French Communist Party to work with socialists and moderates against the growing Fascist threat. This shift permitted the election in May 1936 of the left-leaning Popular Front, with Blum as France's first Jewish prime minister.

The Popular Front lived up to its promise to carry out major social reforms; it won the hearts of workers by introducing collective bargaining, a forty-hour work week and a paid annual vacation. Blum was the Front's intellectual leader, but two other ministers, who both happened to be Jews, were also forceful modernizers. As minister of education and fine arts, Jean Zay not only raised the age at which a child could leave school from twelve to fourteen, he also created the new Musée d'Art Moderne and promoted physical education and sports; and Georges Mandel, the interior minister, oversaw the banning of Fascist *ligues* like the Croix-de-Feu. But like so many Third Republic governments, the Popular Front was also a fragile coalition that included Radicals and Communists as well as socialists. The traditional pacifism of the left prevented Blum from ordering full-scale rearmament in the face of the mounting German threat. At the same time, bowing to conservatives inside the coalition, he disappointed the left—and, no doubt, himself—by refusing to send arms to the besieged Republican government in Spain, which in July 1936 faced a military uprising led by General Francisco Franco.

The extreme right and conservative newspapers gave Blum no respite. They did not like his policies and they did not like being governed by a Jew. When he took office in June 1936, Xavier Vallat, a right-wing deputy who later headed Vichy's General Commission for Jewish Questions, recognized a historic occasion. "For the first time, this old Gallo-Roman country will be governed by a Jew. I dare say aloud what this country is thinking in its heart of hearts; it is preferable to have a man at the head of this country whose origins lie in its soil rather than a subtle Talmudist."[6] *Gringoire* picked four adjectives to describe Blum: Marxist, circumcised, Anglophile and Freemason. Maurras went further, insulting Blum as "this old Semitic camel" and threatening him with death. "It shall be necessary to eliminate Blum physically only on the day he leads us into the godless war he dreams of against our Italian comrades-in-arms. On that day, it is true, he should not be spared."[7] For this, Maurras was jailed for eight months, beginning in October 1936.

But anti-Semitism per se was not punished. In three essays published as *Le Péril juif* (The Jewish Peril), the writer Marcel Jouhandeau added to the chorus by complaining that Jews now controlled the government as well as banking, the press, publishing, music and education. "M. Blum is not one of ours and, what is the toughest, M. Blum is master of my country and no European can ever know what an Asiatic is thinking," he offered. After barely one year as prime minister, Blum was forced to step down. He returned to the post for three weeks in March 1938, but six months later, the Popular Front collapsed. With this, a good part of the left joined much of the right in believing that the Third Republic was beyond salvation, that only some radical new kind of regime could lead France out of the morass.

Beyond the political limelight, both Berlin and Moscow were working at winning over France's opinion makers. On the German side, an important player was Otto Abetz, a former art teacher who later served as Hitler's ambassador to occupied France. In the 1920s, he took the initiative of forming a Franco-German cultural exchange group called the Sohlberg Circle. Already fluent in French, on one of his many trips to France he met the newspaper editor Jean Luchaire, whose secretary, Suzanne de Bruyker, he married in 1932. Two years later, the Sohlberg Circle was formalized as the France-Germany Committee, with Abetz, still only thirty-one, as the German representative.

Tall, blond and sociable, Abetz used the post to befriend conservative French writers and journalists, among them Drieu La Rochelle, Brasillach and Jacques Benoist-Méchin. Initially, the committee even drew moderates eager to improve relations with Germany, among them Blum, who resigned his membership only in 1937—the same year Abetz joined the Nazi Party. Potential allies of the Nazis were invited to Germany to admire the achievements of the Third Reich, some even to attend the Nazi Party's mass gatherings in Nuremberg. After watching Hitler preside over a flag ceremony in 1937, Brasillach was so struck by its near-religious ritual that he compared it to the Eucharist. "Anyone who fails to see the consecration of the flags as analogous to the consecration of bread is unlikely to understand anything about Hitlerism," he wrote in *Je suis partout*.[8] Thanks to

Abetz, Jouvenel was able to interview Hitler for *Paris-Match* in 1936, extracting from the Führer a reassuring invitation to the French: "Let us be friends." Less publicly, Abetz was also subsidizing right-wing newspapers. It was almost as if he were rehearsing the occupation: his intellectual friends of the 1930s would all become prominent collaborators after 1940.

Still, Abetz had little need to import Hitler's hatred of Jews. Fed by L'Action Française and other Fascist groups, French anti-Semitism was given a fresh boost and a grotesque form of literary legitimacy by none other than Céline, who had gained enormous celebrity with *Voyage au bout de la nuit.* He had followed up in 1936 with another book of equal brilliance, *Mort à crédit* (Death on the Installment Plan), a kind of prequel to *Voyage* that opens with his alter ego, Dr. Ferdinand Bardamu, practicing medicine among poor Parisians and then flashes back to his childhood and adolescence. And once again it was the author's voice—raging, pessimistic, cynical, humorous, anti-heroic, desperate—that gave the book its immense punch. Then, quite suddenly, Céline turned this voice into a blunderbuss of anti-Semitism. As a doctor treating shopworkers, prostitutes, single mothers and the like, he had a genuine empathy for the underprivileged (and a deep distaste for the bourgeoisie). He also considered himself a man of the left—until he visited the Soviet Union in 1936. Upon his return, he published *Mea Culpa,* a twenty-seven-page pamphlet denouncing Communism. And it was then that he embraced the far right.

The following year, Céline published another "pamphlet," in reality a long essay, called *Bagatelles pour un massacre* (Trifles for a Massacre), in which he showed his new face. Echoing his horror at World War I, he accused Jews, Communists and Freemasons of driving France toward another war—another "massacre"—with Germany. His main target, though, were Jews, who were, he wrote, all-powerful in finance, politics and the arts, "vermicular, persuasive, more invasive than ever" but, above all, warmongers. "It's the Jews of London, Washington and Moscow who are blocking a Franco-German alliance," he said. And he went on: "I don't want to go to war for Hitler, I insist, but I don't want to wage war against him for the Jews." His conclusion: "Rather a dozen Hitlers to an all-powerful Blum."[9] Gide, for one, was incredulous, noting in his journal, "Surely it's a joke. And if it's not a joke, Céline must be completely mad."[10] But Céline knew exactly what he was doing, writing to a friend, "I have just published an abominably anti-Semitic book, I am sending it to you. I am enemy no. 1 of the Jews."[11] After *Bagatelles pour un massacre* sold eighty thousand copies, he followed up in 1938 with another anti-Semitic diatribe, *L'École de cadavres* (School of Corpses), which sold almost as well.

Moscow was no less active. Initially, its principal agent was Willi Münzenberg, a founding member of the German Communist Party who served as a Comintern agent in Paris and elsewhere in western Europe after 1933. Although many French intellectuals were already in the Communist Party, Münzenberg's talent was to draw non-Communists into the anti-Fascist struggle, notably by creating seemingly respectable front organizations. These fellow travelers included exiled German and Austrian writers, as well as French intellectuals alarmed by Hitler's rise to power. Malraux, a writer with a penchant for romantic adventure, did not join the Communist Party, but he nonetheless traveled to Moscow in August 1934 to attend the All-Union Congress of Soviet Writers. He annoyed his official hosts by rebuking them for imposing Socialist Realism on Soviet writers, noting that "your classic writers give a richer and more complex picture of the inner life than the Soviet novelists,"[12] yet he remained useful to Moscow. In June 1935, he helped to organize the First International Writers' Congress for the Defense of Culture, which was held in Paris. And while Moscow largely controlled its deliberations, the congress was able to present a dazzling panoply of writers—Gide as its honorary chairman, along with E. M. Forster, Bertolt Brecht, Aldous Huxley, Waldo Frank, Heinrich Mann and many others—as friends of the Soviet Union and foes of Nazi Germany.

There were tensions. Ilya Ehrenburg, a Russian journalist and Soviet agent involved in organizing the congress, had earlier written a provocative pamphlet calling Breton and the Surrealists *pédérastes.* On the eve of the congress, Breton met and repeatedly slapped Ehrenburg, which resulted in the Surrealists being excluded from the gathering. René Crevel, a poet who had been expelled from the Communist Party along with Breton and Éluard, tried to have this ban lifted; when his efforts failed, in despair, he committed suicide.* Eventually, a statement by Breton was read to the congress by Éluard, but late at night, after most delegates had left. A more important

---

*Another explanation offered for his suicide was that he had been diagnosed with an acute case of renal tuberculosis, which, he told friends, was incurable.[13]

issue related to the fate of Victor Serge, a Belgian-born French-language writer who joined the Bolshevik Revolution and was now in a labor camp in the Urals. Ehrenburg worked to keep the Serge case out of debate, but several intellectuals, including Gide, signed a letter calling for his release, which Gide himself delivered to the Soviet embassy in Paris. One year later, Serge was freed and, although France under Prime Minister Laval refused him a visa, he was allowed to travel to Belgium.

Soon, though, the dominant reality for the European left was the Spanish civil war. Nazi Germany and Mussolini's Italy moved quickly to arm Franco's Nationalist forces, but only the Soviet Union was willing to help the Republican government in Madrid. For that reason, even non-Communist leftists were ready to close ranks around Moscow. French anti-Fascist intellectuals, all the more embarrassed by the Popular Front's refusal to help the Spanish Republic, felt called upon to act. Along with numerous British, American and Latin American intellectuals, a French delegation led by Aragon traveled to Madrid and Valencia in July 1937 to attend the Second International Writers' Congress for the Defense of Culture. A few French writers even volunteered to fight alongside the Republicans. Among these was Malraux, who, using old planes obtained in France, put together a rudimentary Republican air force called Escadrille España. Although the squadron's military impact was minimal, it served as a symbol of widespread French sympathy for the Republican cause.

A more lasting protest against the horrors of the Spanish war came from Picasso. Although he never left Paris, as Spain's most celebrated artist, he agreed at the start of the civil war to be named director of the Prado Museum. In early 1937, he was invited to paint a major work for the Spanish pavilion at that summer's Paris International Exhibition. Although he was undecided on a theme, it was suddenly provided for him by the bombing of the Spanish Basque town of Guernica by German and Italian warplanes on April 26. By early July, *Guernica*, his mural-sized work in black, white and shades of gray, was displayed prominently in the Spanish pavilion; with its shocking evocation of death and destruction, it brought home what was taking place beyond France's southern border. The massively obtrusive German and Soviet pavilions, facing each other almost menacingly beside the Seine, were in turn harbingers of what lay ahead. After the international exhibition, *Guernica* toured Europe and the United States to help raise funds for the Spanish Republic. When the civil war ended with Franco's victory, the painting remained in the Museum of Modern Art in New York until democracy was finally restored to Spain in the late 1970s.

German and Italian support for Franco eventually sealed the fate of the republic, but while the conflict continued, Moscow used it to smother anyone on the left who refused to toe the Soviet line. Its argument, successfully imposed on European Communist parties, was that any criticism of Moscow was commensurate to supporting Fascism. Its main victims were Trotskyites and anarchists fighting in Spain, a brutal sectarianism witnessed—and later denounced—by George Orwell and Arthur Koestler. But Moscow also hoped that, in the name of solidarity with the Spanish Republic, non-Communist leftists in Europe would not speak out against Stalin's growing heavy-handedness at home. In one high-profile case, this approach failed dramatically.

Although Gide had never before been politically active, by the early 1930s he was openly expressing sympathy for Communism and admiration for the Soviet Union. Such was his international prestige that Moscow was understandably delighted when the writer, then in his late sixties, finally accepted an invitation to visit the Soviet Union in June and July of 1936, by chance just weeks before the opening of the infamous Moscow trials. The voyage began with Gide addressing Maxim Gorki's funeral in Red Square and pledging to defend "the destiny of the Soviet Union." Over the next four weeks, traveling in great comfort, with the Russian-born publisher Jacques Schiffrin as his interpreter, Gide was showered with honors as a valued friend of the regime. On his return to Paris, he immediately wrote his account of the trip, *Retour de l'U.R.S.S.* (Back from the USSR).

It was not what his Soviet hosts had expected. Gide's message was clear: he had wanted to find confirmation of what, three years earlier, he had described as "my admiration, my love, for the U.S.S.R."[14] He found some positive things to recount, and he expressed his conviction that the Soviet Union "will end by triumphing over the serious errors that I point out,"[15] but his final verdict was devastating. He noted that artists could only follow the party line. "What is demanded of the artist, of the writer, is that he shall conform; and all the rest will be added to him."[16] His fiercest criticism focused on the total lack of freedom in the Soviet Union: "And I doubt whether in any other country in the world, even Hitler's Germany, thought be less free, more bowed down, more fearful (terrorized), more vassalized."[17]

Gide's manuscript fell into the hands of Communist intellectuals, who hurriedly leaned on him to soften his attack on Moscow, arguing that it would damage the Republican cause in Spain. He nonetheless went ahead with publication. The book, which was quickly translated into English, naturally pleased the right, but it also shocked many non-Communists on the left, among them Simone de Beauvoir, Sartre's young companion. In her memoir *La Force de l'âge* (The Prime of Life), she recalled, "We had never imagined the U.S.S.R. to be a paradise, but we had also never seriously questioned the construction of socialism. It was inconvenient to be required to do so at the very moment that we felt disgusted by the policies of the democracies. Was there nowhere on earth where we could cling to hope?"[18] In 1937, in response to all the hand-wringing on the left, Gide published a fresh, more nuanced reflection on the trip, *Retouches à mon retour de l'U.R.S.S.* (Afterthoughts, Back from the USSR). But by then, he had become a nonperson for much of the left.

He would not be alone for long. Both the Communist repression of the dissident left in Spain and, even more, the violent purges of the Moscow trials were eroding loyalty to the Soviet Union. Oddly, perhaps, Trotskyism did not catch on in France, even though Trotsky himself was in exile near Paris between 1933 and 1935.* Rather, it was the turmoil in Moscow that cast a deep shadow over the European left. As early as October 1936, for instance, Münzenberg was summoned back to Moscow and, after fierce interrogation, he suddenly feared for his life. Arguing that he was needed to organize the Comintern's operation in Spain, he somehow obtained an exit visa and resumed his work from Paris. His usefulness to Moscow, however, was waning and, in May 1937, he was expelled from the German Communist Party. He continued his anti-Fascist activities, using some of the front organizations he had himself created, but he wisely ignored another summons to Moscow. Instead, in 1938, he founded a German-language journal, *Die Zukunft,* and, while remaining an

---

*Having been drummed out of the Communist Party, Breton finally met Trotsky in 1938 in Mexico, where they signed a manifesto, *For an Independent Revolutionary Art.* Two years later, Trotsky was murdered in Mexico City by a Soviet agent.

anti-Fascist, he took to denouncing Stalinism. In 1938, Koestler, who had been close to Münzenberg, also left the German Communist Party in disgust at the Moscow trials.

Remarkably, in France, the violent sniping within the ranks of the left and between left and right was taking place in seeming oblivion to Germany's massive military buildup and blatant territorial ambition. It was as if winning ideological arguments were more important than strengthening France's resolve to defend itself. As early as October 1935, France had responded meekly to Italy's invasion of Ethiopia, boosting Hitler's confidence that he, too, could act with impunity. In March 1936, France did nothing when Germany remilitarized Rhineland in violation of the Treaty of Versailles; two years later, when Berlin annexed Austria in what became known as the Anschluss, France again declined to act. Even confronted by Germany's growing military might and expansionism, France's political establishment remained divided over rearmament, with its aged army high command insisting that the country was safe behind the two-hundred-mile-long Maginot Line of defenses running along its eastern border.

A young tank commander, Colonel Charles de Gaulle, was almost alone in calling for the creation of new armored divisions. In any event, among both intellectuals and politicians, memories of the carnage of World War I were still feeding pacifism and the belief that Hitler could be appeased. In 1936, a rare reminder that France was ignoring the approaching cataclysm came in a popular song by the bandleader Ray Ventura, "Tout va très bien, Madame la Marquise." In it, an aristocrat's servants keep reassuring her by telephone that all is well: true, her favorite mare died, as the stables were destroyed when the château burned down, and her husband committed suicide, but don't worry, *tout va très bien, Madame la Marquise.*

In Munich on September 30, 1938, France's prime minister Daladier and Britain's prime minister Neville Chamberlain gave Hitler the green light to occupy Czechoslovakia's Sudetenland. When Chamberlain arrived home, he waved the agreement and promised "peace for our time." When Daladier returned to Paris, he later recalled, he quite expected to be lynched; instead, he, too, was acclaimed as a hero. A few writers on the left denounced the Munich Agreement, but they were in a minority. Pacifists were further reassured on December 6 by a Franco-German declaration pledging peaceful relations. Even in March 1939, when Germany swallowed the rest of Czechoslovakia, the consensus in Paris was that no Frenchman should be asked to die to defend the Czechs.

The British and French governments, however, were shaken and finally offered to guarantee the independence of Poland, the next country in Hitler's sights. This, too, had little public support. In an article in *L'Oeuvre* in May 1939, headlined "To Die for Danzig?," Marcel Déat said no one could stop Hitler from seizing the Baltic enclave. "To start a European war because of Danzig would be a little too much," he said, adding, "We will not die for Danzig." Even then, few people in France believed that their own country's survival was at stake. The American ambassador, William Bullitt, was less sanguine. "In considering the question of the defense of the United States and the Americas," he wrote to President Roosevelt in April 1939, "it would be extremely unwise to eliminate from consideration the possibility that Germany, Italy and Japan may win a comparatively speedy victory over France and England."[19]

Certainly, nothing in the social and cultural life of Paris in the spring and summer of 1939 could have persuaded Bullitt that France was ready for war. Costume and masked balls were as lavish as ever; nightclubs were putting on new shows; theaters and movie houses were full; plans were going ahead to open the new Musée d'Art Moderne; the fiftieth anniversary of the Eiffel Tower was being celebrated; and new books were being published, including Sartre's *La Nausée* and Drieu La Rochelle's *Gilles*. In April, the defeat of the Spanish Republic brought a flood of some 450,000 refugees into France, yet Franco's victory had long been expected. Then, on August 23, 1939, to the astonishment of the French government, Germany and the Soviet Union signed a nonaggression agreement, the so-called Molotov-Ribbentrop Pact. One week later, Germany invaded Poland. On September 3, a few hours after Britain did so, France declared war on the Third Reich and began mobilizing its armed forces. The lives of the artists and intellectuals of Paris had finally—and abruptly—changed: within days, they were undergoing military training for a war they had hoped never to see. And, for a few brief months, ideological foes found themselves shoulder to shoulder in defense of France.

CHAPTER 2

Not So Droll

THE DECLARATION OF WAR disrupted Max Ernst's bucolic existence in southeastern France, where he was sharing a stone farmhouse with his latest love, Leonora Carrington. She, too, was a Surrealist painter, although, at twenty-two, something of a beginner. Two years earlier, she had met Ernst in London and, like many women before and after, she had been swept off her feet by the dashing silver-haired painter, twenty-six years her senior. Ernst was still married to Marie-Berthe Aurenche, but he evidently preferred Leonora. And after some stormy scenes in Paris, including one where the possessive young Leonora slapped the jealous and aggrieved Marie-Berthe, Ernst and Carrington settled in Saint-Martin-d'Ardèche, north of Avignon. Leonora had admired Ernst as an artist from the moment she had seen his work, while he was fascinated by how she had created her own Surrealist vision in her teens, in the unlikely setting of a prosperous northern English family. Their farmhouse soon became a Surrealist menagerie, with Max sculpting animal-like deities and Leonora painting walls and ceilings with her own strange fauna.

Ernst was particularly happy to be away from the political squabbles tearing at the Surrealist movement, although his own relations with Breton remained good. In the summer, friends would take the train down from Paris, curious to see how Ernst and his beautiful muse were faring in their rustic Surrealist laboratory.

The declaration of war ended their idyll. One morning in early September 1939, two uniformed French gendarmes came to arrest Ernst. Although he had lived in France for seventeen years and had been denounced as a "degenerate" artist by the Nazis, he remained a German and, as such, an *étranger nondésirable*—an undesirable foreigner—to the French. He was immediately driven forty miles to the northwest to a castle in Largentière, which served as a temporary holding center for German and Austrian nationals in the area. A few weeks later, he was moved to an abandoned brick factory outside Aix-en-Provence, known as the Camp des Milles. From there, he sent word to Jeanne Bucher, his dealer in Paris: *Chère Jeanne, S.O.S., Max.* Held with several hundred other detainees, Ernst hardly found the situation comfortable, but he was not abused and was allowed to work. Further, he was brought paint, clothes and food by Leonora, who turned to Éluard for help. Finally, in December, thanks to the intervention of Albert Sarraut, a former prime minister, Ernst was freed and could return to Leonora and their simple peasant life in Saint-Martin-d'Ardèche.

That the French authorities found Ernst so easily suggested that they kept tabs on the many thousands of foreigners who had been flooding into France from central Europe. In truth, they did, but on September 10 Daladier's government also set up a new structure to deal with the foreigners. All citizens of the Reich were ordered to register with the police. Some were immediately sent to internment camps; others were told not to leave their homes. In the weeks that followed, around twelve thousand German and five thousand Austrian "undesirable foreigners" were detained and spread among dozens of internment camps, some hurriedly improvised, others in the foothills of the Pyrenees already holding tens of thousands of Spanish refugees who had fled Franco's victory earlier in the year. Unknowingly, France's democratic government was preparing the way for the German occupation. A year or so later, when arrests of Jews, Communists, Freemasons, resistance fighters and other perceived enemies began, a network of concentration camps was ready to receive them.

Over the same period, Britain also interned several thousand "enemy aliens," as would the United States two years later, when over 100,000 Japanese Americans were detained. But most of the politicians, university professors, union leaders, journalists, artists and intellectuals held in France in 1939 were either Jews or known opponents of the Nazi regime and, as such, posed no threat to France. After the Molotov-Ribbentrop Pact, foreign Communists were arguably more credible candidates for internment, but in practice French authorities made no such distinction. Only internees with well-placed French friends in political or artistic circles had a chance of obtaining early release. But since a majority of these exiles had fled Germany or Austria with few belongings and were living in France as nearly destitute refugees, few had the right connections. Instead of internment, younger refugees were given the option of joining the French Foreign Legion; the Russian-born painter Nicolas de Staël was one who did, although he was sent to Tunisia and saw no action. Gide found the roundup of guiltless foreigners to be a dismaying spectacle, and he described France's behavior as "morally deficient." According to his close friend Maria van Rysselberghe, "he suffered to see France suddenly being inhospitable to those whom it had initially protected."[1]

These included an impressive catalog of artists and intellectuals. At the Camp des Milles, for instance, along with Ernst were the artists Hans Bellmer, Max Lingner, Hermann Henry Gowa and Wols, the German writers Lion Feuchtwanger, Alfred Kantorowicz and Thomas Mann's son Golo, as well as several German journalists, an opera producer and two Nobel laureates in medicine, Tadeus Reichstein and Otto Meyerhof. Hannah Arendt, the German Jewish philosopher, was arrested with the Marxist philosopher Heinrich Blücher (whom she married in 1940) and sent to an overcrowded camp for women at Gurs, in southern France. Thomas Mann's brother, Heinrich, had the misfortune of being sent to Le Vernet, south of Toulouse, which soon earned the reputation of being the harshest camp, with brutal guards and little food. Koestler, who had narrowly escaped execution by Franco's forces during the Spanish war, was picked up in Paris—although born in Hungary, he was raised in Austria—and also sent to Le Vernet, leaving his English girlfriend, the young sculptor Daphne Hardy, almost penniless in his Paris apartment. Koestler, whose memoir *Scum of the Earth* includes extensive descriptions of the miseries of life at Le Vernet, was freed from the camp in January 1940 after Jean Paulhan, the editor of the *Nouvelle Revue Française,* testified to his "loyalty towards France." Gustav Regler, a German novelist who had been wounded while fighting for the Spanish Republicans, returned to France from Florida, where he had been convalescing in Hemingway's home. He offered his services to the French army and was instead also sent to Le Vernet. Walter Benjamin, the German Jewish philosopher and literary critic, was arrested and held in the camp of Vernuche, near Nevers in Burgundy, for three months before being allowed to return to Paris.

By the end of 1939, close to half of the "undesirable foreigners" had been freed, but a new wave of arrests of Germans and Austrians was ordered on May 13 after the Wehrmacht entered French territory and anti-German hysteria again gripped France. That same month, Erwin Blumenfeld,* a German Jewish photographer who went into exile in France in 1936, was taken to Le Vernet in a train crowded with hundreds of other refugees. Years later, he described their reception:

> We had to undress, in broad daylight, on the main street, and line up naked behind our luggage. The inhabitants of Le Vernet passed by without looking at us. While we were searched, even to our prostate, for hidden treasures, like money, weapons and drugs, a horde of emaciated anthropoid apes entered the camp at the double: skeletons with hollow eyes stepping out of *The Triumph of Death* by Brueghel. I thought I was hallucinating: neither France nor I could fall this low. Someone took the negro Fenster's bugle. Another fellow had to hand over his Cross which he had won in the Foreign Legion fighting for France.[2]

Soon, with the Germans deep inside France, Blumenfeld noticed that Nazi internees were suddenly receiving better treatment than the rest. He added: "Schwarz, who had his nose broken at Dachau, said it was worse here. At least German cruelty was exercised in a punctual and orderly manner."

Ernst, who was still with Carrington in Saint-Martin-d'Ardèche, was again arrested after a deaf-mute neighbor denounced him for

---

*Blumenfeld managed to escape France in 1941 and made it to the United States, where he became a successful fashion photographer for *Vogue* and *Harper's Bazaar.*

sending light signals to the enemy. A single gendarme with a rifle
came for him, and he was taken to the internment camp of Loriol in
the Drôme, then once again to the Camp des Milles. One month
later, as German troops were occupying Paris, Ernst was allowed to
leave the camp—along with hundreds of other detainees—and he
hurried back to Saint-Martin-d'Ardèche by foot, hoping to find
Leonora. She had vanished. After his arrest, she had fallen apart.
Later she wrote, "I wept for several hours, down in the village; then I
went up again to my house where, for twenty-four hours, I indulged
in voluntary vomiting induced by drinking orange blossom water
and interrupted by a short nap."[3] After three weeks, an English
friend and a Hungarian refugee arrived and, alarmed by her condition, persuaded her to leave with them by car for the Spanish border.
They eventually reached Madrid and made contact with the British
embassy. When Ernst arrived at their house, he found it locked. He
broke in to recover some of his and Carrington's paintings before
slowly making his way to Marseille.

Many other foreign interns were also released or escaped before
the German army reached their camps, although Walter Hasenclever,
a German playwright in the Camp des Milles, chose suicide, taking
an overdose of sleeping pills on June 22. Carl Einstein, a German art
historian, escaped from a camp near Bordeaux; then, on July 5, finding himself trapped at the Spanish border, he jumped to his death
from a bridge. The fate of Münzenberg, the former Comintern agent,
was murkier. He was arrested in Paris on May 14 and sent to a camp
south of Lyon. Five weeks later, the camp commander ordered some
prisoners, including Münzenberg, to march to another camp, but
since no military guard accompanied them, they were now free.
Münzenberg's body was found four months later. The cause of death
was hanging, although it was never clear whether he was a suicide or,
as many still believe, a victim of the Soviet secret police. Koestler was
luckier. After being briefly rearrested in late May, he fled Paris with
Hardy. He then signed up for the Foreign Legion under a false name
to avoid further arrest. At first, Hardy followed him as he shunted
between army barracks and mounting disarray. Finally, Hardy found
a place on one of the last ships leaving Bordeaux for England, where
she arranged for the publication of Koestler's political masterpiece,
Darkness at Noon, which she had translated from German. Koestler
himself joined thousands of other foreigners trying to leave France,

and he, too, eventually reached England through Casablanca and Lisbon.

One paradox is that, while these "undesirable foreigners" were already victims of the conflict, the rest of France was still coming to terms with the idea of war. By October 1939, France had some 2.6 million men mobilized, many undergoing training, some stationed along the Maginot Line, even more joining the British Expeditionary Force in the north, where the German attack was expected. With memories of World War I still fresh, Paris was initially swept by fear. Trainloads of children were evacuated to the provinces, gas masks sold out, *métro* stations were readied to serve as air-raid shelters, anti-aircraft balloons were hoisted above the city, evening blackouts were ordered and sirens were tested. Because of the disruptions, theaters and movie houses were temporarily closed. Many movie productions were halted, since most actors and technicians had been mobilized. Pointing to the Molotov-Ribbentrop Pact, Daladier's government also dissolved the French Communist Party and denounced its members as unpatriotic, prompting the party leader, Maurice Thorez, to desert the army and head for Moscow.

Strangely, those other fifth columnists, Hitler's French sympathizers, fared better. Those who openly called on France to break with Britain and make a deal with Germany were sanctioned, as were vocal pacifists, like the writer Giono, who was jailed for signing a "Peace Now!" petition. The Surrealist poet Péret, no friend of Berlin, was also imprisoned for making defeatist remarks. But no move was made to disband pro-Fascist parties. Censorship of newspapers kept pro-German views out of the public eye, although Daladier picked an unlikely propagandist when he named the playwright Jean Giraudoux as minister of information. Giraudoux's own democratic credentials were hardly immaculate. In 1939, he had published the texts of five xenophobic lectures in *Pleins pouvoirs* (Full Powers), in which he defined the concept of French nationality so narrowly that it could be interpreted as anti-Semitic. Certainly, there was no ambiguity when he included "hundreds of thousands of Ashkenazis escaping from Polish or Romanian ghettos" among the foreigners "swarming in our arts and in our old and new industries, in a kind of spontaneous generation reminiscent of fleas on a newly born puppy."[4] He also proposed a Ministry of Race to control immigration, adding that "we are in full agreement with Hitler in proclaiming that a policy only achieves its highest plane once it is racial." For all that, though, he was an ineffective propagandist, at least compared with Paul Ferdonnet, a French journalist broadcasting over Radio Stuttgart, the Nazis' international broadcast station.

Still, in one critical area, Daladier's government was prepared. Already in September 1938, after Germany occupied the Sudetenland, the *Mona Lisa* and some other masterpieces were temporarily sent to the Château de Chambord in the Loire Valley. One year later, when war was declared, the Louvre had a plan in place to empty much of the museum. In less than one month, 3,691 paintings were taken down, carefully packed and trucked in thirty-seven convoys to the Château de Chambord, although the *Mona Lisa* would soon be moved to Louvigny, in the western Loire Valley. The Louvre had good reason to be pleased with its operation. Veronese's gigantic painting *The Marriage at Cana* was removed from its frame and rolled up, while Géricault's *The Raft of the Medusa,* only slightly smaller, was placed inside a large wooden container for transportation. The museum was obliged to leave behind many of its statues and sculptures, placing them in a basement before an air-raid shelter could be built. But exception was made for two Greek treasures, *The Winged Victory of Samothrace* and the *Venus de Milo,* which would spend the war in the Château de Valençay. In several cases, the Louvre was helped by the loan of Comédie Française trucks, which normally carried stage décor. After the evacuation was completed, with only empty gilded frames left in the painting galleries, the museum was closed.

A few weeks later, however, as the promised conflict with Germany began to resemble a "phony war" or a *drôle de guerre,* as the French tagged it,* Paris as a whole relaxed. Schoolchildren returned home, restaurants and nightclubs reopened, and theaters, movie theaters and opera houses again came alive, albeit without many young performers who were at the front. Sacha Guitry, playwright, director, actor and full-time celebrity, was busy: he organized a charity ball for the ambulance service; he presented a new play, *Florence;* and he broadcast a New Year message to French soldiers. A boisterous song written for British troops stationed along the German border, "We'll Hang Out Our Washing on the Siegfried Line," became just as popular in translation, "On ira pendre notre linge sur la ligne

---

*The Germans called it a "Sitzkrieg," or sitting war, to contrast with a "Blitzkrieg."

Siegfried." Édith Piaf, Josephine Baker and Maurice Chevalier traveled north to entertain the troops. Chevalier even had a hit song, "Ça fait d'excellents français" (That Makes for Excellent Frenchmen), which somewhat mockingly portrayed France as a united country: it listed all the unlikely professions and political currents, from bankers to bakers, from rightists of L'Action Française to Communists, who were expected to defend France.

In a sense, he had a point. The Communist poet Aragon and the ex-Communist poet Éluard, as well as the Fascist novelist Brasillach and the anti-Semitic journalist Rebatet were all now in uniform, as were most artists and intellectuals of an age to serve. Breton and Céline were both assigned to the medical corps, the composer Olivier Messiaen was a medical auxiliary and the philosopher Raymond Aron was placed in a meteorological unit. Michel Déon, who would be elected to the Académie Française in 1978, was just twenty when he joined the infantry. "I was among those French who otherwise would never have met peasants, workers or waiters," he recalled of the experience. "That helped a lot in my life of writing."[5] Marcel Carné, the movie director, found himself digging trenches near the Maginot Line, punishment for his portrayal of the army in *Le Quai des Brumes,* where Jean Gabin, now also a soldier, played a deserter. But because actual fighting did not seem imminent, many had time to write letters and keep journals. Officers among them were also given leave to visit Paris and catch up with gossip.

"When I saw how these intellectuals were reacting, that is when I understood they were not worried by the war," observed Stéphane Hessel, the son of the German writer Franz Hessel; Stéphane was raised in France and later became a distinguished French diplomat. "Protected by the Maginot Line, they thought Germany would not invade, that Germany would collapse with economic problems, that the French and British fleets still ruled the world, that the United States would enter the war sooner or later, that even the Soviet Union would not stay out. So intellectual life flourished around people like Joyce, Breton, Duchamp."[6]

The Left Bank, though, was not as jolly as it had been. Working on her first novel, *L'Invitée* (She Came to Stay), Simone de Beauvoir had already learned that she liked to write in cafés and would alternate between Le Dôme in Montparnasse and Café de Flore in Saint-Germain-des-Prés, but she was often almost alone. Across the boulevard, the Brasserie Lipp was still crowded, but now with

elderly politicians and their young mistresses rather than the traditional artist clients. The Latin Quarter seemed strangely deserted,
since university students at the Sorbonne were among the first to be
mobilized. Gaston Gallimard, the head of France's most prestigious
publishing house, Éditions Gallimard, even closed up his Left Bank
offices at 5 rue Sébastien-Bottin and left town. Fearing that Paris
could be bombed if hostilities broke out, he moved his files and
much of his staff to a family mansion at Sartilly, near the Atlantic
coast in western Normandy, and kept on publishing. Jean Paulhan,
who, like Gallimard, was in his late fifties and too old for the army,
was expected to shuttle between Paris and Sartilly to put together the
monthly *Nouvelle Revue Française*. And he did: the journal's last
issue before the occupation was dated June 1940.

As a Spaniard, Picasso was not an *étranger nondésirable*, but as an
opponent of Franco, he was understandably nervous. In the days
before war was declared, accompanied by his mistress Dora Maar, he
headed by car to Royan in southwestern France, where, not accidentally, another mistress, Marie-Thérèse Walter, was waiting with their
three-year-old daughter, Maya. He placed the two women in different hotels and then rented the top floor of a beachfront villa as a studio. He also found himself looking after Breton's wife, Jacqueline
Lamba, and her daughter. On leave from his unit, Breton visited
them at the resort and, on one occasion, learning that he was broke,
Picasso gave him a drawing to sell.

From Royan, Picasso made frequent trips to Paris. He had to prepare his first American retrospective, Picasso: 40 Years of His Art,
which, remarkably, opened on time at the Museum of Modern Art in
New York in December 1939. He also had to ensure that his French
residence papers were in order. When war was declared, he and
Matisse were offered asylum in the United States, but they both
turned it down. As a foreigner, though, Picasso was more vulnerable
than Matisse. He therefore decided to seek French nationality and, on
April 3, 1940, he filed his application. He was interrogated by a police
commissioner near his Paris home at 23 rue La Boétie, and the initial
verdict was positive: "Good information. Favorable recommenda-
tion." Then, in late May, with German troops already on French soil,
his application was rejected. A confidential report said he had been
"identified as an anarchist" in 1905 and had "retained extreme ideas
evolving towards Communism."[7] The following month, now virtu-

ally stateless, Picasso watched German troops pass through Royan on their way to Bordeaux.

Other artists also used the phony war to prepare for the worst. Piet Mondrian, the Dutch abstract master, had already left for England in 1938 and then moved to New York when war was declared. In 1940, Dalí and his wife, Gala, followed Mondrian to New York, while Miró returned to Franco's Spain. Matisse, Bonnard and Maillol had long ago chosen to live and work far from Paris and, as such, were relatively safe. But others stayed in Paris, struggling in a depressed art market to raise funds to move to the provinces or abroad.

Then, for some, an angel of sorts appeared. The American heiress Peggy Guggenheim had been living in London and had exhibited Cocteau, Kandinsky, Picasso, Braque and Tanguy in her new Mayfair gallery, Guggenheim Jeune. She also frequently visited Paris, where Duchamp introduced her to the art world. In early 1940, she was back in Paris, but this time with a mission. "My motto was 'Buy a picture a day' and I lived up to it," she later wrote in her memoir, *Out of This Century.*[8] With Victor Brauner, Alberto Giacometti, Jean Hélion, Man Ray and Constantin Brancusi, she bought directly from the artists, ignoring their complaints about the low prices she was offering. Other art was acquired on the market or through Duchamp's connections. Shortly before the Germans reached Paris, she shipped her collection to Grenoble, in southeast France, and then, many months later, out of the country. By then, Peggy Guggenheim's trove also included works by Kandinsky, Klee, Picabia, Braque, Mondrian, Miró, Ernst, Carrington, Dalí, Chirico, Tanguy and Léger. This collection would serve as the foundation stone for the museum she opened on Venice's Grand Canal in 1951.

Writers who were neither called up nor arrested as *étrangers nondésirables* also lived in uncertainty. Irène Némirovsky, a novelist born in Kiev in 1903, had come to France as a teenager when her wealthy Jewish parents fled the Bolshevik Revolution. In the 1930s, after the success of her novel *David Golder,* which was soon made into a movie, Irène became part of the Paris literary scene, with many right-wing writers among her friends. In the late 1930s, she and her banker husband, Michel Epstein, converted to Catholicism; nevertheless, they were subsequently refused French nationality.

As a precaution, fearing that she and Michel might be interned, Némirovsky sent her two small daughters, Denise and Élisabeth, to

Issy-l'Évêque, a quiet village in south Burgundy that was home to the children's governess and where Irène and her family had spent the previous two summers. At the same time, she told a French magazine featuring women authors that she was writing articles for foreign newspapers "which make known the magnificent morale of France, which portray the quiet determination of combatants, the quiet courage of women."[9] She also wrote articles for *Marie-Claire,* offered excerpts of a new novel, *Les Chiens et les loups* (The Dogs and the Wolves), to *Candide,* and published short stories in *Gringoire,* a political and literary weekly that was now opposed to war with Germany. Even after German soldiers entered France, Némirovsky kept hoping for a French counterattack. Once defeat looked unavoidable, she left Paris to rejoin her children in Issy-l'Évêque, which would become her home for the next two years.

Gide, who was in the south of France, chose to stay out of the limelight. "No, decidedly, I shall not speak on the radio," he wrote in his journal on October 30, 1939. "I shall not contribute to pumping oxygen into the public. The newspapers already contain enough patriotic yappings. The more French I feel, the more loath I am to let my mind be warped. If it regimented itself, it would lose all value." But the entry also strongly suggested that, if he did choose to speak or write, he was not sure what position he would take. "I do not want to blush tomorrow for what I should write today," he noted, adding: "My unseasonable thoughts, until better times, I will store up in this notebook." Some three months later, on February 7, 1940, he worried about the consequences of war: "One must expect that after the war, and even though victors, we shall plunge into such a mess that nothing but a determined dictatorship will be able to get us out of it." Then, on May 21, with German forces advancing rapidly into France, Gide despaired of the French, writing, "O incurably frivolous people of France! You are going to pay dearly today for your lack of application, your heedlessness, your smug reclining among so many charming virtues."[10]

Drieu La Rochelle, the Fascist writer, had been wounded in World War I and was exempted from army duty on health grounds, which allowed him to continue writing fiction and for the *Nouvelle Revue Française.* But while he was outwardly self-confident, his private war journal, published decades after his suicide in 1945, portrays him as confused and insecure in the countdown to open war. Jews remained an obsession, and he repeatedly speculated about whether his longtime friend and ideological foe, Aragon, was Jewish.[11] A tall, good-looking man, he wrote boastfully of how women had always loved him, then expressed shame that he had never been a "real man" of courage.[12] He even recalled that he had married his second wife, Olesia Sienkiewicz, "persuaded by the idea that she was a lesbian and could never truly love me."*[13] But when Drieu La Rochelle managed to look beyond himself, he took France's pulse accurately. "The war has changed nothing, quite the contrary," he wrote in December 1939. "The French are more divided than ever, behind the façade of general agreement resulting from their lethargy."[14]

Sartre was also writing, but from the front. Stationed as an army meteorologist at Marmoutier, less than twenty miles from the German border, he exchanged almost-daily letters with Beauvoir, who also came to visit him. He filled notebooks with reflections on literature, history, politics and philosophy; these would serve as the groundwork for his existentialist treatise *L'Être et le néant* (Being and Nothingness), published in 1943. He also offered acute observations of military life, mocking an order to denounce anyone who displayed defeatist tendencies, an order that he promptly violated by questioning the usefulness of the war. "And what are we fighting for?" he wrote on October 20, 1939.

> To defend democracy? There is no such thing anymore. To preserve things as they were before the war? But it was the most complete disorder. There are no more parties or coherent ideologies. Only social discontent everywhere. Manipulated by capitalists? But they have nothing to gain from this war. They delayed it as long as they could; they are the authors of Munich. They accepted the dismemberment of Czechoslovakia for fear of communism. And their interest in September 1939 was 'to allow Hitler to save face,' as one senior official said on August 30, 1939. They fear Stalin more than Hitler and now, here they are, at war with Hitler, not Stalin.[15]

Interviewed more than thirty years later, Sartre was still more radical: "In 1939, 1940, we were terrified of dying, suffering, for a cause

---

*A more persuasive reason for marrying Olesia was that she was rich and helped to maintain Drieu La Rochelle long after their divorce. To his credit, though, while he hated his Jewish first wife, Colette Jeramec, he saved her from deportation.

that disgusted us. That is, for a disgusting France, corrupt, ineffi-
cient, racist, anti-Semite, run by the rich for the rich—no one wanted
to die for that, until, well, until we understood that the Nazis were
worse."[16]

One man who might have hoped to be in uniform, given his self-
image as a swashbuckling warrior, was André Malraux. His involvement in the Spanish war had boosted the celebrity he had garnered
in the 1920s and 1930s, first as an adventurer who was arrested for
stealing statues from Angkor Wat in Cambodia, then for his prize-
winning book *La Condition humaine.* But in 1939, when he volunteered to join the French air force on the back of his running the
Escadrille España, he was turned down on the not unreasonable
grounds that he could not pilot a plane. He then offered to join a
mechanized unit and was told to wait until contacted. The call finally
came in April 1940, when he was ordered to join a tank regiment at
Provins, fifty miles southeast of Paris. A man who had boasted the
rank of *commandant* in Spain was now a modest private calling himself Georges Malraux. Two months later, the fact that he was not
immediately identified as *André* Malraux, a renowned left-leaning
anti-Fascist, probably saved him from long imprisonment.

On the political front, developments elsewhere in Europe were
fast undermining hopes that France could avoid an open war with
Germany. On September 17, 1939, as part of its understanding with
Germany, the Soviet Union invaded Poland and annexed one-third of
its territory to Belarus and Ukraine. But neither France nor Britain
was ready to declare war on Moscow. Then, on November 30, 1939,
with its western flank secured by the nonaggression pact with Germany, the Soviet Union invaded Finland. Finnish resistance proved
far greater than expected and, in the weeks that followed, Britain and
France felt obliged to offer assistance. In practice, little of this arrived
before the Soviet Union and Finland signed an armistice in March
1940.

For French rightists, obsessed more by Communism than Fascism, France's failure to confront Moscow over Finland was unfor-
givable. This led Pierre Laval and another former prime minister,
Pierre-Étienne Flandin, to oust Daladier's government on March 19,
although its replacement, headed by Paul Reynaud, brought little
extra clarity. While Reynaud had for years demanded rapid French
rearmament, he was nonetheless forced to give the job of minister of
national defense and war to Daladier, the man widely blamed for

France's military weakness. Reynaud at least understood that Berlin, not Moscow, was France's principal foe. But he had no time to act on this. On April 9, Germany invaded Denmark and Norway, with Denmark surrendering almost immediately. Norway put up a brave fight, prompting Reynaud to persuade Britain to join France in sending military reinforcements. By May 2, Germany had driven out the allied forces and seized Norway.

Was Paris ready for what would follow? Hardly. At the end of April, a Swiss journalist, Edmond Dubois, reported that the city's nightlife still offered 105 movie houses, 25 theaters, 14 music halls and 21 cabarets. On May 8, the Paris Opera presented the world premiere of Milhaud's new opera, *Médée.* And even two days later, when Hitler launched his offensive against western Europe, Parisians still presumed that the French army would stop him. But Germany swiftly occupied neutral Luxembourg, Belgium and the Netherlands; then, instead of turning south, where most French and British troops were concentrated, the Wehrmacht launched a tank blitzkrieg through the supposedly unpassable mountains of the Ardennes. By entering France to the west of the Maginot Line but to the east of the main Allied emplacements, German armored divisions caught the French army command by surprise. And in doing so, they cut off the British Expeditionary Force, France's northern army and some Belgian units. The disaster was marginally mitigated by Operation Dynamo, by which some 340,000 soldiers, including 140,000 French, were evacuated to Britain from Dunkirk between May 26 and June 4. But France was now forced to watch helplessly as the German army, supported by the Luftwaffe, advanced largely unopposed into France. On June 10, seeing an opportunity to profit from the German success, Italy declared war on France.

Complicating the retreat of the French army was the exodus of millions of civilians, first from Belgium, then from northern France and finally from Paris and all major cities in the center of the country. Over a period of barely four weeks, some eight to ten million people fled south. These included many of France's cultural lights, not only Jews like Milhaud, the playwright Tristan Bernard and the philosopher Henri Bergson, but also Colette, Drieu La Rochelle and many other literary figures. Gaston Gallimard and Paulhan, accompanied by their wives, quickly left Normandy and found refuge at the home of a poet friend near Carcassonne, in the far south. In her novel *Suite française,* written in 1942 and not published until 2004, Irène

Némirovsky provided a gripping description of the exodus. She was already with her family in Issy-l'Évêque when it occurred, but using other testimonies and her own imagination, she put together her story of rich and poor scrambling desperately and often selfishly for their lives. Early in her book, capturing the mood of the wealthy bourgeoisie, an art collector expresses his incredulity at everything happening around him: "I cannot bear this chaos, these outbursts of hatred, the repulsive spectacle of war. I shall withdraw to a tranquil spot, in the countryside, and live on the bit of money I have left until everyone comes to their senses."[17]

Initially what set off the flight was fear that the Germans would act as everyone believed they had done in occupied French territories during World War I—that is, pillaging, raping and killing indiscriminately. Once people began to flee, panic accelerated the process. If a neighbor or the baker or, still worse, the local mayor was seen piling belongings into his car, it was hard not to follow his example. This process was multiplied a thousand times in Paris, above all when ministries were seen filling trucks with documents and furniture, which were then carried off into the night in convoys. On June 10, President Albert Lebrun, Prime Minister Reynaud, President of the Senate Jules Jeanneney and much of the Chamber of Deputies slipped out of town before dawn or in the evening, after dark. Accompanying Reynaud in his car was the newly promoted General de Gaulle, who four days earlier had been named undersecretary of war. That night, the government reassembled in Orléans.

Signs that Paris was closing down were everywhere. June 10 was also the day that the senior high school examinations called the *baccalauréat* were due to start. Beauvoir went to the Lycée Camille Sée, where she taught, to discover that *le bac* had been canceled. "I returned to the Latin Quarter and found students of the Lycée Henri IV, all having a good laugh; for many of these youths, it was like a holiday, an exam day without exams and with disorder and free time. They walked along the rue Soufflot in a cheerful mood, they seemed to be amusing themselves enormously."[18] That very evening, Beauvoir herself joined the exodus south. Michel Francini, still only nineteen but already a music-hall performer, said he left the city only after Reynaud called on Parisians to flee, on June 12. "If I hadn't heard Reynaud on the radio, I'd have stayed," he said decades later. Instead, he was given a taste of the fear and confusion gripping much of the country: "I had an exodus of thirteen days. I knew my father had gone to Agen, but it's five hundred miles away. So I left not knowing where I was going. I walked for miles, I'd see a train, get on it and sometimes find it was going the wrong way. I arrived in Agen on the eve of my father leaving for Pau. The Italians were bombing us, too," he recalled. "All the time, people were saying, 'The Germans are coming, the Germans are just behind us.' I was starving, I had just a bit of bread. I went to a farm and asked for some water and was refused. They wanted to sell it to me for two francs."[19] It seems unlikely that fugitives were enormously consoled by *chansonniers* like Tino Rossi, who caught the mood with "Quand tu reverras ton village" (When You Next See Your Village) and "Le Petit refugié" (The Little Refugee).

Almost everyone faced chaos. Once the fighting reached northern France, escape by train became impossible. Those with cars or trucks were usually the first to leave, but they were soon slowed down by traffic jams or bomb craters. Those with horse-drawn carts or bicycles were then followed by people on foot, many of them pushing heavily laden prams. As they passed through empty villages, abandoned dogs and cats met them, scrounging for food. In some places, patients from psychiatric hospitals could be seen wandering about in a daze. And all along, there was both the fear and the reality of strafings by Stuka and Messerschmitt fighter planes, which by then were unchallenged in the air. Every attack sent people tumbling from their cars or dropping their bicycles as they sought protection in ditches; many were killed or wounded. Solidarity was in short supply. A few improvised field hospitals were set up, there were cases when villagers gave food and water to passing refugees, but more often the instinct for survival ruled. The lucky travelers headed toward provincial homes where family or friends waited to receive them. Most found themselves hungry and homeless, refugees in their own country. French soldiers whose units had disintegrated were left roaming the countryside in shock, not knowing where to find their families. Foreigners who had escaped internment camps understood only that they had to head south.

As the Wehrmacht encircled the French army in the north and headed south, it took some two million prisoners, among them Sartre, Messiaen, Desnos, Anouilh, Brasillach and the country's future president François Mitterrand. The German army was ill-prepared to handle so many prisoners and, in the confusion, many escaped, including Desnos and Anouilh. Others were taken to Germany and spent the next five years as prisoners of war. Sartre, Messiaen and Brasillach, however, were released in 1941; Mitterrand escaped later the same year. But there were also many fatalities. Around 100,000 French soldiers and civilians died in the fall of France, among them Paul Nizan, an admired writer who had left the French Communist Party to protest the Molotov-Ribbentrop Pact and was killed in the fighting. Another was Saint-Pol-Roux, a seventy-nine-year-old Symbolist poet who died as a result of a common rather than a political crime: a drunken German soldier burst into his home near Brest, killed his servant, raped his daughter and assaulted Roux so viciously that he died in a hospital a few hours later. To the south of Paris, the Germans caught up with Malraux's tank unit and, after a short battle, he was wounded and captured. He was fortunate not to be shipped to Germany and managed to escape four months later with the help of his brother Roland. Aragon, who won medals for bravery, avoided capture when he found a place among French troops evacuated to England from Dunkirk. Many of these were quickly sent back to France in the hope that they could still resist the German advance. But after Aragon's unit landed in Brest, it was soon overwhelmed. He escaped and slowly made his way southeast until he again met up with his Russian-born wife, the writer Elsa Triolet.

Saint-Exupéry, whose 1931 novel *Vol de Nuit* (Night Flight) made him famous as both a writer and an aviator, saw the war from the air. Injuries sustained in earlier plane crashes prevented him from becoming a fighter pilot, so instead he was assigned to an air force reconnaissance unit based at Orconte, about 130 miles east of Paris. When the Battle of France erupted, the Luftwaffe quickly won air supremacy, just as German tanks dominated the land war. Saint-Exupéry's squadron suffered badly. In *Pilote de guerre,* published in the United States as *Flight to Arras,* he recalled that France had only fifty three-man air reconnaissance crews and that, of twenty-three in his Group 2-33, seventeen had vanished by the end of May 1940. In military terms, this was disastrous, since the French army had almost no firsthand information of the whereabouts and movements of the Wehrmacht. Saint-Exupéry's description of the country's mood was still more somber: "Throughout the closing days of the campaign, one impression dominated all others, an impression of absurdity. Everything was cracking up all round us. Everything was caving in. The collapse was so entire that death itself seemed to us absurd.

Death, in such a tumult, had ceased to count." After France's defeat, he was demobilized in Algeria and returned to France to be reunited with his beautiful Salvadoran wife, Consuelo.

Other cultural figures also ended up in the south of France. Much of the movie industry, notably Jewish producers, headed to Nice and Marseille, home to film studios, and to Cannes, with its many comfortable hotels. Others with money in their pockets went to Alpine resorts, like Megève. Paul Derval, who ran Les Folies Bergère, arrived in Biarritz to find the singer Mistinguett and the actresses Elvire Popesco and Suzanne Flon. Guitry opted for Dax, in southwestern France, although unlike Provence, where Matisse, Bonnard and Chagall sought refuge, that region was soon occupied by German forces. Only a few writers chose to stay in Paris, among them the eccentric conservative Paul Léautaud, who refused to abandon his beloved dogs and cats. He watched as the city quickly emptied, noting that even the Louvre was unguarded. A few days later, he wrote in his *Journal littéraire:* "I am completely indifferent to the defeat, as indifferent as I was when I first saw a German soldier the other morning." One simple reason was that, as a convinced anti-Semite, he believed that a British victory would be equivalent to a Jewish victory. Another writer, Marcel Jouhandeau, who would have liked to have left, stayed at the insistence of his domineering wife, Elise. As a result, he provided an eyewitness account of the fall of Paris. On June 10, he wrote: "It seems that everyone is leaving on a long journey and here we are, alone in an ocean of abandoned homes. Those who will arrive speak a different language. We will understand it no better than that of birds and domestic animals."[20] On June 13, General Pierre Héring declared Paris an open city, saving it from further bombardment. At six a.m. on June 14, with Paris already in German hands, Jouhandeau noted almost casually, "When I cross Avenue Malakoff, I find myself before some German non-commissioned officers photographing Luna Park."[21]

The occupation of Paris indeed took place almost silently. The city had lost 60 percent of its population and, apart from German vehicles, its streets were empty. German troops took up positions in front of ministries and army buildings, while senior officers installed themselves in the city's best hotels, starting with the Crillon in the place de la Concorde and soon also the Meurice, Lutetia, Raphaël and George V. The German military command, the Militärbefehlshaber in Frankreich, or MBF, set up its headquarters in the Majestic Hotel, close to the Arc de Triomphe. The Luftwaffe, in turn, took over the French Senate, setting aside an apartment overlooking the Luxembourg Gardens for Air Marshal Hermann Göring himself. The swastika was raised where the French tricolor once hung, even above the Eiffel Tower — although at least there blocked elevators forced the German soldiers to climb to the top. In 1914, the Kaiser's army had planned to take Paris in forty-two days but failed; Hitler's army had done so in thirty-five days. And yet France as a nation had still to surrender. On June 16, the government left the Loire Valley for Bordeaux, where Reynaud argued in favor of moving it — as well as the navy and surviving army and air force units — to French possessions in North Africa. With this in mind, twenty-seven deputies, including Daladier and two former Popular Front ministers, Georges Mandel and Pierre Mendès-France, left Bordeaux for Casablanca on board the *Massilia*. But the new army chief, General Maxime Weygand, appointed in late May in place of General Maurice Gamelin, vetoed any suggestion of restationing the remnants of the army in North Africa, prompting Reynaud to resign.

He was in turn replaced by Marshal Philippe Pétain, the hero of Verdun, who just weeks earlier had been recalled from his post as ambassador to Spain and named deputy prime minister. For most of the French population, it was a reassuring appointment. Pétain had emerged from World War I with enormous prestige as an officer who combined victory with treating his troops humanely. When he was elected to the Académie Française in 1929, the vote was unanimous. Further, although he finally married when he was sixty-four, he had a reputation as a ladies' man, with a twinkle in his eye to prove it. Even at the age of eighty-four, he seemed to be the right man for the moment. The following day, in an emotional speech in which he acknowledged Germany's military superiority, Pétain offered himself as a "gift" to France to alleviate its woes. "In these painful hours, I think of the unfortunate refugees who, in a state of extreme destitution, hurry along our roads. I offer them my compassion and my concern. It is with a heavy heart that I tell you today that the fighting must end." And he confirmed that he had sought out the Germans to prepare a cessation of hostilities.

Even though Pétain did not actually say "armistice," this was the word that set off immediate rejoicing across the country. To this day, older French people can remember where they were — and how they felt — when they learned of Pétain's decision. And few would claim that, at that moment, they felt humiliated. "I was on a train, I was totally miserable, and someone shouted, 'Armistice!' " Francini, the music-hall performer, recalled. "What a relief, what joy! The nightmare is over, we all thought. I was not a *pétainiste,* but I asked myself, if it wasn't Pétain, who would it have been?" Those in army units retreating chaotically felt no different. "If you were on the road, with almost no weapons, and a man you respect takes the microphone, you said yes," Michel Déon remembered. "We all breathed a sigh of relief. We could not go on, physically, morally. We had no more ammunition. I have never seen a country on its knees like that. Some officers led little pockets of resistance, but I had no officer."[22] The eight days between Pétain's speech and the entry into effect of the cease-fire only made things worse: many French soldiers who became prisoners of war were captured during this period. A German military intelligence report dated August 15, 1940, based on interviews with imprisoned French officers, observed: "A large percentage of them are old, broken men, thoroughly dejected and demoralized in spirit." It quoted a German general saying that, after the retreat of a French division was interrupted by destroyed bridges, "all its officers and equipment halted along the road and waited until it was captured." The report added that many French enlisted men "complain bitterly of the conduct of their officers."[23]

One senior French officer, however, was defiant. As soon as Pétain had spoken to the nation, de Gaulle flew to London. The following day, he broadcast a stirring message over the BBC telling the French not to lose hope, that their defeat was not final, that France was not alone. He called on French soldiers in England after Dunkirk and others still in France to join him, and he concluded with appropriately uplifting words: "Whatever happens, the flame of French resistance should not and will not be extinguished." De Gaulle was taking a tremendous gamble. From a military point of view, his action was more than insubordination; for a two-star general, this was high treason. Further, he was largely unknown in France and, in any event, few people heard his message when it was first broadcast. Nonetheless, June 18, 1940, would be recorded as the day that de Gaulle entered French history.

On June 22, the armistice was signed in the same railroad carriage and in the same forest clearing near Compiègne, north of Paris, where the World War I armistice had been signed on November 11, 1918. It was an occasion that Hitler himself could not resist witnessing. The agreement carved up France. A so-called unoccupied zone,* with a population of some thirteen million, was placed under French rule and covered the southern half of France except for Atlantic coastal areas, while the occupied zone, with its twenty-nine million inhabitants, embraced three-fifths of French territory and was under direct German military rule. Other territorial changes not mentioned in the armistice were carried out de facto: the long-contested provinces of Alsace and Lorraine were again annexed by Germany, as they had been between 1871 and 1918; and a small area of northwestern France, including the city of Lille, was attached to Germany's military command in Brussels. Under a separate agreement signed with Rome on June 24, the Alpine region of southeastern France came under Italian control. The armistice allowed France to maintain a 100,000-man army without heavy weapons, such as tanks, while the French navy was to stay anchored in its peacetime ports. France was required to pay a massive 400 million francs per day—worth about $8 million at the time but with a buying power of around $120 million today—to maintain the occupation army, an article that would permit Germany to plunder the French economy. Finally, French prisoners of war would continue to be held in Germany, pending a final peace treaty between the two countries.

When the armistice went into effect, on June 25, Pétain again addressed the nation by radio, explaining why he had accepted it and what it meant. Instead of lamenting the French army's disastrous strategy, he suggested that France had only itself to blame for its situation: "Our defeat was a result of our laxity. The spirit of enjoyment destroyed what the spirit of sacrifice had built." Then, quickly ensuring that no competing government in exile could be set up in North Africa, he ordered that the politicians who had left on the *Massilia* be returned to France and jailed. On July 3, Britain even helped to unite France behind him: fearing that French naval vessels at anchor in the Algerian port of Mers el-Kébir would fall into German hands, Churchill ordered their destruction, leaving thirteen hundred French sailors dead.

By then, Pétain had decided to establish his government in the spa resort of Vichy in central France, just south of the demarcation line now dividing the country. Vichy's appeal was not only that it had

---

*This became known as *la zone no-no*, for *la zone non-occupée*, but was also a play on the words *non-non*.

many elegant hotels and one of France's best telephone exchanges; unlike nearby Clermont-Ferrand, which had been considered as a possible headquarters, Vichy also had no industry or troublesome Communist unions. Most of the country's political and economic leaders and a good number of establishment intellectuals converged on the town. On July 10, in a joint session of the Chamber of Deputies and the Senate held in Vichy's opera house, the Third Republic was buried and Pétain was given full powers. The vote was 569 in favor and 80 against, with 17 abstentions. The following day, Pétain named himself chief of the French state—the new *état français* that replaced the Third Republic—and appointed himself as head of the government and Pierre Laval as his deputy and successor. As Pétain and Laval saw things, all that was left was to start building a new France of family, Catholic and rural values, one cleansed of Jews, Communists and Freemasons. And to set the tone, France's traditional motto— *"Liberté, égalité, fraternité"*—was abandoned in favor of *"Travail, famille, patrie,"* or "Work, family, fatherland."

· CHAPTER 3 ·

Shall We Dance?

EVEN WITH half the population of Paris scattered around the country, there was soon a consensus that the city's cultural life should resume. For musicians, dancers and actors, it was a matter of necessity. They needed to work and saw no reason not to. They bore no responsibility for the country's disaster, and they had no power to redress the situation. Further, the Germans had no cause to take offense at mainstream theater, movies, ballet, opera, classical music or cabaret. The new Vichy government, which retained responsibility for national cultural institutions, was also eager to show that, while crushed militarily, France was not defeated culturally.

In fact, culture was the one area where the French could still feel pride. And it was not unreasonable to expect artists to lift the public's spirits until better days came along. This suited the Germans perfectly: they were sure to face fewer problems if the French, particularly Parisians, were kept entertained. Hitler even enjoyed the idea of the French wallowing in their degeneracy. "Does the spiritual health of the French people matter to you?" Albert Speer recalled Hitler asking. "Let's let them degenerate. All the better for us."[1]

The Germans' priority, then, was simply to make Parisians feel that life was returning to normal. On July 23, Joseph Goebbels, the powerful *Reichsminister* of public enlightenment and propaganda, traveled to Paris to gauge its mood. The Wehrmacht soldiers seemed happy enough: the city's brothels and cabarets were already catering to them, and some restaurants even offered menus in German. But Goebbels still pronounced the city sad and ordered more cheer. By September the mood had improved and many Parisians made their way home. Although they found a city festooned with swastikas where German soldiers goose-stepped down the Champs-Élysées at twelve-thirty every afternoon and patrolled an eleven o'clock curfew every night, the Paris of yore was still recognizable.

Behind the Germans' apparent laissez-faire, however, they had a more radical strategy in mind. Driving it was a deeply held German inferiority complex toward a culture that for the previous two centuries had dominated Europe. Over the same period, Germanic culture had produced its share of great artists, writers and, above all, musicians, yet it was Paris—not London, not Rome, not Vienna and certainly not Berlin—that defined style and taste for the region. The Nazis had trouble explaining how all this could be done by a culture that it saw as degenerated by Jews, blacks and Freemasons. Nonetheless, it was this leadership and this power that Hitler and Goebbels coveted, so the order went out: no cultural activity taking place in France should radiate beyond the country's borders.

In November 1940, Goebbels spelled this out in instructions to the German embassy in Paris: "The result of our victorious fight should be to break French domination of cultural propaganda, in Europe and the world. Having taken control of Paris, the center of French cultural propaganda, it should be possible to strike a decisive blow against this propaganda. Any assistance to or tolerance of this propaganda will be a crime against the nation."[2] At the same time, he saw an opportunity for German culture to infiltrate French society and, above all, its intelligentsia. For Goebbels, cultural collaboration meant distracting the public at large and impressing French artists and intellectuals with Germany's eternal glory and the achievements of the Third Reich. It also offered a message back home: that France had been vanquished culturally and intellectually as well as militarily.

To implement this, Goebbels left nothing to chance. He set up a complicated new structure called the Propaganda Abteilung, or Propaganda Department, which was answerable to him but also formed part of the German military command in France. With a staff of around twelve hundred, it was headed throughout the occupation by a stern infantry officer, Major Heinz Schmidtke, and had the twin responsibilities of propaganda and censorship. Much of this work was done through the Propaganda Staffel, which had fifty bureaus across the occupied zone, with its most important office in Paris at 52 avenue des Champs-Élysées. This department was divided into six sections, each with a specific responsiblity: press; radio; cinema; culture, which included music, theater, fine arts, music hall and cabaret; literature; and active propaganda. Assigned to the Propaganda Staffel were some two hundred Sonderführer, literally "special leaders," who in this case were in the main former journalists, critics or propaganda experts recruited by the Wehrmacht to manage French culture. In a report written on September 14, 1940, Sonderführer Fritz Werner, who was responsible for classical music, echoed Goebbels: "Over recent centuries, the French have become masters in the art of penetrating other peoples with their cultural policy." He described French culture as a wall that stood between France and Germany and that needed to be dismantled to facilitate entente. The answer, he said, was for French culture "to renounce being (too) obtrusive."[3]

The Propaganda Abteilung had little difficulty controlling the mass media, since newspaper editors were either convinced Fascists or eager to please the Germans. In any event, newspapers were subject to censorship—anything remotely critical of Germany or the occupation was excised—and were expected to promote Nazi interests. A still stronger propaganda tool was Radio-Paris, a new French-language station with studios at 116 bis avenue des Champs-Élysées, which was run by a Dr. Bofinger, imported from Radio Stuttgart. Its political broadcasts were designed to whip up hatred for Jews, Communists, Freemasons and the British. These were in turn answered daily by the BBC's French service in London, known as Radio-Londres, in a program called *Les Français parlent aux Français.** But if Parisians ignored the political programs on Radio-Paris, they were

---

*Using the tune of "La Cucaracha," Radio-Londres quickly invented a ditty that was soon on everyone's lips: *"Radio-Paris ment, Radio-Paris ment, Radio-Paris est allemand,"* literally "Radio-Paris lies, Radio-Paris lies, Radio-Paris is German."

drawn to its cultural and entertainment programs, which included classical and popular music, live theater and chat shows discussing cooking, children's health and topics of interest to women. Further, Parisians had little choice in what they listened to. They risked arrest if caught tuning in to the BBC, which was also frequently jammed. And while Vichy operated Radiodiffusion Nationale, the prewar government radio now known familiarly as Radio Vichy, its signal was often too weak to reach Paris and northern areas of the occupied zone.

The Propaganda Staffel was less assured in handling France's cultural elites, particularly in determining how tolerant it should be in managing the performing and creative arts. Since decisions had to be taken quickly as to whether, say, the screenplay for a new movie would be approved or paper be issued for the printing of a specific book, much depended on which German official was considering the case. Some were almost proudly philistine; others were surprisingly flexible. In fact, on more than one occasion, German cultural officials approved books, movies and plays that Vichy wanted banned on moral grounds.

The Propaganda Abteilung, however, also faced competition from the German embassy, notably from Otto Abetz, the newly appointed ambassador. As Berlin's prewar representative on the France-Germany Committee, he had understood the prestige enjoyed by artists and writers in France, and he was now eager to reach out to them. As an appendix to the embassy, he installed a new German Institute in the elegant eighteenth-century Hôtel de Monaco at 57 rue Saint-Dominique, on the Left Bank, which until just weeks earlier had been the Polish embassy. Abetz also brought with him numerous Germans with knowledge of France, including Friedrich Sieburg, a former Paris correspondent for the *Frankfurter Zeitung*, who in 1930 published *Dieu est-il français?* (Is God French?), portraying France as charmingly trapped in the past. Friedrich Grimm, a jurist and broadcaster who was named legal attaché in the embassy, was also an experienced propagandist. The institute's director, Karl Epting, was another old Paris hand. He had previously run the German student-exchange bureau in Paris, while his number two, Karl-Heinz Bremer, was a historian who had taught German at the École Normale Supérieure in Paris before the war. Also enthusiastically Francophile was Gerhard Heller, a former student of French literature and now the Sonderführer in charge of lit-

erature at the Propaganda Staffel. And in 1942, after the embassy
assumed charge of all cultural activities, leaving only censorship to
the Propaganda Abteilung, Heller, too, came under Abetz's control.
Abetz and Epting proved a good team: political events and intimate
dinners were held at the embassy, while lectures, small concerts and
receptions for visiting artists were hosted by the institute. And
French cultural figures would be seen at both. Ordinary Parisians
eager to get to know the occupiers could in turn learn German at the
institute.

Abetz and Epting also worked with Laval and Vichy's delegate in
Paris, Fernand de Brinon, to create the Groupe Collaboration. The
organization's very name explained its function. As the successor to
the France-Germany Committee, it became a kind of pro-German
cultural and intellectual club and, by early 1944, had over 42,000
members across France, among them a good number of writers,
musicians and painters. It was organized into sections addressing the
economy and society, science, literature, the law and the arts, with
the arts section in turn divided into theater, visual arts and music.
Presided over by Alphonse de Châteaubriant, a writer who was the
editor of the new collaborationist weekly, *La Gerbe,* it sponsored
concerts by German orchestras, hosted receptions for visiting German luminaries and organized conferences across France. For German soldiers and for Parisian speakers of German, Epting's institute
opened a German bookshop, Rive-Gauche,* on the corner of the
boulevard Saint-Michel and the place de la Sorbonne, in the heart
of the Latin Quarter. While the Propaganda Abteilung devoted much
of its time to propaganda and censorship, then, the embassy and
the institute set out to seduce the leading lights of French culture.
In time, French intellectuals were invited to contribute articles to
the institute's two journals, *Cahiers de l'Institut Allemand* and
Deutschland-Frankreich. Then, from 1941, at Goebbels's insistence,
the institute began arranging for delegations of French artists and
writers to visit Germany. All this was possible, of course, because
France's cultural life had returned to close to normal with almost
unseemly haste.

Sacha Guitry, whose artistic talent was matched only by his vanity,
was among the first to reach Paris. He missed his elegant home on

---

*On more than one occasion, small bombs placed by *résistants* blew out the
bookshop's windows.

avenue Élisée-Reclus, beside the Eiffel Tower, as well as the exquisite art collection it contained. He also missed his adoring public. And before leaving Dax, in southwestern France, he was further persuaded that he should return to Paris when a German officer recognized him—presumably from his movies—and hailed him as a French cultural treasure. Once he reached Paris, he announced his presence by requesting an audience with General Harald Turner, the administrative governor of Greater Paris. Guitry's immediate plan was to reopen the Théâtre de la Madeleine with his play *Pasteur,* casting himself in the title role. For this, he needed the approval of censors at the Propaganda Staffel, who insisted on cuts, including the final scene, where "La Marseillaise" is sung. Furious, Guitry appealed to Turner, and on July 31, barely six weeks after the fall of Paris, the play was performed as written. Turner even led the audience in rising for "La Marseillaise" and then visited Guitry in his dressing room. Offering his compliments, the general asked Guitry what he could do for him. "For me, nothing, thank you," the Frenchman reportedly replied, "but perhaps the return of some prisoners." And as a result, eleven prisoners of war were indeed released.[4]

For his next production, Guitry decided to celebrate French culture through a staged tribute to notable late greats: Rodin, Monet, Renoir, the playwrights Edmond Rostand and Octave Mirbeau, the composer Saint-Saëns, his own father, the actor Lucien Guitry, and the legendary actress Sarah Bernhardt. Accompanied by early film footage, Guitry proclaimed his own text, including Mirbeau's deathbed words: "Never collaborate!" When the Propaganda Staffel stepped in after eleven performances, though, it was to demand that Bernhardt, a Jew, be excluded. Guitry refused to comply and canceled the show. With Guitry back on stage, however, other *théâtres de boulevard* were soon presenting light comedies inoffensive to the German censors. Visitors arriving from the unoccupied zone in the fall were often surprised by and disapproving over how normal Paris seemed. In response to complaints heard in Vichy, a columnist in *La Gerbe* asked why the *vichyssois* should consider Parisians to be bad citizens just "because we try to forget our sorrows, and their piteous burden, by going to see a show."[5] The columnist might have further annoyed those trapped in the bourgeois dullness of Vichy by noting that music halls and cabarets were also doing a roaring business.

The Comédie Française raised a different issue. Like the Paris Opera and other pillars of French culture, this historic theater remained Vichy's responsibility. The Germans could censor its productions, but Vichy wanted to ensure that it not go dark or worse, as in the case of the Grand Palais, which was turned into a temporary parking lot for German military vehicles. Because the Comédie Française had stayed open until five days before the occupation, most of its actors were in town. The company's provisional administrator, the respected director Jacques Copeau, therefore quickly arranged a performance at a Paris school to show that the company was still active. Then, on September 7, the theater's own curtain finally rose again, albeit with a bizarre program designed by Vichy. It began with a lecture by Abel Bonnard, a right-wing poet and member of the Académie Française, who later became Vichy's education minister. This was followed by readings from a series of traditionalist French authors. Copeau also addressed the audience in fervently *pétainiste* terms, proclaiming that there was hope because France was confessing, condemning and amending its errors and because, "in spite of all the disasters, we maintain a secret but unshakeable faith in the deep powers of the homeland, in the soul of the race, in the lasting strength and survival of the French spirit."[6] The show was repeated on September 15 before the company returned to its traditional repertoire, with plays by Corneille, Shakespeare and Mérimée.

The opera world was even quicker off the mark. In 1939, the Paris Opera at the Palais Garnier and the Opéra-Comique at the nearby Salle Favart were brought under the same administration, with the immensely experienced Jacques Rouché in charge. In the late summer of 1940, it was his job to reopen both theaters, all too aware that senior German officers found opera more to their liking than French-language theater. Further, in the eyes of the Germans, the Palais Garnier had now acquired a special aura. On his only visit to Paris early on the morning of June 23, Hitler had asked to see the opera house before any other building. Accompanied by his chief architect, Albert Speer, and his favorite sculptor, Arno Breker, he took a three-hour tour of an empty and silent Paris that also included Napoleon's tomb at Les Invalides, the Panthéon, Notre-Dame cathedral and other tourist sites, but the opera house, Speer later wrote, was "Hitler's favorite." It appears that the Führer had studied Charles Garnier's neo-Baroque extravaganza as an art student and even knew his way around the building on his first visit. Speer added, "He seemed fascinated by the Opera, went into ecstasies about its beauty, his eyes glittering with an excitement that struck me as uncanny."[7]

On August 24, before an audience packed with uniformed German officers, the Paris Opera reopened with the same production of Berlioz's *La Damnation de Faust* that was being staged when the house closed on June 5. It is not known whether Rouché made a point of picking a French composer for the first production, but *La Gerbe*'s music critic Louis Humbert applauded the decision as conciliatory. After all, he noted, Berlioz loved Germany and had been influenced by Beethoven, Weber and Glück when composing this opera based on Goethe's play. The production was followed by a reprise of Massenet's *Thaïs* and, somewhat oddly, in late October, by Beethoven's operatic ode to freedom *Fidelio*, with a German favorite, the French soprano Germaine Lubin, in the role of Leonora.

By the fall, the opera house was offering shows on Wednesday and Saturday evenings and Sunday afternoons. Its ballet company also returned to the stage under the direction of Serge Lifar, the dancer discovered by Diaghilev's Ballets Russes twenty years earlier. For the ballet's opening performance, on August 28, one-third of the seats were occupied by Germans, including Ambassador Abetz and General Otto von Stülpnagel, the German military commander. At the Opéra-Comique, another French opera, Messager's *La Basoche,* was chosen to open the season on August 22. Soon operetta, also much loved by the Germans, was being presented by several theaters, including the Châtelet, the Mogador and the Bouffes Parisiens. French instrumentalists and singers could entertain the German military elite without assuming political risks, so long as programs did not include music by Jewish composers. This was quickly made clear to Jean Wiener, a Jewish composer who presented himself at the Propaganda Staffel in the fall of 1940. A German officer told him, "If I don't see your dirty name on a poster, perhaps I will leave you in peace. Do you understand?" When Wiener recognized the man as a well-known German musicologist, the reply was rapid: "I don't know you. Get out!"[8]

Movie theaters, on the other hand, reopened immediately after the fall of Paris—no fewer than one hundred by early July. In the main, they showed French movies because of the German ban on British and American films, films made by Jewish directors and films starring Jewish or anti-Nazi actors. German-language films were screened in the Rex, Marignan and Paris theaters, now designated Deutsches Soldatenkino and open only to German soldiers. For French moviegoers, the main change was the end of double features. But French

moviemaking as such had stopped, not least because most top producers, directors and actors had fled Paris during the exodus and
were in no hurry to leave the Côte d'Azur.

Nine months earlier, the declaration of war had forced cancellation
of the inaugural Cannes Film Festival, but the resort was now once
again the informal capital of French cinema, with a trio of beautiful
young actresses—Danielle Darrieux, Micheline Presle and Michèle
Morgan—as its glamorous icons. "We were totally carefree," Darrieux recalled with some embarrassment decades later. "We'd have
our feet done, we'd go to the beauty parlor all the time. We were very
young, very pretty and fashionable stars, we didn't give a damn about
what was happening up north."[9] Darrieux and many other movie
celebrities spent the rest of 1940 at the Grand Hôtel, which the photographer Jacques-Henri Lartigue likened to "an ocean-liner immo-
bilized by the war." The hotel's manager was the father of Louis
Jourdan, the young screen idol who was now engaged to Presle. "It
was extraordinary," Presle recalled. "We'd meet the producers on the
terraces, we'd go out on boats for picnics on the islands. We were far
from the war. And then people began to leave, the producers, most of
the producers were Jewish."[10] A photograph taken on the beach that
summer shows Morgan and Darrieux sitting cheerfully on the knees
of the producer Gregor Rabinovitch, with a smiling Presle standing
behind them. "He was as happy as a king," Darrieux remembered.
He was also among the first Jewish producers to leave France.

The novelist and director Marcel Pagnol, who had his own studio
in Marseille, was one of few to resume work, completing his film *La
Fille du puisatier* (The Well Digger's Daughter), which had been
interrupted in May. And, in a move he would later regret, he added a
scene in which a family crowds around a radio, listening respectfully
to Pétain's armistice speech of June 17.* In the weeks that followed,
other low-budget films, mostly forgettable, also went into production in Marseille and Nice. But until early 1941, the studios in Paris
remained silent. And by then, the French industry had lost a number
of key players. Among those who used the excuse of job offers from
Hollywood to leave France were the directors Jean Renoir, René
Clair and Julien Duvivier and the actors Jean Gabin, Charles Boyer,
Michèle Morgan and Jean-Pierre Aumont. Of these, only Gabin and

---

*Although German censors had this scene removed when the movie was shown in
the occupied zone, its inclusion was later viewed as a collaborationist act.

Aumont would return before the end of the war, Gabin as a soldier in a tank unit participating in the liberation of France, Aumont as a soldier who fought with Allied forces in Italy before reaching France.

Cinema was also one of the art forms most directly affected by the Statute on Jews, the first major anti-Semitic measure of Pétain's Vichy regime, which was promulgated across all of France on October 3, 1940. The statute's purpose was far broader than a restriction on moviemaking. It excluded Jews—defined as anyone with three Jewish grandparents—from the government, the civil service, the judiciary, the armed forces, the press and the teaching profession. Those returning to work in these fields had to sign a document, as Simone de Beauvoir recalled: "At the Lycée Camille Sée—as in all the *lycées*—I was made to sign a paper where I swore under oath that I was not Jewish nor affiliated to Freemasonry; I thought it repugnant to sign, but no one refused: for most of my colleagues, as for myself, there was no way of doing otherwise."[11]

The only Jews allowed to hold on to their jobs were World War I veterans, holders of the Légion d'honneur and those who had rendered "exceptional services" to France in literature, science or art. A few university professors, like the historian Marc Bloch, successfully applied for this exemption, but it would bring them little protection later in the occupation. Almost immediately, there was also pressure to dismiss Jews from the Comédie Française and the Paris Opera, which, as national institutions, were considered to be extensions of the government. But cinema was the only cultural area to be singled out by the statute. Responding to constant prewar Fascist campaigning against Jewish "control" of the movie industry, specifically against the power of foreign Jewish producers, the statute ruled that Jews could not be producers, distributors or directors of movies or owners or managers of movie theaters.

The Statute on Jews did not, of course, come out of the blue. French anti-Semitism, which had grown in the 1930s from a right-wing obsession into a far wider sentiment, was boosted in June 1940 when Jews became one of several scapegoats for France's defeat. The charges now thrown at them by Fascists in Paris and Vichy were many: that even French Jews were not really French because they owed allegiance more to Judaism than to France; that foreign-born Jewish refugees, about one-third of France's 300,000-strong Jewish community, were fifth columnists; that Jews had pushed France into war with Germany; that Jews had infiltrated the government and the armed forces; that Jews had too much financial and cultural power in France.

Fearing the consequences of a German victory, most prominent French Jews had fled Paris by June 14, 1940, but they had left behind legions of impoverished eastern European Jews who had sought refuge in France and had nowhere to go (and would later become the principal victims of internments and deportations to Nazi death camps). In mid-July, Germany expelled almost 18,000 Jews from its newly annexed province of Alsace into the unoccupied zone. At the same time, having ordered all Jews to register with the French police, where their identity cards were stamped in large letters with the word *JUIF,* Vichy revoked the naturalization of more than 7,000 Jews who had become French citizens since 1927. It further canceled the French citizenship granted to Algerian Jews in 1870. Vichy even abrogated a 1939 law against the incitement of hatred so that anti-Semitic campaigning by the press was now authorized.

In reality, the collaborationist press needed little encouragement. Typically, the mass-circulation daily *Paris-Soir* welcomed the Statute on Jews with the headline "The Purification Begins"; the subhead explained, "JEWS AT LAST EXPELLED from all public jobs in the country." The article noted gleefully, "Foreign Israelites can be interned." One month later, collaborationist newspapers were applauding a new requirement that Jewish-owned shops identify themselves with a bilingual sign in the window; it would need to declare both *Jüdisches Geschäft* and *Entreprise Juive.* Vichy went on to do far worse, but the Statute of Jews illustrated the French government's willingness to take anti-Semitic measures of its own initiative and without German pressure. More ominously, it also signaled that Germany could count on Vichy's support in persecuting Jews.

In the summer and fall of 1940, though, while the campaign to "cleanse" French culture of Jewish influence was under way, Hitler and his air minister, Marshal Göring, had their eyes on more valuable jewels, those of the art collections of French Jewish collectors and dealers. On June 30, Hitler had already issued an order that all art in France, public and private, be "safeguarded" pending negotiations on a peace treaty. What this meant was unclear, with different arms of the Reich interpreting it to suit their own interests.

One German opponent of art seizures was a respected art historian, now a Wehrmacht lieutenant, Count Franz Wolff-Metternich, who headed the French branch of the Kunstschutz, the German army body charged with protecting art during military conflict. But while he and Jacques Jaujard, the director of French museums, insisted that the planned expropriations violated the 1907 Convention of The Hague, they faced far stronger forces. Otto Kümmel, the director of Berlin's museums, had already prepared a list of artworks central to German culture that were held abroad. That encouraged Goebbels to demand that France return any art "taken" from Germany since 1500, notably during the Napoleonic Wars. Acting on behalf of Ribbentrop's Foreign Ministry, Abetz tried to gain the initiative, hurriedly ordering the confiscation of art belonging to numerous Jewish collections and its transfer to the Hôtel de Beauharnais, the eighteenth-century mansion at 78 rue de Lille, on the Left Bank, which housed the German embassy. His argument was this art would serve as a surety against the reparations that France would be required to pay as part of an eventual peace treaty. The German military command, though, was reluctant to engage in banditry; at Metternich's insistence, it responded that the seizure of any art was illegal and refused to cooperate.

Then, on September 17, Abetz, Metternich and the army were overruled by Hitler: he gave responsibility for confiscating all art "formerly" owned by Jews* to the Einsatzstab Reichsleiter Rosenberg, or ERR, an office run by Alfred Rosenberg, the Nazi Party's chief ideologue. Initially, the looted art was stored in the Louvre, in three galleries of the Department of Eastern Antiquities, but this was soon overflowing. The nearby Jeu de Paume, a nineteenth-century gallery on the place de la Concorde, was then chosen to be the main transit camp for art being sent east. Although Abetz managed to hold on to scores of paintings, claiming they were to decorate the Foreign Ministry, he nonetheless had to watch as four hundred cases of artworks were transferred from the embassy to the Jeu de Paume.

Von Stülpnagel, the German army commander, was troubled. In a confidential letter to his commander in chief, he condemned the confiscation of Jewish-owned art as damaging to "the esteem" of the German state. "I myself am of the opinion that it ought to stop now," he said.[12] But the issue was out of his hands. The ERR's Special Staff for Pictorial Art, now charged with finding, collecting, cataloging and shipping off to Germany any art owned by Jews, was well

*On July 23 Vichy revoked the nationality of any French citizen who had fled France.

briefed on the collections to be targeted first. These included those of the Rothschild family, Alphonse Kann, the David-Weill family, Lévy de Benzion, Georges Wildenstein, the Seligmann family, Jacques Stern, Alfred Lindon and the art dealers Léonce and Paul Rosenberg. Most of these wealthy Jews had already fled, dispersing their collections in châteaus and hideaways around the country. In a few cases, it would take the ERR up to three years to find them.

The legal justification invented to cover this organized theft was that Jews were now "stateless," and therefore the art was "ownerless." Not satisfied with these princely seizures, the ERR then went after less well known Jewish-owned collections, which were traced, an ERR report later noted, in part through "the address lists of the French police authorities." These works, too, were stored in the Jeu de Paume. When Göring paid his first visit there on November 3, 1940, looking decidedly proprietorial in a broad-brimmed hat and vast overcoat, he was stunned by what he saw and what, in effect, he was being offered. For Göring's inspection, the Jeu de Paume had been arranged like a nineteenth-century museum, with hundreds of paintings covering the walls of two floors, plus a good many more displayed on racks. By the end of the year, Hitler had approved the first shipment of Jewish-owned art to enrich the collection of his planned museum in Linz, the Austrian city where he spent his childhood. The first thirty-two paintings, which were destined for Linz, came from the Rothschild collection and included Vermeer's *The Astronomer*. They were shipped in early February on a train owned by the Luftwaffe, which Göring had helpfully provided. Naturally, there was room for fifty-nine artworks chosen for Göring's own private museum at Carinhall.

The Paris art market, in the doldrums during the 1930s, was also revived by the occupation. Hôtel Drouot, the government-owned and Vichy-run auction house, resumed normal business on September 26, 1940, and, in response to the arrival of moneyed Germans benefiting from an artificial exchange rate,* Parisians began selling off paintings and art objects as never before. Jewish-owned galleries were quickly Aryanized or bought by Aryans following sequestration. The Bernheim-Jeune gallery was sold for a ridiculously low price to a renowned collaborationist. Kahnweiler, who was a Ger-

---

*In June 1940, the exchange rate went from 12 francs to 20 francs for every deutschmark, a 67 percent revaluation of the German currency.

man citizen, had already lost one gallery in World War I when French government auctioneers sold it as enemy property; now the dealer was being persecuted as a Jew, although he was able to "sell" his gallery to the writer Michel Leiris and his wife, Louise, who was Kahnweiler's sister-in-law. The André Weil Gallery was taken over by Louis Carré, while Wildenstein passed ownership of his gallery to his manager, Roger Dequoy. Emmanuel David was able to keep his gallery open, thanks to the protection of friends in the Propaganda Staffel.

These galleries also soon counted German officers and dealers among their clients. A few firms specialized in modern paintings that had been seized from Jewish families and that, declared "degenerate" by Hitler, proved of no interest to the Nazis. The market for more traditional French artists also flourished. In the fall, the Louis Carré gallery exhibited works by Matisse and Maillol, while in November, the Salon d'Automne at the Orangerie displayed works by French masters, from Renoir to Rodin. For this salon, living artists had to swear they were French but not Jewish. Other art fairs, such as the Salon des Indépendants and the Salon du Dessin et de la Peinture à l'Eau, soon followed.

Once again, the favored argument among the French was that France's cultural institutions should stay alive. On September 17, 1940, the Carnavalet and Cernuschi museums in Paris reopened. Then, after a ceremony on September 29 attended by Field Marshal Gerd von Rundstedt, who had led seven panzer divisions during the invasion of France, the Louvre reopened some of its sculpture galleries, although its painting galleries remained empty and closed. The museum was open for only five hours on Tuesdays, Thursdays and Saturdays and two hours on Sunday, with entry free for Germans. Most visitors were Wehrmacht soldiers and they could also buy a German-language guidebook; Metternich insisted on adding German-language signs telling them not to smoke and not to touch art objects. At the Orangerie, beside the place de la Concorde, where Monet's large-format *Nymphéas* (Water Lilies) frescoes remained, a retrospective of Monet and Rodin brought crowds.

The first strictly propagandistic exhibition, Franc-Maçonnerie dévoilée (Freemasonry Unveiled), targeted Freemasonry, which had been banned by Vichy in August 1940 as a "secret society." Abetz even claimed that 900,000 people visited the show, which opened at the Petit Palais in Paris in October 1940. It would be the first of several major propaganda exhibitions: France Européenne at the Grand Palais from June to October 1941 claimed 635,000 visitors; Le Juif et la France supposedly drew 155,000 people to the Palais Berlitz from September 1941 to January 1942; and, finally, Le Bolchevisme Contre l'Europe, which opened at the Salle Wagram in March 1942, boasted 370,000 visitors. After Paris, these exhibitions routinely toured other French cities.

In the world of publishing, the Nazis seemed inspired more by ideology than greed—and here, too, they found willing collaborators. While three Jewish-owned publishing houses, Calmann-Lévy, Nathan and Ferenczi, were soon Aryanized and renamed, other French publishers were eager to resume business. Among these, Bernard Grasset and Robert Denoël had shown where their sympathies lay in the 1930s by publishing right-wing authors, including, in Denoël's case, Céline's anti-Semitic tracts. Now Grasset and Denoël, both friends of Abetz's, were willing conduits for German literature entering France.

Other publishers also recognized the risk of being excluded. From his hideaway in the south of France, Gaston Gallimard feared that his publishing house's liberal record could make it a Nazi target. And, with the Germans already intervening in publishing, Gallimard's own authors encouraged him to return to Paris. As early as August, the occupation forces had issued the so-called Bernhard List of 143 books to be withdrawn from circulation; these included Jewish authors and anti-Nazi books. In September, when a further one thousand or so books were banned under the new "Otto List," the French publishers' association, the Syndicat des Éditeurs, offered to cooperate under the guise of keeping French culture alive. In an agreement signed with the Propaganda Staffel, the publishers pledged not to publish any book banned in France or Germany and to assume responsibility for any new books they would put out. The Syndicat noted, "Affected are books which, through their lying and tendentious spirit, have systematically poisoned French public opinion; particularly targeted are publications by political refugees and Jewish writers who, betraying the hospitality that France has offered them, have unscrupulously promoted a war which they hoped would benefit their egotistical aims."[13] For their part, the Nazis were happy: without self-censorship, they would have needed a small army of French-speaking experts to review thousands of manuscripts.

Gallimard made his own Faustian bargain with the German

embassy. Abetz is said to have remarked that France's three powers were banking, the Communist Party and the *Nouvelle Revue Française.* And he soon fixed his eyes on the prestigious literary and political journal, which had been founded by Gide, Copeau, the writer Jean Schlumberger and Gallimard himself in 1909. Since 1925, the *NRF,* as it was widely known, had been edited by Jean Paulhan, a position that automatically made him one of the most powerful figures in the Paris intelligentsia. In its traditional form, with its pages open to a broad range of political opinions, it was not acceptable to Abetz. But the German envoy was willing to allow it to resume publication if—and only if—it was edited by his friend Drieu La Rochelle. Without much hesitation, Gallimard agreed. With the journal's first postoccupation edition circulating in December 1940, Éditions Gallimard was not only back in business, but had also gained some freedom to publish books by authors not known for their Nazi sympathies.

Thirty years later, Sartre would say, "During the occupation, we had two choices: collaborate or resist."[14] In truth, the options—and dilemmas—facing individual artists were far more varied, as Sartre himself demonstrated. A few Jews, like the the playwright Bernstein, the novelist Maurois and the composer Milhaud, wasted no time in leaving France for the United States. In contrast, the writer Paul Morand and the historian Paul Hazard, who had just been elected to the Académie Française, chose to return to occupied France from abroad. Some viewed the defeat as resolving the problems of the 1930s rather than creating new ones. Paul Claudel, a diplomat, playwright and conservative, happily said good-bye to the Third Republic, which, he maintained, had devoured the country like a rampant cancer. In his diary entry for July 20, 1940, he lamented France's loss of independence but listed developments he considered positive. "Freedom after 60 years under the yoke of the radical and anti-Catholic party (teachers, lawyers, Jews, Freemasons). The new government calls on God and returns the Grande Chartreuse* to the monks. Hope to be released from universal suffrage and parliamentary rule as well as from the evil and idiotic domination by teachers who since the last war have covered themselves with shame. Restoration of authority."[15] In December 1940, he even penned an ode to

---

*The Grande Chartreuse is an isolated monastery in southeastern France that was closed by the government in 1903 and returned to the Carthusian order by Pétain.

Pétain with these instructive lines: "France, listen to this old man who cares for you / And talks to you like a father." Claudel, though, would be among many French citizens who changed their views. The young poet Claude Roy made a bigger leap, switching from L'Action Française to the Communist Party.

Writers who were in the unoccupied zone had the option of remaining there. As a high-profile Communist, Aragon wisely stayed in the south, although he later led intellectual resistance across the region. Similarly, Malraux, renowned as an anti-Fascist, did not leave the Côte d'Azur until he joined the armed resistance in early 1944. On the other hand, right-wingers like Drieu La Rochelle, who had also fled the fighting, were not unhappy with the outcome; some offered their services in Vichy, while the majority returned to Paris. Many moderates also made their way back to the capital, among them Mauriac, who initially believed—"despite everything," as he put it to the essayist Jean Guéhenno—that the French had no choice but to support Pétain. Although he would later join the resistance, in June 1941 he made the mistake of asking Epting to approve publication of his novel *La Pharisienne* and then petitioning Heller for extra paper for a second printing. In a dedicated copy of the book sent to Heller, Mauriac wrote, "To Lieut Heller, who took interest in the fate of *La Pharisienne*, with gratitude."[16] On the other hand, Cocteau, that artistic polymath and social butterfly, refused to stop being Cocteau. In August 1943, he noted in his journal, "At no price should one let oneself be distracted from serious matters by the dramatic frivolity of war."[17] He had unwaveringly followed this principle over the previous three years.

For almost everyone else, it was a period of great uncertainty. Saint-Exupéry, for instance, visited Pétain before deciding to leave France and, even in the United States, he had ambivalent feelings toward de Gaulle. Others felt a need to analyze the reasons for France's defeat, as the playwright Henry de Montherlant did in *Le Solstice de juin* from the safety of a café in Marseille. And at this stage, the commonplace, even among moderates, was that France's prewar decadence—decadence now becoming the scapegoat for all of the country's troubles—had invited defeat. The right, of course, had a more detailed list of culprits.

Gide, who stayed in the unoccupied zone until leaving for Tunisia in 1942, also tried to make sense of political events, although he did so in the privacy of his journal. And, somewhat typically, this quintessential man of letters wavered. He applauded Pétain's first speech and disapproved of another, one week later. He was impressed by the German victory, noting, "We have been prettily maneuvered, without even being aware of it, by Hitler, the sole master of the circus ring, whose sly and hidden smartness surpasses that of the great captains."[18] Almost echoing Pétain, he also saw France inviting its own defeat: "All my love for France could not keep me from being aware of our country's state of decay. To my constant awareness of that decay is merely added a great melancholy. It was obvious that that was leading us to the abyss."[19] At one moment, he regretted that he was far from the fray. "The 'intellectual' who aims first and foremost to take shelter loses a rare opportunity to learn something," he noted.[20] But he also had no yearning to be in Paris.

A few months later, he was still confused, writing, "My torment is even deeper: it comes likewise from the fact that I cannot decide with assurance that right is on this side and wrong on the other."[21] He added: "Oh, I should like to be left alone, to be forgotten! Free to think in my own way without its costing anyone anything and to express without constraint or fear of censure the oscillation of my thought."[22] On May 21, 1941, Gide was reminded that the French right included him among France's problems. The newly formed Légion Française des Combattants, or French Legion of Veterans, forced cancellation of a lecture on the poetry of Henri Michaux that Gide was scheduled to give in Nice. "I like being a 'victim' of the Legion," he later wrote. "I do not like the fact that it should be for so small a reason."[23] Yet, more than one year after the fall of France, Gide remained anguished: "Proud of being French. . . . Alas, for months, for years now, France has hardly given us any reason to be proud."[24]

Gide can perhaps be forgiven for offering pieces for the first and third issues of Drieu La Rochelle's *Nouvelle Revue Française,* since he subsequently recognized his error and broke his ties with the journal in an article in *Le Figaro.* But, in reality, with only a few exceptions, French writers seemed all too eager to continue publishing, even if that meant bowing to censorship.

One who refused to do so was Guéhenno. True, he did not need to publish to stay alive, since he had a job as a teacher in a Paris lycée. But, from the very beginning of the occupation, in contrast to the hesitations of, say, Gide and Mauriac about Pétain, Guéhenno never wavered. His *Journal des années noires* opens with his reaction to

Pétain's June 17 speech proposing an armistice. "There we are, it's over," he wrote in disgust, adding: "I will never believe that men are made for war. But I also know that they are not made for slavery."[25] Two days later, he heard de Gaulle's speech from London. "What joy in this ignoble disaster finally to hear a voice with some pride," he noted.[26] He returned to Paris from Clermont-Ferrand in early September and resumed teaching, but his gloom deepened. After the Statute on Jews was decreed, he wrote, "I am filled with shame."[27]

Guéhenno was far from cheered when the *Nouvelle Revue Française* announced Gide, Giono and Jouhandeau for its first issue and Valéry and Montherlant for its second. On November 30, 1940, he wrote, "The species of the man of letters is not one of the greatest of human species. Incapable of surviving for long in hiding, he would sell his soul to see his name in print. He can stand it no longer. He quarrels only about his importance, the size of the print in which his name appears, its ranking in the table of contents. It goes without saying that he is full of good reasons. 'French literature must continue.' He believes that he is French literature and thought and that they will die without him."[28] A few months later, Guéhenno even took a swipe at Gide: "A perhaps admirable desire to enrich himself, to improve himself, always leads him. But I cannot identify myself with this irresponsible life, one lacking all commitment. Everything for him is literature, an occasion for pleasure."[29]

One notably droll observer of the intellectual and political scene was Jean Galtier-Boissière, a journalist who founded the satirical weekly *Le Crapouillot* in 1915 while he was fighting in the trenches. In 1940, he refused to reopen the newspaper and tried to survive as a bookseller. Throughout the war, he kept a journal, later published as *Mon journal pendant l'occupation,* comprising a vivid mixture of anecdotes, encounters, rumors, jokes and throwaway lines. For instance, of General Weygand, the humbled French army commander, he quipped, *"Veni, Vidi, Vichy."* Then there was the chance meeting of a German and a Frenchman. The German: "You look very cheerful for being conquered." The Frenchman: "You look very sad for being the conqueror."

Since Galtier-Boissière knew many writers and artists, both collaborationists and *résistants,* his insights into that world are particularly telling. And, by his own account, he always spoke his mind, including his early conclusion that Germany would lose the war. Four months into the occupation, one guest at a dinner party in his apartment on the place de la Sorbonne was Drieu La Rochelle, who was full of praise for Ambassador Abetz. "Drieu is certain of the rapid German victory," Galtier-Boissière observed. "I tell him I expect a long war and an English victory. He shrugs his shoulders with a superior smile and treats me like a fool. 'My dear Drieu, I'll bet that you will be shot.' 'And you?' he asks. 'Me too! But in my case . . . by mistake.'"[30] Jokes at the expense of the Germans became his form of entertainment. "Hitler telephones Mussolini: 'Are you in Athens?' 'Sorry, I can't hear you well.' 'I asked if your troops have reached Athens?' 'I hear you very badly, my dear Adolphe, you must be calling from far away . . . perhaps London?'"[31]

Most writers, then, went ahead and published books and plays, while some moderates and a few who were later identified with the resistance wrote for daily and weekly newspapers and journals, both in Paris and in the unoccupied zone. Yet even if they wrote articles about culture in, say, *La Gerbe,* they risked having their names appear alongside anti-Semitic diatribes. *Comoedia,* another literary-political weekly, was perhaps the only place in the occupied zone where noncollaborationist writers could appear unscathed, although there were more outlets in the unoccupied zone, including several literary journals and, notably, the literary supplement of *Le Figaro,* which had moved to Lyon.

For the most part, though, the Paris press served as mouthpieces for the Germans in exchange for subsidies from the German embassy. Some dailies had huge circulations: *Le Matin,* which reappeared on June 17, was soon selling over half a million copies daily; *Le Petit Parisien* close to 700,000; and *Paris-Soir* almost one million. The Nazis were also intent on obtaining or influencing ownership of the printed media, with the German embassy and the Propaganda Abteilung competing for control. Eugène Gerber, the editor of *Paris-Soir,* was backed by the Propaganda Abteilung in expanding his empire to include several popular women's weeklies, including *Pour Elle* and *Notre Coeur.* Jean Luchaire, Abetz's friend from the 1930s, brought out a new daily, *Les Nouveaux Temps,* and later headed the Association de la Presse Parisienne. Abetz also supported the German businessman Gerhard Hibbelen, who took over the Jewish-owned Société Parisienne d'Édition and built up a press group that included fifty newspapers around France.

Further, both Abetz and the Propaganda Abteilung subsidized smaller dailies and weeklies that made a point of denouncing known or suspected Jews, among them *Gringoire, L'Appel* and the particularly vile *Au Pilori. Aujourd'hui* demonstrated that no other path was available: initially it was edited by Henri Jeanson, a respected journalist who thought that an independent newspaper was possible; in December 1940, he was replaced by Georges Suarez, such an avowed collaborator that he was shot soon after the liberation. Others, like *L'Oeuvre, Le Cri du Peuple* and *Le Réveil du Peuple,* were organs of French Fascist parties and took delight in demanding that Vichy support Germany more enthusiastically.

The flag carrier of the collaborationist press, though, was the much-feared weekly *Je suis partout,* which had been founded in 1930 and became openly Fascist and anti-Semitic starting in the mid-1930s. Robert Brasillach, its editor in chief since 1937, was released from a prisoner-of-war camp in April 1941 to return to his post. Initially pro-Vichy, *Je suis partout* joined in verbally lynching the former prime ministers Blum, Daladier and Reynaud as responsible for France's humiliation. As the occupation advanced, however, *Je suis partout* embraced all the Nazi causes and, most infamously, used its pages to denounce individual Communists and to identify prominent Jews who were hiding in the unoccupied zone. At the same time, the weekly provided extensive coverage of the arts, although its theater critic Alain Laubreaux and its music critic Lucien Rebatet often preferred the roles of inquisitors, quick to identify their every enemy as tools of international Judaism. In this, they enjoyed considerable independence, even excoriating celebrities like Guitry and Cocteau who were on good terms with Abetz and the German Institute.

In the early months of the occupation, of course, Fascist writers and journalists faced no intellectual opposition. With the Communist Party neutralized by the Molotov-Ribbentrop Pact of August 1939, only a few intellectuals dared imagine resistance. This in turn underlined the importance of the first open expression of revolt. On November 11, 1940, high school and university students marked the anniversary of France's victory in World War I by trying to march to the Tomb of the Unknown Soldier at the Arc de Triomphe. Jorge Semprun, a Spanish-born writer who later joined the resistance and ended up in Buchenwald, was just sixteen at the time. "We got to the place de la Concorde without much trouble," he recalled. "Around the Rond-Point of the Champs-Élysées, there were several hundred of us, there were some posters and shouts. Then the French police blocked the avenue. Along the avenue George V, armed German troops appeared and the demonstration broke up quickly. I managed to escape into the George V *métro* station."[32] Françoise Gilot, who later became Picasso's mistress, was less lucky. A nineteen-year-old law student at the time, she cycled from her home in Neuilly to join the demonstration, but was caught by the French police. "They took our names," she recalled. "Some of the students were jailed for a few days. I was sent home. But after that, until my father managed to get my name off the list, I had to go daily to the Kommandantur in Neuilly to sign my name. I became a kind of hostage."[33] The German military command closed the Sorbonne until December 20.

These courageous youngsters were exceptions. Most Parisians had accepted the reality of the occupation and were following Pétain's counsel that collaboration with Germany was best for France. In late October, Hitler traveled to Hendaye, on France's border with Spain, for talks with Generalísimo Franco. On his way south, he stopped at Montoire, in the Loire Valley, for a meeting with Laval, who was also Vichy's foreign minister. On October 24, returning home, Hitler stopped again at Montoire for his only meeting with Pétain. Six days later, in a radio broadcast, Pétain told the French: "It is with honor and to maintain French unity — a unity dating back ten centuries — in the context of the active construction of the new European order that I enter today on the path of collaboration." He said this offered the hope of alleviating the suffering of the French, improving the conditions of French prisoners of war, reducing the cost of the occupation and facilitating movement across the demarcation line. He concluded by stressing that he had taken this decision entirely by himself. "It is I alone whom history will judge. Until now, I have spoken to you as a father. I speak to you today as your leader. Follow me. Remain confident in eternal France." With "collaboration" still not a dirty word, it became an acceptable response to the occupation, although not to Galtier-Boissière. "Collaboration is: give me your watch and I'll tell you the time," he quipped.[34] But for the most part, as the historian Henri Amouroux later put it, the French had become "forty million *pétainistes.*"

Yet as Pétain defined collaboration, it was of little interest to the Nazis. Hitler's one gesture of reconciliation was to order the transfer of the remains of Napoleon's son, the duke of Reichstadt, known as L'Aiglon, from Vienna to Les Invalides in December 1940. "A big brouhaha over the return of the ashes of Napoleon II," Galtier-Boissière wrote in his journal on December 15, 1940. " 'A chivalrous

act by the Führer.' But disrespectful Parisians say they would prefer
coal to ashes."[35] In reality, it was amply clear that Hitler had no
intention of "rewarding" Pétain with a peace treaty, if for no other
reason than that the very idea of punishing France—for the reparations it had extracted after World War I, for its defeat in 1940, for its
arrogance—was popular in Germany. Instead, simply by keeping
alive the idea of a peace treaty, Berlin obtained all the collaboration it
needed: Vichy's cooperation in sending French raw materials, industrial products and workers to Germany and, before long, in rounding up Jews for deportation.

Pétain's last chance of negotiating a less arduous collaboration was
in the June 22 armistice. But with most French desperate for a cease-
fire, Pétain's hand was too weak. Among the German demands
accepted by Vichy, one in particular terrified the large community of
German and Austrian exiles in France, many of them writers and
university professors, most of them Jews: Article 19 committed
France to hand over any subject of the Reich requested by Germany.
Those *étrangers nondésirables* who had just escaped from internment
camps knew they had to leave France as soon as possible. Their
options were limited: to seek asylum in Switzerland (although it was
unclear if Germany would respect Swiss neutrality); to cross the
Pyrenees into Franco's Spain and then continue on to neutral Portugal and beyond; to scramble aboard a boat heading for North Africa;
or to find a country willing to accept them and obtain a Vichy exit
permit. Hiding out in third-rate hotels along a stretch of the Mediterranean between Marseille and Nice, these fugitives from injustice felt
their despair mount. Then, quite unexpectedly, a glimmer of hope
appeared. On June 25, the very day the armistice went into effect, an
Emergency Rescue Committee was formed in New York with the
mission of bringing leading writers and artists to the United States.
The man charged with organizing this was a dapper Harvard graduate and literary journalist by the name of Varian Fry. For many, he
would be their unlikely savior.

· CHAPTER 4 ·

L'Américain

FRY WAS just thirty-two when he arrived in Marseille on August 14, 1940, with the names of some two hundred prominent cultural figures and $3,000 strapped to his legs. His motivation was touchingly straightforward, as he wrote after the war in his memoir *Surrender on Demand:** "I knew that among those trapped in France were many writers, artists and musicians whose work had given me much pleasure. I didn't know them personally, but I felt a deep love for these people and gratitude for the many hours of happiness their books and pictures and music had given me. Now they were in danger. It was my duty to help them, just as they—without knowing it— had often helped me in the past." Having visited Berlin in 1935 and having personally witnessed the beating of two elderly Jews, he knew that the threat to these artists was real. He volunteered to use

---

*First published in 1946, this autobiography was also later issued as *Assignment Rescue.*

his vacation time to evacuate them. He thought the job could be done in one month.

Fry at least had reason to believe he enjoyed strong backing at home. The list of names in his pocket had been drawn up by the Emergency Rescue Committee with the help of the exiled writers Thomas Mann and Jules Romains, the theologian Jacques Maritain and Alfred H. Barr Jr., the director of the Museum of Modern Art in New York. Further, Eleanor Roosevelt, the American First Lady who was never slow to defend human rights, had pressed the State Department to grant "emergency visas" to these gifted refugees. But once Fry had crossed Portugal and Spain and had finally reached Marseille, things looked a good deal bleaker. Although fluent in French and German, he had no connections. His instructions were to "save" two hundred people. "But how was I to do it?" he wondered. "How was I to get in touch with them? What could I do for them once I had found them? Now that I was in Marseille, I suddenly realized that I had no idea how to begin—or where."[1]

Remarkably, things fell into place quite quickly. Fry's first contact was Frank Bohn, who had been sent to Marseille by the American Federation of Labor to rescue fugitive European labor leaders. And Bohn already knew how to get people out of France. If they had an overseas visa, they could usually obtain a transit visa through Spain to neutral Portugal and perhaps even a French exit visa, which would allow them to leave France legally. In the early weeks after France's defeat, some people were also given permission to leave by ship for North Africa. This was the ideal arrangement. Others traveled clandestinely to the Spanish border and managed to cross Spain into Portugal without proper documents. There was also the option of using fake passports and visas available at a price in Marseille. In the case of renowned refugees, however, the use of falsified papers increased the risk of their being arrested and ending up in the hands of the Gestapo. Still, Fry now knew what was involved. Through Bohn, he found a room in the Hôtel Splendide on the boulevard d'Athènes and began sending letters to those refugees with known addresses.

Within a week, word spread along the Côte d'Azur that an American with cash in his pockets and visas at the ready had arrived in Marseille, "like an angel from heaven," as Fry put it.[2] His presence was even mentioned in two local newspapers, *Le Petit Provençal* and *Le Petit Marseillais,* bringing streams of refugees to the Hôtel Splendide and prompting the local police to summon him for questioning.

Fry's cover was a letter from the International YMCA saying he had come to help refugees obtain overseas visas and to give them some money to live on. But he now knew he was being watched, and he worried about leaving incriminating documents in his room, lest they be seized in a police raid. His one shield was that he was an American; the United States had recognized the Vichy regime and was not yet at war with Germany. What Fry—and the French authorities—soon learned, however, was that the American consul general in Marseille, Hugh S. Fullerton, strongly disapproved of his activities.

Help came from a motley group of American do-gooders, European refugees and French volunteers, among them Miriam Davenport, an art student in Paris who had befriended the fugitive German poet Walter Mehring on her flight south; Mary Jayne Gold, a wealthy playgirl who was both generous and flighty; Charles Fawcett, an artist-cum-adventurer; Albert O. Hirschman, a fearless German Jewish anti-Fascist and, later, a distinguished American economist, whom Fry nicknamed "Beamish"; an elegant Austrian, Franz von Hildebrand, who spoke English with an Oxford accent; Lena Fishman, a Polish Jew who became Fry's secretary; Daniel Bénédite, a leftist French Protestant, who would take over the operation after Fry's expulsion from France in September 1941; and several others who were themselves refugees. A young American vice consul, Hiram Bingham IV, also surreptitiously provided Fry with visas and travel documents for fugitives, until his disapproving boss moved him out of the visa section in the spring of 1941.

The Marseille of Fry's early months was bustling with cultural life. The government radio network, Radiodiffusion Nationale, had moved there, along with its orchestra and a small army of actors to perform its radio plays. Artists as varied as the composers Reynaldo Hahn and Paul Paray, Josephine Baker and the movie director Pagnol were working there. The Spanish cellist Pablo Casals, who had decided not to leave France, began giving concerts in Marseille and continued to do across the south until late 1942, when the Germans took over the unoccupied zone. The literary journal *Les Cahiers du Sud* resumed publication and, even though it was subject to Vichy censorship, it published many anti-Fascist writers. For a while, it even served as an informal hostel for refugee writers, with its offices, on many evenings, turned into dormitories. Theater activity resumed, the opera house reopened and an unknown singer called Yves Montand had his stage debut. So many middle-class and wealthy Parisian Jews had gone there during the exodus—and stayed—that the anti-Semitic writer Lucien Rebatet renamed the city Marseille la Juive—Marseille the Jewess.

For Fry, however, it was also a no-man's-land of Gestapo spies, corrupt French police and refugees galore—perhaps as many as 150,000 out of a population of 650,000. It was a place where exiles might be exchanging gossip in a port café one day and hiding in fear of arrest the next, where Chinese visas and fake Polish and Czech passports were for sale, where British soldiers who had missed the Dunkirk evacuation were trying to bribe their way onto ships heading to North Africa, where it was even possible to send and receive mail from abroad. France was defeated and Vichy officially governed the unoccupied zone, but Marseille remained something of a safe haven for German and Austrian artists and intellectuals who were Article 19 targets for arrest and deportation to the Reich.

Some independent lawyers helped Fry obtain visas and safe conducts through official channels. Fry also knew a few police officers who were willing to challenge or ignore the new rules. And when all else failed, he tapped the shadier sides of Marseille. He and his team were soon at home in this netherworld. At one point, Fry agreed to serve as a secret agent for London in order to facilitate the escape of British soldiers. On another occasion, his team turned for help to Corsican gangsters who, Fry noted, were also involved in "white slavery, black market dealings and smuggling dope."[3] Fry and Beamish quickly learned the ways of spies: they would send messages to New York hidden inside tubes of toothpaste carried by refugees who had permission to leave France legally. Every means was justified in order to save lives.

Fry's memoir reveals his anxieties and disappointments, but to outsiders he invariably seemed reassuringly calm. "There was in him a delightful mixture of earnest resolve and of wit, of methodical, almost formal demeanour and playfulness," Hirschman recalled long after Fry's death in 1967. "His sartorial elegance (his hallmark was a striped dark suit with bow tie), together with his poker face, were tremendous assets to him in dealing with the authorities."[4] Indeed, since Fry feigned working strictly within the law, he never hesitated in demanding that French officials rectify their assorted illegal acts. At the same time, he felt burdened by his inability to help everyone. He quickly decided to go beyond his initial two hundred names since some on the list had already left France and a few, like Willi Münzenberg, were dead.

To manage the escalating demand for his services, in October Fry moved his operation to larger quarters at 60 rue Grignan and formalized it as the Centre Américain de Secours. By May 1941, he had received letters from 15,000 refugees and had taken on 1,800 cases, representing 4,000 people. Further, there were still refugees interned in the nearby Camp des Milles and other camps in the unoccupied zone. Just those gathered in Marseille represented extraordinary talent. "In our ranks are enough doctors, psychologists, engineers, educationalists, poets, painters, writers, musicians, economists and public men to vitalize a whole great country," noted Victor Serge, the former Communist writer who was now on the run from both Moscow and Berlin. "Our wretchedness contains as much talent and expertise as Paris could summon in the days of her prime; and nothing of it is visible, only hunted, terribly tired men at the limit of their nervous resources."[5]

By the end of 1940, Fry and his team were channeling refugees out of France at an impressive rate. Some escapees were young and willing to take risks; others were old, weak and, occasionally, a tad self-important. Fry himself, for instance, traveled as far as Lisbon with Heinrich Mann, his wife and his nephew Golo, as well as the German novelist Franz Werfel and his wife, Alma Mahler-Werfel, who was carrying scores belonging to her late husband, Gustav Mahler. One frequent guide was Dina Vierny, the twenty-one-year-old muse and model of the sculptor Aristide Maillol, almost sixty years her senior. She would wait in a red dress near the Banyuls-sur-Mer railroad station, close to France's border with Spain, and lead refugees—first those sent by Frank Bohn, then those dispatched by Fry—along secret mountain paths to safety. Vierny herself was a Russian-born Jew (as well as a Trotskyist sympathizer) and, as such, vulnerable to Vichy's decree of October 4 ordering that all foreign-born Jews be interned or placed under house arrest. In 1941, she was detained by French police in Banyuls-sur-Mer, but Maillol obtained her release and sent her to pose for Bonnard and Matisse on the Riviera to distance her from the border. When she returned, she resumed her clandestine work. Every ten days or so, she would travel to Marseille to coordinate her activities with Fry and his team.

Hans and Lisa Fittko were not members of Fry's committee but proved immensely brave and useful allies. Fugitives from Nazi Germany, both had been interned during the phony war, Hans at Vernuche, where Walter Benjamin was also held, and Lisa at Gurs, where Benjamin's sister, Dora, had been sent. In June 1940, the Fittkos managed to escape and, after meeting up again in Marseille, Lisa traveled to Banyuls-sur-Mer to explore ways of leaving France overland. By good fortune, the town's mayor, Vincent Azéma, an anti-Fascist, showed her the best route over the Pyrenees. For the next eight months, until they were themselves forced to flee in April 1941, the Fittkos led over one hundred refugees into Spain without anyone being caught.

However, one early flight ended tragically, albeit through no fault of their own. Hans asked Lisa to lead Benjamin into Spain and, on the morning of September 25, 1940, accompanied by two other refugees, Henny Gurland and her teenage son Joseph, the group set off to check their intended route. Although only forty-eight, Benjamin was soon exhausted and, when the time came to return to Banyuls-sur-Mer for the night, the philosopher insisted on sleeping on the ground where they had stopped. The following morning, Lisa and the others rejoined Benjamin and, taking turns in carrying his heavy black briefcase, they eventually crossed into Spain. With the Spanish fishing village of Portbou now within sight, Lisa began her long walk back to Banyuls-sur-Mer. When Benjamin and the others reached Portbou, however, they were refused official entry into Spain, although they were allowed to spend the night in a local hotel. Depressed and despairing of ever escaping, Benjamin apparently took an overdose of morphine and died the following morning. Before losing consciousness, he gave a note to Henny Gurland, which she memorized before destroying. As she later recounted, it said: "In a situation presenting no way out, I have no other choice but to make an end of it. It is in a small village in the Pyrenees, where no one knows me, where my life will come to an end."[6]

Not everyone on Fry's list was eager to leave. Fry went to see Gide and his daughter Catherine* at Cabris, near Cannes, and his offer of assistance was turned down. Fry learned that the writer was being wooed by the Nazis but was refusing to collaborate. "He knew the

---

*Although a homosexual who apparently never consummated his 1894 marriage to his cousin Madeleine, in 1923 Gide fathered a child, Catherine, with Élisabeth van Rysselberghe, the daughter of his confidante, Maria van Rysselberghe, widely known as La Petite Dame.

possible consequences of his decision," Fry later wrote. "He nevertheless refused to leave France. It was his home, and he was determined to stay."[7] (Gide did, in fact, move to Tunisia in May 1942.) Fry
traveled to see Matisse at his studio at Cimiez, overlooking Nice, and
also failed to persuade him to leave France. A similar answer came
from Malraux, who was living with his mistress, Josette Clotis, and
their baby at Villa La Souco in Roquebrune-Cap-Martin, overlooking the Mediterranean near the Italian border. Malraux reiterated his
anti-Nazi and anti-Vichy views but chose to stay in France; Fry did,
however, give him some money and later managed to send him
American royalties for *Man's Fate,* the English translation of *La
Condition humaine.*

Gide, Matisse and Malraux were, of course, French and were not
Jewish. Writers and artists who were German and/or Jewish had
strong reasons to leave France. One who refused to do so, however,
was Gertrude Stein, that stern matriarch of American expatriate writers. She and her companion, Alice B. Toklas, both Jews, had spent the
summer of 1939 in their house in Bilignin, a village in a region east of
Lyon called Bugey, which had been their favorite retreat for the previous fifteen years. When war was declared, they made a quick trip to
Paris to collect warm clothes as well as Cézanne's portrait of his wife
and Picasso's portrait of Stein, but they did not return to the capital
until after its liberation. They survived the occupation relatively
untroubled. Before the United States entered the war, in December
1941, the Germans did not consider them "enemy aliens," while their
village was in the unoccupied zone until a year later. Further, Stein
was a strong anti-Communist who never hid her admiration for
Pétain. And she had at least one friend in a high place: her French
translator, Bernard Faÿ, a specialist in American studies, was named
by Vichy as director of the Bibliothèque Nationale in place of a
respected Jew, Julien Cain.

In 1941, Faÿ and Stein agreed to publish a selection of Pétain's
speeches in English in the United States, for which Stein wrote a
preface, comparing Pétain with George Washington as "first in war,
first in peace and first in the hearts of his countrymen." No doubt to
her later relief, the project sank when the United States joined the
Allies. After the war, during his trial for collaboration, Faÿ claimed
that he protected Stein and Toklas from arrest and prevented the
Germans from seizing the art remaining in their new apartment at
5 rue Christine in Paris. Still, the occupation was not without hardship

for the two women, who had to walk to distant villages to buy food on the black market. At one point, they also received a message telling them to flee to Switzerland. "No, I said," Stein recalled in *Wars I Have Seen,* "they are always trying to get us to leave France, but here we are and here we stay."[8]

Samuel Beckett also chose to remain in France; or, rather, he returned to Paris in late 1939, reportedly saying he preferred "France at war to Ireland at peace." As a citizen of neutral Ireland, he enjoyed some degree of protection, but he detested the Nazis and decided to join the exodus of Parisians heading south. Having briefly considered leaving for Ireland, he was also part of the mass return to Paris. Soon, he and his companion, Suzanne Dechevaux-Dumesnil, were involved with the resistance, Beckett translating intelligence reports into English for dispatch to London, Suzanne as a messenger. By the summer of 1942, fearing arrest, they had gone into hiding; after obtaining false papers, they left Paris by train for Lyon. From there, they walked to Roussillon, north of Aix-en-Provence, where Beckett worked on a farm and eventually participated in resistance actions with the local maquis.

That other famous Irishman, James Joyce, was already ailing in 1940 and, while he fled Paris ahead of the Germans, he was then stuck for months in eastern France before being allowed to enter Switzerland; he finally reached Zurich, but he died there in January 1941. Two British writers had different responses to the German invasion. Somerset Maugham, long a resident of the Riviera, left France almost immediately for the United States. But P. G. Wodehouse and his wife, Ethel, who were living in Le Touquet on the Channel coast, were interned as enemy aliens. In June 1941, the writer was released from a camp in Germany and taken to Berlin, where he made five broadcasts, which, while jovial and anecdotal, prompted outrage in Britain. In 1943, the Wodehouses were allowed to return to Paris, and they remained there until the liberation. In a subsequent investigation, Wodehouse was found to have acted more foolishly than treacherously, but he was non grata in Britain and spent the rest of his life in New York.

Simone Weil was among the more unusual refugees, even by the eccentric standards set by many fugitives. Born into an agnostic Jewish family, with a brilliant mathematician for a brother, Simone proclaimed herself a Bolshevik at the age of ten. Like many of France's brightest students, she attended the École Normale Supérieure in

Paris in her late teens. And she remained true to her radical beliefs. After graduating, she combined teaching philosophy with doing manual labor, as a way of sharing the lives of workers. By the mid-1930s, she had begun to lose faith in Communism and turned toward Anarchism and Syndicalism.* She even traveled to Spain to offer her services to the Republican cause, but was too nearsighted to be useful. Then, in 1937, she had a mystical experience in the chapel of Saint Francis of Assisi in Assisi and, soon afterward, embraced Christianity, although she was not baptized. When Paris fell, she and her family fled south, where she continued writing, now increasingly on questions of faith. She acquired false papers under the name of Simone Werlin, but apparently made no effort to contact Fry. Eventually, she and her family left by ship from Marseille and reached New York in June 1942. Almost immediately, however, Weil began planning to go to Britain to be closer to France. At the end of that year, she reached London and found work with de Gaulle's Free French Forces. Suffering from tuberculosis and refusing food or medical treatment, she was thirty-four when she died in Ashford, on August 24, 1943. Almost all the philosophic writings that later brought her renown were published posthumously.

Most prominent refugees had nowhere to turn for help except Fry. Among German Jews led to safety through Spain were the Nobel laureate in medicine Otto Meyerhof, the psychiatrist Bruno Strauss and the writers Lion Feuchtwanger, Hannah Arendt and Konrad Heiden, who was Hitler's biographer. And among Jewish musicians who escaped thanks to Fry's organization, the harpsichordist Wanda Landowska and the pianist Heinz Jolles were the best known.

Mehring, Miriam Davenport's poet protégé and a vocal anti-Nazi, had several frights before he left France. He had a permit to cross Spain but worried that he might be recognized and turned over to the Gestapo. Fry's answer was to give him a false Czech passport, persuaded that Mehring looked far too scruffy to be taken for a distin-

---

*It was in the Weil family apartment beside the Luxembourg Gardens on December 30, 1933, that Trotsky presided over the founding meeting—a preconference, he called it—of the Fourth International, which was formally created in June 1936. As Adolf Holl recounts in *The Left Hand of God,* in July 1936, in a letter to Victor Serge, Trotsky said he had known Simone well: "For a period of time she was more or less in sympathy with our cause, but then she lost faith in the proletariat and in Marxism. It is possible that she will turn toward the left again."

guished poet. "In fact, he was so small that we called him *Baby*," Fry
recalled. "He had only one soiled, unpressed suit, the same one he
was wearing when he arrived in Marseille. He looked more like a
tramp than a poet—or a baby."9 Mehring never reached Spain. At
the French border, he was arrested and sent to the nearby Camp
Saint-Cyprien. Somehow Fry obtained his release, but the terrified
Mehring then refused to leave Fry's room in the Hôtel Splendide,
claiming illness. Finally, Fry found him a place on a ship leaving Marseille. As he was embarking, Mehring went before a French police
official who drew out a folder that listed his name beside a prohibition for him to leave France. The official withdrew to consult, then
returned and announced laconically that there must be two Walter
Mehrings—and approved the poet's departure.

Jacques Schiffrin, the Russian-born Jewish publisher who accompanied Gide on his Soviet tour in 1936, was no less eager to escape
the Nazis. As a man totally integrated into the Parisian literary scene,
he also had good reason to expect support from his peers. In 1923, he
founded the Éditions de la Pléiade to publish Russian classics in
French; eight years later he added modern French classics to what
was renamed La Bibliothèque de la Pléiade. In 1933, with Schiffrin in
financial difficulties, the Pléiade series was absorbed into Éditions
Gallimard, but it remained a prestigious imprint. Schiffrin's role in
creating it, however, was soon forgotten.

In the summer of 1940, Schiffrin moved his family to Saint-Tropez
after German officers occupied their Paris apartment. Then, in November, he received a curt letter from Gaston Gallimard informing
him that he was being separated from his job as editor of the Pléiade
series. Gallimard lacked the courage to give the real reason—that
Schiffrin was Jewish—and instead said it was because of a reorgani-
zation "along new lines of our publishing house."10 But Schiffrin's
friends in New York had ensured that his name was on Fry's list.
Finally, on May 6, 1941, he learned that he and his family could travel
on a ship from Marseille to Casablanca on May 15. In a letter to Gide
five days later, he described the kind of uncertainty lived by most
refugees: "Since arriving in Marseille, we have undergone a new kind
of torture. Arrangements are made and then unmade in the same day.
That is, once we have gotten all the necessary papers, visas, tickets,
passports, etc., the next step fails and all is lost. To save what seems
lost forever, I drag myself through the streets in the hope that I will
meet someone who knows someone."11 When the Schiffrins reached

Casablanca, they were interned by the Vichy government; they finally made it to New York more than three months after leaving Marseille.

The Surrealists were perhaps the most visible group of artists in Marseille, creating something of a world of their own in a crumbling mansion called Villa Air-Bel, outside the city. Bénédite had found it while looking for a place where Fry could escape the twenty-four-hour pressure of living in downtown Marseille. With its eighteen bed-rooms, once-elegant salons and big kitchen, Villa Air-Bel proved ideal. In October 1940, Fry was joined there by some of his team— Bénédite and his wife, Mary Jayne Gold and Miriam Davenport—as well as by Serge. The most prominent guest, though, was André Bre-ton, who arrived with his wife, Jacqueline Lamba, and their daughter, Aube. As a result, in the months that followed, Villa Air-Bel was turned into something of a Surrealist commune, with Breton as the presiding guru. "They were having a good time," according to Stéphane Hessel, who spent time in Air-Bel before joining the Free French Forces in London, "but at the same time they were frightened. Fright is an incentive to the good life: enjoy life while you can."[12]

Early in December 1940, their lives were disrupted when French police set about searching the house and triumphantly discovered an old pistol belonging to Breton. As it happens, Fry and the others had already heard that Pétain was planning an official visit to Marseille, and Hirschman had responded accordingly. "I always make it a prac-tice to clear out when the head of a Fascist state comes to town," he told Fry.[13] But the rest of them, plus some visitors, were at Villa Air-Bel when the police arrived, and it was soon apparent that they would be detained. By nightfall, along with some 570 other *nondési-rables,* they were placed in the hold of the S.S. *Sinaïa,* a cargo vessel docked in the port of Marseille. After two uncomfortable nights, Fry and Gold sent a letter to the captain reminding him that he was hold-ing two Americans illegally. The captain promptly invited them to his cabin, apologized profusely and, blaming Vichy for turning his ship into a prison, offered them each a glass of cognac.

Finally, on the fourth day of their detention, Fry and his team were freed. One gauge of the number of refugees in Marseille in late 1940 is that it required four ships, four forts and three movie the-aters, as well as regular jails and prisons, to accommodate them all. One of these briefly detained was a bookseller: in his display win-dow, he had placed photographs of Pétain and Admiral François

Darlan on either side of a copy of Hugo's *Les Misérables.* "In all, twenty thousand people had been arrested," Fry noted dryly. "The Marshal's visit had been a huge success."[14]

With the Surrealists still awaiting their visas, Villa Air-Bel kept drawing curious visitors, many of them from Breton's own circle of artists and poets, among them Wilfredo Lam, André Masson, Max Ernst, Jacques Lipchitz, Benjamin Péret, Remedios Varo, Roberto Matta, Jean Arp and Marcel Duchamp, all of whom would eventually leave France. "Many Surrealists would come there every day and we cheated the anxieties of the hour as best we could," Breton later wrote.[15] For example, he organized debates and put the artists to work on collective drawings; one elaborate set of playing cards changed the traditional four suits to Love, Dream, Revolution and Knowledge. Many of the gatherings were photographed; one series of pictures shows an outdoor exhibition of Ernst's recent work, which Saint-Exupéry's wife, Consuelo, helped him hang on trees. "The entire Deux Magots crowd came, and they were mad as ever,"[16] Fry later wrote, singling out with amusement Oscar Domínguez's "fat and elderly, but rich, French girlfriend"; Péret's poems, which resembled writings on the walls of public toilets; and the one-eyed Romanian painter Victor Brauner, whose women and cats also had only one eye. "André [Breton] would get out his collection of old magazines, colored papers, pastel chalks, scissors and pastepots and everybody would make montages," Fry went on. "At the end of the evening, André would decide who had done the best work, crying *Formidable! Sensationnel!* or *Invraisemblable!* at each drawing, montage or cut."[17]

Another visitor to the villa was Peggy Guggenheim. After she fled Paris on June 11, she rented a house on Lac d'Annecy, east of Lyon, where she also sheltered the German-born artist Jean Arp and his Jewish wife, the painter Sophie Taeuber. While preparing to ship her newly acquired art collection from Grenoble to New York, she was asked to pay the ship fare to the United States for Breton's family, Ernst and Pierre Mabille, the Surrealists' doctor. She agreed to do so for the Bretons and Max Ernst, then typically requested a painting from Ernst in exchange. With her friend Victor Brauner also in need of help, Peggy decided to visit Villa Air-Bel. But she was so disturbed by the threatening mood of Marseille that, after giving Breton and Fry some money, she rushed back to Grenoble. By the time she returned to Villa Air-Bel many weeks later, the Bretons, Serge, Lam, Masson, the writer Anna Seghers and the anthropologist Claude

Lévi-Strauss were safely on board a crowded ship en route to the Caribbean. But Peggy found one consolation: Ernst was still in residence and, in the course of trying to extract more paintings from him, she seduced him. As she recollected later, "Soon I discovered that I was in love with him."[18]

The weeks that followed brought danger and melodrama. Beginning to feel at risk as a Jew, Peggy started making plans to leave France, but she also wanted to take her new lover. On several occasions, she accompanied Ernst to the American consulate in Marseille in the hope that the Guggenheim name would impress. In the end, help came from the Museum of Modern Art in New York, where Ernst's son was working. In an affidavit, Alfred Barr testified to Ernst's "active dislike of all totalitarian forms of government," and an emergency visa was finally issued. On May 1, 1941, twenty months after he was first interned in France as an *étranger nondésirable,* Ernst crossed into Spain with his canvases rolled up in a suitcase. Astonishingly, even the French border official who inspected his baggage proclaimed him a great artist and waved him through. Then, in Lisbon, another surprise awaited him in the fetching form of Leonora Carrington, whom he had not seen for a year and who had spent several months in a psychiatric hospital in northern Spain. This upsetting news also awaited Guggenheim when she reached Lisbon a few days later. Worse, Peggy quickly understood that Ernst was still in love with Leonora and concluded that she had lost him. But Leonora, having agreed to marry a Mexican diplomat, Renato Leduc, kept her word, albeit puzzled by Max's behavior. More than forty-five years later, she told an interviewer: "I felt there was something very wrong in Max's being with Peggy. I knew he didn't love Peggy."[19]

On July 13, Peggy and her contingent of one ex-husband, his ex-wife, seven children and Ernst left Lisbon by plane for New York, where they joined Breton and other Surrealist exiles. Five months later, Peggy married Ernst. It was, she told him, his best insurance against being deported as an enemy alien. But the marriage did not last.

When Ernst left Marseille, several other artists on Fry's list were still awaiting overseas visas. Marc Chagall, however, had been hesitating. Although a Russian-born Jew, he had acquired French nationality in 1937 and felt safe in his stone farmhouse at Gordes, east of Avignon. In a letter to a French official, he noted that he had chosen France as his adopted country in 1910, adding "Since that date, my

artistic career has unfolded entirely in France. I have always been
very honored to be considered as a French painter."[20] On March 8,
1941, Fry and Bingham spent the weekend with Chagall and his wife,
Bella, and delivered a formal invitation to the United States from
Barr, but the painter again said he was happy where he was.

The following month, a roundup of Jews accused of black market
activites in the unoccupied zone alarmed the Chagalls, and they
rushed in alarm to find Fry in Marseille. During a police raid on the
Hôtel Moderne on April 9, Chagall was among several Jews arrested
and driven off in a police van. Quickly informed by Bella Chagall,
Fry responded with typical panache, sternly warning the French
police official responsible that "Vichy would be gravely embarrassed,
and you would probably be severely reprimanded" for arresting "one
of the world's greatest painters."[21] Barely thirty minutes later, Chagall was released. Even then, though, he insisted on traveling with all
of his paintings. On May 7, accompanied by 1.5 tons of baggage, the
Chagalls left France on a train through Spain to Lisbon, where they
boarded a ship for the United States.

The exodus continued. The Russian-born Jewish sculptor Lipchitz, who had to be warned repeatedly by Fry of the dangers he
faced, left Marseille one week later; Péret and his artist lover, Remedios Varo, reached Mexico in late 1941; Duchamp made it to New
York in June 1942; and Arp and Taeuber, who were refused American visas, fled to Switzerland in November 1942. Willy Maywald, a
German fashion photographer who arrived in France in 1931, had to
wait even longer. He was interned in several camps during the phony
war before escaping in May 1940. While awaiting a visa from Fry, he
stayed with friends in Cagnes-sur-Mer, between Nice and Cannes,
where he opened a workshop making shoes and raffia objects to earn
money for himself and other refugees. Only in December 1942 did
he finally make it into Switzerland.

One loyal supporter of Fry's was the Countess Lily Pastré, the
wealthy heiress of the Noilly Prat fortune. She also opened her
Château de Montredon, in a southern neighborhood of Marseille, to
artists, actors and musicians, with Casals and the Romanian Jewish
pianist Clara Haskil among those giving concerts. On July 27, 1942,
Pastré hosted an unusual performance of *A Midsummer Night's
Dream,* directed by the actor Jean Wall and Boris Kochno, Diaghilev's former assistant and librettist, with costumes made from Pastré's curtains by a young Christian Dior. Accompanying music was

provided by the Orchestre National de la Radiodiffusion Française, conducted by Manuel Rosenthal. Pastré also sheltered fugitives, helping both Haskil and the Arps to reach Switzerland. After the Germans took over southern France, they occupied part of her château, although the lively countess continued to support culture in Marseille.

Some refugee artists never left France. Sonia Delaunay, a Ukrainian-born Jewish painter whose French husband, the painter Robert Delaunay, died in October 1941, survived the war in hiding in Grasse, near Cannes. The French photographer Willy Ronis, who was also Jewish, left Paris during the exodus and found work with a theater troupe traveling around the unoccupied zone. When Germany occupied the south, he, too, went into hiding. The artists Bellmer and Wols, who had been in the Camp des Milles with Ernst, also survived the war, as did Brauner and Jacques Hérold, both Romanian Jews, who could find no country willing to receive them.

Others were unluckier. Chaïm Soutine, a Lithuanian-born Jew who was a leading painter of the interwar years, had been living in Paris since 1937 with a German Jew, Gerda Groth. She was interned in the women's camp at Gurs in May 1940, and they never again saw each other. Instead, in March 1941 Soutine left Paris with Marie-Berthe Aurenche, Ernst's former wife, for Champigny-sur-Veude, in central France. Forced to wear a yellow star after May 1942, he nonetheless continued painting. But in summer 1943, his health failed and he was rushed to Paris, where he died on August 9. (Picasso, Cocteau, the poet Max Jacob and Groth were among those attending his burial at the cemetery of Montparnasse.) Both Tristan Tzara, the founder of the Dada movement, and the actor Sylvain Itkine joined the resistance, although Itkine was murdered by the Gestapo days before the liberation of France in August 1944. Fry particularly mourned two prominent German socialists, Rudolf Hilferding and Rudolf Breitscheid, who were arrested by French police and who, despite Fry's intense lobbying, were handed over to the Nazis. The official account was that Hilferding hanged himself in a Paris prison in 1941, while Breitscheid was killed by Allied bombing at Buchenwald in 1944. Fry believed that both men died at the hands of the Nazis.

By the summer of 1941, Fry's own troubles were mounting, with pressure on him to abandon his operation now coming as much from the State Department and the Emergency Rescue Committee in New

York as it was from the French police. From his first days in Marseille, he had come to expect little help from the American consul general. On one visit in late 1940, Fullerton advised him to leave France before he was arrested and showed him a State Department cable criticizing his activities. In January 1941, the diplomat refused to renew Fry's passport unless he agreed to return to the United States. The American embassy in Vichy was no more welcoming. When Fry went there to lobby for more visas, he recalled, the chargé d'affaires "was always too busy to see me."[22]

Fry received no more help when Admiral William D. Leahy became ambassador, in January 1941. On one occasion, a third secretary informed him that the French police had a dossier on him. "I told him the police had a dossier on everybody," Fry replied.[23] Meanwhile, probably under pressure from the State Department, the Emergency Rescue Committee was sending Fry ambiguous signals. It regularly transferred money to him, but it grew impatient with his demands that it extract more emergency visas from the State Department. In late 1940, an American journalist named Jay Allen even arrived in Marseille and claimed that the committee had appointed him to be Fry's replacement. Fry and his team simply ignored him.

More disturbingly, Fullerton was sharing his disapproval of Fry with the local French authorities, and this made it far easier for them to remove this high-minded irritant. On July 10, 1941, Fry was summoned by Marseille's new hard-line police chief, Maurice de Rodellec du Porzic, who, as Fry later recounted, began by noting that "you have caused my good friend the Consul-General of the United States much annoyance." He went on to say that both the United States government and the emergency committee had asked Fry to return home "without delay." When Fry demurred, the police chief said that if he did not leave of his own free will, he would be arrested and forced to reside in a small town "where you can do no harm." Finally, Fry agreed to leave on August 15, but he asked why de Rodellec du Porzic was so opposed to him. "Because you have gone too far in protecting Jews and anti-Nazis" was the reply.[24] The following day, Fullerton gave Fry a new passport valid only for travel to the United States.

The August 15 deadline came and went, but two weeks later Fry was arrested and accompanied to the border town of Cerbère. His team went along, too, and gave him a farewell lunch in the station restaurant before he took the train into Spain. Daniel Bénédite, who had often proved his valor, took over the operation, and hundreds more refugees were helped out of France before the Centre Américain de Secours was closed by the French police in June 1942. The number of people saved by Fry and his team is estimated at around two thousand, ten times more than the number he came to save in August 1940.

In the United States, Fry criticized American immigration policies and warned of the darkening fate of European Jews in a December 1942 article in the *New Republic* entitled "The Massacre of Jews in Europe." The only immediate consequence was that the FBI opened a file on him. After that, he faded from public view, wrote his memoirs and became a high school teacher. Dina Vierny, for one, did not forget him: in 1967, just months before Fry's death, Vierny persuaded André Malraux, by then culture minister, to name Fry as a *chevalier* of the Légion d'Honneur. More than thirty years later, she still remembered him fondly: "I knew this man. He didn't have the physique for the job; as a St. George facing the dragon, he was modest. It never occurred to him for a second that he could be a hero, a true American hero. He stayed in France for only 389 days, but he tried through every means, often illegal, to save people without thinking of the danger he incurred. The man was charming, educated, curious, considerate, thinking only of his task. Later, he regretted not having been able to save more people."[25]

With such artistic, literary and intellectual wealth leaving France (or being forced into hiding), it now looked as if the fields of arts and letters were being surrendered to Vichy supporters and Nazi sympathizers. Was this exodus justified? Jewish and anti-Nazi activists among the European refugees clearly had no alternative. But many French artists—the directors and actors who left for Hollywood and the Surrealists who were helped by Fry—made a more personal choice. "I don't think they felt ashamed to leave," Hessel said of the artists who ended up in New York. "They felt they had to save their art, their reputation and their contribution to art in the world."[26] But their flight did invite charges of cowardice and selfishness from those who remained and still greater abuse from right-wingers who disparaged them as *les mauvais français emigrés en Anglo-Saxonnie,* the bad French emigrants to the Anglo-Saxon world. Indeed, as the occupation moved toward its first anniversary, with Paris bustling with cultural life and most art forms flourishing, it could be argued that those who had gone had merely left room for new talent to replace them. And there were many ready to do so.

CHAPTER 5

Paris by Night

BY THE SPRING OF 1941, Parisians had adjusted surprisingly well to the occupation, fortunately perhaps, since it was also evident that no one was hurrying to their rescue. The United States was reluctant to enter the war. The Soviet Union had a nonaggression pact with Germany. And while Britain had held off a German invasion in the summer of 1940 to the surprise of most of the French, "plucky little England" still posed no threat to the Reich. Indeed, German and Vichy propaganda had been skillfully reminding the French that Britain was their historic enemy. And, it was noted, there were fresh reasons to distrust *la perfide Albion:* the perception that Britain had sacrificed France to save its own forces at Dunkirk; Churchill's decision to bomb French navy vessels moored at Mers el-Kébir in Algeria; and Britain's support for a failed Gaullist attempt to take over Vichy-run Senegal in September 1940.

The beneficiary, by default, was Pétain, who at this stage appeared to most French people to be the only alternative to supporting either the Germans or the British. The problem was that the marshal himself could do nothing to change the lives of Parisians. In fact, he never set foot in Paris between June 1940 and April 1944, four months before the city's liberation. The reality was that the Germans were in charge, and most Parisians chose to make the best of things. And this meant seeking distraction wherever they could.

The 1930s had generated an extraordinary array of music halls, cabarets, nightclubs and bordellos, and almost all had reopened by Christmas 1940. In many of them, notably music halls, it was also possible for Parisians to enjoy themselves without having German uniforms beside them. The reason was simple: stand-up comics and *chansonniers* performed their numbers in French, often peppered with argot, which few German soldiers could understand. Naturally, given the risk of being denounced, direct criticism of the occupation forces was unwise, but that made the double entendre all the funnier. One song, for instance, punned on the word *occupation,* which also means "job" in French:

> *With us our biggest problem*
> *Was the absence of occupation*
> *And we complained we had none*
> *Well, now I believe we have one.*[1]

Another instructed listeners to read between the lines:

> *So in what we say, it's up to you*
> *To look for what we mean*
> *And think: "If he has not said it*
> *I understand . . . what he meant to say."*

All stage texts and lyrics had to be approved by the Propaganda Staffel, but German officials were surprisingly flexible where Germany was not involved. They allowed the comedian Jacques Grello to mock the mudslinging of collaborationist newspapers when he observed that surely one of them must be telling the truth, but which? And Jean Rigaux was authorized to make fun of the Italians, who were occupying part of southeastern France. The story is also told of two comedians, Raymond Souplex and Jean Rieux, who were summoned by the Propaganda Staffel and asked for the text of a pre-war sketch ridiculing Hitler. They claimed they had no text and were therefore ordered to act it out. When they did so without cuts, the

German officer congratulated them on being honest.[2] Less fortunate was Rieux's colleague Georges Merry, with whom in November 1940 he wrote a revue for the Théâtre des Nouveautés called *Occupons-Nous* (another pun on the occupation, this time meaning "Let's keep busy"). Later in the war, Merry was arrested for using a radio variety show to send coded messages to a resistance group; deported first to Buchenwald, he died at the Mittelbau-Dora concentration camp, in Germany.

In practice, much of the comic material written for the stage simply satirized the daily lives of Parisians as they went about juggling ration cards and the black market, riding bicycles after years behind the wheel or trying to make old clothes look presentable. Little wonder that middle-class Parisians felt at home in music halls. They knew many of the songs, they knew some of the jokes, they could have a night out—even a *warm* night out in the winter—and forget their troubles. Michel Francini, a music-hall actor who was back in Paris by mid-July, recalled performing mainly for French audiences, starting with his first job after the occupation, the revue *1900*, which opened at the Théâtre de l'Étoile on September 10, 1940. "Crowds of people came," he said. "Why? To go out. There hadn't been deaths in Paris. It was a French revue. And the public was almost entirely French. It lasted five or six months. Then I did a cabaret show in Reims for two weeks, where there were three French and two hundred Germans. They didn't find me funny, but they liked the girls."[3]

Certainly, for many German soldiers, to see half-naked dancing girls was the best reason for going out at night. And to do so in Paris was one of the unspoken rewards for soldiers who were allowed to spend a few days of R & R in the jewel of the occupied cities. For tips on where to go, soldiers could turn to the German-language newspaper *Pariser Zeitung*, which noted that Tabarin offered the most erotic show. And if by the end of an evening they wound up in a brothel, this, too, fitted into the Paris of their dreams. The city's best-known brothels, Le One Two Two, at 122 rue de Provence, on the Right Bank, and Sphinx, on the Left Bank, were probably out of their price range. There German officers, French collaborators, clandestine resistance agents, black market operators and artists of all kinds, including women, met for drinks, gossip, spying and entertainment (with no requirement that visitors use the sexual services on offer). Ordinary German soldiers, on the other hand, could choose among a score of less upmarket brothels where Wehrmacht doctors monitored the health of the prostitutes.

It was also possible to meet women more casually, as the celebrated German novelist Ernst Jünger noted in his journal. On May 1, 1941, just three weeks after being assigned to Paris by the Wehrmacht, he recorded meeting Renée, a shopgirl in a department store: "Paris offers meetings like that without barely having to seek them; one realizes that the city was founded on an altar of Venus." Jünger took her to dinner and then to the movies. "There I touched her breast," he wrote. "A burning glacier, a hillside in spring which hides in their thousands the seeds of life, perhaps also white anemones." Then, in front of the Paris Opera, they went their separate ways, "no doubt never to see each other again."[4] But, with that, Jünger, the immensely serious author of the World War I novel *Storm of Steel*, had discovered another of the delights of Paris.

German officers with money in their pockets usually preferred cabaret; there they could enjoy dancing girls in audaciously revealing feathered costumes, along with a well-known singer or two and, if lucky, a champagne dinner with a beautiful Frenchwoman. Germans with regular French girlfriends were not that numerous: photographs from the era often show uniformed soldiers watching a show with no women at their table. When the ABC reopened, it initially played exclusively to German soldiers. At Les Folies Bergère, where Germans often made up 80 percent of the audience, Paul Derval was quick to offer programs in German as well as French. Some performers would include a popular German song, such as "Lili Marlène" or "Bei mir bist du schön," and invite the occupiers to sing along. The Germans were not unlike today's tourists, almost filling nightspots themselves yet still imagining they were having a very French experience.

During much of the occupation, cabarets and music halls did booming business, with Pigalle-Montmartre, Montparnasse and the Champs-Élysées the busiest neighborhoods: by one count, there were 102 nightclubs in Paris, with forty-nine cabarets in Montmartre alone. So busy were performers that some appeared in at least two shows a night, hurriedly cycling between theaters or clubs. For some cabaret managers, it was as if *la belle époque* were back. Les Folies Bergère and Le Casino de Paris could be counted on to present the splashiest shows and biggest stars. In 1942, Les Folies Bergère boastfully called its new revue *Trois Millions* because it cost three million francs; this was followed by the still more lavish *Quatre Millions*. It was at Le Casino de Paris that Maurice Chevalier made his occupation debut, in September 1941, in a new revue called *Toujours Paris*. This was hardly an original title, since dozens of other revues also exploited the city's name, among them: *Paris je t'aime; Amours de Paris; Pour toi, Paris; Tout Paris; Bravo Paris; Paris en fleurs; Paris-Printemps;* and even *Paris, ich liebe dich.* In 1941 and 1942, the ABC went beyond song and dance with two revues called *Chesterfollies*, which added burlesque, clowns and acrobats to the mix. At Le Lido, Jacques Tati, later best known for his *Monsieur Hulot* character, was making his name with mime and parody routines. Other cabarets and theaters popular with German officers were L'Alhambra, Le Palace, Le Bobino, Le Shéhérazade and Les Variétés. The best cabarets, where good food and vintage wine were always available, stayed open all night, enabling revelers to ignore the curfew.

This meant that there was plenty of work for actors, singers and musicians—except, of course, Jews. One cabaret assured its German clients that all its performers were entirely Aryan; another announced that Jews were not welcome. In this atmosphere, then, even before Vichy's Statute on Jews in October 1940, most Jewish performers chose to stay in the relative safety of the unoccupied zone. "There were lots of Jews in show business," Francini recalled. "We'd learn that Jewish friends were not coming back. When Jews left, others took their places, directors, producers, they took advantage of their absence."[5] One popular Jewish cabaret singer who hesitated before leaving France was Marie Dubas. She returned to France from a tour of the United States and Portugal to find herself under attack from the collaborationist press. *Paris-Soir,* which accused her of marrying a French air force officer and converting to Catholicism in order to return to the stage, demanded, "Doesn't she know that the Jewish problem is not religious? It's racial." Dubas's Paris apartment was requisitioned by the Wehrmacht, but she nonetheless resumed her career in Lyon, Nice and other towns in the unoccupied zone. Finally, in October 1942, with the Vichy regime now also deporting Jews from the territory it controlled, she obtained a visa to leave for Switzerland. Her new audiences were refugees like herself. For them, she sang "Ce soir, je pense à mon pays" (This Evening, I'm Thinking of My Country).

Of the top non-Jewish cabaret stars, the only one who did not resume her career in Paris was Josephine Baker. Now holding dual American and French citizenship, she was performing at Le Casino de Paris in early May 1940, but she stopped when the Germans entered France. Instead, she sang to French soldiers on the Maginot Line before driving south to the Château des Milandes, in Dordogne, which she had rented in 1938 (and would buy in 1947). She was joined there by Captain Jacques Abtey, a French military intelligence officer whom she had met in Paris and who was in touch with de Gaulle's forces in London. Using La Baker's fame as a cover, with Abtey posing as her secretary, they traveled to Lisbon carrying information about German military movements written in invisible ink on Josephine's music scores. Having delivered their secrets to French agents, they were ordered back to Marseille, where Baker reprised her role in Offenbach's *La Créole* at the city's Théâtre de l'Opéra. Then, again on orders from London, in January 1941 they flew to North Africa, which, while under Vichy rule, offered greater security. Although Josephine was ill for much of the next twenty months,* when American troops landed in Morocco in November 1942 she quickly offered to entertain them. In the twenty-two months before Paris was liberated, she performed from Casablanca to Beirut, always stressing that she did so as a member of the Free French Forces. She was later awarded the Croix de Guerre and the Médaille de la Résistance with the rosette.

Baker's prewar colleagues were happy to be back on stage in Paris, none more than the legendary Mistinguett. Born as Jeanne Bourgeois in 1875, she had been a cabaret diva since the turn of the century and had become a silent movie star soon afterward, as famous for her well-insured legs, exuberant ostrich feathers and sultry voice as for her parade of young lovers. Chevalier was her lucky dance partner at Les Folies Bergère in 1911; she promptly seduced him — and made his career. And as she grew older, she held on to her fans — and her lovers — through the sheer force of her personality. During the occupation, by now in her mid-sixties, La Miss performed almost without interruption, succeeding Chevalier at Le Casino de Paris in November 1941. She was also renowned for shamelessly complain-

---

*One story, endlessly repeated although never confirmed by Baker, is that she fell ill after a private dinner with Göring during which he tried to poison her for belonging to the resistance by putting cyanide in her wine. The unlikely story even has Baker escaping through a laundry hatch and being rescued by her resistance colleagues.

ing to her audiences that she was hungry and extracting gifts of butter, wine and foie gras from her undoubtedly hungrier public. Like everyone else, she sang to audiences with German soldiers, although, unlike Chevalier, Tino Rossi, Charles Trenet, Léo Marjane and Édith Piaf, she never traveled to Germany to perform before French prisoners of war. After the liberation of Paris, now sixty-nine years old, she seemed quite pleased by suggestions that she had had some German lovers, responding disdainfully, *"Ça, c'est différent, ça, c'est l'amour!"* ("That's different, that's love!")

With the movie industry in Paris slow to resume production, cabaret managers sought out popular actors and actresses to appear on stage, among them Viviane Romance and Ginette Leclerc. Suzy Solidor, a singer and prewar screen star, opened her own cabaret, Chez Suzy Solidor, where she sang "Lili Marlène" and other German songs nightly to a uniformed public. But the French public responded most to its beloved *chansonniers.* Trenet, already nicknamed affectionately *le fou chantant* (the Singing Madman), returned to the stage in February 1941. He had a velvety baritone voice and a gentle, smiling presence, and he also wrote many of his own songs, including "Boum!," "Douce France" ("Sweet France") and, most famously, "La mer" (later recorded by Bobby Darin as "Beyond the Sea"). Trenet's performances at Les Folies Bergère, the ABC and the Gaieté Parisienne, with German soldiers in the audience, were invariably well received. Yet, strangely, while he seemed incapable of offending anyone, *Paris-Soir* decided to pick on him, first announcing falsely that he had died, then accusing him of being Jewish, claiming that "Trenet" was an anagram for "Netter," a common Jewish name in France. Trenet hurriedly set about proving he was not Jewish and, feeling all the more vulnerable as a homosexual, he agreed to a request to perform for French prisoners of war in Germany in September 1943. After the liberation of France, he moved to the United States for several years, until all was forgiven and forgotten.

Piaf, "the Little Sparrow," was no less active. In May 1940, she appeared in her first play, *Le Bel indifférent,* which Cocteau had written for her. And by late summer, she was allowed to tour the production in occupied France. The following year, she also starred in Georges Lacombe's movie *Montmartre-sur-Seine,* as a singer whose life was little different from her own. "My real job is to sing, to sing no matter what happens," she was reported to have said in 1940. Throughout the occupation, she drew large crowds during

tours of the Côte d'Azur and performed almost everywhere in
Paris—at the ABC, Le Bobino, Les Folies Bergère, Le One Two
Two, Le Moulin Rouge (where in 1944 she fell in love with the young
Yves Montand) and even at the elegant Salle Pleyel, one month
before the city was liberated.

Naturally, there were Germans in her audience. And she sometimes responded to their presence, according to Simone Berteaut, a
childhood friend who was later sporadically part of Piaf's circle and
falsely claimed to be the singer's half sister. On one occasion, Berteaut
said, Piaf performed a popular German melody to rude French slang,
which pleased both occupier and occupied. On another, for which
Berteaut was not the only witness, she dedicated a song to French
prisoners of war—"Où sont-ils mes petits copains?" (Where Are All
My Close Pals?)—and then suddenly appeared wrapped in the
French colors. There is also evidence that she helped to hide and
maintain three Jewish cabaret musicians, Michel Emer, Marcel
Blistène and Norbert Glanzberg (who may also have been one of her
lovers).[6]

But it was a different story that shielded her from any charge of
collaboration after the liberation of France. Having been chosen as
their "godmother" by POWs at Stalag III-D, outside Berlin, she
traveled there twice for concerts. Acclaimed even by the Germans on
her first visit in 1943, she persuaded the camp commander to allow
her to be photographed with him and with "her" soldiers, as she
called them; those photographs survive. The plan concoted by her
secretary, Andrée Bigard, who was in the resistance, was for the photographs to be enlarged. Each POW's image was then cut out and
attached to a false document identifying him as a French worker in
Germany. When Piaf returned to the camp early the following year,
the documents were secretly delivered so that, should any POW succeed in escaping, he would have a German identity card to protect
him. And, by all accounts, some did escape. "No," Piaf said after the
war, "I was not in the Resistance, but I helped my soldiers."[7]

Of all the *chansonniers,* Chevalier's immense popularity at home
and abroad put him most in the spotlight. During the phony war, he
had entertained French soldiers on the Maginot Line and, somewhat
ostentatiously, he donated his old Packard car as scrap metal for the
war effort. Then, after France's defeat, he withdrew with his companion, Nita Raya, a Romanian Jewish actress, to the comfort of La
Bocca, his villa near Cannes, where swimming and playing tennis

seemed more real than war. Feeling safe in the unoccupied zone, he performed regularly in Nice and other nearby towns. And when he was asked his political opinion, his instinct, like that of most of his fans, was to support Pétain. In an interview with *L'Éclaireur de Nice* in December 1940, he said, "Since we are lucky enough to be able to venerate a man and fully understand what he expects of us, I involve him privately in all the decisions I'm compelled to make. I ask myself: what would he say if he were in my shoes? How would he behave if he were beneath my straw hat? That's why, for the coming year, I can only make the same wish that our Great Man among the Greats would make."[8]

In September 1941, Chevalier was persuaded by Henri Varna, the manager of Le Casino de Paris, to appear in the new revue *Paris Toujours*. He was nervous about returning to Paris but, with a crowd of fans, reporters and show-business friends meeting his train at the Gare d'Austerlitz, his arrival was as warm as he could have hoped. He flashed his smile and expressed delight to be home. When offered a car ride, he even took the *métro* so that, he said, he could again connect with Parisians. (He in fact rode five stops, then joined the waiting car.) Predictably, with his jaunty style, charming smile and twirls of his boater, Chevalier was a great success, although the ever-skeptical Galtier-Boissière was less impressed, noting, "At the Casino de Paris, Chevalier takes his turn to sing before an audience of uniforms that has come only to look at the arses."[9] Less wisely, Chevalier not only accepted the sponsorship of *Paris-Soir* for two concerts in a working-class district but also performed at a charity gala attended by German officers and organized by Radio-Paris. Reminded of Chevalier's popularity, German producers invited him to perform in Berlin, but he refused. Instead, at Vichy's urging, he agreed to sing to French prisoners of war at Stalag XI-A, Altengrabow, the very same camp where he had spent twenty-seven months during World War I.

In late November, he traveled to Berlin by train with his young accompanist, Henri Betti. They spent the night there and were driven the following day to Altengrabow for a concert before some three thousand POWs. Chevalier's only payment, he said, was the release of ten Frenchmen from Ménilmontant, the Paris neighborhood where he was born. He also turned down a fresh invitation to perform at La Scala in Berlin, but his trip nonetheless served German propaganda. His Altengrabow concert was rebroadcast in Germany and by Radio-Paris in France. Further, *Signal,* the German illustrated weekly that circulated in occupied countries and sold some 700,000 copies in France alone, ran photographs of him in Berlin without mentioning that he had performed only for French POWs.

His image abroad suffered accordingly. In August 1942, a Free French broadcast from London included Chevalier's name on a list of prominent collaborators who deserved death. Despite this, he played Le Casino de Paris again in October. But when he returned to La Bocca, the German army had taken over the unoccupied zone, and he brought Nita Raya's Jewish parents to his home to protect them. He gave a number of concerts in the south, but stayed away from Paris. In February 1944, the Jewish humorist André Isaac, who was now at Radio-Londres and working under the stage name Pierre Dac, issued a new death threat against Chevalier, which he took seriously. Then in May, he learned that he had been sentenced to death by a special tribunal of de Gaulle's provisional French government in Algiers. Now fearing both the Gestapo and the resistance, he left La Bocca with Nita and her parents for a hideaway in the Dordogne and stayed there until France was liberated. He narrowly escaped being killed by the maquis before fleeing to Toulouse, where he was briefly arrested. Josephine Baker was not alone in condemning his wartime conduct. In her autobiography, *Josephine,* she wrote, "Maurice was one of those Frenchmen who believed that the Germans had won the war and that it was time things returned to normal—on German terms."[10] But Chevalier was lucky. When he came to answer charges of collaboration, he could count on well-placed friends to speak up for him, none more important than Louis Aragon, the Communist poet. And he was exonerated.

For the French public, whether listening to their favorite singers on stage or on Radio-Paris, the emotional connection often came through the words of their songs. Two broad themes emerged, one around love, the other around France. Léo Marjane, Mistinguett's prewar rival, ended the war having to explain why she performed for German troops and broadcast on Radio-Paris,* but many of her songs—like "J'attendrai" (I Will Wait) and "Attends-moi, mon amour" (Wait for Me, My Love)—spoke for the hundreds of thou-

---

*Although Radio-Paris was a German-run propaganda station, Chevalier, Suzy Solidor and Yvonne Printemps were among the many artists who also performed on its popular variety shows, for which they were well paid.

sands of women whose husbands, boyfriends or sons were prisoners of war or, later, forced to work in Germany. Her biggest hit, "Je suis seule ce soir," would be played almost nightly on Radio-Paris. It begins:

> *I am alone tonight*
> *With my dreams*
> *I am alone tonight*
> *Without your love.*

It continues:

> *I am alone tonight*
> *With my sorrows*
> *I have lost hope*
> *That you will return.*

And it ends:

> *In the fireplace, the wind cries out*
> *In silence, the roses lose their petals*
> *The clock chimes every quarter-hour*
> *Measuring the gloom with its gentle sound.*

Trenet's no less melancholic hit, "Que reste-t-il de nos amours?" (What Is Left of Our Loves?), also looked back nostalgically to a happier time:

> *What is left of our loves?*
> *What remains of those sweet days?*
> *A photo, an old photo of my youth.*

In their songs about France, the *chansonniers* spoke of the country's eternal charms, none more than Lina Margy's "Ah le petit vin blanc" (Ah, the Little Glass of White Wine) and Pierre Dudan's "Café au lait au lit" (Morning Coffee in Bed). Trenet's instant hit "Douce France" evoked childhood memories, then proclaimed:

> *Yes, I love you*
> *And I give you this poem*

Yes, I love you
In joy and in grief
Sweet France.

For those French citizens trapped in the provinces, he wrote "Si tu revois Paris, dis bonjour aux amis"—If you get to Paris, say hello to my friends. And Mistinguett offered the consolation that the Eiffel Tower was still in place: "La Tour Eiffel est toujours là!" But it was Chevalier who assumed the role of chief cheerleader, with songs that echoed Pétain's message of "let's love and rebuild France." "Ça sent si bon la France" (France Feels So Good) presents a long list of French people and places worthy of affection, from "this old bell tower in the setting sun" to "this brunette with eyes of paradise." Even more *pétainiste* is "La chanson du maçon" (The Builder's Song), which imagined all the French singing as one as they built their new house—that is, France. And it ended: "We would be millions of builders / Singing away on the rooftops of our houses." In "Notre Espoir" (Our Hope), Chevalier recalled that he once sang of love and of joy, but now he lacks words so he improvises with sounds, like "Tra la la la la-la" and "Dzim pa poum pa la." Then he added: "My hope is that the sky will become blue again / And that we'll sing in peace in our old France."

A more surprising favorite of the Paris nightlife was Django Reinhardt; as a Gypsy, the gifted Belgian-born jazz guitarist could easily have joined hundreds of thousands of other Gypsies in Nazi death camps. Yet despite official Nazi disapproval of jazz as a product of "degenerate" black American culture, its popularity in the 1930s continued throughout the occupation. Reinhardt was in London with his Quintette du Hot Club de France when war was declared in 1939, but he turned down the option of exile and immediately returned to Paris. Then, after the German occupation, he continued to play at the Hot Club de France and other nightspots, drawing French as well as German jazz fans. (One Luftwaffe officer, Dietrich Schulz-Koehn, even published his own secret jazz newsletter.)

The Hot Club, run by Charles Delaunay, who was also active in the resistance, sponsored jazz concerts and festivals at such mainstream locations at the Salle Gaveau and the Salle Pleyel. Even Radio-Paris, in its eagerness to win over French listeners, broadcast jazz in its many variety programs. Perhaps this was made easier by the absurd claim in André Coeuroy's *Histoire générale du jazz* in

1942 that jazz had its origins in Europe. Reinhardt himself, though, evidently did not feel too secure in occupied Paris. Sometime in late 1943, he decided to flee to Switzerland, but he was caught at the border by German guards. By luck, the officer in charge was a fan, and he returned Reinhardt to Paris, where, in 1944, he opened his own club, Chez Django Reinhardt.

While Django was the city's most famous jazz musician, he was only one of hundreds working in music halls and cabarets. Among these, Johnny Hess stood out for the bizarre sociopolitical movement he indirectly sponsored. Hess and Ray Ventura were responsible for introducing the catchy big band rhythms of swing to France in the late 1930s. And although Ventura, who was Jewish, left with his popular band for South America soon after the occupation, it was swing that ruled the Paris night scene during the early 1940s. (After the war, Trenet said that "La Mer" was not a hit in France when he first sang it in 1943 because it "lacked swing.")

But there was more. As early as 1938, Hess threw into his lyrics for "Je suis swing" the meaningless word *zazou*. It soon caught on as a nickname for swing fans and, during the occupation, it came to represent a broader form of cultural protest, in which Zazou men wore long hair and long jackets, women wore short skirts and heavy shoes and everyone wore dark glasses and carried an unfurled umbrella. Their desire to stand out was seen as a provocation, which pleased them all the more. After Jews were obliged to wear yellow stars after May 1942, some Zazous made their own and scribbled *Swing* or *Zazou* across them. Having already annoyed the authorities, the movement was then blessed in 1942 by Hess with a song, "Ils sont zazous," in which he described their attire in detail, adding with apparent approval, "And above all / They look disgusted."

Still, if the Zazous dressed with attitude, many Parisians were more concerned with remaining stylish—and staying warm—at a time that crucial ingredients likes wool, silk and leather were in short supply or, rather, being sent to Germany. They knew that by looking good, they not only felt better but also showed the Germans that the French spirit was intact. The result was a triumph of improvisation and imagination as both designers and *parisiennes* circumvented the multiple new obstacles to elegance. Already during the phony war, fashion houses and magazines like *Marie-Claire* were quick to adjust, endorsing the grays and blues of military uniforms and suggesting the right clothes to wear in air-raid shelters or how best to carry a gas mask. During the exodus of May and June 1940, the women's pages of some newspapers also recommended what to pack: notably, comfortable clothes and flat shoes. After Paris fell, however, the Germans elbowed their way to the front of shops' lines and set about emptying the city's inventory. And with the deutschmark artificially overvalued by the occupier, they could afford to do so. Soldiers crowded into Les Galeries Lafayette, Printemps and other department stores to buy lingerie and perfume, the ultimate proof to wives and fiancées back home that they had conquered Paris. More senior officers headed for haute couture shops, often carrying photographs of their *Frauen* to determine what size clothes to buy.

What the Third Reich really wanted, though, was to inherit Paris's place as the creative heart of haute couture. And, as early as late August 1940, Goebbels ordered leading French designers to prepare to move their operations to Berlin and Vienna. There they would be assured of the materials needed for their work and be guided toward a style more pleasing to German women. "Parisian fashion must pass through Berlin before women of taste can wear it," proclaimed the German weekly *Signal.* In his memoir, Ambassador Abetz claimed that he challenged Berlin in a report: "It will not be through the temporary, mechanical and forced suppression of French fashion that it will be possible to arrive at the creation of a truly German fashion, but only through the development of the creative spirit and artistic taste of German fashion itself."[11] Subsequently, Lucien Lelong, the designer who headed the the industry's guild, the Chambre Syndicale de la Couture, managed to block the German move to "deport" haute couture. "It stays in Paris or it is not at all," he claimed to have said before traveling to Berlin to make his case. Once there, he explained that, while the Paris fashion industry was renowned for its famous designers, it comprised thousands of independent dressmakers and tens of thousands of artisans skilled in working with an array of fabrics, leathers, perfumes, jewelry and other accessories. Finally, preferring not to provoke unnecessary French discontent so early in the occupation, the Germans abandoned the plan. But they never gave up their dream of promoting Berlin as a fashion capital.

As it happens, Paris's two leading interwar designers chose not to work under the Germans. But while Elsa Schiaparelli moved to New York, Coco Chanel remained in Paris and emerged from the occupation with her image badly bruised. Between trips south, Chanel, who was fifty-six when Paris fell, shared her suite at the Ritz Hotel with

Hans Gunther von Dincklage, a Wehrmacht officer thirteen years her junior who was also said to be a Nazi spy. During the course of the war, she also tried to recover control of her company from an exiled Jewish family, the Wertheimers, who had acquired a majority share in 1924. Finally, in 1943, Chanel became party to an absurd plot, supposedly involving Hitler's foreign intelligence chief, Walther Friedrich Schellenberg, in which she would convey a secret message to Churchill. Nothing came of it, but Chanel still had much to answer for at the moment of liberation. She was briefly arrested and, after some well-placed connections obtained her release, she moved to Switzerland, where she lived until 1954. A third—Jewish—fashion designer had no such option. Fanny Berger (as Odette Bernstein was known professionally) had her *salon de mode* at the upmarket address of 4 rue Balzac, beside the Arc de Triomphe, but in July 1941 she was forced to sell it to an Aryan former employee. She managed to evade the large roundups of Jews in the summer of 1942, but in September that year she was arrested while trying to cross the demarcation line to the south. She spent nine months in an internment camp at Beaune-la-Rolande, in the Loire Valley, before being sent to the transit camp of Drancy, outside Paris. In late July 1943, she was deported to Auschwitz and immediately killed. She was forty-two.

A number of other Jewish designers fled Paris, once again leaving more space for others. Those who stayed kept working, among them Jeanne Lanvin, Nina Ricci, Robert Piguet, Jacques Fath, Maggy Rouff, Marcel Rochas and Lelong, who from 1942 had Christian Dior and Pierre Balmain as his principal designers. In haute couture's first postoccupation shows in October 1940, the industry aimed to hold on to its wealthier and show business clients, imagining what clothes would be suitable for taking the last *métro* after attending the opera. Some designers helped Vichy's propaganda effort by printing scarves portraying Marshal Pétain in uniform and others showing him being acclaimed by cheering crowds.*

Nazi officers with money in their pockets were also important clients. But the designers did not ignore working *parisiennes*. The bicycle, for instance, was now the most practical and best way of moving around town and, while some younger women were happy

---

*The Royal Air Force in turn printed scarves for its pilots with maps of France, Belgium and Luxembourg.

to wear short skirts, the more modest could soon choose from a range of different *jupes-culottes,* or divided skirts. The importance of turning heads while riding along the Champs-Élysées was underlined by a fashion show in October 1941 in which designers nominated bicycle outfits for three titles, *Élégance pratique, Élégance sportive* and *Élégance parisienne.* Dressing for all weathers was still more important for those riding bicycles or tandems known as *vélo-taxis,* which pulled one- and two-seat carriages, usually no more than baskets precariously attached to two wheels. Since this rustic form of transportation offered no protection, passengers, too, had to dress for the elements.

Other changes were imposed by shortages. Wood replaced leather for the soles of shoes, adding close to one inch to women's heights and spawning inventive designs for heels and colorful strips of cloth for appearance. The loud clack that shoes made on sidewalks even inspired Chevalier to serenade the wooden soles in "La Symphonie des semelles de bois." Similarly, since silk stockings were almost impossible to find, women feigned wearing stockings by staining their calves with a special lotion, marketed by Elizabeth Arden; some even painted a vertical line down the backs of their legs for verisimilitude. Furriers could no longer obtain mink and half of France's sheepskins were being shipped to Germany, but they did their best with the skins of seals, rabbits and even cats. For some of the many Paris furriers who were Jews, their profession even became a lifesaver: the Wehrmacht so badly needed fur for winter combat uniforms that it released some 350 Jewish furriers from the Drancy concentration camp in Paris and exempted others from arrest so they could continue working "without contact with the public."

Women's magazines were full of articles suggesting ways of beating restrictions and rationing—by, for example, giving old clothes a new look, turning a blanket into a child's overcoat or transforming men's trousers into warm dresses. (And with so many Frenchmen in Germany as prisoners of war or forced laborers, there was no shortage of unused trousers in wardrobes.) At the same time, because of the growing shortage of traditional textiles—not only wool and silk but also velvet, satin and lace—designers began experimenting with artificial fibers, notably rayon and fibranne, which could be extracted from cellulose. In fact, long before it was known that the Nazis were using hair taken from their death-camp victims, there was an attempt to mix hair with fibranne to make fabric.

Yet for all this, haute couture survived, with spring and autumn shows amply covered in women's and fashion magazines. The first chance prosperous Parisians had to wear tuxedos and long dresses under the occupation was for a gala organized at the Paris Opera on December 20, 1940, for Pétain's charity, Secours National–Entr'aide d'Hiver. And while occasions to dress up were less numerous than before the war, receptions at the German Institute for visiting German dignitaries, as well as other charity galas, invariably brought out the finery.

Perhaps the easiest—and cheapest—way for a woman to draw attention to herself, however, was to wear a jaunty hat. Photographs taken by André Zucca in the streets of central Paris suggest that red and black were the preferred colors. In fact, whether designed by professionals or improvised at home, hats—of all colors, sizes and angles—became the most distinctive fashion emblem of the occupation. They also offered the most imaginative displays of French craftsmanship: there were hats variously made with celluloid, thin slices of wood and newspapers. Nowhere were hats more spectacular than at the races at the Hippodrome de Longchamp and the Hippodrome d'Auteuil, in the Bois de Boulogne. In contrast to the smaller hats for daily use, here they were extravagantly large, often topped by an immense feather or two. Collaborationist newspapers made a point of photographing the most inventive designs as a way of showing Parisians happily at play—alongside smart German army uniforms. The implicit message was that if Parisians could afford to spend an afternoon betting on horses, surely life was much as before. Evidently, these same papers paid little attention to the growing struggle of the majority of Parisians to keep warm and adequately fed.

That money continued to divide Parisians was well illustrated in the restaurant life of the city. Most people could afford to eat only at home. What they acquired with ration cards was supplemented by extras bought on the black market and, for those with generous relatives in the countryside, by an occasional shipment of a chicken or a leg of lamb. But many family-run bistros stayed open, with some willing to risk fines or closure by offering two menus: one official, the other black market; one cheap, the other pricey. So even in seemingly modest establishments, like Picasso's regular haunt, Le Catalan, on the rue des Grands-Augustins, on some days it was possible to have oysters followed by *gigot d'agneau*. (There were even moments when oysters were so plentiful that their shells were used for fuel.)

More elegant restaurants favored by the German military elite and the wealthy of Paris did not bother with such fictions. At establishments like Maxim's, La Tour d'Argent, Prunier, Drouant, Laurent, Le Pavillon de l'Élysée and Fouquet's, everything was available at the right price, starting with the best champagne and ending with vintage cognacs. Of these, Maxim's, a few steps from the place de la Concorde, had the most loyal German clientele, including Göring on his frequent art-raiding visits to Paris. It was also at Maxim's that German officers could be seen hosting leading collaborators, like the newspaper editor Jean Luchaire and such celebrities as Sacha Guitry.

Could the nightlife of Paris have been any different? It was, of course, the Germans who decided how it should be; they wanted to be entertained and they wanted Parisians to be distracted. And since music halls, cabarets, brothels and restaurants were closely monitored, Paris by night posed neither a political nor a security threat to the occupiers. But Parisians also wanted this nightlife to continue: it was part of the city's identity, it provided a sense of normality and it gave jobs to many thousands of actors, singers, dancers and strippers, as well as to seamstresses, furriers, cooks and waiters. True, the sight of Parisians enjoying themselves during the occupation never ceased to surprise outsiders, whether they were visitors from the provinces or Gaullist agents on secret missions from London. But for many Parisians, having suffered the humiliation of defeat, this was one way of demonstrating to themselves—and perhaps also to the Germans— that all was not lost.

· CHAPTER 6 ·

Resistance as an Idea

IN THE FACE OF defeat and occupation, then, the French responded successively with anger, despair, resignation and accommodation. With the notable exception of those Fascist writers who cheered the Nazi victory, most French artists and intellectuals reacted in much the same way. Initially, at least, they, too, looked to Marshal Pétain to shield France from the worst in what promised to be a long ordeal. Feeling powerless, they adopted *attentisme,* an on-the-fence posture, which allowed them to get on with their lives—to write, to paint, to perform, to teach—while waiting to be saved by some external force, presumably the United States. And yet within weeks of France's defeat, a few isolated intellectuals and professionals in Paris dared to think differently: they refused to accept France's humiliation as an immutable fact. They had no experience in either politics or insurgency, but almost instinctively they embraced the *idea* of resistance as an alternative to *attentisme.* They believed that long before an armed struggle was viable, the French had to learn to *think* resistance, to reject open collaboration, to believe that opposition to the occupation was possible. The most surprising feature of these early *résistants,* however, was that they were not anti-Fascist politicians, writers or journalists who had engaged in the ideological battles of the 1930s. In the main, they were little-known ethnologists whose study of human behavior through the ages had led them to spend years far from France.

After the war, this rebel circle came to be known as the Réseau du Musée de l'Homme, the Museum of Man network, because it was at the museum's newly opened Art Deco headquarters on the place du Trocadéro that some of the first conspirators came together. Their improbable leader was Boris Vildé, a Russian-born linguist who had already lived in Estonia and Germany before arriving in Paris in 1933. Still only twenty-five, he was befriended by Gide, who introduced him to Paul Rivet, then director of the Musée de l'Ethnographie, the forerunner of the Musée de l'Homme. This meeting inspired Vildé to study ethnography, and by 1939 he was working as an ethnologist in the Europe Department of the museum. When war was declared, he joined the French army as an artillery officer. After he was wounded and captured by the advancing Wehrmacht in June 1940, he quickly managed to escape. On July 5, he reappeared at the Musée de l'Homme, haggard and hobbling, but asserting that he was determined to do something. The following month, he was joined by another ethnologist, Anatole Lewitsky, and his girlfriend, Yvonne Oddon, the museum's librarian. They also recruited René Creston, a sociologist at the museum, while the venerable Rivet, already in his late sixties, offered the plotters his blessing and counsel.

Across Paris and beyond, a few other individuals were also seeking out friends and acquaintances with the idea of generating some response to the Germans. One who did so "just to remain sane," as she put it, was Agnès Humbert, a curator at the Musée des Arts et Traditions Populaires, which by chance was next door to the Musée de l'Homme. When she returned to Paris on August 5, she immediately went to see Jean Cassou, an admired art historian who was the director designate of the planned Musée d'Art Moderne. He, too, felt a need to act, and they formed a tiny cabal comprising the writers Claude Aveline and Marcel Abraham (who was Jewish), the publishers Albert and Robert Émile-Paul* and Christiane Desroches, an Egyptologist at the Louvre.

*The Émile-Pauls were the only publishers who refused to sign the self-censorship agreement with the Propaganda Staffel.

Together, they assumed the grandiose name of Les Français Libres de France, the Free French of France, but their ambitions were modest: to meet once a week to exchange news picked up on the street or heard on the BBC and to write subversive pamphlets and tracts to be distributed around Paris. Their first sheet, written by Cassou in September and left on café benches and public toilets, already distinguished them from those intellectuals who still hoped that Pétain could "save" France. It was called *Vichy fait la guerre* (Vichy Wages War). Using information from the BBC, it specifically denounced Pétain's regime for ordering its troops to fire on British and Gaullist naval forces trying to "liberate" Senegal, the French colony in West Africa. The following month, after collaborationist newspapers began attacking Cassou as a Communist and a Jew (his wife was Jewish), he and Humbert were both fired from their jobs by Vichy.

Meanwhile, Germaine Tillion, another ethnologist from the Musée de l'Homme, who had just returned to Paris from assignment in Algeria, was similarly dismayed by what she found. Unaware of Vildé's initiative, she made contact with Paul Hauet, a retired colonel who was already helping French prisoners of war escape from German camps in France. At the Palais de Justice, several lawyers, among them Albert Jubineau, André Weil-Curiel and Léon Maurice Nordmann, also began to mobilize their friends, while even some French employees in the United States embassy decided to act.* Soon word reached Paris of another small circle of spontaneous *résistants* led by Sylvette Leleu, a schoolteacher in Béthune, in northwestern France. Still another group appeared in Brittany.

Vildé was quick to recognize that these tiny groups needed to coordinate their activities, which also involved helping British soldiers and airmen escape France through Spain or through Brittany. Adopting the nom de guerre of Maurice, Vildé began traveling secretly to Lyon, Marseille and Toulouse to make contacts and gather information about German military positions and movements. This intelligence was then transmitted to London through the United States embassy office in Paris. For security reasons, Vildé kept many of his clandestine activities to himself, although it later transpired that he had supplied London with details of the German submarine base at

---

*The embassy itself moved to Vichy, but it kept offices in Paris until the United States entered the war, in December 1941. The embassy in Vichy stayed open until November 1942, when allied forces invaded North Africa.

Saint-Nazaire and of German anti-aircraft defenses in Strasbourg. By October 1940, he had also pulled together the various groups into a loose network, which was named the Comité National de Salut Publique, or National Committee of Public Safety. What they had in common was their opposition to the Nazis and to Vichy and their support for de Gaulle, who at that point was more symbol than true war leader. Humbert, who incautiously kept a journal in which she detailed her every meeting, suggested on October 20 that they were at best amateurs: "How bizarre it all is! Here we are, most of us on the wrong side of forty, careering along like students all fired up with passion and fervour, in the wake of a leader of whom we know absolutely nothing, of whom none of us has even seen a photograph."[1]

The new committee's next step was to publish a clandestine newspaper—one of the first of the occupation—called *Résistance.* Describing itself as the official bulletin of the committee, it published its first edition on December 15, 1940—just four pages printed on a Roneo, or mimeograph, machine belonging to the Musée de l'Homme. Cassou, Abraham and Aveline formed the newspaper's editorial committee and, Humbert noted mischievously, "I am the typist, naturally."[2] Its first front-page editorial, written by Vildé himself, began:

> Resist! That is the cry that comes from your hearts, in the distress that the disaster of the Fatherland has left you. It is the cry of all you who do not resign yourselves, of all you who want to do your duty. But you feel isolated and disarmed, and in the chaos of ideas, opinions and systems, you ask what is your duty. To resist is already a way of protecting your heart and your mind. But above all, it is to act, to do something that translates into positive actions, into calculated and powerful actions. Many have tried and have often been discouraged by feeling powerless. Others have joined together. But often these groups have also felt isolated and powerless. Patiently, with difficulty, we have found and united them. They are already numerous (more than an army for Paris alone), those passionate and determined men who have understood that organization of their effort is necessary, that they need a method, discipline, leaders.[3]

The editorial went on to urge people to form groups, name leaders, learn discipline and secrecy and prepare for when they would be called on to fight. Vildé further stressed that the committee's members were all independent actors who had never participated in the squabbles of party politics. He concluded: "We promise we have only one ambition, one passion, one will: to see a pure and free France reborn."

The committee then set about distributing the newspaper—in her journal, Humbert describes carrying one hundred copies through the streets of Paris in her briefcase—as well as continuing their efforts to help British and occasionally other foreign soldiers reach London. Just two weeks later, a second edition of *Résistance* appeared, this time with six printed pages. Its main document was the text of de Gaulle's June 18, 1940, appeal to the French, which appeared under the headline "The Hour of Hope." It also referred to other clandestine newspapers, notably *Pantagruel,* put out by a music publisher, Raymond Deiss.

Humbert, who at times seemed to think she was acting in a thriller, began to scent victory. "We must start drawing up lists of these turncoats, these cowards, these imbeciles," she wrote of the *pétainistes* she kept meeting. "The Fourth Republic will have nothing to do with people like that—or rather it will know what to do with them!"[4] When she saw French porters carrying the bags of German officers, this once-gentle mother of two became still more outraged. "We simply have to stop them, we can't allow them to colonize us, to carry off our goods on the backs of our men while they stroll along, arms swinging, faces wreathed in smiles, boots and belts polished and gleaming. We can't let it happen. And to stop it happening, we have to kill. Kill like wild beasts, kill to survive. Kill by stealth, kill by treachery, kill with premeditation, kill the innocent. It has to be done, and I will do it later."[5]

Instead, their conspiracy began to fall apart. In early January 1941, the first arrest was made—of the lawyer Nordmann, who was caught distributing *Résistance.* The network kept operating, issuing the third edition of its newspaper at the end of that month, with several thousand copies printed and many now distributed anonymously by mail. Vildé was in the south of France at the time, trying to build support for his group. He had been to see his old friend Gide; then he turned to Malraux, confident that the self-proclaimed hero of the Spanish civil war would be ready for more action. But Malraux gave Vildé the answer that he would give to other resistance recruiters: since resistance without a good supply of weapons was pointless, he planned to await the American entrance into the war. "That's all very nice," he told Vildé, "but it's not serious." In mid-February, there was a more serious setback: having reportedly received tips from two employees at the Musée de l'Homme, the Gestapo raided the museum and, after interrogating a dozen staff members, arrested Lewitsky and Oddon. Fearing that his own role would soon be revealed, the museum's director, Rivet, fled to the unoccupied zone and later sought refuge in South America. *Résistance*'s three editors— Cassou, Aveline and Abraham—also decided to leave Paris for the south, passing the reins to a strong-minded intellectual activist, Pierre Brossolette.

There were also other new recruits, including Pierre Walter and Georges Ithier, two friends of Vildé's. The most prominent was Jean Paulhan, the former editor of the *Nouvelle Revue Française,* who continued to work at Éditions Gallimard and who agreed to set up the Roneo machine in his home. The fourth and fifth editions of *Résistance,* both published in March, were printed in his apartment on the rue des Arènes, in the 5th arrondissement. But on March 26 Vildé himself was arrested, betrayed by Albert Gaveau, a double agent who had joined the network.* And in mid-April both Humbert and Walter were detained by German police. By the summer of 1941, a total of nineteen members of the network were in the hands of the Gestapo, held first in the Cherche-Midi and La Santé prisons in Paris and later at the nineteenth-century jail in Fresnes, south of Paris.

In May, Paulhan was also arrested. In Humbert's journal, she notes that she was interrogated about Paulhan and denied even knowing his name. But the Germans knew that Paulhan had kept the Roneo machine at his home. Paulhan's good fortune was that while he had never hidden his anti-German views, he had remained on good terms with Drieu La Rochelle, the Fascist writer who succeeded him as editor of the *Nouvelle Revue Française.* And thanks to Drieu La Rochelle, Paulhan was freed. On May 20, he wrote to his savior: "My Dear Drieu, I fully believe that it is thanks to you alone that I was able to return tranquilly this evening to the rue des Arènes. So thank you. I embrace you. Jean Paulhan."[6] Two days later, in another letter to Drieu La Rochelle, Paulhan recounted his experi-

---

*Gaveau, whose mother was German, was arrested in November 1945 and sentenced to twenty years of hard labor.

ence. His interrogator, a German captain, said that he knew Lewitsky had handed Paulhan the Roneo machine and added that he had promised Lewitsky that Paulhan would be released once the machine's whereabouts were established. Paulhan told Drieu La Rochelle that after five days in La Santé, he had admitted: "1. that L. had indeed given me a case containing the Roneo; 2. that after learning of L.'s arrest, I had thrown it into the Seine (in little pieces)."[7] Then, to Paulhan's surprise, he was released.[*]

Other members of the Réseau du Musée de l'Homme were less fortunate. One reason was that after Germany invaded its former Soviet ally in June 1941, the French Communist Party was at last free to join the resistance. And its first action was the assassination of a German naval cadet at a *métro* station in Paris on August 21, 1941. This and similar killings led to German reprisals, with scores of hostages executed. One victim was Honoré d'Éstienne d'Orves, an aristocratic Gaullist naval officer whose early resistance efforts had been betrayed by an infiltrated German spy in January that year. When the Musée de l'Homme prisoners went on trial in Fresnes in January 1942, then, harsh punishments were expected. In his prison journal on October 21, Vildé had recorded a visit by the trial's French prosecutor, who pledged "to have my head," a threat that he readily believed and dismissed as unimportant. "And yet," he said, "I love life, God, I love life. But I am not afraid of dying. To be shot would in a sense be the logical conclusion to my life."[8]

On February 17, the court's German judge pronounced guilty verdicts and death sentences for seven men, including Vildé, Lewitsky, Walter, Ithier and Nordmann, and three women, among them Oddon, although the women's sentences were immediately commuted to deportation. Humbert and another woman were condemned to five years' imprisonment in Germany, while others in the dock were given lighter sentences. The following day, Walter's lawyer raised Humbert's hope for reprieves. Echoing the lawyer's words, she noted in her journal, "The Germans could not ignore demands for clemency for Vildé from distinguished names such as François Mauriac, Paul Valéry and Georges Duhamel. And once Vildé's sentence was commuted, the others would automatically follow. Gaveau, the despicable informer on whom I have never clapped

---

[*]Unintimidated by the experience, Paulhan would go on to play a central role in the writers' resistance movement.

eyes, would be found wherever he might be and 'dealt with.' "[9] But on February 23, the seven men were shot at Fort Mont-Valérien, west of Paris. Only Vildé's final request was honored: he was the last to be executed.

Almost coincidentally, another early group of intellectual resisters was broken up by the Gestapo. Led by a high school teacher of German literature, Jacques Decour, it began as a protest against the arrest of the prominent French physicist Paul Langevin in October 1940. Joining Decour were Langevin's son-in-law, Jacques Solomon, a radiologist, and Georges Politzer, a Hungarian-born Marxist philosopher. Langevin himself was released after forty days and placed under house arrest in Troyes, in the Champagne region, until he was able to escape to Switzerland in 1944. Nonetheless, in late 1940 these *résistants* founded two clandestine newspapers, *L'Université Libre* and *La Pensée Libre*, which were among the first to call on intellectuals not to collaborate with the occupiers. All three men were members of the Communist Party, which, despite the German-Soviet nonaggression pact, decided to create a series of anti-Fascist "national fronts."

From this was born the Front National des Écrivains—the National Writers' Front—but it struggled to win over non-Communist writers. Then, in the summer of 1941, after the German invasion of the Soviet Union, Decour won party backing to reach out to non-Communists and, with Jean Paulhan as a key ally, he cofounded the Comité National des Écrivains, which would have its own underground newspaper, *Les Lettres Françaises*. But before its first issue was printed, Decour and Politzer were arrested, with Solomon arrested one week later. Solomon and Politzer were shot by the Germans on May 23, Decour on May 30, 1942.

Just as *Les Lettres Françaises* would eventually be brought out by a new team, remnants of the Museum of Man network also kept up their activities. It was no longer possible to publish *Résistance*, but Germaine Tillion led surviving members in gathering information of use to the Free French Forces in London until, in August 1942, she, too, was arrested and deported to Germany.* Brossolette, the newspaper's last editor, turned to organizing other resistance groups in the occupied zone and, after meeting de Gaulle in London, became a liaison officer in France between Gaullist groups and British secret

---

*Both Tillion and Humbert survived.

agents of the Special Operations Executive, which carried out sabotage and espionage in Nazi-occupied territories. Arrested in February 1944 while returning from another trip to London, Brossolette was tortured at length in the Gestapo's infamous Paris headquarters at 84 avenue Foch. On March 22, although handcuffed, he managed to open the window of his room and jump out; he died a few hours later. Others from the Musée de l'Homme network were luckier. Aveline and Abraham, who were in the unoccupied zone when the network was dismantled, joined other resistance groups and survived the war without detention. Cassou, who was hiding in Toulouse, was arrested in December 1941. While in jail, he composed thirty-three sonnets—in his head, since he had no paper—and these were published in secret in 1944. In the spring of 1943, he resumed his underground activities.

As an institution, though, the Musée de l'Homme would pay a high price for its early association with the resistance. In all, twenty-eight members of its staff would be remembered as *morts pour la France et pour la liberté,* some shot like Vildé, others killed fighting in the resistance, and at least one, Deborah Lifchitz, a Jewish ethnologist specializing in Ethiopia and Mali, sent to her death in Auschwitz. At the same time, apart from publishing *Résistance* and providing some intelligence to London, the *réseau* was never more than a minor irritant to the occupiers. For instance, it carried out no assassinations or acts of sabotage. If its leaders were given harsh punishments, then, it was principally to dissuade others from following their example. Yet paradoxically, at least with the seven *réseau* members executed at Mont-Valérien, it was their readiness to fight and to die that would prove the more lasting example. Their clandestine activities had minimal impact compared to the impression caused by their much-publicized deaths. Many other *résistants* would die, while a good number of artists and intellectuals later joined the underground battle against the Germans. But the Réseau du Musée de l'Homme stood out, not only because it was a ragtag army of highly educated people who were thoroughly ill-equipped to take on the Wehrmacht, but also because, at a time when most of the French were coming to terms with the occupation, they were almost alone in acting on their belief in the *idea* of resistance.

CHAPTER 7

Maréchal, Nous Voilà!

SINCE WORLD WAR II the name Vichy has become shorthand for collaboration with the Nazis, yet until Pétain installed his government
there, in July 1940, it referred to a popular spa with a far more benign
reputation. In the early 1860s, Napoleon III built a large villa in the
resort so he could spend time with his mistress, Marguerite Bellanger, in the guise of taking the resort's pungently sulfurous waters.*
Inevitably, the imperial presence accelerated change. A train connection to Paris followed, and Vichy was soon a fashionable retreat for
upper-class Parisians seeking a cure. A delightful park took shape
beside the Allier River, more imperial-style villas were built, and
stylish hotels, restaurants and the ever-popular Grand Casino sprung
up around the town's central gardens. The Opéra de Vichy, which

---

*The story is told that in 1863 Empress Eugénie accompanied her husband to Vichy,
where Bellanger was staying in a nearby chalet. During a promenade, Bellanger's
dog ran up to the emperor, clearly recognizing him. Eugénie saw this as proof of her
husband's affair with the actress and never returned to the resort.

opened in 1902, presented a full season of opera and ballet, with even Richard Strauss conducting his own *Salome* there in 1935.

Five years later, Vichy also seemed like a good shelter for many Parisians fleeing the advancing German army. And soon Pétain and his future deputy, Pierre Laval, spotted the town's suitability as a seat of government. Situated in the center of France, only thirty miles from the demarcation line dividing occupied and unoccupied zones, Vichy was just a few hours away from Paris by road or rail. In this haven of tranquillity, undisturbed by the sound of Wehrmacht boots, Pétain could play his chosen role of head of state of *all* France.

Surprisingly, the fiction that Vichy spoke for the entire nation—and not just for the unoccupied zone—was widely accepted. No fewer than forty governments sent representatives there, including the United States, China, Japan and, until June 1941, the Soviet Union. Distant lands untouched by the war were also represented, among them Afghanistan, Thailand, Iraq, Turkey and most of Latin America, as well as neutral Ireland and even the Vatican. This suited the owners of Vichy's plusher mansions, which, instead of being left empty and abandoned, were snapped up by major embassies. For example, the Villa Ica, the new home of the United States embassy on the suitably named boulevard des États-Unis, was owned by the American millionairess and Riviera socialite Florence Gould. Other delegations rented suites in the no less aptly named Hôtel des Ambassadeurs.

Naturally, most diplomats yearned for Paris, even occupied Paris, but they tempered the tedium by playing tennis, attending endless receptions and dinners and arranging clandestine erotic distractions. Latin American diplomats were known for giving the best parties, some continuing long after the eleven o'clock curfew. The belief that Pétain was important brought foreign journalists to Vichy, among them correspondents of United Press, Associated Press, *Chicago Tribune* and *The New York Times*. For entertainment, there were also visits by Paris opera, ballet and theater companies, while Piaf sang at one of the many galas organized to support Pétain's official charities. The Germans, meanwhile, kept a low profile, monitoring events from a rambling building close to the river. Otto Abetz, Hitler's ambassador, spent most of his time in Paris.

Pétain set up his new home and office on the fourth floor of Vichy's best hotel, the Hôtel du Parc, which overlooks the town's central gardens and had the Hôtel Majestic as an annex. On Sundays, dressed with customary elegance and accompanied by his wife, Eugénie, also known as *la maréchale,* Pétain would watch the changing of the guard from the balcony of his hotel before being driven to attend mass at the Church of Saint-Louis, where a crowd was usually waiting to applaud him. Laval worked on the third floor, although he preferred to spend his nights fifteen miles away in Châteldon, the medieval village where he had been born in 1883 and where he now owned the local château. The floor below was occupied by Vichy's Foreign Ministry, which Laval also headed, while other ministries were scattered around town: the Army Ministry — the June 1940 armistice had allowed France to keep a 100,000-man lightly armed force in the unoccupied zone — was at the Grand Hôtel Thermal; the Hôtel Carlton found room for the Finance, Justice and Labor Ministries; the Youth Secretariat was based at the Opéra itself.

Swelling the population of Vichy to 130,000 were some 30,000 *fonctionnaires,* many drawn to the town by the prospect of job security and the appeal of not living under German occupation. Theirs would be a safe war, but not one exempt from the discomfort of chilly winters — that of 1940–41 was one of the coldest in memory — and frequent food shortages. Ministerial posts in Pétain's first cabinet went to retired military, former ministers in prewar conservative governments and members of Maurras's ultranationalist party, L'Action Française. A few *pétainistes* already enjoyed close ties with the Nazis, among them Fernand de Brinon, who represented Vichy in Paris from December 1940. But Fascist intellectuals, believing more in Hitler's new Europe than in Pétain's National Revolution, showed little interest in staying in Vichy. For instance, Marcel Déat, a socialist-turned-Fascist who became editor of *L'Oeuvre,* left Vichy after Pétain ignored his call to form a regime modeled after that of the Salazar dictatorship in Portugal. In 1941, he created his own collaborationist party, Rassemblement National Populaire, and never abandoned hope that it would become Vichy's official party. Lucien Rebatet, the virulently anti-Semitic journalist, worked briefly for Vichy's Radiodiffusion Nationale before returning to Paris and rejoining the pro-Nazi weekly *Je suis partout.* As he later noted in his book *Les Décombres,* "Everyone with any fascist or anti-Jewish convictions left for Paris."[1] But there was no shortage of politicians, businessmen and artists looking for jobs or favors in Vichy.

Among them was Charles-Édouard Jeanneret-Gris, the celebrated Swiss-born architect better known as Le Corbusier. He left Paris a few days ahead of the Germans and headed for Vichy. "I must fight here where I believe it is necessary to put the world of construction on the right track," he wrote at the time.[2] In other words, this was the artist speaking; to exercise his profession, he had to be close to power. And he was not put off by Vichy's actions on other fronts: on October 1, 1940, two days before Vichy decreed the Statute on Jews, Le Corbusier noted that Jews were going through "a very bad time," but he added, unsympathetically, that "it does seem as if their blind thirst for money had corrupted the country."*[3] Le Corbusier's real dream was to be hired by Vichy to execute an urban renewal plan for Algiers, and he flew there in the summer of 1940 with this in mind. He was also named as a consultant on reconstruction of areas damaged during the German invasion and was later placed in charge of a new housing program. But not one of his dreams was realized. In April 1942, Le Corbusier again flew to Algiers, but his plan for the city was rejected. "Some inventors have ideas and receive a kick in the backside," he lamented.[4] On July 1, 1942, he left Vichy forever, and in October he reopened his studio in Paris. In two years, all he had achieved was a reputation for being uncomfortably close to Vichy.

Le Corbusier's mistake was to project his hopes and ambitions onto the majestic figure of *le maréchal* without knowing what Pétain had in mind for France. He was not alone among artists and intellectuals. The pianist Alfred Cortot was among the very few who chose to live and work in Vichy, but a good many shared the regime's anti-Communist attitude and identification with Catholicism and, initially at least, offered it their support. Some, like the writers Marcel Jouhandeau, Jacques Chardonne, Ramon Fernandez and Henry de Montherlant, did so publicly. Others, like Gide and Mauriac, did so discreetly, more in hope than conviction; and both were soon disillusioned. But in the summer of 1940, they were hardly out of step with the vast majority of French people who wanted to believe that, like some Old Testament prophet, Pétain would lead them out of captivity. They felt reassured that in this old soldier France's brave heart continued to beat, that the military hero of yore would again save France's honor. It helped that Pétain looked the part of the patriarch. His stolidly upright image was endlessly promoted through posters,

---

*Friends of Le Corbusier's would later insist that he was not anti-Semitic, but that he had a strong dislike of Freemasons.

statuettes, scarves, paintings, newspaper articles, books, radio broad-casts and newsreel footage of crowds cheering him on visits to towns and cities in the unoccupied zone.* And when he spoke to the French by radio, his vision of a National Revolution built on those old-fashioned values of work, family and fatherland—*travail, famille, patrie*—was spelled out in simple and comprehensible phrases. The French had good reason to believe that Pétain knew what he was doing.

The reality was far more complicated. While Vichy worked on a day-to-day basis with Abetz and the German embassy in Paris, it also had to deal with the German military command, the Armistice Commission based in Wiesbaden, the Propaganda Abteilung and, later, with the Gestapo and the SS. Further, although Pétain's regime was based in Vichy and the Germans denied its request to move to Versailles, it also had responsibilities in the occupied zone, not only for major cultural and educational institutions but also for security and the economy. To maintain order, it counted on France's tradi-tional network of *préfets,* appointed officials with the power of gov-ernors who owed their loyalty to the central government, not to the citizens. While *préfets* were de facto police chiefs in their *départe-ments,* they also provided Vichy with crucial information about Ger-man behavior and the population's reaction to the occupation.

Vichy nonetheless felt under constant pressure from the Germans, who disapproved of any excessive displays of nationalism and banned various Vichy organizations from operating in the occupied zone. Its biggest headache, though, was managing its economic relationship with the Germans. Not only was Vichy required by the armistice to pay 400 million francs daily† to cover the cost of the occupation, but it also had to organize the economy so as to satisfy Germany's enor-mous demand for industrial and agricultural products and raw mate-rials. Pétain himself was pulled in different directions. While he publicly endorsed collaboration with Germany after his meeting with Hitler in October 1940, he continued to promise a National Revolu-tion designed to build a new and stronger France.

In practice, at least until Germany took over southern France, this

---

*Galtier-Boissière noted with delight that he bought a portrait of Pétain—to hang in his toilet.

†Adjusted to contemporary purchasing power, this is equivalent to paying Germany $43.8 billion per year.

meant subservience to the Germans in the occupied zone and a degree of autonomy in the unoccupied zone. For instance, although subject to Vichy censorship, literary journals like *Poésie, Confluences, Les Cahiers du Sud* and *Fontaine* published work by such known anti-Fascists as the poets Aragon and Éluard. The Vichy region also had a busy press, which included nine newspapers and thirty weeklies that had fled Paris, among them *Le Figaro, Le Temps, La Croix* and a new Lyon edition of *Paris-Soir,* as well as numerous regional dailies, such as *La Dépêche de Toulouse.* And these publications enjoyed some freedom: the intellectual journal *Esprit,* which the philosopher Emmanuel Mounier moved to Lyon, was a rare case of a publication being closed by Vichy. Even Maurras, known for his dislike of Germany, found ways of expressing skepticism toward the occupiers in his movement's newspaper, *L'Action Française.* Michel Déon, then a follower of Maurras's, today an *immortel* of the Académie Française, recalled the mood in Lyon at the time: "You could not think that France was on the right path, but you were waiting, totally powerless in a world war. In the south, you were free, you could speak, even in the press. Although there was censorship, there was also criticism. You became an egoist. I will live! I will eat! In the south, we could think of nothing but victory."[5]

Inside the Vichy regime, there was continuous tension between those favoring outright collaboration and those backing the National Revolution. And, as a stranger to the murky world of political maneuvering, Pétain was himself ill-prepared to rule the governments he headed. In each, men of assorted ideologies and ambitions spent enormous energy wrestling for supremacy and settling scores dating back to the Third Republic. Disenchantment often followed: in time, many French rightists gave up on Vichy and either accepted a new German-ruled Europe or joined the resistance. One who broke with Pétain was François Mitterrand. Having escaped from a German prison camp in late 1941, he held a middle-level post in the Vichy regime dealing with prisoners of war before joining the resistance in mid-1943.

On one early occasion, though, Pétain asserted his will. He disliked Laval, not least for the way his deputy would disrespectfully arrive late for their meetings and blow cigarette smoke in his face. More importantly, the marshal instinctively distrusted this man, who seemed to personify the cynicism and amorality of the Third Republic. Laval could, in fact, boast consistency in one area: as far back as

1919, his desire to avert a fresh confrontation with Germany had led him to vote against the Treaty of Versailles, convinced that it would feed German resentment and bring trouble. Now he was ready to reach out to the Germans: on July 19, 1940, in Paris, he was the first Vichy official to meet Abetz. But this only reinforced Pétain's suspicion of Laval.

On December 13, 1940, after learning that Laval was engaged in unauthorized negotiations with the Germans, Pétain jumped at the chance to be rid of him. He asked all his cabinet members to offer their resignations, then accepted that of Laval and ordered his house arrest. In a brief radio broadcast, Pétain said, "I have resolved to make this decision for compelling political reasons. It in no way alters our relationship with Germany. I remain at the helm. The National Revolution will continue to move forward." Laval was replaced by a triumvirate comprising former prime minister Pierre-Étienne Flandin, General Charles Huntziger and Admiral François Darlan. For Pétain, it was a daring move, but one that displeased Berlin. Abetz rushed to Vichy with an armed guard to free Laval and accompany him back to Paris. While still in Vichy, according to what Galtier-Boissière heard, Abetz demanded to see Flandin, who claimed to be unwell. When Abetz insisted on a meeting, in order to maintain the pretense of his illness, Flandin received the ambassador in bed. "A true Molière farce," Galtier-Boissière observed.[6] Two months later, the Germans pushed out the triumvirate, leaving Darlan alone as Pétain's deputy and newly assigned political heir. But while Darlan proved himself eager to collaborate with the Germans, offering numerous concessions during a meeting with Hitler in May 1941, Laval remained the Nazis' favorite. In April 1942, to Pétain's considerable discomfort, Laval returned to power, this time with the title of prime minister, as well as its power.

This change also marked a turning point in Washington's relations with Vichy. After France's defeat, the United States was first represented in Vichy by a chargé d'affaires, Robert D. Murphy, who worked hard to bolster Pétain as a counterweight to the Germans. In early 1941, after Murphy was sent as President Roosevelt's personal envoy to Vichy-ruled North Africa, Admiral Leahy took over as ambassador. The appointment to the post of a senior American naval officer was, of course, no coincidence: not only would he be dealing with another naval officer, Admiral Darlan, as Vichy's de facto prime minister, but Washington was also eager to keep the French fleet in the port of Toulon from being seized by Germany. In fact, until December 1941, when the United States entered the war, Washington and Vichy shared a common objective: each wanted the other to stay out of the conflict. And even after the United States entered the war, its relations with Vichy remained cordial. But the return of Laval to power signaled a change. Leahy was withdrawn and, barely six months later, the Allies invaded North Africa, prompting Vichy to break ties with Washington. By then, Laval, who had never believed in Pétain's revolution, had embraced Nazi-defined collaboration as the only path left for Vichy.

Yet in some cultural and social areas, the National Revolution—while neither national nor revolutionary—spawned changes that would survive the end of the war. At first, the program seemed devoted entirely to the glorification of Pétain. And with Paul Marion, a former Communist and journalist, as information minister, the marshal found someone adept at effecting this. But once Pétain had been aggrandized and the usual suspects blamed for France's defeat, Vichy identified the key ingredients of its new moral renovation: mothers, children, families, crafts and folk culture, farming and sports. And these, by no coincidence, were all categories closely associated with France's deeply conservative Catholic church, which was still smarting over its loss of power since the "republican and secular" school reform of 1905. Pétain himself was hardly devout, but he enjoyed the backing of most Catholics, including many intellectuals, and he was happy for the Catholic hierarchy to believe that he was inspired by its values. One underlying theme was that "rural" was good and "urban" was bad, with nothing more patriotic than tilling the land. One song among many, "La Terre de France," promoted this:

> We work, we work,
> We work with confidence.
> We are putting right, we will restore
> The prestige of France.

The implicit message behind this propaganda was that the decadent leftist intellectuals of Paris—that is, those who supported the Popular Front—had also contributed to the country's mess. Certainly, the proposition that the French would be better off using their bodies more than their minds was one that both Vichy and the church could endorse.

Vichy could equally count on church backing for the central role given to women in the "new" France, both as pillars of the family and as procreators of legions of much-needed French—and Catholic—babies. Thoroughly persuaded that a woman's place was in the home, for instance, Vichy banned women from working in the public sector, although it did not consider how mothers with husbands in prison camps in Germany were meant to sustain their families. To keep women on a narrow path, Vichy also made divorce more difficult and threatened abortionists with death.* At the same time, Pétain elevated women to near saintly status: reflecting France's perennial alarm over its low birthrate, he encouraged them to have numerous children, offering a special medal, the Médaille d'honneur de la famille française, in different categories: bronze for at least five children, silver for seven or more, and gold for upwards of ten. He also instituted Mothers' Day, to be celebrated on May 25 every year. On the first such fête, in 1941, a poster carried Pétain's message to children: "Your mother has done everything for you. The Marshal asks you to thank her politely." For the 1943 Mothers' Day, Elyane Célis recorded an appropriately syrupy song, "Être maman," with such heartwarming lines as "To be a mother is to be prettier."

Pétain himself was now the nation's new father, even though he had no children of his own. Soon, across the unoccupied zone, children began their school day singing "Maréchal, nous voilà," Vichy's unofficial anthem. Four stirring verses each ended with the refrain:

> *Marshal, here we are!*
> *Before you, the savior of France*
> *We swear, we your lads*
> *To serve and follow your steps*
> *Marshal, here we are*
> *You have given us new hope*
> *Our nation will be reborn*
> *Marshal, Marshal*
> *Marshal, here we are!*

---

*On July 30, 1943, Marie-Louise Giraud, a laundress from near Cherbourg who was found guilty of performing twenty-seven abortions, became one of the last women to be guillotined in France.

Later in the occupation, the resistance came up with numerous parodies of this song, one replacing the refrain with *"Général, nous
voilà,"* referring to de Gaulle, another warning Pétain that he would
pay for his collaboration, *"Maréchal, tu payeras."* But elderly French
people raised in the unoccupied zone still remember the song's official words. Less well known is that its lyricists, André Montagard
and Charles Courtioux, plagiarized the tune from a Polish Jewish
composer, Casimir Oberfeld, who was later deported from France to
Auschwitz, where he died.

Borrowing from both the Popular Front and the Third Reich,
Vichy emphasized physical education for children and teenagers and
quadrupled the prewar sports budget. Jean Borotra, the former
Wimbledon tennis champion who was general commissioner for
sports until ousted by Laval in April 1942, took the lead in promoting sports as a new nationalist creed. He organized athletics meetings
in both Paris and the unoccupied zone, as well as cycling races in
Vichy and rowing regattas on the Allier River. He even invited those
active in sports to swear the Oath of the Athlete: "I promise on my
honor to practice sports disinterestedly, with discipline and loyalty,
in order to improve and thus best serve my country."[7] The regime's
greatest success was in giving sports and physical education a new
status in schools and universities. Borotra himself fared less well after
he lost his Vichy post. Known as an ardent Anglophile, he was suspected of secret contacts with British agents and arrested in November 1942. Deported to Germany, he was held at Sachsenhausen,
Buchenwald and other camps before being freed by American troops
at Itter, in Austria, in May 1945. After returning to France, though,
he still had to answer for his association with Vichy.

The need to improve young people—or at least to keep them out
of mischief—was evidently high among Vichy's priorities. And here
the example of the scouting movement run by the Catholic church
proved vital. It had experience with recruiting teenagers, organizing
them into teams, teaching them independence and, above all, inculcating them with moral and patriotic values. Unsurprisingly, then,
it fell to former scout leaders to create and lead several youth organizations on behalf of Vichy. The first, Les Chantiers de la Jeunesse,
or Building Sites for Youth, was founded in July 1940 to replace military service, which was banned by the armistice. Under a former
scoutmaster, General Joseph de La Porte du Theil, Les Chantiers
organized isolated camps across the unoccupied zone where twenty-

year-old men were required to spend eight months living under a regime of military discipline. Wearing uniforms, they learned to march, hold flag ceremonies and pay homage to Pétain. More usefully, they also did forestry and agricultural work. Somewhere between 300,000 and 500,000 youths passed through these camps during the occupation. From 1943, though, Les Chantiers also served Germany's interest since, upon completing their stints in the camps, many young men were automatically sent to Germany under a compulsory work program. In January 1944, when General La Porte du Theil resisted German orders to press-gang all those in the camps to work in Germany, he was arrested and himself interned in Germany. In practice, though, many youths escaped the camps and joined the rural resistance known as the maquis.*

A similar organization, Les Compagnons de France, also founded in July 1940 by a former scout leader, Henri Dhavernas, targeted boys between fourteen and nineteen. It, too, had a paramilitary structure, with tents, uniforms, flag ceremonies, campfires and the like. And Pétain himself attended its inaugural ceremony, applauding the movement's intention of replacing peasants who were now prisoners of war by working on farms and repairing roads and bridges. Les Compagnons also engaged in cultural activities, including theater and music. And while the group was meant to be loyally *pétain-iste,* it never excluded Jews and it often sheltered youths fleeing to the south from the occupied zone. In February 1941, Dhavernas was replaced by Guillaume de Tournemire, who by the end of 1942 was himself engaged in the resistance. Increasingly, Vichy sensed that it had lost control of the movement until finally, in January 1944, Les Compagnons were dissolved. Many of its members then joined the maquis. All that survived were Les Compagnons de la Musique, a choir that gained popularity around France. After the liberation, adopted by none other than Édith Piaf, it survived under a new name, Les Compagnons de la Chanson.

The experiment with quite the most lasting cultural impact, however, was Jeune France, or Young France, which was launched by Vichy's Youth Secretariat in December 1940 with the idea of promoting cultural activities around the country, including in the occupied zone. What most distinguished the movement was that its

*The word *maquis* means scrub, bush or overgrown heath, while *prendre le maquis* means to take to the bush or to go into hiding.

leaders were not only anti-Communist Catholics who believed that the National Revolution could serve a purpose, but they were also well educated and independent-minded. The man behind Jeune France was Pierre Schaeffer, another Catholic and former scout who had graduated from the prestigious École Polytechnique and had experimented in electroacoustical sound at Radiodiffusion Nationale before the war. Now, still only twenty-nine, seeing an opportunity to broadcast culture in a way of interest to young people, he proposed the creation of Radio Jeunesse, or Radio Youth, which by August 1940 already had a fifteen-minute daily slot on Radio Vichy. Its tone was thoroughly patriotic, including speeches by Pétain and readings of the nationalist poet Charles Péguy. But along with an inspirational message, it also presented live theater, choral music, poetry and interviews with artists.

The success of Radio Jeunesse enabled Schaeffer to win over Vichy to the more ambitious idea of Jeune France. Working with other former scout leaders, Schaeffer set out to mobilize artists of all genres—poets, painters, actors, movie directors and designers—under the banner of preserving "the great traditions" of French culture. Each of Jeune France's sections—theater, literature, radio and cinema, music and visual arts—had representatives in Paris and in the unoccupied zone. New cultural centers, Maisons Jeune France, were also set up in Lyon, Toulouse, Marseille, Bordeaux and Le Mans, as well as Paris. These centers, forerunners of a similar network created around France in the 1960s, not only organized cultural events and debates but also held night classes on everything from choral singing to costume design.

The idea of bringing culture to the masses conformed with the philosophy of the National Revolution, yet in practice Jeune France's very openness spawned a sense of freedom among many artists. In May 1941, under its aegis, the artist Jean Bazaine ignored official disapproval of "degenerate" art and organized a show of abstract art at the Galerie Braun in Paris under the deceptively innocent title of Vingt Jeunes Peintres de Tradition Française (Twenty Young Painters of the French Tradition). That same year, Jeune France hosted the so-called Rencontres de Lourmarin, where poets and musicians were invited to work together on new projects. A great lover of theater, Schaeffer also used Vichy's budget to finance Étienne Decroux's mime school, which would have Marcel Marceau among its early students.

Schaeffer was particularly keen on theatrical and musical events held before large crowds, preferably outdoors. And who better to stir a patriotic audience than Joan of Arc? With a colleague, Pierre Barbier, he created a ten-tableau musical pageant devoted to the martyred heroine called *Portique pour une fille de France* (Portico for a Daughter of France), which on May 11, 1940, was performed simultaneously in Lyon, Marseille and Toulouse before crowds of upwards of twenty thousand in each city. Arthur Honegger's oratorio *Jeanne au bûcher* (Joan at the Stake), based on Paul Claudel's text, was first presented at the Lyon Opera on July 4, 1941, also sponsored by Jeune France. Other cultural events were organized around the Fête de Jeanne d'Arc, which took place annually on the second Sunday in May: the Orchestre National de la Radiodiffusion Française performed Paul Paray's *Messe solennelle pour Jeanne* in May 1941 and Gounod's *Messe pour Jeanne d'Arc* in May 1942.

Jeune France took seriously its commitment to tour productions and exhibitions. Here, its greatest impact was in theater, with some twenty different companies performing 770 times around France during the movement's seventeen months of existence. The repertory tended to be rich in Molière, Racine and other French classics, but Greek drama was also popular. In Paris, again with Honegger's music, Jean-Louis Barrault directed an outdoor performance of Aeschylus's *The Suppliants* among the sprouting weeds of the abandoned Roland Garros tennis stadium, while Jean Vilar, who would become France's leading postwar theater director, adapted Hesiod's *Works and Days* outdoors in Melun, where peasants and artisans paraded with their work tools as extras. But the very enthusiasm that Jeune France awakened among young artists condemned it to failure. Under pressure from hard-liners in Vichy, Jeune France was closed down in March 1942, although its influence would survive the occupation.

One other organization was also punished for its success. In December 1940, a former army officer, Pierre Dunoyer de Segonzac, founded the École Nationale des Cadres de la Jeunesse, literally the National School for Youth Leaders. Based in the Château of Uriage, a small mountain spa near Grenoble, the École d'Uriage, as it was known, was unapologetically elitist in its aim to build a new generation of leaders for postwar France. Among its teachers were Mounier and Hubert Beuve-Méry, a Catholic journalist who in December 1944 would found the afternoon newspaper *Le Monde*. Guided by these and other intellectuals, Uriage's orientation was Catholic, nationalist and anti-Communist, as well as both *pétainiste* and anti-German. The four thousand men and women who attended its courses, which lasted between three and twelve weeks, underwent an intense program of political, intellectual and moral education, after which they were supposedly imbued by the "spirit of Uriage." But this freethinking was not to Vichy's liking, and the school was closed by Laval in December 1942. After that, many of its graduates, as well as de Segonzac, Mounier and Beuve-Méry, joined the resistance. Meanwhile, a more artistic experiment was taking place in Oppède-le-Vieux, north of Aix-en-Provence, where the renowned architect Bernard Zehrfuss drew together musicians, painters, sculptors and architects into a commune of sorts, which, surprisingly, received a subsidy from Vichy. Among those who spent time there in 1941 was Saint-Exupéry's wife, Consuelo, herself a writer. But by 1942, this, too, was looked on with suspicion by Vichy: Zehrfuss obtained permission to travel to Barcelona and used the opportunity to join the Free French Forces.

The closure of both Jeune France and the École d'Uriage in 1942 illustrated how the realities of the occupation were replacing the conservative idealism of the National Revolution. In Pétain's one attempt to build a popular base for his regime, he recruited veterans of World War I to form the Légion Française des Combattants. It grew quickly, numbering some 590,000 by early 1941 and later incorporating nonveteran volunteers. Along with Vichy's *préfets*, the legion worked to ensure an orderly occupation, one that enabled Germany to wind down its security presence in France. (In mid-1942, for instance, Germany had fewer than three thousand police officers stationed in France.) However, while the legion could summon large crowds to welcome Pétain on his visits around the unoccupied zone, it was never effective in helping him resist German pressure. In practice, as he repeatedly discovered, his bargaining power was minimal. And it was further weakened when he resisted Nazi demands that France declare war on Britain. Soon, Vichy was doing little more than responding to events beyond its control.

The first of these was Operation Barbarossa, Germany's invasion of the Soviet Union on June 22, 1941. In time, it would require France to send still more manufactured goods and raw materials to Germany, followed by mass recruitment—first voluntary, then enforced—of Frenchmen to work in German factories. But the most immediate consequence was the mobilization of France's Moscow-line Communist Party to start resisting the occupation. The party's first shot, literally, was fired in the Barbès-Rochechouart *métro* station in Paris on August 21, 1941, killing a German naval cadet.

Similar murders followed, with a furious Führer ordering the execution of fifty hostages for every German killed. As if in anticipation, hundreds of Communist and Jewish hostages were already being held in French prisons. After a German soldier in Bordeaux and an officer in Nantes were killed in late October, forty-eight hostages were shot. In late November, another ninety-five were executed. Public outrage and condemnations by the Catholic church forced Vichy to protest and, it claimed, it obtained some reprieves. Yet in the nine months after the Communist Party took up arms, 471 hostages were shot. After one year of relative calm, the occupation was degenerating. Resistance attacks and executions continued, even after the Germans warned that, in reprisal, "close male relatives, brothers-in-law and cousins of the agitators above the age of eighteen years will be shot" and that female relatives would be condemned to hard labor. In September 1942, after several German soldiers were killed in an attack on Le Rex, a Paris movie theater patronized exclusively by German troops, 166 more hostages were shot.

Long before then, Pétain began to sense that much of the French population was beginning to lose confidence in him. In fact, on August 12, 1941, even before the first German soldier was murdered, he broadcast an urgent appeal for national unity. "I have serious things to tell you," he began. "From several regions of France, I have felt an ill wind blowing in recent weeks." He acknowledged that his National Revolution had not yet become reality, but he blamed followers of the ancien régime and those working for foreign interests. Recalling his role in World War I, he went on: "I know from experience what is victory; today I see what is defeat." He concluded by urging, "Remember this: a defeated country, if it is divided, is a country that dies; a defeated country, if it knows how to unite, is a country that is reborn."

Yet within months, Vichy's internal divisions would be further exposed by the trial of prewar French political leaders. For Pétain, the ultimate purpose of the trial was to blame the Third Republic for France's defeat and to legitimize his own regime. In October 1941, tired of waiting for the trial, Pétain himself summarily condemned the former prime ministers Blum and Daladier as well as the former army chief General Maurice Gamelin and two other politicians. The last prime minister before the defeat, Paul Reynaud, and his interior minister, Georges Mandel, were acquitted, although both were then handed over to the Nazis and sent to camps in Germany. Then, in February 1942, the five found guilty by Pétain were brought before the Supreme Court of Justice in Riom, near Clermont-Ferrand, for a fresh trial, now public. Part of the prosecution's case was that Blum's Popular Front had carried out social reforms—such as paid holidays and a forty-hour week—that had weakened France's will to fight. Gamelin refused to answer any questions, which was perhaps wise since, ten days before France declared war on Germany, he had told the National Assembly, "The day war is declared against Germany, Hitler will collapse."[8] But Daladier skillfully demonstrated that senior military officers—and not politicians—were to blame for the debacle.*

Ending his testimony on March 6, Daladier went further, turning away from the judges and addressing the public: "Germany suffered its first defeat with England and its second with Russia. There is no doubt that Germany will be defeated; it is inevitable. We must not let our confidence waver."[9] In mid-March, after twenty-four hearings and four hundred witnesses, Hitler ordered Abetz to halt the trial. He had hoped it would show that France, and not Germany, was responsible for the war; instead it had become an embarrassment. On April 14, the trial was suspended and those in the dock were sent to camps in Germany. Blum was taken to Buchenwald and Dachau, where, somewhat surprisingly, he was treated well and lived in relative comfort. All five survived the war.

The French public was not enthusiastic about the growing armed insurgency, criticizing both the Communists for provoking reprisals and the Germans for carrying them out. But for Vichy, initially even more than the political opposition coming from de Gaulle's Free French Forces, the emergence of the Communist-led Francs-Tireurs

---

*Outside *pétainiste* and right-wing circles, Daladier's view was widely shared. As early as June 28, 1941, having read *Les Causes militaires de notre défaite* by a Colonel Michel Alerme, Galtier-Boissière scoffed at the author's attempt to blame the Third Republic. "In truth, it is the result of the incapacity of the Superior War Council that French troops found themselves in the situation of savages carrying bows and arrows in the face of cannons and machine-guns," he wrote in *Mon journal pendant l'occupation* (p. 55).

et Partisans, or FTP, posed a different problem: this organization of guerrillas and partisans challenged Vichy's claim to be the only viable alternative to the German occupiers. Vichy's response was to step up its anti-Communist propaganda, even doing Berlin the favor of portraying Moscow as the main threat to the "new" Europe. Still more eager to fight Communism were French Fascists in Paris, led by Jacques Doriot, head of the Parti Populaire Français, and Marcel Déat, the journalist who had also recently founded his own party. Immediately after the German invasion of the Soviet Union, they began working with the German embassy and the Wehrmacht to create the Légion des Volontaires Français Contre le Bolchévisme to send French volunteers to fight on the Eastern Front. The initiative was backed by Vichy's Paris delegate, Brinon, and, more astonishingly, by Cardinal Alfred Baudrillart. In practice, the LVF, as the legion became known, contributed little to the Nazi war effort. Most of its seven thousand or so volunteers were killed, and the few survivors were incorporated into a French Waffen-SS brigade in 1944. Nonetheless, for propaganda purposes, it became a powerful symbol of French collaboration.

But if Bolshevism was the new enemy, Vichy was all too ready to continue collaborating with Germany in tackling the old enemy, the Jews. In the year following its Statute on Jews of October 1940, it issued a stream of laws and decrees targeting Jews. In some cases, they complemented Nazi diktats, including one ordering the takeover or Aryanization of Jewish-owned businesses in the occupied zone, an action extended to the unoccupied zone in 1941. With Jewish businesses, though, Vichy had its own reason to act before the Germans did: in this way, at least in the unoccupied zone, it ensured that the companies passed into the hands of French trustees or owners, rather than Germans. But, in general, Vichy was also eager to strip Jews of all influence. When, in March 1941, Germany nudged Darlan into creating a special department for Jewish affairs, the General Commission for Jewish Questions, he named an infamous prewar anti-Semite, Xavier Vallat, as its head. Vallat in turn proudly told Theodor Dannecker, who ran Adolf Eichmann's Jewish Office in Paris, "I have been an anti-Semite for much longer than you."[10] In June 1941, a second Statute on Jews was decreed, banning Jews from a series of professions, including medicine, law and architecture. Darlan's notorious justice minister, Joseph Barthélemy, then added new restrictions on Jewish activities, such as acting in movies, the theater and music halls. These measures affected the occupied zone as well as the Vichy area.

As early as October 1940, Vichy had claimed the right to intern foreign Jews and, soon, many thousands were being held in camps in the south. The following year, instead of waiting for foreign Jews in the occupied zone to present themselves to the authorities, Vichy instructed the French police to go in search of them. The first big *rafle,* or roundup, of Jews, carried out by French police in Paris on May 14, 1941, resulted in another thirty-seven hundred refugees, mainly Polish, being sent to internment camps. Among the intellectuals of Paris, Jean Guéhenno was unusual in taking note of this escalation of official anti-Semitism. "On rue Compans," he wrote, "several men were taken. Their wives, their children begged the police, they shouted, they cried. The humble people of Paris who watched these harrowing scenes were filled with disgust and shame."[11]

A second *rafle* in Paris, between August 20 and 25, rounded up forty-two hundred men, but this time one-third were French Jews and they were sent to an unfinished housing estate in Drancy, outside Paris, which would soon become the main transit camp for Jews being deported to the east. Among those arrested was the philosopher Jean Wahl,* prompting Guéhenno to observe sourly, "But he is a major criminal: he is Jewish."[12] The third *rafle,* this time of mainly French Jews, is recorded on a plaque near the École Militaire in Paris. On December 12, 1941, it states, French police and German military police arrested 743 prominent French Jews and held them in a stable of the École Militaire before sending them to the Royallieu camp at Compiègne, where some died of hunger and cold. The survivors were among the 1,112 Jews aboard the first deportation train to leave France for Auschwitz on March 27, 1942.

In the spring of 1942, with Hitler's "final solution" now moving ahead, Vichy was expected to help. In April, after Laval returned to power, Vallat was replaced at the General Commission for Jewish Questions by Louis Darquier de Pellepoix, a still greater fanatic who was totally loyal to the Germans. As part of their European strategy for eliminating Jews, the Nazis decided that 100,000 Jews should be deported from France. And since they needed French police to carry

---

*Wahl was lucky: after spending three months in Drancy, where he wrote seventy poems, he was released and eventually made his way to the United States.

out the arrests and French trains to transport the deportees, they
began preparing a new *rafle* with René Bousquet, Vichy's secretary-
general for police.* They agreed that, as a first step, 40,000 foreign
Jews between the ages of sixteen and forty would be sent east,
including 10,000 from the unoccupied zone. Laval then proposed
that children under sixteen also be included, so that they would not
be separated from their parents. Laval even turned down an American offer to take 1,000 Jewish children, arguing that they were not
orphans. The roundup, which was postponed from July 14 to avoid
Bastille Day, began before dawn on July 16 and continued the following day, with at least 4,500 French police, aided by volunteers
from Doriot's Fascist Party, arresting 12,884 Jews, including 4,051
children. Most were taken in convoys of buses to a sports stadium
called the Vélodrome d'Hiver, where they were held in grim conditions before being transfered to camps at Beaune-la-Rolande and
Pithiviers as well as to Drancy prior to deportation.†

The *rafle du Vél'd'Hiv'*, as this roundup became known, shocked
many Parisians and brought protests from the United States embassy
in Vichy and, more significantly, from five prominent Catholic
bishops, led by Archbishop Jules-Gérard Saliège of Toulouse. On
August 23, as part of his sermon, Saliège read a short text that was
distributed as a leaflet and later read on the BBC French service.
"Children, women, men, fathers and mothers treated like a lowly
herd; members of the same family separated from each other and
shipped off to an unknown destination; our age was destined to see
this dreadful spectacle," he said. Referring to two nearby internment
camps, he added, "In our diocese, moving scenes have occurred in
the camps of Noé and Récébédou. The Jews are men, the Jewesses
are women. The foreigners are men and women. One cannot do what
one wishes to these men, to these women, to these fathers and mothers. They are part of the human race; they are our brothers like so
many others. A Christian cannot forget this."[13] As an institution,
though, the Catholic hierarchy remained silent. And the arrests continued across the occupied zone, with 6,500 foreign Jews interned in

---

*Bousquet escaped punishment after the war and enjoyed a stellar career in banking
before his past caught up with him; in 1991, he was indicted for crimes against
humanity. Two years later, he was murdered in his home by a lone gunman with
known psychiatric problems.

†In practice, children were separated from their parents. Many were held at Beaune-
la-Rolande, fifty miles south of Paris, before being deported on their own.

the unoccupied zone also sent to Drancy. By the end of 1942, 36,802 Jews, including 6,053 children, had been deported from France.

Among these were the novelist Irène Némirovsky and her husband, Michel Epstein. They had already left Paris and joined their two daughters in Issy-l'Évêque when German troops entered the small town in Burgundy on June 17, 1940. Since their first visit two summers earlier, Irène and Michel had always stayed in the Hôtel des Voyageurs and, while a dozen German officers had moved in, the couple had not been asked to leave. In fact, Epstein, who spoke German, sometimes played billards with the soldiers, who, in this quietly bucolic area of Saône-et-Loire, had little to do. The Epsteins' two children, Denise, eleven at the time, and Élisabeth, three, attended the local school, while Irène, weather permitting, would walk to nearby woods—the Bois du Sapin or the Bois de la Maie—where she could write in peace. One favorite spot was L'Étang Perdu, a "lost pond" hidden among the trees. "She would go off into the countryside and write all day, all day, all day," Denise reminisced. "Only later did I understand she was upset to have been abandoned by the literary world that had once feted her."[14]

The Epsteins stood out in the town, not because they were the only Jews but because they were educated Parisians. "Irène was chic, elegant, tall, thin," recalled Gérard Morley, the son of a local *résistant,* who was ten at the time. "You could see that she was not from Issy, that she was from a different class. We knew she was a writer because she gave my mother a copy of her book *Deux.*"[15] A photograph of Élisabeth's class at school also underlined this difference: Élisabeth was the only child wearing shoes; all the others were in clogs. But the Epsteins were no longer well off. Michel had lost his job at a Paris bank and, as early as October 1940, Éditions Fayard had canceled a book contract with Irène. Surprisingly, though, Horace de Carbuccia, the right-wing editor of *Gringoire,* which was based in Marseille, agreed to publish her under a pseudonym, and he ran eight of her short stories between December 1940 and February 1942 before deciding he was taking too great a risk. Further, while unable to publish her, Robert Esménard at Éditions Albin Michel in Paris stood by her, paying her regular advances against future books.

In late June 1941, following the German invasion of the Soviet Union, the Wehrmacht detachment in Issy was reassigned to the new war front and, after holding a party at the local château, the occupiers left as abruptly as they had arrived. Irène, who was planning a five-part epic called *Suite française,* inspired by *War and Peace,* had already completed the first volume, *Storm in June,* covering the exodus from Paris. She set the second volume, *Dolce,* in an occupied town like Issy, where she imagined an unconsummated love story between a refined German officer billeted in a private home and a young woman whose husband is a prisoner of war. Her story ends when the Germans are sent to the Eastern Front.* Around that time, she also wrote *Chaleur du sang* (Fire in the Blood), a family drama set in a town in Burgundy, which was finally published in 2007. In early 1942, the Epsteins left the Hôtel des Voyageurs and rented half of a large unfurnished house overlooking the town's war memorial. That spring, while Irène and her family were now required to wear yellow stars, she continued to fill her notebooks, using minuscule handwriting to conserve her paper. She and her husband were not in hiding, and they made no effort to enter the unoccupied zone just twenty miles to the south, yet the little news that reached them was beginning to alarm them. "My mother's face was pale," Denise said. "There was no longer a smile. My father, who used to sing, was very silent."[16]

Then, on July 13, two gendarmes knocked on their front door with an arrest warrant for Irène. "When they came for her, there were no tears," Denise remembered. "It was a silent adieu. She asked me to look after Papa and she told Élisabeth she was going on a trip. I am sure she knew she was leaving forever."[17] Desperate to obtain her release, Michel contacted friends in publishing and even wrote to Abetz stressing Irène's "hatred for the Bolshevik regime."[18] He was unaware that already on July 17 she was aboard a train carrying nine hundred other Jews from the camp at Pithiviers to Auschwitz. One month later, she died there, perhaps from typhus. She was thirty-nine. Epstein's own luck ran out on October 9. He, too, was arrested by gendarmes and died in an Auschwitz gas chamber on November 6. The only good fortune was that Denise and Élisabeth survived, first hidden by a local teacher when gendarmes came to look for them, then taken by a governess to southwestern France, where they hid for eighteen months in a convent. In their suitcase, they carried the unfinished manuscript of *Suite française,* which would be published sixty-two years later.

---

*The three unwritten volumes planned for "her" *War and Peace* were *Captivité, Bataille* and *La Paix.*

Even after the major *rafles* of 1942, French police and officials
continued to implement this Nazi policy, with Bousquet himself
again playing a role in what became known as the Battle of Marseille
in January 1943, when French police destroyed part of the old city
and arrested some 2,000 people for deportation. Of the 76,000 Jews
eventually sent from France to death camps, barely 2,000 survived.
After the war, Vichy officials claimed they believed the Jews were
being sent to work in Germany, but by 1943 they could not ignore
strong rumors, if not actual confirmed reports, that Jews were being
murdered en masse in Poland. In November 1943, *Les Étoiles,* an
underground newspaper published by writers in southern France,
reported on the horrors of Auschwitz and noted, "Periodically, as a
reprisal, groups of 200 and 300 at a time are asphyxiated in 'gas
chambers.' "[19]

Further, Vichy did nothing to alleviate the hardship and hunger
that resulted in the deaths of at least 3,000 Jews in French internment
camps. The record of the French as a whole was more heartening.
Three-quarters of the Jews trapped in France in 1940 escaped deportation and, while many lived through the occupation in depradation
and fear, most survived because they were in some way protected — or
at least not denounced — by their French neighbors. In the Massif
Central, for instance, Protestant pastors and families in Le Chambon-
sur-Lignon and other mountain communities assumed huge risks in
shielding thousands of Jews from arrest. Many Jews also found safety
in the southeastern region of France that was under Italian occupation between November 1942 and September 1943. But if a far greater
proportion of Jews made it through the war in France than in, say, the
Netherlands, there was also a geographic explanation: as a relatively
large country with tens of thousands of remote villages and hamlets
and a mountain range running through its heart, France offered many
places to hide. Some communities in rural France never saw a German
soldier during the entire occupation.

While many French citizens were either opposed or indifferent
to the persecution of Jews, Pétain himself felt that his popularity
depended more on his handling of the prisoner-of-war problem. As a
result, in May 1942, when Berlin demanded that 350,000 Frenchmen
be sent to work in Germany to replace German workers sent to fight
on the Russian Front, Vichy proposed a one-for-one worker-POW
swap. Instead, although Laval managed to reduce the initial demand
to 250,000 French workers, Berlin imposed a far tougher deal: three

skilled workers for every freed prisoner of war. Vichy was forced to accept. The return of the first POWs in August, under what was known as *la relève,* or "the relief," was celebrated as a Vichy triumph, but the number of volunteers fell far below the required target. This was resolved the following month with a new law obliging all men between the ages of eighteen and fifty and all women between twenty-one and thirty-five to carry out any duties defined by Vichy. Companies were ordered to identify all staff members who were not indispensable, and the shipment of workers to Germany stepped up. By the end of 1942, the quota of 250,000 had been met and 90,000 prisoners of war had been freed. One consequence was a further slowdown of economic activity in France at a time of dire shortages of such necessities as food, clothes and coal. The only consolation for Vichy was that, at least in the occupied zone, Hitler, not Pétain, was blamed for the mounting misery of most of the French nation.

Soon, however, Pétain's standing was further eroded by events beyond his control. On November 8, 1942, United States troops landed in Vichy-ruled Morocco and Algeria. Washington had hoped to drive a wedge between Vichy and Berlin by placing French troops stationed in North Africa under General Henri Giraud, who had escaped a German POW camp and had pledged loyalty to Pétain. By chance Admiral Darlan, the former deputy prime minister, was in Algeria at the time and, assuming command, he quickly signed a cease-fire with the Americans. Meanwhile, Laval rushed to Munich in the hope of persuading Hitler that Vichy's forces in North Africa were resisting the Allied invasion. Unimpressed, Hitler ordered the Wehrmacht into the unoccupied zone and, soon after dawn on November 11, the twenty-fourth anniversary of the armistice sealing Germany's defeat in World War I, German troops were driving past Pétain's hotel in Vichy. Almost simultaneously, Italian troops occupied the Savoie and half the Riviera as well as Corsica.

With Vichy rapidly losing control of North Africa and the rest of its African empire, some in Pétain's circle urged him to fly to Algiers to preserve the tattered fiction of an independent French government, but he refused. Instead, under German pressure, he reluctantly broke diplomatic relations with the United States. In a radio broadcast, he said that until then he had thought his darkest days had been in June 1940. Guéhenno was not impressed. "Here he is in despair at the very moment that all the French begin to have hope," he noted in his journal. "Never has a head of state been more ignorant, more deaf, than his people."[20]

Still, one act of rebellion rescued a modicum of French pride. On November 27, as German and Italian troops entered the naval base in Toulon, orders were given to scuttle the French fleet to prevent it from falling into German hands: seventy-seven vessels were sunk or destroyed, including three battleships, seven cruisers and fifteen destroyers. The situation of the French in North Africa, though, remained confused. On December 24, Darlan was assassinated in Algiers by a monarchist involved in a bizarre plot to bring Henri, Comte de Paris, the Orléanist pretender to the French throne, to power; instead, the murder enabled the Americans to appoint Giraud as his successor. A protracted power struggle between Giraud and de Gaulle followed. Forced to share the presidency of the Free French Forces and of the French National Liberation Committee with Giraud, de Gaulle would need several months before he could assume undisputed French leadership of the battle to liberate France.*

In Vichy, while Pétain retained the title of head of state, Laval now ran the government, paying little heed to the aged marshal. Berlin allowed Vichy to maintain some of the trappings of government, albeit at a price: more than ever, it required the French police, its rural gendarmerie and its newly created paramilitary *milice,* or militia, to carry out repression on its behalf. However, events far from France had a greater impact on the occupation. As the Allies consolidated their hold on North Africa, the six-month-long Battle of Stalingrad, in southern Russia, ended on February 2, 1943, with the surrender of the German army. In his journal, Galtier-Boissière recorded the latest joke making the rounds: "Churchill and Stalin are up to their necks in excrement; Hitler is only up to his knees. 'So how do you do it?' the two asked Hitler. 'I'm on Mussolini's shoulders.' "[21] Yet if Stalingrad would prove to be a key turning point in the war, Parisians still found it difficult to imagine the occupation coming to an early end. Their one consolation remained an intense cultural scene that, since the fall of 1940, had done much to lift the city's spirits.

---

*Astonishingly, during some of this period, many Jews interned by Vichy remained in camps in Morocco and Algeria.

Vivace Ma Non Troppo

WHILE PARISIANS ignored Germany's efforts to market its literature, theater and cinema, they responded warmly to its music. And why shouldn't they? There was no language barrier and, further, they already knew and liked German music.* After all, Bach, Handel, Mozart, Beethoven, Mahler and so many other German greats stood at the heart of all classical music. And just as Hitler's barbarities could hardly be blamed on German composers, not even on that infamous anti-Semite and Romantic nationalist Richard Wagner, the Third Reich could in no way claim credit for their genius.

The Nazis, however, thought otherwise. In 1941, Goebbels proclaimed the Germans to be "the first musical people on earth" and, as such, natural heirs to the great composers of the past.[1] He also understood that music was the one area where Germany could impress the French and successfully export its culture. As a result, confident that

---

*Here, "German" music embraces the pre-1871 German principalities and imperial Vienna as well as modern Germany and Austria.

they would be well received by the French public as well as by cultivated Wehrmacht officers, Berlin mobilized German conductors, orchestras, opera companies and choirs to carry German music to Paris and the French provinces throughout the occupation. And to show French musicians bowing before German music, a score of French composers and critics were invited to Vienna in late 1941 for commemorations of the 150th anniversary of Mozart's death.

Of course, not all German music was German enough. By the mid-1930s, the Nazis had banned the works of dead Jewish composers like Mendelssohn, Meyerbeer and Mahler and living avant-gardists like Paul Hindemith, Arnold Schönberg, Alban Berg and Kurt Weill. Then, in 1938, inspired by Entartete Kunst, or Degenerate Art, an exhibition held the previous year in Munich, they organized a similar show called Entartete Musik, or Degenerate Music, in Düsseldorf. In 1940, expanding the blacklist to occupied France, they then included French Jewish composers, notably Paul Dukas, who had died five years earlier, and Darius Milhaud, who was already in the United States. In practice, though, works by Dukas and Mendelssohn—though not Milhaud—were performed and occasionally broadcast in the unoccupied zone. Further, Jacques Offenbach, a German-born Jew who had made his name in France in the mid-nineteenth century, remained immensely popular, with his operettas performed in the south and his cancan music heard nightly in Paris cabarets.

For the French, the particular appeal of classical music was that its abstract nature provided a unique respite from reality. When German military bands or choirs performed at lunchtime on the steps of the Paris Opera, crowds quickly gathered, not to approve the occupation but drawn by the magnet of music. And when German brass bands played in the Luxembourg Gardens, Parisians sunning themselves nearby could forget for a moment that those were the trumpets of a conquering army. Indeed, if anything, the real danger of classical music was that it risked humanizing the Nazis: If so many uniformed Germans attended concerts or operas because they, too, loved music, did this make them less than monsters? Could a man whose eyes filled with tears upon hearing Mozart also be an assassin? Was a country that had given the world Bach and the Berlin Philharmonic all bad? In truth, the emotions stirred by music are accessible to all. Hitler admired Bruckner as well as Wagner, while Mussolini was himself a musician, a violinist. After attending a Berlin Philharmonic performance of Beethoven's Ninth Symphony to celebrate Hitler's fifty-third birthday on April 20, 1942, Goebbels wrote: "It was interpreted perfectly and with thrilling effect. I have never heard it played with such fervor. The public was deeply moved. Around me, I see soldiers and workers with tears in their eyes."[2] In *Dolce,* the second volume of Irène Némirovsky's unfinished epic, *Suite française,* a lonely Frenchwoman opens her heart to a German officer billeted in her home when he plays the piano.

Looking to market German music, the Propaganda Staffel pushed Vichy into restarting the musical life of Paris. The city's musicians were equally eager to return to work. Orders went out to reopen the opera houses and concert halls, along with the Conservatoire de Paris, the country's leading music college, all still Vichy's responsibility. Four symphonic orchestras also revived their tradition of holding Sunday afternoon concerts, each in its own venue: the Association des Concerts Lamoureux in the Salle Pleyel; the Association des Concerts Pasdeloup in the Salle Gaveau; the Association des Concerts Pierné* in the Théâtre du Châtelet; and the Société des Concerts du Conservatoire in the Salle du Conservatoire.

In July 1941, the composer Francis Poulenc wrote to the exiled Milhaud, "Musical life is intense and everyone finds in it a way of forgetting the present sadness."[3] Initially, though, orchestras were short of musicians: a good number were prisoners of war, others were Jews who felt safer in the unoccupied zone, and a few were Parisians who had fled the city during the exodus and were awaiting German permission to return. Paris also lost one orchestra: the Orchestre National de la Radiodiffusion Française, which took refuge in Rennes during the phony war, moved to Marseille in June 1940 and was now dependent on Vichy (it returned to Paris only in March 1943, four months after the unoccupied zone was taken over by the Germans). But in October 1941, Paris gained another: Radio-Paris, the German-run French-language radio station, founded the Grand Orchestre de Radio-Paris, which soon drew good audiences for its twice-weekly free concerts at the Théâtre des Champs-Élysées. And since Vichy was required to finance the operation of Radio-Paris as part of its

---

*Previously known as the Orchestre Colonne, it took the name of the composer Gabriel Pierné in 1940 because its founder, Édouard Colonne, was Jewish.

innumerable economic burdens, it also ended up paying the wages of the eighty-member Radio-Paris orchestra.*

Evidently, Vichy could not ignore the Germans. For instance, Vichy's secretary-general of fine arts, Louis Hautecoeur, named the heads of cultural institutions, but only after consulting the Propaganda Staffel. Similarly, while Vichy increased the prewar cultural budget, it had to reimburse theaters for the tickets given to the occupation forces: 20 percent of seats at the Paris Opera and the Opéra-Comique were reserved for the Wehrmacht, with other tickets sold at a 50 percent discount.

Vichy's strongest musical asset, though, was its star performer, the concert pianist Alfred Cortot, who was acclaimed across Europe, including in Germany. Although Swiss-born, he had moved to France as a child and now, at the age of sixty-three, was a convinced *pétainiste*. Working first as an adviser to Hautecoeur and, from May 1942, to the education minister, Abel Bonnard, he was the only important artist to play an official role in the regime. In 1942, he was named president of the Comité Professionel de la Musique, and the following year he headed what became known as the Cortot Committee, a kind of advisory group made up of musical heavyweights, both moderates and *pétainistes*. He took his position seriously, using it to promote music education and to reorganize the music profession. He also gave his blessing to an excellent program called Les Jeunesses Musicales de France, or Musical Youth of France, designed to introduce young people to classical music: as many as fifty thousand students participated in the 1942–43 season, with members attending dress rehearsals at the opera and given free tickets to concerts.

At the same time, Cortot kept performing, offering recitals across France and, more compromisingly, playing with German orchestras, in France and in Germany. In June 1942, he traveled to Berlin to perform Schumann's Piano Concerto, with Wilhelm Fürtwangler conducting the Berlin Philhamonic. At a reception upon his return to Paris, Max d'Ollone, the head of the music section of the Groupe Collaboration, congratulated him for his "useful act of collaboration" as the first French artist to perform in Germany since the occupation. Six months later, Cortot gave more concerts in Berlin and five other German cities. And it was for this musical collabora-

*These wages, which were twice as high as those paid to musicians at the Paris Opera, served to woo some instrumentalists from the Orchestre National.

tion, more than for his work in Vichy, that he had to answer after the liberation.

The French delegation attending the 1791–1941 Mozart commemorations in Vienna, where it was received by Richard Strauss, was celebrated as another example of cultural collaboration. Led by Hautecoeur, the delegation included Jacques Rouché, who was overall head of the Paris Opera and the Opéra-Comique, the Fascist critic Lucien Rebatet, the prominent Swiss composer Arthur Honegger, the collaborationist French composers Florent Schmitt and Marcel Delannoy as well as critics and journalists, including Robert Bernard, the Swiss-born editor of *L'Information Musicale,* the Nazi-authorized music weekly. The visitors could hardly not be impressed by a program of not fewer than sixty-five concerts.

As with similar delegations of artists, writers and movie stars, not all those accepting German invitations were Nazi sympathizers; the most frequent justification for making the trip was the promise that, in exchange, some French prisoners of war would be released. But there is also no record of anyone being freed—or of anyone turning down the invitation to Vienna to protest measures now being applied against Jewish musicians. By then, most Jews had lost their jobs in the orchestras of Paris. Eighteen Jewish-owned music publishers had been closed or Aryanized. The Jewish composer and conductor Manuel Rosenthal, who was released from a prisoner-of-war camp in February 1941, was told in July that year that he could no longer conduct the Orchestre National de la Radiodiffusion Française. Soon afterward, Paul Paray, another composer-conductor, left for Monaco rather than conduct the same orchestra stripped of its Jewish instrumentalists. The composer Reynaldo Hahn, born in Venezuela of a German Jewish father, was certified as an Aryan, but he wisely spent the war in Marseille. The Society of Authors, Composers and Editors of Music, known by its French acronym of SACEM, even asked its 12,500 members to declare in writing that they were not Jewish. Later, however, after Vichy froze royalties due to Jewish composers, SACEM secretly gave money to some composers who were in hiding and to the wives of others who had been deported. Of those deported, at least fifteen died in Auschwitz and other Nazi camps.

Even if music lovers regarded classical music as a deeply personal experience, then, the world of music could not escape being politicized. And with the Nazis using music as a propaganda tool, anti-Nazis also felt called upon to respond. But what could they do?

They had already suffered losses in their ranks. Three promising young French composers—Jehan Alain, Maurice Jaubert and Jean Vuillermoz—had been killed in the Battle of France. Along with Milhaud, the revered music teacher Nadia Boulanger, although not herself persecuted, was living in New York, where she began a long and influential relationship with American composers.

Raymond Deiss, the publisher of Milhaud, Poulenc and other French composers, took the lead. Just four months after the occupation, acting entirely on his own initiative, he started printing a protest sheet with the Rabelaisian name of *Pantagruel*. In the first issue, he called on his countrymen to support General de Gaulle, who, he assured them, would triumph with the support of the British people, "whose unbreakable phlegm and determination are legendary." Over the next year, he issued sixteen numbers of his sheet before he was arrested and deported to Germany. Two years later, largely forgotten in France, he was decapitated in a prison in Cologne. Maurice Hewitt, who had been a member of the Capet String Quartet before the war and in 1939 founded the Hewitt Chamber Orchestra, recorded works by Rameau during the occupation. At the same time, already in his late fifties, he joined a British-run resistance group helping Allied airmen to escape France through Spain. Arrested in December 1943, he was deported to Buchenwald, where he organized concerts. After his release in 1945, wearing prison-camp clothes, he conducted a performance of Fauré's *Requiem* in memory of French deportees.

But for the tiny minority of musicians who took a stand, the battle against the Germans was fought mainly in the musical arena itself. Already in late 1941, an underground newspaper, *L'Université Libre,* recognized that it was illogical to boycott all German music, but it urged French musicians not to betray their own roots by collaborating with the occupier. Some were already doing so, such as the composers Delannoy and Schmitt, who had joined d'Ollone in the Groupe Collaboration; the conductor and composer Eugène Bigot, who attended dinners organized by the group; and Joseph Canteloube, who had offered his services to Cortot in Vichy. The following summer, the conductor Roger Désormière and the composer Elsa Barraine decided to form a resistance group linked to the Communist Party; they called it the Comité du Front National de la Musique.*

---

*It was later variously called Comité des Musiciens du Front National, Front National des Musiciens and, finally, Front National de la Musique.

They were subsequently joined by an impressive list of musicians: the composers Honegger, Poulenc, Georges Auric, Louis Durey, Alexis Roland-Manuel, Rosenthal and Henri Dutilleux; the soprano Irène Joachim; Claude Delvincourt, director of the Conservatoire de Paris; and Charles Munch, the permanent conductor of the Société des Concerts du Conservatoire, the country's top orchestra.

This gathering of talent was, however, just that: a musical elite with little political experience and, it soon transpired, no ability to shift the musical rank and file from the safety of its artistic neutrality. It published a clandestine newsletter, *Le Musicien d'Aujourd'hui,* which in October 1942 spelled out its aims: to keep alive banned music, such as that of Milhaud, through private performances; to help musicians who were captives in Germany or who, as Jews, were in hiding; and to boycott pro-Nazi events and encourage spontaneous protests, such as playing "La Marseillaise" in the presence of Germans.* As an opposition force, though, the front remained peripheral: as of March 1944, it had fewer than thirty members, and only eight issues of *Le Musicien d'Aujourd'hui* were circulated, the last two reaching a larger audience as part of *Les Lettres Françaises,* the writers' underground publication.

What most mobilized the front was what it called "the systematic strangling of French music by Nazi propaganda." As Auric later wrote acidly in an unsigned article in *Le Musicien d'Aujourd'hui:* "If music has no country, musicians do. And we're going to put our orchestras and conductors, our virtuosos, our singers, at the service of the monumental works of the German school . . . all this with the pretext of covering up the so-called insufficiency of French musical culture."[4]

In fact, French music was being widely performed, but in the main this comprised symphonic works by Berlioz, Debussy, Fauré and Ravel and operas by Bizet, Gounod and Massenet. Living composers, on the other hand, felt they were being overlooked, perhaps for political reasons. And they were hardly beginners. In the interwar years, six of them—Milhaud, Honegger, Poulenc, Auric, Durey and Germaine Tailleferre—had become known as Les Six, a nod to the nineteenth-century Russian composers known as the Five. Although their styles were different, they were friends of much the

---

*"La Marseillaise" was frequently performed in the unoccupied zone but was banned in the German-run area.

same age who had all sympathized with the left-leaning Popular
Front in the mid-1930s. Now they saw they had to fight to be heard.

They were helped by Vichy, which felt a need to challenge the perceived superiority of German music. Over four years, the regime
commissioned works from fifty-seven composers, including those in
the Front National de la Musique and, above all, those returning to
France from prison camps. Some of these works were performed
publicly, and many were recorded. It was also possible to present new
compositions privately, in homes or cultural salons. One forum was
before students at the École Normale de Musique, although composers reached a wider audience at the new Concerts de la Pléiade,
created by the publisher Gaston Gallimard and the movie producer
Denise Tual. These were held in the Conservatoire or the Galerie
Charpentier before invited guests and, so long as the audience did not
exceed forty people, no official permission was required. Here,
Poulenc and others could hear their new works performed by top
instrumentalists and singers. Occasionally, programs included works
by Milhaud and other banned composers. The concerts were hardly
clandestine, though, since Francophile Germans also attended.

Honegger, who carried a Swiss passport but had spent all but two
years of his life in France, needed no extra push. Early in the occupation, he had to prove that he was not Jewish. But while he joined the
Front National de la Musique, he was viewed with some suspicion
by other members because he had accepted the German invitation to
Vienna and wrote music reviews for the German-approved cultural
weekly *Comoedia.** In 1943, the front decided to exclude Honegger
from its meetings. Yet, throughout the occupation, he maintained the
high profile he had enjoyed in the 1920s and 1930s. Always a prolific composer, he saw his instrumental works regularly performed
by most orchestras. His oratorio *Jeanne au bûcher,* with text by
Claudel, was presented in Lyon in 1941 and then toured the country,
while his opera *Antigone,* with a libretto by Cocteau, was finally
presented by the Paris Opera in 1943, sixteen years after it was first
rejected. He also wrote the music accompanying Claudel's epic play
Le Soulier de satin, which was produced at the Comédie Française in
late 1943.

---

*Although subject to German censorship, *Comoedia* provided ample and objective
coverage of the arts and included Sartre, Valéry, Claudel and Cocteau among its
occasional contributors.

Part of Honegger's appeal was that his style bridged the French and German music traditions. The perception that he had become close to an official French composer was reinforced by the honors that came his way around his fiftieth birthday, in 1942, with Vichy's *L'Information Musicale* devoting an entire issue to the occasion. But he was not a collaborationist; in fact, he helped some Jewish composers. Rather, like his colleagues, he simply wanted his music to be heard and appreciated—and was more successful than the others in doing so.

None of Les Six carried the stigma of being a "degenerate" composer. Although they had made their name at the time that Schönberg, Berg and Anton Webern were founding the Second Vienna School, they did not adopt twelve-tone serialism. Poulenc was particularly admired for his captivating melodies. Only twenty-three when he wrote the ballet *Les Biches* for Diaghilev, in 1922, he was openly homosexual and considered an enfant terrible in the 1920s and early 1930s. But in 1936, while visiting the shrine of the Black Virgin in Rocamadour in southwestern France, he had a religious conversion that profoundly affected his life and resulted in a body of sacred music (including his fine postwar opera, *Dialogues des carmélites*). During the war, while his opposition to the occupation never wavered, he wrote works for both public and private performance. In a letter to a friend in December 1941, he did not sound unhappy: "The musical life in Paris is intense. Munch puts on beautiful concerts and everyone tries to keep alive the spiritual atmosphere of our good city. Picasso paints alone and wonderfully. Braque too. Éluard writes masterpieces. In the spring, there will be a concert devoted to my works given by the Société Nouvelle de Musique de Chambre de Paris."[5]

In 1942, Poulenc's ballet *Les Animaux modèles,* inspired by La Fontaine's *Fables,* was presented at the Paris Opera. Knowing there would be many Germans in the audience, he mischievously borrowed a few bars of an Alsatian song, "Non, non, vous n'aurez pas notre Alsace-Lorraine" (No, No, You Will Not Have Our Alsace-Lorraine), a reference to German annexation of France's easternmost regions between 1871 and 1918 and again in 1940. He also wrote scores for many poems, including some by Louise de Vilmorin and Aragon. One outstanding work was *Figure humaine,* a twelve-voice cantata based on resistance poems by Éluard, including "Liberté"; it was first performed in 1944 at the home of the wealthy socialite

Marie-Laure de Noailles. Poulenc also put to music "Un soir de neige," Éluard's homage to the poet Max Jacob, who died in Drancy in 1944.

Olivier Messiaen, nine years Poulenc's junior, was no less devout a Catholic but was a more experimental composer. Only thirty-two when he was captured by the Wehrmacht in June 1940, Messiaen spent the next eleven months in Stalag VIII-A in Görlitz, in eastern Germany. It was there that he completed his *Quatuor pour la fin du temps* (Quartet for the End of Time), first performed on January 15, 1941, inside the camp itself. Before an outdoor audience of freezing POWs and interested German guards, Messiaen played an old piano and was joined by three other prisoners, the cellist Étienne Pasquier, the violinist Jean Le Boulaire and the clarinetist Henri Akoka. In May 1941, Messiaen was released and was named by Vichy to be professor of harmony at the Conservatoire de Paris, a position previously held by a Jewish musician. He also recovered his place as organist at the Église de la Sainte-Trinité, a post he held until his death in 1992. Paris first took note of him when he presented his *Visions de l'Amen* for two pianos on May 10, 1943, at a Concert de la Pléiade that included Poulenc, Valéry, Cocteau, Braque and Mauriac in the audience. Messiaen was the only prominent composer not to have a work commissioned by Vichy, but he emerged as an influential teacher: among the students at the *conservatoire* whom he converted to serialism was Pierre Boulez, who after the war would become a leading avant-garde composer in his own right as well as an admired conductor of both classical and modern music.

When Boulez arrived in Paris from Lyon in September 1943, he was only eighteen and would not learn of the activities of the Front National de la Musique until after the liberation. In hindsight, though, he said he did not feel that German music was smothering French music. "Radio-Paris had its own orchestra which celebrated Richard Strauss's eightieth birthday in May 1944," he recalled. "But the Germans in charge of culture tried to seduce rather than impose their will. I remember hearing Messiaen for the first time at the École Normale de Musique; Poulenc was at the Concerts de la Pléiade. Honegger was the big French composer. He was very popular." While attending the Conservatoire de Paris, Boulez took counterpoint lessons with Honegger's wife, Andrée Vaurabourg. In June 1944, he finally met Messiaen. He recalled, "I showed him some work and asked to join his harmony class, which I did in September, after the liberation."[6] The two composers would become friends and, in the furious debates over musical style in late-1940s Paris, Boulez was Messiaen's strongest defender.

The experience of another young composer illustrated how difficult it was for many musicians to make ends meet. Henri Dutilleux was twenty-two in 1938 when he won the prestigious Prix de Rome to study at the Villa Medicis, the French academy in Rome, following the path of many of France's great composers. But when he arrived in Rome in February 1939, he found Mussolini's Fascism in full flower. And in early April, it celebrated Franco's victory in the Spanish civil war. "I wasn't keen to be there at that time," he recalled, "and I left in July." Soon he was mobilized as a stretcher bearer with an air force squadron based near Rennes. "During the phony war, music continued," he said. "We thought we were protected by the Maginot Line. I spent some time in Paris. I played piano a bit in a brasserie, I took some lessons, I worked with some singers."

When Germany invaded, his unit went south to Bordeaux, where the French government had fled. As he remembers it, "We thought there was a possibility of continuing the war in North Africa. We were almost sorry that Pétain asked for an armistice. It was the beginning of the French turning against the French." Demobilized in Toulouse, Dutilleux reached Paris in time to attend the reprise of a famous production of Debussy's *Pelléas et Mélisande* at the Opéra-Comique, conducted by Roger Désormière, with Jacques Jansen and Irène Joachim in the title roles. "It was one of the most intense moments I have known," Dutilleux said. He then returned to Toulouse for some months before going to Nice, where winners of the Prix de Rome were summoned to resume work. "I didn't want to be in a golden cage," he recalled. "It was not the right moment. My brother was a prisoner of war, friends had been killed. I wrote a piece for the bassoon and then left for Paris."[7]

Without a job, he was forced to freelance. "I gave some lessons in counterpoint and in harmony, I accompanied dancers and singers, I played jazz in some brasseries," he said. "I even orchestrated some Chopin waltzes, which was criminal of me." One break came in early 1942 when he was invited by the Paris Opera to accompany the chorus in rehearsals for the first French production of Hans Pfitzner's opera *Palestrina*. He noted, "I didn't like the opera, but it was well written, with heavy counterpoint. I'd get grumbled at by some of the singers for making mistakes. I'm not a very good pianist." He was

not asked to stay on. But, through Irène Joachim, he was invited to
join the Front National de la Musique, along with the pianist
Geneviève Joy, later his wife. "We belonged to a chain of resistance,"
he said. "Our aim was to fight collaboration. We said it was all right
to play in front of Germans, but not for Radio-Paris. Many musicians agreed to play and sing on Radio-Paris, saying they had to live,
but they shouldn't have done so."

During the last months of the occupation, Dutilleux found work
at Radiodiffusion Nationale, better known as Radio Vichy, which
had returned to Paris. There his job was to commission music to
accompany radio plays and other spoken programs. At the same
time, he began working with Pierre Schaeffer,* the former head of
Jeune France, who was now running the experimental Studio d'Essai
and preparing programming for the liberation by recording banned
music by the likes of Schönberg, Berg and Milhaud. Two poems that
Dutilleux put to music—"La Geôle" (The Jail), based on a sonnet by
Jean Cassou, and "Chanson de la deportée" (Song of the Deported
Woman) by Jean Gandrey-Réty—were first performed in public
after the liberation.

Also keeping alive the spirit of French music was the Conservatoire de Paris under Delvincourt. Vichy had named him to succeed
Henri Rabaud in April 1941 because it felt reassured by his ties to the
right-wing Croix-de-Feu in the 1930s. When he arrived, two Jewish
teachers, Lazare Lévy and André Bloch, and twenty-five Jewish students had already been forced to leave, and in September 1942, under
pressure from Vichy, most "half-Jewish" students were also expelled.
But the occupation gradually transformed Delvincourt. Whether or
not there is truth to the version that he secretly arranged for private
tuition for Jewish students, the composer Roland-Manuel, himself
Jewish, later said that not one Jewish student under his care at the
conservatoire was deported.†

Delvincourt also brought important changes to the conservatoire,
notably in its teaching methods. In 1942, by now thoroughly disenchanted with Pétain, he adopted the pseudonym of Monsieur Julien

---

*After the war, through his revolutionary work in electroacoustic research, Schaefer
became known as the "father" of musique concrète.

† Michel Tagrine, a Jewish violinist, who won year-end prizes at the conservatoire in
1941 and 1942, would become one of the music world's few martyrs: only twenty-
two at the time, he died fighting in the Paris insurrection on August 25, 1944.

and joined the Front National de la Musique, which occasionally met in his office at the *conservatoire*. In 1943, after young men were ordered to work in Germany, he won a reprieve for sixty of his students by forming a youth orchestra called the Orchestre des Cadets du Conservatoire. The following year, when this cover no longer protected the students, he summoned them before dawn one day. After distributing false identity cards, ration tickets and work papers provided by an organ teacher, Marie-Louise Boëllmann-Gigout, who was in the resistance, he told them to disappear. "Delvincourt was admirable at the Conservatoire where not one student left for Germany," Poulenc wrote to Milhaud after the liberation.[8]

Désormière led still more of a double life. A member of the Communist Party and the driving force behind the musicians' resistance group, he was also the chief conductor at the Opéra-Comique. This required some compromises. He had to work with two successive *pétainistes* as directors of the theater, Max d'Ollone and the tenor Lucien Muratore. He also conducted a benefit concert at the opera where Cortot was the soloist, although in this case the good cause was musicians in distress. But he was free to promote French music, organizing the premieres of several French operas, among them Delannoy's *Ginevra** and Emmanuel Chabrier's *L'Étoile,* and programming only two Germanic operas—Mozart's *Die Entführung aus dem Serail* in 1941 and Richard Strauss's *Ariadne auf Naxos* in 1943—during the entire occupation.

As a conductor, Désormière also won accolades in 1941 for the first complete recording of Debussy's opera *Pelléas et Mélisande,* again with Jansen and Joachim. As a *résistant,* while taking delight in attacking d'Ollone and Muratore in unsigned articles for *Le Musicien d'Aujourd'hui,* he helped the Jewish composers Jean Wiener and Rosenthal, who were in hiding. Wiener, a leading composer of movie music in the 1930s, was even able to continue working because Désormière signed his scores for seven new movies; Wiener was later properly credited. After the liberation of Paris, Désormière was on a four-man team running the Opéra-Comique before he was named director of the Paris Opera.

It was all the more to Désormière's credit that the Opéra-Comique was not swamped by visiting German opera companies and orches-

---

*Joachim, who sang the title role, subsequently refused to perform excerpts on Radio-Paris.

tras. The German Institute, which managed these tours, organized no fewer than seventy-one concerts by German orchestras around France between May 1942 and July 1943. In fact, just three weeks after the occupation, the Berlin Philharmonic played in Paris and Versailles, and it returned to Paris and other cities several more times, conducted successively by Hans Knappertsbusch, Eugen Jochum and Clemens Krauss.* In June 1943, it performed Beethoven's nine symphonies in a series of sold-out concerts at the thirty-five-hundred-seat Palais de Chaillot in Paris. But if the Berlin Philharmonic could usually count on appreciative audiences, one concert under Krauss in Lyon in May 1942 ended in chaos when thousands of people protested outside the Salle Rameau, singing "La Marseillaise." More frequently, French music lovers scrambled to buy tickets for German orchestras. In 1941, the Berliner Kammerorchester under Hans von Benda offered its own Mozart festival, including a free concert in the gardens of the Palais-Royal. The Vienna Boys' Choir was another popular visitor to many cities, while the choir of Ratisbon Cathedral sang in Notre-Dame in Paris. Even the Luftwaffe Orchestra toured France.

Unsurprisingly, Wagner, Hitler's favorite composer, was the most performed German opera composer in occupied Paris, accounting for fifty-four performances at the Paris Opera, compared with thirty-five for Mozart. In 1943, the Mannheim National Theater brought a production of *Die Walküre* to mark the fiftieth anniversary of the opera's first performance in Paris, while the Paris Opera reprised its production of *Der fliegende Holländer* thirty-six times and that of *Das Rheingold* on thirteen occasions. Other German and Austrian composers were also well represented. For instance, the Deutsche Opernhaus of Berlin presented the rising soprano Elisabeth Schwarzkopf in Johann Strauss's *Die Fledermaus,* with all seven performances of the popular operetta reserved for the Wehrmacht. Franz Lehár traveled from Vienna to conduct his operetta *Das Land des Lächelns* (The Land of Smiles) at the Gaieté-Lyrique theater and, on the same trip, conducted a concert uniting the German army, navy and air force orchestras at the Palais de Chaillot. The Paris Opera also revived several prewar productions of German operas, starting in December 1940 with Beethoven's only opera, *Fidelio,*

---

*Fürtwangler was the only leading German conductor not to perform in occupied France.

itself an odd choice since it is a stirring paean to freedom.* Later seasons included *Le Nozze di Figaro* and other operas by Mozart, Richard Strauss's *Der Rosenkavalier* and Handel's *Alceste.* Along with Pfitzner's *Palestrina,* there was the French premiere of *Peer Gynt* by Werner Egk, a Nazi favorite who won a musical competition linked to the 1936 Berlin Olympics. In all, 31 percent of opera performances were of works by German composers. The most performed composer, though, was Verdi, with ninety-four performances, including fifty-five of *Rigoletto* and thirty-two of *Aïda.* Gounod ranked second, with seventy-eight performances of *Faust,* making it the single most performed opera during the occupation. These endless reprises evidently reflected the Paris Opera's need to save money by reusing existing stage sets and costumes.

One instant celebrity was the dashing young conductor Herbert von Karajan, a member of the Nazi Party since 1933 and the new music director of the Berlin Staatsoper and its orchestra, the Staatskapelle. On several occasions, he filled the Palais de Chaillot, but it was a trip sponsored by Hitler himself in the spring of 1941 that thrust him into the limelight: for the first time, the Berlin Staatsoper was to perform on the revered stage of the Paris Opera. On May 18 and 20, von Karajan conducted *Die Entführung aus dem Serail.* Then, for performances of Wagner's *Tristan und Isolde* on May 22 and 25, he brought together something of a dream team: the heralded German "heroic" tenor Max Lorenz and the great French soprano Germaine Lubin.

Lubin, a longtime admirer of Pétain's, was also a Nazi favorite. When she had performed *Tristan und Isolde* at the Bayreuth festival in 1938, Hitler had been in the audience. She was then introduced to him in a restaurant after the show; she told a journalist that this was the highlight of her visit. Later, the Führer sent her a bouquet of red roses and a photograph of himself in a silver frame inside a red leather casket stamped with an eagle and a swastika. One performance of *Tristan und Isolde* was reserved entirely for Wehrmacht officers; the other was also sold out. Lubin in particular was acclaimed. Cocteau promptly wrote to her: "Madame, what you have done for Isolde was

---

*Beethoven proved useful to both sides in the war: while the BBC opened its French news bulletins with the first four notes of Beethoven's Fifth Symphony, also the letter *V* in Morse code, the Berlin Philharmonic frequently performed Beethoven's Ninth Symphony, with its rousing "Ode to Joy" vocal finale.

such a marvel that I lack the courage to remain silent." Presiding over
the occasion was Wagner's British-born daughter-in-law, Winifred
Wagner, an ardent admirer of Hitler's who became friends with
Lubin in Bayreuth. She later boasted that she personally intervened
with Hitler to obtain the release of Lubin's son from a German POW
camp. In fact, days before the *Tristan und Isolde* performance in
Paris, Hitler reportedly again stepped in, this time to free Lubin's
Jewish singing teacher, after the soprano refused to sing while he was
in jail. Winifred Wagner was in turn delighted that Lubin's latest
lover was none other than her old friend Hans Joachim Lange, a
Wehrmacht officer who was posted to Paris.[9] Lubin's days of glory,
though, were numbered. After the war, her public identification with
the Nazis, whether by attending receptions in the German embassy
or performing in Germany, brought an end to her career.

Reviewing music for the German-language newspaper *Pariser
Zeitung* was an unlikely critic who, over a seven-year period, found
himself on all sides of the conflict. In 1938, given the choice of leaving his Jewish wife or losing his job in Germany, Heinrich Strobel
moved to France, where he wrote for the *Deutsche Allgemeine
Zeitung* and resumed work on his biography of Debussy. When, in
1939, France declared war on Germany, he was interned as an "undesirable foreigner" in the Camp des Milles. After the German victory,
he stayed in France and, in 1942, began writing for the *Pariser
Zeitung* and gave lectures at the German Institute. What served him
well later, though, was that he reviewed French music with sympathy
and understanding. As a result, after the war, the French military
appointed him to run the Südwestfunk, the Southwest Radio, in
Baden-Baden, which was the capital of the region of Germany occupied by France. In the following years, Strobel not only loyally promoted modern French music but he also created an experimental
studio that encouraged research into electroacoustic music.

Jacques Rouché had the trickier job of running the Paris Opera.
The director of the opera since 1913, Rouché was seventy-seven
in 1939 when he took over the Réunion des Théâtres Lyriques
Nationaux, which included both the Paris Opera and the Opéra-
Comique. After Hitler's visit on June 23, 1940, however, it was the
Paris Opera that most interested the Germans and became a "must"
for visiting Nazi dignitaries. In 1940, Rouché was forced to dismiss
thirty Jewish musicians from the orchestra, decimating its string section, although he kept paying them secretly for another two years

and even retained a Hungarian Jewish decorator, Ernest Klausz, until late 1943.[10]

In theory, Rouché was answerable to Vichy, but his principal headache was managing German officials, who constantly tried to influence the opera's programming and, even with their quota of free tickets, frequently demanded more. On the other hand, he had no worries about filling the house. Michel Francini, the music-hall actor, recalled that his father, who worked in the opera house's administration, complained loudly about armies of German boots damaging the Palais Garnier's sweeping marble staircase.[11] French opera lovers followed these boots, Jean Guéhenno observed caustically in his journal: "Every evening at the Opera, I am told, German officers come in large numbers. During the intervals, as is the custom in their country, they stroll around the foyer, in three and fours, all going in the same direction. The French, despite themselves, unconsciously join the procession and keep in step. The boots impose the rhythm."[12]

Adding to Rouché's troubles, from late 1942 he faced increased meddling by Vichy's new education minister, Abel Bonnard, whom he tried to appease by sending copies of laudatory letters he had received from Ambassador Abetz. But there was also labor unrest within the company, often promoted by the clandestine Front National de l'Opéra, which had been organized by an upholsterer, Jean Rieussec, and included just twenty members, in the main technicians rather than musicians. After the war, when Rouché was accused by this group of collaborating with the Nazis, he was not helped by rumors that his wife had had an affair with a German officer. "In Paris, musical life resumes as best it can, very disturbed by questions of the purge," Poulenc wrote to Milhaud in March 1945. "There is also a terrible crisis at the Opera. We lament the departure of dear Rouché. The social indiscretions of his wife and the fascism of Lucienne* have, as you can imagine, complicated things."[13] But Poulenc, Désormière and Auric jumped to Rouché's defense and he was acquitted. Now eighty-two, he was happy to retire. Today, he is remembered as a skilled manager who "saved" the Paris Opera in the interwar years and did what he could to protect it during the occupation.

---

*The pianist Lucienne Delforges, a close friend of Céline's, was an infamous Nazi sympathizer who fled France in 1944 and performed for Vichy officials "exiled" in Germany.

Serge Lifar, the flamboyant ballet master at the Paris Opera, had an easier war. An infamous self-promoter, he was quick to ingratiate himself with the Germans, so much so that after the war he claimed that he had persuaded them to confirm Rouché in his post in 1940. It helped that, while the Germans considered themselves masters of opera, they recognized ballet to be a French specialty. Nazi officers loved going to the ballet, and a few found mistresses among the beautiful young ballerinas who paraded in the gilded *Foyer de la danse* behind the main stage.

If ballet held its own during the occupation, however, this was also a measure of Lifar's enormous talent. Born in the Ukrainian capital of Kiev, then part of the Russian Empire, he was just eighteen when he joined Diaghilev's Ballets Russes in Paris in 1923, and he soon became the company's star dancer as well as a rising choreographer. In 1930, he joined the Paris Opera Ballet, starting as a principal dancer, then becoming ballet master. By the late 1930s, he had transformed the company, professionalizing it as never before. When France declared war on Germany in September 1939, he saved his male dancers from being sent to the front by hurriedly organizing a trip to Australia and, in the spring of 1940, a tour of Spain and Portugal. The troupe had just returned to Paris when the German army arrived, but Lifar seemed unfazed: he resumed dance classes in the historic rehearsal room in the coupole of the Palais Garnier. By August 1940, when the opera house reopened to the public, he was ready to present an exciting program of ballets.

Lifar was at the center of everything: management, choreography, performance. In fact, as a dancer or a choreographer (or both), his name was listed on the program for 272 of the 837 performances presented at the Paris Opera during the occupation. For his dancing partners, he had a rich choice of prima ballerinas, among them Lycette Darsonval, Solange Schwarz and Yvette Chauviré, as well as younger dancers like Janine Charrat, Ludmilla Tchérina and Renée "Zizi" Jeanmaire. And it was Lifar who named Serge Peretti an *étoile* in 1941. As important was his work as a choreographer: between 1940 and 1944, he created fifteen new ballets, including *Sylvia, Boléro, Istar, Les Mirages, Suite en blanc* and *L'Amour sorcier,* with music by French composers for all but *Joan de Zarissa* by Egk, in which he had the title role. In the spirit of Diaghilev, Lifar also involved other artists in his new ballets. For Poulenc's *Les Animaux modèles,* he invited the painter Maurice Brianchon to design the sets and Désormière to conduct the performance in which he danced — to his own choreography — alongside Peretti, Schwarz and Chauviré.

Then as now, one of the secrets of the Paris Opera Ballet's success was its ballet school, which put its students, long nicknamed *les petits rats,* through the kind of tough regime needed to prepare them for a career on the stage. Some *petits rats* from that time would later become famous: Roland Petit as a choreographer, Juliette Gréco as a singer and Jean Babilée, just twelve when he entered the school in 1935, as one of France's great postwar dancers, famous above all for his soaring leaps. "I loved the work," he recalled decades later, "all the girls around me, appearing as an extra in operas. It was marvelous."[14] In 1940, as the Wehrmacht approached Paris, he left for a family farm in the south of France, accompanied by his friend Petit. But while Petit soon returned to Paris, Babilée instead joined the Ballet de Cannes, where, now seventeen, he was given lead roles in *Les Sylphides* and *Le Spectre de la rose.* In early 1942, he decided to return to Paris and, too old for the ballet school, he was auditioned by Lifar and accepted into the corps de ballet.

Babilée nonetheless knew he was taking a risk: he had borrowed his stage name from his mother, but the name on his identity papers — Gutmann — was that of his Jewish father. Inside the Palais Garnier, he was soon reminded of that. "One day in the dressing room we all shared, someone painted a large yellow star and the word *Juif* on my mirror," he said. "I purposefully ignored it, but it stayed there for three days. Then one afternoon the school's dresser saw it and said, 'Aren't you ashamed of yourselves, boys?' And he wiped it off."

More dangerous were the German patrols, not least because the Nazi Kommandantur, or commander's office, was in the place de l'Opéra. "Once I was stopped and asked for my papers," Babilée remembered. "The German saw 'Gutmann' and asked, German? I nodded and he let me go." He had a narrower escape during the mass roundup of Jews known as the *rafle du Vél' d'Hiv'* in July 1942. He was staying in a cheap hotel on the rue du Sentier when he was awakened at six a.m. on July 16 by someone banging on his door.

"There was a huge Frenchman in a leather overcoat," Babilée recalled. "He asked for my papers, put them in his pocket and told me to get a blanket and a bag and go downstairs. I looked out of the window and saw a parked bus. I had no way out. I dressed and started going down the stairs slowly. I suddenly heard footsteps. The same guy was hurrying back up. 'Are these your papers?' I nodded. 'With this name, it's too dangerous. Go back to bed.' "

In early 1943, like hundreds of thousands of other young men, Babilée received a summons to work in Germany. The director of the opera, Marcel Samuel-Rousseau, refused him a certificate stating that he was on contract to the opera house. "He said Germany would do me good," Babilée related. A German doctor then rejected his claim to be excused on medical grounds. "I decided I would not go and would leave my papers at a friend's house," Babilée said. "As I came out of the *métro*, I saw two German soldiers at the exit. I turned and ran, I heard cries as they followed me. I jumped over the gate to the platform and got into a *métro* car as it was leaving. My coat caught in the door." The next day, he fled Paris and spent the rest of the war with the maquis in the Touraine region. After the liberation, he refused to return to the Opera Ballet and instead joined the new Ballets des Champs-Élysées, which Roland Petit had just created. "I was disgusted with the Opera," he said.

Lifar, in contrast, sought out the Germans. He missed Hitler's dawn visit to the Palais Garnier, but eight days later he gave a guided tour of the opera house to Goebbels, who was presumably eager to share the Führer's delight in the building. And for the opening of the ballet's 1940–41 season on August 28, the audience was packed with Germans. On September 3, the first anniversary of the declaration of war, Lifar accepted an invitation from the German embassy to perform with some of his dancers at a reception given for the German army commander in chief, Field Marshal Walther von Brauchitsch. Two years later in Berlin, Lifar had a chance to meet Hitler, who—at least according to Lifar—invited him to participate in celebrations planned for the Nazi conquest of Moscow: certainly, as a Ukrainian, Lifar would have welcomed the breakup of the Soviet Union.

With such expressions of German approval, Lifar's position at the Paris Opera was unchallenged. This translated into a tripling of his salary during the war years, as well as total artistic freedom. Yet even he was not safe from vicious attacks by the collaborationist press, with the anti-Semitic weekly *Au Pilori* accusing him of being a Jew whose real name was "Rilaf," an anagram of "Lifar." The terms of his denial were not to his credit. He noted that he had studied at the Imperial Lycée in Kiev, which excluded Jews; that he had belonged to an anti-Jewish youth movement during the Russian Revolution; that his origins excluded all possibility of Jewish blood; and that he was of pure Aryan blood. He added: "As for my ideas about Jews, they are well known."[15]

After the war, the complaint against Lifar was not that German officers flocked to the opera house to see him dance; it was that he could not resist being flattered and fêted by the occupier offstage. He would be seen dining among Wehrmacht uniforms at Maxim's and drinking with Nazi officials at receptions at the German embassy or the German Institute. Along with many other cultural figures, he attended the splashy opening of the exhibition of Arno Breker's sculptures at the Orangerie in 1942, which included a short piano concert by Cortot and the German virtuoso Wilhelm Kempff and a song by Lubin. Lifar also traveled to Vichy to perform with Schwarz, and he dedicated one of his Paris premieres to Marshal Pétain. In his memoir, *Ma vie,* published two decades after the war, it is apparent that the passage of time had not tempered his vanity. He boasts, "My authority among the Germans enabled me to come to the assistance of a large number of artists. I gave special importance to ensuring that nothing unpleasant happen to my friend Pablo Picasso."[16] Recalling the compulsory work program in Germany, he also claimed to have protected his dancers: "It was in this way that I saved Serge Peretti, Jean Babilée and many others," he recalled.[17] This was not how the moment was remembered by Babilée, who saved himself by joining the maquis. "He says absolutely anything that comes into his head," Babilée said of Lifar. "He was a mythomaniac. I admired him enormously as an artist, he was amazing, but he was rather an ordinary human being. He didn't save me at all."

At the liberation of Paris, Lifar was condemned not as an artist but, as Poulenc put it in a letter to Milhaud, for acting with "an infantile imprudence because of his taste for publicity."[18] Further, his strong anti-Communism hardly endeared him to Communist-run purge committees charged with punishing collaborationist artists. Yet such was his talent that he was quickly recruited by the Nouveau Ballet de Monte-Carlo, which had been founded in 1942 by Paris Opera dancers who had refused to return to Paris.* In late 1944, Lifar was banned from working in ballet in France for life, but the follow-

---

*They were relatively safe in Monte Carlo, although Léon Blum's brother, René, who had created the Ballet de l'Opéra de Monte-Carlo in 1931, was arrested in Paris during a roundup of prominent Jews in December 1941; he was held in various French camps before being deported to Auschwitz, where he died in April 1943.

ing year the sentence was reduced to a one-year suspension. This did little to disrupt his career. In 1945, he was already dancing in Monte Carlo. In 1946, he performed in London, although there he was received with boos. In 1947, he was rehired by the Paris Opera Ballet; he remained its director of dance until 1958. By then, his rubbing shoulders with the Nazis had been reduced to a footnote in the history of the company.

CHAPTER 9

A Ripped Canvas

BY 1941, the Nazis had turned their art-looting operation into a smooth-running machine, one all too often oiled by French informers offering tips on where Jewish-owned art could be found. Mandated to run this crime ring was the Einsatzstab Reichsleiter Rosenberg, or ERR, which set up its Paris headquarters in the former library of the Universal Israelite Alliance in Pigalle. Once a Jewish collection was identified in an urban mansion or a remote château, the ERR moved in. Its agents, many of them art historians and young curators, would then spend days, even weeks, photographing and preparing an inventory of art objects to be dispatched to the Jeu de Paume, the museum-turned-depot in central Paris. Of primary importance were northern European—and, above all, Germanic— paintings and statues from before the nineteenth century, the kind of "pure" art that Hitler wanted for his future museum in Linz and Göring for his private collection at Carinhall. The final choice was usually made by Göring, who personally visited the Jeu de Paume to inspect this veritable Ali Baba's cave on twenty-one occasions during twelve different trips to Paris.

On each visit, Göring singled out works by Rembrandt, Vermeer, Cranach the Elder, Van Dyck and other Old Masters that he considered merited a place in Linz or Carinhall. He had little affection for Impressionism and none for "degenerate" modern paintings, but he recognized that they had a market value, so they, too, were kept and stored separately in the Jeu de Paume, pending their exchange for classical art. Neutral Switzerland, which had sold "degenerate" art removed from German museums before the war, was open to all kinds of business. Large numbers of looted paintings were sold there. Similarly, it proved a good place to negotiate exchanges. In July 1941, twenty-two Impressionist paintings stolen in Paris were bartered for six northern Renaissance works through the Fischer Gallery in Lucerne; twenty-seven similar deals followed over the next three years.

Unsurprisingly, no objection to this ransacking was heard from the Vichy government. Not only had it institutionalized anti-Semitism through its Statute on Jews in October 1940; even earlier, it had stripped French Jews who had fled France of their nationality, creating the convenient legal fiction that their possessions—in this case, their art—had been abandoned. The principal opposition to this was voiced by Jacques Jaujard, a dapper *fonctionnaire* who at least had the support of Count Metternich's Kunstshutz, the German army unit responsible for protecting artworks in times of war. After a career as a senior curator at the Louvre Museum, Jaujard was now the director of National Museums. Backed by the Consultative Committee of National Museums, he tried hard to protect Jewish-owned art that had been given to the Directorate of National Museums either as a gift or for safekeeping. But the Germans had already ruled that any transfer of ownership of art to the French government after September 1939 was invalid. Further, this battle interested neither of Pétain's deputies, Laval or Darlan.

Ignoring protests from Jaujard, the Germans felt free to seize 130 cases of art from the David-Weill collection that had been bequeathed to the French government and were stored at the Château de Sourches. A similar fate awaited other Jewish-owned art collections guarded by French curators in the Château de Chambord and the Château de Brissac, in western France. Jaujard even created the Comité de Liquidation et Séquestration to buy threatened works under a law authorizing the government to preempt any sale or export. It recorded a few successes but, after Laval returned to office in April 1942, it was frequently overruled by Abel Bonnard, the education minister, or by Louis Darquier de Pellepoix, the unhinged anti-Semite who took over the General Commission for Jewish Questions and who himself had an appetite for looted art.

One important collection managed to remain undiscovered until after Germany took over the unoccupied zone. Built up by Adolphe Schloss in the nineteenth century, it comprised 333 centuries-old Dutch paintings and was hidden by his heirs in the Château du Chambon, in central France. The Germans had been searching for it since late 1940 and, thanks to French police and an infamous informer named Jean-François Lefranc, in April 1943 they finally tracked it down and arrested two members of the Schloss family.

Soon afterward, the collection was seized at Chambon by armed members of the Rue Lauriston gang, a band of French criminals who freelanced for the Nazis and themselves became known as the French Gestapo. The convoy carrying the art was halted by French gendarmes, and the paintings were taken to a Banque de France vault in Limoges. Abel Bonnard then stepped in, ordering that the collection be handed over to the Germans. Complicated negotiations followed, with Jaujard insisting on his power of preemption. In the end, while France was allowed to keep 49 of the paintings, the remaining 284 were never fully accounted for and, to this day, have not all been found. As payment for his help in finding the collection, Lefranc was given 22 paintings, which he promptly sold. After the remaining 262 oils were transferred to the Jeu de Paume, where Darquier de Pellepoix was part of the reception committee, only 230 were recorded as having been shipped to Germany, with 32 presumably misappropriated by ERR officials.

These maneuvers took place almost secretly because the ERR's pompous Paris chief, Baron Kurt von Behr,* who liked to feign military rank by wearing a grandiose uniform of the German Red Cross, had declared the Jeu de Paume off-limits to all French officials, including Jaujard. The single exception was Rose Valland, a frumpy-looking forty-two-year-old spinster who had studied at the École du Louvre and liked to paint as a hobby. She had worked since 1932 as a

*To escape arrest and prosecution, von Behr and his wife committed suicide at the end of the war.

curator of foreign modern art at the Musée National des Écoles
Étrangères Contemporaines, which at the time occupied the Jeu de
Paume. When the Nazis took over the gallery in October 1940, Jaujard ordered her to stay on to administer the building. The Germans
acquiesced, presumably because Valland seemed harmless.

In reality, along with Jaujard, Valland would become one of the art
world's few heroes of the occupation. By good fortune, she knew
shorthand. And she used it to keep a record of all art entering and
leaving the building, noting its provenance and likely destination,
even establishing which trains were carrying looted artworks to Germany. One scribbled note sent to Jaujard on January 3, 1943, said
that "75 bottles of champagne, 21 bottles of cognac, 16 Flemish and
Dutch paintings left the Jeu de Paume at the request of M. Göring to
celebrate his birthday."[1] To prevent these convoys from being blown
up by railroad saboteurs, she passed this information to Jaujard and,
through him, to resistance groups. Further, because Valland never
disclosed to the ERR officials that she spoke German, she was able to
eavesdrop on their conversations and report their plans to Jaujard.
Still more daringly, when the Germans photographed their art booty,
she would "borrow" the negatives overnight to make prints for
Jaujard.

On four occasions, Valland was ordered to leave, but each time she
talked her way back into the building a few days later. In the summer
of 1943, she was the only French witness to the burning in the Jeu de
Paume garden of between five hundred and six hundred "degenerate" paintings by Picasso, Miró, Léger, Ernst and others. "Impossible
to save anything," she noted in a message to Jaujard on July 23.[2] On
occasion, she also stood her ground. For instance, when ordered to
sign an oath not to reveal anything of what she knew or saw, she
refused, arguing that as a *fonctionnaire,* or civil servant, she was forbidden to sign any agreement with a foreign power. Once, in February 1944, when she was seen copying an address, von Behr's deputy,
Bruno Lohse,* warned her against violating the rules of secrecy. Valland recalled, "Looking me in the eyes, he said I could be shot. I
replied calmly that no one here is stupid enough not to know the
risks they are running."[3]

But Valland could do nothing to prevent art from leaving France.

---

*After the war, Lohse admitted that he had kept—and later sold—some of the
Schloss paintings destined for Germany.

The record shows that between April 1941 and August 1944, 4,174 cases, containing some 20,000 works of art, were shipped from the Jeu de Paume to Germany. With bureaucratic exactitude, the ERR itself claimed in August 1944 to have confiscated 203 collections and seized 21,903 art objects. Robert Scholz, an ERR official and art critic, exuded pride in his report covering art seized between March 1941 and July 1944, stating, "The extraordinary artistic and material value of the seized art works cannot be expressed in figures. The paintings, period furniture of the 17th and 18th centuries, the Gobelins, the antiques and renaissance jewelry of the Rothschilds are objects of such a unique character that their evaluation is impossible, since no comparable values have so far appeared on the art market." He went on to mention "absolutely authenticated signed works" by Rembrandt, Rubens, Frans Hals, Vermeer, Velázquez, Murillo, Goya and Sebastiano del Piombo along with such French masters as Bouchard, Watteau and Fragonard. "This collection can compare with those of the best European museums," he boasted.[4]

Still, on the eve of the liberation of Paris, with the Germans determined to empty the Jeu de Paume, Valland was able to save what would have been the last convoy of art. She learned on August 1, 1944, that five cars of train No. 40,044 were being loaded with 148 cases of art, much of it modern art that until then had been ignored by the Nazis. She tipped off the resistance, which kept the train from leaving Aulnay, on the outskirts of Paris. Then, after Paris was freed, the train itself was liberated by a unit of the French army led by Alexandre Rosenberg, the son of the exiled art dealer Paul Rosenberg. For her bravery, Valland was named an *officier* of the Légion d'Honneur and was awarded the Médaille de la Résistance in France, the Officer's Cross of the Order of Merit by West Germany and the Presidential Medal of Freedom in the United States. She died in 1980 at age eighty-two.

The Nazis' reach, however, extended beyond Jewish art collections. Soon after the fall of Paris, the Germans demanded to know the whereabouts of the 3,691 paintings taken from the Louvre in 1939 and dispersed around the country. Some of these were moved several times: having been taken from Chambord to Louvigny in November 1939, the *Mona Lisa* went to the Abbey of Loc-Dieu, east of Bordeaux, in June 1940; to the Ingres Museum, in nearby Montauban, in October 1940; and finally, in March 1943, to the Château de Montal, in southwestern France, where the treasure spent the rest of the war under the bed of a Louvre curator. Other paintings had a more settled time, stored in a single château—for the most part, Chambord—throughout the occupation, their whereabouts known to German investigators. When paintings had to be moved, word was sent to London by the resistance to warn Allied bombers to avoid the convoys; confirmation that the message had been received would come from the BBC with the code words "Mona Lisa is smiling."

The German authorities, though, were divided over how to respond to art owned by French museums. Count Metternich did his best to carry out the Kunstschutz's mandate of safeguarding monuments and artworks in a time of war, but Ambassador Abetz wanted to give Hitler a free hand to choose whatever art pleased him. At the same time, Berlin seemed reluctant to ignore totally the 1907 Convention of The Hague, which protected French museum collections. In the end, because of both firm opposition by French curators and an uncharacteristic Nazi wish to appear to be acting legally, surprisingly little art was transferred from French government hands to Berlin.

The most scandalous exception involved a treasure from Belgium, the early-sixteenth-century Ghent Altarpiece by Hubert and Jan Van Eyck. This extraordinary polyptych panel painting, also known as *Adoration of the Mystic Lamb,* had been sent to France shortly before Germany occupied Belgium in May 1940. But because it included some panels recovered from Germany under the Treaty of Versailles after World War I, Hitler himself wanted the entire altar. The operation to seize it in July 1942 was carried out secretly, with an envoy of the Führer's demanding it from curators guarding art kept in the Château de Pau, in the French Pyrenees. The chief curator in Pau refused to release it, but he was overruled by Laval. Belgian curators, who learned of the heist only after the altarpiece reached Neuschwanstein Castle, in Germany, felt deeply betrayed by France. The painting was returned to Ghent after the war, but it had suffered damage.

With other art coveted by the Nazi leaders, Germany suggested circumventing the Convention of The Hague through diplomatic art exchanges. And here there was a recent precedent. In 1940, to encourage General Franco to maintain Spain's neutrality, Pétain approved the return of Murillo's *Immaculate Conception,* the fourth-century B.C.E. bust known as the *Lady of Elche* and some other antiquities in exchange for *La Reine Marie-Anne d'Autriche* by Velázquez and his studio and El Greco's *Portrait of Antonio de Covarrubias.* The Louvre considered it a poor exchange for France.

Among the Germans, the first to propose a swap was von Ribbentrop, who wanted Boucher's *Diane au bain.* The painting was even taken to Germany, but it was returned to Paris after Berlin museum officials refused to offer Watteau's *L'Enseigne de Gersaint* in exchange. Göring was more successful. He demanded ten early German works of art and obtained nine of them, including a late-fifteenth-century wooden statue by Gregor Erhart of Mary Magdalene, known in France as *La Belle allemande.* France received nothing in return.

In one high-profile case, however, where the Kunstschutz again took France's side, Jaujard and his colleagues fared better. By threatening to resign en masse from their posts, they blocked the transfer of a priceless eleventh-century gold bas-relief known as the *Basel Antependium,* which Bonnard had promised as a personal gift from Pétain to Hitler. This did not please Vichy: in early 1944, Georges Hilaire, who had replaced Louis Hautecoeur as secretary-general for fine arts, began planning to fire Jaujard. He was unable to do so before the liberation. Indeed, thanks to Jaujard's good relations with the Kunstschutz, in July 1944 Metternich's successor, Baron Bernhard von Tieschowitz, obtained the release from Drancy of Jaujard's former secretary, Suzanne Kahn, who, as a Jew, faced likely deportation.

Already busy plundering the French economy, the Nazis were still not satisfied. Valuable books appealed to them. As early as October 1940, ERR officials seized the Turgenev Library, created by Russian exiles in Paris in 1875, and sent some 100,000 books to Berlin. Tens of thousands of books were taken from the Symon Petliura Ukrainian Library and the Polish Library, as well as 28,000 volumes from the "ownerless" private collection of the Rothschilds. The ERR also shipped off 40,000 books from the library of the Universal Israelite Alliance, which it now occupied. Among Jewish artists and intellectuals, the libraries of Léon Blum, André Maurois, Marc Bloch and Tristan Bernard were pilfered, as were those of the musicians Arthur Rubinstein, Darius Milhaud and Wanda Landowska. Pianos stolen from Jewish families were stored in the basement of the new Musée d'Art Moderne in the Palais de Tokyo.

Then, in December 1941, Alfred Rosenberg, the ERR's chief, won Hitler's approval for the Möbel-Aktion—literally, Furniture Plan— under which furniture and other possessions found in "abandoned"

Jewish homes in occupied countries would be seized and sent to Germany. Initially, the objects were intended for use by the Nazi authorities in occupied lands to the east, but as Allied bombing of Germany intensified, they were also given to homeless Germans. Over the next thirty months, according to the ERR, M-Aktion trucks carried away everything from 38,000 Jewish homes in Paris alone and from a further 31,000 elsewhere in France. The Germans opened several internment camps inside Paris where some seven hundred Jewish captives sorted out the booty into different categories, while others repaired furniture, watches, shoes and clothes. Photographs taken in M-Aktion warehouses confirmed that nothing was considered worthless: piled up alongside beds, clocks, wardrobes, tables and chairs were collections of crockery, coat hangers, bottles, clothes, bed linens, fur coats, lamps, bicycles, children's toys, even food. In a report dated August 8, 1944, von Behr boasted that the efficiency of his office had enabled it "to succeed in providing for the use in Germany even of things which appeared to have no value, such as scrap paper, rags, salvage, etc."[5]

Flush with money, much of it provided by the French treasury, the Germans were also ready to buy art, sometimes privately, not infrequently at Drouot auctions, but most often through commercial art galleries. And, as always, Hitler and Göring were the best clients. Hans Posse, a German curator who until his death in 1942 was charged with filling the museum in Linz,* was in touch with numerous German dealers who were always on the lookout for rare objects or good bargains. Prominent among these was Karl Haberstock, who did extensive business in France before the war and was quick to return after June 1940. One of his first actions was to travel down to Aix-en-Provence to negotiate with Georges Wildenstein with a view to buying some of the dealer's classical art in exchange for allowing modern paintings to be sent to the United States. Serving both Hitler and Göring, Haberstock grew immensely rich during the occupation.

No less striking was how many wealthy French people jumped at the chance to sell family treasures. Some went out of their way to invite German dealers or buyers to inspect their homes for paintings or objects of interest. Early in the occupation, the Galerie Charpentier presented a show of medieval and Renaissance objects from pri-

---

*At the end of the war, some eight thousand paintings were found in storage in Linz.

vate collections; Göring bought everything on display. In 1942, one Paris newspaper estimated that there were seventy galleries in operation and most were doing better than at any time since the 1920s. These included several businesses formerly owned by Jews, some of which had deftly managed their own Aryanization, such as the Kahnweiler*—now Leiris—gallery and the Wildenstein and André Weil galleries. For these and other galleries, the Germans were valued clients. And since few galleries showed any concern for the provenance of the art they were selling, it was not long before paintings looted from Jewish collections were on the market.

In theory, Jewish-owned art of no interest to the Germans was to be sold to benefit French war widows and orphans; in practice, these works simply fed the booming art market. In 1943, Picasso bought a landscape by Le Douanier Rousseau from Martin Fabiani's gallery. After the war, he was visited by Germaine Wertheimer, who had just returned from exile in New York with her husband, Pierre, one of the owners of Chanel. "I was there when she came in and said, 'This is a painting of mine,' " recalled Françoise Gilot, the young artist who became Picasso's mistress in early 1944. "Picasso immediately said, 'Okay, I'll give it back to you and I'll ask Fabiani for my money.' "[6]

There was also a good market for art that had not been stolen from Jews. That included works by many living artists, among them Bonnard, Raoul Dufy, Georges Rouault, Matisse, Braque and the Fauvists Derain, de Vlaminck and Van Dongen. Drouot even occasionally auctioned paintings by Picasso, that most "degenerate" of artists, as well as by Chagall and Modigliani, both Jews, and Léger, now exiled in New York. But Germans would also monitor and censor shows in galleries. "You couldn't have an exhibition of paintings without Germans coming in to check, not in uniforms, but in civilian clothes," Gilot said. "I happened to be in one gallery, which had big exhibitions, when they came in and said, 'Picasso no, Matisse no, Van Dongen yes.' They would remove from the walls everything they didn't want." That same art, however, simply went into drawers or cupboards and could be seen or bought privately. "I liked Max Ernst's work a lot," she went on, "so I'd go to Jeanne Bucher's gallery before six p.m. and then, after it closed, she would show me her Ernst paintings."

---

*Kahnweiler survived the war by hiding out in Saint-Léonard de Noblat, near Limoges in southwestern France.

Bucher was particularly daring. Already in her late sixties when Paris fell, she had been known as the high priestess of avant-garde art since establishing her first gallery, in 1926. In April 1941, she reopened for business in a house at 9 ter boulevard du Montparnasse and, during the occupation, she organized no fewer than twenty exhibitions. Although she preferred to seek out emerging painters like Nicolas de Staël, Jean Bazaine, Édouard Pignon and Charles Lapicque, she was no less admired by established artists. On July 21, 1942, Bucher even presented paintings and gouaches by Wassily Kandinsky, the Russian abstract art pioneer and Bauhaus teacher who had moved to Paris from Berlin in 1933 and was now living quietly in Neuilly. The show, however, was closed a day later by the Germans. One group show, in 1943, included paintings by Braque, Gris, Léger and Picasso; another, in 1944, had drawings and engravings by Bonnard, Braque, Dalí, Dufy, Picasso and others. Never one to be intimidated, on January 6, 1944, Bucher organized a group show with works by Kandinsky, César Domela and de Staël. Artists who crowded into her gallery for the opening included Braque, Picasso, Dora Maar, Pignon and Bazaine. Then, in June 1944, to highlight women artists, she showed paintings by Maar and Vera Pagava.

German officers also visited the Jeanne Bucher gallery, often to buy, sometimes to laugh at modern art. On one occasion, the story is told, Bucher indignantly asked some Germans why they bothered to look at a painting they thought was "bad." Furious, she found a photograph of one of Arno Breker's sculptures, threw it on the floor and stamped on it, shouting, "That's German art. So, look what I do to it!" When one of the Germans asked if he could keep it, she replied, "No, it will come in useful next time."[7] She also encouraged other mavericks, such as Maurice Panier and Noëlle Lecoutour, the owners of the small L'Esquisse gallery, who had parallel lives in the resistance. After Bucher exhibited Kandinsky in January 1944, she offered her show to L'Esquisse, with the addition of works by Alberto Magnelli. And, suprisingly, after Panier and Lecoutour sent out printed invitations, Abstract Painters opened on February 15 without a hitch. But the following day, German officers arrived, looked around and announced ominously that they would shortly return. Alarmed, the gallery owners suspended the show. They called de Staël to pick up his paintings, while Domela grabbed the Kandinskys and spent the next few hours on a bicycle delivering them back to the artist in Neuilly.

Many other shows went ahead unperturbed by the Propaganda Staffel, whose director for visual arts, a certain Dr. Lange, was considered a Francophile and, it was said, ensured that artists were supplied with coal in winter. Even Braque, who steered clear of the Germans, exhibited twenty-six paintings and nine sculptures in the 1943 Salon d'Automne. Louis Carré sold Matisse and several Fauvists, while René Drouin threw the spotlight on the *art brut* innovator Jean Dubuffet and Jean Fautrier, whose later *Hostages* series were among the few wartime paintings to address the political situation.

Because they were unknown to the Germans, many younger artists were also free to exhibit their work. Some were featured in Vingt Jeunes Peintres de Tradition Française, the Galerie Braun show in 1941. Organized by Bazaine as part of Vichy's Jeune France initiative, it brought together twenty painters who were anything but traditional and who would develop French abstract art after the war. Among them were Lapicque, Jean Le Moal, François Desnoyer and Alfred Manessier. Some of these and others also showed their latest work in Étapes du Nouvel Art Contemporain in the Berri-Raspail Gallery in 1942 and in Douze Peintres d'Aujourd'hui at the Galerie de France in 1943. And despite the shortage of most necessities of life, with some ingenuity they were able to find painting supplies. "I'd go to the flea market and buy a worthless oil painting for just the price of the canvas," Gilot remembered. "I'd then turn it around and paint on the other side. We could still find good paper. Paint colors were more difficult, but you'd get an address and find them there. And brushes you could find."

A key promoter of younger artists was Gaston Diehl, an art critic who in October 1943 founded the Salon de Mai in a café in the Palais-Royal. At that point, it was more of a club than an event, but it enabled artists to share their distaste for the Nazis and their support for "degenerate" and other modern art. Finally, in May 1945, the first Salon de Mai was held, starting a tradition that continues to this day. A few artists went further. André Fougeron, a former anarchist who joined the Communist Party in 1939, was a painter of Socialist Realism and, as such, was naturally drawn to politics. In 1941, soon after escaping from German captivity, he set up a clandestine printing shop in his studio to publish *L'Art Français,* the art world's principal underground journal, as well as to design other clandestine newspapers, such as *L'Université Libre* and, later, *Les Lettres Françaises.* Fougeron also played a key role in founding the Front National des

Peintres et des Sculpteurs, which near the end of the occupation became the Front National des Arts.

Pignon, in turn, provided a safe house for resistance meetings that was also available as a hideout for Aragon on his secret visits to Paris. The American painter Harry Bernard Goetz helped found the semi-clandestine Surrealist review *La Main à Plume,* which published poetry and art and was tolerated by the Propaganda Staffel.* As a *résistant,* however, Goetz not only had a gift for making false identity papers but also printed resistance posters, which he and his Dutch wife, Christine, would paste on walls. The painter and illustrator Jean Lurçat, who was involved in the resistance in the Lot region from early in the occupation, became best known for his design of Aubusson tapestries with resistance themes, among them one using Éluard's poem "Liberté." Paul Goyard, an artist in his late fifties, was arrested in 1944 for running a clandestine printing operation and sent to Buchenwald; he survived. Boris Taslitzky, a Communist artist, also survived deportation, leaving a powerful testimony in 111 drawings made in Buchenwald. And as a cover for his resistance activities, the Gaullist representative Jean Moulin opened the Romain Gallery in Nice in February 1943 and filled it with borrowed art, including loans from Matisse, Pierre Bonnard and Rouault.

While most artists enjoyed the freedom to work, at least in the privacy of their studios, the line dividing acceptable and unacceptable art remained clear. This was apparent when the long-planned Musée d'Art Moderne finally opened in 1942. With 650 works on display, the artists represented included Matisse, Bonnard, Rouault, Picabia, Édouard Vuillard, Braque, Maillol and even Léger and Tanguy, who were in exile in New York. On the other hand, Picasso, Modigliani, Miró, Ernst, Klee, Duchamp and Chagall were excluded. And Jean Cassou, the man originally named to be the museum's director, was also absent; by then, he was in jail in Toulouse for his resistance activities.

For the Germans, of course, the enemy camp also included foreign Jewish artists, a handful of whom had been unable to find a country willing to receive them and were living in constant fear of arrest. Of

---

La Main à Plume also kept up the great Surrealist tradition of infighting, well illustrated by its attacks on Éluard, including a letter addressed to him as *Vieux Canaille,* or Old Villain.

these, Victor Brauner, Jacques Hérold and Wols spent the occupation
in hiding in the south of France, while the Lithuanian Chaïm Soutine
died of natural causes in a Paris hospital in August 1943. But others
perished at the hands of the Nazis. Five Jewish artists long resident in
France—the Ukrainian Vladimir Baranov-Rossiné, the Pole Henri
Epstein, the Belarusan Jacques Gotko and the Germans Adolphe
Feder and Otto Freundlich—were deported and died in Nazi camps.
Freundlich, who had moved to France in 1925, long before Hitler
took office, nonetheless represented everything the Nazis disliked:
one of his sculptures was even featured on the cover of the program
for the Degenerate Art exhibition in Munich in 1937. In 1939, he was
interned as an "undesirable foreigner," but after France fell he found
a safe haven in Saint-Paul-de-Fenouillet, a mountain village near Perpignan. On February 23, 1943, however, supposedly after a tip-off
by an informer, French police arrested him and delivered him to the
Germans. He was immediately deported to the Lublin-Majdanek
camp in Poland, where he was killed on March 9.

At the other extreme, there were artists who willingly identified
with the Germans, specifically by accepting an invitation by Goebbels to visit the Third Reich in the fall of 1941. Later, some of the
eleven who made the trip said they accepted in exchange for the
release of some French prisoners of war, although no such gesture followed. Others said they were encouraged by Vichy to make the journey. But, like Braque, they could have refused. Instead, two days
before their departure, they attended a splashy reception given at the
Propaganda Staffel's office on the Champs-Élysées. Then, on the
evening of October 30, after being photographed at the Gare de l'Est
alongside uniformed German officers, they took an overnight train
to Germany.

Although the Nazis had condemned Fauvism as "degenerate,"
they were evidently impressed by the high level of the French delegation, which included the leading Fauvist painters Derain, Vlaminck, Van Dongen and Othon Friesz; the graphic artist André
Dunoyer de Segonzac; and the sculptors Charles Despiau, Henri
Bouchard, Paul Belmondo (father of the actor Jean-Paul Belmondo)
and Paul Landowski, the director of the École Nationale des Beaux-
Arts. The two-week junket took them to Munich, Vienna, Dresden,
Düsseldorf, Nuremberg and Berlin, where they visited museums,
met German artists and attended formal dinners. In Berlin, they
were shown models and designs for Albert Speer's new Berlin—

"Germania," as it was to be called—and they visited the studio of Hitler's pet sculptor, Arno Breker. And, as per the new practice, upon their return to Paris they were welcomed by the collaborationist press. Galtier-Boissière noted, "Vlaminck, Van Dongen and Despiau, back from Berlin, expound enthusiastically in interviews. Derain and Segonzac try to be forgotten."[8] In his memoirs, Derain said he deeply regretted making the trip, but Dunoyer de Segonzac and Bouchard told reporters they were impressed by Nazi support for artists, while Despiau confided to a friend that the voyage had done him good.

Breker's involvement in the Berlin program was hardly accidental. Not only was he Germany's most prestigious contemporary artist, but he had lived in Paris between 1927 and 1934 and already knew several of the artists in the French delegation. The French artist to whom Breker was most closely tied, though, was the sculptor Aristide Maillol. Breker was twenty-seven and Maillol sixty-six when they first met in Maillol's hometown of Banyuls-sur-Mer in 1927, and a close friendship was immediately born. Both men were figurative artists, but while Maillol favored round, sensual female forms, Breker preferred large neoclassical male statues. Happy to learn from Maillol, Breker immediately began making his new friend's work known in Germany.

By the mid-1930s, Breker's own reputation was also growing in Germany and, while he opposed repression of modern art, the neo-Fascist monumentalism of his work came to the attention of Goebbels and Hitler. Soon he was commissioned to create sculptures and reliefs for new Nazi ministries and, by 1939, he was close to being an official artist. When Hitler visited the newly conquered Paris in June 1940, he summoned Breker—and Speer—to join him. For this historic visit, Breker later recalled, the Führer said, "I want to be surrounded by artists."[9]

In 1942, Breker enjoyed a different form of consecration when a huge retrospective of his work opened at the Orangerie in Paris. Organized by his old friend Jacques Benoist-Méchin, a pro-Nazi journalist who had joined the Vichy regime, the show was supported by an honor committee that included senior Vichy officials as well as the Fascist writers Brasillach and Drieu La Rochelle. While preparing the show, Ambassador Abetz arranged for Breker to stay in Helena Rubinstein's Aryanized apartment on the Île Saint-Louis, and Laval offered him a lunch at the Hôtel de Matignon, the prime

In late August 1939, days before Nazi Germany invaded Poland and set in motion World War II all the paintings in the Louvre's Grande Galerie and other exhibition rooms were hurriedly evacuated, for the most part to the Château de Chambord in the Loire Valley. *(Roger-Viollet)*

TOP On May 10, 1940, after eight months of "phony war," Germany invaded Western Europe and quickly outmaneuvered the French army. In the panic, millions of French families fled south, on trains, in cars, on bicycles and finally on foot.
(LAPI/Roger-Viollet)

LEFT At dawn on June 23, 1940, nine days after Paris fell, Hitler paid his only visit to the city. Claiming he wanted to be accompanied by artists, he posed in front of the Eiffel Tower with the architect Albert Speer, left, and the sculptor Arno Breker, who remained his favorites throughout the war.
(U.S. National Archives)

TOP Under the June 1940 armistice, southeast France remained unoccupied. Much of show business gathered in Cannes and, for a while, enjoyed itself. Three leading actresses, left to right, Michèle Morgan, Micheline Presle and Danielle Darrieux, posed on the beach with Gregor Rabinovitch, a Jewish movie producer who was soon forced to flee France. *(Courtesy of Madame Micheline Presle)*

RIGHT After France's defeat, the nightlife of Paris quickly resumed, with Wehrmacht officers and soldiers often making up most of the audience for saucy cabaret shows. *(Roger Schall)*

Varian Fry, an American journalist who was sent to Marseille by the New York–based Emergency Rescue Committee, helped some two thousand artists, intellectuals and other refugees to escape occupied France. Here he sits in his office beside André Breton's wife, Jacqueline Lamba, while, right to left, Breton, André Masson and Max Ernst look on. *(Varian Fry Papers, Rare Books & Manuscript Library, Columbia University)*

On October 24, 1940, returning from a meeting in Hendaye with Spain's Generalísimo Franco, Hitler stopped at Montoire in the Loire Valley to receive Marshal Pétain, the "head of state" of the Vichy regime. A few days later, Pétain endorsed collaboration with the German occupiers. *(Roger-Viollet)*

The Nazi propaganda chief, Joseph Goebbels, considered music to be the best way of demonstrating Germany's cultural superiority over France. Many German orchestras and choirs toured France, some of them giving lunchtime concerts on the steps of the Paris Opera. *(LAPI/Roger-Viollet)*

On September 29, 1940, the Louvre was reopened in the presence of Field Marshal Gerd von Rundstedt, seen here with a French curator, although only statues and sculptures were on display and the paintings galleries remained closed. *(LAPI/Roger-Viollet)*

Herbert von Karajan, a frequent visitor to occupied Paris, posed with the French soprano Germaine Lubin after conducting her in a Berlin Staatsoper production of Wagner's *Tristan und Isolde* at the Paris Opera in May 1941. *(LAPI/Roger-Viollet)*

CLOCKWISE FROM TOP RIGHT Rose Valland, seen above in uniform after the war, was stationed throughout the occupation at the Jeu de Paume, where she kept a secret record of art looted from Jews. Air Marshal Hermann Göring, with a walking stick and trilby, would frequently visit the gallery to pick art for Hitler and for himself. The paintings shown here were considered "degenerate" and were either destroyed or exchanged for pre-twentieth-century art. *(top right: Collection C. Garapont/Association la Mémoire de Rose Valland; bottom left and right: Archives des Musées Nationaux)*

An exhibition called The Jew and France, which opened at the Palais Berlitz in Paris in the fall of 1941, included a section claiming that Jews were "masters of French cinema." *(LAPI/ Roger-Viollet)*

Among the most virulently anti-Semitic French writers were Louis-Ferdinand Céline, left, at the opening of the Institut d'Études des Questions Juives in Paris, and Lucien Rebatet, shown signing copies of his memoir, *Les Décombres. (left: Roger-Viollet; right: Albert Harlingue/ Roger-Viollet)*

Goebbels frequently invited French artists to Germany to underline cultural cooperation between the two countries. Among French movie stars leaving the Gare de l'Est for Berlin in March 1942 were, left to right, Viviane Romance, Danielle Darrieux, Suzy Delair and Junie Astor. *(LAPI/Roger-Viollet)*

In October 1941, a high-level delegation of French artists leaving the Gare de l'Est for Germany included the leading Fauvist painters Maurice de Vlaminck, Kees van Dongen and André Derain. *(LAPI/Roger-Viollet)*

In November 1941, a group of French writers returned to Paris by train after attending a European writers' congress in Weimar. In uniform on the left is Gerhard Heller, the German official in charge of literary censorship; beside him in a trilby is Pierre Drieu La Rochelle, a leading collaborationist writer; next to him in a white raincoat is Robert Brasillach, the editor of the pro-Nazi weekly *Je suis partout*; and on the far right, wearing glasses, is Karl-Heinz Bremer, the deputy director of the German Institute in Paris. *(LAPI/Roger-Viollet)*

Many popular French singers, including Maurice Chevalier, left, and Édith Piaf, right, traveled to Germany to perform in camps holding some of the 1.6 million French prisoners of war. *(left: Roger-Viollet; right: Ulstein Bild/Roger-Viollet)*

The opening of Arno Breker's sculpture exhibition, top, at the Orangerie in May 1942 drew senior Vichy officials as well as many French artists and intellectuals who would later be accused of collaboration. Among those in attendance were the dancer Serge Lifar, seen here, at left, in costume for the ballet *Joan de Zarissa* by the German composer Werner Egk, and, at right, the artist and poet Jean Cocteau. *(top: LAPI/Roger-Viollet; bottom left: André Zucca/BHVP/Roger-Viollet; bottom right: Ulstein Bild/Roger-Viollet)*

Jean Paulhan, a literary critic and book editor, seen at left in a dark suit with the artist Georges Braque, was a pivotal figure in the intellectual resistance and a cofounder of *Les Lettres Françaises*, a clandestine newspaper published by writers. The Communist poet Louis Aragon was an important resistance figure in southern France. (*left: Roger-Viollet; below right: Rue des Archives*)

The American socialite Florence Gould, shown in a portrait from the late 1930s, held a weekly literary salon in occupied Paris. It was attended by both collaborationist and resistance writers as well as by some Germans, among them the renowned novelist Ernst Jünger, who was stationed in Paris with the Wehrmacht and is seen here on horseback leading a parade. *(top: Florence Gould Foundation; bottom: Marbach/Rue des Archives)*

The Kiev-born Jewish writer Irène Némirovsky spent her last beach vacation in 1939 with her daughters, Denise and Élisabeth, and her husband, Michel Epstein. From May 1940, the family lived in the Burgundy town of Issy-l'Évêque, where she wrote her best-known work, *Suite Française*, published only in 2004. In July 1942, she was arrested by French gendarmes and deported to Auschwitz, where she died one month later. *(Fonds Irène Némirovsky/IMEC)*

Late in the occupation, the young writer Marguerite Duras joined the resistance along with her husband, Robert Antelme, right, and her lover Dionys Mascolo. Antelme was subsequently arrested and deported to Germany, but he survived the war. *(Collection Jean Mascolo/Sygma/ Corbis)*

The popular writer Colette spent much of the occupation in her apartment in the Palais-Royal, where her Jewish husband, Maurice Goudeket, was forced to hide every night in a maid's room in the building's attic. *(Pierre Jahan/ Roger-Viollet)*

Pablo Picasso, who spent the occupation in Paris, wrote a surrealist play, *Le Désir attrapé par le queue* (Desire Caught by the Tail), which was performed privately in Michel Leiris's home on March 19, 1944. Brassaï recorded the occasion in a photograph that shows, among others, Simone de Beauvoir holding a book to Picasso's left, Albert Camus engaging with the dog below him and Jean-Paul Sartre, with a pipe to Camus's right. Some Picasso paintings are displayed in the background. *(Estate Brassaï-RMN)*

Two of France's most popular actors, Arletty and Jean-Louis Barrault, were the stars of Marcel Carné's movie *Les Enfants du paradis*, which was shot largely during the occupation but released only after the liberation of France. By then, Arletty was in disgrace for having had a German lover. *(Rue des Archives/RDA)*

The writer Albert Camus, left, who joined the resistance in late 1943 and edited the clandestine newspaper *Combat*, is seen here after the liberation of Paris with the resistance leader Jacques Baumel and the writer André Malraux, who is wearing a French army uniform. *(René St. Paul/Rue des Archives)*

A week before the liberation of Paris on August 25, 1944, the French Communist Party called for an insurrection and thousands of young Parisians took up arms, building barricades and harassing the retreating German forces. *(Roger-Viollet)*

General Charles de Gaulle, who for more than four years had led the French fight against Germany, first from London, then from Algiers, returned to Paris on liberation day, August 25, 1944. The following morning, he walked down the avenue des Champs-Élysées and was acclaimed by Parisians. *(Roger-Viollet)*

After the liberation of France, writers and artists were among tens of thousands of men and women brought to trial on charges of collaborating with the enemy. The writer Robert Brasillach, left, was condemned to death and shot on February 6, 1945. Sacha Guitry, right, was jailed for sixty days, but legal proceedings against him continued until August 1947, when his case was shelved. *(Top Foto/Roger-Viollet)*

minister's official residence. Soon it was apparent that this was to be *the* cultural event of the year: the turnout for its opening on May 15, 1942, included *le tout Paris* willing to be associated with anything German. Most of the artists who had traveled to Germany were present, as were celebrities like Arletty, Guitry, Lifar, Cocteau and Drieu La Rochelle. So immense were Breker's statues that Guitry quipped to Cocteau, "If they all have erections, we won't be able to move around."[10] Opening speeches by Bonnard and Benoist-Méchin were followed by a concert given by Alfred Cortot, Wilhelm Kempff and Germaine Lubin. Breker also received a handwritten note of congratulations from Pétain. For Breker, though, the guest of honor was Maillol. The old man had been reluctant to make the trip, but Gerhard Heller, the German officer in charge of literature at the Propaganda Staffel, took a car and driver to Banyuls-sur-Mer to collect him.

The Breker spectacle was not over. A few days later, another reception in his honor, this one at the Musée Rodin, drew still more cultural luminaries, including the collaborationist writers Paul Morand and Céline, the playwright Giraudoux and others, like Guitry, who had been at the Orangerie. In the cultural weekly *Comoedia,* Cocteau also published a "Salut à Breker," which began "Hail Breker" and gave seven reasons for his admiration, including "because the great hand of Michelangelo's *David* has shown you your path." Cocteau was promptly made to understand that he had gone too far. In a letter expressing his "painful surprise," the poet Éluard reminded him that "Freud, Kafka, Chaplin have been banned by the very same people who honor Breker." But if Cocteau was willing to exhibit himself in this way, it was also out of gratitude to Breker. The previous year, his lover, Jean Marais, had punched the pro-Nazi theater critic Alain Laubreaux for his criticism of Cocteau. Fearing a reprisal from the Gestapo, Cocteau had turned to Breker for protection. In his journal on May 6, 1942, a few days before the Orangerie opening, Cocteau recalled the German's loyalty: "At the time that all the Germanophile press was insulting me, Arno Breker, Hitler's sculptor, offered me the chance of calling him by a special telephone to Berlin in the event that anything serious happened to me or to Picasso."[11]

Breker later also claimed to have obtained the release from the prison in Fresnes of Eugène Rudier, whose foundry had cast Rodin's bronzes and who subsequently went to Berlin to cast Breker's

bronzes, and of the poet Patrice de la Tour du Pin, who was a prisoner of war in Germany. What seems certain is that in 1943 he did
help to free Dina Vierny, Maillol's model. In late 1940, Maillol had
saved her from jail for leading Jews and other refugees along secret
mountain trails into Spain. Now she had again been arrested, this
time in Paris, with the risk that she would be unmasked as an anti-
Fascist foreign Jew. As Vierny later told the story, during a visit to
Paris, Breker found Maillol incapable of working, as he put it, "without Dina," who by then had spent six months in Fresnes. Breker
consulted Belmondo, who assured him that Vierny was innocent of
the charges of trafficking in gold and helping refugees. A few days
later, a German officer delivered Dina to a restaurant in Montparnasse where Breker and Maillol awaited her.[12] That same year, Breker
traveled to Banyuls-sur-Mer to do a bronze bust of Maillol.

Noticeably absent from anything resembling the official art world
were Dufy, Rouault, Bonnard, Matisse and Picasso. All were men
who had first made their names in the early years of the century and,
in the cases of Bonnard, Matisse and Rouault, were now over seventy. All felt they still had something to contribute to art, yet they
saw no role for themselves in France's political drama. All but
Picasso also chose to live in the south of France. Dufy, whose colorful oils owed much to the early influence of Les Fauves, lived first
in Nice, then in Perpignan and finally in the small village of Mont-
saunès, west of Carcassonne. He kept busy painting and designing
tapestries. He also began working with the Paris dealer Louis Carré,
while exhibitions of his work were held during the war years in
Lyon, Brussels and New York, as well as Paris. Rouault, a Fauvist-
turned-Expressionist, moved to the Riviera, spending the occupation
in the tiny resort of Golfe-Juan east of Cannes. He was increasingly
consumed by Christianity, a surprisingly common trait among
wartime artists, and his work, like that of Bonnard, Matisse and
Dufy, seemed to pay no heed to the *années noires* being lived by most
French.

Pierre Bonnard, who in his youth was a central figure of Les
Nabis, had long since opted for a quiet life of introspection. When
war was declared in 1939, he and his wife, Marthe, withdrew to Villa
Le Bosquet in Le Cannet, on the Côte d'Azur, where Bonnard continued to paint bucolic landscapes and, above all, nudes. Although
mobilized as a war painter in 1917, now in his mid-seventies, he
seemed barely touched by the new conflict. His only interest was

painting, and he continued to portray the aged Marthe, naked or in her bath, as if she were still a young beauty. In 1941, Maillol sent Vierny to pose for Bonnard, mainly to keep her out of trouble. Bonnard immediately began work on *Nu sombre,* a Gauguinesque portrait of the naked Dina that he would complete only in 1946. One reason for the delay was that Marthe's death, in January 1942, plunged him into deep mourning. With Bonnard running out of money, alone and isolated much of the time, a young printer, Aimé Maeght, came to his rescue, bringing him food and painting materials as well as selling some of his oils. At the same time, Maeght, who would become a renowned art dealer after the war, was making false documents for the resistance. When the war ended, Bonnard lived just long enough—until January 1947—to enjoy his new international celebrity.

Matisse, too, preferred to paint joy over sorrow, but during the occupation this meant overcoming his failing health, the turmoil within his family and the discomfort imposed by war. In early 1939, after years of stormy marriage, his wife, Amélie, filed for separation, with the result that Matisse's unsold art and other valuables were stored in the Banque de France in Paris pending their division into equal parts. The catalyst for Amélie's action was the arrival in their lives of a strong-minded young Russian woman, Lydia Delectorskaya, whose care and attention Matisse soon found indispensable. After a final meeting at the Gare Saint-Lazare in July 1939, Matisse never again saw Amélie, while Lydia became his secretary, protector and companion (though not mistress), an arrangement that lasted until his death in 1954. During the phony war, Matisse left his Paris studio for Nice, where he occupied an entire floor of the Hôtel Regina, in the neighborhood of Cimiez. In the spring of 1940, he even planned to escape for a few weeks by taking a boat to Brazil. Yet when Germany invaded France, he was in Paris, and it took him and Lydia six weeks to return to Nice, via Bordeaux, Carcassonne and Marseille.

Throughout the journey and during the months that followed, Matisse suffered terrible stomach pains. In late 1940, he turned down a visa for the United States offered by Varian Fry, explaining in a letter to his son Pierre, in New York, "If everything of any worth flees, what will remain of France?" But his health continued to deteriorate and, in January 1941, he was rushed to Lyon for an emergency colostomy. Fearing that he might not survive, he wrote a letter that

he instructed Pierre to give to Amélie should he die. In an accompanying letter, he complained that Amélie "called in question everything about me—my honesty, my affection for my family, and all the
rest." He added, "I shall not of course go into that. I shall simply tell
her that I continued to love her." But he survived the operation, the
letter was never delivered and five months later he returned to
Cimiez with Lydia. Too weak to paint, he concentrated on drawing.

To cheer him up, Maillol also sent him Vierny, with a note saying,
"I lend you the vision of my work, you will reduce her to a line."[13]
And, indeed, Matisse did some exquisite nude line drawings of Mail-
lol's model. At one point, Vierny insisted that she had to return to
Bonnard, who was still at work on *Nu sombre*. Later she recounted
Matisse's response: "No question of your returning to Bonnard!
You're going to interrupt my flow. Look, I'm going to draw Bon-
nard, here he is; I stick him on the drawing, he's behind you now.
Let's talk no more of this and continue."[14]

Matisse had also begun making the paper cutouts that he published in 1947 as *Jazz* and would occupy him during his final years.
Yet while consumed by his work, he was not cut off from the world.
Through visiting art dealers and collectors, he knew that his paintings were being shown—and bought—in Paris. Rouault called on
him, and he traveled to Le Cannet to see Bonnard. He also struck up
an unlikely friendship with the resistance poet Aragon, who wrote
the preface to Matisse's collection of drawings *Thèmes et variations*.
Further, he was aware of the desperate situation of Jewish painter
friends and constantly worried that the French police might arrest
Lydia as an enemy alien. After Germany took over the unoccupied
zone and Italian troops marched into Nice in late 1942, fearing that
the war would soon reach the Côte d'Azur, Matisse, Lydia and their
cook moved to a small country house, grandly called Villa Le Rêve,
outside Vence, twenty miles to the west. With no telephone and no
car, Lydia headed off daily by bicycle to find food for the household.

Matisse's family was also dispersed. Pierre was in New York, where
he organized the 1942 show Artists in Exile for Mondrian, Chagall,
Ernst, Léger and other painters who had left France. Matisse's other
son, Jean, was in nearby Antibes but deeply involved with the maquis,
training young resisters in the art of sabotage. Matisse knew that
Amélie and their strong-minded daughter, Marguerite, were living in
the family home at Issy-les-Moulineaux, outside Paris. He did not
know that both had joined the Communist resistance group Francs-

Tireurs et Partisans, Marguerite as a courier and Amélie typing intelligence reports to be smuggled to London. Then, on April 13, 1944, both women were arrested by the Gestapo, Marguerite in Rennes and Amélie in Paris. Learning of the arrests one week later, Matisse appealed for help to the dealer Fabiani and Guitry, both on good terms with the Germans, but to no avail. Amélie spent the rest of the occupation in jail in Fresnes and was freed when Paris was liberated. Marguerite had a narrower escape. After undergoing weeks of torture, she was deported—along with hundreds of other women prisoners—just as Allied forces were advancing into Brittany. By good fortune, her train, destined for the Ravensbrück concentration camp, was stopped at the German border on August 4 by Allied bombing. In the confusion, she escaped and made her way to safety. In the final days of the war, even Matisse was in danger: with Allied forces landing on France's southern coast in mid-August, three bombs exploded near the Villa Le Rêve. Yet it was probably only in January 1945, when Marguerite visited her father and recounted her experiences, that the true horror of war was brought home to him.

Picasso, too, could have sought the tranquillity of the Côte d'Azur or, indeed, exile in the United States or Mexico, but after he drove to Paris from Royan with two carloads of paintings on August 23, 1940, he left the city only once during the occupation. He knew that, as a Spaniard who had supported the defeated Spanish Republic and had been refused French nationality, his situation was precarious. Further, while Spain remained neutral, Franco had good relations with both Hitler and Pétain and was in a position to demand Picasso's arrest and extradition to Spain. The artist's only option was to keep a low profile and set about organizing the logistics of his life and his women. When he left for Paris, his mistress, Marie-Thérèse Walter, stayed in Royan with their daughter, Maya, until the end of the year, but Picasso's more public partner, Dora Maar, followed him by train the same day. At the time, he had two Paris homes, but fuel shortages during the first winter of the occupation prompted him to close his Right Bank apartment, on the rue La Boétie, and settle into his Left Bank duplex, at 7 rue des Grands-Augustins, a stone's throw from the Seine. There, he was around the corner from Maar's home on the rue de Savoie and conveniently close to his old hangouts of the Café de Flore and the Brasserie Lipp in Saint-Germain. Marie-Thérèse and Maya then moved into an apartment on the boulevard Henri IV on the Île Saint-Louis, a fifteen-minute walk away; Picasso would usually visit them on Thursdays and Sundays. His Paris had shrunk to the size of a village.

But he was not allowed to forget the German presence. In the fall of 1940, as the Germans set about scavenging France, they decided to inspect all bank vaults, including those of the Banque Nationale pour le Commerce et l'Industrie on the boulevard Haussmann, where Picasso and Braque rented strong rooms. Picasso was in the bank vaults when his two strong rooms were opened for German officers. The officer in charge seemed so confused by what he saw that Picasso pointed to Braque's adjacent strong room and said it contained still more of his unsold work. With that, the officer ended the inspection.[15]

German officers also visited Picasso's studio on the rue des Grands-Augustins, and it was there that the famous—and perhaps apocryphal—exchange took place about *Guernica,* his 1937 painting protesting the Luftwaffe's bombing of the eponymous Basque town. As Picasso often told the story, offered a postcard of *Guernica,* one German asked, "Did you do this?" To which Picasso replied, "No, you did!"

Other Germans would also knock on his door, curious to meet the man already considered the world's most important living artist. Gerhard Heller was taken to meet Picasso by the Gallimard editor— and secret *résistant*—Jean Paulhan in June 1942. In his memoir, Heller recalled his excitement: "We rang. Picasso himself came to open. I recognized his familiar silhouette: small, stocky, wrapped in a sort of blanket kept in place by a leather belt, a cap on his bald head and fiery eyes that pierced us. Very pleasant, very simple, he led us into his apartment, then into vast lofts with oak beams. Everywhere there were paintings, piled up, hanging, leaning on each other, upside down; he showed them, one by one, saying little, awaiting our reaction. I felt as if I were drunk."[16] One month later, Picasso was visited by the novelist Ernst Jünger, also stationed in Paris with the Wehrmacht. In his journal entry for July 22, 1942, sounding no less excited than Heller, Jünger described Picasso's apartment in detail. After much discussion about art, Jünger then quoted Picasso as saying: "The two of us, just as we're sitting here, we could negotiate peace this very afternoon. This evening men could smile."[17] It was a remark that Jünger loved to repeat.

The one time that Picasso left Paris was in early 1943, when he visited one of his oldest friends, the poet Max Jacob, with whom he had shared a room decades earlier. Jewish by birth, Jacob had converted to Catholicism in 1909 and was living in the monastery of Fleury in Saint-Benoît-sur-Loire, although he knew that his conversion would not shield him from Nazi persecution. The painter and the poet spent much of the day together, visiting the basilica and walking beside the Loire. Whether Picasso sensed his friend's pessimism is not known, but Jacob, who defiantly wore a yellow star while helping priests during mass, was increasingly resigned to being arrested. His brother Gaston had already been deported, and in January 1944 his sister and brother-in-law were also sent to their deaths in Auschwitz.

On February 24, 1944, Jacob was himself arrested by the Gestapo. He managed to smuggle a letter to Cocteau in which he begged for Sacha Guitry's help.* Cocteau also appealed to Heller to intervene. In his memoir, Heller claimed that he lobbied Ambassador Abetz and the German secret service and eventually obtained an order for Jacob's release. But the poet died of bronchial pneumonia in Drancy on March 6 before he could be rescued. Picasso's behavior at that time was hard to explain. Pierre Colle, a Paris art dealer who was Jacob's literary executor, said that Picasso had refused to add his voice to those calling for Jacob's release. On the other hand, Georges Prade, an infamous *pétainiste,* said he told Picasso that his signature on a letter to the Germans would be counterproductive. Still, on March 18, along with Derain and a handful of Jacob's friends, Picasso attended a commemorative mass at the Church of Saint-Roch in Paris. And on March 21, Picasso joined a larger group of some fifty mourners, including Braque, Éluard, Mauriac, Maar, Coco Chanel and Paulhan, at a second mass in the same church.

Certainly, Picasso would have been informed, not only about the darkening plight of Jews in France and the internment of tens of thousands of Spanish Republicans, but also about the growth of the resistance. André Dubois, who used his senior post in the Interior Ministry to protect many intellectuals and refugees, would stop by frequently. Among others who kept Picasso up to date were Sartre, Cocteau, the poets Jacques Prévert and Robert Desnos, the photographer Brassaï and, even after he joined the resistance in 1944, André

---

*Jacob's note read: "Dear Jean. I write to you in a train carriage with the agreement of the gendarmes who surround us. We will soon be at Drancy. That's all I have to say. When Sacha was told about my sister, he said: If it were him, I could do something. Fine, so it is me. I embrace you. Max."

Malraux. Annie Ubersfeld, a young *résistante* who later became a respected theater teacher, said that as early as 1942 Picasso gave money to the resistance and occasionally hid fugitives in his apartment. "You can't imagine what risks he took," she recalled many decades later.[18]

But Picasso also had to take precautions. Gilot, who was introduced to her future lover by the actor Alain Cuny at Le Catalan in May 1943, said she knew Picasso always gave money to Spanish exile causes and may also have helped the resistance, adding, "But whatever people did, you never talked about it, because the more people who know something, the more the danger." After she began almost daily visits to Picasso in his studio, she noticed that at least once a month Germans would knock on his door. She recalled, "They'd never be in uniform when they came, a group of five or six. And Pablo would ask me to follow them to make sure they didn't plant any documents they could 'find' later. He was always concerned about that. There was also a very good photographer, a German, a homosexual, not a Nazi, Herbert List, who would come very often. And each time, Pablo told me to follow him around to see what he was doing."

When Picasso met Gilot, who, at twenty-two, was forty years his junior, he was still involved with both Dora Maar and Marie-Thérèse Walter. But while Gilot did not become his mistress until nine months later and the pair did not live together until after the war, she became a close observer of his routine. "He did not get up very early," she recalled. "And he would have people like me come to see him between eleven-thirty a.m. and one-thirty p.m. He would have a light lunch and then work all afternoon and evening. And then he would have a light dinner. He was not a big eater."

Nonetheless, Picasso usually went out for his meals, invariably accompanied by his Spanish secretary, Jaime Sabartés, and, until his death in March 1942, by the Spanish painter Julio González. Thanks to the black market, even small bistros like Le Catalan and others on the rue Dauphine that he frequented were not short of food. (Le Catalan was once closed for a week after it was found serving meat on a meatless day.) But, apart from attending openings at Jeanne Bucher's gallery on the boulevard du Montparnasse, Picasso rarely ventured far from his neighborhood. "He had a car, but I did not see him use it," Gilot said. "You had to get gasoline from the Germans, so that was seen as an act of collaboration. If he had to go anywhere, like the Leiris Gallery, he'd take the *métro* because that was the most neutral thing. It was anonymous. On buses, you could be noticed." The right-wing writer Paul Léautaud bumped into Picasso on the rue Jacob one morning in April 1944. Léautaud noted in his journal: "He crossed the road to join me. He has let his hair grow down to his collar. His hair is all white. He does not have the face of an old man at all. From behind, you could take him for one. Strange thing. Until now I didn't realize how small he is. He has a charming face and a teasing manner."[19]

Throughout the occupation, Picasso continued working. In 1941, he was even inspired to write a short six-act play, *Le Désir attrapé par la queue* (Desire Caught by the Tail), penned in the Surrealist tradition of "automatic" writing and therefore close to unintelligible. Still, for its first reading, on March 19, 1944, in the home of Michel and Louise Leiris, his neighbors on the rue des Grands-Augustins, the play had an impressive cast that included Sartre, Raymond Queneau, Maar and Beauvoir, with Albert Camus as the Chorus, introducing the characters and describing the imagined décor. The occasion was recorded by Brassaï.

Picasso's paintings and drawings were also sold discreetly at the Leiris Gallery and occasionally at Drouot auctions. Was his art as detached from the war as that of Bonnard and Matisse? Heller, though hardly an expert, wrote of the paintings he saw that "in the cruel decomposition of forms, in the tragic violence of colors, the horror of the war (while never directly expressed) was present in a manner difficult to bear."[20] Certainly, while the violence of *Guernica* did not reappear in his painting until after the liberation, there is ample anguish, even tragedy in *L'Aubade* of 1942 and in numerous still lifes, some of red, gray and black skulls baring their teeth, others of skulls and leeks suggesting skulls and crossbones. Picasso also made one hundred drawings for his best-known sculpture of the period, *L'Homme au mouton* (Man with a Lamb). In 1945, he explained: "I did not paint the war because I am not one of those artists who goes looking for a subject like a photographer, but there is no doubt that the war is there in the pictures which I painted then. Later on perhaps the historians will find them and show that my style changed under the war's influence."[21]

Although Picasso kept away from the Paris art scene, avoiding the visibility of, say, Braque, his shadow nonetheless continued to haunt those Fauvist artists who blamed Cubism for sinking their move-

ment. Vlaminck, in particular, seemed to be troubled that he had
been more celebrated in 1900 than in 1940. Now, perhaps aware of
Picasso's vulnerability as both a foreigner and a "degenerate" artist
and confident of his own good standing with the Germans, he saw a
chance for revenge. Using the platform of *Comoedia*, the same cultural weekly where Cocteau had published his paean to Breker,
Vlaminck turned on Picasso on June 6, 1942. Amid a series of gratuitous insults, among them describing Picasso as having "the face of a
monk and the eyes of an inquisitor," Vlaminck pronounced him
"guilty of having led French painting into the most deadly impasse,
into indescribable confusion." Bazaine promptly responded to the
charges in the *Nouvelle Revue Française* and André Lhote did so in
Comoedia. Unsurprisingly, this diatribe harmed Picasso less than
Vlaminck, who was among the artists suspended from exhibiting
their work after the liberation.

Once Paris was free again, though, Picasso's stance during the
occupation was also examined. Having joined the French Communist Party in the fall of 1944, he was now conveniently on the same
side as those carrying out the purges of collaborators. But he also had
no cause for concern. He never claimed to have been in the resistance, but he had also done nothing to encourage the enemy. Unlike
Cocteau, Lifar and Guitry, he had not socialized with the Germans;
unlike Vlaminck, Derain and Van Dongen, he had not traveled to
Germany as a guest of the Nazis. Gilot, who was perhaps the only
one of Picasso's women ever to criticize him and, in 1953, the only
one ever to leave him, came to respect his posture. "What would have
changed if Picasso, who certainly was no good with armaments, had
thrown a grenade? Nothing. No, his position was being against the
Germans and staying in Paris. For people of my generation, that
symbol was very important. Just by being there and not losing your
dignity, you could do certain things. Someone like Derain, why did
he go to Germany? That was sheer stupidity."

Distraction on Screen

THE GERMAN OCCUPATION is remembered as a golden age of French cinema, but the truth is more nuanced: of the 220 films made in France between June 1940 and August 1944, only a handful were memorable and the most popular of all, Marcel Carné's masterpiece, *Les Enfants du paradis,* was released only after the liberation of France. Yet the movie industry had good reason to feel upbeat. It had a captive audience, one that was eager to flee the ennui of daily life into the laughter and tears of the screen (and, in winter, into the warmth of a crowded theater). By 1943, movie attendance was 40 percent higher than in 1938. As important, "enemy" films, first British, then American, were banned, so that, with the exception of German movies, which few French filmgoers wanted to see, foreign competition largely disappeared. Even within the industry, there was less competition. Some major talent left for the United States. And, perhaps unintentionally, the Germans made further room in the industry by expelling Jewish producers, directors and actors from the profession and banning French films made before 1937. Henri-

Georges Clouzot, Robert Bresson, Jacques Becker, Jean Delannoy and Claude Autant-Lara would be among directors who made their names during the occupation.

The key variable was how the Nazis defined their interests. They would allow nothing anti-German or excessively nationalistic to appear on French screens, but even Goebbels regarded cinema as a good way of keeping the French distracted. A movie buff himself, he also had a soft spot for French stars: one famous photograph taken in July 1939, barely one month before war broke out, shows him posing with Fernandel and Elvire Popesco while visiting the Berlin set of Albert Valentin's *L'Héritier des mondésir.* Less predictably, while dozens of French films were made in Germany in the 1930s, Goebbels now wanted Germany to make commercially successful French films in France itself. The man he sent to Paris to execute this mandate was Alfred Greven, a forty-year-old World War I veteran and Nazi Party member. A longtime producer at the Berlin-based studio Universum Film AG, or UFA, he was a cultivated man who spoke fluent French and admired French cinema. He also knew many French producers, directors and actors who had worked for UFA in Berlin. Once in Paris, he created a new German-owned studio, Continental Films, and assumed control of both a distribution affiliate and a company managing theaters once owned by Jews. Under his guidance, he imagined French cinema—or at least his films—assuming the dominant position in Europe enjoyed by Hollywood before the war.

The industry as a whole fell under the responsibility of a section of the Propaganda Staffel called the Referat Film, run by a taciturn German officer known to the French only as Dr. Diedrich. This unit was in charge of authorizing screenplays, production schedules, distribution, film crews and actors. It also issued a list of two hundred films that could not be shown, some for being anti-German, others for having Jewish actors or directors, a dozen for being so pro-Nazi as likely to provoke French fury. One obvious target of censorship was any film made by Max Ophüls, a German-born Jewish director who had fled to France in 1933 and had recently sought refuge in Switzerland. Soon the list of banned films was expanded to include those of directors who had left for the United States, like Jean Renoir, Julien Duvivier and René Clair. A few films in production before the fall of France were abandoned. Delannoy's *Macao* had to be reshot because its male lead, the Austrian actor Erich von Stroheim, was a renowned anti-Nazi who was already in the United States. Two years later, the film was released as *L'Enfer du jeu,* with von Stroheim's scenes now played by Pierre Renoir, a son of the painter and the older brother of Jean Renoir.

In the fall of 1940, the only moviemaking was taking place in the unoccupied zone: in Marseille, where Marcel Pagnol, who was also a novelist and playwright, completed *La Fille du puisatier;* and in Nice's Victorine Studios, where Abel Gance, best known for his silent movie *Napoléon,* began shooting *Vénus aveugle,* which he dedicated to Pétain. But both men were soon disillusioned: Pagnol chose to destroy his only other film, *La Prière aux étoiles,* while Gance, whose father's family had Jewish roots, moved to Spain after making *Le Capitaine Fracasse* in 1943.

The French movie world itself was slow to adjust to the new regimes, those of the occupier and of Vichy, which also assumed a right to censor screenplays and movies. Having fled Paris in June 1940, many producers, directors and actors chose to remain in that welcoming stretch of Mediterranean coast between Marseille and Nice. Then, in October, Vichy's Statute on Jews confirmed what many had feared: that Jews could no longer work in cinema, an industry that French Fascists had long claimed was dominated by Jews. Lucien Rebatet, the anti-Semitic critic of *Je suis partout,* claimed that 82 of 110 new French films in 1938 were produced by Jews. In 1941, he returned to the subject in a book called *Les Tribus du cinéma et du théâtre,* the *tribus,* or "tribes" being Jews.

According to one study, Jews accounted for only 15 percent of all movie-industry workers—some 9,000 out of 60,000—but these included the owners of more than forty movie theaters, as well as a score of important producers, some of whom had also done business in Germany before the war. The theaters were quickly taken over or Aryanized, but experienced foreign-born Jewish producers like Gregor Rabinovitch, Arnold Pressburger, Joseph Bercholz, Serge Sandberg and Simon Schiffrin could not easily be replaced.* The story is told that the French poet and screenwriter Jacques Prévert warned Greven that his cause was lost: "Because you have no Jew with you. Look at Hollywood. You can't make movies without

---

*All managed to flee France and survive the war, although Pathé's former head, Bernard Natan, who was in jail for fraud when the Germans took Paris, died in Auschwitz.

them." Subsequently Greven asked the screenwriter Jean Aurenche if he knew any Jewish writers who would be willing to write for him. As Aurenche recalled the conversation, Greven explained: "I read very few interesting screenplays. You know why? Because there are no more Jews in France or Germany. And many of the best screen-writers and directors were Jews."[1] Greven heeded his words, at least in one noteworthy case. Although he knew that Jean-Paul Le Chanois was a Jew with the family name of Dreyfus, he hired him to write the screenplays for four Continental movies: *Picpus, La Main du diable, Vingt-cinq ans de bonheur* and *Cécile est morte!* Two more Jews, Henri Calef and Jacques Cohen, also worked as screenwriters in the unoccupied zone.

By early 1941, Boulogne-Billancourt and a score of other Paris studios had reopened and, along with Pathé-Cinéma, Gaumont and numerous smaller French companies, Continental Films at last started making movies. In 1941 alone, Greven's firm produced eleven films, starting with two thrillers made by experienced directors, *L'Assassinat du Père Noël* (The Murder of Father Christmas) by Christian-Jaque and *Le Dernier des six* (The Last of Six) by Georges Lacombe. Its third production was *Premier rendez-vous,* directed by Henri Decoin, who had made several prewar films for UFA in Berlin and whose strongest card was that he was married to France's biggest star, Danielle Darrieux. "We were in Cannes together, but then he went to Paris and called me from there to join him," she later recalled.

> It didn't seem strange to make a film for Continental because I'd already made so many films in Germany before the war. They'd make French and German-language versions of the same movies. It was funny because if they were shooting the German version first, we'd peep to see how they were doing it. My very first film, *Le Bal,* made by a German called Wilhelm Thiele, was like that. Everyone said, "Ah, the little girl." I was fourteen, and after that I made lots of films in Germany. Later, I'd hear things, that homosexuals were being arrested, that Hitler was evil, but I was really very naïve.[2]

After *Premier rendez-vous,* where she appeared opposite the rising screen heartthrob Louis Jourdan, Darrieux made two more movies for Continental Films, *Caprices,* directed by Léo Joannon, and *La Fausse maîtresse* by André Cayette.

From the comfort of his new office at 104 avenue des Champs-Élysées, Greven set about recruiting other top directors and actors. The immensely experienced Maurice Tourneur would be the most active of Continental's directors, with six films, while Richard Pottier made five, Cayette four, Decoin three and both Christian-Jaque and Clouzot two each. Among actors, along with Darrieux, Greven hired both established and rising stars, including Fernandel, Robert Le Vigan, Pierre Fresnay, Edwige Feuillère, Jean-Louis Barrault, Harry Baur, Albert Préjean, Raimu, Suzy Delair, Michel Simon, Ginette Leclerc and Martine Carol. Of these, only Le Vigan displayed overt sympathy for the Nazis; the others presumably never imagined that exercising their profession in this way could damage their reputation. In that sense, it was Carné's good fortune that no Continental movie ever carried his name. "After I was demobilized," he later recounted, "Greven summoned me and asked me to make films for Continental Films. I demanded in exchange that the screenplay be chosen by mutual accord and that the film be made in France. I was called to Matignon* and told that I would not be allowed to make films. Then Continental agreed to the two clauses and I signed, but I made no film for Greven. Instead I signed up with an independent producer to make three films."[3]

Still, those working for Continental enjoyed many advantages, not the least of which was job stability: directors were given three-movie contracts and were confident that financing would be forthcoming, while technicians were hired for one year. Continental's screenplays were also waved past German censors, while Greven himself ensured that productions were supplied with film stock, clothes for costumes and even electricity for studio work. French producers, in contrast, had to negotiate their scripts with the Referat Film, which also supervised the actual shooting of films and decided if the final version could be released. Dr. Diedrich, who often appeared unannounced at studios, was himself not short of opinions. "In the past, French films had a negative quality and were made by Jewish producers who assumed no moral responsibility and were in effect vile speculators," he said in a speech to the industry in September 1941. But the French people, he went on, could now look forward to "wholesome films, which are worthy of the

---

*The Hôtel de Matignon, the traditional home and office of French prime ministers, was used by Laval and other senior Vichy officials during the occupation.

artistic heritage of the country and carry the stamp of the new order."[4]

The Germans also occasionally banned or censored parts of films made in Marseille and Nice that Vichy had already approved. Vichy would in turn prohibit movies made in the occupied zone, which it considered damaging to France's moral welfare. The formation in late 1940 of a new professional organization, the Comité d'Organisation de l'Industrie Cinématographique, COIC,* served both French and German interests. Headed by Raoul Ploquin, a producer who had worked with Greven in Berlin, its aim was to give a structure to France's disorganized movie industry. In 1944, for instance, it founded the country's first film school, the Institut des Hautes Études Cinématographiques, IDHEC. Yet the COIC's first action was to remind the industry that the Statute on Jews had excluded Jews from all jobs in cinema. In practice, since Jews could not obtain COIC's new professional card, they could not work in the industry.

Until November 1942, Vichy's Information Secretariat had responsibility for monitoring movie production in the south. What Vichy wanted was a French cinema that promoted the family, rural and Catholic values of the National Revolution. Or, as Ploquin put it in August 1941, the aim was to raise the artistic and moral level of French cinema "by not allowing morbid and depressing films to poison the soul of the French public."[5] That said, both Vichy and the Propaganda Staffel cheerfully approved three poisonous propaganda films: *Les Corrupteurs,* a twenty-nine-minute anti-Semitic documentary by Pierre Ramelot shown in 1942 before Decoin's popular *Les Inconnus dans la maison* (which also had suggestions of anti-Semitism); *Forces occultes,* an anti-Freemason and anti-Semitic diatribe in the form of a full-length feature made in 1943 by Jean Mamy[†] under the name of Paul Riche; and an anti-Communist documentary, *Français, vous avez la mémoire courte* (People of France, You Have a Short Memory). To reach a larger public, Vichy also drummed out its political message through Gaumont's *France actualités,* the fifteen-minute newsreels that preceded every feature film and were devoted to glorifying Pétain and the National Revolution. It was not long before audiences responded to it with whistles and shouts of abuse.

---

*Similar *comités d'organisation* were created for most industries, trades and art forms.

†In March 1949, Mamy became the last person to be executed as a collaborator.

Then, after orders were issued for the theater lights to stay on during the newsreels, many cinemagoers made a point of arriving just in time for the opening credits of the feature film.

Naturally, the Germans hoped that the French would embrace German movies. Indeed, in 1941, some 20 percent of movies in Paris theaters were German. But very few drew French audiences. One that did was Josef von Báky's lighthearted fantasy *Münchhausen,* an early color film about a baron granted immortality, which Goebbels commissioned to celebrate the twenty-fifth anniversary of UFA. More disturbingly, also popular with some French was *Jud Süss,* or *Le Juif Süss,* a grotesquely anti-Semitic adaptation of a novel by the German Jewish writer Lion Feuchtwanger; it was directed by Veit Harlan and featured the veteran German actor Heinrich George. Such was its success that when George came to Paris to perform at the Comédie Française, French movie figures joined in fêting him at Maxim's.

Otherwise, apart from a German-made short documentary, *Le Péril juif,* distributed in France in 1941 to coincide with the exhibition Le Juif et la France,* the Nazis left propaganda to their own newsreel, *Actualités mondiales.* These weekly bulletins, which were made in Germany for distribution in the language of each occupied country, brought social and cultural news from the Third Reich, mockery of Germany's "Jewish-dominated" enemies and triumphant images of the Wehrmacht's fighting machine. Watching a German newsreel soon after he arrived in Paris, Ernst Jünger was struck by the violence of the images. "They showed our offensives in Africa, Serbia and Greece. The mere display of these tools of destruction provoked cries of horror." He even added a note to remind himself to study where "propaganda blends with terror."[6] Until November 1942, *Actualités mondiales* were shown only in the occupied zone; after November 1942, a new version of *France actualités,* combining German and Vichy propaganda, was shown across the country.

Greven himself showed little interest in propagating the Nazi message, although he organized a splendid reception at Ledoyen on May 20, 1941, to welcome Zarah Leander, a Swedish-born actress

---

*This 1941 exhibition in Paris had a section devoted to cinema, which showed photographs of Jewish producers under a banner reading, LES JUIFS, MAÎTRES DU CINÉMA FRANÇAIS, "Jews, Masters of French Cinema."

who was then the toast of Germany. Even the Referat Film and Dr.
Diedrich were often surprisingly tolerant in authorizing movies that
left audiences feeling good about France. For instance, one line in
Delannoy's historical drama *Pontcarral, colonel d'empire* would
often prompt applause from audiences: "Under such a regime, monsieur, it is an honor to be condemned!"

Such laxity did not please Goebbels. In his private journal, he
complained bitterly about another film, *La Symphonie fantastique.*
This romantic screen biography of the French composer Hector
Berlioz, directed by Christian-Jaque, with Jean-Louis Barrault in the
lead role, was even made by Continental Films. "I am furious,"
he wrote on May 15, 1942, "because our Paris bureaus are showing
the French how to portray nationalism in their films. I have given
very clear orders that the French should produce only films that are
light, empty and if possible kitsch. I think they'll find it enough.
There is no need to develop their nationalism."[7] He need hardly have
worried. Most of the French movies of this period were indeed light
comedies, costume dramas, fantasy films, love stories or thrillers.
Indeed, one-third of them were adaptations of novels and plays:
seven were borrowed from Balzac and no fewer than nine from the
Belgian-born writer Georges Simenon, who spent the war in Vendée,
in western France. A good many were also set in the past, like Guitry's *Le Destin fabuleux de Désirée Clary,* Autant-Lara's *Lettres
d'amour* and René Le Hénaff's *Le Colonel Chabert.*

That said, one of the most popular films of the occupation years,
Carné's *Les Visiteurs du soir,* or *The Devil's Envoys,* as the film was
later called in English, ended with a scene that could easily be interpreted as a nationalist gesture. Even before its release, there was a
buzz of excitement that France's best-known director after Renoir
was making his first movie in three years. After walking out of Continental Films, Carné had signed up to make three films for André
Paulvé, but the first, *Juliette, ou La Clef des songes,* based on the Surrealist play by Georges Neveux, fell through after Greven vowed
to keep it out of theaters. Paulvé then urged Carné to contact
Prévert, who had written four of Carné's prewar hits and who was
living on the Côte d'Azur. Prévert teamed up with Pierre Laroche to
write *Les Visiteurs.* Seeing the chance to rebuild his prewar team in
Nice, Carné then recruited the designer Alexandre Trauner, a Hungarian Jew, who was hiding in Tourrette-sur-Loup, near Vence, also
in the unoccupied zone. To make this possible, a non-Jewish de-

signer, Georges Wakhévitch, agreed to "sign" Trauner's work. Joseph Kosma, another Hungarian Jew who was living discreetly outside Cannes, was then invited to compose the score, although in the end much of it was written—and all of it signed—by Maurice Thiriet. Finally, for his lead roles, Carné chose the ever-popular Arletty, who starred in his *Hôtel du Nord* and *Le Jour se lève,* as well as Marie Déa, Jules Berry and Alain Cuny (the actress Simone Signoret and the director Alain Resnais, two future pillars of French cinema, were among the extras).

Shot near Nice, the film is an entertaining romp set in the Middle Ages in which good narrowly defeats evil. As Anne and her fiancé, the chevalier Renaud, preside over a prenuptial banquet,* they are joined by two minstrels, Gilles and Dominique, who are in fact envoys of the Devil. Gilles sets about seducing Anne, while Renaud and Anne's father, the Baron Hugues, court Dominique. Learning that Gilles has inconveniently fallen in love with Anne, the Devil arrives to forestall a happy outcome by depriving Gilles of his memory. When Gilles again sees Anne and his memory returns, an angry Devil turns them into stone statues. The film's final scene would become its most famous: although the lovers now seem lifeless, their hearts can still be heard beating. It took no great leap of imagination to understand that the Devil was Hitler and, yes, France's heart was still beating. "I would not swear that Jacques and I had thought of that," Carné conceded in his autobiography, *La Vie à belles dents.* "But in any event we accepted that interpretation since it responded to a real need on part of the public when the film was released in late 1942."[8]

A more political movie was *Le Corbeau* (The Raven), which Clouzot made for Continental in 1943. His first film for the studio, *L'Assassin habite au 21,* had been well received and Greven was eager for another film noir. Clouzot chose a 1937 screenplay by Louis Chavance called *L'Oeil du serpent* (The Eye of the Snake), inspired by the story of a woman who for five years sent poison-pen letters around the town of Tulle. Clouzot then reworked the screenplay and cast two popular actors, Pierre Fresnay and Ginette Leclerc, in the lead roles.

In the screen version, anonymous letters signed "Le Corbeau" are

---

*The banquet scene entered movie lore because Carné ordered platefuls of fruit to be injected with carbolic acid to dissuade hungry extras from eating them between scenes.

sent to a village doctor and other prominent locals, accusing the doctor of having an affair with the wife of the hospital psychiatrist and of carrying out illegal abortions. Other people are also targeted by letters, feeding ever-mounting distrust, jealousy and paranoia. Before the troublemaker is identified, one letter provokes a suicide and another prompts the doctor to leave the village. However, what might in normal times have been a straightforward thriller carried a darker message in 1943. At the urging of both the Germans and Vichy, some French citizens had taken to sending anonymous letters to the authorities denouncing members of the resistance, Jews, black marketers or simply detested neighbors. But instead of applauding this exposé of the moral turpitude of informers, *L'Écran Français,* the clandestine newspaper of the small movie resistance group, saw it differently, complaining that it fueled the Nazi view that "the inhabitants of our towns are nothing but degenerates, ripe for slavery" and implied that the French should follow "the moral rules of the virtuous Nazi."[9] Clouzot was not easily forgiven. After the liberation, *Le Corbeau* earned him a two-year ban from filmmaking.

Yet just as Clouzot would go on to make numerous acclaimed films, not least *Le Salaire de la peur* (The Wages of Fear), other directors who shaped postwar French cinema also made impressive debuts during the occupation. The most gifted was Robert Bresson, who in the 1950s would direct *Pickpocket* and *Journal d'un curé de campagne* (Diary of a Country Priest). Having spent a year as a German prisoner of war, he was immediately noticed in 1943 with his first feature film, *Les Anges du péché* (Angels of Sin). With a screenplay by Bresson and the playwright Jean Giraudoux, the movie tells of a secluded order of nuns who dedicate themselves to rehabilitating women from prison. (Before that, Giraudoux wrote his first screenplay for *La Duchesse de Langeais,* a film directed by Jacques de Baroncelli.)

Others less new to cinema also made films noted for their originality, among them Becker's *Dernier atout, Falbalas* and *Goupi mains rouges* and Autant-Lara's *Douce.* Jean Grémillon's *Le Ciel est à nous* (The Sky Is Ours) managed to warm the hearts of both Vichy and the resistance with its true-life story of Andrée Dupeyron, a French aviatrix who in 1938 had participated in the Paris-to-Baghdad air race in a plane built in her auto mechanic husband's garage.* In the same

---

*Around the same time as the movie was made, the Dupeyrons were sheltering an American airman shot down over France.

issue as it denounced *Le Corbeau, L'Écran Français* said Grémillon's film presented "characters full of French vigor, of genuine courage, of moral standing, where we find a national truth that does not wish to and cannot die."[10]

Another movie that merited its immense popularity was *L'Éternel retour* (The Eternal Return), a gripping modern rendering of the legendary love story of Tristan and Isolde, which united the talents of Delannoy as director, Jean Cocteau as writer and Georges Auric as composer. Even Cocteau's enemies recognized the many qualities of the movie, which was presented in a gala performance in Vichy attended by Pétain himself. After the war, though, there were some who saw the triumph of Aryanism in the two striking blonds, Jean Marais and Madeleine Sologne, cast in the lead roles of Patrice and Nathalie.

Then as now, of course, most moviegoers were drawn less by directors than by well-known actors. And keeping track of the lives and loves of screen celebrities were new movie magazines like *Vedettes, La Semaine, Ciné-Mondial* and *Toute-la-Vie.* In the nightlife of Paris, too, the stars were more important than their movies. None caused a greater stir when she swept into Maxim's than Danielle Darrieux, at the time unchallenged as France's biggest female star. After her marriage to Decoin had ended in late 1940, she had fallen in love with a dashing Latin diplomat, Porfirio Rubirosa, who was appointed the Dominican Republic's ambassador to France after the breakdown of his marriage to the daughter of the Dominican dictator, Rafael Leónides Trujillo. In theory, Rubirosa was posted to Vichy, but he spent most of his time in Paris. In fact, he and Darrieux met because they had apartments in the same building in Neuilly. "He was divine, he was as good as a god," she recalled almost seven decades later. "We'd go out every night. He'd say, 'Put on your evening dress,' and we'd go dancing at Jimmy's. Django Reinhardt's orchestra would play, Henri Salvador would sing. Shéhérazade was another favorite place. Then we'd have dinner at Maxim's or at the Ritz. He liked the bar at the Ritz before lunch. Were there Germans in uniform? I don't know and I didn't care. It was such a crazy period."

Darrieux's carefree life ended abruptly. After Pearl Harbor brought the United States into the war, Trujillo also declared war on Hitler and ordered the arrest of German diplomats in Santo Domingo. Within days, German officers came for Rubirosa and sent him to a special concentration camp for foreign diplomats at Bad Nauheim, north of Frankfurt in Germany. Darrieux was heartbroken, but a few months later Greven offered her a chance to visit her lover. *Premier rendez-vous,* Darrieux's first movie for Continental, was a romantic comedy about a pretty girl in her late teens who escapes from her orphanage to meet a man who has placed an ad in a newspaper.* The movie was to open in Berlin and Greven wanted Darrieux's glamorous presence to draw attention to the film—and to Franco-German cultural collaboration. "I told him, No way," she recalled. "But he said, 'You should think of your family.' My mother had a Polish grandfather and he seemed to be suggesting there were Jews in my family. It was blackmail. I said I'd go on one condition: 'I'll stay one day in Berlin and go and see Rubi.' He agreed, and that's what happened." To accompany her, Greven then organized a delegation of movie stars, among them Viviane Romance, Suzy Delair, Junie Astor and Albert Préjean. Photographs in both French and German newspapers and magazines showed the actresses in jaunty hats and fashionable attire as they left the Gare de l'Est on the overnight train for Berlin on March 18, 1942. Movie magazines noted that only Darrieux was not required to share a compartment.

After the opening of *Premier rendez-vous,* Goebbels hosted an official dinner for his French guests, which was also attended by leading German actors. The following morning, as the other French actors began a tour of various German cities, Darrieux was taken by car to meet Rubirosa. "When I saw my Rubi arriving in his cashmere overcoat looking very smart, it was marvelous," she remembered. "We were left alone, but we were together for a short time. Did we make love? I presume so, or else what was the point of going there?" A few months later, Rubirosa was freed, and he tracked down Darrieux in Perpignan, where she was making *La Fausse maîtresse,* her third film for Continental. On September 18, 1942, they were married at Vichy's city hall. "Greven sent Cayette and Clouzot down to tell me I had to return to Paris because I had a contract to make one film a year for Continental," Darrieux said. "I told them I was finished, I would make no more films, I was going to stay in the 'free' zone. They said I'd be in trouble, but I said I didn't care. I was stay-

---

*The oddest thing about the movie is that, while there is a shot of a calendar displaying May 1941, nothing else indicates that the story is taking place during the occupation.

ing with Rubi." They were sent to the Alpine resort of Megève under a form of internal exile called *résidence surveillée,* although Darrieux recalled that it was not unpleasant since the region was under Italian control: "We had a chalet, we gave parties, we drank, we ate, we played bridge, we were completely relaxed."

At the end of 1943, with the Germans now controlling all of France, the couple decided to leave Megève. "We learned there was a fellow who made false papers and we had some made under the names of Denise and Pierre Robira, so as not to change our initials because his initials were on his elegant suitcases," Darrieux recalled. With a well-known race-car driver at the wheel, they headed north and settled under their new names in Darrieux's country home at Septeuil, west of Paris. "There was always food in the countryside. It was the people in Paris who suffered. I was able to buy eggs just to wash my hair," she said. But now the war was also far closer. At one point, Darrieux and Rubirosa were forced to provide accommodations to a German officer, although after the D-Day landings in June 1944, he suddenly disappeared. On another occasion, a Canadian air force plane crashed near their garden and they helped to bury the six victims. Darrieux recalled, "Two days later, the mayor's daughter said we should hide because the Gemans wanted to shoot forty people, so we fled into the woods with our dog and stayed with a French family for eight or ten days." Soon afterward, American troops arrived in Septeuil.

Other leading lights of the French movie world had a less agitated time. A few actresses would be seen in Paris nightclubs on the arms of German officers. Of these, Arletty was the best known: she was the mistress of a Luftwaffe officer, Hans Jürgen Soehring, throughout the occupation. While making seven movies during the occupation, she was also seen at social events at the German embassy or the German Institute. She was no less careless in her choice of French friends, who included the collaborationist writers Drieu La Rochelle and Céline and the pianist Alfred Cortot.[11]

Mireille Balin, who in 1941 was featured on the cover of *Vedettes* with her then lover, the popular singer Tino Rossi, fell for a Wehrmacht officer, Birl Desbok, with whom she spent the rest of the war. Corinne Luchaire, a star in the 1930s whose newspaper editor father, Jean Luchaire, was one of Abetz's close friends, had a child with her Austrian lover, a Luftwaffe captain named Wolrad Gelrach. But the line defining collaboration was often blurred. Suzy Delair, who joined Darrieux on the trip to Berlin, helped protect two Jewish actors; and Michèle Alfa, whose lover was an officer at the Propaganda Staffel, obtained the release of the veteran actor Charles de Rochefort from an internment camp and hid some resistance leaders. In reality, most actors and directors were glad just to have work and, with sixty films made in 1941, sixty-seven in 1942 and another sixty in 1943, this was usually possible.

Micheline Presle, who was only seventeen when Paris fell, had left for Saint-Jean-de-Luz during the exodus and then joined Louis Jourdan, her fiancé, in Cannes. She spent the first two years of the occupation untroubled in the south, making three movies in Nice, two of them with Jourdan, *Parade en 7 nuits* and *Félicie Nanteuil,* both directed by Marc Allégret. In late 1942, she moved back to Paris and made three more movies, albeit none for Greven's company. But she never became part of the Paris nightlife. "I detested the Germans and did my best not to see them," she recalled. "It wasn't an act of heroism, it wasn't active resistance, it was an attitude. I'd play cards at a friend's house or I'd meet a group of young people like myself at cafés. We'd talk, but we were careful. A very good friend of mine, Joël Le Tac, was in the resistance, but I didn't know. He'd go away for a while—only later did I learn he often traveled to London—and then he'd come back. No questions. Only when he was arrested did I understand. I managed to get some food to him at La Santé prison, then he was deported to Dachau. But he survived."

By early 1944, such were the power shortages that only late at night was electricity made available for movie productions. "I was making *Falbalas* with Jacques Becker and we'd take the *métro* home in the morning," she said. "There were often members of the *milice* on the *métro,* and one in particular struck me. After the war, I found myself standing in line for something and he was in front of me. I said to him, 'I remember you very well.' He didn't reply."[12]

Elina Labourdette, another young actress (she was twenty-one in 1940), also steered clear of the social scene. "I didn't know one German during the whole war," she recounted much later. Initially, she stayed in the south—her parents owned a house in Opio, north of Cannes—and appeared in a play, *Les Jours heureux,* which toured the unoccupied zone. Even after she returned to Paris, she had no difficulty in obtaining a permit to cross the demarcation line to the south. The two movies she made during the occupation—*Le Pavillon brûle* in 1941 and *Des jeunes filles dans la nuit* in 1943—were both shot in

Paris for French producers, not Continental Films. In *Le Pavillon brûle,* she recalled, she was the fiancée of a miner played by Marais, Cocteau's boyfriend. "I already knew Cocteau through my parents, and he invited me to dinner," Labourdette said. "He told me that Jean was very nervous about the love scene we would shoot the following day. Well, I was nervous, too. I can't tell you how many times we shot the scene. The director said we were behaving like at a first communion. In the end, we hardly kissed."

One good friend was Bresson, who cast Elina in *Les Dames du Bois de Boulogne* in 1944. "Once I was dining with Bresson at home—I lived on the Île de la Cité overlooking Notre-Dame—and a friend of my parents', an Austrian Jew, called in a panic. She'd heard there would be a *rafle* of Jews the following day. Both Robert and I had an *Ausweis* to be out during the curfew. We went to pick her up with her luggage, and she spent the next two years in our maid's room. Later we got her out of Paris, and she spent the rest of the war hiding in the south."[13]

Harry Baur, in contrast, did not survive the war. Born in 1880, he was a giant of French theater and cinema in the interwar years, with more than seventy movie roles, including memorable performances in Raymond Bernard's *Les Misérables* and Tourneur's *Volpone.* During the occupation, *Je suis partout* and collaborationist weeklies accused him of being a Freemason and a Jew, attacks that led him to accept roles in two of Greven's movies—*L'Assassinat du Père Noël* and *Péchés de jeunesse* (Sins of Youth)—as a form of protection.

In 1942, Baur also agreed to return to Germany, where he had shot several movies in the 1920s and 1930s, to appear in the German-speaking lead role of Hans Bertram's musical comedy *Symphonie eines Lebens* (Symphony of a Life). While in Berlin, he was also invited to Goebbels's dinner for Darrieux and other French stars. Yet almost simultaneously, Baur's Jewish wife was arrested in France on suspicion of being a British agent. When he protested loudly, he was in turn arrested and tortured by the Gestapo. Finally, after four months in the Prison du Cherche-Midi, on Paris's Left Bank, Baur was released, ailing and reduced to half his normal weight. On April 8, 1943, he died at home, but the cause of death was never established. As word of his death spread, the consensus was that he had been murdered. Only his family and close friends dared to attend his funeral at Saint Vincent Cemetery in Montmartre.

The Baur case was nonetheless something of an exception, since the movie industry and show business in general were not targets of Nazi repression. Still odder, then, was the case of Robert Hugues-Lambert, who was chosen to play the title role in Louis Cuny's movie *Mermoz* only because he resembled Jean Mermoz, a famous French aviator. Near the completion of filming, in 1943, he was arrested in a gay bar, Le Sans-Soucis, and sent to Drancy, where he is said to have recorded his last lines for the movie through the barbed-wire fencing of the camp. He was later deported to the Gross-Rosen camp, in Germany, where he died of exhaustion in March 1945. What seemed puzzling about this case was that, while homosexuality was officially prohibited, many in the literary and artistic world were gay, not only Cocteau and Marais but also infamous collaborationists like Brasillach and Abel Bonnard.* Further, numerous gay bars in occupied Paris were popular with German soldiers. In fact, one explanation offered for Hugues-Lambert's arrest is that he was denounced by a jealous German lover.

As a rule, however, the relative freedom enjoyed by the French movie industry meant that its key players had little motivation to join the resistance. And if they wanted to play an active role, what exactly could they do? It was a question that Carné contemplated. "I have never handled a gun in my life," he recalled. "Also, I'm very sensitive to physical pain and I thought, If I am caught and tortured, I'm likely to tell everything I know. So I found a way of working."[14]

Nonetheless, in 1943, when the prospect of a German defeat was spawning new resistance groups across France, a handful of directors, actors and screenwriters formed the Comité de Libération du Cinéma Français. Among them were the directors Becker, Louis Daquin and Jean Painlevé, the assistant director Jean-Devaivre, the screenwriters Charles Spaak, Bernard Zimmer and Jean-Paul Le Chanois, the critic Georges Sadoul and the actor Pierre Blanchar. In the main, they saw themselves as preparing cinema for after the war. They also singled out those thought to be collaborators, criticizing them in *L'Écran Français,* which they first printed in mimeograph form in December 1943 and then, from March 1944, was included in *Les Lettres Françaises.*

---

*Galtier-Boissière gave Bonnard the nickname of Gestapette, uniting *Gestapo* with *tapette,* French slang for "homosexual."

In the case of Le Chanois and Spaak, their very cover was that they were writing for Continental. In fact, Spaak adapted Simenon's novel *Les Caves du "Majestic"* for Greven from jail. Devaivre, who also worked for Continental, was among the very few in the industry to participate actively in armed resistance, ending the war in a Burgundy maquis. Le Chanois, who was both a Communist and a Jew, left the most important legacy of the cinema resistance when he spent several weeks in early 1944 filming the Vercors maquis in southeastern France—and its fiercest battle with German forces—for *Au coeur de l'orage* (Heart of the Storm), a documentary released after the liberation. Le Chanois's unit, which was called the Réseau de Résistance du Cinéma Français, or French Cinema's Resistance Network, then filmed the insurrection in Paris in the days before Allied troops entered the city. *La Libération de Paris,* as the documentary was entitled, was in Paris theaters barely one week later.

More by accident, *Les Enfants du paradis* opened many months after the liberation. The idea for the film was nonetheless born in early 1943, during a visit Carné made to Nice to discuss his next movie with Prévert. While walking along the city's elegant promenade des Anglais, Carné bumped into Jean-Louis Barrault, the actor-director. When Prévert joined them on a café terrace, Barrault then entertained them with theater stories. One was about the great nineteenth-century French mime Baptiste Deburau, who accidentally killed a drunk with his cane, prompting *le tout Paris* to show up for his trial: at last, they would hear him speak.

Carné immediately saw a movie idea, although he worried that if Barrault played Deburau, audiences would not be surprised to hear his all-too-familiar voice. Carné decided to pursue the idea anyway, ignoring Prévert's lack of enthusiasm. He returned to Paris and went to the Musée Carnavalet to gather material on Deburau's Théâtre des Funambules and the nearby boulevard du Temple or, as it was appropriately known, the boulevard du Crime. With that, Prévert finally started writing and, as before, Trauner was brought in to design the set (this time Léon Barsacq agreed to "sign" his drawings), and Thieret and Kosma composed the score. At one point, Barrault's involvement seemed in doubt because he was also directing and acting in Claudel's *Le Soulier de satin,* scheduled for the Comédie Française in December 1943. Carné even considered replacing him with the still uncelebrated mime Jacques Tati. But then Barrault became available, the boulevard du Crime was built at Nice's Victorine studios and, in August 1943, filming began on what was then France's most expensive movie ever.

The central role of Garance was given to Carné's screen darling, Arletty, who, in her mid-forties, remained as seductive as ever. In the story, four men are vying for her affections: Baptiste Debureau, played by Barrault; Frédérick Lemaître, a struggling actor played by Pierre Brasseur; Pierre François Lacenaire, a sleazy crook played by Marcel Herrand; and Édouard de Montray, an aristocrat played by Louis Salou. In the role of Nathalie, who pines for Debureau, Carné cast the Spanish-born Maria Casarès, who was just twenty-one at the time. The film, which runs three and a quarter hours, is divided into "Boulevard du Crime" and a second episode, "L'Homme blanc," which takes place six years later. The same characters appear in each, although in "L'Homme blanc" Debureau and Lemaître are now the stars of their respective theaters, one for mime, the other for traditional theater. The plot involves Garance in every possible permutation of love and betrayal as her various suitors fight for her favor. The film is also an homage to theater, celebrating the emotion and drama of life on and off the stage, with a particular tribute to the magic of mime. Indeed, *paradis* refers here to the cheaper balcony seats — "the gods" in an English theater — where the poorest and most devoted theater lovers sit. Yet in the end, it was the combination of Prévert's powerful screenplay and Carné's skillful direction that made *Les Enfants du paradis* so beloved a movie.

Without Carné's determination, the film might never have been completed. Just as the cameras began to roll in Nice, Allied forces landed in southern Italy and, on September 8, accepted Italy's surrender.* This not only prompted Germany to take over the southeastern region of France under Italian control; it also threatened the financing of *Les Enfants du paradis,* which had been planned as a French-Italian production. Carné and his crew and cast were summoned back to Paris, where the Germans took Paulvé off the film and, after a three-month delay, handed the production to Pathé. Some filming was then done in Paris, but by the time Carné resumed work in Nice in early 1944, storms had badly damaged the film's outdoor décor.

*The war in Italy would in fact continue — against German troops — until April 29, 1945.

There were other complications. In the countdown to the long-expected Allied invasion of France, political tensions were rising. Le Vigan, the Nazi sympathizer who had a part in *Les Enfants du paradis,* fled France for Germany, forcing Carné to replace him with Pierre Renoir. More ominously, both the Gestapo and Vichy's *milices* were hunting down Jews and members of the resistance as never before. One morning, two French policemen in civilian clothes arrived on the movie's set looking for an extra whose wife, they said, had suffered an accident and was about to have a leg amputated. Carné hesitated, aware that the story could be true or could be a trap. Finally, concluding that if the extra was on the run, he could easily hide in the crowd, Carné took a megaphone and called out the man's name. "Perhaps he was in the resistance, perhaps he was a Jew, but we never heard of him again," the director recalled five decades later. "He was certainly shot, perhaps also tortured. The police must have been working for the Gestapo. Why did he come forward? When his name was called, he should have suspected, he should have.... I have never forgiven myself. I will relive that scene for the rest of my days."[15]

Filming was completed following the liberation and, on March 9, 1945, almost two years after it was born as an idea, *Les Enfants du paradis* had its premiere at the Palais de Chaillot, in Paris, and was proclaimed an immense success. Of all the movies made during the occupation, it would be the only one to assume an important place in the history of cinema. The paradox was that it was just the kind of film that the Germans wanted France to make: quality entertainment with no hint of politics or nationalism. By presenting it after the liberation, Carné ensured that it would be remembered as a purely French film, untainted by the occupation. But he made it only because the Germans allowed him to do so.

· CHAPTER 11 ·

Mirroring the Past

PARISIANS FOUND IT REASSURING to see that, along with concert halls and movie houses, their theaters were quick to reopen. It made them hope that their lives had not been totally deformed, that another part of the French way of life had survived, that the reality of defeat could occasionally be forgotten in the illusory world of the stage. As curtains rose again and directors and actors were called back to work, a glimmer of optimism also returned to the professionals of the theater world, especially those who had been in uniform and had not earned a decent wage for months. And, as with other art forms, the new powers were satisfied. Vichy wanted the capital's main stages—in this case the Comédie Française, the Théâtre de l'Odéon and Théâtre National Populaire at the Palais de Chaillot—to resume their activities as soon as possible, both as a symbol of continuity and to dissuade the Wehrmacht from occupying them. And the Germans, still surprised to have taken the city with barely a shot fired, wanted Parisians to believe that daily life was going on much as before.

So almost everyone welcomed the arrival of the 1940–41 theater season, with its promise of popular revivals and new plays. No one thought to suggest that an evening at the theater was an act of collaboration, even if Germans were also in the audience. Rather, theatergoing was viewed as a healthy antidote to depression.

What is more surprising is that, as with cinema, the occupation would be remembered as a theatrical golden age. Even with the need to rush home on the last *métro* before the curfew, the popularity of theater as an escape mechanism was immense: box-office revenues jumped by 163 percent between 1941 and 1943. Most productions were straightforward entertainment—historical dramas, romantic comedies or bedroom farces of the kind that had long defined the city's *théâtre de boulevard.* "You can't be a Nazi in theater," said Annie Ubersfeld, a theater lover and young *résistante* at the time. "You cannot be so excessively dominating in a theater, you can't have a virulent Nazi approach. It just doesn't work in theater. Anyway, most theater was *théâtre de boulevard,* where the issue was whether the heroine went to bed with someone or remained a virgin."[1]

As in the prewar years, this lighter fare was accompanied by productions of Corneille, Molière, Racine and Shakespeare* as well as the Irish-born playwrights Richard Brinsley Sheridan, George Bernard Shaw and John Millington Synge. But what most marked the period were new plays by writers who are now considered pillars of twentieth-century French theater, among them Paul Claudel, Jean Giraudoux, Henry de Montherlant, Jean Anouilh, Jean Cocteau, Jean-Paul Sartre and the ever-prolific Sacha Guitry. Even Albert Camus, first and foremost a novelist and essayist, would have a play staged in 1944.

For the public at large, of course, celebrity actors were an important part of the attraction. Some, such as Raimu, Robert Le Vigan, Harry Baur, Marie Bell, Elvire Popesco and Cécile Sorel were veterans of the Paris stage; others drawn to the theater, like Jean-Louis Barrault and Edwige Feuillère, were already well known across France for their movie roles. At the same time, the occupation spawned a new generation of leading men in their twenties—Jean Marais, Louis Jourdan and Gérard Philipe among them—who alternated between stage and screen. And while movie contracts were

---

*Interestingly, the Germans treated Shakespeare as a universal dramatist rather than an English poet.

more lucrative and promised greater fame, theater offered special kudos, above all for appearances in serious drama. In all, with fifty-four theaters open in Paris, the acting profession was kept busy.

The Nazis interfered little beyond ensuring that French theater was "cleansed" of Jews. Some twenty theaters said to be run by Jews were quickly Aryanized (and the Théâtre Sarah Bernhardt renamed the Théâtre de la Cité), while the Comédie Française and the Odéon were required to dismiss fifteen Jewish actors. Jacques Copeau, the director who was then provisional general administrator at the Comédie Française, noted in his journal on July 26, 1940, that the Nazis had already asked for the names of his Jewish actors. And he added: "The Germans have declared, so I am told, that while they are in Paris not one Israelite playwright or composer will be performed, not one Jewish actor will appear on the screen."[2] Louis Hautecoeur, Vichy's secretary-general for fine arts, urged him to play for time and not cast Jews in the first productions of the occupation. But Copeau came under more German pressure and, fearing reprisals against the theater, asked his Jewish actors to resign. Thanks to commercial theaters, though, there were still Jews on the stage and a good many more in the audience. Then things changed radically. In early 1942, an eight p.m. curfew was imposed on Jews in Paris, making it risky for them to attend shows. In May, they were required to wear yellow stars. In July, they were prohibited from entering all theaters. And in the fall of 1942, Jews were formally banned from appearing on stage. Jewish playwrights were blacklisted early in the occupation, although every new production—text, cast and even décor—was subject to censorship, with texts scanned for any anti-German or excessively nationalistic sentiments.

But the Germans did want the show to go on. From the moment the Théâtre de l'Oeuvre reopened on July 11, 1940, the Propaganda Staffel was particularly enthusiastic about the distracting qualities of théâtre de boulevard, home to endless crowd-pleasing revivals. It also occasionally approved dramas or controversial passages in plays that Vichy had initially banned. Most significantly, it was tolerant of most new plays, even of plays like Anouilh's Antigone and Sartre's Les Mouches and Huis clos, which their authors later claimed carried barely disguised messages of resistance.

The theater scene was covered in depth by the collaborationist press, notably the relatively independent cultural weekly Comoedia, but also by literary-political weeklies like La Gerbe, Gringoire and the proudly Fascist *Je suis partout,* which boasted Alain Laubreaux and Lucien Rebatet as its widely feared reviewers. For these two critics, whose reviews also appeared in other collaborationist publications, such as *Le Petit Parisien* and *Le Cri du Peuple,* the quality of the play was often less important than the identity of its author; they had their favorites, like Anouilh and Montherlant, while playwrights who had alienated them in the ideological and aesthetic battles of the 1930s could expect no mercy. In fact, German-approved newspapers even savaged playwrights who, in the eyes of the Free French Forces in London, were already close to collaborators. After press attacks on Guitry, claiming he was Jewish, the Germans asked him to prove that he was Gentile. To the relevant family certificates, he mischievously attached a statement from the chief rabbi of Paris expressing regret that he could not count Guitry among his Jewish community.

For all of Laubreaux's power and self-importance, however, one of his maneuvers backfired. *Les Pirates de Paris,* a play by a certain Michel Daxiat set against the infamous Stavisky affair of the mid-1930s, opened at the Théâtre L'Ambigu-Comique in March 1942. In *Je suis partout,* Laubreaux gave it a warm review, noting that "the public will watch, will be entertained and will reflect." He added: "For the first time, we have a play where a Jew is called a Jew and where the Jew stands out clearly against a background of a regime of filth and decadence."[3] What Laubreaux naturally failed to mention was that he was the author of the play, under a pseudonym. The play, which other critics rightly considered mediocre, closed after one month.

Still, unlike cinema, which lost some leading directors and actors to Hollywood, almost every significant theatrical figure stayed in France. One exception was Henri Bernstein, the Jewish playwright of popular *boulevard* comedies, who wisely left for New York. Another was Louis Jouvet, a leading director and actor who during the interwar years had drawn public attention to Giraudoux's plays. He resumed work in Paris in the fall of 1940 with a new production of Molière's *L'École des femmes* at the Théâtre de l'Athénée; because of his prestige, he was assured sympathetic support by the German embassy. But Jouvet was already thinking of leaving France and, as a first step, he agreed to appear in a screen version of *L'École des femmes* directed by his old friend Max Ophüls, who was in exile in Switzerland. With the production under way, however, Ophüls began a secret affair with Jouvet's companion, the Belgian actress

Madeleine Ozeray, who was also in the movie. When the liaison was discovered by Jouvet, the scandal sank the film project. Forced to choose between her two lovers, Ozeray decided to stay with Jouvet and, shortly afterward, she joined him and his company on a long-scheduled tour of Latin America. In the main, they performed French classics, although in Rio de Janeiro they created Giraudoux's one-act play *L'Apollon de Bellac*. Ozeray finally left Jouvet in Buenos Aires, but the company carried the French flag across the continent until France was liberated. In late 1944, Jouvet was once again running the Théâtre de l'Athénée.

Had he stayed in Paris, Jouvet might well have succeeded Copeau at the Comédie Française. Copeau had been appointed in May 1940 after the theater's general administrator, Édouard Bourdet, was injured in an accident. By the end of the year, after Copeau had reopened the theater, Bourdet was ready to return. But the Germans wanted neither man. Instead, Copeau was replaced by Jean-Louis Vaudoyer, a poet and novelist, who held the post until March 1944. Although dependent on Vichy's subsidy, Vaudoyer proved a skilled manager—no easy task, given the theater's tradition of internal power struggles and a regulation that allowed permanent members of the troupe (the *sociétaires*) to decide which actors on contracts (the *pensionnaires*) could join their exclusive group. Several *sociétaires* were openly *pétainistes* and accepted invitations to recite poetry or verse on political occasions, while a few used their status as *sociétaires* to disguise their involvement in the resistance.

One Romanian-born Jewish *sociétaire*, Jean Yonnel, widely heralded as the company's greatest tragedian, was initially forced to resign, but the Propaganda Staffel then concluded that he was indispensable. In October 1941, he appeared in Racine's *Bérénice* and, six months later, in Goethe's *Iphigénie en Tauride,* a production he also directed. He went on to play leading roles in two of the company's stellar creations of the period, *La Reine morte* and *Le Soulier de satin.* "The Germans named him an honorary Aryan," recalled Michel Francini, who was working in music halls at the time. "Yonnel's name was on posters. After Jews were ordered to wear yellow stars, he went on stage wearing one. He was given an ovation."[4]

Although censors were ready to cut words or phrases from plays, even classics, the Germans viewed the Comédie Française with reverence; the free seats reserved for Wehrmacht officers at every performance were invariably taken, while the German Institute was eager to see German plays performed in the House of Molière. In theory, foreign companies were not allowed onto the theater's stage, but this rule was twice ignored. In February 1941, prompting the official press to hail the first example of theatrical collaboration, Heinrich George brought Berlin's Schiller Theater to Paris for two German-language performances of Schiller's *Kabale und Liebe* (Intrigue and Love). George, a star of the German stage who had recently been seen in France in the anti-Semitic movie *Le Juif Süss,* proved a good diplomat, too: he gave Molière's bust a Nazi salute and responded to the play's warm reception by noting that in this case "the genius of art" was the only conqueror. But not everyone was pleased. Béatrice Bretty, a Jewish *sociétaire* who had resigned, later recalled her shock at learning that "the German actors had been received with flowers, champagne, toasts and speeches."[5]

The National Theater of Munich came next. In April 1942, it brought Goethe's *Iphigenie auf Tauris,* which was twinned on successive nights with the Comédie Française's production of the same play, *Iphigénie en Tauride,* directed by Yonnel. While the German-language newspaper *Pariser Zeitung* said the two versions symbolized "an exemplary coexistence between two peoples," Laubreaux declared that the mediocrity of the French production more than justified Vaudoyer's dismissal. Behind Laubreaux's attack was not only his ambition to run the Comédie Française himself but also his perception that the theater was doing too well in maintaining its independence. Indeed, the following year Vaudoyer tried hard to resist German pressure to celebrate the eightieth birthday of Gerhart Hauptmann, a German playwright who won the Nobel Prize in literature in 1912. But after the Palais de Chaillot presented Hauptmann's *Rosa Bernd* and the Odéon put on his *Le Voiturier Henschel* (The Wagoner Henschel), the Comédie Française was left with little choice. In May 1943, it staged Hauptmann's *Iphigenie in Delphi* in a new French translation, albeit portraying it as part of an *Iphigénie* series following the earlier versions by Goethe and Eurypides. It would be the last German play given by the company during the occupation.

Writing in the German Institute's *Cahiers Franco-Allemands* in 1943, Laubreaux lamented that, in contrast to classical music, opera and cinema, Franco-German exchanges in theater were minimal. And in truth, no French theater delegation ever traveled to Germany as guests of the Reich. For this, Vaudoyer could claim some credit.

After the war, he noted that, by allowing just two German companies onto the stage of the venerable Salle Richelieu, he had obtained the release of fifteen employees who were prisoners of war and protected others from compulsory work in Germany.

For the most part, by ensuring that French classics featured prominently, Vaudoyer stayed true to the Comédie Française's mission as France's national theater. In December 1940, still during Copeau's regime, Barrault, newly hired by the theater, appeared in the title role of Corneille's *Le Cid.* Plays by Molière — *Le Bourgeois gentilhomme, Le Misanthrope, Tartuffe* and *Le Malade imaginaire* — were always popular, as were Corneille's *Horace* and Racine's *Phèdre* and *Bérénice.* Seeing France defended by its great playwrights, Galtier-Boissière savored the latest quip: "How will the war be won? With American gold, British tenacity . . . and the Comédie Française."[6] Prewar productions of Shakespeare's *Hamlet* and *Twelfth Night* were also revived, but it was not until late 1942 that the company staged its first new play, Montherlant's *La Reine morte.*

A closet homosexual with a penchant for chasing young boys, Montherlant was a solitary figure in his late thirties, best known as a novelist and essayist. In *L'Équinoxe de septembre,* he had taken a brave stand against the September 1938 Munich Agreement, in which France and Britain had surrendered the Sudetenland to Hitler. But after the French defeat, he, too, surrendered. In *Le Solstice de juin,* a book of essays published in early 1941, he blamed the Third Republic for France's humiliation and welcomed the conquering Germans as if they were virile medieval knights. Per chance, one of these handsome Germans was Karl-Heinz Bremer, Montherlant's former translator and now Epting's deputy in the German Institute. In one shocking essay, "Les Chenilles," Montherlant describes urinating on caterpillars, many of whom die and a few escape: it was his metaphor for Germany's victory over the hapless French. At the end of *Le Solstice de juin,* Montherlant spelled out his philosophy: "To do everything possible to wipe out the enemy. But once he has demonstrated that he has the stronger hand, to join forces with him with the same conviction."[7] Put differently, he believed in collaboration. After spending a few months in the unoccupied zone, he returned to Paris in May 1941 and wrote regularly for Drieu La Rochelle's *Nouvelle Revue Française,* as well as for *La Gerbe, Comoedia* and the daily *Le Matin.*

Since Montherlant's earlier plays had all flopped, Vaudoyer took something of a risk when he commissioned him to write a historical drama for the Comédie Française. Montherlant took his inspiration from a sixteenth-century Spanish playwright, Luís Vélez de Guevara, and set his story in Portugal, where King Ferrante wants to marry off his son Pedro to the Infante of Navarre. When the king discovers that Pedro has secretly married Inès de Castro, who is carrying his child, the affront to his authority leads him to order Inès's death, a sentence that then brings on his own death. With Yonnel as Ferrante, Barrault as Pedro and Madeleine Renaud as Inès, this star-laden cast helped to ensure a splashy opening on December 8, 1942.

Seeing no apparent parallel between the plot and contemporary events, the collaborationist press felt free to praise the play for its poetic depiction of the passion and tragedy unfolding in Ferrante's court. Yet, illustrating how carefully texts were studied for hidden meanings, the clandestine newspaper *Les Lettres Françaises* complained that the play celebrated the victory of "reasons of state" over human feelings. "And there lies the secret of the official support given to *La Reine morte*," it said. For Montherlant, though, it was above all a family drama. So, too, was his next play, *Fils de personne,* produced at the Théâtre Saint-Georges in June 1943, in which a father seeks out his twelve-year-old son, whom he abandoned before birth. Still, for all the intellectual resistance's disapproval, Montherlant's reputation only grew. In a list prepared in 2000, among the 133 plays most performed at the Comédie Française since 1680, Montherlant's *La Reine morte* and *Port-Royal,* staged in 1954, were the only ones written in the twentieth century.

By choosing a historical theme in *La Reine morte,* Montherlant followed the wartime practice of setting dramas (and movies) in the past. While this often allowed them to be staged without interference by censors, it also encouraged audiences to view them as allegories. This was almost too easy in the case of Joan of Arc. Having stood up to the English invaders, the fifteenth-century French saint proved to be an all-purpose heroine. For anti-Nazis, she was the personification of French honor and courage, an inspiring example of resistance to humiliation and occupation. For the Germans and Vichy, she served to remind the French that England was their traditional enemy, a country that as recently as 1940 had again betrayed France. "Martyr of National Unity, Joan of Arc is the symbol of France," proclaimed a Vichy poster. Beyond the pageants and oratorios put on around France by Vichy's Jeune France organization, then, Paris, too, underwent a Joan mania.

Oddly, the occupation produced almost no new plays about Jeanne La Pucelle, as she was known in France, but producers had many to choose from. The first to be presented in Paris, in December 1940, was Shaw's *Saint Joan*. Two others, *Jeanne d'Arc* and *Le Mystère de la charité de Jeanne d'Arc*, written years earlier by the literary nationalist Charles Péguy, were adapted by his son Marcel in 1941. Honegger's oratorio *Jeanne au bûcher*, written in the 1930s, was toured widely by Jeune France after its premiere in 1942. This work was apolitical; other plays leaned toward Vichy's point of view, among them Jean Jacoby's *Scènes de la vie de Jeanne d'Arc* and Marcelle Vioux's *Jeanne d'Arc*. One play that pleased everyone was Claude Vermorel's *Jeanne avec nous*, which he wrote in 1938 and which ran for eight months in Paris in 1942. It was applauded by the collaborationist press, with Rebatet hailing Vermorel's Joan as a "patroness of French Fascism." Yet in time, both for its staging and its text, it was considered the first resistance play of the occupation: not only did English soldiers click their heels, but the Inquisition that condemned Joan behaved remarkably like Vichy.[8] In her memoir, Simone de Beauvoir said that, in applauding Joan's "proud response" to the English, "we demonstrated without ambiguity against the Germans and against Vichy."[9]

Guitry also saw historical drama as an excellent vehicle for glorifying France, an objective he pursued even while socializing with German officers and diplomats. Already in the fall of 1940, after reopening his Théâtre de la Madeleine with *Pasteur* and his tribute to distinguished French artists, he followed with *Florence* and *Le Roi Louis XI*, both plays that made audiences feel good about France. Then, before the year was over, he appeared in *Le Bien-aimé*, a new comedy in which the absolutism of Louis XV could be interpreted as an allegory for that of the Nazis. The story is told that a German general visited Guitry in his dressing room after the show. "So, Monsieur, after two hours you're not defeated," the officer said. Guitry replied, "That, General, is exactly the impression I hoped to give."[10]

Next came *Le Soir d'Austerlitz*, which he renamed *Vive l'empereur* after objections from the Propaganda Staffel. In this comedy set on the eve of Napoleon's victory at Austerlitz in 1805, Guitry, who had been married five times, celebrated adultery. In *N'écoutez pas mesdames*, though, there is a veiled reference to Jews whose property had been Aryanized when one character notes, "In truth, no, I am not an antiquarian. I am helping out someone who, at this time, is experiencing misfortune."[11] Two of Guitry's plays were vetoed by the Propaganda Staffel. *Mon auguste grandpère* (My August Grandfather), his pointed response to the charge that he was Jewish, mocked anti-Semitic legislation put in place by Vichy. And *Le Dernier troubadour* (The Last Troubadour), which was to star Charles Trenet and the young soprano Géori Boué, was a musical comedy in which the first and third acts take place during the German occupation and the second act jumps back four centuries to the time of Joan of Arc and the English occupation. Here, at least, the German censor offered an explanation: "Impossible! It will give too much pleasure to the Gaullists."[12]

Despite these setbacks, Guitry remained an irrepressible showman. At the same time as he was being insulted by Rebatet and Laubreaux, he was the life of the party at German dinners and receptions. While he was being condemned to death by the Free French Forces, he published a paean to Pétain in the form of a luxurious art book — which had Cocteau, Colette, Cortot and Giraudoux among contributors — and then followed it up with a documentary, *De 1429 à 1942 (de Jeanne d'Arc à Philippe Pétain),* which had its premiere at the Paris Opera in May 1944, a time when even loyal *pétainistes* had given up on Vichy.

But Guitry could not have ignored the fact that he was fast losing friends. In April 1944, *La Scène Française,* the clandestine newspaper of the resistance organization Front National du Théâtre, turned its guns on him in an article headlined "In the Filth of Collaboration," noting, "Sacha Guitry sees only himself. And since he is very satisfied with himself, he is a happy man. Outside events barely touch him."[13] When called on for help, though, Guitry came through. In May 1941, he organized a fund-raising gala in the Comédie Française, called *Le Triomphe d'Antoine,* to support the revered theater director André Antoine, in his early eighties, ailing and living in poverty. In October 1943, he and the actress Arletty also used their friendship with Abetz to obtain the release of the seventy-seven-year-old Jewish playwright Tristan Bernard* and his wife from Drancy.

---

*Renowned for his wit, Bernard made a remark to his wife after their arrest that quickly did the rounds. Galtier-Boissière recorded it in his journal: "My dear friend, our position is improving. Yesterday we lived in anguish; from now on, we will live in hope" (p. 213).

If Guitry behaved as if he were larger than life, it was partly because he was richer than most. His elegant home on avenue Élisée-Reclus, which he inherited from his actor father, Lucien, resembled a small museum. On display were paintings by Monet, sculptures by Rodin, Baroque decorative art, books in the thousands and valuable manuscripts. He also collected theater souvenirs, such as a diadem worn by Sarah Bernhardt and large floppy shoes worn by a famous circus comedian. This was the setting for sumptuous lunches and dinners for guests from both political and artistic worlds. Ernst Jünger, the German novelist, was not alone in being impressed. Upon his arrival for lunch on October 15, 1941, Guitry offered him the gift of signed letters by the playwright Octave Mirbeau, the novelist Léon Bloy and the composer Debussy for his autograph collection. Salad was served in a silver bowl and ice cream in a golden bowl once owned by Bernhardt. Jünger recorded his impressions of Guitry in his journal: "Once again, I was astonished by his tropical individuality which blossomed above all when telling anecdotes in which his meetings with kings played a remarkable role. The various people in question were also depicted in mime to illustrate his words. Also excellent, from a theatrical point of view, was how he played with his thick tortoise-shell glass throughout the conversation."[14]

While Guitry could not resist being part of *le tout Paris,* Giraudoux had withdrawn from public view after his unhappy experience as information minister during the phony war. Nonetheless, he was France's leading playwright of the interwar years, and his prestige was immense. Like that of many intellectuals, his political position following France's defeat also evolved. As early as July 1940, his son Jean-Pierre joined de Gaulle in London, although it would be another year before Giraudoux lost all faith in Pétain. By 1943, it is said, he was sending secret reports on intellectual life in Paris to London. His first writing projects during the occupation were screenplays—for *La Duchesse de Langeais,* adapted from Balzac, and for *Les Anges du péché.* Then, in October 1943, he returned to the stage with *Sodome et Gomorrhe,* a new play that was presented at the Théâtre Hébertot and had Feuillère and Philipe in the lead roles.

Set once again in the past, in this case the biblical past, the play's story unfolds against the background of God's destruction of Sodom and Gomorrah, but its focus is on a squabbling husband and wife whose inability to love each other brings on the debacle. Although Giraudoux was known for his verbosity, here his language explored with precision the impossibility of love between a man and a woman, a theme that perhaps mirrored his own oft-broken heart. In *Je suis partout* Robert Brasillach mocked the play as vaudeville on the Dead Sea, and Cocteau compared its solemnity with that of a mass, but Giraudoux's admirers remained loyal: *Sodome et Gomorrhe* filled the Hébertot for eight months. He wrote one other play during the occupation, *La Folle de Chaillot* (The Madwoman of Chaillot), but he would not see its premiere in December 1945; he died on January 31, 1944, at the age of sixty-one. The official cause of death was food poisoning, but such was his stature that a popular—and unlikely—rumor had him poisoned by the Gestapo.

By then, the Hébertot was one of the city's liveliest commercial theaters. Earlier in the occupation, Feuillère had won ovations there as the courtesan Marguerite Gautier in Alexandre Dumas fils's *La Dame aux camélias.* This was followed in April 1941 by Cocteau's *La Machine à écrire* (The Typewriter), a thriller about anonymous hate mail in which Marais, his lover, played the two roles of twin brothers. Vichy's representative in Paris, Fernand de Brinon, immediately ordered the play closed as immoral, but he was overruled on grounds of "artistic freedom" by the Propaganda Staffel.

The *scandale* was not yet over, however. After Rebatet, in *Je suis partout,* denounced Cocteau's "inverted"—or homosexual—theater, Laubreaux followed up with a campaign of abuse against both Cocteau and Marais. A few weeks later, introduced to Laubreaux at a restaurant, Marais spat in his face; when the critic tried to strike back with a cane, the actor hit him. Marais even followed him into the street, grabbed his cane and threw it away, while Laubreaux cried out for help.

That Cocteau was a favorite target of Fascists became still clearer when he revived *Les Parents terribles* (The Awful Parents), a dark comedy with Marais again in a lead role. It purported to denounce family decadence but was itself pronounced decadent. At the play's opening at the Théâtre du Gymnase in late 1941, Fascist provocateurs organized a riot, including setting off stink bombs, which led the Paris police hurriedly to ban the play. Marais's own production of Racine's *Andromaque,* at the Théâtre Édouard VII in 1944, was in turn closed after Vichy's paramilitary *milice* threatened to attack the theater.

Given Cocteau's dissolute reputation, then, the Comédie Française's Vaudoyer again showed daring in April 1943 when he presented Cocteau's new play, *Renaud et Armide,* which the author himself directed. But instead of scandal, Cocteau offered a tragic love story in alexandrine verse inspired by operas of Wagner and Glück and close to the plot of Dvořák's *Rusalka:* Renaud, the king of France, loves the fairy Armide; she appears to him, but he cannot touch her; finally she begs to become human even knowing that with Renaud's first kiss she will die; and she does. It was the perfect story for romantic Germans in the audience.

For Jean Anouilh, the occupation was marked by untroubled success. Only thirty when Paris fell, he carefully avoided taking any political position, which served him well until the liberation. After he presented two plays in the fall of 1940, *Bal des voleurs* and *Léocadia,* both Laubreaux and Rebatet proclaimed him to be the best young playwright around. And nothing more controversial followed. *Le Rendez-vous de Senlis* was a satire of bourgeois manners, and *Eurydice* was a modern rendering of the legend of Orpheus and Eurydice, which ran at the Théâtre de l'Atelier for three months.

However, when Anouilh returned to the same theater in February 1944 with *Antigone,* he dared for the first time to address affairs of state. What led him to this subject was a very political incident. On August 27, 1941, during a ceremony for French Fascists leaving to fight alongside the Germans in Russia, a young man, Paul Collette, shot and wounded Laval, at the time out of office but still a Nazi favorite. Collette, who also wounded the collaborationist journalist Marcel Déat, had a lucky escape: arrested, beaten and condemned to death, he was reprieved by Pétain, deported to Germany and, remarkably, survived the war. What interested Anouilh as a playwright, however, was not the fight against evil as such. Rather, it was his belief that, echoing *Antigone,* Collette's individual, heroic and futile gesture represented the quintessence of tragedy.

Following the plot of Sophocles' verse classic, Anouilh's play opens with Antigone in the court of her uncle, King Creon, who has assumed the throne after her two brothers, Eteocles and Polynices, killed each other in a battle for power. Defying Creon's order that Polynices be left unburied, Antigone is arrested in the act of burying her brother. She defends her action and, even in face of death, she refuses to repent. Creon condemns Antigone to be buried alive, then discovers that his son, Haemon, has chosen to die alongside the woman he loves. What made the play seem topical—what brought the story into the 1940s—was not only its modern dress and its contemporary prose (which included mention of cigarettes and night-clubs) but also the confrontation between freedom and order person-ified by Antigone and Creon. Strangely, at the time at least, the play sparked no debate as to whether *Antigone* was a work of resistance or collaboration, although a case could be made for either claim. For those opposed to Germany and Vichy, Antigone challenged the abusive power of the state; for collaborators, Creon demonstrated that strong rulers must be obeyed. Audiences also saw the play under very different circumstances: it had 645 peformances, beginning during the occupation and ending long after the liberation.

Revisited today, the play still offers ammunition to both sides. Introducing the drama, the Chorus's description of the guards would fit that of French police officer working for the Nazis: "At the same time—they are policemen; eternally innocent, no matter what crimes are committed; eternally indifferent, for nothing that happens matters to them. They are quite prepared to arrest anybody at all, including Creon, should the order be given by a new leader." Antigone, in turn, speaks as someone willing to die for her beliefs: "I can say no to anything I think vile, and I don't have to count the cost." And, responding to Creon's offer of a deal, she elaborates: "I will *not* be moderate. I will *not* be satisfied with the bit of cake you offer me if I promise to be a good girl."

Creon, in contrast, echoes Pétain's belief that he is sacrificing himself for France after the disasters of the Third Republic: "There had to be one man who said yes. Somebody had to agree to captain the ship. She had sprung a hundred leaks; she was loaded to the waterline with crime, ignorance, poverty." He goes on, again using words that Pétain might have chosen to justify creating the Vichy regime: "Was it a time, do you think, for playing with words like yes and no? Was that a time for a man to be weighing the pros and cons, wondering if he wasn't going to pay too dearly later on?" Even after Antigone and Haemon have died, Creon defends his sense of duty: "They don't know it, but the truth is the work is there to be done, and a man can't fold his arms and refuse to do it. They say it's dirty work. But if we didn't do it, who would?"

Earlier, inspired by Giraudoux and Cocteau, Sartre also tapped Greek mythology for his first play, *Les Mouches* (The Flies). In it, he reworked the story of Orestes, staying close to the perennial Greek themes of freedom, humanity and revenge. Having left his native city as a child fifteen years earlier, Orestes returns to Argos to find a

pestilent city engulfed by flies, a symbol of its remorse over the murder of King Agamemnon by his wife, Clytemnestra, and her lover,
Aegisthus.

Only when Orestes meets his sister Electra, who is a servant of the
ruling couple, does he understand his mother's crime. While Electra
begs him to avenge their father's death, Zeus tells him to leave, since
the people of Argos have long accepted Aegisthus as their king. But
once Orestes decides to kill Aegisthus and Clytemnestra, even Zeus
cannot stop him. "Once freedom lights its beacon in a man's heart,
the gods are powerless against him," Zeus laments. With Clytemnestra dead, Orestes is abandoned by Electra, whose only reason for living was to hate her mother. At Zeus's insistence, she repents her role
in the double murder, but Orestes stands his ground, telling the god,
"You should not have made me free." He adds, "Suddenly, out of the
blue, freedom crashed on me and swept me off my feet." The people
of Argos, though, do not follow him. Instead, by choosing exile,
he assumes their sins, fears and remorse and then frees them from the
torture of the flies, saying, "Farewell, my people. Try to reshape
your lives. All here is new, all must begin anew."

Was *Les Mouches* a resistance play? Like every other play at the
time, its text and cast were subject to approval by the Propaganda
Staffel, which also required a pledge that no Jews were involved in
the production. The premiere took place on June 3, 1943, in Charles
Dullin's theater, formerly the Théâtre Sarah Bernhardt, with German
officers in the audience and at a reception given by Dullin and Sartre
after the play. Writing in *Je suis partout*, Laubreaux was dismissive,
making no reference to any political message and simply noting that
"Sartre is characterized by an absolute and total absence of dramatic
sense."

Sartre's friends and admirers thought otherwise. Beauvoir recalled
her reaction at the dress rehearsal: "I was moved as soon as the curtain was raised. It was impossible to misunderstand the meaning of
the play; falling from Orestes's mouth, the word Freedom exploded
with a blinding clap."[15] The writer Jorge Semprun, who at nineteen
was already in the resistance, had a similar response. "*Les Mouches* is
a song to liberty," he said many years later. "I went to see it with a
group because we had heard it was anti-Nazi. Many barely knew
Sartre. He was an important figure only for a minority."[16]

Defending the play almost thirty years later, Sartre said that
French critics did not understand that Orestes represented the resis-

tance and his mother and her usurping lover the Germans: "I wrote it to convince the French that, yes, to murder a German is to be guilty of murder, but morally it is the right thing to do, though he who does commit the murder will find no moral solace in the act."[17] Evidently, having submitted *Les Mouches* for German approval, Sartre was still eager to suggest that he had outfoxed the censors. Certainly, it is not hard to imagine that some in the audience at the Théâtre de la Cité were moved by Orestes' discovery of his humanity and his language extolling freedom. Yet it was also apparent that Orestes' act of freedom—killing his mother and her lover—was rejected by the people of Argos, who preferred the existing order. The real problem, it seems, is that few people saw the play: it closed after fifty performances.

Sartre's second play of the occupation, *Huis clos* (No Exit), which deals more generically with the despair of the human condition, was also approved by the Propaganda Staffel. And again there were numerous Germans in the audience when it opened at the Théâtre du Vieux-Colombier on May 27, 1944, less than two weeks before D-Day. Sartre asked Camus to direct and take the male lead in it, but Camus withdrew, arguing that professionals would do a better job. Meanwhile, the two actresses cast in the play, Olga Barbezat and Wanda Kosakiewicz, were arrested—they were not deported and both survived—and substitutes were hurriedly found. Later Sartre explained that, once again, his aim was to demonstrate that "honor and integrity demand resistance to the Germans, no matter the consequences."[18]

Yet while in *Les Mouches* Orestes saw himself as a liberator, the message of *Huis clos* was one of resignation, not rebellion. The play, which Sartre initially set in an air-raid shelter, opens in a Second Empire sitting room in hell. Three persons newly dead are trapped inside it, forever sleepless and condemned eternally to one another's company: Garcin, a former journalist and army deserter, has been executed by a firing squad; Estelle, who murdered the baby she had with her lover, has died of pneumonia; and Inès, a sadistic lesbian, was suffocated when her lover switched on the gas that killed them both. As their lives pass before them, they lie, they confess, they judge each other; Inès tries to seduce Estelle, who tries to seduce Garcin, but there is no love left in any of them. In this dance of hate, Garcin concludes, "Hell is—other people!" The response of critics was mixed, with conservatives denouncing the play's immorality and

Claude Jamet, in *Germinal,* noting that Sartre and Anouilh were the best playwrights of the day. Interestingly, while *Huis clos* had a lasting life in postwar theater, it was not remembered as a resistance play. In the context of Sartre's oeuvre, it was above all a popular staging of his existentialist philosophy.

Camus, who was embarked on his own existentialist journey, also had a play performed for the first time during the occupation (the first play he wrote, *Caligula,* was presented in 1945). Although Camus moved to Paris only in late 1943 and immediately joined the resistance, he had achieved a degree of celebrity with his first novel, *L'Étranger* (The Stranger). His digression into theater with *Le Malentendu* (The Misunderstanding) therefore stirred interest.

Presented at the Théâtre des Mathurins in early June 1944, the play recounts how Jan returns home with his new wife after many years away. His mother and his sister, Martha, run an inn, where, in the hope of saving enough money to leave the region, they drug, rob and murder their overnight guests. Jan's misfortune is that they do not recognize him until he, too, has been killed. Discovering his identity, his mother also dies, while Martha, distraught over losing her mother, hangs herself. Unsurprisingly, the play was condemned as a fête of pessimism, so inappropriate for the moment that France was living. But, like *Huis clos,* it is more an examination of the human condition than a commentary on the times. Camus himself never claimed it as a resistance play, placing it instead among the works that made up his *cycle de l'absurde.* The play brought one unexpected reward for the author, however: he began a passionate affair with Maria Casarès, the striking Spanish-born actress who played Martha.

Most Parisian theatergoers preferred a lighter diet, à la Guitry, and they had much to choose from. As early as July 1940, the Théâtre des Ambassadeurs promised "three hours of uncontrollable laughter" in *Nous ne sommes pas mariés* (We Are Not Married), a comedy exploring a man's hesitations over whether to cheat on his mistress. The collaborationist weekly *La Gerbe* lamented that "it is this comedy that is meant to show the Germans what the theater of Paris is worth." But there would be dozens more like it. Soon afterward, *Histoire de rire* (A Chance to Laugh) by Armand Salacrou had crowds applauding Alice Cocéa and Pierre Renoir in another tale of marital fireworks. Marcel Achard and the Comédie Française's former director Édouard Bourdet were also on safe ground writing romantic comedies: Bourdet's *Père* (Father) ran for 409 performances at the Théâtre de la Michodière during the occupation. Brasillach gave these plays the nickname of *comédies sans tickets*— comedies without ration coupons—because they studiously ignored the travails of daily life. In any event, they were quickly approved by the Propaganda Staffel.

Vichy, though, occasionally stepped in. With *La Parisienne,* a popular comedy first produced in 1895, it objected to a heroine who had two lovers. But since much was at stake—it was an expensive production, with Cocéa as the heroine and Balenciaga the costume designer—a simple solution was found: the play was renamed *Clotilde du Mesnil.* Another comedy, *Échec à Don Juan* by Claude-André Puget, was also almost banned, this time because the Germans concluded—erroneously—that its author was Jewish. The problem was resolved when Cocéa—also appearing in this play— turned for help to her friend Suzanne Abetz, the wife of the German ambassador.

No less than in peacetime, theater managers were principally interested in selling tickets and, for this, they covered the walls of Paris with posters advertising their productions and stars. Since conflicts with the Propaganda Staffel could cost them money, they were also careful about what they presented. Along with the lightest of modern comedies, they sought out evergreen French comedies by, say, Molière and Beaumarchais and French translations of plays by "safe" authors like Ibsen, Lope de Vega and Schiller. There were also new translations from English of several Irish plays—Sheridan's *The School for Scandal* and Synge's *The Playboy of the Western World* as well as Shaw's *Saint Joan.* Shakespeare's comedies and tragedies—at least *Hamlet*—were also presented in commercial theaters; his history plays, which frequently involve fighting the French, were not considered appropriate.

New plays, on the other hand, entailed risks, both financial and political. And this was no less true when Vaudoyer programmed Claudel's massive religious epic *Le Soulier de satin* (The Satin Shoe) for the Comédie Française. Here, though, the principal risk was not political: the Propaganda Staffel approved a production in December 1942.

A far greater complication was Claudel himself. Now in his mid-seventies, retired after a stellar career as a French diplomat, he was a playwright whose writing was shaped by his fervent Catholicism. His poetic language was influenced by Rimbaud and the Symbolists, while his plays, often set in distant lands in distant times, were unwavering explorations of the challenges of faith. Politically, he was conservative, which led him to oppose the Popular Front in the mid-1930s and to write an "Ode au Maréchal Pétain" in December 1940, reportedly in exchange for a pension. But he had always hated Fascism—he was horrified by Hitler's *Mein Kampf* when it came out in France in 1934—and he was soon disillusioned with Vichy; in December 1941, he wrote a letter to the chief rabbi of France expressing disgust at the persecution of "our Israelite compatriots." Settled in the village of Brangues, near Lyon, he viewed the cultural life of Paris with aloof disdain. In fact, among his targets was the Comédie Française, which as recently as October 1940 he had described as a cemetery of forgotten plays, a view no doubt influenced by its reluctance to produce *Le Soulier de satin,* written almost two decades earlier.

Once Vaudoyer decided to present the play, however, financial risks arose. As written, the play ran for close to eleven hours over two evenings—and its grumpy author would not hear of abridging it. At one point Brasillach even accused Claudel of trying to delay the production until the liberation of Paris. Then Barrault became involved. He wanted both to direct and to appear in the play and, after making several visits to Brangues, he finally extracted a five-hour version from the playwright. Honegger agreed to compose accompanying music, but differences arose over a set designer. Claudel rejected Rouault, while Barrault refused Claudel's choice, the Spanish painter José María Sert. According to one version, Picasso was approached, only to retort: "Me, work for Claudel? I'd rather die!"[19] Derain and Braque also turned down the commission before the choice eventually fell on Lucien Coutaud, one of the artists in Galerie Braun's exhibition of young French painters in 1941. With rehearsals under way, the Comédie Française had to make or find costumes and wigs for thirty-seven named roles, plus extras, who appear in no fewer than thirty-three different scenes. The production could at least boast crowd-pulling actors: along with Barrault and Marie Bell, major roles were also given to Yonnel, Pierre Bertin and Renaud.

When the curtain finally went up, on the afternoon of November 26, 1943, everyone of any importance in Paris and beyond—supposedly as many as four hundred German officials and army officers, along with Vichy politicians, poets and intellectuals, even wealthy businessmen—had found a seat in the theater. What most of them thought of the play is not known, but they could be forgiven for losing their way amid the endless twists and turns of the plot. Set in sixteenth-century Spain, *Le Soulier de satin* takes its name from the satin shoe that the married Dona Prouhèze places before a statue of the Virgin, asking to be crippled if she surrenders to sin. The problem is that she is in love with the handsome Don Rodrigue. The plot itself resembles a geography lesson as it spills out of Iberia into the New World, North Africa and even Japan. And it is rife with the tragedies of love. Prohèze and Rodrigue are separated when he is named viceroy in the Americas. Meanwhile, Prouhèze's husband dies and she is forced to marry a Spanish rebel in Morocco. Rodrigue returns for a brief and passionate reunion with Prohèze before she is killed when the Spanish navy puts down the Moroccan rebellion. Rodrigue then ends up as a prisoner in Japan and devotes his life to God. Since the play appeared to have no contemporary resonance, it alarmed neither the Nazis nor Vichy. Parisians, on the other hand, seemed delighted by this swashbuckling romance, laced with a touch of morality play.

One who never forgot the opening was Dominique Delouche, much later a film director but only twelve at the time. "I went with my mother," he recalled. "We queued for three hours to get seats at the very top. I wanted to be an actor, and I lived in a world of fiction. I wasn't bored for one second. I was fascinated. There were quite a lot of Germans in the audience, but not as many as at the opera or ballet. Claudel was there. At the interval, I went to Marie Bell's dressing room. I can't remember how I got there. There were flowers, photographers. I squeezed in. Bell embraced Claudel and she praised his text. 'It is rare to have a text like this,' she said. Claudel looked pleased."[20] Delouche did not remember Claudel appearing on stage at the end, but other accounts had the aged playwright taking as many as fourteen curtain calls, the last few with only German officers still left in the auditorium. The play itself had mixed reviews—criticism from Laubreaux, praise from Brasillach—but that mattered little: it had fifty-seven sold-out performances before the production was suspended by electricity shortages in June 1944; it then returned for a further twenty performances in November 1944; and it was revived for thirty-one performances in April 1949. The play's success under German occupation was not held against Claudel after liberation. When he died, eleven years later, he took with him the knowledge that *Le Soulier de satin* had entered theater lore as the most important theatrical event of the war years.

For Vaudoyer, it would be a final triumph. From the moment he had taken over the Comédie Française, he had been under attack from Laubreaux and others in the collaborationist press. More recently, Abel Bonnard, Vichy's education minister, had also begun undermining him. Finally, on March 23, 1944, Vaudoyer resigned. A battle to succeed him immediately followed. Guitry, Bourdet and even Cocteau were mentioned as possible candidates, while Laubreaux, who had long coveted the job, was blocked when leading actors threatened to resign. Finally, on July 28, Vichy chose the playwright Jean Sarment, who had been head of the theater section of the Groupe Collaboration. But by then the Comédie Française had closed its doors. Elsewhere in the city, only a handful of theaters were still working. "We had no electricity," recalled Héléna Bossis, whose actress mother, Simone Berriau, was running the Théâtre Antoine, "but we could open the roof. It was strange because the public was in the light and the stage was dark. The theater was almost empty, but we played until mid-August. We closed because some people wanted to take over the theater because we'd worked during the occupation. It was dreadful."[21] On August 25, the city was liberated. A few weeks later, just as they had in the summer of 1940, the theaters of Paris gradually returned to life.

CHAPTER 12

Writing for the Enemy

OF ALL THE FRENCH ARTISTS forced to live under Nazi rule, it was inevitable that writers should take the clearest stances—and assume the greatest risks. Painters, composers, movie directors and actors could go about their work without either applauding or lamenting France's humbled condition; at most, they would later be judged by the company they kept. But France's writers had long presumed a right to opine on politics and, particularly since the 1930s, the public had grown used to hearing them hold forth. During the occupation, of course, only those on the far right were free to do so, and they carried on with their customary bombast, adjusting to the moment by variously praising Pétain, fueling anti-Semitism, justifying the occupation, even defending Hitler. In doing this, they were also writing their own sentences. After the liberation, there could be no ambiguity about their proselytizing: it was all in print. Paradoxically, the same was true for writers in the opposing camp. Although their clandestine newspaper *Les Lettres Françaises* and their underground books had had relatively few readers, the magic of the printed word—

in this case, denouncing the Nazis and Vichy—empowered them to judge their now-ostracized peers. The wheel of fortune had spun quickly. In just over four years, both sides had tasted the privileges and perils of being a writer in a land where words can speak louder than actions.

Yet despite their intense verbal cross fire, the line separating villains and heroes was often blurred. Those who ended up on the losing side included outright Fascists as well as Vichy supporters, anti-Semitic nationalists and cynical opportunists. Floating in the middle were old-fashioned conservatives, ardent Catholics and anti-Communists. And among the victors were many Communists and a smaller number of men and women who were inspired more by principle than ideology. During the occupation, positions also changed, above all as early *pétainistes* gave up on Vichy, with some siding openly with the Nazis and others opting for outright resistance. At the same time, personal ties could often override political differences.

From the beginning, Pierre Drieu La Rochelle and André Malraux were political foes, but they remained friends; in 1943, Drieu La Rochelle became godfather to one of Malraux's children. Similarly, the *résistant* Jean Paulhan never broke with the collaborationist writer Marcel Jouhandeau, even after Jouhandeau's wife denounced him to the *Feldgendarmerie,* the Wehrmacht's military police. Then there was the unspoken understanding between the collaborationist writer Ramon Fernandez and Marguerite Duras. Fernandez lived above Duras on the rue Saint-Benoît in Saint-Germain-des-Prés and never reported resistance meetings taking place in her apartment, while she tried to ignore noisy gatherings of Fascists chez Fernandez on Sunday evenings. They even shared a cleaning woman. For their part, Guitry and Cocteau were willing to use their German connections to help other writers in trouble. In a few cases, though, friendship became poisonous: Drieu La Rochelle's wartime hatred of Aragon can only be explained by the intensity of their prewar ties.

In reality, politics aside, writers of renown in occupied Paris had much in common. Some were independently wealthy, others worked in publishing houses, many earned a steady income writing for an array of newspapers, and a number taught in senior high schools; few shared the winter cold or year-round food shortages suffered by other Parisians. Many were of bourgeois extraction and had attended the same schools or colleges, not least that home of intellectual excellence the École Normale Supérieure. They could be seen lunching or dining in the Brasserie Lipp or attending the Concerts de la Pléiade or socializing at salons organized by wealthy hostesses. They read and criticized one another's work, they gossiped furiously, they formed cliques, they insulted their enemies in private and shook hands with them in public. Several who joined the literary resistance even had cordial relations with a handful of "good" Germans—considered "good" because, while openly anti-Semitic and perhaps Nazi Party members, they were Francophiles. Whether Ambassador Abetz could be counted among them remains debatable, but he spoke French, had a French wife and probably helped free some writers from jail. Certainly, almost all the Paris literati came to know Gerhard Heller, the affable thirty-something Sonderführer who was the chief literature censor, initially in the Propaganda Staffel, then, from mid-1942, in the embassy itself. Karl Epting, the director of the German Institute, and his assistant, Karl-Heinz Bremer, both fluent in French, were also considered sympathetic to French culture.

Wandering through the Paris world of letters was a still more unlikely German, Ernst Jünger, who was posted to Paris as a Wehrmacht captain in April 1941. Still in his mid-forties, Jünger had made his name with his semiautobiographical novel *Storm of Steel,* inspired by his experience in World War I, for which he had received Germany's highest honors for bravery. After he had been demobilized, he had studied etymology, but the immense success of *Storm of Steel* earned him a prestige and authority to speak out on public affairs. He was hardly a liberal. He criticized the Weimar Republic, he wrote an essay called "On Nationalism and the Jewish Question," suggesting that Jews threatened German unity, and he endorsed the Nazi cult of courage and death. But he never joined the Nazi Party, and he declined an invitation to head the German Academy of Literature. At a stretch, his 1939 novella *On the Marble Cliffs* could be read as an allegory for the tyranny of the Third Reich. Certainly, by the time Jünger reached Paris, he found anti-Semitism distasteful and he positively disdained Hitler, to whom, in his journal, he gave the bizarre name of Kniébolo. And although he shared his political views only with his private diary, he, too, was soon considered a "good" German by many leading writers in Paris.

Working from the Wehrmacht headquarters in the Hôtel Majestic and living in the nearby Hôtel Raphaël, Jünger seemed to have plenty of time for himself, going to the theater or cabaret when he was not a guest at expensive restaurants or private homes. On a few occasions he was assigned military duties: in his diary entry for May 29, 1941, he describes in detail supervising the execution of a German army deserter.[1] With his reputation as a serious novelist serving as his calling card, however, he became something of an attraction at social events. Invited to dinner by Vichy's Fernand de Brinon, Jünger met Arletty and Guitry, who in turn invited him to lunch at his mansion. At the writer Paul Morand's home, he met the publisher Gaston Gallimard as well as Cocteau, who became a close friend. He visited Arno Breker before the German sculptor's large show at the Orangerie, and he was received by Picasso. He also often found himself holding literary discussions with writers who he suspected were in the resistance.

Still, anyone reading the press after the fall of Paris would find no such nuances: collaborationists held court unchallenged, with some right-wing writers and journalists savoring the ultimate I-told-you-so. Had they not warned that the Third Republic was rotten to the core, had they not cautioned that Jews, Communists and Freemasons were leading France into an unnecessary war, had they not anticipated that Britain would be an unreliable ally? Now France was paying the price. And it could start building a healthy new society only once it had acknowledged its errant ways and eliminated its enemies within.

Persuaded by Vichy's promise of a National Revolution, at least until Laval's return to power in April 1942, even some moderate writers pinned their hopes on Pétain. Jean Zay, the Popular Front's education minister, was struck by how many writers had betrayed themselves. In his memoir *Souvenir et solitude* he wrote, "Alas! How much kneeling and renunciation there is in French letters in 1941. If a few great writers save honor by the dignity of their silence, how many others, and not the least among them, rush to serve the new gods, curiously forgetting their past and their own works!"[2] Prewar Fascist intellectuals were at least consistent in celebrating the Nazi victory. For them, just as Vichy's lessons of Catholic piety seemed irrelevant, its aged leader and his mediocre government were clearly incapable of saving the country. Rather, they believed that defeat had opened the way to a different future, one where France would take its place in Hitler's new Europe. There, with Jews stripped of their power, international Communism defeated and the Anglo-American world neutralized, a Fascist France with its empire intact would eventually recover its stature and dignity. Put differently, the Nazis did not have to recruit them; they were true believers. With few exceptions, the Fascists of the 1930s remained Fascists throughout the occupation.

Many of their ideas—of Nazi might, of British perfidy, of a global Jewish conspiracy, of Communist treachery—were trumpeted by mass-circulation dailies like *Paris-Soir, Le Matin* and *Le Petit Parisien,* which were directly under German control. These messages were in turn reinforced by Radio-Paris, the Nazis' official French-language broadcaster, albeit contradicted daily by the equally propagandistic BBC in London. However, a more sophisticated form of collaboration was developed by a half-dozen weeklies, which, while subject to German censorship, competed for educated readers. Describing themselves as "political-literary," itself an apt label for many French intellectuals, these publications followed editorial lines that were variously pro-Vichy, pro-German and anti-Semitic, but they also made room for literary voices.

One such weekly was *La Gerbe,* which was founded in 1940 by Alphonse de Châteaubriant, the writer who also headed the Groupe Collaboration. Cocteau, Guitry, Fernandez, Drieu La Rochelle, Anouilh and even Colette were among its contributors. Financed by the German embassy, *La Gerbe* paid well, which presumably won over writers who might otherwise have objected to its unwavering hostility toward Jews, Communists, Freemasons and Britain. In one absurd example of commercial interest trumping ideology, Éditions Denoël, which had accepted German investment, published an advertisement in *La Gerbe* for a book of short stories by Aragon's wife, Elsa Triolet, a Russian-born Jew who was hiding in southern France. Two prewar right-wing weeklies opted to move to the unoccupied zone—*Candide* to Clermont-Ferrand and *Gringoire* to Marseille—although this did nothing to moderate their views. Even so, in 1941 and early 1942, *Gringoire*'s editor, Horace de Carbuccia, published several short stories by Irène Némirovsky under a pseudonym, despite the fact that as a Jew she was banned from appearing in print. Was Carbuccia acting out of compassion? It is more likely that he simply needed well-written material.

The most influential of these weeklies was the openly pro-Nazi *Je suis partout,* edited by Robert Brasillach. A graduate of the École Normale Supérieure who soon made his name as a novelist, poet, journalist and polemicist, Brasillach embraced Fascism after the failed right-wing uprising of February 6, 1934. Writing first in *L'Action*

Française, the newspaper of Maurras's ultranationalist movement, Brasillach came to see Hitler's National Socialism as a purifying alternative to the decadence of the Third Republic. In 1937, still only twenty-eight years old, he became editor in chief of *Je suis partout,* which by then shared both his pro-German and his anti-Semitic views. That same year, he attended the Nazi Party congress in Nuremberg and came away hypnotized by the regimented rituals of Fascism and, it seems, by the strapping young Aryan warriors at the Führer's command. Clearly influenced by this visit, Brasillach's novel *Les Sept couleurs* presented a romantic view of Fascism through a prism of eroticism and mysticism.

When war was declared, Brasillach joined the French army, but he was captured and spent the next ten months as a POW.* But the Germans, knowing him to be a friend, authorized the publication of his 1939 memoir, *Notre avant-guerre* (Before Our War), in which—erroneously—he traced the rise of French anti-Semitism to the moment that a Jew, Léon Blum, became prime minister in 1936.† According to Brasillach, "The movie industry almost closed its doors to Aryans. Radio took on a Yiddish accent. The most peaceful people began to look askew at those with curly hair and hooked noses, who were everywhere to be seen. This is not polemic, it is history."[3] He also provided a fanciful definition of Fascism: "It is a spirit. It is above all a non-conformist spirit, anti-bourgeois with an element of irreverence." He added, "It is the true spirit of friendship, which we would like to raise to a national friendship."[4] In April 1941, at Abetz's request, Brasillach was released and returned as editor in chief of *Je suis partout.*

Closed by the French government in May 1940 for opposing the war with Germany, the weekly had already resumed publication in late February 1941. Two months later, it was apparent that Brasillach's enthusiasm for the Third Reich was undiminished. Writing most of his newspaper's editorials, he called for Blum, Paul Reynaud, Édouard Daladier and other Third Republic politicians to be sentenced to death; he singled out Jews who he said should be arrested; he applauded Germany's seizure of the unoccupied zone in Novem-

---

*During much of this time, he was in camps reserved for French officers and was not unduly uncomfortable. While a prisoner of war, he wrote his play *Bérénice.*

†The catalyst for twentieth-century French anti-Semitism was evidently the Dreyfus affair.

ber 1942; and he called for summary execution of all *résistants*. After the *rafle du Vél'd'Hiv'* in July 1942, Brasillach wrote, "We must remove the Jews in a block, and not keep the young ones." A frequent guest at German embassy receptions, he was particularly close to Bremer, the handsome number two at the German Institute, whom he likened to "the young Siegfried" of Wagner's *Ring* cycle and who may also have been Brasillach's lover.* In August 1943, after a dispute with *Je suis partout*'s owner, Brasillach left the newspaper, but he immediately found a fresh outlet for his venom in *Révolution Nationale*. A Propaganda Abteilung report noted approvingly at the time: "Encouraged by his entourage, he has resumed his valuable political work."[5]

With a circulation that exceeded 300,000 in 1944, the newspaper's new editor was Pierre-Antoine Cousteau, the older brother of the explorer Jacques-Yves Cousteau and an obsessive Anglophobe. Under Cousteau, *Je suis partout*'s political voice became shriller, endorsing the violence of the new *milice,* but the weekly also continued to cover the arts scene in Paris. Lucien Rebatet, its talented music and cinema critic, was also known for his vicious turns of phrase, which he used against anti-Nazi writers. To portray Paulhan as a friend of Jews, for example, Rebatet called him "an Aryan ashamed of his foreskin and baptism." Like Brasillach, Rebatet had passed through L'Action Française on his way to Fascism and a compulsive anti-Semitism. Unlike Brasillach, this son of a provincial notary carried with him a hatred of the Paris bourgeoisie.

In June 1940, the first instinct of Rebatet, still only thirty-seven years old, was to applaud Pétain's armistice to end the fighting. He wrote, "I was moved to tears with enthusiasm and tenderness for this old chief who had achieved this disengagement. With his great voice of a grandfather, France, for the first time in so many years, assumed its national sovereignty."[6] But after he failed to find a good job in Vichy, he turned against Pétain. Back in Paris, he complemented his column in *Je suis partout* by also writing in *Le Cri du Peuple,* published by Jacques Doriot's extremist Parti Populaire Français, and *Le Petit Parisien.* In his constant search for scapegoats for France's troubles, he accused the Catholic church of succumbing to international

---

*Bremer was later sent to the Russian Front, where he died in 1942. In an obituary in *Je suis partout,* a heartbroken Brasillach addressed Bremer: "Once peace came, we wanted to go walking together, to go camping, to find twin landscapes, the fraternal cities of our two countries."

Jewry when some bishops protested deportations of Jews. A measure of Rebatet's audience was that his vitriolic memoir *Les Décombres* (The Ruins), published in July 1942, sold over sixty-five thousand copies in the occupied zone alone. In it, he boasted of his Fascism. "I have never had a drop of democratic blood in my veins," he said, recalling that twenty-two years earlier he had written, "I aspire to a dictatorship, a severe and aristocratic regime."[7] Along with endless anti-Semitism, he also mocked his former mentor Maurras as a "false Fascist" for not backing Germany. And he expressed his fervent hope for an outright German victory in the European war. Unsurprisingly, Radio-Paris declared *Les Décombres* to be the book of the year for 1942.

A more moderate publication was *Comoedia*, which described itself as "the entertainment, literature and arts weekly" and largely avoided controversial subjects. Launched in June 1941 by an experienced journalist, René Delange, it had no ties to a similarly named weekly that circulated between 1907 and 1937, but it benefited from the earlier *Comoedia*'s good image. Delange proved a skilled operator: he proclaimed the weekly's total independence at the same time as declaring that his "main aim is to work toward total Franco-German collaboration in the domain of culture." He gave another nod to the occupier by offering a "European" page each week to German cultural news. Yet while every edition of *Comoedia* required German approval, Delange nonetheless provided an objective account of cultural events in occupied Paris. The Propaganda Abteilung would occasionally censor articles or references to Jewish artists, but it never demanded that *Comoedia* publish outright propaganda or even positive reviews for collaborationist artists. This was as close to freedom of the press as the occupation would know.

As a result, with the respected writer Marcel Arland as *Comoedia*'s book editor, many artists and intellectuals felt comfortable publishing there, even some who otherwise followed the resistance diktat of "no writing for occupied-zone newspapers." Certainly few refused *Comoedia*'s request for an interview or an essay if they had a new play, movie or book coming out in Paris. This explained the appearance in its pages of the playwrights Montherlant, Claudel and Anouilh, the actor-director Barrault, the composer Honegger and the movie directors Carné and Pagnol. The collaborationist writers Jouhandeau and Jacques Chardonne were frequently published there, but so also were the *résistant* poets Éluard and Desnos and the liter-

ary critic Paulhan. Colette, the only woman to write for *Comoedia,*
contributed short stories, while Arland was the first critic to pro-
claim Camus's *L'Étranger* a masterpiece. Sartre, too, wrote for the
weekly, which his companion Simone de Beauvoir proclaimed to be
"a real newspaper" after Arland praised her first novel, *L'Invitée.*[8]
For the newspaper's first edition, Sartre reviewed a new translation
of *Moby-Dick.* He was interviewed before the premiere of his first
play, *Les Mouches,* in 1943. And early in 1944, he wrote an appreciation of the playwright Jean Giraudoux, who had just died. In all,
although Delange was called before a purge committee after the
liberation, he served both readers and writers without inordinate
compromise.

The *Nouvelle Revue Française* failed to strike such a balance. Better known simply as the *NRF,* it had been France's leading intellectual
journal since its foundation in 1909. With Paulhan as its editor from
1925, it had also long opened its pages to all political currents, but it
suspended publication in June 1940 as the Germans approached
Paris. Now, as a key symbol of "normality," Ambassador Abetz
wanted it back in circulation, and he proposed his prewar friend
Drieu La Rochelle as its new editor.

The choice of Drieu La Rochelle was hardly accidental. Born in
1893, he had emerged as an important new writer in the 1920s and,
while initially focusing on fiction and poetry, he was noticed in the
1930s for his political essays. Like many of his generation, having
begun on the left, he embraced Fascism after the February 1934
right-wing riots. That same year, while visiting Berlin, he met Abetz,
who was courting French intellectuals through his France-Germany
Committee. In 1935, at Abetz's invitation, Drieu La Rochelle
attended the Nazi Party congress in Nuremberg and visited the
"model" labor camp at Dachau. Already disenchanted by French
democracy, he joined Doriot's Fascist Parti Populaire Français and
continued to publish books with Gallimard and occasional articles
in the *NRF.* On the eve of war, he published his best-known novel,
Gilles, a portrait of France's decadence during the interwar years as
viewed by his alter ego, Gilles Gambier, who, like his creator, ends
up a Fascist. Throughout this period, he remained in touch with
Abetz. On August 10, 1940, the two men met again in Paris and the
ambassador initially suggested that Drieu La Rochelle found a new
political-literary journal, which, he pledged, would not be subject to
censorship. A week later, they decided instead that the *NRF* should

be revived by Drieu La Rochelle, who three months earlier had vowed never again to set foot in what he described as a nest of Jews, Communists, Surrealists and fellow travelers.

The journal's owner, the publisher Gaston Gallimard, had little choice but to accept. His building at 5 rue Sébastien-Bottin, on the Left Bank, was closed on November 9 after German agents found anti-Hitler books in stock. Further, not only had Gallimard refused to accept German capital into his company, but the firm was also reputed to favor leftist authors. Before the war, he had often been attacked by the extreme right; now he was an easy target. On October 10, 1940, Paul Riche* wrote in *Au Pilori* of Gallimard and the *NRF:* "A band of scoundrels has operated in French literature from 1909 to 1939 under the orders of a bandit chief: Gallimard. Thirty years of abject and underhand propaganda in favor of anarchy, revolutionaries of all colors, the 'antis'—anti-Fascist, anti-national, anti-everything. Thirty years of literary, spiritual and human nihilism! Gallimard and his gang have prepared the leaders of a distinguished mob rule."[9]

Still, in exchange for ceding the *NRF* to an ally of the Nazis, Gallimard could return to business. In a letter in late October 1940, Paulhan noted, "Gaston G. sees it as a kind of protection for his entire company."[10] Heller was eager to use his position at the Propaganda Staffel to make this happen. While studying French literature in Toulouse before the war, he had come to admire many French writers. Now he was well placed to meet them. He was also fully aware of the importance of both Gallimard and the *NRF.* In his memoir, *Un Allemand à Paris* (A German in Paris), published in French in 1981,[†] he said he obtained permission for Éditions Gallimard to reopen and accompanied a German military police officer to remove the seal on its building. He recalled, "I climbed to the first floor to the office of Paulhan—I learned that later—which would become that of his successor. I took the telephone and called: 'Monsieur Drieu, I am at rue Sébastien-Bottin: the building is open, everything is in order.' "[11]

---

*Paul Riche was the pseudonym of Jean Mamy, who in 1943 directed *Forces occultes,* a movie attacking Freemasons and Jews, and who in 1949 was executed.

†A number of French scholars consider this memoir, which Heller wrote with a French author, Jean Grand, thirty-six years after he left Paris, to be self-serving and highly selective. Nonetheless, after the war, Heller devoted himself to translating French literature and in 1980 was awarded the Grand Prix du Rayonnement de la Langue Française by the Académie Française.

Aware that the *NRF*'s best-known writers might object to his appointment, Drieu La Rochelle invited Paulhan to stay on as coeditor. Paulhan turned down the offer, but he agreed instead to cooperate in "saving" the *NRF.* It was a peculiar arrangement. Sitting in adjacent offices in Gallimard, Drieu La Rochelle knew that Paulhan was an anti-Nazi. Yet Heller recalled being told by Drieu La Rochelle in early 1941, "Make sure nothing ever happens to Malraux, Paulhan, Gaston Gallimard and Aragon, no matter what allegations are brought against them."[12]

In May of that same year, Drieu La Rochelle himself used his Nazi connections to free Paulhan from jail after the Gestapo discovered his ties to the Musée de l'Homme resistance group. Paulhan in turn kept his word by inviting many respectable authors to write for the "new" *NRF.* The first three editions included two excerpts from André Gide's journal, poems by Paul Valéry and Éluard and an essay by the composer Georges Auric, who, like Éluard, would later join the resistance. Even Mauriac initially believed that the rebirth of the journal would demonstrate "a continuity of the French spirit," though he changed his mind after seeing the first issue.

But while Drieu La Rochelle's *NRF* was never openly anti-Semitic, the moderates were soon turned off by its collaborationist tone. In his *Journal des années noires,* the critic Jean Guéhenno described its first edition in December 1940 as "lamentable, even from a literary point of view." He added, "It would appear that most of these gentlemen have lost almost all of their talent."[13] This issue included an article by Chardonne called "L'Été à la Maurie" (Summer in La Maurie), which describes German soldiers being welcomed in a French village, where a wine-growing peasant offers cognac to a courteous Wehrmacht colonel. "I can only have the highest praise for your soldiers," he tells the colonel, "and I think all the village has the same opinion. In fact, your soldiers don't appear to be unhappy with the welcome they have received." Paulhan described the piece as "abject" and Gide considered it offensive.

In another article, entitled "Lettre à un américain," Alfred Fabre-Luce* celebrated the fact that Europe's "new horizons" were giving

---

*For all his collaborationist instincts, however, Fabre-Luce found himself in trouble with the Germans. After publishing the first two volumes of his *Journal de la France* in the unoccupied zone, he decided to publish the third privately. Predictions of a German defeat and the observation that "the Jew has become a symbol of human suffering" earned him four months in prison.

birth to "a different race" of Frenchmen. Soon, these writers and other collaborationists like Morand, Jouhandeau, Chardonne, Montherlant, Giono, Fernandez, the philosopher Alain, Châteaubriant and Abel Bonnard were filling the pages of the *NRF*. The journal's circulation never exceeded ten thousand but, for Abetz, it was a model of intellectual collaboration.

Drieu La Rochelle, however, was unhappy with the review—and with his life. Admirers like Abetz and Heller were impressed by his tall, striking appearance and his dogmatic opinions, but his *Journal, 1939–1945,* published in 1992, forty-seven years after his death, revealed a man consumed by both self-hatred and hatred of the world. "My disdain for myself is intolerable and leads me into sordid adventures," he mused to himself.[14] Others fared little better, including Vichy's prime minister, "this revolting Laval, this half Jew half Gypsy, this trash made behind a caravan."[15]

More surprisingly, while publicly defending Nazi Germany, Drieu La Rochelle concluded early on that Hitler faced defeat. On December 22, 1941, he wrote, "I am sure that the situation in Russia is very serious and for once I believe the English radio." He added, "So Hitler has not only the genius but also the stupidity of Napoleon."[16] On November 7, 1942, he wrote, "I am beginning to think that a German victory will be very difficult."[17] And he asked himself, "If the Germans are beaten, what will happen to me? Could I subsist until the moment that the new Communist-democratic drama begins? Or should I commit suicide before then?"[18] By this time, boycotted by France's best writers, the *NRF* was losing subscribers. Already, in the October 1942 issue, Drieu La Rochelle had written with a tone of self-pity, "Almost all French intelligentsia, almost all French lyricism is against us." He was ready to resign, noting, "Thank God, I have been given enough pretexts. I'm sick of smiling at Paulhan and Arland, who both hate me. In his heart, Paulhan is as Communist as he is Gaullist, while Arland is above all against me."[19]

Gaston Gallimard was alarmed. Fearing that the Nazis might move against his publishing house if Drieu La Rochelle were to leave, he urged Paulhan to form an editorial committee acceptable to the Germans to ease the editor's workload. Long negotiations followed, with Paulhan convinced that the *NRF* could be rescued only if it became a purely literary journal supported by weightier names like Gide, Mauriac, Valéry and Claudel. But Gide was living in

Tunisia, Mauriac belonged to the writers' resistance group, and Valéry and Claudel refused to help. With no agreement forthcoming, Drieu La Rochelle increasingly felt he was wasting his time, time he could more usefully devote to his own writing. On March 15, 1943, he noted in his journal, "I have again announced that I am leaving the *Revue* and this time it should work: I have exhausted my rage and I have nothing more to prove."[20] The last edition came out on July 1. Twelve days later, Drieu La Rochelle wrote, "At last the *NRF* is truly dead. Poor old Paulhan holding to his heart the debris of French literature (Surrealists, Jews, professors who believe they are as free as Baudelaire or Rimbaud)."[21]

Still, Éditions Gallimard suffered no reprisals. The rules of the game for the publishing world had been in place since the late summer of 1940 when René Philippon, the president of the Syndicat des Éditeurs, and the Propaganda Staffel agreed on a regime of self-censorship that would prevent publication of new books by Jewish or anti-German authors. The small print added that if French publishers were uncertain about the suitability of a new book, they could send the manuscript to the Propaganda Staffel for approval or rejection. The Nazis had also long since "cleansed" the publishers' backlists. In the summer of 1940, after the "Bernhard List" named 143 prohibited titles, including works by German exiles like Thomas Mann, Erich Maria Remarque and Stefan Zweig, some 20,000 books were seized. In late September, the new "Otto List"* —which probably took its name from Otto Abetz—named 1,060 titles, many by French authors, including Gide, Mauriac, Julien Benda, Georges Duhamel, Aragon and, most absurdly, Flaubert (whose *Madame Bovary* suddenly recovered its nineteenth-century reputation for immorality). Oddly perhaps, *Mein Kampf* was also banned, but apparently only because a French translation had been published in 1934 without the authorization of Hitler's publisher.

After the Otto List, a far wider sweep followed, with German military police raiding seventy publishing houses, closing eleven of them, and confiscating over 700,000 books. But the Nazis were not yet satisfied. In July 1942, the Propaganda Staffel issued an updated Otto List of 1,070 titles; some books on the first list were removed as mistakes, and others were added. Then, in May 1943, a third list was

---

*There is evidence that the Otto List was drawn up with the participation of some French publishers eager to please the Germans.

issued, naming 1,554 authors, including 739 "Jewish writers in the French language."

In his memoir, Heller said that a total of 2,242 tons of books were burned. He noted, "I was able to visit the place where these books were stocked before their destruction. It was a vast garage on the avenue de la Grande-Armée. In the sad light coming through dusty windows, I saw piled up, torn, dirty books, which for me were the objects of a veritable cult. A mountain of horror, a dreadful sight which reminded me of the autos-da-fé in front of Berlin University in May 1933."[22] Heller said he could not resist taking some of these banned books and hiding them in the Propaganda Staffel, even joking that his office had become an annex to the French National Library. He did not identify the books he smuggled out, but from this imprisoned library he could have chosen works by Heinrich Heine, Mann, Zweig, Freud, Jung, Marx and Trotsky and, among French Jewish authors, by Max Jacob, Benda and Blum.

In practice, many booksellers as well as riverside *bouquinistes* hid banned books and sold them under the counter to trusted clients. But the Germans also frequently raided stores looking for illegal titles. Until December 1941, Shakespeare & Company, on the rue de l'Odéon, was shielded by Sylvia Beach's American nationality, but things changed after the United States entered the war. Shortly after Christmas, a German officer appeared at the bookstore and, not for the first time, tried to persuade Beach to sell him her only copy of Joyce's *Finnegans Wake*. When she refused, he announced that all her books would be confiscated that afternoon. In the hours that followed, she and friends hid all of her stock in an empty apartment four floors above the shop. By her own account, she even had the name of the store painted over and its bookshelves dismantled so that, when the Germans returned, they found nothing.

But Beach's troubles were not over. In late September 1942, she was arrested as an "enemy alien" and, along with some three hundred other American women, was interned in Vittel, a spa in the Vosges Mountains, where many British were already being held. Astonishingly, after six months, she was freed, albeit embarrassingly thanks to the intervention of an old writer friend and new collaborationist, Jacques Benoist-Méchin. She returned to Paris and, for the rest of the occupation, tried to go unnoticed. She avoided a fresh internment, but she also accepted that the two-decades-long adventure of Shakespeare & Company was over.*

French publishers, who had no interest in testing German tolerance, learned quickly to operate inside the new straitjacket. And this was no less true of Aryanized Jewish publishers, like Calmann-Lévy, now Éditions Balzac, and Ferenczi, which reappeared in 1942 as Le Livre Moderne.† One exception was Éditions du Seuil, then a small Catholic publisher, which initially suspended operations because one of its partners, Jean Bardet, was a prisoner of war and the other, Paul Flamand, joined Vichy's cultural movement Jeune France.

Many other publishers, however, went out of their way to ingratiate themselves with the Germans, none more than Bernard Grasset, then France's most powerful publishing figure, who saw himself as the ideal interlocutor between the Nazis and the publishing industry. In one letter to a friend on August 3, 1940, he boasted, "As far back as one goes on the two sides of my family, you will not find a Jew or Jewess." In another letter the following day, he offered this: "The occupiers are essentially racist. I have a clear tendency to be one. In brief, on a number of points that I will call 'doctrine'—'doctrine' as opposed to 'politics'—I share many of their sentiments."[23] Later that year, Grasset summed up France's situation in a collection of essays he published and prefaced *À la recherche de la France:* "The French find themselves entirely in the hands of a nation that has risen to the summit of unity and strength, and by the virtue of one man."[24] Robert Denoël, whose publishing house was initially closed by the Nazis, went further by selling part of his company to Germans. Hachette, on the other hand, was almost immediately requisitioned by the Nazis because of its large distribution network.

Industry-wide issues were handled by the Comité d'Organisation du Livre, one of the many organizing committees created by Vichy to manage the economy. But publishers also had direct relations with the Germans, with potentially troublesome manuscripts sent for Heller's verdict. In his memoir, Heller recalled being impressed by

*Before her death in 1962, Beach authorized a new English-language bookstore on the Left Bank to use the name of Shakespeare & Company.

†Although Calmann-Lévy's Jewish owners were quickly sidelined, a power struggle to control it ensued, with Bernard Grasset proposing that French publishers pool their resources to acquire it, before it was absorbed into the media empire of the German businessman Gerhard Hibbelen.

Camus's *L'Étranger* and offering to obtain additional paper for its publication. Thus, when it suited them, the Germans overruled French institutions they had themselves approved, such as the commission created by French publishers in 1942 to manage the perennial shortage of paper.* Many publishers—Stock, Flammarion, Payot and Plon among them—also lobbied the German Institute for German books that they could translate. The inimitable Grasset could not resist lobbying for the right to publish Goebbels's memoir, *Vom Kaiserhof zur Reichskanzlei* (From the Kaiserhof to the Chancellery), in translation. "It is in your interest as it is in ours that we ensure Dr. Goebbels's masterly work the distribution it deserves," he wrote to Goebbels's publisher, Eher Verlag.[25] The institute followed up by creating the Franco-German Translation Committee, which listed over one thousand German books worthy of translation, including a collection of Hitler's war speeches. Numerous contracts were signed, although fewer than half the books on the list were ever published.

Most publishers focused on the French market, which expanded rapidly in the early years of the war. In fact, although the paper shortage meant smaller print runs, the number of new titles increased annually until 1943. In his memoir, Abetz even claimed that in 1943 France published more new books than either the United States or Britain—further proof, he said, that Goebbels's order to dismantle French culture had been ignored.

Escapist books were the most popular. Simenon published ten thrillers between 1940 and 1944, while Marcel Aymé's popular science fiction stories included *Le Passe-muraille* (Walker Through Walls). Colette's three novellas published during the war—*Le Képi, Chambre d'hôtel* and *Julie de Carneilhan*—sold well, as did historical novels, adventure travel stories and cookbooks with tips on how to make the best of rationing. No less than in theater, nostalgia for better times fed an appetite for biographies of great French figures of the past, not only the inevitable Joan of Arc and Napoleon, but also Louis XIV, Richelieu, Molière, Voltaire, Fragonard and Diderot.

Contemporary events were also covered. A number of books offered analyses or personal accounts of France's defeat, such as Henry Bordeaux's *Les Murs sont bons,* Bertrand de Jouvenel's *Après la défaite* and Chardonne's *Chronique privée de l'an 1940.* Here, too,

*The commission's secretary was none other than a young Marguerite Duras.

the Germans occasionally meddled: they authorized Montherlant's *Le Solstice de juin* after it was banned by Vichy, and they promoted Paul Mousset's *Quand le temps travaillait pour nous,* which won the 1941 Renaudot Prize. Long-forgotten authors also published myriad anti-Semitic tracts, including a practical handbook, *Comment reconnaître un juif?* (How to Recognize a Jew?). A still greater harvest comprised books praising Pétain, among them Georges Suarez's *Le Maréchal Pétain,* José Germain's hyperbolic *Notre chef, Pétain,* René Viard's *De Charlemagne au maréchal Pétain* and Guitry's special edition of *De 1429 à 1942,* paying homage to French heroes from Joan of Arc to Pétain.

More surprisingly, many books by authors who were either *attentistes* or were linked to the resistance appeared during the occupation. New plays by Anouilh, Montherlant and Sartre were routinely published before their premieres. Sartre brought out his long existentialist treatise *L'Être et le néant,* while Beauvoir published *L'Invitée,* a stormy love story set on the eve of World War II. Initially censored, Mauriac's *La Pharisienne* was published thanks to the German Institute's Epting, while no one raised objections to Paulhan's meditation on language, *Les Fleurs de Tarbes* (The Flowers of Tarbes). In the first two years of the occupation, Aragon published a collection of poems, *Le Crève-coeur* (Heartbreak), and two novels, *Les Voyageurs de l'impériale* and *Aurélien.* Still more bizarrely, Elsa Triolet's novel *Le Cheval blanc* (The White Horse) came out in 1943 and *Le Premier accroc coûte deux cents francs* (A First Snag Costs Two Hundred Francs) in 1944. Saint-Exupéry's *Pilote de guerre* (published in the United States as *Flight to Arras*), which he sent to Paris from his exile in the United States, was published in a small edition in the unoccupied zone in 1942, but it was quickly banned by the Germans. His most famous work, *Le Petit prince* (The Little Prince), also written in the United States, was published in New York in 1943 and in France only in 1945. Desnos, too, published several books of poems, including *État de veille,* before he was arrested by the Gestapo in early 1944. And along with *L'Étranger,* Camus published a philosophical essay, *Le Mythe de Sisyphe* (The Myth of Sisyphus),* and the plays *Le Malentendu* and *Caligula.*

Still, if the publishing industry's concern for its survival led it to

---

*With *Le Mythe de Sisyphe,* Gallimard asked Camus—and he agreed—to cut references to Kafka, who as a Jew could not be mentioned positively in print.

collaborate, other institutions linked to the world of letters fared little better. Of these, the Bibliothèque Nationale, on the rue de Richelieu, had perhaps the unhappiest experience. In the summer of 1939, thanks to the foresight of Julien Cain, its general administrator then, the library evacuated its most valuable books and documents. But within weeks of the occupation, Cain* was ousted by Vichy for being Jewish and replaced by Bernard Faÿ, a Catholic monarchist and a historian of American civilization who had translated Gertrude Stein into French. When he took over, Faÿ introduced himself to the staff with these words: "I have been named because I have the confidence of the marshal and the confidence of the Germans."[26] He promptly dismissed all Jews, banned Jews from the library and accepted books seized from Jewish collections.

Faÿ's only positive achievement was to create a new department of music, but his principal obsession was his hatred of Freemasons. He organized conferences around La Franc-Maçonnerie Dévoilée, the exhibition at the Petit Palais in late 1940; he denounced Freemasons in *La Gerbe;* and in 1941 he began publishing an anti-Masonic review, *Les Documents Maçonniques.* After the liberation of Paris, Faÿ was arrested and, despite claiming to have protected Gertrude Stein and Alice B. Toklas, he was sentenced to a lifetime of hard labor. In 1951, while undergoing treatment in the prison hospital, he escaped dressed as a priest and made his way to Switzerland, where he lived until he was pardoned in 1959.

The Académie Française, in contrast, retained its traditional autonomy, which shielded it from direct interference by Vichy. Founded by Cardinal Richelieu in 1635 as the guardian of the French language, it had become renowned in recent times for electing new members on their political, military and ecclesiastical merits rather than their literary talent. Thus, in June 1940, its forty so-called *immortels* included not only Pétain but also Cardinal Alfred Baudrillart, who was rector of the Catholic Institute of Paris, as well as other generals and prelates.

Others who were quick to support Pétain and to collaborate with the occupier were also not outstanding writers, among them: Abel Bonnard, later Vichy's education minister; Charles Maurras, the life-

*In February 1941, after being denounced in *Le Matin,* Cain was arrested. He was held in various French prisons until he was deported to Buchenwald in January 1944. Freed by American forces in April 1945, he returned to his post at the Bibliothèque Nationale, where he remained until 1964.

long leader of L'Action Française, who chose to live in the unoccupied zone; and André Bellessort, the academy's *secrétaire perpétuel,* who until his death in January 1942 wrote a column for *Je suis partout.* These and other right-wingers further abused the academy's prestige: Bonnard, Abel Hermant, Pierre Benoit and Baudrillart joined a *comité d'honneur* of the Groupe Collaboration; Bonnard, Hermant and Baudrillart even gave their blessing—literally in the case of the cardinal—to the Légion des Volontaires Français, created to fight alongside the German army on the Russian Front.

The academy's two Jewish members were lucky to escape such company. Émile Salomon Wilhelm Herzog, better known by his pen name of André Maurois, was in London when France fell, and he moved to the United States before joining the Free French Forces in Algeria in 1943. The other Jewish academician, the venerated philosopher Henri Bergson,* who won the Nobel Prize in literature in 1927, died of natural causes in Paris in January 1941.

A small group of members fought to rescue the academy's honor. Among them, Mauriac and Valéry helped to dissuade the academy from applauding Pétain for embracing collaboration during his meeting with Hitler in October 1940. Valéry's eulogy at Bergson's funeral, in which he surmised that the philosopher had been struck down by the "total disaster" engulfing France, was also hailed as an act of courage. But while the old poet was distrusted by Vichy, which dismissed him as administrator of the Centre Universitaire Méditerranéen, a cultural complex in Nice, Valéry was apolitical by nature and never threw his weight behind the intellectual resistance. In fact, Mauriac was the only academician to join the active resistance, although there were enough silent *attentistes* within the academy to prevent it from becoming a collaborationist covey.

From 1942, following Bellessort's death, the election of Georges Duhamel as *secrétaire perpétuel provisoire* reinforced the academy's independence. Thanks to Duhamel, whose own books had been banned by the Otto List, the academy's 1942 prize for literature went to Jean Schlumberger, one of the founders of the *NRF,* and for fiction to *L'Orage du matin* (Morning Storm) by Jean Blanzat, who was also writing for *Les Lettres Françaises.* In 1943, the literature prize went

---

*Bergson had come close to converting to Catholicism in the 1930s, but in the summer of 1940 he insisted on registering before the French police as a Jew, out of solidarity with other Jews.

to Jean Prévost, a poet who later joined the maquis in southern France. As important, Duhamel, Mauriac, Valéry and several others resisted conservative pressure to fill the seats of twelve academicians who died during the occupation.

The Académie Goncourt had less of a reputation to defend. In fact, even its claim to be an academy seemed pompous since it had no building of its own; its ten members merely gathered for lunch on the first Tuesday of every month in a private room in the Restaurant Drouant in Paris. However, since its foundation in 1900, the Goncourt's annual fiction prize had become the most coveted of numerous French literary prizes. This brought intense lobbying by publishers as they competed to see their friends elected to the jury and their books rewarded. And few years went by without some related scandal spilling into the newspapers. While the Femina and Interallié juries suspended their prizes during the occupation, then, it was characteristic of the Goncourt to carry on. Because its jurors were scattered around France, the academy did not meet until December 1941. It then retroactively awarded the 1940 fiction prize to a writer in a German prison camp, his name to be chosen later. Meeting under the occupation, however, the academy's traditional personal and generational squabbles were enriched by ideological differences.

No Goncourt *académicien* joined the resistance, a few avoided taking a position and several would later have to answer for collaboration. The dominant figure was Guitry, who used his connections with the Germans to strengthen his hand within the Goncourt jury. And he had as an ally the novelist René Benjamin, an early admirer of Mussolini's, who devoted a book and numerous odes to Marshal Pétain. Through their campaigning, the 1941 Goncourt Prize went to *Vent de mars* by Henri Pourrat, also a loyal *pétainiste*. Another right-wing member was the writer Jean Ajalbert, a proud member of Doriot's Parti Populaire Français, who unsuccessfully promoted Rebatet's *Les Décombres* for the 1942 prize. They joined forces to block the election to the academy of André Billy, the respected literary critic of *Le Figaro*.* At least this dispute was not over politics— Billy had in the past dared to criticize the books of some Goncourt jurors—but it did nothing to improve the Goncourt's standing. In the December 1943 issue of *Les Lettres Françaises,* an anonymous

---

*Le Figaro moved to Lyon in June 1940 and suspended publication after Germany took over the unoccupied zone in November 1942.

writer pronounced his verdict on the Goncourt jury: "It is inadmissible that, after the victory, men who in the midst of this enemy occupation adopted a spirit of treason should exercise the least influence over the French public."[27]

With writers no less than other artists, however, it was often trips to Germany as invited guests of the Third Reich that drew public attention to their collaboration. With photographers recording their every move, they would be waved off with a reception at the German Institute or the Propaganda Staffel, they would be wined and dined by Goebbels in Berlin and they would be interviewed on their return to Paris.

Of the writers on two separate trips to Germany, none needed persuading of the virtues of occupation. Heller was in charge of invitations and organization and accompanied the delegations. The first trip was ordered by Goebbels, who wanted writers from all "friendly" countries to attend the First European Writers' Congress in Weimar in late October 1941. For this voyage, the French delegation included *la crème de la collaboration*—Drieu La Rochelle, Brasillach, Bonnard, Fernandez, Jouhandeau, Chardonne and André Fraigneau. In contrast, Montherlant, Arland, Giono, Benoit and Morand, although far from being *résistants*, found excuses not to go.

Jouhandeau may also have wavered. He noted in his *Journal sous l'occupation* that he consulted his closest friend—Paulhan—and was told, "You're the only person who can make this journey without my holding it against you." Soon after leaving Paris, Jouhandeau was still trying to justify himself. "If anyone saw this journey to Germany as a follow-up to my reflections on the Jewish question, they'd be wrong," he wrote, referring to *Le Péril juif,* his anti-Semitic tract of the late 1930s. "I only want to prove in this way that a Frenchman is not necessarily a Germanophobe, even under the present circumstances. Still further, I would like to make my body a fraternal bridge between Germany and us."[28] Here, at least, Jouhandeau appears to be speaking metaphorically, but, as a well-known homosexual,* he may also have been signaling his hopes.

---

*Jean Guéhenno was not the only opposition writer who cited Jouhandeau, Brasillach, Montherlant, Bonnard, Lifar and Cocteau as evidence that homosexuals were more likely to be collaborationists. This theory often blended with the view that, like a woman, France surrendered to Germany's masculine force. At the same time, even in artistic circles, there was widespread homophobia, with *pédéraste* frequently used as a generic insult.

In the event, he spent much of the voyage in the company of an attractive young German poet, Hans Baumann, although it transpired that he was really infatuated with Heller. In a later book, *Le Voyage secret,* which Paulhan described as "pitifully idiotic," Jouhandeau wrote of Heller, "Without him, I am only darkness and desert, with no hope of dawn or vegetation."[29] Referring to him as X, he added, "Without X, I would never have come, but when I decided to follow him, I did not know what I was doing. I only came to trust him later. Had I known, I would not have gone. I left with his hand over my eyes."[30]

While the Weimar conference was the formal purpose of the voyage, it was also designed to exhibit the glories of the Reich. In the end, Drieu La Rochelle, Brasillach, Bonnard and Fraigneau traveled directly to Weimar later in October. But Chardonne, Jouhandeau and Fernandez left the Gare de l'Est on October 4, 1941, for an extended tour of Germany and Austria. Chardonne became the spokesman of the trio, Jouhandeau was the cultural tourist and Fernandez the bon vivant who impressed the Germans with his consumption of alcohol. They opted out of touring Strasbourg, the French city now annexed by Germany, but they visited Aachen, Cologne, Bonn, Frankfurt, Mainz, Heidelberg, Freiburg, Lindau, Munich, Salzburg, Vienna and Berlin. In the German capital, they were received by Goebbels, who warned them that a Russian victory would bring Communism to all Europe. Jouhandeau seemed reassured when Goebbels added that, after the German victory, "each people of the European community would preserve its own physiognomy and individuality."[31] The French group then joined their colleagues as well as other European writers in Weimar, where Goebbels personally invited them to a wreath-laying ceremony at the tombs of Goethe and Schiller. Then, as Goebbels had planned, they founded the European Writers' Union.

On November 4, the Propaganda Staffel welcomed them back to Paris with a reception at which they could share their experience with journalists. Many would also do so in the press. Jouhandeau, for instance, wrote in the December 1941 issue of the *NRF:* "I saw a great people at work, so calm in its labor that one was unaware of the war." Heller had good reason to be proud, as he noted in a year-end report: "The participation of the French writers in the voyage to Germany and poetry meetings of Weimar has had a considerable echo in the Paris daily press and in periodicals. Exploitation of the voyage will continue."[32]

The voyage had indeed been noticed, including by the intellectual resistance. On December 16, 1941, the clandestine Communist weekly *L'Université Libre,* whose editors would be shot by the Gestapo a few months later, addressed a long public letter to "Bonnard, Fernandez, Chardonne, Brasillach, etc., former French writers" and signed it "French writers." As if anticipating the charges these writers would face three years later, it said, "While in Paris the Gestapo was imprisoning five members of the Institut de France, you went as 'invited guests' of the German Institute to Weimar and Berlin to receive your orders from Mr. Goebbels. Is this your concept of patriotism?" The letter concluded, "You have chosen abdication, treason, suicide. We, free French writers, have chosen dignity, fidelity, the battle for the existence and glory of our French writing."[33]

One incident during the train ride taken by Chardonne, Jouhandeau and Fernandez might also have made them question the wisdom of their voyage, although the only reference to this "meaningful and moving meeting" can be found in Heller's memoir. He recalled that when their train made an unscheduled stop in the German countryside, the three writers heard French being spoken. Leaning out of the train windows, they saw a dozen Frenchmen, their heads shaved and their tattered coats painted with the letters KG, for *Kriegsgefangenen,* or prisoners of war, in striking contrast with the well-dressed and well-fed writers. "They are somewhat ashamed of their privileged situation in the face of the misfortune of their compatriots," Heller wrote. "They try to engage in conversation, but they do not know what to answer when the others ask them what they are doing on the train. Only a few words are exchanged before we leave: they sufficed to move deeply the French in our group."[34]

The following year, Heller led another group of French writers to Weimar for the Second European Writers' Congress, although only Drieu La Rochelle, Chardonne and Fraigneau were again on the delegation. Two lesser-known writers, Georges Blond and André Thérive, were added to fill the ranks after Brasillach and Jouhandeau turned down fresh invitations. Heller also made a new attempt to persuade Montherlant to join the group, visiting the playwright in his apartment on the quai Voltaire overlooking the Seine. Montherlant again declined, although blaming his decision on his nervous disposition rather than a reluctance to collaborate. "I have provided ample public and private proof of my hope and my faith in an improvement in Franco-German relations," Heller quoted him as saying. "I have done so before and since this war, most recently by collaborating with your review *Deutschland-Frankreich.*"*[35]

This second writers' voyage brought Heller closer to Chardonne, a friendship that proved crucial to the writer a few months later when his son Gérard was arrested for resistance activities in Tunisia and sent to the Sachsenhausen camp, outside Berlin. In his memoir, Heller said that, in lobbying for the man's release, he stressed that Chardonne had joined the second voyage to Weimar "when so many others pulled out." After his son was freed, Chardonne thanked Heller in a letter, saying, "I will be thankful to you for the rest of my life."[36]

One highly original writer—and decidedly unorthodox personality—who surfaced during the occupation was Jean Genet. He would make his name as a novelist, essayist and playwright only after the war, but it was a meeting with Cocteau in February 1943 that marked the beginning of his transition from petty criminal to acclaimed writer. By then, at the age of thirty-two, Genet had served no fewer than nine prison terms, in the main for shoplifting books and manuscripts, but at the same time he had been writing poems, plays and semiautobiographical novels dwelling in great detail on his homosexual affairs. It was one of these unpublished novels, *Notre-Dame des Fleurs* (Our Lady of the Flowers), that so impressed Cocteau that he quickly persuaded Robert Denoël to publish it— without German permission and for sale under the counter. Even then, only thirty copies were printed and the author's name was omitted from the cover. Genet, who cheerfully described himself "as a thug and a poet,"[37] was again jailed in May 1943 for stealing books and, in September, just one month after his release, he was back in prison. Cocteau stood by him, using his contacts to ease Genet's discomfort. When Genet was released in March 1944, his prison life finally came to an end: during the occupation alone, he had spent twenty-one months behind bars. But from then, his troubles with the law arose from what he wrote—"pornography," according to a later charge—and not what he did.

In contrast, a more dangerous nonconformist—the doctor known as Louis-Ferdinand Céline—prospered during the occupation. His hatred of Jews probably exceeded that of other leading Fascist writers, but his attitude toward the Germans swung between admiration

Deutschland-Frankreich was published by the German Institute in Paris.

and disdain. What gave special weight to his views was that, following *Voyage au bout de la nuit* in 1932, he was considered the most innovative French writer of his generation. He was also stubbornly independent. Although invited to Weimar, for instance, he would never have agreed to be just another collaborationist shepherded by his German masters. Similarly, while many writers received subsidies from the German Institute, Céline never took money from the Nazis. He also refused to sell articles to newspapers, preferring to expound his views in angry letters. In brief, as an outsider in both literary and political circles, he felt free to say and write what he wished. For instance, although he shared many of their views, he dismissed the editors of *Je suis partout* as a "feverish club of ambitious little pederasts." He also delighted in offering gratuitous advice to the Germans.

In his journal, Jünger recorded a typical conversation with Céline: "He said how surprised he was that, as soldiers, we do not shoot, we do not hang, we do not exterminate the Jews—he is astonished that someone in possession of a bayonet does not make unlimited use of it."[38] On another occasion, Céline visited Heller and wrote "NRF" on his door. "Everybody knows that you're an agent of Gallimard and the private secretary of Jean Paulhan," he told the German officer before handing him two pairs of goggles—to be used, he said, "when German cities go up in flames and smoke."[39]

Yet while Céline's language was often too vulgar to be used in Nazi propaganda, he was held in awe by some German officials, none more than Epting, who admired him as much for his literary style as for his exemplary anti-Semitism.* When Céline claimed he was being threatened by Gaullists, the Germans allowed him to carry a gun. When he attended the opening of the Institut d'Études des Questions Juives in Paris in May 1941, they felt honored. When he criticized the Nazis, they were upset but bit their tongues. In one famous dinner at the German embassy in February 1944, accounts of which vary, Céline supposedly shocked Abetz as well as Drieu La Rochelle and other guests by pronouncing the Germans doomed to defeat and saying that Hitler had been replaced by a Jew. Abetz hur-

---

*One German who did not appreciate Céline's writing was Bernhard Payr, a literature representative in Alfred Rosenberg's bureau of Nazi indoctrination. While Payr also applauded Céline's anti-Semitism, he was shocked by his obscenities, all of which "reduce to nothing the author's intentions, which are certainly good" (Loiseaux, *La Littérature de la defaite de la collaboration*, p. 181).

riedly ordered the servants from the room, while his guests accused
Céline of being anti-German. This he denied and, to prove it, he
instigated his artist friend Gen Paul to do his much-practiced imita-
tion of Hitler. The Nazis were not amused.

Céline did, in fact, have one reason for resentment toward the
Nazis. In the 1930s, he began sending his royalties from *Voyage* to
the Netherlands and Denmark in the form of gold coins and bars.
But when the Germans seized his stash of 184 ten-florin gold coins in
Amsterdam, he was furious. In October 1941, he wrote to Brinon,
"That they should act like this against Gaullists and Jews—all the
better—but with their few friends, those who have been condemned,
hunted, persecuted, defamed for their cause, not just today but
between '36 and '39, that's the last straw."[40]

Actually, he had one further gripe, albeit one common to all
authors who cannot find their books on sale. In October 1941, after
visiting the exhibition Le Juif et la France at the Palais Berlitz, Céline
was angry to discover that the show's bookshop was carrying neither of his prewar anti-Semitic best sellers, *Bagatelles pour un massacre* and *L'École des cadavres*. Both were nonetheless reprinted
during the occupation, *Bagatelles* in 1941 and 1943 and *L'École* in
1941 and 1942. Céline also completed his anti-Semitic trilogy in 1941
with *Les Beaux draps* (The Fine Mess), which he dedicated to "the
hangman's rope" to be used on Jews and others responsible for
France's humiliation. In this book, there is no hint that the Jews are
already being persecuted in France and across Europe; rather, he portrays them as all-powerful, still using their wiles to obtain everything
since "they want everything, they want more, they want the moon,
they want our bones, they want our guts in hair curlers to present on
the Sabbath, to dress with flags at carnival time."[41] He also had no
time for the Catholic church, since it was "founded by 12 Jews." He
even took an implicit swipe at Vichy's leaders, noting that they also
had no wish to die: "How many went pale when it came to paying
the check? Start counting on your little fingers. And no doubt it is
still not over. The spectacle is permanent."[42] *Les Beaux draps,* again
published by Denoël, sold some forty thousand copies, although it
was banned in the unoccupied zone—not for its anti-Semitism but
for its rudeness to Vichy.

In December 1941, Céline was among those asked by the daily
L'Appel to answer the question, Should Jews be exterminated?
"I've had enough of repeating myself on the Jewish question," he

responded. "Three definitive books suffice, I believe. But what about the others? All the other writers? For years, I have wanted to know the opinion of Duhamel, de Monzie, Bergery, Montherlant, Colette, Chateaubriant, Mauriac, Bordeaux, Guitry, Déat, Luchaire, Morand. What silence!" His publisher agreed that Céline had said all that could be said in those three books. In *Cahier Jaune,* a new anti-Semitic journal, Denoël wrote, "His three books contain a capital lesson. If we wish to restore France, we can find in them wise counsels, useful reflections, a good method. It's all there. You have only to take it."[43]

What sparked and what kept alive Céline's anti-Semitism? His biographers have offered various clues: he was born during the Dreyfus affair to a father who disliked Jews; he came to resent his Jewish boss when he worked at the League of Nations; he was deeply hurt when Elizabeth Craig, an Irish dancer whom he loved, left him for "a Jewish gangster," as he put it. He traveled to Hollywood hoping to win her back and to sell the movie rights to *Voyage* but was twice rejected, by Craig and by "the Jewish barons of finance."[44] By 1936, when *Mort à crédit* received mixed reviews, he had a ready answer: his critics were Jews. Then, the following year, with the publication of *Bagatelles,* Céline, now forty-two, proclaimed anti-Semitism as his new mission in life. By then, seeing Hitler's escalating persecution of Jews, he was also persuaded that Jews—French, British, American and even Russian—were intent on waging war against the Reich. After his experience in World War I, this was a nightmare that he refused to relive.

Yet Céline's anti-Semitism was both paranoid and hysterical. When Desnos criticized *Les Beaux draps* in the weekly *Aujourd'hui* in March 1941, Céline responded with typical excess: "Why doesn't Mr. Desnos instead yell out, 'Death to Céline, Long live the Jews!' Since June, it seems to me, Mr. Desnos (and your newspaper) is untiringly carrying out a philo-yid campaign."[45] Instead, he suggested that *Aujourd'hui* publish Desnos's photograph, "his face and profile."

At the same time, throughout the occupation Céline worked as a doctor treating the poor in municipal clinics in the Paris suburbs of Sartrouville and Bezon, traveling most days by motorcycle from the small apartment in Montmartre that he shared with his dancer wife, Lucette Almanzor, and their cat, Bébert. Yet for all his verbal and written bravado, he was terrified by Allied bombing of the outskirts of Paris in April 1944, and he lobbied the German embassy to give him a visa to leave the country. On June 17, 1944, barely a week and a half after D-Day, Céline, Lucette and Bébert left Paris for Baden-Baden, in western Germany, on their way to exile in Denmark—and, Céline hoped, to recover his hidden gold. In his journal, Jünger observed Céline's departure with disgust: "Curious to see how people capable of demanding the heads of millions of men in cold blood worry about their dirty little lives. The two facts must be connected."[46] It would be nine years before Céline returned to France.

CHAPTER 13

Chez Florence

WITH THE PARISIAN ELITES enjoying their cultural and social lives as best they could, the peculiarly French institution of the salon once again became fashionable. Born in the seventeenth century, when aristocratic ladies of leisure opened their homes to men of power and letters, the salon served as a kind of neutral territory where politics and art could be discussed in genteel surroundings by people who might otherwise avoid one another. Such a formula was evidently suited to the occupation. The key to drawing worthy guests lay with the hostess, often an attractive and cultivated woman of means who lived alone—perhaps a widow—and who maintained her place in society through a salon. In the early 1940s, several Paris hostesses were well practiced in this art. Marie-Laure de Noailles, the interwar muse of the Surrealists, threw lavish parties and held concerts at her large home on the place des États-Unis—and still had time for a love affair with a Wehrmacht officer. Princess Marie-Blanche de Polignac, heiress to the Jeanne Lanvin fashion house and a leading socialite, was an important patron of musicians and artists. Marie-Louise Bousquet, the editor of the French *Harper's Bazaar,* who had long held court in her sumptuous apartment overlooking the place du Palais-Bourbon, chose to offer musical evenings.

For German guests, too, these soirées offered a good opportunity to socialize with prominent cultural figures. Indeed, it was at one such concert, given by the cellist Pierre Fournier in early 1941, that Gerhard Heller met Marcel Jouhandeau, later to be his traveling companion on the writers' visit to Germany. Heller in turn introduced Ernst Jünger to Madame Boudot-Lamotte's salon* on the rue de Verneuil, where one evening in February 1942 they — and *le tout-Paris intellectuel*—heard Cocteau read his new play, *Renaud et Armide.*

The most memorable salon of the war years, however, was that of a beautiful American named Florence Gould, who was born to French parents in San Francisco in 1895. Her father, Victorien Maximilien Lacaze, had moved to the United States sixteen years earlier as a penniless immigrant and had prospered as the publisher of a French-language newspaper in the Bay Area. After the 1906 San Francisco earthquake, fearing for the safety of his two young daughters, Lacaze sent Florence and Isabelle to boarding school in Paris. By her late teens, Florence was back in the United States, where she married for the first time. But she was already divorced when she returned to Paris in 1917, hoping that her promising soprano voice could lead to a career as an opera singer. Instead, in 1923, she met—and became the third wife of—Frank Jay Gould, the son of Jay Gould, the American robber baron and railroad magnate.

Frank had two homes, an apartment in Paris to facilitate his dalliances and a large villa at Maisons-Laffitte, to the northwest of the city. Florence soon lured him away to Cannes. Until the mid-1920s, rich Parisians who wintered along the Côte d'Azur would flee its summer heat. But the Goulds—along with some British aristocrats, Russian exiles and American millionaires—now helped to turn Cannes into the year-round fun capital of the Riviera. They bought two villas—one, Le Patio, in Cannes; the other, La Vigie, in nearby Juan-les-Pins—and filled them with fine art. Frank also added to his fortune by investing in new hotels and casinos along the Côte d'Azur. However, as a recovering alcoholic who was eighteen years

---

*Boudot-Lamotte's daughter Madeleine was Gaston Gallimard's secretary and therefore also knew many writers.

older than his new wife, Frank could not match Florence's social energy. Young, striking and athletic, she introduced waterskiing to Cannes and took tennis lessons from the legendary champion Suzanne Lenglen. She was also at the heart of the Riviera's party life, which Frank tended to avoid. Often in bed by eleven p.m., he left Florence to enjoy herself with her many admirers. According to one story that did the rounds, Frank's only rule was that she join him for breakfast every day.

Florence also liked the nightlife of Paris, where Frank bought her an apartment at 2 boulevard Suchet, beside the Bois de Boulogne. When war was declared, she sent food packages to French soldiers and volunteered as a nurse in a Paris hospital (she would arrive in her blue convertible Bugatti), but she was back in Juan-les-Pins when the Germans entered Paris. Although the Goulds had boat tickets to return to the United States, she refused to leave. Frank would spend the war years in Juan-les-Pins. By early 1941 Florence had returned to Paris. And since the boulevard Suchet apartment and the Maison-Laffitte villa had been requisitioned by the Wehrmacht, she settled into the luxurious Hôtel Bristol, on the rue du Faubourg Saint-Honoré.

Now forty-five, although looking far younger, she was soon inviting friends and acquaintances for lunches, teas and dinners at the hotel, which seemed unaffected by the new food shortages in Paris. That the Bristol was supplied by the black market was taken for granted. Colette once accepted Florence's invitation for afternoon tea on one condition: "I will come if you replace the petits fours with Camembert and the tea with champagne."[1] Florence's evenings might also include dinner at Maxim's, the floor show at Chez Carrère or an appearance at Marie-Louise Bousquet's salon. It was there that she met—and became instant friends with—Jouhandeau. It was also chez Marie-Louise that she came to know Heller.

On March 28, 1942, with no small pride, Heller brought Jünger to meet Florence and Jouhandeau at the Bristol. It was the eve of the novelist's forty-seventh birthday, and they had a lively discussion about literature over a delicious dinner, Jünger noted in his war diaries.* Then there was a blackout. "Air-raid alert," Jünger noted in his journal. "Sitting around a lamp, we drank 1911 champagne while

---

*In the first edition of his journal, he does not name Florence, referring to her instead as Lady Orpington or Armance.

the planes buzzed overhead and the noise of the cannons shook the city. Small like ants. We talked about death."[2]

It was around that time that Bousquet suggested that Florence host her own salon, one devoted to literature. Florence was hardly an avid reader, but she liked the idea of presiding over a gathering of witty and intelligent authors. As she once put it, "I may not know much about literature, but I know a lot about writers."[3] In April 1942, she rented a large apartment on the third floor of 129 avenue Malakoff, near avenue Foch in the 16th arrondissement. Its decoration demonstrated that everything was still available—at a price. She chose silk-covered furniture and Persian carpets for the sitting room and several black lacquer tables for the dining room. Naturally, she also had a cook and a butler. Her new friend Jouhandeau, who lived one block away, on the rue du Commandant-Marchand, effectively became her cohost. The salon was even scheduled for Thursdays because that was the one day of the week that Jouhandeau was not teaching in a Paris high school. And it was convened around lunch so that the meal and a prolonged *après-déjeuner* would not be cut short by the curfew. Florence herself was, of course, the main attraction, with her green eyes often hidden behind dark glasses, her strings of pearls, large emerald ring and yapping Pekingeses completing a portrait of sophisticated wealth. And to her guests, she offered not only her stylish beauty, sparkling personality and comfortable home, but also excellent food—obtained, naturally, on the black market. No one ever worried that her supply of vintage wine and cognac could run out.

To Florence's close friends, like Bousquet, Cocteau and the Académie Française's Pierre Benoit, who fell in love with her when they first met in late 1935, Jouhandeau added his own crowd, including his closest friend (and secret *résistant*) Jean Paulhan; *Comoedia*'s editor in chief, René Delange, and its book editor, Marcel Arland; and the painter Marie Laurencin. Jouhandeau, who had acquired an intense affection for Heller, also invited the blue-eyed young German to the avenue Malakoff apartment. Among other guests were the playwrights Montherlant, Guitry and Giraudoux and the decorator Christian Bérard. Each in turn occasionally brought along friends for what resembled auditions to join Florence's salon. On some occasions, Florence had as many as fifty guests. There were moderate collaborators, *attentistes,* at least one *résistant* and a few Germans, but none of France's most viciously Fascist writers—Brasillach, Drieu La Rochelle, Rebatet or Céline—ever attended.

One soap opera that provided background noise to the lunches was Jouhandeau's endless complaining about his overbearing wife—except when she was present. Heller, who described her as "a kind of bloodthirsty, proud and cruel tyrant," was not alone in feeling sorry for the writer.[4] Now in her fifties, Élise Jouhandeau had enjoyed a successful career as a dancer, using the stage name of Caryathis, before she married Marcel in 1929. Since then, while failing in her principal mission to woo him away from homosexuality, she had pushed him further to the right, encouraging him to write his notorious anti-Semitic pamphlet, *Le Péril juif,* in the late 1930s. In April 1942, perhaps out of jealousy of her husband's "best friend," Élise even denounced Paulhan to the German military police, an unpardonable act since Paulhan had already been arrested once by the Germans. By good fortune, the complaint was not passed to the Gestapo and the case was dropped.

Ernst Jünger, an interesting addition to the group, was brought by Heller on March 4, 1943. Dressed in the uniform of a Wehrmacht captain, he was charmed to see Florence again and, he noted in his journal, they continued their conversation of one year earlier about death. After another lunch a week later, he quoted her poking fun at Jouhandeau's wife: "It's a fact, I feel comfortable in a state of matrimony because I have been married twice and have been very happy. The only exception that I'd make would be for Jouhandeau because he likes awful women."[5]

Did Florence also make a real exception for Jünger? The novelist certainly appreciated women and, despite the absence of solid evidence, some historians have stated categorically that they became lovers.[6] More certain is that Jünger, whose wife, Gretha, remained in Hannover, had a serious relationship with Sophie Ravoux, née Koch, a German-born doctor whose mother was Jewish and whose husband was a prisoner in Dachau. In his journal, where Jünger variously referred to Sophie as La Doctoresse, Dorothée or Charmille, he described spending long hours with her. But he also made frequent visits to Florence's home, where he celebrated his forty-eighth and forty-ninth birthdays with her (as he had his forty-seventh birthday at the Hôtel Bristol). On one occasion, she gave him a letter from Thornton Wilder to add to his collection of autographs. On another, she told him she had given her husband a copy of his novel *On the Marble Cliffs,* which had just been translated into French. After reading it, Frank had responded, "There's someone who goes from dreams to reality." Jünger observed that this, "for an American multimillionaire, is not a bad judgment."[7]

Among Florence's many rumored lovers, however, one was particularly close to her heart: Ludwig Vogel, an engineer who worked for a powerful German aircraft manufacturer, Focke-Wulf, and who moved in Luftwaffe circles in Paris. It is not known how or when they met but, using a false name, she joined him on two trips to Germany to visit the company's main factory in Friedrichshafen.[8] Vogel usually called on Florence outside the customary hours of her Thursday salon, but on one occasion Jünger met him at her home and they discussed the outlook for the war. In a journal entry in August 1943, Jünger said that a German aeronautical engineer named Vogel told him that the Luftwaffe had phosphorus bombs but Hitler had chosen not to deploy them. Using his nickname for the Führer, Jünger commented in his journal, "That would be worthy; but given Kniébolo's character, somewhat surprising."[9]

Jünger made no suggestion that Vogel might be Florence's lover, but her friendship with Germans of influence was no secret. One Nazi with a notably sinister reputation who would visit her was SS-Standartenführer Helmut Knochen. He was Paris commander of the Security Police, itself part of the Security Service, and as such played a central role in organizing the deportation of Jews to death camps. Knochen, for one, knew all about Vogel. During questioning by French police after the war, he named the German engineer as one of Florence's lovers.

At Florence's salon, conversation moved easily between literature and gossip, between politics and war news. In his journal for August 4, 1943, Jünger noted that over lunch he had learned from Florence that Mussolini had just resigned—he had in fact resigned on July 25—and his portraits were already being burned. That day, the guests also discussed the week-long Allied bombing of Hamburg and the reports of some 200,000 victims, "which is probably highly exaggerated," Jünger added.[10] One evening a few weeks later, Jünger found Jouhandeau very upset because he had been singled out on a Free French broadcast from London. Jünger noted, "He had spent a sleepless night because it seems that his name was on a list of people to be executed. In recounting his fears, he had the air of a little boy watching a policeman write down his name in a notebook."[11]

Occasionally, political differences surfaced. Giraudoux, a frequent guest whose son had joined de Gaulle in London, once warned Paulhan against Heller: "Beware. Don't you see it's a bait?"[12] Another guest, Paul Morand, was openly *pétainiste* at a time when Vichy seemed to many to be a lost cause. He returned from his diplomatic post in London after Paris fell and from 1942 headed Vichy's commission for movie censorship. In his favor, Morand was a lively raconteur who was often accompanied by his elegant wife, the Romanian princess Hélène Soutzo, who years earlier had been part of Proust's inner circle. Later Morand became Vichy's ambassador to Romania and then, shortly before the liberation, ambassador to Switzerland.

On one occasion, during a visit to Paris by Horace de Carbuccia, the editor of *Gringoire,* Florence's guests for dinner included Colette, who was still writing short stories for *Gringoire.* This time, she was accompanied by her Jewish husband, Maurice Goudeket, who normally stayed out of view. Also present was a German,* Colette noted in a letter to a friend: "An electric atmosphere. Maurice suddenly became imprudently magnificent, and there was no further conversation between him and the German."[13]

More often the mood over lunch and postprandial cigarettes and cognac was relaxed, as if culture weighed more than politics. One day, Claude Mauriac, who, like his father, François, was a *résistant,* was summoned to a nearby café by Jouhandeau, who then took him without warning to Florence's apartment. There, he later recounted in his memoir *Le Temps immobile,* he was shocked to find Heller in his Wehrmacht uniform and the German playwright Curt Langenbeck in German naval attire. But he was gradually won over by Heller.[†] "I had before me a young man barely older than myself, drinking steadily, laughing and smiling, good humored and amiable, with nothing to remind that he was German, above all a conquering and highly placed German," Mauriac wrote, adding that he was even

---

*This was possibly Heller, since Colette would have considered Jünger's name worth mentioning.

†Forty years later, during a live television broadcast of the literary program *Apostrophes,* Heller reminded Claude Mauriac that they had met at Florence's apartment, but Mauriac said he could not remember.

tempted to romanticize that moment: "An American, two Germans and three Frenchmen. Far above the massacres, the lies, the blood, there was this little island of civilized people."[14]

Quite the most eccentric of Florence's guests was the conservative writer Paul Léautaud. Now in his early seventies, he had long preferred the company of myriad dogs and cats in the Paris suburb of Fontenay-aux-Roses to that of fellow writers in Left Bank cafés. But he had some friends in literary Paris, among them Paulhan, who arranged for his first invitation to lunch at the avenue Malakoff apartment on November 22, 1943. That evening, Léautaud penned a vivid description of Florence, albeit giving her thirteen years less than her age: "Pretty, pressing up against you when she talks to you, around 35 years old, nut-brown hair, tall, slim, supple, svelte, in an old-fashioned skirt more elegant than today's fashion, unusual eyes, when we were having coffee, sitting beside me, as I spoke of cats as my favorite animals, her face next to mine: 'I have the eyes of a cat, look at me.' Unusual eyes, I repeat, in which, if they have something of a cat, or rather a she-cat, it is a kind of amorous languor and warmth."[15] After his second lunch chez Florence on March 2, 1944, he offered a sketch of himself: "Truly, let me say immediately, I have no taste for these meetings. These shouts, this need to talk, this feeling of being invited as a rare object." He added, "I am used to being alone, eating alone, my nose in my plate, reading a newspaper if I have one, or eating with someone I need hardly have to talk to."[16]

Nonetheless, he rarely turned down an invitation. In fact, some of Florence's lunch guests suspected that he tolerated their company only so he could take leftover food to his animals. Certainly, unlike, say, Paulhan and Jouhandeau, Léautaud was poor, working for a meager wage in a collaborationist publishing house, Mercure de France, and writing occasionally for collaborationist weeklies to supplement his paltry royalties. His best-known novel, *Le Petit ami,* had been published forty years earlier, and his most recent, *Passe-temps,* fifteen years earlier. But he also took pleasure in exhibiting his poverty, occasionally appearing unshaven, often dressed in scruffy old clothes, once wearing slippers. And he evidently enjoyed having an audience for his sharp barbs, from which few people were spared—certainly not the Jews, but not even those around the table. In his *Journal littéraire,* he described Marie-Louise Bousquet as "odious"; Dr. Arthur Vernes, a scientist and occasional guest, as "an idiot and pretentious"; and Cocteau as "complicated, affected and false." Léautaud, who often noted that he had declined prelunch champagne, later compared the salon's raucous afternoon debates, fueled by liquor, with those of "a bordel or an orgy."[17]

Heller, for one, was intrigued by Léautaud, noting, "Despite his maliciousness, his ferocious words, his apparent insensitivity to all humans, Jünger and I felt some sympathy for this old fellow whose whole life seemed to be expressed by two loves: for literature and for animals."[18] But even Heller could not understand how, as Germany's defeat became probable, Léautaud held on to his belief that "France's political interest lay in a German victory and *entente* [with Germany]."*[19] Jünger raised Léautaud's precarious economic condition with Vichy's Abel Bonnard, albeit adding in his journal, "True, Léautaud is a cynic who is satisfied with his armchair and the company of his cats and by whom one risks being rudely rebuffed."[20] A few days later, he described Léautaud arriving for Florence's lunch dressed in a 1910-style suit and wearing a thin tie knotted like a shoelace. But Jünger also spoke warmly of him: "He says many fewer useless things than all of his colleagues whom I have so far observed."[21] The appreciation was mutual. "There are no frontiers for me in matters of the spirit," Léautaud wrote, "and these two Germans have moreover displayed sentiments of sympathy for France and the French." Jünger took particular delight in Léautaud's dry humor. When he mentioned that Victor Hugo was one of the authors he had always neglected, Léautaud retorted: "You can continue doing so."[22]

By all public appearances, Florence's life seemed undisturbed by the fact that the United States was at war with Germany. Thanks to her German connections, she had a very rare permit allowing her to use her car at night during the curfew in Paris—at a time when very few Parisians were allowed to drive at all. She also had a permanent pass to cross the demarcation line to and from the unoccupied zone to visit her husband at Juan-les-Pins. Once she shipped some artworks, including a Goya and a Jordaens, from the Côte d'Azur villa to her avenue Malakoff apartment.

After the war, however, it became apparent that her life had been far more complicated. Sometime after June 1941, she found herself caught up in Göring's art-looting fever. According to a report prepared by the

---

*In his journal, though, Léautaud said he looked forward to the end of hardship promised by an Allied victory, even noting—overoptimistically—that he had no need to store coal for the coming winter.

German army command in 1942, the cellars of the Gould villa in Maisons-Laffitte were searched for weapons.[23] While nothing incriminating was found, "a valuable triptych and two precious single pieces," all antiquities carved in ivory, were seized by an agent of the Einsatzstab Reichsleiter Rosenberg, or ERR, as the Nazi art police was known. The report went on: "Mrs. Gould declared on the spot that she wanted to contribute the entire stock of wine for the soldiers on the Eastern Front; all the copper and brass, which filled an enormous cellar room, was to go to German war industry." The report said that agreement was subsequently reached with the ERR that the triptych would be dedicated to Göring, who would in turn donate it to the Cluny Museum in Paris, to which the Goulds had intended to will it. In gratitude for Göring's gesture, Florence then offered him the two single ivory pieces as a gift. But this was not enough, according to the ERR's representative in Paris, Kurt von Behr. The report said: "It has finally been possible to show the three pieces to the Reich Marshal; he was informed of the above offer by von Behr. The Reich Marshal, however, liked all three pieces and ordered that all three be brought to Germany." In subsequent talks with Gould and her lawyer, the report's author noted, "they beseeched me to refrain from any further undertaking in this matter in order to avoid any difficulties for Mrs. Gould such as the possibility of her being sent to a concentration camp." The author added that he made further inquiries, suggesting that Göring was perhaps unaware that private property was involved: "Everywhere I met with a regretful shrug of the shoulders."*

Florence had good reason to be worried. In September 1941, Vichy's General Commission for Jewish Questions concluded that Frank Gould's name was Jewish and, as a result, it appointed administrators to manage his Aryanized companies in both the occupied and the unoccupied zones. "I was all the more alarmed because my husband's fortune awakened covetousness," Florence told French investigators after the war.[24] "If he were declared Jewish, his property would be confiscated, he would certainly be arrested and eventually deported." It was eighteen months before Gould could demonstrate, with baptism certificates and other documents sent from the United States through Switzerland, that he was of Presbyterian Irish extraction. In March 1943, Vichy lifted the Aryanization order against

---

*The report's critical tone reflected the German army command's well-known disapproval of the ERR's looting of art.

Gould's property, but almost immediately the Germans seized control of the same property, including the hotels and casinos on the Riviera, on the grounds that Gould was now an "enemy alien." Three successive German administrators then ran the companies until the liberation.

Florence, though, showed no outward sign of alarm, and there is no hint in Jünger's journal or Heller's memoirs that she mentioned either of these problems to them. In Paris, apart from her weekly salon, she maintained a busy schedule. She would be seen at the Concerts de la Pléiade at the Galerie Charpentier. Thanks to Paulhan, she was also introduced to modern art; together, they visited art galleries as well as the studios of Picasso, Braque, Jean Fautrier and Jean Dubuffet. (She later invited Dubuffet to some of her lunches, and she commissioned him to paint portraits of several guests.) On more than one occasion, accompanied by the actress Marie Bell, Florence traveled across Paris to Montmartre to visit Céline. Once, in mid-March 1943, as she left his apartment, she slipped and broke her leg. In a letter to a friend after the war, Céline recalled—not entirely accurately—her visits and that accident:

> Madame Frank J. Gould the wife (the 5th! I also knew very well the 2nd) of the old multimillionaire of the American railroads, she is a former manicurist, French by birth (Lacaze) whimsical and not dumb, snobbish, and she wished me *all the best in the world,* she would force herself on our modest home, with Marie Bell (of the Comédie Française) they would bring their own dinner! I who never receive anyone was forced to receive her! She wanted by any means to buy my manuscripts. I refused not wanting to owe anything to the American multimillionaire. But she was neither unpleasant nor stupid—In a hurry, at night and drunk, she even broke her leg at the bottom of my staircase on rue Girardon—I refused to visit her in her bed as she had invited me to look after her! By telegram.[25]

In the letter, sent from jail in Denmark, where he fled in 1945, Céline confessed his reason for remembering her. "What could she do for me now?" he asked.

Still, after her accident, others did visit her. Jünger stood at the head of her bed and heard her opinion of Céline: "She said that the reason this writer was always short of money, despite the importance of his income, is that he gives it all away to street girls who come to consult him" as a doctor.[26] Heller, who accompanied Jünger, recalled different details. The doorbell rang, he wrote in his memoir, and in walked a man in civilian clothes whom Florence welcomed as "Colonel Patrick." Imagining that Florence might be hiding a British or American airman, Heller and Jünger were silent. When the conversation resumed, however, the man turned to them and said, "But, gentlemen, we can talk in German."[27] He introduced himself as head of the Lyon branch of the Abwehr, the German intelligence service linked to the Wehrmacht. Heller offered no explanation as to why this officer was visiting Florence.

Florence herself left no written record of the war years but, despite the Nazis and anti-Semites she received, there was never any suggestion that she herself expressed pro-German or anti-Jewish opinions. Certainly, those in her circle appear to have had nothing but fond memories of the salon. Although Heller regretted not being able to say farewell to her, Jünger lunched with her on August 10, 1944, and noted, "Perhaps this is the last Thursday."[28] On August 13, he went for a final walk along the Seine with his mistress, Sophie. The following day he left Paris. Two weeks later, Allied troops entered the city, but somehow the Thursday salon survived. Florence was lucky: many Frenchwomen had their heads shaved and were publicly humiliated for courting Germans. During the days of the insurrection in Paris, she was apparently able to distract attention from her eclectic circle of friends by making a donation to the Forces Françaises de l'Intérieur, the united resistance movement.[29] Some of her French guests, though, were temporarily absent: Benoit was jailed for six months, while Jouhandeau went into hiding for several months before agreeing to face interrogation. For others, the lunches soon resumed, now with occasional American guests, as if the war had been no more than a passing storm. In late 1945, Heller received a letter that, he recalled, read, "Come quickly, the Thursdays await you."[30] It was signed by Florence, Paulhan, Léautaud, Jouhandeau and Arland.

Before Florence could turn the page, however, she had the tricky job of explaining why she had invested in a Nazi-financed bank in Monaco during the weeks before the Allied landings in southern France on August 15, 1944. When interrogated on the subject by a French investigating magistrate in March 1945, she said in sworn testimony that she was blackmailed into becoming a partner in the newly constituted Banque Charles.[31] If she had refused, she said, her husband's companies would have had to pay a far larger sum to the Aerobank, a Luftwaffe-controlled bank that was behind the Banque Charles. Given the expectation of an Allied invasion of the Riviera, she also feared for the safety of her husband—"67 years old and in delicate health"—in Juan-les-Pins. As part of the agreement, she said, her husband and her sister were promised refuge in Monaco, a supposedly neutral principality. She added that she sent 5 million francs, her share of the bank's capital of 80 million francs,* only once she had confirmation that Frank and Isabelle were in Monaco. Florence noted, "Had I acted freely and with a pecuniary interest, would I have committed the folly of interesting myself in a German bank at a moment when no one, neither in Europe nor America, believed any more in a German victory? I was obliged and forced to invest these funds, I paid a kind of ransom to the enemy, and I am certain, that by doing so, I fulfilled my duty towards my husband; I had then and still have today the conviction that I did nothing against the interests of the Allies." And with that, it seemed, the investigation was over.

But three years later, with the discovery of new documents revealing a far more complex operation, the case was reopened. A fresh report by the prosecutor's office of the Département de la Seine, dated September 20, 1948, said that Johannès Charles, a Swiss banker, obtained a license to open a bank in Monaco from the enclave's ruler, Prince Louis II, in 1943.[32] From the beginning, Karl Schaeffer, the Paris representative of the Reichsbank, was involved in what was planned as a German bank controlled by the Aerobank disguised as an international bank working in a neutral country. The report said the bank's purpose was not to help the German war effort but, rather, to channel German money abroad in anticipation of a Nazi defeat in the war. Along with Florence, the other investors were a German banker by the name of Gaussebeck and a French Fascist, Guillaume Lecesne, although both were front men for other interests. Documents also showed that Prince Louis expressed willingness to participate in the bank and that Schaeffer and Charles met Frank Gould in Nice on August 11, four days before the Allied landings. At that point, the report confirmed, only Charles and Florence had deposited their share of the bank's capital. The Allied landings sank the project.

---

*In 1944, 80 million francs was worth around $1.6 million, equivalent to close to $20 million in 2010 dollars.

After this new investigation, the prosecutor's office again decided not to press charges, but it seemed unconvinced that Florence had acted under duress. Its conclusion was harsh: "But this Franco-American appears to have enjoyed singular protections during the occupation, and if it is not certain that she committed the crime of intelligence with the enemy, it is certain that we have no reason to congratulate her for her attitude."

Florence herself never wavered in insisting that everything she did was to protect her husband. In any event, by the late 1940s she was again the reigning patroness of the Paris literary scene. Although she now spent more time in the Côte d'Azur, her literary lunches continued in her 16th arrondissement apartment. Then, after her husband's death, in 1956, she moved into an apartment in the Hôtel Meurice overlooking the Tuileries Gardens, where she now held court on Thursdays. As before, she remained loyal to her old friends, like Jouhandeau and Léautaud, financing their publications and using her influence to promote favored candidates for election to the Académie Française. In 1963, when it was Paulhan's turn to become an *immortel,* he scribbled at the top of his acceptance speech: "This little speech for Florence, who does what she wants with me, even making me an academician."[33] A few years later, when Jünger translated Léautaud's wartime memoirs, *In Memoriam,* he dedicated the book to Florence. Younger writers, too, were in her debt, among them Alain Robbe-Grillet and Françoise Sagan. She also created numerous literary prizes, including the Max Jacob Poetry Prize, named after the Jewish poet who died at Drancy in March 1944. The United States named her a commander of the Veterans of Foreign Wars in 1954, and she was appointed a Chevalier of the Légion d'Honneur in 1961. Since her death in 1983, thanks to her legacy, the Florence Gould Foundation has continued to play a central role in Franco-American cultural relations. Over the years, Florence's wartime salon and her questionable choice of friends have been quietly forgotten.

"On the Side of Life"

IN THE END, even if writers refused to accept the occupation, what were their options? Since it was evident that the Nazis would not be driven out by the power of the pen, many anti-Fascist writers felt the best strategy was simply to provide the French with some intelligent diversion. At the same time, given their prestige in France, at least some writers felt honor-bound to resist, but how? Until Germany invaded the Soviet Union in June 1941, Communists found their hands largely tied by the Molotov-Ribbentrop Pact. France's most prestigious writers were also hardly of an age—André Gide was seventy-one, Paul Valéry sixty-nine—or physical condition to engage in active warfare. Even putting out clandestine newspapers was dangerous, and sometimes fatal, as the leaders of the Musée de l'Homme network and the cofounders of *L'Université Libre* and *La Pensée Libre* discovered in 1942. Initially, then, resistance by writers was more of a process than a sudden decision.

Yet, gradually, more and more chose to be "on the side of life," as Jean Paulhan put it, answering complaints that *résistants* were dying in vain. "You can squeeze a bee in your hand until it suffocates," he wrote in February 1944. "It won't suffocate without stinging you. That's precious little, you will say. But if it didn't sting you, bees would have been extinct a long time ago." Many writers chose to sting with words, some did so in the armed resistance, a few gave their lives for their beliefs. When the liberation came, the world of letters had its heroes and martyrs, too.

What few were willing to do, though, was to abandon writing. The majority of writers also wanted to continue publishing, whether out of economic necessity or vanity or perhaps believing they were keeping alight the flame of French literature. Among non-Fascist writers alone, those who gave their manuscripts to publishers authorized by the Germans ranged from the poets Aragon and Éluard to the novelists Colette and Camus. Some distinguished between publishing books, which was considered acceptable, and writing for the collaborationist press, where their names might appear alongside pro-German or anti-Semitic columns. Nonetheless, a few wrote for weeklies like *Comoedia* and *Gringoire* because they needed the money. Others had salaries—Paulhan and, later, Camus worked at Éditions Gallimard; Guéhenno, Sartre and Beauvoir taught in lycées; and Desnos was a journalist for the collaborationist daily *Aujourd'hui*—and they, too, wrote books for publication. Even the most distinguished names of the literary establishment were slow to show leadership. Gide and Valéry provided texts for early editions of Drieu La Rochelle's *Nouvelle Revue Française,* while Mauriac published *La Pharisienne* in 1941. Yet, by the end of the war, most of these writers—Claudel, Colette and Beauvoir were exceptions—were identified with the resistance.

One who stood by his early decision not to publish in any officially approved outlet was Guéhenno, an essayist who taught at the Lycée Henri IV. He wrote only for the clandestine newspaper *Les Lettres Françaises* and the underground publishing house Éditions de Minuit. In his *Journal des années noires,* which was published in 1946, he was deeply disapproving of those who published under their own names. "Why write now? It is impossible to question how ridiculous it is to pursue such a personal profession. These times call for modesty."[1] He went on: "Now is the time to write for nothing, for pleasure. Here we are, reduced to silence, to solitude, but perhaps also to seriousness. Whether our cell is to be filled with light depends entirely on ourselves."[2] He also worried that the idea of keeping

French literature alive played into the German hands. "What," he asked, "should we think of those writers who, to be sure not to displease the occupying authority, decide to write about everything except for the one thing the French are thinking about. Even more, those who out of cowardice favor this authority's strategy of making everything in France appear as it was before." Surprisingly, he did not lose hope. "But French thought in fact continues. Against them, despite them. The republic of letters holds its ground, after all, quite well. The 'collaborators' are rare, a few old unsatisfied troubadours, always eager for glory or money."[3]

In truth, the collaborators were not so rare, but France's best writers were not among them. Further, with relatively few exceptions, the best stayed in France. Georges Bernanos, a conservative, had already immigrated to South America in 1938, and he spent the war years in Brazil, where he edited a pro–Free French journal. Benjamin Péret, a Surrealist poet, was guided out of France by Varian Fry and ended up living in Mexico until 1948. Jules Romains, a writer and poet who was elected to the Académie Française in 1946, went first to the United States, but then also chose to live in Mexico.

The exiled writer with the most tormented relationship with France, however, was Saint-Exupéry. Dismayed by France's humiliation but unwilling to join de Gaulle in London, he went instead to the United States, where he wrote *Pilote de guerre* and *Le Petit prince*. But it is a short text called *Lettre à un otage* (Letter to a Hostage), addressed to a Jewish friend he believed to be trapped in France, that most reveals his anguish. A small-format book of just seventy-two pages, it was published in French by Brentano's in 1943, with a first printing of one hundred copies. In it, Saint-Exupéry recalls his own departure from Lisbon by sea and imagines occupied France as a silent boat, its lights extinguished, exposed to the perils of the sea. "That night," he says, "he who haunts my memory is 50 years old. He is sick. He is Jewish. How will he survive the German terror?"[4] Later, Saint-Exupéry addresses this friend: "If I fight again, I will fight a little for you. I need you so I can better believe in the coming of this smile. I need to help you to live." He adds, "You who are so French, I feel you twice threatened with death, as a Frenchman and as a Jew."[5] Finally, when the writer-aviator speaks of the entire French population as "forty million hostages," he seems to be announcing his decision to return to Europe to fight the Germans.

Gide, too, left France. He regretted offering an excerpt from his journal to the collaborationist *NRF,* but he was not made to be a resistance leader. In May 1942, he moved to Tunisia, which, although Vichy-ruled, offered him a degree of detachment from the war. Then, six months later, after the Allies occupied Algeria and Morocco and the Germans and Italians took over Tunisia, Gide was given a real taste of enemy occupation. Finally, in May 1943, the Allies freed Tunisia and he, too, was free to move to Algeria, where he sponsored a new literary review, *L'Arche.* He dined there on June 26 with General de Gaulle. "I shall not find it hard to hang my hopes on him," he noted that same evening.[6]

Gide's close friend Roger Martin du Gard, the Nobel literature laureate in 1937, opted for still greater silence. In 1940, having finally published the epilogue of his best-known work, the eight-volume family epic *Les Thibault,* he moved first to Nice, then to Cap d'Antibes. There, he devoted himself to a new novel, *Le Lieutenant-colonel de Maumort,* but he published nothing until after the liberation. For his part, Mauriac, who stopped writing for any German-approved publisher after 1941, was by 1942 engaged in the intellectual resistance.

André Malraux also chose to withdraw from public life. After his prewar campaigns against Fascism and his support for the Republicans in the Spanish civil war, he had come to personify the *intellectuel engagé.* But in 1941 and 1942, he turned down several invitations to join the resistance, arguing that only the Allied armies could free France. Instead, he spent much of the war in a quiet corner of the Côte d'Azur, publishing one book, *La Lutte avec l'ange,** in Switzerland and following his half brother Roland into the armed resistance only in early 1944. Working with British agents in the Dordogne, Malraux assumed the name of "Colonel Berger" and made several secret visits to Paris. On July 22, while driving with a British officer, Major George Hiller, Malraux was arrested and jailed in Toulouse, but he was freed by resistance fighters one month later, just as the Germans were withdrawing from the city. After the liberation of Paris, he compensated for his late arrival in the resistance by joining the French army.

A handful of writers were nonetheless ready to act, helping British soldiers to flee France and collecting intelligence to be sent to Lon-

---

*This was Malraux's last novel, republished in France in 1948 as *Les Noyers de l'Altenburg* (The Walnut Trees of Altenburg).

don. As a professional group, though, they were in need of leadership. Two men emerged to provide it: Paulhan, the literary critic who as the longtime prewar editor of the *NRF* knew most French writers, and Aragon, the Communist poet who broadened the movement by reaching outside Communist ranks. Other figures emerged, some as activists, others as symbols, but these two men played pivotal roles, recruiting new members, serving as points of communication and remaining coolheaded in difficult moments.

Their lives could hardly have been more different. Aragon, who at first struggled to reconnect with his Communist colleagues in the occupied zone, stayed in Nice until the Germans took over the south; he then hid for a year in Lyon and, again forced to flee, he and his Russian-born Jewish wife, Elsa Triolet, spent the final months of the occupation under the assumed names of Élisabeth and Louis-Lucien Andrieux in Saint-Donat-sur-l'Herbasse, fifty miles south of Lyon. Throughout, he wrote prolifically and, from mid-1941, remained in constant touch with fellow resisters in both Paris and southern France. Paulhan, in contrast, lived a double existence. An elegant intellectual in his mid-fifties, he was jailed in May 1941 after the Gestapo discovered his involvement in the Musée de l'Homme network, but he was freed thanks to Drieu La Rochelle and promptly resumed his resistance activities. At the same time, he maintained an aura of respectability: he lived with his wife on the rue des Arènes in the 5th arrondissement, he went to work daily at Gallimard and he was a regular at Florence Gould's Thursday lunches. "I admire Jean Paulhan's gift to lighten life all around him," Guéhenno, who knew of his resistance work, wrote in his journal. "What a delightful companion and how he would have helped me to live in this prison."[7] Even Gerhard Heller, who befriended many French writers, described Paulhan as "my master" in his memoir.

But if Paulhan and Aragon became the pillars of the intellectual resistance, the idea of organizing writers came even earlier from Jacques Decour, a Paris lycée teacher who, with George Politzer and Jacques Solomon, founded *L'Université Libre* and *La Pensée Libre,* both sponsored by the Communist Party. These newspapers were aimed specifically at academic and intellectual elites. In February 1941, with its ninety-six pages giving it the appearance of a traditional literary journal, *La Pensée Libre* called on them "to revive the authentic traditions of our national culture in order to lead, along with writers, thinkers, scholars and artists of all occupied countries, the great battle of enlightenment against obscurantism, which is the intellectual climate of the New Europe." To carry this flag, the Communist Party then formed the Front National des Écrivains, or National Writers' Front. But despite its grand name, it had almost no members, with several non-Communist writers refusing to write— even anonymously—for La Pensée Libre. Conversely, the Communist Party was not happy with Aragon's decision to publish poetry under his own name, in the belief that he should channel his energy into subversive work. Nonetheless, Aragon's first important initiative after the Soviet Union entered the war was to convince Decour to reach outside Communist ranks. And, with this in mind, during a secret trip to Paris in late June 1941, he put Decour in touch with Paulhan.

This bore fruit a few months later when Decour, Paulhan, Mauriac and several others cofounded the Comité National des Écrivains, or CNE, to represent all anti-Fascist writers. While Aragon agreed to set up a southern branch in the unoccupied zone, in Paris Decour took responsibility for publishing a new writers' newspaper, Les Lettres Françaises, and began writing the first issue single-handedly. But on February 19, 1942, after the second—and last—issue of La Pensée Libre was printed, Decour was arrested by French police and was handed over to the Germans. He was shot on May 30, one week after Solomon and Politzer. The Communist Party passed the job of putting out Les Lettres Françaises to a man known as Claude Morgan, the pseudonym used by the son of Georges Lecomte, a member of the Académie Française. As Lecomte, he worked at the Louvre looking after provincial museums. As Morgan, he had to start from scratch, since Decour's sister had destroyed all the texts Decour had prepared. Further, with no contact with Paulhan and the fledgling CNE, Morgan wrote the first six-page issue of Les Lettres Françaises entirely on his own. Printed on a mimeograph machine in September 1942, it opened with the manifesto of the Front National des Écrivains and included an homage to Morgan's predecessor: "Adieu à Jacques Decour."

Soon help came from Édith Thomas, an anti-Fascist writer who had just returned to Paris from the unoccupied zone. In the October 1942 issue of Les Lettres Françaises, also duplicated rustically on a mimeograph machine, Thomas wrote the main editorial, "Criez la Vérité" (Shout Out the Truth). In it, addressing the literary community, she described seeing a deportation train crowded with Jews, including children:* "The thin arms of children clung to the bars. A hand sticking out waved like a leaf in a storm. When the train slowed down, voices cried out, 'Mummy.' And nothing replied except the grinding of axles. You can then say that art has no country. You can then say that the artist should know how to isolate himself in his ivory tower, to do his job, nothing but his job. Our job? To be dignified, one must tell the truth. And the truth is total or it doesn't exist." Silence, she warned her fellow writers, meant complicity in the Nazi crimes.[8]

As crucially, Thomas introduced Morgan to Paulhan and other CNE members, and the November issue carried a statement signed by the Comité National des Écrivains. By early 1943, Morgan was able to publish poems by Éluard and Aragon and articles by Paulhan, Sartre, Michel Leiris and Jacques Debû-Bridel, a conservative nationalist once close to L'Action Française. Finally, in October 1943, after printing nine issues on mimeograph machines, with the words "Founder: Jacques Decour, shot by the Germans" handwritten under *"Les Lettres Françaises,"* Morgan found a clandestine printer willing to take on the job. The next four issues were four pages each. In March 1944 the newspaper expanded to eight pages and incorporated *L'Écran Français, La Scène Française* and *Le Musicien d'Aujourd'hui,* representing the cinema, theater and music resistance groups. Some articles were even laid out by *résistants* working in the German-language *Pariser Zeitung.* Distribution of the monthly involved mailing copies in unmarked envelopes, placing other copies in apartment mailboxes, leaving some in cafés and circulating some among friends. The print run of four thousand in 1943 jumped to some twelve thousand in the months before the liberation.

Les Lettres Françaises became the CNE's principal raison d'être, but its members also met to exchange news and gossip, to debate their responses to new books, to plan denunciation of Fascist writers and to prepare for the end of the occupation. Morgan, Thomas, Aragon and Éluard were among its Communist members, but it also included moderates like Mauriac and Paulhan. Inevitably, a certain amateurism prevailed. Mauriac's son Claude recalled a secret meeting at his parents' house attended by Mauriac, Paulhan, Guéhenno and others. "With the air of inquisitors, they were drawing up—'for victory day'—lists of those to be banned. Jean Paulhan said (with a cer-

---

*The first Jewish children were deported after the *rafle du Vél'd'Hiv'* in July 1942.

tain irony) that there was no need to change the law, since the existing crime of 'flagrant treason' would allow them to judge the accused
quickly and without investigation."[9]

The committee—or at least a handful of its twenty-two members
in Paris—would occasionally meet in Paulhan's office at Gallimard,
literally next door to that of Drieu La Rochelle. If just two or three
writers needed to confer, La Closerie des Lilas, a restaurant on the
corner of the boulevard du Montparnasse, was also a favorite. Then,
from February 1943, the *comité* began meeting regularly in Thomas's
apartment at 15 rue Pierre-Nicole, near the Val-de-Grâce church, in
the 5th arrondissement. The appeal of this address was that the
building had no concierge, although the writers nonetheless took a
risk by meeting in the same place every time. And they took other
risks. When talking by telephone, they were meant to use codes, but
Mauriac later admitted that he would forget the codes and wind up
naming names. On one occasion, Thomas recalled, all twenty-two
members in Paris came to her apartment, parking no fewer than fifteen bicycles below it. She begged her friends to be more cautious.

By 1943, many of the writers of the CNE were also participating
in an extraordinary venture of clandestine book publishing. Its gene-
sis was almost accidental. In late 1941, Jean Bruller, a journalist and
satirical illustrator who chose to work as a carpenter during the
occupation, read Ernst Jünger's *Jardins et routes* (Gardens and Highways), his journal of the conquest of France. Impressed by Jünger's
sympathetic portrayal of France, Bruller wrote a novella, which he
called *Le Silence de la mer* (The Silence of the Sea) and signed Vercors,* taking the name from a mountainous region of southeastern
France where he had once convalesced. His plan was to have it published by his friend Pierre Lescure, a secret British agent who was in
contact with *La Pensée Libre.*

When the Germans confiscated the newspaper's printing press
(and arrested its editors), Lescure and Bruller instead formed their
own underground publishing house, appropriately called Éditions
de Minuit, or Midnight Publishing. They found a printer, Claude
Oudeville, who was able to print Vercors's novella, albeit only eight
pages at a time, while Bruller turned to a childhood friend, Yvonne
Paraf, to bind the books by hand. The first 350 copies of *Le Silence*

---

*Later in the war, the maquis of Vercors would become one of the strongest rural
resistance forces.

de la mer were ready in February 1942, but distribution was suspended when Lescure was forced into hiding. Finally, in September 1942, the first underground book of the occupation was released. Copies reached London, where Cyril Connolly translated the story into English; further copies were made and sent to France by RAF transport planes delivering weapons to the resistance.

Le Silence de la mer was striking because its tone in no way resembled the anti-German and anti-Vichy drumbeating of *Les Lettres Françaises*. The story is told in the first person by a man who lives with his niece in an unidentified provincial town. Billeted in their house is Werner von Ebrennac, a well-educated German officer descended from French Huguenot exiles. Each evening he talks to them, but they remain silent. He says he has always admired France from afar, but on his deathbed his father had told him, "You must never go to France until you can enter with boots and helmet."[10] He apologizes, insisting on his love for France. On subsequent visits, he reveals that he is a composer; he peruses the house library, admiring Shakespeare, Dante, Cervantes, Molière, Voltaire; he recounts the tale of the Beauty and the Beast; he recites from *Macbeth;* he talks about Bach. Often he addresses the niece, to whom he seems attracted. And each visit ends with: "I wish you a good night."[11]

One day the officer announces that he must travel to Paris. Upon his return, he asks them to forget everything he has said during the previous months. In Paris, he met German soldiers who felt different about France. They told him, "We're not mad or stupid: we have the opportunity to destroy France and we will. Not only its power, also its soul. Above all, its soul. Its soul is the biggest threat. This is our job at this moment: Don't fool yourself, my dear. We will corrupt it with our smiles and tenderness. We will turn it into a groveling bitch."[12] The officer then discloses that, disgusted by what he heard, he has asked to be transferred to the Russian Front and will be leaving the following morning. Once again, he wishes his hosts good night. Then, looking intently at the young woman, he adds, "Adieu." Long seconds later, breaking her silence for the first and last time, she whispers, "Adieu."*

Le Silence de la mer raised some difficult issues, notably whether silence was the proper response to the occupation and whether a

---

*By coincidence, this story echoes that of *Dolce,* the second volume of Irène Némirovsky's unfinished *Suite française,* which also portrays a "good" German officer billeted in a private home in a provincial town.

German officer should be portrayed sympathetically in print. But, while not knowing the real name of its author, the Free French Forces in London approved of the book, and *Les Lettres Françaises* hailed it as "the most moving, the most deeply human book that we have had the opportunity to read since the beginnings of the German occupation."[13]

Encouraged by the response, Bruller decided to publish more books through Éditions de Minuit. Yvonne Paraf, who kept Vercors's identity secret until the end of the war, crossed the demarcation line into the unoccupied zone to collect the manuscript of *À travers le désastre* by the exiled philosopher Jacques Maritain, who had already published it in the United States as *France, My Country, Through the Disaster.* This appeared under the Éditions de Minuit imprint in October 1942. Then, early in 1943, Bruller made contact with Paulhan and suddenly gained access to Paulhan's entire resistance circle. This was reflected in the third book, *Chroniques interdites* (Banned Chronicles), published in April 1943, which included a tribute by Paulhan to Jacques Decour. Over the next sixteen months, another twenty-one small books were published under a variety of pseudonyms. Triolet published her novella *Les Amants d'Avignon* as Laurent Daniel; Mauriac offered an essay, *Le Cahier noir,* as Forez; Debû-Bridel paid tribute to English literature in *Angleterre (d'Alcuin à Huxley),** under the name of Argonne; Guéhenno published *Dans la prison,* adapted from his private journal, as Cévennes; and Morgan published a novella, *La Marque de l'homme,* as Mortagne. John Steinbeck's short novel about occupation and resistance in an unnamed country, *The Moon Is Down,* was also issued by Éditions de Minuit shortly before the liberation, as *Nuits noires.* It was described as the first complete French translation to distinguish it from *Nuits sans lune,* an edition published in Switzerland in 1943 in which key sections had been eliminated.

Poetry, however, proved best suited to the conditions of the occupation. A poem required little paper, it was easily remembered and recited, it could be copied by hand and left on a café table, it could be broadcast by the BBC and, above all, it carried a sharp emotional punch. Further, resistance poetry enjoyed a monopoly since no col-

*The title refers to Alcuin of York, an eighth-century English poet and theologian, and to Aldous Huxley.

laborationist writer ever tried to express his Fascism in verse. Aragon was particularly skilled at publishing poems in which resistance messages were disguised as literary, historical or lyrical references. "Contraband in literature is the art of awakening forbidden sentiments with authorized words," he explained after the war.[14]

Another poet, Pierre Seghers, kept quality poetry alive in the unoccupied zone through his review, *Poésie '40,* which changed its date with each year. Edited at his home in Villeneuve-lès-Avignon, outside Avignon, it was subject to Vichy censorship yet enjoyed considerable freedom. Seghers made a point of including poems by French prisoners of war mailed from German camps and of sending copies of *Poésie* to these camps. He later recalled being moved by a letter he received in early 1942 in which a POW recounted how, inspired by *Poésie,* he and his friends put out a monthly poetry review in their prison camp. "Your review does me good," the letter writer said. "That's all. All French people should know the place that those of us who have nothing give to poetry, and the faith we all have in the future of French poetry." He ended: *"Monsieur Seghers, courage, courage, courage, courage."* The following year, Seghers devoted an entire issue of *Poésie '43* to *Poètes Prisonniers.*

Other important outlets for poetry were *Le Figaro*'s literary supplement and René Tavernier's *Confluences,* both in unoccupied Lyon; *Les Cahiers du Sud* in Marseille; and Max-Pol Fouchet's *Fontaine* in Algiers. In Paris, *Les Cahiers d'Art* managed to combine intellectual resistance—its office on the rue du Dragon in Saint-Germain-des-Prés was often used to edit *Les Lettres Françaises*—with publishing poetry, both privately and with German approval.

Scores of poets emerged during the occupation, but Aragon and Éluard, both in their mid-forties, were the most prolific and the most influential. And thanks to the occupation, they even patched up a bitter quarrel dating back to 1933, when Éluard (along with André Breton) was expelled from the Communist Party and Aragon was drummed out of the Surrealist movement. Until then, Éluard and Aragon were the leading Surrealist poets. In contrast, their verse during the occupation was clear, direct and emotive. The principal difference was between their signed poems and those published anonymously or under a pseudonym; those that passed German censorship evoked the deep melancholy and malaise of the times, while their resistance poems were often violent in denouncing the Nazis and their French vassals. Both men were also lucky never to be jailed,* not least because their individual styles could be recognized in some of their clandestine poems.

Aragon was the first to bring poetry to Éditions de Minuit with a raging verse epic called *Le Musée Grevin*. But by then, as part of his "clandestine literature," he had already published one collection with Gallimard in Paris, *Le Crève-coeur,* in 1941 and another in Switzerland, *Les Yeux d'Elsa* (Elsa's Eyes), in 1942. In "Les Lilas et les roses" (The Lilacs and the Roses), written immediately after France's defeat in June 1940 and published in *Le Crève-coeur,* Aragon contrasts spring with the pain of defeat. It opens:

> Oh month of blossomings month of metamorphoses
> May that was without clouds and June stabbed
> I will never forget the lilacs and the roses
> Nor those whom spring has folded in her arms.

The poem then evokes soldiers, tanks, panic and death, and continues:

> All is quiet The enemy rests in the shadows
> We learn this evening of the surrender of Paris
> I will never forget the lilacs and the roses
> Nor the two loves that we have lost.

In "La Nuit d'exil" (The Night of Exile), Aragon imagines faraway Paris:

> We will never again see that distant paradise
> Les Halles l'Opéra la Concorde and the Louvre
> Those nights you remember when the night would conceal us
> The night that comes from the heart and has no morning.

As the occupation advanced, this tone of resignation was replaced by more combative verse. In 1943, Aragon published "Ballade de celui qui chanta dans les supplices" (Ballad of He Who Sang on the

---

*Aragon and Triolet were briefly detained while crossing the demarcation line in June 1941, but they were not properly identified and after ten days were allowed to travel on to Paris.

Torture Rack) in *Les Lettres Françaises* and dedicated it to Gabriel Péri, a young Communist shot in December 1941 after refusing to reveal resistance secrets.

> And if it had to be done again
> I would take the same road
> The voice rising from the chains
> Speaks to the men of tomorrow.

While Aragon the poet was writing prolifically, Aragon the Communist was busily organizing doctors and lawyers, as well as writers, into resistance groups in the south. From February 1943 to March 1944, he also put out his own clandestine monthly, *Les Étoiles,* which began with a call for intellectuals to unite and later informed readers about broader resistance activities. It, too, occasionally included poems by Aragon, under different pseudonyms.

Éluard was slower to embrace resistance, with *Livre ouvert* (Open Book), a collection published privately by *Cahiers d'Art* in 1941, reflecting his gloom. He also published some poems for Seghers's *Poésie '41.* One typical verse read: "I don't hear the monsters speak / I know them they've said everything." Then, in June 1942, *Fontaine,* in Algiers, published what would become the best-known French poem of the war years, "Liberté." If it resembles a love poem, it is because Éluard first wrote it for his wife, Nusch, under the title of "Une Seule pensée" (A Single Thought). And it was authorized for publication only because Vichy's censors in Algiers did not read the full poem. In twenty-one four-line stanzas, Éluard describes the delights of life, from his school days to his travels, from moments of sickness to others of love. And, as celebration, he ends twenty of the verses with the words "I write your name." But in *Fontaine*'s text, instead of naming Nusch, he changed the last word of the poem:

> And through the power of one word
> I restart my life
> I was born to know you
> To name you—Freedom.

Three months later, Éluard included "Liberté" in a collection of poems published privately in Paris. More importantly, Fouchet sent a copy of the poem to London, where it was printed on single sheets by the Gaullist *Revue du Monde Libre;* the RAF then dropped tens of thousands of these over occupied France.

In late 1942, having returned to the Communist Party, Éluard joined the CNE and soon afterward wrote an homage to Paris for *Les Lettres Françaises* called "Courage." It opens:

> Paris is cold Paris is hungry
> Paris no longer eats chestnuts in the street
> Paris is wearing yesterday's old clothes
> Paris sleeps standing airless in the *métro.*

In April 1943, Bruller recruited Éluard to prepare Éditions de Minuit's first poetry anthology, *L'Honneur des poètes* (The Honor of Poets). Among its twenty-two authors were Aragon, Seghers, Thomas, Tavernier, Bruller and Éluard himself, as well as three POWs, all using pseudonyms. In an unsigned preface, Éluard wrote, "In face of the peril confronting humanity today, we poets have come together from all corners of French territory. Under threat, poetry once again regroups, it finds anew a precise meaning to its latent violence, it cries out, accuses, waits."[15] In May 1944, while now spending much of his time in hiding, Éluard was able to edit another collection, *Europe,* for Éditions de Minuit; it included poems by many of the same *résistants* as well as those written by poets in other occupied countries.

One unusual book published by Bruller was *33 sonnets composés au secret* (33 Sonnets Composed in Solitary Confinement), attributed to Jean Noir. The poems had, in fact, been written by Jean Cassou, the modern art curator who had fled Paris after the Germans broke up the Musée de l'Homme network in 1941. He continued his resistance activities in Toulouse, where he was arrested by French police in December 1941. He was released in February 1942, but soon afterward returned to jail until early 1943, when he could finally rejoin the resistance. It was during his first stretch behind bars that he composed these sonnets in his head, memorizing them until the last few days of his detention, when he was finally given pencil and paper. "For those two months I had composed half a sonnet a night," he recalled years later.

In May 1944, Cassou's sonnets, dedicated to "My companions of

prisons," were published by Éditions de Minuit. The lengthy introduction by Aragon, as François La Colère, added drama to Cassou's
achievement: "On this night when the prisoner absolutely refuses to
acknowledge hunger, thirst, cold, the pain of indignity, the humiliation of man by man, the poem is his great act of defiance thrown at
the contempt that he suffers. The poem is his superhuman effort to
remain a human being, to reach those regions of mind and heart
which everything around him denies and debases."[16]

While later proclaimed as "sonnets of the resistance," the poems
are in fact more sonnets than resistance, reflecting the scattered
memories, images and thoughts coming to a man in prison in the
solitude of the night. In one sonnet, the sounds he hears mix with
those he remembers.

> Life's distant sounds, celestial, tucked away;
> Horns hooting, children going home to tea,
> The church bells pealing for a festal day,
> Cars blindly heading for infinity.[17]

In another, he imagines the joy of poets returning to earth:

> They'll recognise in masks maniacal,
> Dancing the farandole in carnival,
> Their finest verse, free from the agony
> That gave it birth: and then, in happiness,
> As evening falls they shall depart, and bless
> Long love and glory, wind, and blood, and sea.[18]

Paris, too, is remembered, "her blood-draped monuments, her sky /
at sundown, aircraft-grey: all this again / I've seen again."[19] The
occupation itself is suggested only when he anticipates that "days are
reborn at daybreak."[20]

> When hate and scorn have shattered every wall,
> Heart close to breaking, what remains at all
> But to hate hate, scorn scorn, no less?[21]

The lyrical quality of many of these sonnets led Henri Dutilleux, Darius Milhaud and Manuel Rosenthal each to set one to music. Cassou

himself survived the war. Badly wounded in a clash with a German unit during the liberation of Toulouse, he recovered and returned to Paris to run the Musée d'Art Moderne until 1965.

Robert Desnos was unluckier. Born in 1900, he was caught up in the turmoil of the Surrealist movement before being expelled by Breton in 1929 for, among other things, refusing to join the Communist Party. But he remained on the left, supporting the Republicans in the Spanish civil war and horrified by the rise of the Nazis. Mobilized in September 1939, he evaded capture in June 1940 and returned to Paris to work on the newspaper *Aujourd'hui.* After its editor was jailed for refusing to attack Jews, Desnos stayed on under its new Fascist editor, Georges Suarez, focusing on literary issues and avoiding politics. But *Aujourd'hui* also proved an important listening post: after Desnos joined the Agir resistance group in 1942, he was well placed to pass on information gathered in the newsroom. He also continued to write poetry, contributing a poem called "Le Veilleur du Pont-au-Change" (The Watchman of the Pont-au-Change) to the collection *Europe.* In one verse, he salutes the resistance:

> Hail to those who sleep
> After tough clandestine labor,
> Printers, bomb-carriers, derailers, arsonists,
> Distributors of tracts, contrabandists, messengers,
> Hail to all you who resist, children of twenty with spring-like
>   smiles,
> Men as old as bridges, robust, portraits of the seasons,
> I hail you at the dawn of a new morning.

But by the time *Europe* came out, in May 1944, Desnos was in a German concentration camp. In his journal, Galtier-Boissière recalled telephoning Desnos and his wife, Youki, on the morning of February 22, 1944. "Youki Desnos cuts me off brusquely: 'Call me in 15 minutes, will you.' A quarter of an hour later, she tells me with an upset voice: 'The German police came in when you were calling. They've taken Robert.' "[22] The artistic community was mobilized to obtain his release, with Youki even winning the promise of Heller's help. At one point, Desnos wrote to Youki that he still hoped to avoid deportation: "I had a close call with the last departure and I sure hope not to be on the next. I am here with very good and pleasant people: Communists, Gaullists, royalists, priests, nobles, peasants. It's an extraordinary hotchpotch."[23] But the collaborationist press, led by Laubreaux, continued to campaign against him, accusing him of being a Communist. In late April, he was put on board a train convoy heading east. In the year that followed, he was repeatedly moved between camps until he reached Terezin, in Czechoslovakia. It was there that he died of typhus on June 8, 1945, one month after V-E Day.

René Char took a different path. A former rugby player who became a Surrealist poet, he was just thirty-three when Paris fell. But instead of returning there after he was demobilized, he chose to contemplate his options in his birthplace, L'Isle-sur-la-Sorgue, east of Avignon. He quickly decided to continue writing but not to publish. "My reasons are dictated to me partly by the rather unbelievable and detestable exhibitionism that too many intellectuals have shown since June 1940," he wrote to his old friend Francis Curel.* In another letter to Curel, Char hinted at the need to go further: "True, poems should be written, the anger and sobs of our deadly mood should be traced with silent ink, but we should not stop at that. To do so would be pathetically inadequate."[24] In December 1940, after French police searched Char's house, he was warned that he would soon be arrested. In February 1941, he traveled to Marseille to meet Breton, Wilfredo Lam and other Surrealists who were waiting at Villa Air-Bel for visas to leave France, but he never thought of following them.

Instead, he moved to the safety of Céreste, a mountain village thirty miles to the east of L'Isle-sur-la-Sorgue. It was there, shielded by the silence of his neighbors, that he gradually built up a resistance group, first in nearby villages, then farther afield, eventually linking his units to the Armée Secrète, the Secret Army, which unified some resistance groups in 1943. By then, his maquis had been swollen by the arrival of young men escaping compulsory work in Germany. Char was put in charge of the region's parachute-landing section, which meant collecting, storing and distributing weapons, money and documents dropped by the RAF. Soon, his group had grown to some two thousand men and, as the SS and the *milice* stepped up their activities in the south, his fighters saw more and more action. In July 1944, he was flown to Algiers to help prepare the landing of

*Curel was himself arrested in July 1943 and deported to Austria, but he survived the war.

Allied forces along France's southern coast. One month later, he guided American troops to liberate the area where his forces had been resisting.

Throughout the war, while cut off from the intellectual resistance in Paris, Char kept notes, published in 1946 as *Feuillets d'Hypnos* (Leaves of Hypnos),* which included aphorisms, prose-poetry and straightforward description. His aphorisms were born of the resistance struggle: "Acquiescence illuminates the face. Refusal gives it beauty" and "Eternity is hardly longer than life" and "The fruit is blind. It's the tree that can see" and "A man without faults is like a mountain without ravines. He doesn't interest me."[25] Char's most powerful notes refer to the combat itself, with particular poignancy on June 22, 1944, "a horrible day," when he witnessed the execution of one of his fighters, a twenty-three-year-old poet named Roger Bernard. "I had only to pull the trigger of my automatic rifle and he could be saved!" Char wrote, noting that the SS troops were unaware of his hidden fighters. "To the eyes all around me that implored me to give the signal to open fire, I responded no with my head." It was a dreadful decision to make, he said. "I did not give the signal because this village had to be saved *at all cost.* What is a village? One village like another? Perhaps he realized that, at the very last moment?"[26]

The Germans also killed Émile Cavagni, whom Char called "my best brother-in-arms," adding, "He carried his 45 years upright, like a tree of liberty. I loved him without effusion, without pointless gravity. Unshakeably."[27] Char's description of a resistance ambush was more brutal: "The small enemy column immediately retreated. Except for the machine-gunner, who had no time to become dangerous: his stomach exploded. The two cars allowed us to escape."[28]

Other intellectuals paid with their lives for their resistance. Jean Cavaillès, a philosopher who was thirty-six when war was declared, was captured by the Wehrmacht in June 1940 but managed to escape. While teaching in Clermont-Ferrand later that year, he met Emmanuel d'Astier de la Vigerie, a former naval intelligence officer, and together they formed a resistance group, Libération-Sud, and published a newspaper, *Libération.* When Cavaillès was assigned to teach at the Sorbonne in Paris, he formed Libération-Nord. The Gaullist

*In Greek mythology, Hypnos is the god of sleep. By taking this name, Char saw himself watching over the long night of the occupation.

resistance then ordered him to create an intelligence network across northern France, before sending him south again. In September 1942, he was arrested by French police, but he escaped three months later. As a measure of his stature, he was summoned to London to meet de Gaulle. On August 28, 1943, he was again arrested, this time in Paris. After being tortured and held in Fresnes and Compiègne, he was shot on February 17, 1944.

Jean Prévost, also in his late thirties in 1940, moved more slowly into armed resistance. A prolific writer who was working at *Paris-Soir* in Lyon, he was brought into the southern CNE by Aragon in 1942. He was briefly in the public spotlight when, thanks to Mauriac and Duhamel, he won the Académie Française's literature prize in 1943 for his doctoral thesis on Stendhal, *La Création chez Stendhal: Essai sur le métier d'écrire et la psychologie de l'écrivain.* But by then, under the nom de guerre of Capitaine Goderville, he was involved in the Vercors maquis in southeastern France. On August 1, 1944, he and four colleagues died fighting the Germans.

Two leading lights of the Paris intelligentsia, both Jews, also died as *résistants.* Marc Bloch, a brilliant historian who in 1929 cofounded the review *Annales d'histoire économique et sociale* with Lucien Febvre, insisted on joining the army in 1939 despite being fifty-three and the father of six children. After France fell, he wrote his analysis of the debacle, *L'Étrange défaite* (The Strange Defeat), which was published posthumously in 1946. After Vichy's first Statute on Jews, in October 1940, he was banned from teaching, but he appealed the order and was allowed to work in the unoccupied zone, first in Clermont-Ferrand, then in Montpellier. He also had a temporary falling-out with Febvre, who insisted on resuming publication of their review, which was possible only without Bloch's Jewish name appearing. After Germany took over the unoccupied zone, Bloch entered the resistance in the Lyon region with the Francs-Tireurs et Partisans group, which then joined the United Resistance Movements. On March 8, 1944, he was arrested by the Gestapo and tortured. On June 16, along with other *résistants,* Bloch was shot.

Also in his mid-fifties, Benjamin Crémieux was a literary critic and secretary-general of the French PEN Club in the interwar years. A striking figure with a long black beard, he appears in many photographs of writers of the era. He was also close to the prewar *NRF,* where in 1924 he published the first serious study of Proust, two years after the writer's death. Like Bloch, he sought refuge in the unoccupied zone before joining the Combat resistance group in 1943 under the nom de guerre of Lamy. Arrested by the French *milice* in Marseille on April 27, 1943, he was tortured by the Gestapo but revealed nothing about his group. Held successively in Drancy, Fresnes and Compiègne, he was deported to Buchenwald, where he died of exhaustion on April 14, 1944.

The maquis and other armed units hardly needed the encouragement of written words, but they quickly embraced "Le Chant des partisans" (The Song of the Partisans), a fiery poem put to music, which was soon being sung and whistled as the anthem of the resistance. It was written in London by two novelists, Joseph Kessel and his nephew Maurice Druon,* who had joined the Free French in 1942 and were working on propaganda broadcasts. In 1943, d'Astier de la Vigerie asked them for a song to unify the different resistance groups that otherwise had little in common. "D'Astier kept insisting and we kept replying, 'We're thinking,' " recounted Druon, who was elected to the Académie Française in 1966 and later became its *secrétaire-perpétuel.* "Then, one Sunday, we started writing. We had chosen a piece of music by Anna Marly, who was Russian and who had borrowed the tune from a Russian song. The resistance liked it immediately. The BBC played it. The RAF dropped copies of it."[29] Accompanied by a catchy motif, repeated so often that it became hard to forget, the song's four stanzas were designed to stir courage. In the first verse it warns:

> Tonight the enemy
> Will learn the price of blood
> And tears.

It then summons the fighters:

> Hey! Killers!
> To the bullet and the knife,
> Kill quickly!

---

*Before reaching London via Spain and Portugal, Druon, who was living in the unoccupied zone, had his first play, *Mégarée,* performed at the Grand Théâtre de Monte Carlo.

And it climaxes with the pledge to keep on fighting no matter the setback:

> Friend, if you fall,
> A friend comes from the shadow
> To take your place.
> Tomorrow black blood
> Will dry in the heat of the sun
> On the highways.
> Whistle, companions,
> In the night of Freedom
> They're listening . . .

For many writers in Paris, however, armed combat seemed almost an abstraction. For instance, Colette, long one of France's most popular writers, did her best to ignore politics even though she lived under the shadow of official anti-Semitism. Already in her late sixties in 1940 and suffering from rheumatoid arthritis, she was married to Maurice Goudeket, "the Jew who doesn't know he's one," as she put it. In the exodus of June 1940, they ended up in a château in Corrèze belonging to the writer's daughter. But the couple missed Paris and, after much difficulty, they obtained passes to cross the demarcation line. In September 1940, they returned to their apartment in the Palais-Royal and she resumed writing, penning a weekly column for *Le Petit Parisien* and offering short stories to German-approved weeklies like *Comoedia* and the anti-Semitic *Gringoire* and *La Gerbe*. In late 1941, she published a revised version of *Le Pur et l'impur* (The Pure and the Impure), as well as the new novella *Julie de Carneilhan*, in which she painted Jews and Third Republic politicians in a light that upset some friends and must have pleased the occupiers. Colette herself seemed almost oblivious to the occupation. She remained a pillar of *le tout Paris*, dining out in pricey restaurants with artist and writer friends from opposing political camps, while her neighbor Cocteau would entertain her at home with wit and gossip.

Then political reality stepped in. On December 12, 1941, in the first *rafle* of prominent French Jews, Goudeket was arrested by the Gestapo and taken to Compiègne. By good fortune, one of Colette's admirers was Suzanne Abetz, the German ambassador's French wife, who persuaded her husband to order Goudeket's release seven weeks later. Subsequently, Colette also wrote a letter of thanks to Epting at the German Institute. Goudeket promptly acquired false papers to enter the unoccupied zone and was staying with friends in Saint-Tropez when the major Vél'd'Hiv' roundup of Jews took place in Paris. In late 1942, he nonetheless returned home, and for the rest of the occupation he spent every night in a maid's room above Colette's apartment. Colette herself continued writing, publishing her much-loved *Gigi* in 1944, but she now went out little and increasingly complained about her health. When Paris was freed, the fact that she had initially written for collaborationist weeklies was soon forgotten. Colette remained Colette.

Certainly some writers experienced cold and hunger and others risked arrest and deportation, but for many the war was largely one of words. Indeed, not a few gave less importance to clandestine outlets than to publishing openly. This was the case with Jean-Paul Sartre. As early as the fall of 1940, a group of students from the École Normale Supérieure, Sartre's old school, began publishing a tract called *Sous la Botte* (Under the Boot). "I had my father's old Underwood," Dominique Desanti, then twenty, recalled decades later. "I was the only one who knew how to type on a stencil. We'd distribute the sheets in the *métro* or outside factories. We'd take information from the BBC; we spoke about the French bourgeoisie, which had fled."[30]

After Sartre was released from prison camp on medical grounds in April 1941, the philosopher Maurice Merleau-Ponty introduced him to these students and, together, they formed a group called Socialisme et Liberté (Socialism and Freedom), which briefly published a one-page newspaper under the same name. "For us, Sartre was already a great man," Desanti said, pointing to his 1938 novel, *La Nausée.* But after a trip south, where Gide and Malraux refused to endorse Socialisme et Liberté, Sartre lost interest in the venture. In September 1941, he began teaching at the Lycée Condorcet, where he took the place of a Jewish teacher who had been dismissed months earlier. Meanwhile, the students persevered, even after one of their number was arrested and deported to Birkenau, where she died. One of the final issues of *Sous la Botte,* in mid-1942, carried an unsigned essay by Sartre denouncing the order that Jews wear yellow stars. But by fall 1942, the group had dispersed.

Sartre, who was initially excluded from the CNE by Decour, was

finally invited to join in early 1943, and in April that year he published an anonymous article for *Les Lettres Françaises* called "Drieu
La Rochelle, or Self-Hatred." He wrote two more short pieces for
Les Lettres Françaises in 1944, but nothing for Éditions de Minuit.
Rather, his focus was on his own writing, which included his existentialist tome *L'Être et le néant,* the plays *Les Mouches* and *Huis clos*
and an unproduced screenplay.

Meanwhile, Simone de Beauvoir, having published her first novel,
was suspended from her teaching post in June 1943 for "inciting a
minor to debauchery"—more specifically, for seducing one of her
students, Nathalie Sorokine, whose mother complained to the authorities. The following February, Beauvoir began presenting a series
of programs on the history of the music hall on Radio Vichy, which
had moved to Paris. By then, she was still further from the resistance
than Sartre; she later explained that she felt no need to attend CNE
meetings since she was represented by Sartre, who, in any event, considered them boring. But both found time to become Left Bank
celebrities. In January 1944, the illustrated weekly *Toute la Vie* carried photographs of writers and artists in Saint-Germain-des-Prés
cafés, with Sartre shown writing in the Café de Flore. In her memoir
La Force de l'âge, Beauvoir painted a typical scene in the Flore:
"Slowly, over the course of the morning, the room filled up; by the
cocktail hour, it was full. Picasso smiled at Dora Maar, who was
holding a large dog; Léon-Paul Fargue remained silent, Jacques
Prévert chatted; there were noisy debates at the tables of the movie
directors who, since 1939, met there almost every day."[31] Sartre and
Beauvoir lived in the Hôtel La Louisiane, on the nearby rue de Seine,
but they did much of their writing in the Flore, with its wood-fired
stove a particular attraction in winter.

In the spring of 1944, a new diversion appeared in the form of all-
night parties, nicknamed *fiestas,* attended by many writers and occasionally by Picasso and Maar. "Amorous dissipation had little place
in these saturnalia," Beauvoir wrote. "It was above all drink that
broke the routine. With alcohol, we did not hold back; no one among
us objected to getting drunk; some made it almost a duty; Leiris,
among others, applied himself with zeal and succeeded admirably."[32]
Many years later, Sartre also remembered the parties fondly:
"Because of the curfew, which lasted until six or even seven in the
morning, we often partied until then so none of us would get caught
sneaking home during the night. We started having these *fiestas,* as

we called them, just to have fun, not in conjuction with some illegal editorial meeting or whatever."[33] On the night of the D-Day landings, the *fiesta* was hosted by Charles Dullin, the director of the Théâtre de la Cité, and included Sartre, Beauvoir, Camus, his actress girlfriend Maria Casarès, Michel and Louise Leiris and Raymond Queneau. "We played records, we danced, we drank and soon we were wandering all over the place as usual," Beauvoir recalled.[34]

While Camus livened up the *fiestas* with his nifty *paso doble,* however, he was more seriously engaged with the resistance than Sartre. But his path to editorship of the clandestine newspaper *Combat*—linked to the resistance group of the same name—was long and winding. Born in 1913 in Algeria, then a French *département,* in the 1930s Camus was a struggling journalist of little means and poor health (he contracted tuberculosis in his late teens). He was twenty-one when he married Simone Hié, but the marriage soon foundered. In 1935, he joined the French Communist Party, but he was expelled two years later in one of its trademark purges. His point of stability was his friendship with Pascal Pia, a fellow journalist ten years his senior, who hired Camus for the newspaper *Alger Républicain* and later for *Le Soir Républicain.* But the French government closed both in January 1940, leaving Camus and Pia unemployed.

Then, thanks to vacancies created by journalists drafted into the army, both Pia and Camus found work in Paris in the mass-circulation daily *Paris-Soir.* The newspaper's last Paris issue before Paris fell came out on June 11. Led by its powerful owner, Jean Prouvost, a small legion of executives, editors and reporters fled south, with Camus driving one of the cars in the convoy. By September, with Prouvost now running propaganda in Vichy's Information Ministry, *Paris-Soir* was being edited and printed in Lyon. But even with its *pétainiste* line, it was struggling. Three months later, with the newspaper reduced to four pages, Camus was dismissed. He married Francine Faure, a pianist and longtime girlfriend, and went home to Algeria.

In his luggage, Camus carried three manuscripts, the fruit of several years' work: *L'Étranger,* an existentialist novel; *Le Mythe de Sisyphe,* a philosophical essay; and *Caligula,* a play. His dream was that his "three absurds," as he called them, could be published in a single volume and, while earning his keep by teaching in Oran, he worked to achieve this. But Edmond Charlot, a local publisher and friend, had neither the paper nor the money for such a large book.

So, in April 1941, Camus mailed the manuscripts to Pia in Lyon, who sent them to Malraux, who in turn recommended them to Gaston Gallimard. Because of the difficulty in communicating between Paris and Algeria,* it would be months before Camus agreed to the inevitable—that the "absurds" would have to be published separately. *L'Étranger* came out in June 1942, *Le Mythe de Sisyphe* in October 1942 and *Caligula* in May 1944. And it was of course *L'Étranger* that made Camus the toast of literary Paris.

Camus himself, however, was still in Oran and was again ill. His Jewish doctor, Henri Cohen, whose practice would soon be closed by Vichy, ordered him to stay in bed until he could convalesce in a climate milder than Algeria's. Finally, in August 1942, Camus moved to a property owned by his wife's family in Le Chambon-sur-Lignon, a mountain village just seventy-five miles south of Lyon, which would become famous for sheltering thousands of Jews during the occupation. In the months that followed, while he worked on a new novel, *La Peste* (The Plague), and a new play, *Le Malentendu,* Camus's health slowly improved.

Until then, he was largely an outsider to France's drama. In the late 1930s, he had opposed the idea of war, a position taken by many on both left and right, and more recently he had expressed disgust at Vichy's subservience to the Nazis. When he returned to France, he learned that Pia was now involved with Combat, a resistance group active in a broad stretch of eastern France. He met other members of Combat and occasionally attended meetings of Aragon's southern CNE at the Lyon home of Tavernier, the editor of *Confluences.* Camus even obtained a pass to visit Paris in January 1943 and, when he returned there in June, he made a point of introducing himself to Sartre at the dress rehearsal for *Les Mouches.*

His health was still far from good, but he was restless and in November he moved permanently to Paris, taking a job as a reader at Gallimard. He remained something of an outsider, though, because until then he had spent little time in Paris and, unlike most of his new colleagues, he was not a graduate of either the Sorbonne or the École Normale Supérieure. He found a small room in a boardinghouse just three hundred yards from Gallimard and began working there under

---

*Until November 1942, when the Allies landed in North Africa and Germany took over the unoccupied zone, postal services worked efficiently within the Vichy-run territories, but important mail crossing the demarcation was usually hand-carried.

the avuncular eye of Paulhan. But *L'Étranger* had won him admirers, and soon he was drawn into Sartre's circle at the Café de Flore, directing the reading of Picasso's play *Le Désir attrapé par la queue* at Leiris's apartment in March 1944, even agreeing—then refusing—to direct Sartre's new play, *Huis clos.*

Camus also attended some of the CNE meetings and wrote an essay for *Les Lettres Françaises* in May 1944. But a turning point came when Pia introduced him to the editors of *Combat,* the clandestine newspaper founded in December 1941 that now represented the United Resistance Movements. By early 1944, it was printing a remarkable 250,000 copies every two weeks in fifteen different locations and somehow distributing them across the rest of France, often by rail disguised as cargo. As a contributor and, later, as *Combat*'s editor in chief, Camus commissioned and edited articles and wrote at least two himself. His first, in March, was headlined "À guerre totale résistance totale" (To Total War Total Resistance) and reminded readers that every *résistant* becomes a role model: "Every Frenchman can choose: he will be for us or against us." In May, a second article, "Ils ont fusillé des français" (They Shot Frenchmen), denounced the execution of eighty-six men after the resistance derailed a German troop carrier. By the spring of 1944, Camus had several lives: a member of Gallimard's prestigious Reading Committee, an *habitué* of the Café de Flore and a *résistant* known in underground circles as Albert Mathé.

Another latecomer to the resistance was Marguerite Duras. Born and raised in Indochina, the setting for her most famous novel, *L'Amant* (The Lover), she was seventeen when she arrived in France in 1931 to complete her studies. At university, she met a young poet named Robert Antelme, whom she married in September 1939, three weeks after war was declared. By then, she had been working for over a year as a secretary in the Ministry of Colonies, but she left that job in November 1940. She was already intent on becoming a writer and, although both Gallimard and Denoël turned down her first novel, *Les Impudents,* it was eventually published by Plon in 1943. Duras also suffered the pain of losing her baby at birth in May 1942.

Antelme's wartime career took a stranger path. He worked first in the Préfecture de Police in Paris and then as an information officer for Pierre Pucheu, Vichy's minister of industry; when Pucheu took over the Interior Ministry, Antelme became his private secretary. Given Antelme's later involvement in the resistance, his association with one of Vichy's most odious figures seemed all the more strange: Pucheu was accused of handing over French hostages to be shot by the Nazis and later executed by the provisional French government in Algiers.

Duras, on the other hand, found work with the Comité d'Organisation du Livre, the Vichy-created publishers' association, and in January 1943 she became the secretary of its Nazi-approved committee assigning paper for new books. It was at the Comité d'Organisation du Livre that she met the collaborationist writer Ramon Fernandez, through whom she rented an apartment in his building at 5 rue Saint-Benoît, half a block from the Café de Flore. And it was at meetings of the paper committee that she met Gallimard's representative Dionys Mascolo, who became her lover.*

To this day, it remains unclear exactly when or how Duras, Antelme and Mascolo joined the resistance group headed by François Mitterrand, who until early 1943 had worked in a Vichy department charged with repatriating French prisoners of war. Years later, Duras recalled that on Mitterrand's first visit to her apartment, she was shocked to see that he was smoking English cigarettes; that would place the meeting in early March 1944, after Mitterrand returned from a secret trip to London. What seems beyond doubt is that Duras, Antelme and Mascolo began working with Mitterrand's network by, among other things, hiding *résistants* in Duras's apartment, below that of Fernandez.† Then, on June 1, Antelme was arrested and deported, first to Buchenwald, then to Dachau.

What followed is one of the murkiest episodes in Duras's life. With Antelme initially held at Fresnes, she sought permission to send him food. In doing so, she met a Frenchman, Charles Delval, who was working with the Gestapo and claimed to have ordered Antelme's arrest. Attracted by the young woman, Delval invited her to dinner, and they subsequently shared numerous meals in expensive restaurants. After the liberation, Duras claimed that she was collecting information for Mitterrand's group; under interrogation, Delval said they discussed literature. In early 1945, Delval was executed, leaving unanswered the oft-asked question of whether he and Duras were

---

*Antelme had in turn taken Anne-Marie Henrat, a colleague at the Interior Ministry, as his mistress.

†Fernandez died on August 2, 1944, thus escaping an inevitable trial for collaboration.

lovers. After V-E Day, Mitterrand miraculously found Antelme among thousands of starving inmates at Dachau; he urgently messaged Mascolo, who drove to Germany to bring the skeletal Antelme home. Antelme survived,* but his marriage to Duras did not.

In the final months of the occupation, then, while some writers were still going about their lives with a degree of normality, others were giving their lives for their resistance or, in the case of the poet Max Jacob, who died in Drancy, for being Jewish. Joining them was Saint-Exupéry, who died when his plane crashed into the Mediterranean on July 31, 1944, during a reconnaissance flight from Corsica over southern France.

In Paris, with Éluard, Mauriac and others increasingly forced to hide, Paulhan had a narrow escape. In his memoir, Heller claimed that in June 1944 he warned Paulhan of a plan to arrest him. "When the undesirable visitors arrived at his place at 7:00 in the morning," Heller recounted, "he escaped over the rooftops and first hid in the loft of a nun's school close to his home. He changed his hideout various times until he went to a house in the suburbs." In a thank-you letter to Heller, Paulhan noted calmly that "my morning visitors returned twice."[35] Paul Léautaud, still unaware of Paulhan's resistance activities, was puzzled by his friend's dramatic flight. "I wonder what imprudence he has committed?" he asked in his journal.[36] Paulhan was, as always, understated, telling another friend, "A morning visit has made us change apartments, has sent us to the suburbs, beyond the reach of visitors. What tranquillity!"[37] Heller said that, a few weeks later, he saw Paulhan standing at a bar and, to avoid any risk to him, gave an almost imperceptible nod of recognition and walked on. They would next meet after the war.

---

*Duras gave a poignant account of his return in *La Douleur*, published in English as *The War: A Memoir*.

The Pendulum Swings

WHETHER COLLABORATORS, *attentistes* or resisters, the French were at least agreed on one thing: that no matter what they did inside France, the country's fate would be decided by others beyond its frontiers. They also understood that the first step would be an Allied counterattack across the Channel. Indeed, throughout the summer of 1943, there were rumors of an imminent Anglo-American invasion. The Germans, too, were expecting one. After British commandos carried out a successful raid against dry-dock facilities at Saint-Nazaire, on the west coast of Brittany, on March 28, 1942, Hitler ordered the construction of the Atlantikwall, a system of coastal fortifications stretching from northern Norway to France's border with Spain. In August 1943, when British and Canadian troops tried to seize the Channel port of Dieppe, the German defenses stood up well; the attack proved a setback for the Allies and further delayed their long-planned invasion of France.

Clearly, the Allies were not yet ready. Further, Washington and London had made it clear that their principal objective was not the liberation of France but the defeat of the Reich. France could well be the first occupied country to be liberated, but that was because it lay on the path to Berlin. Certainly, Roosevelt and Churchill felt they owed no special favor to France and, least of all, to de Gaulle, whose stubborn defense of French honor was driving them to distraction.

Nonetheless, the tide was turning, albeit slowly. After the Allied occupation of Vichy-ruled Algeria and Morocco in November 1942, Hitler moved his army into southern France in anticipation of an Allied attack across the Mediterranean. He also allowed Italy to occupy Corsica and Savoy, as well as the Côte d'Azur as far west as Toulon. But the Allies needed time to consolidate their control of North Africa. Early in 1943, following the Battle of El Alamein, the British drove Field Marshal Rommel's Afrika Korps out of Egypt and Libya and into Tunisia. Hitler then hurried army and air force reinforcements to Tunisia, and it was there that the Germans and Italians made a stand. Finally, in May 1943, the Allies took Tunisia, capturing some 275,000 Axis soldiers. But, rather than invading southern France, Washington and London opted for what seemed to be an easier route—the "soft belly," in Churchill's optimistic words—into the heart of Europe: in July 1943, Allied troops seized Sicily, prompting the ouster and arrest of Mussolini.

Two months later, after the Allies invaded the "toe" of southern Italy, a successor Italian government under Marshal Pietro Badoglio turned its back on Berlin and signed an armistice with the Allies. The Germans were unimpressed, immediately taking over the southeastern area of France under Italian occupation. They also assumed control of the war in Italy, arming Fascist militias, rescuing Mussolini and setting him up as head of a puppet regime. Meanwhile, the Allied campaign in Italy bogged down. Even with the support of Italian partisans, it was not until June 4, 1944, two days before D-Day, that American troops finally entered Rome, which had been declared an "open city."

On the Eastern Front, hope was reborn with the stunning Soviet victory over the Wehrmacht in the Battle of Stalingrad in early February 1943. But here, too, the war was far from over. Germany still occupied a broad swath of western Russia, as well as Belarus and the Ukraine. And while its advance into southern Russia had been halted, the siege of Leningrad (today's Saint Petersburg) lasted until January 1944. The Nazi killing machine was also intact. Having taken the lives of millions of Soviet citizens, including many Jews, following its invasion in June 1941, the German military, notably its feared Waffen-SS units, continued to commit atrocities as it was gradually driven out of the Soviet Union and eastern Europe. In the Soviet Union alone, by the time Hitler was defeated, combat, massacres and starvation had killed an estimated twenty-three million people, roughly half of them civilians, including one million Jews. At the same time, in 1943 and 1944, as word of large-scale killing of Jews began to reach the west, Hitler continued to execute his "final solution" of European Jews, with railroad cattle cars full of deportees arriving in Poland's death camps almost daily.

In France, despite growing confidence that Germany now faced defeat, the mood remained grim. With the demarcation line eliminated in March 1943* and the German army and the Gestapo now present across all of France, the notion that Pétain was the father-protector of the nation was no longer credible.

Vichy remained responsible for the economy, internal security, education and culture. But it was now Prime Minister Laval, not Pétain, who was in charge—not that the Germans paid him much heed. He was brushed aside by Hitler when he tried to forestall a German takeover of southern France in November 1942. Laval also lost an important ally and interlocutor when Ambassador Abetz was withdrawn and replaced by his deputy, Rudolf Schleier, from December 1942 to December 1943, supposedly for being too Francophile. But Laval still did his utmost to please Berlin. As early as June 22, 1942, he had declared in a speech, "I hope for a German victory because, without it, Bolshevism would take over everywhere tomorrow." Now he was more persuaded than ever that a German defeat would bring Communism to France.

To forestall this, French industry, which included aircraft manufacturing, was placed ever more at the service of Germany. Laval also offered additional French labor. In 1942, 250,000 Frenchmen had gone to work in Germany in exchange for the release of some 90,000 prisoners of war; on February 16, 1943, a compulsory program, the Service du Travail Obligatoire, or STO, was imposed. This, too, helped the Nazi war effort since it provided replacements for those many German men of all ages who were being drafted into the army and Waffen-SS. By the end of 1943, close to 650,000 Frenchmen and

*Paradoxically, without German controls at the demarcation line, resistance groups were also freer to move around the country.

Frenchwomen were at work in German industries, while many of the 1.4 million POWs were also laboring in factories and farms.

For Pétain, the only consolation was that Laval was now the most hated Frenchman in the country. The old marshal even tried to dismiss Laval in late 1943, perhaps believing that he could again appear to be France's savior, but he was blocked by the Germans.

An occupation that began for many as an accommodation was becoming ever more of a confrontation. The resistance, which had grown only slowly in 1942 despite Communist backing, was now particularly strong in the former unoccupied zone. Its rural maquis, which began as isolated and poorly armed units based in mountainous and wooded areas of southeastern France, was also given an enormous boost by the STO. In fact, Laval's compulsory work program became the resistance's best recruitment tool. If in 1942 Vichy had tried to fill its quota by persuasion and negotiation, giving priority to skilled workers, now French police and German soldiers simply grabbed young men coming out of *métro* stations or movie theaters. The performing arts were inevitably affected. While the Conservatoire de Paris shielded some of its students by forming a youth orchestra, other orchestras, theaters and movie productions lost instrumentalists, actors and technicians to the STO. Two among the many artists caught up in these sweeps were the writer Alain Robbe-Grillet and the singer Georges Brassens, both in their early twenties.

But there was also a strong backlash against the STO. Tens of thousands of young men became what were known as *réfractaires*—those who had fled their jobs or universities and joined the maquis, most often in the Massif Central. Overnight, they escaped forced labor in Germany and wrapped themselves in patriotism. But they also posed huge problems for the resistance. Suddenly, it had to find false papers, food, warm clothes and weapons for large numbers of young men who, for the most part, were ill-prepared for combat.

In his journal, Jean Guéhenno noted with pride that some of his former lycée students were now in the maquis. One came to see him during a visit to Paris. Guéhenno wrote, "He told me about their lives, their admirable fraternity, companions so different from himself, their deprivation; the fight against snow and cold, the war against the Italians, then the Gestapo, the informers. He had become head of a unit, then of a camp. Fourteen of his comrades had been shot."[1] The *maquisards* were not always popular. The main complaint was that maquis attacks on German patrols brought reprisals against unarmed villagers. In some areas, where *maquisards* robbed banks and post offices or forced farmers to hand over food in exchange for worthless bonds, they were also viewed as bandits. But with many middle-aged and older French opting for *attentisme,* the foot soldiers of the maquis also became a symbol of a younger generation's willingness to stand and fight. And many died doing so: in June 1944, some six hundred *maquisards* were killed when German parachutists and gliders carrying troops launched a major attack on the maquis of the isolated Vercors plateau in southeastern France.

Gradually, though, the resistance as a whole was becoming better armed and more united. In this, the British Special Operations Executive and the Free French Forces were important outside players. The SOE, which had had secret agents operating in France since 1941, provided radio tramsitters, weapons, training and money to trusted resistance groups; the Gaullists, alarmed by Communist control of much of the underground, offered a degree of legitimacy to non-Communist *résistants.* The problem they both faced was the sheer number of resistance groups—close to 250 have been identified—that had appeared, many of them not only tiny but also proudly independent.

A crucial turning point came in spring 1943, when eight major resistance groups formed the Conseil National de la Résistance, or National Resistance Council, headed by Jean Moulin, a former *préfet* and de Gaulle's new personal representative in France. But less than one month after the council's first meeting in Paris, Moulin and eight other leaders were arrested in Lyon by the city's infamous Gestapo chief, Klaus Barbie, widely known as the Butcher of Lyon.* The circumstances of Moulin's arrest and subsequent death remain a matter of speculation to this day. Was he, as was later charged, the victim of an informer who had infiltrated his group? And after being tortured, did he commit suicide, as Barbie claimed, or was he murdered?

In any event, while a setback, Moulin's death was not a fatal blow to the resistance, since its main components—groups like Combat, Libération, Francs-Tireurs et Partisans and the Armée Secrète—increasingly coordinated their activities. They suffered losses. Nu-

---

*After the war, Barbie was one of many Nazis who fled to South America. In 1983, he was arrested in Bolivia and extradited to face trial in France. In July 1987, he was sentenced to life imprisonment for crimes against humanity, notably for his deportation of forty-four Jewish children from an orphanage at Izieu. He died in jail in Lyon in 1991.

merous leading *résistants* were arrested by the *milice* and handed over to the Gestapo for interrogation, torture and either execution or deportation. But by D-Day, with its urban support groups included, the resistance was estimated to number around 100,000 men and women.

In response, both Vichy and the Nazis became more aggressive. Their new weapon was the paramilitary *milice*. Founded by Laval in January 1943 to help arrest Jews and fight the resistance, it had also partly been his response to the growing reluctance of French police and *gendarmerie* to do the Germans' dirty work. To give it a more elevated mission, it was said to be defending Christian civilization against the usual evils: Jews, Freemasons, Bolsheviks and democracy. It even had its own newspaper, *Combats* (just one letter away from the resistance monthly *Combat*), and it could count on cheerleading from collaborationist weeklies like *Je suis partout.*

With some thirty thousand full- or part-time members, uniformed in blue coats, brown shirts and large berets, the *milice* was much feared. As part of its psychological warfare, its units would march through towns, swaggering in the knowledge that they could act with impunity. Its leader was Joseph Darnand, an avowed Fascist who in October 1943 pledged his loyalty to Hitler and was awarded the rank of Sturmbannführer, or major, in the Waffen-SS. In December, Laval brought Darnand into his government as deputy minister of the interior, effectively fusing the activities of the French police and the *milice.* Both were answerable to the Germans, although the *milice* carried out its own raids on villages and its own executions. One infamous *milice* leader in Lyon, Paul Touvier, who was finally arrested in 1989 after years of protection by a religious order in Nice, was condemned to life imprisonment in 1994 for ordering the killing of seven Jewish hostages at Rillieux-la-Pape outside Lyon on June 29, 1944. Some *miliciens* also had military training, and they took part in operations against the maquis alongside the Waffen-SS.

In Paris, where the *milice* was rarely seen, a different form of thuggery was provided by what was variously known as the French Gestapo, the Bonny-Lafont gang and the Rue Lauriston gang. It was headed by Pierre Bonny, a former police inspector, and Henri Chamberlin, a.k.a. Lafont, a small-time criminal; they made a tidy fortune on the black market and shared some of their spoils with Nazi officers. In May 1941, they requisitioned the building at 93 rue Lauriston, in the 16th arrondissement, and expanded their operation to hunting *résistants* on behalf of the Gestapo. Soon the very name rue Lauriston was synonymous with kidnapping and torture.* Jews, too, were among their victims, but most of the 23,000 Jews deported from France in 1943 and of the 16,000 deported in the eight months of 1944 were already being held in camps scattered across southern France. As with earlier deportations, a majority were foreign-born. In fact, while foreigners represented one-third of France's Jewish population, they accounted for two-thirds of the 76,000 Jews deported from France, some 2,000 of whom survived. Put differently, the deportation rate was close to 50 percent for foreign Jews and around 13 percent for French-born Jews.

With a simmering civil war under way across much of France, the propaganda war was intensifying. Working closely with the resistance, the BBC's French-language service not only trumpeted acts of sabotage and denounced German repression but also sent daily messages in code, such as the timing of arms shipments. Resistance newspapers proliferated; some were little more than mimeographed sheets, others the well-printed organs of major resistance groups. After the war, the National Library collected examples of a total of 1,015 clandestine publications that circulated at one time or other during the occupation.

Combating the Allies and the "terrorists" of the resistance were collaborationist dailies and weeklies, as well as Radio-Paris and Radio Vichy, all trying to alarm the French with the prospect of a Bolshevik takeover. Michel Francini, the young music-hall performer, was working at the time on a weekly variety program called *Les Ondes joyeuses* (Happy Airwaves) on Radio-Paris. "Everyone turned to Radio-Paris for entertainment," he recalled. "The politics were all lies."[2] One Frenchman in particular, Philippe Henriot, proved a skilled and articulate propagandist for the Nazis. Having found inspiration in the right-wing nationalism of Maurras's L'Action Française in the 1930s, Henriot embraced the Nazi cause after Germany invaded the Soviet Union in 1941. He also became a loyal supporter of Pétain or, more exactly, of Laval. And it was Laval who, ignoring Pétain's objections, named him in January 1944 to be Vichy's minister for information and propaganda.

Henriot's real power, however, came from his oratory, whether at public meetings or in his daily "editorials" on Radio-Paris. Respond-

---

*Bonny, Lafont and six other gang members were executed on December 27, 1944.

ing to him on Radio-Londres was Pierre Dac, an actor and broadcaster, who warned that Henriot's tomb would carry the inscription
DIED FOR HITLER, SHOT BY THE FRENCH. It happened sooner than
Dac expected. Early on the morning of June 28, 1944, a group of
résistants dressed as *miliciens* murdered him in his apartment in the
Information Ministry in Paris. Henriot was the most prominent
Vichy official to be killed by the resistance and, as such, was given a
state funeral in Notre-Dame, conducted by none other than the
archbishop of Paris, Cardinal Emmanuel Suhard. To avenge Henriot,
the *milice* picked an easy target. Georges Mandel, the Jewish politician who had served as the Popular Front's interior minister, was
already being held in Buchenwald. The Germans returned him to
Paris and delivered him to the *milice*. On July 7, he was murdered in
the Fontainebleau forest. Two weeks earlier, another prominent Jew,
Jean Zay, who was education minister in the Popular Front, was
taken from a French jail by the *milice* and also murdered.

From early 1944, Parisians, too, felt the war coming closer. Allied
bombers, which regularly attacked factories and railroad connections in the Paris suburbs, occasionally missed their targets; the
movie studios at Boulogne-Billancourt were hit and badly damaged.
Further, with some stray bombs striking residential neighborhoods,
Parisians grew used to spending nights in basements or *métro* stations. Operas, plays, movies and concerts were frequently interrupted by air-raid alerts and, because of electricity cuts, no movies
were shown on Tuesdays.

On April 26, 1944, Pétain paid his only wartime visit to the city to
express solidarity with Parisians after several days of heavy bombing; he was heartily cheered by a crowd of some ten thousand
Parisians when he spoke from the balcony of the Hôtel de Ville.
After a stirring rendering of "La Marseillaise," sung in public in Paris
for the first time since 1940, Pétain attended a special mass in Notre-
Dame given by Cardinal Suhard. For all too brief a moment, the old
man could again imagine himself as a symbol of national unity. But
two days later, the Nazis forced him to broadcast a message praising
Germany for defending Europe against Communism. He also criticized the resistance and told the French that "it is in your interest to
maintain a correct and loyal attitude toward the occupying troops."
The following month, large crowds welcomed him when he visited
four cities formerly in the occupied zone—Nancy, Rouen, Épinal
and Dijon—for the first time in four years. But it was too late for

Pétain to distance himself from Laval; in the eyes of their enemies in France and abroad, they remained the two pillars upon which Vichy rested.

On June 6, barely six weeks after Pétain visited Paris, American, British and Canadian troops began landing along a bleak and sparsely populated stretch of the Normandy coastline. Simultaneously, resistance groups were mobilized. Now known uniformly as the Forces Françaises de l'Intérieur, or FFI, they set about sabotaging power supplies, bridges and communications networks to disrupt German efforts to send reinforcements. When the first Allied parachutists landed behind the German lines, the resistance was also well placed to provide intelligence on enemy military movements. But it took the Allies seven weeks to gain control of Normandy and Brittany.

During much of June, the Americans fought their way up the Cotentin Peninsula before capturing the strategic port of Cherbourg. To the east, British and Canadian forces struggled until late July to take Caen, although in the process they held down German armored divisions — and also largely destroyed the city; for the first time since 1940, there were large numbers of French civilian casualties. Finally, Allied forces broke out of their enlarged beachhead on July 25 and began moving east at speed. One week later, France's 2nd Armored Division, under General Philippe Leclerc, landed in Normandy and joined the Allies.

Meanwhile, German troops summoned from the south to cut off the Allied advance carried out two particularly shocking acts of reprisal: on June 9, a day after the maquis had killed forty German soldiers, units of the 2nd SS Panzer Division *Das Reich* hanged ninety-five men from lampposts in Tulle in the Corrèze; the following day, about eighty miles to the north, after a report that a German officer was being held hostage, German troops entered the village of Oradour-sur-Glane, rounded up the population, shot 190 men and then burned 247 women and 205 children to death in the local church. Word of the Oradour massacre stunned France, prompting *Les Lettres Françaises* to put out a special issue denouncing the killings. It also strengthened the determination of the resistance, which played an important role in liberating small towns and harassing German units after the Allies landed along the Riviera on August 15.

Thanks to the BBC, Paris was able to follow developments on the war front, learning, for example, of the Normandy landings at the same time as they were announced in London. "Numerous fleets and

11,000 planes have participated in the operations," Jünger noted professionally in his journal. "This, no doubt, is the start of the great offensive that will mark this day in history. I was nonetheless surprised because there had been so many predictions about it. But why this place, this moment? This will be debated for centuries to come."[3] Galtier-Boissière was more excited, writing, "At last, that's it! The landings began this morning in Normandy. There is talk of parachute landings near Rouen. In the street, the faces of passersby display a sweet joy."[4]

With the end of the occupation in sight, artists and writers active in the intellectual resistance began preparing their professions for after the liberation. The Front National du Théâtre, which until then had dwelled mainly on denouncing collaborationist authors and actors in *La Scène Française,* created a twenty-five-member Comité du Théâtre charged with purging and reorganizing French theater after the liberation. Among its members were Sartre, the playwright Armand Salacrou and the actor Pierre Dux, who would run the Comédie Française after the liberation and again in the 1970s. This front and other groups also drew up lists of those of their peers who had betrayed France—and their profession—by collaborating with the enemy. Some groups even planned *comités d'épuration*—purge committees—to judge traitors.

A good number of collaborationists, however, knowing what awaited them, were already far from Paris. Among the first to leave, just eleven days after D-Day, was Céline, who fled to Germany. Others waited until Allied troops had fought their way out of Normandy and were moving north. Some traveled with the first German convoys to evacuate the city. "Good" Germans also packed their bags. Gerhard Heller left Paris at dawn on August 14. That same evening, Jünger checked out of the Hôtel Raphaël. He noted, "Sudden departure at nightfall. I left my room in order, I left a bouquet of flowers on the desk and distributed some tips. Unfortunately, I forgot some irreplaceable letters in the drawer of a wardrobe."[5]

What remained of the Vichy regime also imploded. Since 1943, Vichy itself had become an increasingly gloomy and empty town, with only a handful of countries keeping embassies there. Still believing Pétain could be useful to them, the Germans did not want the marshal to fall into Allied hands and, on August 17, they ordered him to prepare to leave. He was eager to appear to be standing up to the Germans, who went along with the fiction for two days. Then, on the morning of August 20, after making a final radio broadcast, Pétain and his entourage were driven to Belfort, still in France but beside Alsace and Lorraine, the French provinces annexed by Germany in 1940. Once there, he wrote a protest letter to Hitler, recalling his pledge never to leave France.

Laval was also in Belfort, sent there under arrest after he had held talks with the prewar Radical leader Édouard Herriot about reconvening the National Assembly. Other Vichy politicians, including Fernand de Brinon, Pétain's former man in Paris, were summoned to Berlin for talks on forming a new government. Then, starting on September 8, the entire Vichy circus was moved to Sigmaringen, in southwest Germany. Pétain refused to name a government in exile, but he allowed Brinon to become head of a "French Governmental Delegation," which included such notorious Fascists as the *milice* leader Darnand; Marcel Déat, the editor of *L'Oeuvre* and the leader of the rightist Rassemblement National Populaire; and Jean Luchaire, Abetz's close friend and the founding editor of *Les Nouveaux Temps.*

In October 1944, Céline also arrived in Sigmaringen, where he acted as an informal court doctor until he obtained German permission to travel to Denmark in March 1945. An actor friend of Céline's, Robert Le Vigan, was also there, although writers and journalists were more numerous, including Lucien Rebatet and Paul Marion, Henriot's predecessor as Vichy's minister of information and propaganda. Jacques Doriot, the Fascist politician, also set up his own French-language radio and newspaper in Mainau, thirty miles to the south, although he was killed by Allied aircraft while driving to Sigmaringen on February 22, 1945. Ignored equally by Paris and Berlin, the "republic" of Sigmaringen lasted until French troops took the town in April 1945.

Even after the Normandy landings, though, the cultural life of Paris proved resilient. Claudel's *Le Soulier de satin* and Sartre's *Huis clos* continued to draw crowds. Work went ahead on new movies, including *Les Enfants du paradis.* The Berlin Philharmonic was among the German orchestras performing in Paris, while Wehrmacht officers filled the boxes at the Paris Opera and the Opéra-Comique. Between D-Day and the liberation, for instance, there were twenty-seven performances of opera and ballet at the Paris Opera, with the house closing its doors only after a performance of Glück's *Alceste* on August 8. Publishers complained about the shortage of paper, but they still produced new books. Only the art market had gone off the boil: much of the best art, sold by Parisian families or looted from Jews, had already been acquired by Germans who, with the obvious exceptions of Hitler and Göring, now also had less money to invest in paintings. Like most Parisians, artists and writers—or their wives—had learned the tricks of staying alive, using ration cards and the black market to obtain food and fuel, although both were in short supply. Journals kept by writers nonetheless mentioned lunches and dinners in good restaurants and brasseries. Sartre, Beauvoir, Leiris and their fellow partygoers also appear to have had no difficulty finding wine for their *fiestas* in the spring of 1944. And, of course, Florence Gould continued to treat her guests with the best of everything.

In early August, it was still unclear when Paris would be freed. General Dwight Eisenhower, the supreme Allied commander, preferred to advance toward the northeast and, in any event, did not favor a prolonged siege of the city if the Germans chose to make a stand. In contrast, de Gaulle saw the early liberation of Paris as essential to establishing the legitimacy of his provisional government and blocking American plans to create an Allied Military Government for Occupied Territories (for which a new currency had already been printed).

In the end, two unexpected developments played into his hands. General Dietrich von Choltitz, the German commander of Greater Paris, began an orderly retreat of some twenty thousand soldiers and eighty tanks from the city. Seeing trucks full of troops heading for eastern France, Parisians finally dared to defy the occupiers. The first sign of revolt came on August 15 with a strike by the Paris police, which, until then, had disgraced itself by rounding up Jews and arresting *résistants.* The strike spread to *métro* and postal workers and prompted the FFI's Paris leader, Colonel Henri Rol-Tanguy, to prepare for armed action.

The Germans, however, had not given up. Early in August, the Germans loaded art from the Jeu de Paume into five railcars destined for Berlin, although the resistance succeeded in preventing the train from leaving. On August 15, the last train carrying Jewish deportees left Paris unimpeded for the east. On August 16, thirty-five young *résistants* were caught and executed in the Bois de Boulogne. On that same day, though, *Je suis partout* was published for the last time, prompting Galtier-Boissière to rename it *Je suis parti*—"I have left"—instead of "I am everywhere."

By August 19, an insurrection was under way, with sporadic attacks launched against German armored units and as many as six hundred barricades eventually thrown up across city streets. The German forces took up defensive positions inside the Luxembourg Gardens, in the place de la Concorde and Tuileries Gardens, at the Porte Maillot, around the Arc de Triomphe and beside the École Militaire. To this day, many buildings in these districts carry the scars of shells fired by German tanks, while hundreds of marble plaques mark the places were young FFI fighters died.

The days that followed were both chaotic and theatrical. Communist Party posters called for an uprising, using the World War I slang for a German: "For every Parisian, a Boche." During lulls in the fighting, ordinary Parisians brought food and drink to those manning the barricades, then scurried away to safety when battles erupted. "What I liked about the resistance was to be among people whom I didn't know, who were not from my circle, who were from all sectors of life," recalled Annie Ubersfeld, then a young *résistante.* "I was pleased to meet people who were different."[6] One morning, the painter Françoise Gilot bicycled from her home in Neuilly to visit her new lover. But Picasso was not in his studio, so she headed back along the Left Bank of the Seine. Beside the National Assembly, she came across a German tank with its cannon pointing at her. "Either they'll shoot and I'll probably die or they don't shoot," she recounted many years later. "So I must not stop. I went on cycling and I took the pont de la Concorde and they didn't shoot and I thought, 'Phew, that was a close one.' "[7]

Sartre and Beauvoir had left Paris in mid-July for a three-week vacation, but they were back in the city before the insurrection began (prompting some wits to remark later that Sartre joined the resistance on the same day as the Paris police). In her memoir *La Force de l'âge,* Beauvoir gave a good idea of how life went on amid death:

> Fighting had resumed. The morning seemed calm; on the banks of the Seine, you could see fishermen throwing out lines and some young men sunbathing in their swimsuits; but the FFI were hiding behind the balustrades of the embankments, Zette told me, others in nearby buildings, others in the place Saint-

Michel on the steps of the underground station. A German truck passed beneath the window; two young soldiers, both very blond, stood upright holding submachine guns; twenty meters away, death lay in wait for them. One felt like shouting, Beware! There was a burst of gunfire and they fell.[8]

While Beauvoir saw young soldiers, many of the Germans left in Paris were old and neither equipped nor willing to fight. "I was watching from the sixth floor," Francini remembered. "I saw a German, he was about fifty. His car had broken down. He was pushing his car alone and people were shouting insults at him. French flags were flying. He was sweating with fear. I felt sorry for him."[9] Some German tanks were even abandoned in the middle of streets when their crews ran out of ammunition.

Guéhenno saw two German soldiers stationed alone on a bridge. "With grenades hanging from their belts, submachine guns in hand, they were terrified, awaiting inevitable death,"[10] he wrote in his journal, adding, "What were they doing there, on rue Manin, in the middle of this crowd that neither hated nor loved them but thought only of killing them? In the evening, around eight o'clock, they died."[11] Guéhenno concluded that he lacked the soul of a warrior, since he could not celebrate their deaths. "But," he wrote, "I cannot forget all the crimes of the past five years committed by these stupid soldiers. All my heart is with those young boys of Paris who are fighting almost without guns, they're the ones I pity."[12] Three days later, on August 23, his friend B. telephoned him with a less romantic view of the insurrection: "All this fighting in Paris to create the illusion that we alone are recovering our freedom when it is clear that we owe this to others, to the armies that are arriving, all this, in his view, is pointless, a lie and a waste of lives." But Guéhenno had a more nuanced view: "The life of an idea—of freedom—cannot be the same in the minds of the masses as it is in the critical brains of people like my friend B. . . . and myself. The history of peoples is built on such illusions."[13]

Certainly, a feeling of revolution was in the air. Newspaper stands selling *Je suis partout* and *Au Pilori* one day were offering *Combat* and *Libération* the next. The Comité de la Presse Clandestine had been preparing for this moment for months and, as staffs fled collaborationist newspapers, their buildings and presses were taken over by resistance newspapers. *Combat,* for instance, shared the presses of *Pariser Zeitung*, the Wehrmacht's newspaper, with *Franc-Tireur* and *Défense de la France*. Also back on the streets were the Communist Party daily *L'Humanité*, which by the end of 1944 had a circulation of close to 300,000, as well as *Le Figaro*, the conservative daily that had stopped publishing in Lyon when the city was occupied twenty-two months earlier. *Les Lettres Françaises* published its first "aboveground" issue on September 9; during the insurrection itself, Éluard and Seghers distributed old copies of the monthly around the Left Bank.

With fighting continuing across Paris, the new daily press provided a breathless blow-by-blow account of resistance heroism. Edited by Albert Camus and Pascal Pia, *Combat*'s first nonclandestine issue came out on August 21 with the headline "The Insurrection Leads the Republic to Triumph in Paris—Allied Troops Are Six Kilometers from the Capital." Later in the day, Camus was heard on Radio Liberté, a Paris station occupied by the resistance, reading the text of a *Combat* editorial, "De la résistance à la révolution" (From Resistance to Revolution). Assuming the right to speak on behalf of the French, it said, "Having started by resistance, they want to finish with revolution."[14] Not unreasonably, it was a good moment for dreams. Indeed, Camus's contributions to *Combat* during the days before liberation were less reportages than philosophical essays laced with poetic images.

Camus also commissioned Sartre to provide a street-eye view of the insurrection. On August 28, three days after the liberation, *Combat* published the first of his seven reports under the series title of "Un Promeneur dans Paris insurgé" (A Walker in Insurgent Paris). Written in lively journalistic language, with Sartre's personal experience seemingly as important as this turning point in history, the articles evoked the confusion and uncertainty experienced by most civilians, who might be lining up for bread one moment and cowering in doorways the next. Sartre wrote, "There is a geography of insurrection: in certain areas, they have been fighting relentlessly for four days; in others (Montparnasse, for instance), everything is almost disturbingly calm." He went on: "A few people venture all the way to the boulevard Saint-Germain and come back disappointed: the flag with the swastika is still flying over the Seine." Sartre the playwright also observed himself on stage. "Then, suddenly, that Wednesday, the BBC announced that Paris had been freed. A friend and I listened to the news flat on our stomachs because heavy gunfire was just then hammering our building: we couldn't help finding the announcement somewhat surprising, even annoying. Paris had been freed, but we could not leave our building, because the rue de Seine, where I lived, was still blocked."

It seems likely that Beauvoir and Leiris contributed extensively to these articles* since Sartre spent much of the insurrection inside the Comédie Française, the improvised headquarters for the Comité National du Théâtre, the theater world's tiny resistance group. Still, with his byline prominently displayed on the front page of *Combat,* Sartre could start reinventing himself as Sartre *le grand résistant.*

Galtier-Boissière, who walked his dog, Azor, amid the barricades, offered an eyewitness account of life during the insurrection. And since he lived on the place de la Sorbonne, beside the boulevard Saint-Michel, one of the combat zones, he was well placed to do so. He was also fed news by friends in other parts of the city. On August 23, he noted, "At two o'clock, Delattre telephoned me to say the Grand Palais was on fire. Since he seemed genuinely upset, I consoled by assuring him that this was not a major calamity."[15] The following morning, he observed, "The barricades have held firm. Evidently tank shells are useless in urban warfare and produce more noise than damage."[16] By midnight, the first small contingent of French troops reached the Hôtel de Ville and, somewhat prematurely, the bells of Notre-Dame began sounding the liberation. But it was only hours away. Early on Friday, August 25, Galtier-Boissière watched as tanks of Leclerc's armored division rolled down the rue Saint-Jacques, one block from his home: "An excited crowd surrounds the French assault tanks, which are bristling with flags and sprinkled with flowers. On each tank, on each armored car, beside gunners wearing khaki jumpsuits and little rose-colored caps, there are clusters of girls, women, kids, FFIs with armbands."[17] He followed the column to Notre-Dame and noted, "In all its charming confusion, this parade is one hundred times more moving than the solemn victory parade in 1919."[18]

The fighting, however, was not over. That very day, there were still some tank battles between French units and German troops holding out in the Luxembourg Gardens, near the École Militaire and around the city's main railroad stations. The Hôtel Majestic, the Wehrmacht's Paris headquarters, was set afire to drive out remaining sol-

---

*After Sartre's death, Beauvoir explicitly claimed coauthorship of the articles.

diers. "This was the job of the tanks of Leclerc, whom the Allies kindly allowed to cleanse the capital completely," Galtier-Boissière wrote.[19]

De Gaulle had achieved his objective. With the agreement of the American field commander, General Omar Bradley, French troops had entered Paris a few hours before those of the Americans. Further, while some fifteen hundred street fighters and innocent passersby died in the insurrection, General von Choltitz had ignored Hitler's orders to leave Paris in ruins and, at three-thirty p.m. on August 25, he surrendered in a brief ceremony at the Préfecture de Police. Alongside his signature, the document carried that of General Leclerc and, to de Gaulle's annoyance, above it, that of the resistance leader Colonel Rol-Tanguy. Soon German soldiers were being rounded up and taken to the Louvre's main courtyard, where they were held for the next three days.

Later that afternoon, de Gaulle himself arrived in Paris and, standing in the main hall of the Hôtel de Ville, where Pétain had spoken four months earlier, he addressed a vast crowd. Matching the intense drama of the occasion, he hailed Parisians as if they and the French had alone heroically freed the city. And as de Gaulle embarked on rewriting the history of the occupation, he also signaled his determination to have France stand alongside the United States, Britain and the Soviet Union as victors in the war:

Why should we hide the emotion that consumes us all, men and women, who are here, in our home, in Paris, which stood up to liberate itself and has done so with its own hands? No! We will not hide this deep and sacred emotion. These are minutes that go beyond each of our poor lives. Paris! Paris abused! Paris broken! Paris martyred! But Paris liberated! Liberated by itself, liberated by its people with the help of the French armies, with the support and the help of all France, of the France that fights, of the only France, of the real France, of the eternal France! Well, then! Since the enemy that held Paris has capitulated into our hands, France returns to Paris, to its home. It returns bloody, but thoroughly determined. It returns there enlightened by the immense lesson, but more convinced than ever of its duties and of its rights. I speak of its duties first, and I will sum them all up by saying that, for now, they are the duties of war. The enemy staggers, but it is not vanquished yet. It remains on our territory. It will not even be enough for us to be satisfied that we have, with the help of our dear and admirable allies, chased it from our home. We want to enter its territory as is fitting, as victors.

The following day, accompanied by French troops, de Gaulle walked through cheering crowds down the Champs-Élysées, along a path that, for four years, Wehrmacht soldiers had marched daily. It was the first time Parisians had set eyes on this tall, solemn-looking man who had left France as an obscure tank officer and now returned as a national hero. He was still wearing the uniform of a two-star general, his rank in 1940, but from now on he would be known simply as *le général.* At Notre-Dame, there was a brief panic when shots were fired from nearby rooftops, but the snipers were silenced, and a thanksgiving mass went ahead. Cardinal Suhard, non grata for having led the funeral mass for Henriot two months earlier, was asked not to appear in the cathedral and was instead confined to his residence. V-E Day was still nearly nine months away, the horror of the gas chambers was not widely known and France still had to earn its place among the victorious Allies on the battlefields of eastern France and Germany. But for the moment, Parisians had ample reason for celebration.

· CHAPTER 16 ·

Vengeance and Amnesia

EVEN AS PARISIANS finally slept without fearing a knock on their front door, a purge of the past began. No one doubted that it was necessary. France had been betrayed, dreadful crimes had been committed and now, as part of the rite of passage from occupation to liberation, the rule of law should be seen to prevail. But before an appropriate legal structure could be put in place, vengeance erupted spontaneously. While ad hoc military tribunals were ordering the deaths of some seven hundred notorious traitors, in the main Gestapo informers, *miliciens,* police and some French soldiers who had fought alongside the Wehrmacht, there was a wave of extralegal killings, soon known as the *épuration sauvage,* the "savage purge." As towns and villages were liberated, perhaps as many as nine thousand *miliciens,* collaborators and black marketers were summarily executed, both by furious individual citizens and by the resistance, now, at least theoretically, under the single banner of the Forces Françaises de l'Intérieur, or FFI.

Many communities also turned on women accused of *collabora-*

tion horizontale—they had slept with the enemy. Thousands had their heads shaved in public, while some were stripped naked and paraded through yelling crowds. It was not a pretty sight. "I saw a group of thugs who were pushing and kicking a woman with a shorn head," Michel Francini recalled. "She was naked and a swastika had been painted on her breasts. They were drunk."[1] Some of these women were prostitutes, but others had had more stable relationships. And this brought complications. Less than a year later, when the two million or so Frenchmen imprisoned or working in Germany began returning home, some found a new baby in the family.*

Because of their renown, artists, writers and journalists who had either supported Vichy or collaborated with the Germans were soon in the spotlight. There were more opportunists than outright criminals among them, but many had been denounced by name on Radio-Londres, the condemnations occasionally even accompanied by death threats. And it was no secret that, thanks to their ties to the occupying power, they had enjoyed privileges denied to most other French citizens.

Two celebrities in particular had a penchant for drawing attention to themselves. Their contrasting experiences at the liberation were early signs of the capriciousness that would come to characterize much of the *épuration.* One was Cocteau, an artist, poet, playwright and a frequent guest at cultural and social events organized by the German Institute. In his journal entry for August 25, 1944, liberation day itself, he worried about how his friendship with Arno Breker would be viewed, above all about his 1942 article in *Comoedia* praising the German sculptor: "What counts is Breker, the Breker article, the Breker friendship, the only act that can be used to hang me." While looking to Éluard and Sartre to protect him, he wallowed in self-pity, asking, "Why should the destiny of a poet change? My realm is not of this world and the world resents me for not following its rules. I will always suffer the same injustice. People are always thrusting me into scandals, which I hate and which they accuse me of liking and instigating."[2]

At one point on August 25, as Paris celebrated, Cocteau sought the protection of the family of the actress Elina Labourdette, on the

---

*Estimates of the number of children born of French mothers and German fathers— the so-called *enfants de Boche*—during or immediately after the occupation range between 100,000 and 200,000. Some Frenchmen working under the STO program also fathered children with German women.

Île de la Cité. Elina promptly called over her friend Claude Anglès, a young doctor at the nearby Hôtel-Dieu hospital. "I saw a man sitting in the corner looking very shocked," Claude recalled. "It was Cocteau, and he was frightened to death. He thought he was going to have to answer for his ties to the Germans. But he didn't. Cocteau belonged to a group that protected him, while Sacha Guitry, who did one hundred times less than Cocteau, had lots of enemies."[3] In reality, what probably saved Cocteau was that his partner, the dashing young actor Jean Marais, joined the FFI during the insurrection. A few hours later, Cocteau left the Labourdette apartment and was never asked to explain himself.

In contrast, two days earlier, five young FFI members arrived at Guitry's mansion beside the Eiffel Tower and accused him of "intelligence with the enemy," the catchall charge against collaborators. Wearing lime-colored pajamas below a tweed jacket, with a Panama hat on his head, the ever-dapper Guitry was taken on foot to the town hall of the 7th arrondissement, on the rue de Grenelle. Word of his arrest quickly spread and, by good fortune, Alain Decaux,* one of Guitry's young admirers and a new FFI recruit, obtained permission to protect the playwright's home from looters. Guitry himself was then taken to a succession of detention centers that, only days earlier, had held Jews and political prisoners: the Vélodrome d'Hiver, the stadium where thousands of Jews were first held after the July 1942 roundups; Drancy, the main transit camp for Jewish deportees; and the fortress at Fresnes, which usually housed *résistants*.

Tristan Bernard, a Jewish playwright, testified that he was freed from Drancy in 1943 thanks to Guitry, but Guitry's enemies said this only proved his good relations with the Germans. "Is it 'collaboration' to exercise one's profession under the eye of the occupier during an armistice?" he asked in frustration. Yet if Guitry felt deeply wronged, a poll carried out in September showed that 56 percent of those questioned approved of his arrest, with only 12 percent opposed and the rest offering no opinion.

Finally, on October 20, after spending "Sixty Days in Prison" ("Soixante jours de prison"), as he titled his published account of the experience, Guitry was freed on grounds of poor health. But the case against him dragged on for another thirty-four months, focused less

*Decaux went on to have a successful career as a writer and was elected to the Académie Française in 1979.

on his professional life than on his good relations with German officialdom. Guitry became increasingly embittered, complaining, "What I am paying for today is not my activity over four years, but for the success and happiness of 40 years, for which I am not forgiven." Indeed, jealousy may have been a factor: he was an actor, playwright, movie director, theater owner—and rich. When the case was dropped on August 8, 1947, the ruling attributed his behavior to narcissism. It concluded: "Thus his need, like oxygen, of a public; and off-stage, of the adulation and favors of the world and its powerful. He has only known a life of exhibiting himself. It is that which explains and measures his relations with the occupier."[4]

At the time of Guitry's arrest, many of the gun-toting young men roaming Paris were themselves fresh to the resistance. "Heroes have multiplied," Galtier-Boissière observed. "The number of last-minute resisters, armed head to foot, wearing ammunition belts in the style of Mexicans, is considerable. Some heroines, too, revolvers in their belts."[5] At the end of August, however, the provisional government gave FFI members the choice of surrendering their weapons or continuing the war against Germany by joining the French army. Then, from mid-September, it began creating a legal structure to handle the *épuration.* The task was immense: initially, some 900,000 people were arrested, often for only a few days; in the end, 124,613 people answered in court for their activities during the occupation.

The High Court of Justice, which was authorized to order death sentences, was set up to try a small number of senior politicians closely associated with the Vichy regime, several of whom returned to France, voluntarily or by force, after V-E Day. The next level, the Courts of Justice, which dealt with other serious cases of collaboration, were far busier, handing down 6,760 death sentences, almost 60 percent of them in absentia; in the end, only 767 of these sentences were carried out. Finally, the Civic Courts heard cases involving lesser forms of collaborationist and unpatriotic behavior. Those found guilty of *indignité nationale* were sentenced to prison terms or *dégradation nationale,* which prevented them from working in the police forces or as teachers and from holding any other government job.

De Gaulle's own position added new variables. While in exile, he had viewed the resistance as a potential threat to his power and played down its importance. Now, as part of his strategy to reunify the country, he portrayed France as a nation of resisters, with only a small number of genuine collaborators. This meant displaying considerable tolerance toward those "forty million *pétainistes*" of the early 1940s. "If it is urgent to punish true traitors," he said in a speech on October 14, 1944, "it is not a good idea to remove from French society those people who, in the name of legality, were misled to follow the marshal."[6] Put simply, de Gaulle favored punishment but not deep soul-searching.

The trial of Vichy was evidently a priority, not only because of the regime's criminal record, but also because it was important to demonstrate that l'État Français created by Pétain was not a successor to the Third Republic but an entirely illegal regime. Supporting the prosecution's case was Article 75 of the penal code, decreed in July 1939, which defined the crime of treason and required the death sentence for those found guilty. Pétain, who had asked to be repatriated from Switzerland in late April 1945, was brought before the High Court three months later. But while the trial stirred enormous interest in a country that had looked to him in hope not many years earlier, it was largely anticlimactic. After his opening statement, the marshal refused to speak and, now eighty-nine, dozed through most of the hearings. His lawyers argued that he had played a double game, appeasing the Germans while helping the Allies, but evidence of this was thin. Verdicts of guilty of high treason, intelligence with the enemy and *indignité nationale* (which meant losing his military rank) were returned, but his death sentence was commuted by de Gaulle, and Pétain died in prison on the Île d'Yeu, off the Atlantic coast, in 1951.

Laval's trial in October 1945 was more dramatic, with the presiding judge struggling to maintain order as jurors shouted insults at the accused. After he was sentenced to death, Laval tried to kill himself with cyanide, but doctors saved him by pumping out his stomach. He had attempted suicide, he said, so that French soldiers would not be parties to a "judicial crime," but he went to his death courageously. After he was refused the right to give the firing squad the order to open fire, he told the soldiers, "I don't hold this against you. Aim for the heart. Vive la France!"[7]

Of the sixteen others sentenced to death by the High Court, only two—Joseph Darnand, the *milice* leader, and Fernand de Brinon, the government-in-exile leader in Sigmaringen—were executed. Abel Bonnard, the Académie Française member who had served as Vichy's education minister, had fled to Spain and was condemned to death in absentia. Granted asylum by Franco, he returned to France in 1960 for another trial, at which he was given the symbolic sentence of ten years' banishment, retroactive to 1945. Believing that he had been treated unfairly, he returned to Spain, where he died in 1968. Others sentenced to death in absentia included Darquier de Pellepoix, the infamous head of Vichy's General Commission for Jewish Questions, who also spent the rest of his life in Spain.

In the world of culture, all the disciplines set up their own *comités d'épuration,* which were authorized to investigate and interrogate collaborationist artists and writers. They could also recommend cases for trial by Civic Courts and issue professional sanctions, such as a ban on performing or publishing for up to two years. In practice, however, there was much confusion and overlap, since disciplines were often represented by several professional organizations. For instance, six different groups representing writers held hearings, while many institutions, such as the Comédie Française, the Académie Française and the Paris Opera, carried out their own inquiries and purges.

These "trials" could be incestuous affairs since, not infrequently, the judges and the judged knew each other well and may have worked together before the war and even during the occupation. Some may also have rubbed shoulders at German receptions. "I can recall no case where a French intellectual refused an invitation to such receptions in the German embassy in Paris," Abetz told French interrogators after the war. "Even those who declared themselves opposed to collaboration at a political level were in favor, they said, of the confrontation and exchange of ideas in culture."[8] Adding to the disarray was the power struggle between Communists, who dominated most *comités d'épuration,* and moderates, who were reluctant to join a witch hunt. In some cases, personal vendettas translated into political charges; in others, professional envy played a role, since prohibitions to work could remove competitors from the scene; in a few cases, old friendships survived political differences and helped to soften punishments. Ideological feuds also resurfaced: when Aragon denounced Gide for a defeatist journal entry in September 1940, published after the liberation,* it was apparent that the

---

*On September 5, 1940, Gide wrote, "To come to terms with one's enemy of yesterday is not cowardice; it is wisdom and acceptance of the inevitable." He added, "What is the use of bruising oneself against the bars of one's cage? In order to suffer less from the narrowness of the jail, there is nothing like remaining squarely in the middle."

poète de la résistance, as he was soon known, had not forgotten
Gide's 1936 attack on Moscow in *Retour de l'U.R.S.S.*

In all, what looked relatively simple during the occupation proved
immensely complicated immediately after the liberation. Almost
every artist and writer had worked during the occupation, so where
should the line be drawn? What exactly constituted collaboration?
Did it embrace early sympathy for Pétain? Did it include performing
before German audiences? Was it treachery to attend a reception
hosted by Germans? Was it credible when a prominent collaborationist insisted that he was secretly working for British intelligence?
Was there evidence to support claims by some Fascists that they
saved the lives of Jews by warning them of imminent roundups? In
practice, because no consensus ever emerged, the *épuration culturelle*
was rife with inconsistencies; among artists, writers and journalists
with comparable records of collaboration, some were sanctioned,
others were jailed, a handful were even executed, while a good many
were never arrested. Only in hindsight did one pattern appear: the
longer an arrest, trial and sentence could be delayed, the lighter the
punishment. "If Drieu La Rochelle had agreed to hide in a basement
for two years, he'd have been made a minister," Paul Léautaud later
quoted Jouhandeau as saying.[9]

Among the different cultural *comités d'épuration,* that of writers
was the best organized and most radical, just as the Comité National
des Écrivains, or CNE, had been the most effective cultural resistance group. Its *commission d'épuration,* which included Éluard,
Queneau and Jean Bruller (now better known as Vercors), began by
naming twelve traitors in early September 1944, among them Céline,
Drieu La Rochelle, Brasillach, Montherlant, Giono, Jouhandeau and
Châteaubriant. To these were added another 153 "undesirables,"
defined as journalists and writers who had remained loyal to Vichy
after Germany occupied southern France in November 1942. Their
names were then splashed across *Les Lettres Françaises,* which added
the names of a few more "professionally repugnant" writers of its
own choosing. Many of the "most wanted" were the editors of pro-
German newspapers who had not only celebrated Hitler and denounced Jews but had also attacked and insulted the Communists
and Gaullists who were now in power. These cases, however, were
handled by the Courts of Justice, where, to add to the confusion,
many presiding judges had also worked under Vichy. Initially at
least, punishments were severe.

The first to be tried and sentenced to death for his writings was Georges Suarez, the editor of *Aujourd'hui*. Although Youki Desnos spoke up for him, saying he had tried to save her husband, Robert, from deportation, he was executed on November 9, 1944. Paul Chack, a writer and former naval officer who had also written for the collaborationist press, was condemned to death. "You took the side of Germany at the moment the French were uniting against the invader," he was told. He was shot on January 9, 1945. Three other well-known journalists were also executed. Jean Hérold-Paquis, who had broadcast German propaganda on Radio-Paris and was famous for ending his nightly news program with the cry "England, like Carthage, must be destroyed," was executed on October 11, 1945. Paul Ferdonnet, accused of broadcasting Nazi propaganda in French from Radio Stuttgart between 1940 and 1942, was arrested in Germany in May 1945, tried in July and executed in August. And Jean Luchaire, the former editor of *Les Nouveaux Temps* whose old friend Abetz was brought from jail to testify on his behalf, was shot on February, 22, 1946.

Others were luckier. Henri Béraud, a novelist known for his Anglophobia who was the chief editorial writer for *Gringoire*, was also condemned to death in December 1944, but Mauriac came to his defense, arguing that he had not intentionally aided the enemy. He was reprieved by de Gaulle and freed in 1950.* The rabid anti-Semite Lucien Rebatet, who was arrested in Germany on May 8, 1945, was finally brought to trial in November 1946, along with Pierre-Antoine Cousteau, the editor of *Je suis partout* from 1943. Both men were condemned to death, but six months later their sentences were commuted to life imprisonment, and within five years they, too, were out of jail.

Two Fascist writers who were also journalists stood out for the literary prestige they enjoyed. Of these, Drieu La Rochelle, who for thirty months edited the *Nouvelle Revue Française*, harbored no illusions about what awaited him. Since long before the liberation, he had not only anticipated Germany's defeat but also planned his own suicide. On August 10, 1944, he wrote a final letter to his brother Jean in which he defended his philosophy: "In my heart, I stood beyond my nation, beyond all nations—more racist than nationalist.

---

*In another apparent contradiction, Béraud's editor at *Gringoire*, Horace de Carbuccia, was never brought to trial.

I would have preferred to have been English or German or Russian: from the north. France has too much mixed blood from the south for us." Now he was happy to end his days before illness and old age took over. "I am going to kill myself," he wrote. "My death is a freely chosen sacrifice that will protect me from certain stains, certain weaknesses. And above all, I am not interested enough in politics to have it fill (prison, etc.) my final days."[10]

Two days later, Drieu La Rochelle took a heavy dose of barbiturates, but he was found unconscious by his housekeeper and taken to the American Hospital in Neuilly. Gerhard Heller later recalled learning of his friend's condition and hurrying to visit him. "He opened his eyes briefly — 'for the first time,' the nurse tells me — and he whispers, 'Ah, it's you, Heller.' I slip a passport under his pillow."[11] The passport contained visas allowing Drieu La Rochelle to travel to either Spain or Switzerland, but he would never use it. While still in the hospital, he attempted suicide anew by cutting his wrists, but was again saved.

After Paris was freed, hiding occasionally in the home of his first — Jewish — wife, Colette Jeramec, he was apparently shielded from arrest by his friends Malraux and Emmanuel d'Astier de la Vigerie, the resistance leader who was now interior minister in the provisional government. But Drieu La Rochelle knew that he could not escape trial. On March 15, 1945, after switching on his gas cooker and swallowing poison, he died. Galtier-Boissière remembered warning him five years earlier that he would be shot for being pro-German. "The unfortunate has shot *himself*," he noted.[12] Among those attending his funeral in Neuilly were Paulhan, Léautaud and Gaston Gallimard. Malraux, whom Drieu La Rochelle specifically asked to be present, could not return from the war front, where he was serving in the French army.

While Drieu La Rochelle avoided arrest by committing suicide, Robert Brasillach felt constrained to surrender to the Paris police on September 14, 1944, following the arrest of his mother and his brother-in-law, Maurice Bardèche, a fellow Fascist. After being held in a fort at Noisy-le-Sec, a Paris suburb, he was transferred to Fresnes to await the opening of his trial by a Court of Justice on January 19, 1945. The case against him was simple: it consisted of presenting his signed editorials in *Je suis partout* and his later articles in *La Révolution Nationale,* all of which seemed to support the charge of intelligence with the enemy.

As in similar trials, Brasillach's anti-Semitic views were not held against him; his crime was supporting the Germans and denouncing Jews and resisters. In his defense, his lawyer Jacques Isorni read from letters of support from Claudel and Valéry, as well as one from Mauriac, who, the lawyer said, wrote that "it would be a loss to French letters if this brilliant mind were extinguished forever."[13] For the government commissioner, Marcel Reboul, Brasillach's crimes were born of vanity: "Brasillach's treason is above all a treason of the intellectual, a treason of pride. This man grew tired of the jousting of the placid contest of pure letters. He needed an audience, a public role, a political influence, and he was ready to do anything to achieve that."[14] After a trial that lasted just six hours, Brasillach was condemned to death.

Brasillach's case was difficult: he was an admired writer who had gone beyond opinion to finger people who had ended up jailed or deported. The verdict against him nonetheless intensified the debate among writers about how to deal with collaboration by their peers. In public, the issue confronted Camus in *Combat* and Mauriac in *Le Figaro*. Both agreed that the *épuration* was chaotic, but Camus insisted that a genuine purge was necessary if France was to be reborn. Without such justice, he added, "one sees that Mr. Mauriac is right, we will need charity." Mauriac had asked whether, in a world of "pitiless cruelty," human tenderness and mercy should be discarded.[15] In this spirit, Mauriac had already taken a stance by defending Béraud, whose death sentence was commuted immediately before the Brasillach trial.

Responding to Camus on January 7, 1945, in a column headlined "Contempt for Charity," Mauriac again argued the virtues of national reconciliation and the importance of judicial impartiality at a time of high emotions. A few days later, with "Justice and Charity," Camus replied: "On the matter of the purges, every time I have spoken of justice, Mr. Mauriac has spoken of charity. And the virtue of charity is sufficiently singular that, by demanding justice, I have given the impression of advocating hate. In listening to Mr. Mauriac, one truly has the impression that, in these daily questions, it is absolutely essential to choose between the love of Christ and the hatred of men." He continued: "As a man, I will perhaps admire Mr. Mauriac for knowing how to love traitors, but as a citizen I deplore it because this love will inevitably lead us to become a nation of traitors and mediocrities as well as a society of a kind that we do not want."[16]

Mauriac, whose campaign prompted *Le Canard Enchaîné* to nickname him Saint Francis of the Assizes, was not deterred. After the verdict in the Brasillach case, he organized a petition addressed to de Gaulle asking for clemency—not on moral grounds but because Brasillach's father had "died for France" in World War I. Among its sixty signatories were Valéry, Claudel, Anouilh, Paulhan, Colette, the composer Honegger, the painters Derain and Vlaminck and, added at the last minute, Camus. De Gaulle rejected the appeal and, on February 6, Brasillach was shot. But just six months later, Camus, too, had serious misgivings about the purge. On August 30, 1945, he wrote in *Combat:* "We beg the reader's indulgence if we begin today with a basic fact: there can no longer be any doubt that the postwar purge has not only failed in France but is now completely discredited. The word 'purge' itself was already rather distressing. The actual thing became odious."[17] In 1948, he conceded that Mauriac had been right all along.

The trial of Charles Maurras, already seventy-six years old when France was liberated, had an entirely different significance. Although elected to the Académie Française only in 1939, Maurras's political importance dated back to the turn of the century when he had led the campaign against Captain Alfred Dreyfus, the French Jewish army officer wrongfully accused of spying for Germany. In the years that followed, notably after World War I, his movement and its newspaper, *L'Action Française,* came to represent a peculiar blend of anti-Semitism, nationalism, Germanophobia and monarchism. At the same time, Maurras became the ideological mentor of a generation of bright young intellectuals, Brasillach and Rebatet among them, who in the late 1930s embraced Hitler's National Socialism. When France fell in 1940, Maurras moved to the unoccupied zone and backed Pétain's National Revolution. He remained violently anti-Semitic, but also so overtly anti-German that, after Germany took over the unoccupied zone, he feared Gestapo reprisals.

Maurras's arrest in September 1944 set the stage for a sensational trial, which began on January 26, 1945, in the middle of the writers' campaign to save Brasillach. Since he could not be accused of collaborating with an enemy he hated, the formal charge against him was that of demoralizing France. His real crime, however, was that of founding the Fascist movement that had so harmed the country. The prosecution asked for a death sentence but, because of his age and the Brasillach case, Maurras was condemned to life imprisonment. "It's

Dreyfus's revenge," he cried out. He was released in March 1952 on
health grounds and died eight months later.

After Brasillach, no writer was executed. Some who would certainly have faced severe punishment stayed abroad. Alphonse de
Châteaubriant, who had headed the Groupe Collaboration and
edited *La Gerbe,* managed to reach Austria and took refuge in a
monastery in the Tyrol, where he died in 1951. Alain Laubreaux,
Je suis partout's venomous theater critic, found refuge in Franco's
Spain, where he died in 1968. With the CNE and *Les Lettres
Françaises* beating the drum for quick and radical justice against collaborationist writers, however, others did spells in jail before their
cases were judged.

Jean Giono, who had been jailed as a pacifist during the phony
war, was again arrested, in September 1944, and detained for five
months. His offense was to have published articles in some collaborationist outlets and to have written—as he always had done—about
rural life in what now seemed like a *pétainiste* manner. In the end, no
formal charges were brought against him since he had never defended
the Nazis and he claimed to have protected a German refugee and
two Jews. But the CNE still banned him from publishing for two
years. Some of Giono's friends said that his real mistake was to have
fallen out with Aragon and the Communist Party before the war.

The case against Georges Simenon, the popular thriller writer,
dragged on for six years. He was not part of the Paris literary scene,
preferring to stay in Vendée. But because nine of his novels had been
adapted for the screen during the occupation, four by Continental
Films, the German-owned studio, in 1950 he was banned from publishing new works for five years, although the sentence was retroactive and therefore meaningless.

For many writers, uncertainty was their main punishment.
Jacques Chardonne, the novelist and shareholder of Éditions Stock
who had been on two French delegations to Weimar writers' conferences, was jailed for six weeks in 1944, but charges against him were
dropped in 1946. Marcel Jouhandeau, Florence Gould's friend who
had also accepted the German invitation to Weimar, was never jailed,
but he lived for several months in fear of arrest. Even before Paris
was liberated, he had begun to receive threatening telephone calls,
and he had taken Paulhan's advice to go into hiding with his wife. In
his journal, he had started rehearsing his defense: "Ours was a simple
offense of opinion, imprudences which brought us no reward."[18]

After his name appeared on the CNE's list of "undesirables," he fled Paris. Then, when nothing further happened, he returned and resumed teaching. But in May 1945, he was summoned for questioning and found himself in the company of Montherlant. "Before nightfall, they're going to take you to Drancy and me perhaps to Vincennes, and we'll never see each other again," the playwright told him. "They will strangle us in our cells."[19]

The outcome was far less dramatic. While Montherlant was banned from publishing for one year, principally because his 1941 book of essays, *Le Solstice de juin,* was considered pro-German, Jouhandeau's punishment was to be ostracized by writers on the left. This mattered little to him: soon he was again jousting with Léautaud around Florence Gould's Thursday lunch table.

Gradually, though, the thirst for revenge against writers began to ease. One important factor was the recognition that writers and journalists were being punished far more severely than, say, many industrialists who had profited from doing business with the Nazis. "In the *épuration,* it is the journalist, threadbare and mangy, who is the scapegoat," Galtier-Boissière wrote. "One forgets that some of them had only their pen with which to feed their family and wrote only anodyne pieces. Does one reproach the workers at Renault for making tanks for the Wehrmacht? Wasn't a tank more useful to the Fritz than an item in *Le Petit Parisien*?"[20]

Paulhan, who as a central figure of the intellectual resistance had supported the *épuration,* also now believed writers were being singled out unfairly. "The engineers, entrepreneurs and masons who built the Atlantic Wall walk among us undisturbed," he argued. "They keep busy building new walls. They build the walls of new prisons, which hold journalists who made the mistake of writing that the Atlantic Wall was well built."[21] In late September 1944, Paulhan resigned from *Les Lettres Françaises* and gradually began distancing himself from his former colleagues. He worried that, with Communists in the driver's seat, the *épuration intellectuelle* was beginning to resemble a Stalinist purge. His argument that writers had "a right to err" was dismissed by hard-liners. Other moderates, noting widely differing punishments for the same offenses, began to ask if, in a free country, any writer should be condemned for the "crime of opinion." Some were unhappy when ninety-three books by Céline, Rebatet and other collaborators were banned: it reminded them of the Nazis' Otto List.

But if collaborationist writers ended up enduring a tough *épuration,* this was not only because they were opinion makers; it was also because, by giving them importance, resistance writers were underlining their own importance and reinforcing their own social status. They did not want to abandon the view that writers had special responsibilities, a view that de Gaulle himself endorsed. In his *Mémoires de guerre,* recalling his posture toward collaborators, he indirectly explained why he had not saved Brasillach's life: "If [collaborators] had not served the enemy directly and passionately, I commuted their sentence on principle. In the opposite case—the only one—I did not feel I had the right to pardon. For in literature, as in everything, talent carries with it responsibility."[22] Even Drieu La Rochelle had written of the intellectual, "He has duties and rights above those of others."[23]

And yet, for all their political and ethical differences, writers had shared one fundamental need during the occupation: that of seeing their words in print. As a result, since so many *résistants* had also published books with German approval, the purge committee for publishing, which included Sartre, Bruller and Seghers among its members, was largely toothless. And its inability to judge publishers soon prompted Bruller and Seghers to resign in disgust. True, Bernard Grasset, the most actively pro-German publisher, was arrested on September 19 and sent to Drancy. But with Mauriac, Valéry and Duhamel among writers jumping to his defense, he was released six weeks later. Éditions Grasset was banned from selling or publishing books, but this sanction was lifted in May 1946. Robert Denoël, the Belgian national who had published the anti-Semitic ravings of both Céline and Rebatet, as well as books by Aragon and Triolet, was never brought to trial: he was found murdered on a street near the Invalides on December 2, 1945, with the killer's identity and motive never clarified. On the other hand, Gaston Gallimard, who had protected his own business by allowing Drieu La Rochelle to take over the *Nouvelle Revue Française,* had nothing to fear. He had published many writers opposed to the Germans, and twenty of them wrote individual letters to support him. "I believe that any criticism of the Éditions Gallimard would be directed at all the writers who belonged to the intellectual resistance who were published by the house," Sartre wrote, ignoring the question of whether these writers should have been publishing at all.[24] In any event, two "untouchables," Paulhan and Camus, were still on Gallimard's payroll.

Two other literary institutions cleaned up their own houses. The Académie Française expelled Pétain, Maurras, Bonnard and Abel Hermant and filled the numerous seats left open during the occupation. But it remained a conservative body, adding Claudel, Marcel Pagnol, Jules Romains and Édouard Herriot in 1946, Cocteau in 1955 and Montherlant in 1960. Two *résistants* were elected still later, Guéhenno in 1962 and Paulhan in 1963. The Académie Goncourt, in turn, expelled Guitry and René Benjamin and brought in Colette. Soon amnesties, one in January 1951, a second in July 1953, led to the release of almost all jailed collaborators.

A few writers chose to stay abroad, but it was perhaps the return of Céline from Denmark that closed this chapter of France's literary wars. He reached Copenhagen from Sigmaringen on March 22, 1945, although the French government learned of his whereabouts only months later. Finally, in December, France demanded his extradition to face charges of treason. But while Céline spent the next eighteen months in jail in Denmark, he was never sent home. In early 1950, he was tried in absentia, found guilty of *indignité nationale* and sentenced to one year in prison, a heavy fine and confiscation of half his belongings. Barely one year later, he was amnestied and, in July 1951, he and his wife, Lucette, returned to France. They moved to Meudon, a suburb southwest of Paris, where two years later Céline opened a medical practice. Had he been arrested in 1944, he almost certainly would have been executed. A decade later, while he looked like a mad hermit, he was again publishing with Gallimard and his status as one of France's greatest twentieth-century writers seemed secure. For many French citizens, his pro-Nazi and anti-Semitic delirium was simply overshadowed by his genius.

The *épuration* in other cultural areas was, by comparison, relatively gentle, although in music, an art form particularly dear to the Germans, two high-profile cases stood out. The concert pianist Alfred Cortot, who had found time to perform in Germany while working as a musical adviser to Vichy, was arrested by the FFI in his Neuilly home on September 1, 1944. He was quickly released following intercession by Claude Delvincourt, the director of the Conservatoire de Paris and himself a *résistant*. But the following year, the Fine Arts Committee of Inquiry revoked Cortot's position as a professor at the conservatory, while a professional purge committee suspended his right to perform in public for one year. When he resumed his career at the Théâtre des Champs-Élysées in Paris in January

1947, he was booed off the stage. Within two years, though, much of the public had forgiven him.

In contrast, the *épuration* destroyed the singing career of Germaine Lubin, the great Wagnerian soprano. A German favorite, she was arrested by the FFI on the day after the liberation and taken for questioning to the town hall of the 8th arrondissement. Her lawyer obtained her release, but one week later she was again arrested, and this time she was held for two months, first in Drancy, then in Fresnes. In the meantime, she was banned from performing at the Paris Opera. The legal case against her was dropped in January 1945, reopened in March by a Civic Court, then again dropped. She withdrew to her château in the Loire Valley, but in December 1946 she was rearrested and brought to trial, this time before a Court of Justice, which found her guilty of *indignité nationale* and ordered confiscation of her property and condemned her to *dégradation nationale.* Then, in May 1949, Lubin was once more summoned by still another Civic Court in Paris, to answer the charge that she had used her friendship with Hitler to obtain her son's release from a prison camp. The following year, now sixty years old, she offered a recital at the Salle Gaveau. Her loyal fans gave her an ovation, but her voice was failing her and she never again sang in public. Instead, until her death in 1979, she worked as a voice teacher, with the soprano Régine Crespin among her pupils.

The purge of other musicians and dancers focused on those close to the Germans. Serge Lifar, the Paris Opera's ballet director, who both boasted and exhibited his close ties with the Germans, left Paris before he could be arrested. He was banned from the opera, but he had found work in Monte Carlo and returned to his old post as ballet master at the opera in 1947. Perhaps most remarkably, at least to judge by his memoir, *Ma vie,* Lifar never ceased to believe that he had always acted correctly and in the interests of the Paris Opera.

The *étoile* ballerina Solange Schwarz, who had had a German lover, was also banned from the Paris Opera, but she, too, soon resumed her career, first at the Ballets des Champs-Élysées, then at the Opéra-Comique. Even Jacques Rouché, the venerable head of both the Paris Opera and the Opéra-Comique, was interrogated by the FFI, but the composers Francis Poulenc, Georges Auric and Roger Désormière came to his defense and no charges were brought against him. In contrast, Max d'Ollone, the *pétainiste* who had headed the music section of the Groupe Collaboration and served as director of the Opéra-Comique during much of the occupation, emerged unscathed.

The world of popular music was no less exposed than opera and ballet, since *chansonniers* and cabaret dancers had routinely performed before Germans. Like many others, Léo Marjane had sung regularly on Radio-Paris, where her signature "Je suis seule ce soir" had echoed the melancholy of women whose husbands were prisoners in Germany. When she was taken before a Civic Court to answer for performing before Germans, she responded dismissively, "I am myopic." But her career never recovered.

Maurice Chevalier, Tino Rossi, Charles Trenet and Édith Piaf had been denounced by Radio-Londres for visiting Germany, even though it was only to perform before French prisoners of war or STO workers. Chevalier, who had spent the final months of the occupation hiding from both the resistance and the Gestapo, was briefly arrested. Thanks to Aragon, he was released and escaped further punishment, although in exchange he was expected to perform at various Communist Party fund-raisers. He then tried to persuade his American fans that he had never collaborated with the Germans by filming a special message to them in his trademark "Frenchie" English. Rossi was arrested in October 1944 and spent three weeks in Fresnes before he was briefly banned from performing, while Trenet, also suspended from singing in public, went to the United States for two years before returning to enjoy a glittering career. Piaf was hardly bothered: summoned for questioning, she found witnesses to testify that she had helped some prisoners of war escape and was forgiven for entertaining Germans in Paris.

In cinema, it was still more difficult to separate judges and judged since, except for Jews and those few actors and directors who had left for the United States, the entire industry had worked throughout the occupation: no fewer than 220 French movies by 82 different directors had been made and released under German rule. After the liberation, the industry's Communist-dominated *comité d'épuration* decided to focus on those who had worked for Alfred Greven's Continental Films. Bizarrely, among those who had done so were the screenwriter Jean-Paul Le Chanois and the assistant director Jean-Devaivre, who had belonged to the small cinema resistance group that put out the clandestine sheet *L'Écran Français*. Further, while seven of the eight directors named for investigation had worked for Continental, some, like Michel Tourneur, who had made six movies for Greven, were not on the list. Jean Marais, now wearing an FFI uniform, was disturbed by the persecution. "Many of my colleagues who had worked for Continental or Radio-Paris revealed themselves at the liberation to be *résistants*," he wrote in his memoir, *Histoire de ma vie*. "They accused and judged their peers."[25]

One who was admonished for signing a contract with Continental was Marcel Carné, even though he had made no movies for the German firm. On the other hand, after endless hearings, Henri-Georges Clouzot was banned from filmmaking for two years, albeit more because the resistance hated *Le Corbeau* than because he had made it for Continental. The movie was even proscribed at the liberation, although the poet and screenwriter Jacques Prévert testified that it was not "a film of anti-French propaganda." Perhaps because he was so well known, Pierre Fresnay, who had made nine films during the occupation, including four for Continental, was jailed for six weeks, then placed under house arrest.

In a few cases, punishments went beyond professional sanctions. Some directors and editors involved in making propaganda newsreels for *France Actualités* were given prison sentences. One movie director, Jean Mamy, who had also used the name Paul Riche, was even executed. He had made *Forces occultes*, an anti-Semitic and anti-Masonic production, which was arguably the only propagandistic feature film of the occupation. In August 1944, having first gone into hiding, he surrendered to the police after his mother was arrested by the FFI. Inexplicably, he was not brought to trial until late 1948 and, in March 1949, he was the last person shot under the *épuration*.

Some FFI lists included the actors who had traveled to Berlin in 1942 with Danielle Darrieux. Albert Prejean, who had made six movies for Continental, was jailed for six weeks but never charged. Viviane Romance was arrested in Biarritz, held for several weeks, then acquitted by a military tribunal. Darrieux recalled that when she arrived to be questioned, the first man she saw was none other than her former husband, Henri Decoin, who had made three films for Continental. "He said, 'But what the hell are you doing here?' And he said, 'Get the hell out of here right now.' They really didn't know who was who in the purge."[26] Decoin himself was suspended from working for one year because one of his films, *Les Inconnus dans la maison*, was said to have demoralized the French.

Other cases were more serious. Céline's friend Robert Le Vigan had a lot to answer for: a veteran star of stage and screen, he was a convinced Fascist who had voiced his anti-Semitism on Radio-Paris, he had joined Doriot's extreme rightist party and he was suspected of being an informant for the Gestapo. Jean-Louis Barrault, Madeleine Renaud and Pierre Renoir spoke up for him, but he was nonetheless sentenced to ten years of hard labor by a Court of Justice; he was freed on bail in 1948. The veteran actress Cécile Sorel, seventy years old when Paris was liberated, was sentenced to *dégradation nationale* for requesting the gift of an apartment confiscated from a Jewish family. And Alice Cocéa was jailed for three months and banned from working for a year for taking over the lease of the Théâtre des Ambassadeurs, which belonged to the exiled Jewish playwright Henry Bernstein.* Ginette Leclerc, who made eleven films during the occupation, including *Le Corbeau,* suffered more than most: she was jailed for nine months because, with Greven's help, she had opened a cabaret popular with German officers.

Just as women who engaged in *collaboration horizontale* were seen to have offended French honor, actresses who had paraded around Paris with German officers on their arms were singled out. Mireille Balin's Wehrmacht lover was even assassinated when she was arrested by the FFI in September 1944. The actress Corinne Luchaire was carrying the child of her Austrian Wehrmacht lover when she followed her collaborationist father, Jean, to Sigmaringen in 1944; she was later sentenced to ten years of *dégradation nationale.*

The most famous actress to be trapped by the *épuration* was the inimitable Arletty. In her favor, she had made no films for Continental and, with Guitry, she had helped obtain Tristan Bernard's release from Drancy. But from 1941 she was devoted to a young Luftwaffe officer, Hans Jürgen Soehring. She was seen everywhere with him, dining at Maxim's and attending receptions at the German embassy, including one for Göring in December 1941. After the liberation, she went into hiding, but she was arrested two months later and sent to Drancy. "In jail, a young nun tried to bring me closer to God," she later recalled. "I told her that we had already met and it hadn't worked out."[27] Always quick with a bon mot, one morning during her trial she was asked by the prosecutor how she was feeling. "Not

---

*In 1950, Bernstein publicly forgave Cocéa and dropped a lawsuit against the actress Michèle Alfa, who, with her Wehrmacht boyfriend, had occupied his apartment from 1940.

very *résistante,*" she replied. The principal complaint against her, then, was that she had had a German lover, to which she retorted, "In my bed there are no uniforms." She then offered the line for which she is best remembered: "My heart is French but my ass is international." After six weeks in Drancy, she was placed under house arrest at the château of friends in La Houssaye-en-Brie, twenty miles outside Paris. In 1947, she resumed her career with *La Fleur de l'âge,* a new film by her old friend Carné, for whom she had made two of the best films of the occupation, *Les Visiteurs du soir* and *Les Enfants du paradis.* In 1956, with ten movies to her name since the liberation, she was chosen to be a member of the jury of the ninth Cannes Film Festival. Even at the age of fifty-eight, she still knew how to charm the French.

For visual artists, it was relatively easy during the occupation to continue working and even to sell oils or sculptures privately or through a gallery without ever coming into contact with Germans. When German officers came to his door, Picasso was unable to turn them away, but at least some of these uninvited visitors were educated men, like Jünger and Heller. The issue of collaboration arose when artists went out of their way to associate themselves with the occupiers. After the liberation, the Communist-dominated Front National des Arts immediately denounced the dozen artists who had accepted invitations to visit Germany in October 1941, among them the Fauvists Derain, Van Dongen, Vlaminck and Friesz. Several of these same artists had also sat on the Comité d'Honneur for Arno Breker's splashy exhibition at the Orangerie in 1942. Aristide Maillol would probably also have been interrogated about his friendship with Breker, but the octogenarian sculptor died in a car crash while driving to visit Dufy on September 26, 1944. The Front National itself had no power of arrest, but its naming and shaming of artists under investigation was widely reported, above all after Picasso joined the Communist Party and was appointed president of the Front's executive committee.[*]

In June 1946, twenty-three artists, including those fêted in Germany in 1941, were sanctioned with one- or two-year suspensions of

---

[*]Galtier-Boissière was unpersuaded by Picasso's new ideological commitment. In *Mon journal depuis la libération,* he wrote, "The truth known to all artists is that Picasso was in terror of losing his immense fortune. By joining the Communist Party, he obtained an insurance and some are even mentioning the exact size of the premium" (p. 31).

their right to exhibit or sell their works. And while this had little impact on their professional activity, at the very least it bruised their reputations. On the other hand, galleries that had operated during the occupation, even some that had sold art looted from Jewish families, were not sanctioned. Thus, once again, businessmen were held to lower moral standards than artists. In fashion, designers were also treated as businessmen—essential to France's recovery—rather than artists: of the fifty-five cases brought before the *commission d'épuration de la couture*, not one involved a major fashion house. In contrast, it was Chanel's private life that earned her a short spell in jail; friends obtained her release and she wisely moved to Switzerland until 1954.

The debate about theater during the occupation was simplified by the fact that, as with cinema, everything presented before the public had been censored and/or approved by the Propaganda Staffel. On the other hand, the urge to purge was complicated by the fact that playwrights who accepted these rules included not only *pétainistes* like Montherlant, *attentistes* like Anouilh and Claudel and opportunists like Cocteau and Guitry, but also Sartre and Camus, men who after the liberation were identified with the resistance. Further, it was no secret that German officers had attended and applauded performances of both of Sartre's plays.

Among the mainly Communist members of the Front National du Théâtre, there was nonetheless a strong desire to sanction those who had appeared to be too close to the Vichy regime. René Rocher, who had been named director of the Théâtre de l'Odéon by Vichy, was jailed for five months but was then acquitted. The Comédie Française's own purge committee dismissed a number of actors who had freelanced by reciting poetry or famous soliloquies at Nazi-sponsored events. Conversely, the Jewish actress Béatrice Bretty, whose husband, Georges Mandel, had been murdered by the *milice* in 1944, was welcomed back to the theater. Among playwrights, the only appealing target was Montherlant, not for his historical drama *La Reine morte* but for *Le Solstice de juin.* But even his one-year prohibition from publishing was retroactive.

A more interesting debate revolved around whether plays approved by the Nazis contained hidden resistance messages. For some in the Front National du Théâtre, Anouilh was suspect, not only because he was a Laubreaux favorite but also because he was a relative newcomer to theater and did not belong to Left Bank literary circles.

He defended himself, arguing that *Antigone* forcefully articulated his belief in individual freedom. But while he was never sanctioned, the unproved charges thrown at him, all too often by the Communist Party's daily, *L'Humanité,* raised doubts about his position.

Sartre, on the other hand, was better placed to insist that *Les Mouches* and *Huis clos* were both resistance plays. Although his involvement in the intellectual resistance had been minimal, after the liberation he had suddenly appeared as the chronicler of France's calvary. While many other artists and writers were consumed by the *épuration,* he stood back and reinvented the occupation as a kind of tragic historical novel. "Never have we been freer than under the German occupation," he wrote in *Les Lettres Françaises* on September 9, 1944. "We had lost all our rights, starting with that of speaking; we were insulted daily and had to remain silent; we were deported en masse, as workers, as Jews, as political prisoners; everywhere—on walls, in newspapers, on screens—we were confronted by this vile image that our oppressors wanted to give us of ourselves: because of all that, we were free." In this drama, the resistance was the unfailing hero. And since Sartre's "we" embraced both the French and the resistance, it was easy to suppose that he, too, had faced the risk of "imprisonment, deportation and death"—notwithstanding the fact that he, for one, had not "lost all [his] rights" to publish books and present plays. When the article was reprinted as "The Republic of Silence" in the *Atlantic Monthly* in December 1944, the magazine introduced its author as "one of the leaders of the CNE" who "had devoted himself to underground activities with sublime courage," and it ranked him among literary combatants alongside Aragon, Éluard and Paulhan. The construction of Sartre's American image was well under way.

Meanwhile, the artists and writers who had chosen exile began returning to France, the theater director Louis Jouvet in 1945, André Breton in May 1946, others much later. The postwar cultural life of Paris did not wait for them. The Paris Opera reopened on October 23, 1944, with an existing production of Gounod's *Roméo et Juliette;* Picasso was the star of the 1944 Salon d'Automne,* his first exhibition in France since early 1940; Josephine Baker returned to

*Picasso, who had always stayed away from the traditionally conservative Salon d'Automne, was shocked when his seventy-four paintings and five sculptures provoked angry protests from visitors disturbed by their radicalism.

the stage as a resistance heroine; the *théâtre de boulevard* came back to life; *Les Enfants du paradis* finally had its premiere in March 1945; and new newspapers and journals appeared, including *Le Monde* and Sartre's *Les Temps Modernes*. Among some artists and writers who had belonged to the resistance, above all those close to Aragon, now nicknamed the *Le grand inquisiteur*, the urge to settle old scores faded slowly. But once the worst traitors and criminals of the war years had faced justice (or had gone into hiding abroad), most French people seemed happy to embrace the myth of the resistance, to bury the memory of their own ambivalances and to forget the occupation. Artists and writers were among the beneficiaries. Few were those who, within a few years, were not again performing or painting or publishing.

CHAPTER 17

Surviving at a Price

WHAT, THEN, was the cultural legacy of the occupation? Were the "dark years" in fact a golden age for culture, as some remembered them, or were they a time of creative silence and pain? Certainly, despite the taxing circumstances, France's performers and creators kept remarkably busy, offering the public a rich fare of art and entertainment that it could enjoy and understand. In just four years, they also produced some works of lasting quality: several movies, notably *Les Enfants du paradis;* a handful of plays, including *Huis clos;* a few compositions, among them Messiaen's *Quatuor pour la fin du temps;* some hidden paintings and sculptures; and one great work of fiction, Camus's *L'Étranger.* In part, this reflected advantages France enjoyed over other occupied countries, such as a degree of self-government and a residue of German respect for French culture. In Paris, both occupier and occupied wanted an active cultural life—the Germans to distract the locals and themselves, the French to demonstrate that their culture was still alive.

Yet these were hardly normal times. Numerous leading artists left the country, others were forced into hiding, a few chose to remain silent. And those still working in Paris could draw little inspiration from the daily sight of Nazi troops. Not only did fear, censorship and propaganda dampen the creative spirit, but Germany was also ready to smother any new French claim to cultural leadership of Europe. Above all, there was no room for the intense intellectual and artistic debates that had enlivened Paris during the interwar years. Creative artists need the oxygen of freedom to take flight. During the occupation, they had sufficient air to survive, but not to lift off. In that sense, then, the Germans could claim success.

The occupiers did less well, however, with their broader plan to tame French culture and bring German arts to France. While the occupation isolated French artists and writers from the rest of the world, the Germans still liked to parade them through Berlin and other cities as guests of the Reich. They banned and then persecuted Jewish artists, performers and producers, but this left more room for new French talent. They extended their prohibition of "degenerate" art, music and jazz to France, yet modern art was still created, contemporary music was composed and jazz was widely performed. The shortage of textiles, leather and fur hurt the fashion industry, but designers, seamstresses and women at home improvised with flair; understandably, German officers were beguiled by the style and beauty of *les parisiennes*.

Of course, the German embassy and institute had no difficulty in gathering celebrities for diplomatic dinners and receptions. And these guests invariably included Fascist writers and newspaper editors who supported Hitler's new German Europe. But many others attended simply to be in the limelight, to enjoy good wine and food and to ensure that no obstacles stood in the way of their careers. And as opportunists they were not reliable apostles of German culture. In fact, even French Fascists who were happy to endorse National Socialism did little to promote German arts beyond applauding Breker's Orangerie show in 1942. This job was left to the German Institute, which invited some historians and philosophers to give lectures and exchange ideas with their French colleagues. But German movies, plays and books reached few French people. Only in music were the French enthusiastic about German culture—as they had been before 1940 and would again be after the war.

The cultural resistance used every opportunity to work openly as the best way of reaching a broad public. And while artists could hardly be expected to organize an uprising, they could at least assure their audiences that they were not alone in resenting the occupation. A few *chansonniers* with a gift for the double entendre could usually count on chuckles of recognition from streetwise Parisians. Plays by Anouilh and Sartre, while approved by German censors, addressed the question of personal freedom and could be read as allegories. In movies, there was the final scene of *Les Visiteurs du soir,* with a stone statue's beating heart suggesting that France still lived. Some poetry with coded resistance messages was also published openly with the approval of the Propaganda Staffel in Paris and of Vichy in the south. Somewhat accidentally, this included the most influential poem of the occupation, Éluard's "Liberté."

Poetry denouncing the occupation and extolling the resistance, on the other hand, could only circulate secretly. Its function was different. Direct, emotional, patriotic, often violent, it was not written for posterity: it was closer to agitprop than art. After the war, the Surrealist poet Benjamin Péret, who was in exile in Mexico, compared the lyricism of this militant poetry with "pharmaceutical advertising" in *Le Déshonneur des poètes;* the title was chosen as a riposte to *L'Honneur des poètes,* the poetry collection published by Éditions de Minuit in 1943. From the comfort of New York, André Breton also sniped at Aragon and Éluard for sacrificing their art to politics. Yet in occupied France, political poetry was the path that beckoned.

In fiction, two works stood out for their artistic quality. Vercors's *Le Silence de la mer,* published clandestinely by Éditions de Minuit in 1942, portrayed the pain of defeat in a refined literary form. And Irène Némirovsky's *Suite française*—written in 1941 and 1942 and published only in 2004—was a still finer example of fiction in time of war. Significantly, though, no hidden literary chef d'oeuvre appeared immediately after the liberation.

Did this form of cultural resistance worry the Germans? Early in the occupation, alert to any signs of plotting, they moved quickly to dismantle the Musée de l'Homme network in 1941 and to execute the cofounders of *La Pensée Libre* in 1942, even though these *résistants* were doing little more than publishing anti-German propaganda. As the occupation advanced, however, persecution of artists and writers became more haphazard. Several foreign artists, including Otto Freundlich, were arrested and sent to death camps, but as Jews, not resisters. Similarly, Tristan Bernard and Max Jacob were arrested as Jews: Bernard was soon freed, but Jacob died at Drancy. Two Jewish intellectuals, Benjamin Crémieux and Marc Bloch, also died at the hands of the Germans, but both were engaged in the armed resistance. Among those active in Paris, Robert Desnos was one of the few to be arrested and deported (he died of typhus at the Terezin camp in Czechoslovakia), but, again, he had belonged to the Agir resistance group.

From mid-1942, no one involved in the writers' Comité National des Écrivains or in the smaller cinema, art, music or theater resistance groups was detained. One likely explanation is that, while bent on combating armed resistance, the Germans gave little importance to these groups. They were aware of *Les Lettres Françaises* and they had good reason to believe that Paulhan, Mauriac, Aragon and Éluard were involved. In his memoir, Heller said he worried constantly about Paulhan's safety: "Several times at night, I walked up and down the rue des Arènes"—where Paulhan lived—"as a kind of watchman, ready to warn him in case the German or French police arrived."[1] Indeed, in mid-1944, a tip from Heller gave Paulhan time to go into hiding. At the same time, while these literary *résistants* had ample cause to be fearful, they took few precautions; if the Gestapo had chosen to follow them, it could have rounded up a good part of the writers' resistance group in Édith Thomas's 5th arrondissement apartment. But the Germans presumably calculated that ignoring intellectual celebrities would cause them less trouble than arresting them.

The reality is that cultural resistance had a limited reach, if for no other reason than that its numbers were small: albeit including some of France's most respected writers, membership of the writers' CNE, in both Paris and the south, never exceeded forty; the other cultural resistance groups were even smaller. And they all struggled to find the resources—and the printers—needed to put out their clandestine sheets. In its best moments in the weeks before the liberation, *Les Lettres Françaises* was printing twelve thousand copies per month (less than one-tenth of the print run of, say, *Combat*). And with the exception of *Le Silence de la mer,* which was reprinted in London and delivered back to France by the RAF, Éditions de Minuit could usually put out only between five hundred and two thousand copies of each of its books.

After the liberation, Galtier-Boissière was dismissive of this literary resistance. "Poets who wrote a quatrain about Hitler for a confidential sheet—called clandestine—under a pseudonym believe sincerely that they have saved France," he wrote in his journal.[2] In fact, often the public understood that an artist or writer was in the opposition only when he was insulted by the collaborationist press. After the liberation, Mauriac recalled that it was thanks to the "calumnies" of his enemies that he was quickly designated an opponent of the regime. And it was attacks on Aragon by his erstwhile friend Drieu La Rochelle that publicly identified the poet as a resister. But the collaborationist press also fired indiscriminately, frequently targeting Cocteau for his homosexuality and—erroneously—accusing Guitry, Trenet and Lifar of being Jewish. In the end, the French were very aware of the armed resistance but knew little of the artistic and intellectual underground.

What, then, did cultural resistance achieve? Its real importance was not its public impact. Although it was given a structure by the Communist Party, it was born principally as a reaction—ideological, patriotic or moral—by a number of individuals who refused to accept the occupation and felt the need to do something. They then joined like-minded colleagues and found a way of expressing their views in print. Yet even if they aspired to reach a larger audience, their main feat was to preserve a core of decency among practitioners of the arts. Put differently, by following their consciences, they remained true to what they believed were the responsibilities of artists and writers. "The resistance of intellectuals was first of all useful to them, which after all is worth something," Mauriac said after the war.[3] Taking place largely inside the world of artists and writers, this resistance also served to warn collaborationists that they would pay a price for embracing the German occupier. This much, at least, some in France could deduce from fiery clandestine poetry and the stirring "Chant des partisans."

Even then, however, most collaborationists paid little heed to their critics. They were too fully enjoying being in the spotlight, ready to exchange their prestige for whatever benefits were available. And in contrast to the improvised struggle of the resistance press, they were well paid for their articles, and their pronouncements were widely publicized. Still more damaging was the example they set by socializing with the Germans and accepting invitations to Berlin. But, as always, not everything was as it seemed: Parisians would have been surprised to learn that some prominent writers, musicians and movie directors who worked with German approval were also in the resistance. Instead, many French were left with the impression that cultural collaboration had become acceptable.

When the liberation came, then, cultural *résistants* hurried to make it known that, from 1940, there were artists and writers who rejected collaboration and actively opposed the enemy. In doing so, they wanted to rescue both their individual reputations and the prestige of performers and creators as a social class. And now the columns of the city's new or reopened newspapers were open to them. Galtier-Boissière was amused by how quickly they responded. In his journal entry for August 28, he wrote, "First newspaper: a 'message' from Mauriac; second newspaper: a 'message' from Duhamel; third newspaper: a 'message' from Mauriac on the right and a 'message' from Duhamel on the left; fourth newspaper: a 'message' from Duhamel on the right and a 'message' from Mauriac on the left. . . . When you've had to hold back for four years!"[4] Soon Mauriac had a regular column in *Le Figaro,* while other former *résistants* had their own newspapers: Camus as editor in chief of *Combat,* Aragon as editor of *Ce Soir* and Morgan still running *Les Lettres Françaises.*

Sartre, who had begun glorifying the resistance—and, implicitly, himself—in *Les Lettres Françaises,* never altered his simplistic, and duly romanticized, claim that the only options were to collaborate or to resist. Many years later, he told an interviewer: "So every French person had the free choice to be part of the resistance, in their heads anyway, even if they actually did nothing, or to be an enemy."[5] He even suggested that intellectual resisters were more important than saboteurs. "Our job was to tell all the French, we will not be ruled by Germans. That was the job of the resistance, not just a few more trains or bridges blown up here and there."[6]

The cultural resistance was no less intent on exposing collaborationists as deviants from the ethical standards claimed by the creative and performing arts. The greater the scorn that was poured on collaborationists, the greater the credit due to *résistants.* For this, the press was again crucial, giving full coverage to the chain of celebrity artists and writers who were arrested by the FFI and thrown together for a few weeks in Drancy and Fresnes. Meetings of the various cultural *comités d'épuration* were also reported, as were bans on the professional activity of collaborationists. It seemed reasonable to believe that only through this public cleansing ritual could the cultural community recover its standing in society. But even among those claiming the moral high ground, there were soon deep dis-agreements. Specifically, hard-liners, mostly Communists, wanted strong punishment, while moderates—and, in practice, much of the public—were more forgiving. The gap between these two groups, illustrated by the justice-versus-charity debate between Camus and Mauriac soon after the liberation, continued to widen.

Paulhan, who had misgivings about the *épuration* as early as fall 1944, resigned in 1947 from the very CNE that he had cofounded. In 1952, he went further, publishing a critique of the *épuration* in a small booklet called *Lettre aux directeurs de la résistance*. Eight years after the liberation, he was still trying to rescue the resistance from politi-cal extremism. "I am a *résistant*," he began. "I became one from the month of June 40 and I still am, or at least I think I am. And yet this no longer gives me pride. Rather, it fills me with shame."[7] He accused the *résistants* of abusing their power: "Let me tell them that they have fallen into a trap: no less cowardly or treacherous, no less unjust than those among them who, on the torture table, informed on their col-leagues."[8] And he concluded, "I am neither politician nor judge. I am also not a priest. All I see—and this I see clearly—is that horror and disgust will awaken us tomorrow if we close our eyes today. We are owed arrears of justice and law. Let us have them! Then—and this should be possible—let us be kept informed."[9]

Whether or not Paulhan believed that the sins of cultural collabo-ration should be forgiven, by the early 1950s they had been largely forgotten. In 1951, Éditions Gallimard published Rebatet's *Les Deux étandards* (The Two Battle Flags). The following year, it published Céline's *Féerie pour une autre fois* (Fable for Another Time). And in 1953, Gallimard won permission to reopen the *Nouvelle Revue Française*—it was called the "new" *NRF* until 1959 to distinguish it from Drieu La Rochelle's version—and Paulhan returned as its edi-tor, opening its pages to all political currents, as he had done before the war. In his letter to the "leaders of the resistance," however, Paul-han appeared to be addressing less the past excesses of the *épuration* than the current excesses of a Communist Party that remained as Stalinist and doctrinaire as it had been in the 1930s. The party had, of course, changed in one important way: it had emerged enormously strengthened from the occupation, winning 27 percent of seats in a new Constitutional National Assembly in October 1945 and partici-pating in coalition governments until 1947. Even after it left the gov-ernment, its control of the labor movement enabled it to organize general strikes and other actions to destabilize the newly installed Fourth Republic.

In the world of culture, as power shifted sharply to the left, the Communist Party worked hard to impose its thinking on a new postwar generation of artists and creators. Even Éluard, whose wartime poem "Liberté" had inspired resistance, became a servant of the Soviet propaganda machine, penning an "Ode to Stalin" in 1950. Aragon, who remained the party's intellectual commissar, edited its afternoon paper, *Ce Soir,* until it closed in 1953. He then took over *Les Lettres Françaises* as a weekly supplement of the party daily, *L'Humanité.* Still more influential was Sartre, who never actually joined the Communist Party but shared many of its positions. As the pipe-smoking guru of existentialism, he presided over the Left Bank intelligentsia from the benches of the Café de Flore. Those on the left who challenged this conformism could expect no mercy, as Camus was to discover. Briefly a Communist in his twenties in Algeria, he remained firmly on the left, but in 1952 his strong anti-Stalinism brought a rift with Sartre, whom he considered overtolerant of totalitarianism. As a result, he was increasingly ostracized by the left.

For sheer celebrity value, of course, Picasso was the Communist Party's bright new star. In a 1944 interview with the American magazine *New Masses* that also ran in *L'Humanité,* he explained his decision to join the party: "Yes, I am conscious of always having fought as a true revolutionary through my painting, but I have now understood that this is not enough."[10] In a separate interview with *Les Lettres Françaises,* he defended political art, saying, "No, painting is not done to decorate apartments. It is an instrument of war, for attack and defense against the enemy."[11] In early 1945, for the first time since *Guernica,* he painted a political work, *The Charnel House,* his response to the genocide of the Nazi death camps. In 1950, he traveled to Moscow to accept the International Stalin Peace Prize. And the following year, he painted another protest, *Massacre in Korea,* depicting American soldiers shooting Korean civilians. But Picasso was hardly a born apparatchik, and his next venture into political art would prove to be his last. When Stalin died, on March 5, 1953, Aragon begged him for a drawing of the dictator. Picasso, who was in the south of France, could only find a photograph of Stalin as a young man and, with that as a model, his sketch of a Georgian peasant appeared on the front page of *Les Lettres Françaises.* Such was the scandal provoked in Communist ranks by this "disrespectful" image that Aragon was forced into a public mea culpa for the affront. Picasso was unrepentant.

Still, for all this political agitation, the cultural life of Paris slowly resumed. But clearly, much had changed. The liberation was followed by a harsh winter, aggravating fuel and food shortages, while the economy as a whole would begin to recover only when the effects of the Marshall Plan were felt, in the late 1940s and early 1950s. More significant, culturally the city was no longer a magnet for artists and writers from around the world. American writers were the exception: Richard Wright, Chester Himes, James Jones, James Baldwin, William Burroughs, Allen Ginsberg and William Styron were among the dozens to experience the Left Bank expat life in the late 1940s and 1950s. But if these Americans found respite from racism and McCarthyism in Paris, they remained Americans in Paris and contributed little to the city's literary scene. In contrast, European artists and writers who had been so integrated into Paris culture during the interwar years no longer needed a refuge from Fascism (and it would be some years before the city began taking in eastern European writers fleeing Communism). Many of them had also been scattered in the diaspora of the war. And even if some, like Chagall, did return, Paris was no longer at the center of their lives. Soon a question was being posed: Had the city lost its place at the creative heart of modern Western culture?

The clearest sign that cultural power was shifting away from Paris came in the visual arts, with Jackson Pollock and Abstract Expressionism placing New York at the vanguard of contemporary art. In Paris, too, a new generation of painters emerged, including Jean Bazaine, Jean Fautrier and Nicholas de Staël, who were first noticed during the occupation and who created their own abstract movement, known as Lyrical Abstraction. Others went their own way, like Pierre Soulages, who became known as the "painter of black," and Jean Dubuffet, who developed the neoprimitive style known as *art brut*. But they could no longer count on the influential art dealers who had done so much since the late nineteenth century to make Paris the world's art capital. Now the market, the money and the energy were to be found in New York. Instead, Paris became an exporter of modern masters like Picasso, Matisse, Braque and Léger, who represented an earlier era. Even Surrealism's leading artists, Dalí and Miró, had returned home to Spain.

Yet in that other high-profile visual art, fashion, Paris held its own with panache. In March 1945, in a bid to reclaim their crown, leading fashion designers participated in a show called Théâtre de la Mode in an annex to the Louvre. Displayed on thirteen "stages" bathed in theatrical lighting were 228 *petits mannequins,* or dolls, made of sculptured wire and angelic molded heads and standing just twenty-seven inches high. Each doll presented what Balenciaga, Lucien Lelong, Schiaparelli, Nina Ricci, Pierre Balmain and other designers had in mind for the spring–summer season of 1946. After V-E Day, two months later, the show carried the message "Paris is back" to London, Barcelona, Copenhagen, Stockholm and Vienna and, in May 1946, to New York. A generational change then brought radical renewal. With Coco Chanel living in Switzerland after her amorous adventures with a Nazi officer, in the late 1940s Christian Dior's New Look revolutionized haute couture. Overnight the stark wartime look gave way to elegance and femininity.

In other art forms, the record of France's postwar creativity was more nuanced. In theater, although Anouilh was the only new playwright of the war years whose work was widely performed abroad, Paris could soon claim Samuel Beckett as its own. Starting with *Waiting for Godot* in 1952, his stark existentialist plays, often written first in French, would revolutionize Western theater. Messiaen, the leading French composer of the postwar years, was another innovator, although from the 1950s it was Pierre Boulez who became the driving force of experimental electroacoustic music. Both theater and music also built on some of Vichy's legacy. Jean Vilar, a theater director who worked with Jeune France, founded the Avignon Theater Festival in 1947. And as France's culture minister between 1959 and 1969, André Malraux followed Jeune France's example by opening cultural centers across France. The Jeunesses Musicales de France, created during the occupation, also survived: every year, it still presents some three hundred free concerts, attended by close to half a million children and teenagers.

In dance, though, while Diaghilev's Russian dancers and choreographers had brought modernity to Paris early in the century, the initiative passed to New York. With Serge Lifar back at the Paris Opera in 1947 (he remained its ballet master until 1958), classical ballet continued to rule dance in France. And it, too, produced new names, notably Roland Petit as a choreographer and Jean Babilée as an acclaimed dancer. But New York breathed new life into modern dance, thanks to George Balanchine, who had worked there since leaving Paris in the mid-1930s, as well as to Martha Graham, Merce Cunningham, Jerome Robbins and a host of other American choreographers. Together, they created an entirely new vocabulary of contemporary dance that, two decades later, was enthusiastically adopted in France.

Where American influence was most immediately felt—and resented—was in cinema. Even before the war, the French movie industry was unhappy about Hollywood's growing influence and, in the late 1940s, Hollywood was able to exploit the poverty and disarray of much of European cinema. But France was determined to rebuild its industry. And, in the Institut des Hautes Études Cinématographiques,* founded by Vichy in 1944, it had a film school capable of training a new generation of directors, with Alain Resnais among its earliest graduates. Some directors who made their name during the occupation, among them Robert Bresson and Henri-Georges Clouzot (despite the controversy over *Le Corbeau*), also went on to make exceptional movies in the decade that followed. And the Cannes Film Festival, which had canceled its inaugural gathering in September 1939, finally opened in 1946 and quickly became the place where moviemakers most sought recognition.

Perhaps the crucial moment of postwar French cinema came with the founding of the *Cahiers du Cinéma* journal in 1951, because it spawned the New Wave of French movies of the late 1950s. The way was opened by landmark movies like François Truffaut's *The 400 Blows* and Jean-Luc Godard's *Breathless.* And along with such other directors as Resnais, Éric Rohmer, Claude Chabrol, Jacques Demy and Agnès Varda, there came glamorous new stars like Brigitte Bardot and Jeanne Moreau. Almost overnight, it seemed, the Nouvelle Vague revived Paris's reputation as a city of artistic innovation.

Literature had a more turbulent ride. In the late 1940s and 1950s, French fiction was still routinely translated into English and other languages. And as a measure of its continuing prestige, the Nobel Prize in literature went to Gide in 1947 and to Mauriac in 1952. But here, too, the war years brought new writers to the fore, none more prominently than Camus, who followed *L'Étranger* with *La Peste* in 1947, both quickly translated into English. In the 1950s, he also pub-

*In 1986, the school was renamed the École Nationale Supérieure des Métiers de l'Image et du Son and is now known as La Fémis, the acronym for the Fondation Européenne pour les Métiers de l'Image et du Son.

lished *L'Homme révolté* (The Rebel), a historical analysis of the phe-nomenon of revolution in Europe, and *La Chute* (The Fall), his most existentialist novel. In 1957, it was his turn to win the Nobel Prize in literature. By then, a new literary movement had appeared in Paris. Known as the *nouveau roman,* or "new novel," it was driven by a still younger group of writers who were more interested in experi-menting with different styles than pursuing traditional narrative. Among these were Marguerite Duras, Alain Robbe-Grillet, Nathalie Sarraute and Claude Simon (who became a Nobel literature laureate in 1985), as well as the Argentine-born Paris resident Julio Cortázar. But their very obsession with style opened the doors to American, British and Latin American storytellers and, in many ways, French fiction never recovered from the *nouveau roman.**

Rather, it was in the vaguely defined area of thought that France made its deepest mark in the postwar years. With his development of the existentialist ideas of Kierkegaard and Nietzsche, Sartre was for two decades Paris's reigning philosopher. In 1964, he was awarded— and refused to accept—the Nobel Prize in literature, but the Nobel committee's citation reflected his sway: "For his work which, rich in ideas and filled with the spirit of freedom and the quest for truth, has exerted a far-reaching influence on our age."

Sartre was not alone. Simone de Beauvoir's 1949 treatise, *The Sec-ond Sex,* became the cornerstone of modern feminism, while a dis-parate group of men played a central role in rethinking the ways history, literature and society can be analyzed. Variously introducing concepts like structuralism, deconstruction and poststructuralism into the modern language were the Marxist philosopher Louis Althusser, the sociologist and Nietzschean philosopher Michel Fou-cault, the psychoanalyst Jacques Lacan, the anthropologist Claude Lévi-Strauss, the semiotician Roland Barthes and the philosopher Jacques Derrida. They were not glamorous in the manner of painters and actors, for the most part they were not even household names in France, but their intellectual and academic influence was immense, not least in American universities.

Several of these men were, at one time or another, members of the Communist Party, yet they were not heirs to the *intellectuels engagés* of the interwar years or to the cultural *résistants* of the occupation.

---

*In 2006, Irène Némirovsky's *Suite française* was the first French novel to become a major American best seller since Françoise Sagan's *Bonjour tristesse* (Hello, Sadness) and Simone de Beauvoir's *Les Mandarins* more than fifty years earlier.

Rather, it was again Sartre who, by defending such varied causes as Algeria's independence, the 1968 Paris student revolt and the anti–Vietnam War movement, kept alive the idea of the public intellectual until his death in 1980. And even those who crossed swords with him, like Camus and Raymond Aron, were in a sense reacting to the radical positions he took. Did this mean that, despite the betrayal of trust by collaborationists, French society still looked to intellectuals and artists to serve as moral guides? Certainly there were fewer pretenders to this title than before the war, because many had failed the test during the occupation. Yet in a country where politicians are uniformly distrusted, the perception survived that those engaged in artistic and intellectual creation were more committed to a disinterested truth.

The real question, then, was not if but how these influential voices exercised their power. And here, once more, France offers an interesting lesson. Probably no other country better illustrates the perils assumed by a population that is educated to revere theories: it becomes fertile ground for extremism. Some see this as another legacy of the 1789 revolution, the inebriating notion that an idea translated into action can bring sudden, radical and idealized change. Certainly, during much of the twentieth century, many prominent French writers and intellectuals propagated doctrines—monarchism, Fascism, anti-Semitism, Communism, even Maoism—that offered explanations and solutions for everything. If French intellectuals no longer have the authority they once enjoyed, then, it is because these doctrines have failed and these mirages of Utopia have vanished. All for the better, no doubt: politically speaking, artists and writers may now be less prominent, but they are also less dangerous. They can still use their prestige and celebrity to ring alarm bells on national and global issues ignored by the political establishment. It is just that they no longer believe that ideas alone can resolve life's problems.

ACKNOWLEDGMENTS

EVERYONE who has written a book about the occupation of France in recent decades owes a debt to Robert O. Paxton for his pioneering work on the subject. I owe a particular debt to Professor Paxton, who generously agreed to read my manuscript and, in doing so, corrected myriad errors and offered immensely useful ideas to improve the text. I was no less lucky that Robert Gottlieb, editor extraordinaire, was willing to read my manuscript at a stage where his erudite mind and sharp eyes could still shape the final result. My deepest thanks to these two Bobs.

I am also grateful to other experts and friends who read all or parts of this book and saved me from many pitfalls, among them Daphné Anglès, Lenny Borger, Myriam Chimènes, Hector Feliciano, Debra Isaac, Karine Le Bail, Gisèle Sapiro, Yannick Simone and C. K. Williams. As a journalist, I would have felt even more of an intruder in the world of historians had I not been able to interview many who had firsthand experience of the cultural life of Paris during the occupation. I am enormously appreciative of the time, memories and reflections of Claude Anglès, Jean Babilée, Héléna Bossi, Pierre Boulez, Leonora Carrington, Danielle Darrieux, Dominique Delouche, Michel Déon, Dominique Desanti, Michel Francini, Françoise Gilot, Stéphane Hessel, Elina Labourdette, Madeleine Malraux, Micheline Presle, Denise René, Jorge Semprun and Annie Ubersfeld, as well as those of the late Marcel Carné, Maurice Druon, Marguerite Duras and Willy Ronis.

I would also like to record my recognition of the academics and historians who, while too numerous to name outside my bibliography, have done much of the hard work that has made my overview possible. As well, the Institut d'Histoire du Temps Présent and the Institut Mémoires de l'Édition Contemporaine have supported research that has proved enormously useful to me. Without the work of these scholars and institutions, I would not have known where to start. I was also lucky to count on Ginny Power for help in finding the photographs accompanying this book.

I owe special thanks to Ashbel Green at Knopf, who not only planted the seed of this book fifteen years ago but who over the past thirty years has proved both a loyal friend and an immensely patient editor. Susanna Lea, a dear friend long before she became my agent, has never ceased to nudge me and encourage me. My mother, Ina, in her one hundredth year while I was writing this book, was, as always, an inspiration. Finally, my wife, Marlise Simons, has once again allowed me to disrupt our lives by devoting long hours to a book. My fondest gratitude for her patience, endurance and support.

BIBLIOGRAPHY AND NOTES

A number of books proved constantly useful to me during the preparation of this book. For general background, I counted on: *Vichy France: Old Guard and New Order, 1940–1944* by Robert O. Paxton; *France: The Dark Years, 1940–1944* by Julian Jackson; and *France Under the Germans: Collaboration and Compromise* by Philippe Burrin. For a cultural overview, I was helped by *La Vie parisienne sous l'occupation* by Hervé Le Boterf and *La Vie culturelle sous l'occupation* by Stéphanie Corcy. Books covering more detailed aspects of culture during the occupation are listed below.

CHAPTER 1 Everyone on Stage

BIBLIOGRAPHY

Beauvoir, Simone de. *La Force de l'âge.* 1960. Paris: Éditions Gallimard (Folio), 1986.

Bernier, Olivier. *Fireworks at Dusk: Paris in the Thirties.* Boston: Little, Brown, 1993.

Céline, Louis-Ferdinand. *Bagatelles pour un massacre.* Paris: Éditions Denoël, 1937.

Gide, André. *Back from the U.S.S.R.* Translated by Dorothy Bussy. London: Martin Secker and Warburg, 1937.

Guéhenno, Jean. *Journal des années noires.* Paris: Éditions Gallimard, 1947.

Jackson, Julian. *France: The Dark Years, 1940–1944.* New York: Oxford University Press, 2001.

Koch, Stephen. *Stalin, Willi Müzenberg and the Seduction of the Intellectuals.* New York: Free Press, 1994.

Mauriac, Claude. *Le Temps immobile.* Paris: Éditions Grasset, 1993.

Paxton, Robert O. *Vichy France: Old Guard and New Order, 1940–1944.* New York: Knopf, 1972.

Rysselberghe, Maria van. *Je ne sais si nous avons dit d'impérissables choses: Une anthologie des* Cahiers de la Petite Dame. Paris: Éditions Gallimard, 2006.

Weber, Eugen. *The Hollow Years: France in the 1930s.* New York: Norton, 1994.

INTERVIEWS

Jean-Louis Crémieux-Brilhac, Paris, April 4, 2008.

NOTES

1. Guéhenno, *Journal,* p. 205.
2. *The Paris Review, The Art of Fiction No. 28,* Summer–Fall 1962.
3. Weber, *Hollow Years,* p. 229.
4. Bernier, *Fireworks,* p. 164.
5. Interview with Crémieux-Brilhac, Paris, April 4, 2008.
6. Judaisme.sdv.fr/perso/lblum/lblum.htm.
7. Actionfrancaise.net/histoire-biographies-charles_maurras.htm.
8. Minaudier.com/documents/allemagne/allemagne-03-troisiemereich.pdf, p. 35 n. 2.
9. Céline, *Bagatelles,* p. 180.
10. *Nouvelle Revue Française,* No. 295, April 1938.
11. Letter to D. W. Strauss, 1937, cited by *Lire Hors-Série,* No. 7, p. 75.
12. Bernier, *Fireworks,* p. 191.
13. Mauriac, *Le Temps,* p. 143.
14. Gide, *Back from the U.S.S.R.,* p. 11.
15. Ibid., p. 16.
16. Ibid., p. 78.
17. Ibid., pp. 62–63.
18. Beauvoir, *La Force,* p. 330.
19. Bernier, *Fireworks,* p. 311.

CHAPTER 2 Not So Droll

BIBLIOGRAPHY

Beauvoir, Simone de. 1960. *La Force de l'âge.* Paris: Éditions Gallimard (Folio), 1986.

Bernier, Olivier. *Fireworks at Dusk: Paris in the Thirties.* Boston: Little, Brown, 1993.

Carrington, Leonora. *House of Fear: Notes from Down Below.* London: Dutton, 1988.

Daix, Pierre, and Armand Israël. *Pablo Picasso: Dossiers de la préfecture de police, 1901–1940.* Paris: Éditions Acatos, 2003.

Gerassi, John. *Talking with Sartre: Conversations and Debates.* New Haven: Yale University Press, 2009.

Gide, André. *Journals.* Vol. 4, *1939–1949.* Translated by Justin O'Brien. Urbana: University of Illinois Press, 2000.

Giraudoux, Jean. *Pleins pouvoirs.* Paris: Éditions Gallimard, 1939.

Guggenheim, Peggy. *Out of This Century: The Informal Memoirs of Peggy Guggenheim.* New York: Dial, 1946. All page references are to *Out of This Century: Confessions of an Art Addict.* London: André Deutsch, 1997.

Huffington, Arianna Stassinopoulos. *Picasso: Creator and Destroyer.* London: Weidenfeld and Nicolson, 1988.

Jackson, Julian. *France: The Dark Years, 1940–1944.* New York: Oxford University Press, 2001.

Jouhandeau, Marcel. *Journal sous l'occupation.* Paris: Éditions Gallimard, 1980.

Klarsfeld, Serge. *Le Calendrier de la persécution des juifs en France, 1940–1944.* Paris: Les Fils et Filles des Déportés Juifs de France and the Beate Klarsfeld Foundation, 1993.

Koch, Stephen. *Stalin, Willi Müzenberg and the Seduction of the Intellectuals.* New York: Free Press, 1994.

Némirovsky, Irène. *Suite française.* Paris: Éditions Denoël, 2004. (My page references are to the 2007 Vintage edition, translated from the French by Sandra Smith.)

Paxton, Robert O. *Vichy France: Old Guard and New Order, 1940–1944.* New York: Knopf, 1972.

Philipponnat, Olivier, and Patrick Leinhardt. *La Vie d'Irène Némirovsky.* Paris: Éditions Grasset & Denoël, 2007.

Rysselberghe, Maria van. *Je ne sais si nous avons dit d'impérissables choses: Une anthologie des* Cahiers de la Petite Dame. Paris: Éditions Gallimard, 2006.

Saint-Exupéry, Antoine de. *Flight to Arras.* New York: Harcourt Brace, 1942.

Sartre, Jean-Paul. *Carnets de la drôle de guerre, septembre 1939–mars 1940.* Paris: Éditions Gallimard, 1995.

Weber, Eugen. *The Hollow Years: France in the 1930s.* New York: Norton, 1994.

INTERVIEWS

Leonora Carrington, Mexico City, November 20, 2008.
Jean-Louis Crémieux-Brilhac, Paris, April 4, 2008.
Michel Déon, Paris, April 7, 2008.
Michel Francini, Paris, March 13, 2008.
Stéphane Hessel, Paris, April 8, 2008.
Jorge Semprun, Paris, March 26, 2008.

NOTES

1. Rysselberghe, *Je ne sais* p. 508.
2. Klarsfeld, *Le Calendrier,* p. 14.
3. Carrington, *House of Fear,* p. 164.
4. Giraudoux, *Pleins pouvoirs,* p. 65.
5. Interview with Déon, Paris, April 7, 2008.
6. Interview with Hessel, Paris, April 8, 2008.
7. Daix and Israël, *Pablo Picasso,* p. 124.
8. Guggenheim, *Out of This Century,* p. 209.
9. Philipponnat and Leinhardt, *La Vie,* p. 332.
10. Gide, *Journals,* p. 19.
11. Drieu La Rochelle, *Journal,* p. 93.
12. Ibid., p. 97.
13. Ibid., p. 96.
14. Ibid., p. 129.
15. Sartre, *Carnets,* p. 154.

16. Gerassi, *Talking with Sartre*, p. 119.
17. Némirovsky, *Suite*, p. 35.
18. Beauvoir, *La Force*, p. 503.
19. Interview with Francini, Paris, March 13, 2008.
20. Jouhandeau, *Journal*, p. 32.
21. Ibid., p. 40.
22. Interview with Déon, Paris, April 7, 2008.
23. Weber, *Hollow Years*, p. 282.

CHAPTER 3 Shall We Dance?

BIBLIOGRAPHY

Abetz, Otto. *Histoire d'une politique franco-allemande, 1930–1950: Mémoires d'un ambassadeur.* Paris: Éditions Stock, 1953.

Amouroux, Henri. *La Grande histoire des Français sous l'occupation.* Vols. 1–5. Paris: Éditions Robert Laffont, 1976.

Beauvoir, Simone de. *La Force de l'âge.* 1960. Paris: Éditions Gallimard (Folio), 1986.

Berghaus, Günter, ed. *Fascism and Theatre.* Oxford: Berghahn Books, 1996.

Chimènes, Myriam, ed. *La Vie musicale sous Vichy.* Paris: Éditions Complexe, 2001.

Claudel, Paul. *Journal.* Vol. 2, *1933–1955.* Paris: Bibliothèque de la Pléiade, 1969.

Cocteau, Jean. *Journal, 1942–1945.* Paris: Éditions Gallimard, 1989.

Desanti, Dominique. *Sacha Guitry: 50 ans de spectacle.* Paris: Éditions Grasset, 1982.

Feliciano, Hector. *The Lost Museum: The Nazi Conspiracy to Steal the World's Greatest Works of Art.* New York: Basic Books, 1997.

Galtier-Boissière, Jean. *Mon journal pendant l'occupation.* Paris: Éditions La Jeune Parque, 1944.

Gerassi, John. *Talking with Sartre: Conversations and Debates.* New Haven: Yale University Press, 2009.

Gide, André. *Journals.* Vol. 4, *1939–1949.* Translated by Justin O'Brien. Urbana: University of Illinois Press, 2000.

Guéhenno, Jean. *Journal des années noires.* Paris: Éditions Gallimard, 1947.

Heller, Gerhard. *Un Allemand à Paris.* Paris: Éditions du Seuil, 1981.

Loiseaux, Gérard. *La Littérature de la défaite et de la collaboration.* Paris: Éditions Fayard, 1995.

Nicholas, Lynn H. *The Rape of Europa: The Fate of Europe's Treasures in the Third Reich and the Second World War.* New York: Knopf, 1994.

Porcile, François. *Les Conflits de la musique française, 1940–1965.* Paris: Éditions Fayard, 2001.

Speer, Albert. *Inside the Third Reich.* New York: Simon and Schuster, 1970.

Yagil, Limore. *"L'Homme nouveau" et la révolution nationale de Vichy (1940–1944)*. Paris: Presses Universitaires du Septentrion, 1997.

INTERVIEWS

Danielle Darrieux, Paris, January 22, 2009.
Françoise Gilot, New York, April 4, 2009.
Stéphane Hessel, Paris, April 8, 2008.
Micheline Presle, Paris, April 28, 2009.
Jorge Semprun, Paris, March 26, 2008.

NOTES

1. Speer, *Inside the Third Reich*, p. 184.
2. Abetz, *Histoire*, p. 176.
3. Manuela Schwartz essay " La Musique, outil majeure de la propagande culturelle des Nazis," in Chimènes, *La Vie*, p. 90.
4. Desanti, *Sacha Guitry*, p. 332.
5. Amouroux, *Grande histoire*, vol. 2, p. 199.
6. Quoted in Serge Added essay "Jacques Copeau and 'Popular Theatre' in Vichy France," in Berghaus, *Fascism and Theatre*, p. 249.
7. Speer, *Inside the Third Reich*, pp. 171–72.
8. Porcile, *Les Conflits*, pp. 21–22.
9. Interview with Darrieux, Paris, January 22, 2009.
10. Interview with Presle, Paris, April 28, 2009.
11. Beauvoir, *La Force*, p. 532.
12. The Nizkor Project: http://www.nizkor.org/ftp.cgi/imt/nca/ftp.py?imt/nca/nca-06/nca-06-3766-ps.
13. Loiseaux, *La Littérature*, p. 78.
14. Gerassi, *Talking with Sartre*, p. 122.
15. Claudel, *Journal*, p. 321.
16. Heller, *Un Allemand*, p. 146.
17. Cocteau, *Journal*, p. 335.
18. Gide, *Journals*, July 7, 1940.
19. Ibid., September 24, 1940.
20. Ibid., July 17, 1940.
21. Ibid., January 12, 1941.
22. Ibid.
23. Ibid., June 14, 1941.
24. Ibid., July 5, 1941.
25. Guéhenno, *Journal*, p. 15.
26. Ibid.
27. Ibid., p. 57.
28. Ibid., p. 72.
29. Ibid., p. 127.
30. Galtier-Boissière, *Mon journal*, pp. 17–18.
31. Ibid., pp. 34–35.
32. Interview with Semprun, Paris, March 26, 2008.
33. Interview with Gilot, New York, April 4, 2009.
34. Galtier-Boissière, *Mon journal*, p. 28.
35. Ibid., p. 25.

CHAPTER 4 *L'Américain*

BIBLIOGRAPHY

Alexander, Sydney. *Marc Chagall.* New York: G. P. Putnam's, 1978.

Bair, Deirdre. *Samuel Beckett: A Biography.* New York: Harcourt Brace Jovanovich, 1978.

Benjamin, Walter. *Selected Writings.* Edited by Howard Eiland and Michael W. Jennings. Cambridge, Mass.: Harvard University Press, 2003.

Carrington, Leonora. *House of Fear: Notes from Down Below.* London: Dutton, 1988.

Fry, Varian. *Assignment Rescue,* with an introduction by Albert O. Hirschman. New York: Scholastic, 1968. Originally published as *Surrender on Demand.* New York: Random House, 1945.

Guggenheim, Peggy. *Out of This Century: The Informal Memoirs of Peggy Guggenheim.* New York: Dial, 1946. All page references are to *Out of This Century: Confessions of an Art Addict.* London: André Deutsch, 1997.

Holl, Adolf. *The Left Hand of God.* Translated by John Cullen. New York: Doubleday, 1998.

Paxton, Robert O., Olivier Corpet and Claire Paulhan, eds. *Archives de la vie littéraire sous occupation: À travers le désastre.* Paris: Éditions Tallandier, 2009.

Schiffrin, André. *A Political Education: Coming of Age in Paris and New York.* New York: Melville House, 2007.

Stein, Gertrude. *Wars I Have Seen.* New York: Random House, 1945.

Sullivan, Rosemary. *Villa Air-Bel.* London: John Murray, 2006.

Varian Fry à Marseille. Exhibition catalog. Paris: Mona Bismark Foundation, 2000.

Wullschlager, Jackie. *Chagall: A Biography.* New York: Knopf, 2008.

INTERVIEWS

Leonora Carrington, Mexico City, November 20, 2008.
Stéphane Hessel, Paris, April 8, 2008.

NOTES
1. Fry, *Assignment,* p. 8.
2. Ibid., p. 14.
3. Ibid., p. 41.
4. Ibid., p. vii.
5. Wullschlager, *Chagall,* p. 392.
6. Benjamin, *Selected Writings,* p. 445.
7. Fry, *Assignment,* p. 140.
8. Stein, *Wars,* p. 50.
9. Fry, *Assignment,* p. 44.
10. Paxton, Corpet and Paulhan, *Archives,* p. 266.
11. Schiffrin, *A Political Education,* p. 30.
12. Interview with Hessel, Paris, April 8, 2008.
13. Fry, *Assignment,* p. 121.
14. Ibid., p. 137.

15. *Varian Fry à Marseille.*
16. Fry, *Assignment,* p. 111.
17. Ibid., p. 112.
18. Guggenheim, *Out of This Century,* p. 231.
19. Carrington, *House of Fear,* p. 213.
20. Wullschlager, *Chagall,* p. 389.
21. Fry, *Assignment,* p. 163.
22. Ibid., p. 119.
23. Ibid.
24. Ibid., p. 173.
25. *Varian Fry à Marseille,* p. 4.
26. Interview with Hessel, Paris, April 8, 2008.

CHAPTER 5 Paris by Night

BIBLIOGRAPHY

Abetz, Otto. *Histoire d'une politique franco-allemande, 1930–1950: Mémoires d'un ambassadeur.* Paris: Éditions Stock, 1953.

Behr, Edward. *The Good Frenchman: The True Story of the Life and Times of Maurice Chevalier.* New York: Villard Books, 1993.

Baker, Josephine, and Jo Bouillon. *Josephine.* Translated by Mariana Fitzpatrick. New York: Harper & Row, 1976.

Berteaut, Simone. *Piaf: A Biography.* New York: Harper & Row, 1972.

Chimènes, Myriam, ed. *La Vie musicale sous Vichy.* Paris: Éditions Complexe, 2001.

Crosland, Margaret. *Piaf.* London: Coronet Books, 1985.

Galtier-Boissière, Jean. *Mon journal pendant l'occupation.* Paris: Éditions La Jeune Parque, 1944.

Halimi, André. *Chantons sous l'occupation.* Paris: Marabout, 1976.

Jünger, Ernst. *Journaux de guerre.* Vol. 2, *1939–1948.* Paris: Éditions Gallimard, 2008.

Le Boterf, Hervé. *La Vie parisienne sous l'occupation.* Paris: Éditions France-Empire, 1997.

Veillon, Dominique. *La Mode sous l'occupation.* Paris: Éditions Payot, 1990.

Zucca, André. *Les Parisiens sous l'occupation: Photographies en couleurs d'André Zucca.* Exhibition catalog. Paris: Éditions Gallimard, 2008.

Zwerin, Mike. *La Tristesse de Saint Louis: Jazz Under the Nazis.* New York: Beech Tree Books, 1985.

INTERVIEW
Michel Francini, Paris, March 13, 2008.

NOTES
1. Le Boterf, *La Vie parisienne,* p. 47.
2. Ibid., p. 46.

3. Interview with Francini, Paris, March 13, 2008.
4. Jünger, *Journaux*, pp. 213–14.
5. Interview with Francini, Paris, March 13, 2008.
6. Ursula Mathis essay "'Honte à qui peut chanter': La Neuvième Art sous l'Ocupation," in Chimènes, *La Vie*, p. 302.
7. Berteaut, *Piaf*, p. 207.
8. Behr, *The Good Frenchman*, p. 241.
9. Galtier-Boissière, *Mon journal*, p. 99.
10. Baker and Bouillon, *Josephine*, p. 128.
11. Abetz, *Histoire*, p. 176.

CHAPTER 6. Resistance as an Idea

BIBLIOGRAPHY

Boris Vildé: Chef du Réseau du Musée de l'Homme. Pamphlet for the exhibition shown at the Musée National d'Histoire Naturelle and the Musée de l'Homme, 2008.

Humbert, Agnès. *Resistance.* Translated Barbara Mellor. New York: Bloomsbury, 2008.

Paulhan, Jean. *Choix de lettres, 1937–1945.* Paris: Gallimard, 1992.

NOTES

1. Humbert, *Resistance*, pp. 20–21.
2. Ibid., p. 25.
3. *Boris Vildé*, p. 13.
4. Humbert, *Resistance*, p. 26.
5. Ibid., p. 28.
6. Paulhan, *Choix*, p. 214.
7. Ibid., pp. 214–15.
8. *Boris Vildé*, p. 15.
9. Humbert, *Resistance*, p. 106.

CHAPTER 7 *Maréchal, Nous Voilà!*

BIBLIOGRAPHY

Bernier, Olivier. *Fireworks at Dusk: Paris in the Thirties.* Boston: Little, Brown, 1993.

Burrin, Philippe. *France Under the Germans: Collaboration and Compromise.* Translated by Janet Lloyd. New York: New Press, 1996.

Callil, Carmen. *Bad Faith: A Story of Family and Fatherland.* London: Jonathan Cape, 2006.

Cointet, Michèle. *Vichy capitale.* Paris: Perrin, 1993.

Daladier, Edouard. *Prison Journal, 1940–1945.* Translated by Arthur D. Greenspan. Boulder, Colo.: Westview Press, 1995.

Eychart, François, and Georges Aillaud, eds. *Les Lettres Françaises et Les Étoiles dans la clandestinité, 1942–1944*. Paris: Le Cherche Midi, 2008.

Galtier-Boissière, Jean. *Mon journal pendant l'occupation*. Paris: Éditions La Jeune Parque, 1944.

Guéhenno, Jean. *Journal des années noires*. Paris: Éditions Gallimard, 1947.

Jackson, Julian. *France: The Dark Years, 1940–1944*. New York: Oxford University Press, 2001.

Le Bail, Karine. *Musique, pouvoir, responsabilité: La politique musicale de la Radiodiffusion française, 1939–1953*. Paris: CNRS Éditions, 2010.

Mollier, Jean-Yves. *Édition, presse et pouvoir en France au XXe siècle*. Paris: Éditions Fayard, 2008.

Nord, Philip. "Scout's Honor: Catholic Scoutism and Vichy Culture." Paper presented at Between Collaboration and Resistance: French Literary Life Under Nazi Occupation, 1940–1944, a colloquium at the New York Public Library, April 3, 2009.

Paulhan, Jean. *Choix de lettres, 1937–1945*. Paris: Gallimard, 1992.

Paxton, Robert O. *Vichy France: Old Guard and New Order, 1940–1944*. New York: Knopf, 1972.

Paxton, Robert O., Olivier Corpet and Claire Paulhan, eds. *Archives de la vie littéraire sous occupation: À travers le désastre*. Paris: Éditions Tallandier, 2009.

Philipponnat, Olivier, and Patrick Leinhardt. *La Vie d'Irène Némirovsky*. Paris: Éditions Grasset & Denoël, 2007.

Rebatet, Lucien. *Les Décombres*. Paris: Éditions de l'Homme Libre, 2006.

Rioux, Jean-Pierre, ed. *La Vie culturelle sous Vichy*. Paris: Éditions Complexe, 1990.

Weber, Nicholas Fox. *Le Corbusier: A Life*. New York: Knopf, 2008.

INTERVIEWS

Michel Déon, Paris, April 7, 2008.
Denise Epstein, Paris, November 18, 2004.
Gérard Morley, Issy-l'Évêque, April 16, 2009.

NOTES

1. Rebatet, *Les Décombres*, p. 535.
2. Weber, *Le Corbusier*, p. 413.
3. Ibid., p. 425.
4. Ibid., p. 453.
5. Interview with Déon, Paris, April 7, 2008.
6. Galtier-Boissière, *Mon journal*, p. 27.
7. Rioux, *La Vie*, p. 89.
8. Bernier, *Fireworks*, p. 311.
9. Daladier, *Prison Journal*, p. 117.
10. Jackson, *France*, p. 357.
11. Guéhenno, *Journal*, p. 139.
12. Ibid., p. 170.
13. Lesamitiesdelaresistance.fr/lien6/saliege.

14. Interview with Epstein, Paris, November 18, 2004.
15. Interview with Morley, Issy-L'Évêque, April 16, 2009.
16. Interview with Epstein, Paris, November 18, 2004.
17. Ibid.
18. Philipponnat and Leinhardt, *La Vie*, p. 421.
19. Eychart and Aillaud, *Les Lettres*, p. 251.
20. Guéhenno, *Journal*, p. 300.
21. Galtier-Boissière, *Mon journal*, pp. 155–56.

CHAPTER 8 *Vivace Ma Non Troppo*

BIBLIOGRAPHY

Chimènes, Myriam, ed. *La Vie musicale sous Vichy.* Paris: Éditions Complexe, 2001.

Corcy, Stéphanie. *La Vie culturelle sous l'occupation.* Paris: Éditions Perrin, 2005.

Eychart, François, and Georges Aillaud, eds. *Les Lettres Françaises et Les Étoiles dans la clandestinité, 1942–1944.* Paris: Le Cherche Midi, 2008.

Goebbels, Joseph. *Journal.* Vol. 4: *1939–1942.* Paris: Éditions Tallandier, 2009.

Guéhenno, Jean. *Journal des années noires.* Paris: Éditions Gallimard, 1947.

Hamann, Brigitte. *Winifred Wagner: A Life at the Heart of Hitler's Bayreuth.* Translated by Alan Bance. London: Granta Books, 2005.

Huynh, Pascal, ed. Catalog for the exhibition Le IIIème Reich et la musique, shown at the Musée de la Musique, Paris, October 2004.

Langham Smith, Richard, and Caroline Potter. *French Music Since Berlioz.* Farnham, Eng.: Ashgate Publishing, 2005.

Le Bail, Karine. *Musique, pouvoir, responsabilité: La politique musicale de la Radiodiffusion française, 1939–1953.* Paris: CNRS Éditions, 2010.

Le Boterf, Hervé. *La Vie parisienne sous l'occupation.* Paris: Éditions France-Empire, 1997.

Lifar, Serge. *Ma vie.* Paris: Éditions René Julliard, 1965.

Némirovsky, Irène. *Suite française.* Paris: Éditions Denoël, 2004.

Porcile, François. *Les Conflits de la musique française, 1940–1965.* Paris: Éditions Fayard, 2001.

Poulenc, Francis. *Correspondance 1910–1963.* Edited by Myriam Chimènes. Paris: Éditions Fayard, 1994.

Rioux, Jean-Pierre, ed. *La Vie culturelle sous Vichy.* Paris: Éditions Complexe, 1990.

Simeone, Nigel. *Making Music in Occupied Paris.* Hove, Eng.: Musical Times, 2006.

Simon, Yannick. *Composer sous Vichy.* Paris: Éditions Symétrie, 2009.

——. *La SACEM et les droits des auteurs et compositeurs juifs sous l'occupation.* Paris: Mission d'Étude sur la Spoliation des Juifs de France, 2000.

INTERVIEWS

Jean Babilée, Paris, April 17, 2008.
Pierre Boulez, Paris, August 7, 2009.
Henri Dutilleux, Paris, July 22, 2009.
Michel Francini, Paris, March 13, 2008.

NOTES

1. Huynh, *Le IIIème Reich,* p. 15.
2. Goebbels, *Journal,* p. 535.
3. Poulenc, *Correspondance,* p. 511.
4. Eychart and Allaud, *Les Lettres,* p. 159.
5. Poulenc, *Correspondance,* pp. 533–34.
6. Interview with Boulez, Paris, August 7, 2009.
7. Interview with Dutilleux, Paris, July 22, 2009.
8. Poulenc, *Correspondance,* p. 577.
9. Hamann, *Winifred Wagner,* p. 332.
10. Sandrine Grandgambe essay "La Réunion des Théâtres Lyriques Nationaux," in Chimènes, *La Vie,* p. 118.
11. Interview with Francini, Paris, March 13, 2008.
12. Guéhenno, *Journal,* p. 101.
13. Poulenc, *Correspondance,* p. 584.
14. Interview with Babilée, Paris, April 17, 2008; all Babilée quotes are from this interview.
15. Fonds Lifar, Archives of City of Lausanne, Switzerland.
16. Lifar, *Ma vie,* p. 250.
17. Ibid., p. 326.
18. Poulenc, *Correspondance,* p. 577.

CHAPTER 9 A Ripped Canvas

BIBLIOGRAPHY

Arnaud, Claude. *Jean Cocteau.* Paris: Éditions Gallimard, 2003.

Bouchoux, Corinne. *Rose Valland: La Résistance au musée.* Paris: Geste Éditions, 2006.

Brandon, Ruth. *Surreal Lives: The Surrealists, 1917–1945.* London: Macmillan, 1999.

Bucher, Jeanne. Catalog for the exhibition Une Galerie d'avant-garde shown at the Musée d'Art Moderne et Contemporain in Strasbourg, France, 1994.

Calvi, Fabrizio, and Marc J. Masurovsky. *Le Festin du Reich: Le Pillage de la France occupée, 1940–1945.* Paris: Éditions Fayard, 2006.

Cocteau, Jean. *Journal, 1942–1945.* Paris: Éditions Gallimard, 1989.

Cone, Michele C. *Artists Under Vichy.* Princeton: Princeton University Press, 1992.

La Dame du Jeu de Paume: Rose Valland sur le Front d'Art. Catalog for the exhibition shown at the Centre d'Histoire de la Résistance et de la Déportation in Lyon, December 2009.

Dorléac, Laurence Bertrand. *Art of the Defeat: France, 1940–1944.* Translated by Jane Marie Todd. Los Angeles: Getty Research Institute, 2008.

Feliciano, Hector. *The Lost Museum: The Nazi Conspiracy to Steal the World's Greatest Works of Art.* New York: Basic Books, 1997.

Fonkenell, Guillaume, ed. *Le Louvre pendant la guerrre: Regards photographiques, 1938–1947.* Exhibition catalog. Paris: Musée du Louvre Éditions, 2009.

Galtier-Boissière, Jean. *Mon journal pendant l'occupation.* Paris: Éditions La Jeune Parque, 1944.

Gilot, Françoise, and Carlton Lake. *Life with Picasso.* New York: McGraw-Hill, 1964.

Greilsamer, Laurent. *Le Prince foudroyé: La Vie de Nicolas de Staël.* Paris: Éditions Fayard, 1998.

Heller, Gerhard. *Un Allemand à Paris.* Paris: Éditions du Seuil, 1981.

Huffington, Arianna Stassinopoulos. *Picasso: Creator and Destroyer.* London: Weidenfeld and Nicolson, 1988.

Jaër, Muriel. "Jeanne Bucher, grande prêtresse de l'art avant-garde." *Supérieur Inconnu* 19 (October–December 2000).

Jean Cocteau, sur le fil du siècle. Catalog for the exhibition shown at the Centre Pompidou, 2003. Paris: Centre Pompidou, 2003.

Jünger, Ernst. *Journaux de guerre.* Vol. 2, *1937–1948.* Paris: Éditions Gallimard, 2008.

Léautaud, Paul. *Journal littéraire.* Vol. 13, *February 1940–February 1956.* Paris: Mercure de France, 1986.

Le Musée Maillol s'expose. Catalog of exhibition shown at Musée Maillol, 2003. Paris: Éditions Gallimard, 2003.

Nicholas, Lynn H. *The Rape of Europa: The Fate of Europe's Treasures in the Third Reich and the Second World War.* New York: Knopf, 1994.

Spurling, Hilary. *Matisse the Master.* New York: Knopf, 2005.

INTERVIEWS

Leonora Carrington, Mexico City, November 20, 2008.
Françoise Gilot, New York, April 4, 2009.
Véronique Jaeger (Jeanne Bucher's granddaughter), Paris, April 29, 2009.
Denise René, Paris, July 15, 2008.
Annie Ubersfeld, Paris, March 25, 2008.

NOTES

1. *La Dame du Jeu de Paume.*
2. Bouchoux, *Rose Valland,* p. 39.
3. Ibid., p. 42.
4. The Nizkor Project: http://www.nizkor.org/hweb/imt/nca/nca-01/nca-01-14-plunder-01c.html.
5. The Nizkor Project: http://www.nizkor.org/hweb/imt/nca/nca-01/nca-01-14-plunder-01b.html.
6. Interview with Gilot, New York, April 4, 2009; all Gilot quotes are from this interview.

7. Jaër, "Jeanne Bucher."
8. Galtier-Boissière, *Mon journal*, p. 98.
9. www.meaus.com/arno-breker-biography.htm.
10. Cocteau, *Journal*, May 16, 1942, p. 125.
11. Ibid., May 6, 1942, p. 112.
12. Greilsamer, *Le Prince*, pp. 118–19.
13. *Le Musée Maillol*, p. 101.
14. Ibid., p. 102.
15. Nicholas, *The Rape*, p. 124.
16. Heller, *Un Allemand*, p. 118.
17. Jünger, *Journaux*, p. 325.
18. Interview with Ubersfeld, Paris, March 25, 2008.
19. Léautaud, *Journal*, p. 1041.
20. Heller, *Un Allemand*, p. 118.
21. Huffington, *Picasso*, p. 260.

CHAPTER 10 Distraction on Screen

BIBLIOGRAPHY

Arletty. *La Défense: Auto-portrait.* Paris: Éditions Ramsay, 1971.

Aurenche, Jean. *La Suite à l'écran.* Arles: Actes Sud, 1993.

Bertin-Maghit, Jean-Pierre. *Le Cinéma français sous l'occupation.* Paris: Presses Universitaires de France, 1994.

Carné, Marcel. *La Vie à belles dents.* Paris: Éditions Belfond, 1989.

Château, René. *Le Cinéma français sous l'occupation.* Paris: Éditions René Château et La Mémoire du Cinéma Français, 1995.

Corcy, Stéphanie. *La Vie culturelle sous l'occupation.* Paris: Éditions Perrin, 2005.

Desanti, Dominique. *Sacha Guitry: 50 ans de spectacle.* Paris: Éditions Grasset, 1982.

Devaivre, Jean. *Action! Mémoires, 1930–1970.* Paris: Nicolas Philippe, 2002.

Eychart, François, and Georges Aillaud, eds. *Les Lettres Françaises et Les Étoiles dans la clandestinité, 1942–1944.* Paris: Le Cherche Midi, 2008.

Goebbels, Joseph. *Journal.* Vol. 4, *1939–1942.* Paris: Éditions Tallandier, 2009.

Jünger, Ernst. *Journaux de guerre.* Vol. 2, *1939–1948.* Paris: Éditions Gallimard, 2009.

Le Boterf, Hervé. *La Vie parisienne sous l'occupation.* Paris: Éditions France-Empire, 1997.

Presle, Micheline. *L'Arrière-mémoire.* Paris: Éditions Flammarion, 1994.

Ragache, Gilles, and Jean-Robert Ragache. *La Vie quotidienne des écrivains et des artistes sous l'occupation.* Paris: Hachette, 1988.

Rioux, Jean-Pierre, ed. *La Vie culturelle sous Vichy.* Paris: Éditions Complexe, 1990.

Sadoul, Georges. *Histoire du cinéma mondial: Des origines à nos jours.* Paris: Éditions Flammarion, 1999.

Servat, Henry-Jean. *Les Trois glorieuses.* Paris: Éditions Pygmalion, 2008.

Weber, Alain. *La Bataille du film, 1933–1945.* Paris: Ramsay, 2007.

Yagil, Limore. *"L'Homme nouveau" et la Révolution Nationale de Vichy.* Paris: Presses Universitaires du Septentrion, 1997.

INTERVIEWS
Marcel Carné, Paris, December 3, 1994.
Danielle Darrieux, Paris, January 22, 2009.
Elina Labourdette, Paris, August 11, 2009.
Micheline Presle, Paris, April 28, 2009.

NOTES
  1. Aurenche, *La Suite,* p. 115.
  2. Interview with Darrieux, Paris, January 22, 2009; all Darrieux quotes are from this interview.
  3. Interview with Carné, Paris, December 3, 1994.
  4. Yagil, *"L'Homme nouveau,"* p. 170.
  5. Le Boterf, *La Vie,* p. 76.
  6. Jünger, *Journaux,* p. 214.
  7. Goebbels, *Journal,* p. 573.
  8. Carné, *La Vie,* p. 156.
  9. Eychart and Allaud, *Les Lettres,* p. 117.
  10. Ibid.
  11. Arletty, *La Défense,* p. 162.
  12. Interview with Presle, Paris, April 28, 2009; all Presle quotes are from this interview.
  13. Interview with Labourdette, Paris, August 11, 2009; all Labourdette quotes are from this interview.
  14. Interview with Carné, Paris, December 3, 1994.
  15. Ibid.

CHAPTER 11 Mirroring the Past

BIBLIOGRAPHY
Anouilh, Jean. *Antigone.* Translated by Lewis Galantière. London: Metheun, 1951.

Beauvoir, Simone de. *La Force de l'âge.* 1960. Paris: Éditions Gallimard (Folio), 1986.

Berghaus, Günter, ed. *Fascism and Theatre.* Oxford: Berghahn Books, 1996.

Camus, Albert. *Notebooks, 1942–1951.* Translated by Justin O'Brien. New York: Knopf, 1965.

Cohen-Solal, Annie. *Sartre: A Life.* New York: Pantheon Books, 1987.

Copeau, Jacques. *Journal, 1901–1948.* Paris: Seghers, 1991.

Corcy, Stéphanie. *La Vie culturelle sous l'occupation.* Paris: Éditions Perrin, 2005.

Desanti, Dominique. *Sacha Guitry: 50 ans de spectacle.* Paris: Éditions Grasset, 1982.

Eychart, François, and Georges Aillaud, eds. *Les Lettres Françaises et Les Étoiles dans la clandestinité, 1942–1944*. Paris: Le Cherche Midi, 2008.

Galtier-Boissière, Jean. *Mon journal pendant l'occupation*. Paris: Éditions La Jeune Parque, 1944.

Gerassi, John. *Talking with Sartre: Conversations and Debates*. New Haven: Yale University Press, 2009.

Jacobs, Gabriel. "The Role of Joan of Arc on the Stage of Occupied Paris." In *Vichy France and the Resistance: Culture and Ideology*, edited by Harry Roderick Kedward and Roger Austin. London: Croom Helm, 1985.

Joubert, Marie-Agnès. *La Comédie-Française sous l'occupation*. Paris: Éditions Tallandier, 1998.

Jünger, Ernst. *Journaux de guerre*. Vol. 2, *1939–1948*. Paris: Éditions Gallimard, 2008.

Le Boterf, Hervé. *La Vie parisienne sous l'occupation*. Paris: Éditions France-Empire, 1997.

Lottman, Herbert R. *Albert Camus: A Biography*. New York: Doubleday, 1979.

Montherlant, Henry de. *Le Solstice de juin*. Paris: Éditions Grasset, 1941.

Ragache, Gilles, and Jean-Robert Ragache. *La Vie quotidienne des écrivains et des artistes sous l'occupation, 1940–1944*. Paris: Hachette, 1998.

Rioux, Jean-Pierre, ed. *La Vie culturelle sous Vichy*. Paris: Éditions Complexe, 1990.

Sartre, Jean-Paul. *No Exit (Huis clos)*. Translated by Stuart Gilbert. New York: Vintage, 1989.

———. *The Flies (Les Mouches)*. Translated by Stuart Gilbert. New York: Vintage, 1989.

Todd, Olivier. *Albert Camus: A Life*. New York: Knopf, 1997.

INTERVIEWS
Héléna Bossis, Paris, May 2, 2008.
Dominique Delouche, Paris, November 24, 2008.
Michel Francini, Paris, March 13, 2008.
Jorge Semprun, Paris, March 26, 2008.
Annie Ubersfeld, Paris, March 25, 2008.

NOTES
1. Interview with Ubersfeld, Paris, March 25, 2008.
2. Copeau, *Journal*, p. 507.
3. Le Boterf, *La Vie*, p. 140.
4. Interview with Francini, Paris, March 13, 2008.
5. Joubert, *La Comédie-Française*, p. 169.
6. Galtier-Boissière, *Mon journal*, p. 179.
7. Montherlant, *Le Solstice*, p. 952.
8. Jacobs, "The Role of Joan of Arc," p. 115.
9. Beauvoir, *La Force*, p. 581.
10. Le Boterf, *La Vie*, p. 115.
11. Ibid., p. 141.

12. Desanti, *Sacha Guitry*, p. 389.
13. Eychart and Aillaud, *Les Lettres*, p. 132.
14. Jünger, *Journaux*, p. 239.
15. Beauvoir, *La Force*, p. 616.
16. Interview with Semprun, Paris, March 26, 2008.
17. Gerassi, *Talking with Sartre*, p. 114.
18. Ibid., pp. 108–9.
19. Le Boterf, *La Vie*, p. 159.
20. Interview with Delouche, Paris, November 24, 2008.
21. Interview with Bossis, Paris, May 2, 2008.

CHAPTER 12. Writing for the Enemy

BIBLIOGRAPHY

Abetz, Otto. *Histoire d'une politique franco-allemande 1930–1950: Mémoires d'un ambassadeur.* Paris: Éditions Stock, 1953.

Beauvoir, Simone de. *La Force de l'âge.* 1960. Paris: Éditions Gallimard (Folio), 1986.

Brasillach, Robert. *Notre avant-guerre.* Paris: Éditions Godefroy de Bouillon, 1998.

Céline, Louis-Ferdinand. *Les Beaux draps.* Paris: Nouvelles Éditions Françaises, 1942.

———. *Lettres.* Bibliothèque de la Pléiade. Paris: Éditions Gallimard, 2009.

Corcy, Stéphanie. *La Vie culturelle sous l'occupation.* Paris: Éditions Perrin, 2005.

Drieu La Rochelle, Pierre. *Journal, 1939–1945.* Paris: Éditions Gallimard, 1992.

Dufay, François. *Le Voyage d'automne: Octobre 1941, des écrivains français en Allemagne.* Paris: Éditions Plon, 2000.

Eychart, François, and Georges Aillaud, eds. *Les Lettres Françaises et Les Étoiles dans la clandestinité, 1942–1944.* Paris: Le Cherche Midi, 2008.

Fouché, Pascal. *L'Édition française sous l'occupation.* Paris: Éditions Fayard, 2008.

Galtier-Boissière, Jean. *Mon journal pendant l'occupation.* Paris: Éditions La Jeune Parque, 1944.

Glass, Charles. *Americans in Paris: Life and Death Under Nazi Occupation, 1940–1944.* London: Harper Press, 2009.

Guéhenno, Jean. *Journal des années noires.* Paris: Éditions Gallimard, 1947.

Heller, Gerhard. *Un Allemand à Paris.* Paris: Éditions du Seuil, 1981.

Jouhandeau, Marcel. *Écrits secrets I: Le voyage secret.* Paris: Arléa, 1988.

———. *Journal sous l'occupation.* Paris: Éditions Gallimard, 1980.

Jünger, Ernst. *Journaux de guerre.* Vol. 2, *1939–1948.* Paris: Éditions Gallimard, 2008.

Kaplan, Alice. *The Collaborator: The Trial and Execution of Robert Brasillach.* Chicago: University of Chicago Press, 2000.

Lire, Hors-Série. No. 7. *Céline, les derniers secrets.* June 2008.

Loiseaux, Gérard. *La Littérature de la defaite et de la collaboration.* Paris: Éditions Fayard, 1995.

Lottman, Herbert. *The Left Bank: Writers in Paris from Popular Front to Cold War.* Boston: Houghton Mifflin, 1982.

Martinoir, Francine de. *La Littérature occupée: Les Années de guerre, 1939–1945.* Paris: Hatier, 1995.

Mollier, Jean-Yves. *Édition, presse et pouvoir en France au XXe siècle.* Paris: Éditions Fayard, 2008.

Ory, Pascal. *Les Collaborateurs, 1940–1945.* Paris: Éditions du Seuil, 1976.

Paulhan, Jean. *Choix de lettres, 1937–1945.* Paris: Éditions Gallimard, 1992.

Poulain, Martine. *Livres pillés, lectures surveillées: Les Bibliothèques françaises sous l'occupation.* Paris: Éditions Gallimard, 2008.

Ragache, Gilles, and Jean-Robert Ragache. *La Vie quotidienne des écrivains et des artistes sous l'occupation, 1940–1944.* Paris: Hachette, 1998.

Rebatet, Lucien. *Les Décombres.* Paris: Éditions de l'Homme Libre, 2006. First edition: Éditions Denoël, 1942.

Sapiro, Gisèle. *La Guerre des écrivains, 1940–1953.* Paris: Éditions Fayard, 1999.

White, Edmund. *Genet: A Biography.* New York: Knopf, 1993.

NOTES
1. Jünger, *Journaux*, pp. 220–22.
2. Lottman, *The Left Bank*, p. 157.
3. Brasillach, *Notre avant-guerre*, p. 197.
4. Ibid., p. 291.
5. Kaplan, *The Collaborator*, p. 57.
6. Rebatet, *Les Décombres*, p. 447.
7. Ibid., p. 16.
8. Beauvoir, *La Force*, p. 636.
9. Paul Riche, *Au Pilori*, http://www.thyssens.com/01chrono/chrono_1940.php.
10. Paulhan, *Choix*, p. 196.
11. Heller, *Un Allemand*, p. 46.
12. Ibid., p. 48.
13. Guéhenno, *Journal*, p. 77.
14. Drieu La Rochelle, *Journal*, p. 316.
15. Ibid., p. 303.
16. Ibid., p. 280.
17. Ibid., p. 300.
18. Ibid., p. 301.
19. Ibid., p. 289.
20. Ibid., p. 338.
21. Ibid., pp. 348–49.
22. Heller, *Un Allemand*, p. 30.
23. Mollier, *Édition*, p. 66.
24. Lottman, *The Left Bank*, p. 161.
25. Fouché, *L'Édition*, p. 160.
26. Poulain, *Livres pillés*, p. 133.
27. Eychart and Aillaud, *Les Lettres*, p. 104.
28. Jouhandeau, *Journal*, p. 84.
29. Jouhandeau, *Écrits secrets*, p. 21.
30. Ibid., pp. 27–28.

31. Jouhandeau, *Journal*, p. 121.
32. Dufay, *Le Voyage*, pp. 157–58.
33. Ibid., pp. 168–70.
34. Heller, *Un Allemand*, pp. 84–85.
35. Ibid., p. 92.
36. Ibid., p. 87.
37. White, *Genet*, p. 284.
38. Jünger, *Journaux*, p. 255.
39. Heller, *Un Allemand*, p. 153.
40. Céline, *Lettres*, p. 672.
41. Céline, *Les Beaux*, p. 47.
42. Ibid., p. 8.
43. Loiseaux, *La Littérature*, p. 565.
44. *Lire, Hors-Série*, No. 7, *Céline*, p. 76.
45. Céline, *Lettres*, p. 622.
46. Jünger, *Journaux*, p. 716.

CHAPTER 13 Chez Florence

BIBLIOGRAPHY

Abramovici, Pierre. *Un Rocher bien occupé.* Paris: Éditions du Seuil, 2001.

Arnaud, Claude. *Jean Cocteau.* Paris: Éditions Gallimard, 2003.

Aury, Dominique. Preface to *Par le don de Florence Gould.* Paris: Bibliothèque littéraire Jacques Doucet, 1988.

Burrin, Philippe. *France Under the Germans: Collaboration and Compromise.* Translated by Janet Lloyd. New York: New Press, 1996.

Cornut-Gentille, Gilles, and Philippe Michel-Thiriett. *Florence Gould.* Paris: Mercure de France, 1989.

Dufay, François. *Le Voyage d'automne: Octobre 1941, des écrivains français en Allemagne.* Paris: Éditions Plon, 2000.

Gould, Florence. Testimony given in Paris to Investigating Judge Thirion. March 28, 1945.

Heller, Gerhard. *Un Allemand à Paris.* Paris: Éditions du Seuil, 1981.

Jouhandeau, Marcel. *Écrits secrets I: Le voyage secret.* Paris: Arléa, 1988.

———. *Journal sous l'occupation.* Paris: Éditions Gallimard, 1980.

Jünger, Ernst. *Journaux de guerre.* Vol. 2, *1939–1948.* Paris: Éditions Gallimard, 2008.

Léautaud, Paul. *Journal littéraire.* Vol. 15, *Novembre 1942—juin 1944.* Paris: Mercure de France, 1962.

———. *Journal littéraire.* Vol. 17, *1946–1949.* Paris: Mercure de France, 1964.

Mauriac, Claude. *Le Temps immobile.* Paris: Éditions Grasset, 1986.

Ministère Public. Public Prosecutor's Department of the Court of Justice of the Département de la Seine in the case of *Ministère Public contre X . . . pouvant être le personnel dirigeant de la Banque Charles de Monaco*, September 20, 1948.

Nicholas, Lynn H. *The Rape of Europa: The Fate of Europe's Treasures in the Third Reich and the Second World War.* New York: Knopf, 1994.

Paulhan, Jean. *Choix de lettres, 1937–1945.* Paris: Éditions Gallimard, 1992.

Thurman, Judith. *Secrets of the Flesh: A Life of Colette.* New York: Knopf, 1999.

NOTES

1. Cornut-Gentille and Michel-Thiriett, *Florence Gould,* p. 97.
2. Jünger, *Journaux,* p. 296.
3. Aury, Preface to *Par le don,* p. 7.
4. Heller, *Un Allemand,* p. 75.
5. Jünger, *Journaux,* p. 476.
6. Burrin, *France,* p. 205.
7. Jünger, *Journaux,* p. 519.
8. Abramovici, *Un Rocher,* p. 257.
9. Jünger, *Journaux,* p. 566.
10. Ibid., p. 563.
11. Ibid., p. 593.
12. Cornut-Gentille and Michel-Thiriett, *Florence Gould,* p. 109.
13. Thurman, *Secrets,* pp. 436–37.
14. Mauriac, *Le Temps,* p. 223.
15. Léautaud, *Journal,* p. 935.
16. Ibid., p. 1022.
17. Ibid., p. 1723.
18. Heller, *Un Allemand,* p. 65.
19. Ibid.
20. Jünger, *Journaux,* p. 694.
21. Ibid., p. 696.
22. Ibid., p. 697.
23. The Nizkor Project: http://www.nizkor.org/ftp.cgi/imt/ftp.py?imt//nca/nca-06/nca-06-3766-ps.
24. Gould, Testimony.
25. Cornut-Gentille and Michel-Thiriett, *Florence Gould,* p. 99.
26. Jünger, *Journaux,* p. 478.
27. Heller, *Un Allemand,* p. 64.
28. Jünger, *Journaux,* p. 728.
29. Ibid., p. 1299.
30. Heller, *Un Allemand,* p. 66.
31. Gould, Testimony.
32. Ministère Public, *Banque Charles.*
33. Cornut-Gentille and Michel-Thiriett, *Florence Gould,* p. 188.

CHAPTER 14 "On the Side of Life"

BIBLIOGRAPHY

Adler, Laure. *Marguerite Duras.* Paris: Éditions Gallimard, 1998.

Beauvoir, Simone de. *La Force de l'âge.* 1960. Paris: Éditions Gallimard (Folio), 1986.

Betz, Albrecht, and Stefan Martens. *Les Intellecteuls et l'occupation, 1940–1944: Collaborer, partir, résister.* Paris: Éditions Autrement, 2004.

Burrin, Philippe. *France Under the Germans: Collaboration and Compromise.* Translated by Janet Lloyd. New York: New Press, 1996.

Camus, Albert. *Camus at Combat: Writing, 1944–1947.* Edited by Jacqueline Lévi-Valensi. Princeton: Princeton University Press, 2006.

———. *Notebooks, 1942–1951.* Translated by Justin O'Brien. New York: Knopf, 1965.

Cassou, Jean. *33 sonnets composés au secret.* Signed Jean Noir, With an introduction by François La Colère. Paris: Éditions de Minuit, 1943. Published in English as *33 Sonnets of the Resistance.* Introduction by Louis Aragon. Translated by Timothy Adès. Todmorden, Eng.: Arc Publications, 2002.

Cate, Curtis. *André Malraux: A Biography.* London: Hutchinson, 1995.

Char, René. *Feuillets d'Hypnos.* Paris: FolioPlus, 2007.

———. *Oeuvres complètes.* Paris: Éditions Gallimard, 1983.

Cohen-Solal, Annie. *Sartre: A Life.* New York: Pantheon Books, 1987.

Corcy, Stéphanie. *La Vie culturelle sous l'occupation.* Paris: Éditions Perrin, 2005.

Daix, Pierre. *Les Lettres Françaises: Jalons pour l'histoire d'un journal, 1941–1972.* Paris: Éditions Tallandier, 2004.

Duras, Marguerite. *Wartime Writings, 1943–1949.* Translated by Linda Coverdale. New York: New Press, 2008.

Éluard, Paul, ed. *L'Honneur des poètes.* Paris: Éditions de Minuit, 1943.

Eychart, François, and Georges Aillaud, eds. *Les Lettres Françaises et Les Étoiles dans la clandestinité, 1942–1944.* Paris: Le Cherche Midi, 2008.

Galtier-Boissière, Jean. *Mon journal pendant l'occupation.* Paris: Éditions La Jeune Parque, 1944.

Gerassi, John. *Talking with Sartre: Conversations and Debates.* New Haven: Yale University Press, 2009.

Gide, André. *Journals.* Vol. 4, *1939–1949.* Translated by Justin O'Brien. Urbana: University of Illinois Press, 2000.

Guéhenno, Jean. *Journal des années noires.* Paris: Éditions Gallimard, 1947.

Guérin, Raymond. *Retour de barbarie.* Bordeaux: Éditions Finitude, 2005.

Heller, Gerhard. *Un Allemand à Paris.* Paris: Éditions du Seuil, 1981.

Jünger, Ernst. *Journaux de guerre.* Vol. 2, *1939–1948.* Paris: Éditions Gallimard, 2008.

Léautaud, Paul. *Journal littéraire.* Vol. 3, *February 1940–February 1956.* Paris: Mercure de France, 1986.

Le Boterf, Hervé. *La Vie parisienne sous l'occupation.* Paris: Éditions France-Empire, 1997.

Loiseaux, Gérard. *La Littérature de la défaite et de la collaboration.* Paris: Éditions Fayard, 1995.

Lottman, Herbert R. *Albert Camus: A Biography.* New York: Doubleday, 1979.

———. *The Left Bank: Writers in Paris from Popular Front to Cold War.* Boston: Houghton Mifflin, 1982.

Malraux, André. *Anti-Memoirs.* Translated by Terence Kilmartin. New York: Holt, Rinehart and Winston, 1968.

Martinoir, Francine de. *La Littérature occupée: Les Années de guerre, 1939–1945.* Paris: Hatier, 1995.

Mauriac, Claude. *Le Temps immobile.* Edited and with commentary by José Cabanis. Paris: Éditions Grasset, 1993.

Mollier, Jean-Yves. *Édition, presse et pouvoir en France au XXe siècle.* Paris: Éditions Fayard, 2008.

Paulhan, Jean. *Choix de lettres, 1937–1945.* Paris: Éditions Gallimard, 1992.

Paxton, Robert O., Olivier Corpet and Claire Paulhan, eds. *Archives de la vie littéraire sous occupation: À travers le désastre.* Paris: Éditions Tallandier, 2009.

Ragache, Gilles, and Jean-Robert Ragache. *La Vie quotidienne des écrivains et des artistes sous l'occupation, 1940–1944.* Paris: Hachette, 1998.

Rioux, Jean-Pierre, ed. *La Vie culturelle sous Vichy.* Paris: Éditions Complexe, 1990.

Rondeau, Daniel. *Camus, ou Les promesses de la vie.* Paris: Éditions Mengès, 2005.

Saint-Exupéry, Antoine de. *Lettre à un otage.* New York: Brentano's, 1943.

Sapiro, Gisèle. *La Guerre des écrivains, 1940–1953.* Paris: Éditions Fayard, 1999.

Seghers, Pierre. *La Résistance et ses poètes (France 1940–1945).* Paris: Éditions Seghers, 1974.

Thurman, Judith. *Secrets of the Flesh: A Life of Colette.* New York: Knopf, 1999.

Todd, Olivier. *Albert Camus: A Life.* New York: Knopf, 1997.

———. *Malraux.* New York: Knopf, 2005.

Vallier, Jean. *C'était Marguerite Duras.* Vol. 1, *1914–1945.* Paris: Éditions Fayard, 2006.

Vercors. *Le Silence de la mer.* Paris: Éditions de Minuit, 1942. (My page references are to the Albin Michel edition, 1951.)

INTERVIEWS
Dominique Desanti, Paris, March 14, 2008.
Maurice Druon, Paris, June 3, 2008.
Marguerite Duras, Paris, March 26, 1990.
Madeleine Malraux, Paris, June 12, 2008.
Jorge Semprun, Paris, March 26, 2008.

NOTES
1. Guéhenno, *Journal*, p. 73.
2. Ibid., p. 74.
3. Ibid., p. 75.
4. Saint-Exupéry, *Lettre*, p. 32.
5. Ibid., pp. 69–70.
6. Gide, *Journals*, p. 221.
7. Guéhenno, *Journal*, p. 189.

8. Eychart and Aillaud, *Les Lettres,* p. 27.
9. Mauriac, *Le Temps,* p. 42.
10. Vercors, *Le Silence,* p. 28.
11. Ibid., p. 29.
12. Ibid., p. 53.
13. Eychart and Aillaud, *Les Lettres,* p. 52.
14. Betz and Martens, *Les Intellectuels,* p. 206.
15. Éluard, *L'Honneur,* p. 10.
16. Aragon, in Cassou, *33 sonnets,* p. 32.
17. Cassou, *33 sonnets,* pp. 30–31.
18. Ibid.
19. Ibid., pp. 50–51.
20. Ibid., pp. 58–59.
21. Ibid.
22. Galtier-Boissière, *Mon journal,* p. 227.
23. Mémorial de l'internement et de la deportation, Camp de Royallieu, Compiègne, Press Dossier, p. 17.
24. Char, *Oeuvres,* p. 632.
25. Char, *Feuillets,* pp. 29, 36, 51, 17.
26. Ibid., pp. 44–45.
27. Ibid., pp. 49–50.
28. Ibid., p. 39.
29. Interview with Druon, Paris, June 3, 2008.
30. Interview with Desanti, Paris, March 14, 2008.
31. Beauvoir, *La Force,* p, 609.
32. Ibid., p. 657.
33. Gerassi, *Talking with Sartre,* p. 118.
34. Beauvoir, *La Force,* p. 665.
35. Heller, *Un Allemand,* p. 106.
36. Léautaud, *Journal,* p. 340.
37. Paulhan, *Choix,* p. 364.

CHAPTER 15. The Pendulum Swings

BIBLIOGRAPHY

Beauvoir, Simone de. *La Force de l'âge.* 1960. Paris: Éditions Gallimard (Folio), 1986.

Burrin, Philippe. *France Under the Germans: Collaboration and Compromise.* Translated by Janet Lloyd. New York: New Press, 1996.

Camus, Albert. *Camus at Combat: Writing, 1944–1947.* Edited by Jacqueline Lévi-Valensi. Princeton: Princeton University Press, 2006.

Eychart, François, and Georges Aillaud, eds. *Les Lettres Françaises et Les Étoiles dans la clandestinité, 1942–1944.* Paris: Le Cherche Midi, 2008.

Galtier-Boissière, Jean. *Mon journal pendant l'occupation.* Paris: Éditions La Jeune Parque, 1944.

Guéhenno, Jean. *Journal des années noires.* Paris: Éditions Gallimard, 1947.

Heller, Gerhard. *Un Allemand à Paris.* Paris: Éditions du Seuil, 1981.

Jackson, Julian. *France: The Dark Years, 1940–1944.* New York: Oxford University Press, 2001.

Jünger, Ernst. *Journaux de guerre,* Vol. 2, *1939–1948.* Paris: Éditions Gallimard, 2008.

Le Boterf, Hervé. *La Vie parisienne sous l'occupation.* Paris: Éditions France-Empire, 1997.

Paxton, Robert O. *Vichy France: Old Guard and New Order, 1940–1944.* New York: Knopf, 1972.

Paxton, Robert O., Olivier Corpet and Claire Paulhan, eds. *Archives de la vie littéraire sous occupation: À travers le désastre.* Paris: Éditions Tallandier, 2009.

INTERVIEWS
Michel Francini, Paris, March 13, 2008.
Françoise Gilot, New York, April 4, 2009.
Annie Ubersfeld, Paris, March 25, 2008.

NOTES
1. Guéhenno, *Journal,* p. 387.
2. Interview with Francini, Paris, March 13, 2008.
3. Jünger, *Journaux,* p. 713.
4. Galtier-Boissière, *Mon journal,* p. 238.
5. Jünger, *Journaux,* p. 733.
6. Interview with Ubersfeld, Paris, March 25, 2008.
7. Interview with Gilot, New York, April 4, 2009.
8. Beauvoir, *La Force,* p. 679.
9. Interview with Francini, Paris, March 13, 2008.
10. Guéhenno, *Journal,* p. 433.
11. Ibid., p. 434.
12. Ibid.
13. Ibid., p. 436.
14. Camus, *Combat,* p. 13.
15. Galtier-Boissière, *Mon journal,* pp. 271–72.
16. Ibid., p. 272.
17. Ibid., pp. 275–76.
18. Ibid., p. 276.
19. Ibid., p. 282.

CHAPTER 16 Vengeance and Amnesia

BIBLIOGRAPHY
Assouline, Pierre. *L'Épuration des intellectuels.* Paris: Éditions Complexe, 1996.

Baruch, Marc-Olivier, ed. *Une Poignée de misérables: L'épuration de la société française après la Seconde Guerre mondiale.* Paris: Éditions Fayard, 2003.

Beauvoir, Simone de. *La Force de l'âge.* 1960. Paris: Éditions Gallimard (Folio), 1986.

Beevor, Antony, and Artemis Cooper. *Paris After the Liberation, 1944–1949.* New York: Doubleday, 1994.

Betz, Albrecht, and Stefan Martens. *Les Intellectuels et l'occupation*. Paris: Éditions Autrement, 2004.

Camus, Albert. *Camus at* Combat: *Writing, 1944–1947*. Edited by Jacqueline Lévi-Valensi. Princeton: Princeton University Press, 2006.

Château, René. *Le Cinéma Français sous l'occupation*. Paris: Éditions René Château et La Mémoire du Cinéma Français, 1995.

Chimènes, Myriam, ed. *La Vie musicale sous Vichy*. Paris: Éditions Complexe, 2001.

Cocteau, Jean. *Journal, 1942–1945*. Paris: Éditions Gallimard, 1989.

Cohen-Solal, Annie. *Sartre: A Life*. New York: Pantheon Books, 1987.

Corcy, Stéphanie. *La Vie culturelle sous l'occupation*. Paris: Éditions Perrin, 2005.

Decaux, Alain. *Tous les personnages sont vrais: Mémoires*. Parris: Perrin, 2005.

De Gaulle, Charles. *Mémoires de guerre*. Paris: Éditions Plon, 1959.

Desanti, Dominique. *Sacha Guitry: 50 ans de spectacle*. Paris: Éditions Grasset, 1982.

Drieu La Rochelle, Pierre. *Journal, 1939–1945*. Paris: Éditions Gallimard, 1992.

Galtier-Boissière, Jean. *Mon journal depuis la libération*. Paris: La Jeune Parque, 1945.

——. *Mon journal pendant l'occupation*. Paris: Éditions La Jeune Parque, 1944.

Gide, André. *Back from the U.S.S.R.* Translated by Dorothy Bussy. London: Martin Secker and Warburg, 1937.

Guéhenno, Jean. *Journal des années noires*. Paris: Éditions Gallimard, 1947.

Guitry, Sacha. *60 jours de prison*. Paris: L'Élan, 1949.

Jackson, Julian. *France: The Dark Years, 1940–1944*. New York: Oxford University Press, 2001.

Jouhandeau, Marcel. *Journal sous l'occupation*. Paris: Éditions Gallimard, 1980.

Judt, Tony. *Past Imperfect: French Intellectuals, 1944–1956*. Los Angeles: University of California Press, 1992.

Kaplan, Alice. *The Collaborator: The Trial and Execution of Robert Brasillach*. Chicago: University of Chicago Press, 2000.

Léautaud, Paul. *Journal Littéraire*, Vol. 17. Paris: Mercure de France, 1954.

Le Boterf, Hervé. *La Vie parisienne sous l'occupation*. Paris: Éditions France-Empire, 1997.

Letan, Michel. *Pierre Laval: De l'armistice au poteau*. Paris: Éditions de la Couronne, 1947.

Lifar, Serge. *Ma vie*. Paris: Éditions René Julliard, 1965.

Loiseaux, Gérard. *La Littérature de la défaite et de la collaboration*. Paris: Éditions Fayard, 1995.

Lottman, Herbert. *The Left Bank: Writers in Paris from Popular Front to Cold War*. Boston: Houghton Mifflin, 1982.

Ory, Pascal. *Les Collaborateurs, 1940–1945*. Paris: Éditions du Seuil, 1976.

Paxton, Robert O. *Vichy France: Old Guard and New Order, 1940–1944*. New York: Knopf, 1972.

Paxton, Robert O., Olivier Corpet and Claire Paulhan, eds. *Archives de la vie littéraire sous occupation: À travers le désastre.* Paris: Éditions Tallandier, 2009.

Picaper, Jean-Paul, and Ludwig Norz. *Enfants maudits.* Paris: Éditions des Syrtes, 2004.

Rioux, Jean-Pierre, ed. *La Vie culturelle sous Vichy.* Paris: Éditions Complexe, 1990.

Rousso, Henry. *La Collaboration: Les Noms, les thèmes, les lieux.* Paris: MA Éditions, 1987.

Sapiro, Gisèle. *La Guerre des écrivains, 1940–1953.* Paris: Éditions Fayard, 1999.

Weyembergh, Maurice. *Albert Camus, ou La Mémoire des origines.* Paris: De Boeck Université, 1998.

INTERVIEWS

Claude Anglès, Paris, August 8, 2007.
Danielle Darrieux, Paris, January 22, 2009.
Dominique Desanti, Paris, March 14, 2008.
Michel Francini, Paris, March 13, 2008.

NOTES

1. Interview with Francini, Paris, March 13, 2008.
2. Cocteau, *Journal,* p. 537.
3. Interview with Anglès, Paris, August 8, 2007.
4. Desanti, *Sacha Guitry,* p. 441.
5. Galtier-Boissière, *Mon journal pendant,* p. 284.
6. Galtier-Boissière, *Mon journal depuis,* p. 36.
7. Letan, *Pierre Laval,* p. 167.
8. Betz and Martens, *Les Intellectuels,* p. 77.
9. Léautaud, *Journal,* vol. 17, p. 121.
10. Drieu La Rochelle, *Journal,* p. 506.
11. Heller, *Un Allemand,* p. 56.
12. Galtier-Boissière, *Mon journal depuis,* p. 189.
13. Assouline, *L'Épuration,* p. 54.
14. Ibid., p. 53.
15. Weyembergh, *Albert Camus,* p. 167.
16. Assouline, *L'Épuration,* pp. 46–47.
17. Camus, *Camus at* Combat, pp. 249–50.
18. Jouhandeau, *Journal,* p. 278.
19. Ibid., p. 365.
20. Galtier-Boisssière, *Mon journal depuis,* p. 129.
21. Assouline, *L'Épuration,* p. 123.
22. De Gaulle, *Mémoires,* p. 115.
23. Assouline, *L'Épuration,* p. 82.
24. Ibid., p. 100.
25. Château, *Le Cinéma,* p. 458.
26. Interview with Darrieux, Paris, January 22, 2009.
27. Château, *Le Cinéma,* p. 441.

CHAPTER 17 Surviving at a Price

BIBLIOGRAPHY

Assouline, Pierre. *L'Épuration des intellectuels.* Paris: Éditions Complexe, 1996.

Beevor, Antony, and Artemis Cooper. *Paris After the Liberation, 1944–1949.* New York: Doubleday, 1994.

Galtier-Boissière, Jean. *Mon journal depuis la libération.* Paris: La Jeune Parque, 1945.

———. *Mon journal pendant l'occupation.* Paris: Éditions La Jeune Parque, 1944.

Gerassi, John. *Talking with Sartre: Conversations and Debates.* New Haven: Yale University Press, 2009.

Heller, Gerhard. *Un Allemand à Paris.* Paris: Éditions du Seuil, 1981.

Maison Rouge, Isabelle de. *Picasso.* Paris: Le Cavalier Bleu, 2005.

Paulhan, Jean. *Lettre aux directeurs de la résistance.* Paris: Les Éditions de Minuit, 1952.

Sapiro, Gisèle. *La Guerre des écrivains, 1940–1953.* Paris: Éditions Fayard, 1999.

NOTES

1. Heller, *Un Allemand,* p. 105.
2. Galtier-Boissière, *Mon journal pendant,* p. 289.
3. Sapiro, *La Guerre,* p. 62.
4. Galtier-Boissière, *Mon journal pendant,* p. 287.
5. Gerassi, *Talking with Sartre,* p. 122.
6. Ibid., p. 124.
7. Paulhan, *Lettre,* p. 7.
8. Ibid., p. 10.
9. Ibid., p. 54.
10. Maison Rouge, *Picasso,* p. 15.
11. Quoted in *Theories of Modern Art: A Source Book by Artists and Critics,* edited by Herschel B. Chipp (Berkeley: University of California Press, 1973), pp. 487–89.

INDEX

ABC, 93, 94, 96, 97

Abetz, Otto, 20–1, 53–4, 57, 69, 132, 157, 199, 242; art and, 61, 63, 168, 176; Céline's visit to embassy and, 251–2; Drieu La Rochelle's relationship with, 235–6; *épuration culturelle* and, 320, 322; as "good German," 229; haute couture and, 103; prisoner release and, 137, 183, 215, 229, 232, 290; publishing and, 64, 65, 69–70, 235–6, 238, 239, 242; replacement of, 299; Vichy regime and, 118, 121, 123

Abetz, Suzanne, 20, 223, 229, 289–90

Abraham, Marcel, 109–10, 111, 113, 116

Académie Française, 10, 35, 46, 56, 65, 236*n*, 244–6, 268, 287, 288; *épuration culturelle* and, 320, 329

Académie Goncourt, 246–7, 329

Achard, Marcel, 222

Action Française, L', 18, 231–2, 325

actors, actresses, 8–9, 50, 197–202, 207, 227

Actualités mondiales (newsreel), 193

Âge d'or, L' (The Golden Age), 13

Agir resistance group, 284, 341

air force, Canadian, 199

air force, French, 40, 46, 151

air force, Spanish Republican, 23, 40

Ajalbert, Jean, 246

Akoka, Henri, 150

Alain (Émile-Auguste Chartier), 238

Alain, Jehan, 146

À la recherche du temps perdu (In Search of Lost Time; Proust), 10–11

Alfa, Michèle, 200, 333*n*

Algeria, 45, 48, 90, 139, 140*n*, 272, 292–3, 298, 350

Algiers, 99, 120, 139, 140, 279, 281, 285–6, 295

Allégret, Marc, 200

Allemand à Paris, Un (A German in Paris; Heller), 236, 240, 241–2, 249, 250, 273, 296, 341

Allen, Jay, 88

Allied Military Government for Occupied Territories, 308

All-Union Congress of Soviet Writers, 22

Almanzor, Lucette, 253, 254, 329

Alsace, 48, 60, 149, 307

Amouroux, Henri, 71

André Weil Gallery, 63, 171

Anges du péché, Les (Angels of Sin), 196

Anglès, Claude, 317

Animaux modèles, Les (Poulenc), 149, 158–9

Anouilh, Jean, 43, 207, 208, 209, 218–19, 222, 231, 234, 243, 340, 347; *épuration culturelle* and, 325, 335–6

Antelme, Robert, 294–6

Antigone (Anouilh), 208, 218–19, 336

Antigone (Honegger), 148

anti-Semitism, 19–22, 35, 45, 59–64, 73, 205, 224, 259, 266; Babilée's experience of, 159–60; ban on professions and, 133–4, 189, 192, 231, 287; of Céline, 21–2, 64, 250–4, 328, 329; censorship and, 55, 57, 64; of Darquier de Pellepoix, 134, 165; deportation and, xiii, 60, 72, 104, 134–6, 145, 152, 169, 174, 175, 183, 234, 274–5, 301*n*, 303, 340–1; Dreyfus affair and, 15, 232*n*, 253, 325; of Drieu La Rochelle, 38–9, 237; *épuration culturelle* and, 324; Goudeket's experience of, 289–90; L'Action Française and, 15–16, 17, 21, 35; Lifar's experience of, 160–1; in movies, 192, 211, 236*n*, 332; newspapers and, 60, 69–70; performers and, 94, 96, 97, 339; Radio-Paris and, 52, 333; roundups (*rafles*) and, 104, 134–8, 159–60, 161*n*, 275*n*, 289, 290, 308, 317; Statute on Jews and, 59–60, 68, 94, 120, 133, 164, 189, 192, 287; theater and, 59, 208, 209, 210, 214–15, 220, 223; Vichy regime and, xiii, 49, 59–60, 68, 72, 77, 79, 94, 110, 119, 120, 133–8, 152, 164, 165, 189, 215, 244, 287, 293; writers and, 227–34, 239, 240, 243, 247

Antoine, André, 9, 215

appeasement, 26–7, 212

Appel, 70, 252–3

Aragon, Louis, 23, 39, 122, 149, 174,
    228, 237, 243, 270, 328, 331, 340; as
    Communist, 13, 18, 35, 65, 99, 273, 274,
    275, 281, 326, 345–6; Gide denounced
    by, 320–1; Matisse's friendship with,
    180; resistance and, 273, 274, 275,
    279–83, 287, 336, 337, 341, 342, 343;
    Surrealism and, 12, 13, 279, 346
architecture, 119–20, 175–6
Arden, Elizabeth, 105
Arendt, Hannah, 7, 30, 81
Arland, Marcel, 234–5, 238, 247, 258, 266
Arletty, 9, 177, 195, 199, 204, 215, 230;
    épuration culturelle and, 333–4
Armée Secrète (Secret Army), 285, 301
army, British, 34, 41, 76, 90, 110, 272
army, French, 18, 26, 33, 34, 167, 257, 272,
    315, 318, 323; armistice and, 48, 119;
    Dreyfus affair and, 15; entertaining of,
    35, 95, 97; German advance on, 41, 43,
    44; retreat of, 41, 47; troops evacuated
    to England, 44, 47
army, German, 4, 32, 36, 37, 38, 41, 45,
    118, 151, 245, 264, 298, 299, 300, 305,
    312; in Battle of Stalingrad, 140; in
    Issy-L'Évêque, 136; Kunstschutz of,
    60–1, 164, 168, 169; in occupation of
    Paris, 3, 46, 131, 158, 202; orchestra of,
    154; as Paris audience, 91, 92, 157
Aron, Raymond, 35, 350
Arp, Jean, 84, 86, 87
art, artists, 54, 60–4, 163–86, 227, 308;
    attracted to Paris, 4–7, 346; censorship
    and, 171, 234; cultural legacy of
    occupation and, 338–9, 346; Dada in, 12;
    "degenerate," 29, 142, 164, 166, 171,
    173, 175, 186, 339; épuration culturelle
    and, 334–5; Fauvism, 5, 173, 175, 178,
    185–6; German, 161, 172; Gould and,
    263–4, 265; market for, 5, 37, 62–3,
    170–1, 308, 346; protection of, 34, 60–1,
    164, 168, 169; Surrealism in, 6, 12, 22,
    28–9, 83, 84–5, 89, 174
art collections, 37, 55, 84; German seizure
    of, 60–1, 163–7, 263–4, 308, 335
art galleries, 62–3, 128, 170–4, 184, 265, 335
Atlantic coastal areas, ix, 48, 297, 327
À travers le désastre (France, My Country,
    Through the Disaster; Maritain), 278
attentisme, 108, 301, 335
Aubade, L' (Picasso), 185
Aujourd'hui, 70, 253, 270, 284
Aumont, Jean-Pierre, 58–9
Au Pilori, 70, 160, 236, 310
Aurenche, Jean, 190
Aurenche, Marie-Berthe, 28, 87
Auric, Georges, 147–8, 157, 197, 237, 330
Austria, 26, 62, 126, 141n, 248, 285n, 326
Austrian exiles, 22, 29, 30, 31, 72, 76, 201
Autant-Lara, Claude, 188, 194
Aveline, Claude, 109–10, 111, 113, 116
Aymé, Marcel, 242
Azéma, Vincent, 78

Babilée, Jean, 159–60, 161, 347
Bach, Johann Sebastian, 141, 142
Badoglio, Pietro, 298
Bagatelles pour un massacre (Trifles for a
    Massacre; Céline), 21–2, 252, 253
Baker, Josephine, 7–8, 35, 75, 95, 99, 336–7
Bakst, Léon, 6
Báky, Josef von, 193
Balanchine, George, 6, 347–8
Balin, Mireille, 199, 333
ballet, 6, 50, 57, 118, 149, 158–62, 307, 330,
    347
Ballet de Cannes, 159
Ballet de l'Opéra de Monte-Carlo, 161n
Ballets des Champs-Élysées, 160, 330
Ballets Russes, 6, 57, 158
Balmain, Pierre, 104, 347
Banque de France, 165, 179
Banyuls-sur-Mer, ix, 77, 78, 176, 177, 178
Baranov-Rossiné, Vladimir, 175
Barbezat, Olga, 221
Barbie, Klaus, 301
Barbier, Pierre, 129
Bardèche, Maurice, 323
Bardet, Jean, 241
Barr, Alfred H., Jr., 74, 85, 86
Barraine, Elsa, 146
Barrault, Jean-Louis: movies and, 191, 194,
    203–4, 234, 333; theater and, 129, 207,
    212, 213, 224
Barrès, Maurice, 15
Barsacq, Léon, 203
Barthélemy, Joseph, 133–4
Baudrillart, Cardinal Alfred, 133, 244, 245
Baur, Harry, 191, 201–2, 207
Bayreuth festival (1938), 155
Bazaine, Jean, 128, 172, 173, 186, 346
BBC, 47, 52, 53, 110, 135, 155n, 168, 231,
    278, 288, 290, 303, 305–6, 311
Beach, Sylvia, 7, 240–1
Beauvoir, Simone de, 39, 42, 59, 185, 214,
    220, 270, 308; writing of, 25, 35, 235,
    243, 291–2, 309–10, 312, 349
Beaux draps, Les (Céline), 252, 253
Becker, Jacques, 188, 196, 200, 202
Beckett, Samuel, 7, 80, 347
Beckmann, Max, 5
Beethoven, Ludwig van, 57, 141, 154–5
Behr, Kurt von, 165, 166, 170, 264
Belarus, Belarusans, 40, 175, 298
Belgium, 23, 41, 104n, 168
Bell, Marie, 224, 225, 265
Belle allemande, La (Erhart), 169
Bellessort, André, 245
Bellmer, Hans, 30, 87
Belmondo, Paul, 175–6, 178
Benda, Hans von, 154
Benda, Julien, 17, 239
Bénédite, Daniel, 75, 83, 88–9
Benjamin, René, 246, 329
Benjamin, Walter, 7, 31, 78
Benois, Alexandre, 6
Benoist-Méchin, Jacques, 20, 176, 177, 240

Benoit, Pierre, 245, 247, 258, 266
Bérard, Christian, 258
Béraud, Henri, 322, 324
Berg, Alban, 142, 149, 152
Berger, Fanny (Odette Bernstein), 104
Bergson, Henri, 10, 41, 245
Berlin, 8, 11, 12, 73, 80, 103, 307; Chevalier in, 98–9; French artists in, 175–6, 339; French classical musicians in, 144; movies in, 188, 190, 198, 201; movie stars' visits to, 198, 200, 201, 332; writers' visits to, 247, 248, 249, 339, 342
Berliner Kammerorchester, 154
Berlin Philharmonic, 142, 143, 144, 154, 155n, 307
Berlioz, Louis Hector, 57, 147, 194
Bernanos, Georges, 271
Bernard, Robert, 145
Bernard, Roger, 286
Bernard, Tristan, 41, 169, 215, 317, 333, 340
"Bernhard List," 64, 239
Bernhardt, Sarah, 55, 216
Bernheim-Jeune gallery, 62
Bernstein, Henri, 9, 65, 209, 333
Berriau, Simone, 226
Berteaut, Simone, 97
Bertin, Pierre, 224
Betti, Henri, 98
Beuve-Méry, Hubert, 129–30
Bibliothèque Nationale, 79, 240, 244, 303
Bigard, Andrée, 97
Bigot, Eugène, 146
Billy, André, 246
Bingham, Hiram, IV, 75, 86
Bizet, Georges, 147
black market, 86, 106, 184, 196, 257, 302, 308, 315
blacks, 7–8, 51, 101
Blanchar, Pierre, 202
Blanzat, Jean, 245
Blistène, Marcel, 97
Bloch, André, 152
Bloch, Marc, 59, 169, 287, 288, 341
Blond, Georges, 249
Bloy, Léon, 216
Blücher, Heinrich, 30
Blum, Léon, 14, 16, 18–21, 70, 132, 169, 232
Blumenfeld, Erwin, 31
Boëllmann-Gigout, Marie-Louise, 153
Bohn, Frank, 74, 77
Bonnard, Abel, 15, 56, 169, 177, 202, 238, 263; Académie Française and, 56, 244, 245, 329; as education minister, 56, 144, 157, 165, 226; trial of, 319–20; in visit to Germany, 247–9
Bonnard, Marthe, 178, 179
Bonnard, Pierre, 5, 37, 45, 172, 174, 178–9, 185; Vierny's posing for, 77, 179, 180
Bonny, Pierre, 302, 303n
books, 242–3; banning of, 64, 239–40, 243, 245, 327; burning of, 240; valuable, 169, 244

bookshops, 7, 54, 240, 241
Bordeaux, ix, 46, 128, 131, 151
Bordeaux, Henry, 242
Borotra, Jean, 126
Bossis, Héléna, 226
Bouchard, Henri, 175–6
Boucher, François, 169
Boué, Géori, 215
Boulanger, Nadia, 146
Boulez, Pierre, 150–1, 347
Bourdet, Édouard, 210, 222–3, 226
Bousquet, Marie-Louise, 256, 257–8, 262
Bousquet, René, 135, 138
Boyer, Charles, 58
Bradley, Omar, 313
Brancusi, Constantin, 6, 37
Braque, Georges, 5, 37, 149, 150, 172–5, 182, 183, 185, 224, 265, 346
Brasillach, Robert, 15, 17, 35, 70, 176, 202, 223, 225, 259; background and career path of, 231–3; épuration culturelle and, 321, 323–6, 328; Je suis partout and, 18, 20, 70, 217, 231, 232, 233, 323; as POW, 43–4, 70; in visit to Germany, 247–9
Brassaï, 183, 185
Brassens, Georges, 300
Brasseur, Pierre, 204
Brauchitsch, Walther von, 160
Brauner, Victor, 37, 84, 87, 175
Breker, Arno, 56, 161, 172, 176–8, 186, 230, 316, 334, 339
Bremer, Karl-Heinz, 53, 212, 229, 233
Bresson, Robert, 188, 196, 201, 348
Breton, André, 12, 13, 22, 25n, 29, 35–6, 279, 284, 336, 340; emigration of, 84–5; at Villa Air-Bel, 83, 84, 285
Breton, Aube, 83, 84–5
Bretty, Béatrice, 211, 335
Brianchon, Maurice, 158
Brinon, Fernand de, 54, 119, 133, 217, 230, 252, 307, 319
British Expeditionary Force, 33, 41
Brittany, 110, 181, 297, 305
Brossolette, Pierre, 113, 115–16
brothels, 51, 91, 92–3
Bruller, Jean (Vercours), 276–8, 282, 328, 340
Bucher, Jeanne, 29, 171–2, 184
Bullitt, William, 27
Buñuel, Luis, 13
businesses, Jewish-owned, 60; Aryanization of, 64, 104, 133, 145, 171, 189, 208, 264–5

cabarets, 8, 41, 50, 51, 55, 91, 93–7, 101, 142, 331
Café de Flore, 35, 291, 294, 345
Cahiers du Sud, 75, 122, 279
Cain, Julien, 79, 244
Calef, Henri, 190
Caligula (Camus), 292–3
Camelots du Rois, 16, 18

Camus, Albert, 185, 207, 221, 222, 235, 242, 243, 270, 292, 338; *épuration culturelle* and, 324, 325, 328, 344; resistance and, 292–4, 311, 335, 343; Sartre's rift with, 345, 350

Canada, 199, 297, 305

Canard Enchaîné, 14, 18, 325

Candide, 18, 231

Cannes, ix, 45, 58, 97–8, 159, 200, 256–7

Cannes Film Festival, 58, 334, 348

Canteloube, Joseph, 146

Capitaine Conan (Captain Conan; Vercel), 10, 11

Carbuccia, Horace de, 136, 231, 261, 322n

Carinhall, 62, 161, 164

Carné, Marcel, 8, 35, 187, 191, 194–5, 202–5, 234, 332, 334

Carré, Louis, 63, 173, 178

Carrington, Leonora, 28–9, 31–2, 37, 85

Casals, Pablo, 75

Casarès, Maria, 204, 222, 292

Casino de Paris, Le, 93, 94, 95, 98, 99

Cassou, Jean, 109–10, 111, 113, 116, 152, 174, 282–4

Catholicism, 7, 17, 37, 130, 223, 228, 241, 244, 252; conversion to, 81, 94, 183, 245n; Rebatet's views on, 233–4; roundup of Jews and, 135; Vichy regime and, 49, 120, 124–7, 131, 192, 230

Cavagni, Émile, 286

Cavaillès, Jean, 286–7

Cayette, André, 190, 191, 198

Céline (Louis-Ferdinand Destouches), 11, 35, 177, 199, 344; anti-Semitism of, 21–2, 64, 250–4, 328, 329; *épuration culturelle* and, 321, 327, 329; exile of, 254, 265, 306, 307; Gould and, 259, 265–6

censorship, 54–8, 109n, 339; art and, 171, 234; literature and, 7, 148n, 243, 279, 281; movies and, 13, 58n, 187, 188–9, 191, 192, 194–5, 261; newspapers and, 33, 52, 231; publishing and, 64, 67, 75, 122, 235, 239, 243, 281; theater and, 55, 56, 208, 210, 213, 215, 217, 221, 335, 340

Centre Américain de Secours, 77, 89

Ce Soir, 18, 343, 345

Cézanne, Paul, 5, 79

Chabrier, Emmanuel, 153

Chack, Paul, 322

Chagall, Bella, 86

Chagall, Marc, 7, 45, 85–6, 171, 180, 346

Chaleur du sang (Fire in the Blood; Némirovsky), 137

Chamberlain, Neville, 26

Chamberlin, Henri (a.k.a. Lafont), 302, 303n

Chamber of Deputies, French, 13, 18, 42, 49

Champs-Élysées, 51, 52, 70, 93, 105, 175, 314

Chanel, Coco, 103–4, 183, 335, 347

"Chanson de la deportée, La" (Song of the Deported Woman; Gandrey-Réty), 152

"chanson du maçon, La" (The Builder's Song), 101

"Chant des partisans, Le" (The Song of the Partisans), 288, 342

Char, René, 285–6

Chardonne, Jacques, 120, 234, 237, 238, 247–50, 326

Charles, Johannès, 267

Charlot, Edmond, 292

Charrat, Janine, 158

Châteaubriant, Alphonse de, 54, 231, 238, 321, 326

Château de Chambord, 34, 167, 168

Château de Montredon, 86–7

Chautemps, Camille, 14, 18

Chauviré, Yvette, 158, 159

Chavance, Louis, 195

"Chenilles, Les" (Montherlant), 212

Chevalier, Maurice, 8, 35, 94–9, 101, 105, 331

Chiappe, Jean, 18

children: French-German, 316; Jewish, 135, 136, 137, 275, 301n; Vichy regime and, 124, 125, 126; World War II and, 33, 34

Choltitz, Dietrich von, 308, 313

Chroniques interdites (Banned Chronicles), 278

Churchill, Winston, 48, 90, 104, 140, 298

Ciel est à nous, Le (The Sky Is Ours), 196–7

Civic Courts, 318, 320, 330, 331

Clair, René, 58, 188

classical music, 141–62, 338, 347; French, 147–50, 152, 153, 156; German, 141–3, 146, 148, 149, 150, 153–5, 307, 339; Jews and, 142, 143, 146–50, 152, 153, 156–7; royalties for, 145; *see also* opera

Claudel, Paul, 9, 65–6, 129, 203, 234, 270; *épuration culturelle* and, 324, 325, 329, 335; *NRF* and, 238–9; theater and, 148, 207, 223–6, 307, 335

Clotis, Josette, 79

Clouzot, Henri-Georges, 187–8, 191, 195–6, 198, 332, 348

Cocéa, Alice, 222, 223, 333

Cocteau, Jean, 10, 87, 148, 150, 183, 215, 230, 231, 289, 329; collaboration and, 70, 177, 186, 228, 316; Genet's relationship with, 250; homosexuality of, 177, 202, 217, 247n, 342; Lubin's correspondence with, 155–6; movies and, 13, 197, 201; at salons, 256, 258, 262–3; theater and, 96, 177, 207, 217–18, 219, 226, 256, 335; "total art" and, 6; vengeance against, 316–17; World War II and, 66

Coeuroy, André, 101–2

Cohen, Henri, 293

Cohen, Jacques, 190

Colette, 9, 10, 17, 41, 215, 231, 235, 242, 270, 289–90, 325, 329; at salons, 257, 261

collaboration, xi, xii, 14, 21, 108, 184, 186, 228, 306; art and, 175–6, 334–5; Chevalier charged with, 99, 331;

cultural, 51, 54, 58n, 62, 64–5, 70, 99, 144–5, 146, 149, 152, 155–6, 157, 160–2, 175–6, 177, 192n, 198, 199–200, 202, 208–9, 211, 214, 215, 219, 222, 226, 230–1, 234, 237, 241–4, 246–51, 270, 271, 285, 331–4, 342–3; Gide's refusal of, 78–9; homosexuality and, 247n; of Lifar, 160–2; LVF and, 133; newspapers and, 60, 91, 94, 106, 107, 110, 160, 201, 209, 303, 342; Pétain's views on, 71; Rassemblement National Populaire and, 119; vengeance against, 315–37; Vichy and, 14, 54, 70, 71–2, 117, 121–4, 126, 245

Colle, Pierre, 183

Collette, Paul, 218

Combat, 288, 292, 293, 301, 302, 341

Combat, 292, 294, 310–11, 324, 325, 343

Comédie Française, 34, 55–6, 193, 206, 210–13, 217–18, 306, 312; Antoine gala at, 215; classics at, 9, 56, 212; Copeau's running of, 10, 56, 210, 212; épuration culturelle and, 320, 335; Jews dismissed from, 59, 208, 210; Soulier de satin at, 148, 203, 210, 223–6

comédies sans tickets (comedies without ration coupons), 223

comics, stand-up, 91–2

Comintern, 22, 25

Comité de la Presse Clandestine, 310

Comité de Libération du Cinéma Français, 202

Comité de Liquidation et Séquestration, 164–5

Comité d'Organisation de l'Industrie Cinématographique (COIC), 192

Comité d'Organisation du Livre, 241, 295

Comité National de Salut Publique (National Committee of Public Safety), 111–12

Comité National des Écrivains (CNE), 115, 274, 275–6, 282, 287, 290–1, 293, 294, 336, 341, 344; épuration culturelle and, 321, 326, 327

Comité National du Théâtre, 312

Comité Professionel de la Musique, 144

Comité Secret d'Action Revolutionnaire (La Cagoule), 16

Communist Party, French, 16–19, 22, 35, 44, 65, 66, 70, 269, 284, 309, 321, 326, 331, 335, 344–6, 349; dissolution of, 33; expulsions from, 13, 22, 279, 292; Picasso in, 186, 334, 345–6; publications of, 18, 311, 336, 345; purge committees run by, 161, 186, 320, 327, 331, 344; in resistance, 114, 115, 131, 132–3, 146–7, 153, 180–1, 273–4, 275, 281, 300, 301, 342

Communist Party, German, 22, 25, 26

Communists, Communism, 4, 29, 36, 49, 52, 228, 230, 231, 248, 304, 346; Céline's denunciation of, 21; fear of, 39, 40, 299, 301, 302, 303; Gide's views on,

24–5; Moscow's grasp on, 13; Sorbonne and, 17

Comoedia, 69, 148, 177, 186, 208, 212, 234–5, 270, 289, 316

Compiègne, 134, 287, 288, 289

Concerts de la Pléiade, 148, 150, 229

Concorde, place de la, 18, 45, 61, 63, 70, 309

Condition humaine, La (Man's Fate; Malraux), 10, 79

Connolly, Cyril, 277

Conservatoire de Paris, 143, 147, 148, 150, 152–3, 300, 329

Continental Films, 188, 190–1, 193–6, 198, 200, 201, 203, 326, 331–2, 333

Convention of the Hague (1907), 61, 168

Copeau, Jacques, 9–10, 56, 65, 210, 212

Corbeau, Le (The Raven), 195–6, 332, 333, 348

Corneille, Pierre, 9, 207, 212

Corsica, ix, 76, 139, 296, 298

Cortot, Alfred, 120, 144–5, 146, 153, 161, 177, 199, 215; épuration culturelle and, 329–30

Coty, François, 18

"Courage" (Éluard), 282

Courtioux, Charles, 126

Courts of Justice, 318, 321, 323, 330, 333

Cousteau, Pierre-Antoine, 233, 322

Coutaud, Lucien, 224

Craig, Elizabeth, 253

Crémieux, Benjamin, 287–8, 341

Crémieux-Brilhac, Jean-Louis, 17

Creston, René, 109

Crève-coeur, Le (Aragon), 280

Crevel, René, 22

Cri du Peuple, 70, 209, 233

"Criez la Vérité" (Shout Out the Truth; Thomas), 274–5

Croix-de-Feu, 16–19, 152

Cubism, 5, 185–6

Cuny, Alain, 184, 195

Curel, Francis, 285

curfew, 118; in Paris, 51, 94, 201, 207, 258, 263, 291

currency, 14, 15, 48, 62n, 308

Czechoslovakia, 26–7, 39

Dac, Pierre, 304

Daladier, Édouard, 14, 18, 26, 29, 33–4, 40–1, 46, 70, 132, 232

Dalí, Gala, 37

Dalí, Salvador, 6, 12, 13, 37, 172, 346

dance, dancers, 4, 7–8, 331, 347–8; ballet, 6, 50, 57, 118, 149, 158–62, 307, 330

Dannecker, Theodor, 133

Darin, Bobby, 96

Darkness at Noon (Koestler), 32

Darlan, François, 83–4, 123, 133, 139, 140, 164

Darnand, Joseph, 302, 307, 319

Darquier de Pellepoix, Louis, 134, 165, 320

Darrieux, Danielle, 9, 58, 190, 191, 197–201, 332

d'Astier de la Vigerie, Emmanuel, 286, 288, 323
Davenport, Miriam, 75, 81, 83
David-Weill collection, 62, 164
Déat, Marcel, 27, 119, 133, 218, 307
Debû-Bridel, Jacques, 275, 278
Debureau, Baptiste, 203, 204
Debussy, Claude, 6, 147, 151, 153, 216
Decoin, Henri, 190, 191, 192, 332
Décombres, Les (The Ruins; Rebatet), 119, 234
Decour, Jacques, 115, 273, 274, 275, 278, 290
Decroux, Étienne, 128
de Gaulle, Charles, 26, 42, 66, 81, 95, 99, 111, 126, 132, 146, 216, 261, 271, 287, 298, 301, 322; épuration culturelle and, 318–19, 325, 328; Giraud's power struggle with, 140; liberation of Paris and, 308, 313–14; London speech of (June 18, 1940), 47, 68, 112; in North Africa, 272; resistance and, 47, 318–19
Degenerate Art exhibition (1937), 142, 175
Deiss, Raymond, 112, 146
Delair, Suzy, 198, 199–200
Delange, René, 234, 235, 258
Delannoy, Jean, 188, 194, 197
Delannoy, Marcel, 145, 146, 153
Delaunay, Charles, 101
Delectorskaya, Lydia, 179, 180
Delforges, Lucienne, 157
Delouche, Dominique, 225
Delval, Charles, 295–6
Delvincourt, Claude, 147, 152–3, 329
demarcation line, ix, 48, 71, 104, 118, 200, 263, 278, 280n, 293n, 299
Denmark, 41, 252, 254, 265, 307, 329
Denoël, Robert, 64, 241, 250, 252, 253, 294, 328
Déon, Michel, 35, 47, 122
Départment de la Seine, prosecutor's office of, 267–8
De 1429 à 1942 (de Jeanne d'Arc à Philippe Pétain), 215, 243
Dequoy, Roger, 63
Derain, André, 5, 6, 175–6, 183, 186, 224, 325, 334
Derval, Paul, 45, 93
Desanti, Dominique, 290
Desbok, Birl, 199
Désir attrapé par la queue, Le (Desire Caught by the Tail; Picasso), 185
Desnos, Robert, 12, 43, 183, 234, 243, 253, 270, 284–5, 322, 341
Desnos, Youki, 284, 322
Desnoyer, François, 173
Désormière, Roger, 146, 151, 153–4, 157, 159, 330
Despiau, Charles, 175–6
Desroches, Christiane, 109–10
de Staël, Nicolas, 30, 346
Devaivre, Jean-, 202, 203, 331
Dhavernas, Henri, 127

Diable au corps, Le (The Devil in the Flesh; Radiguet), 10
Diaghilev, Sergei, 6–7, 57, 149, 158, 347
Diane au bain (Boucher), 169
Diedrich, Dr., 188, 191–2, 194
Dieu est-il français? (Is God French?; Sieburg), 53
Dincklage, Hans Gunther von, 104
Dior, Christian, 86, 104, 347
Dolce (Némirovsky), 137, 143, 277n
d'Ollone, Max, 144, 146, 153, 330–1
Domela, César, 172
Dominican Republic, 197–8
Doriot, Jacques, 16–17, 133, 135, 233, 235, 246, 307, 333
Dreyfus, Alfred, 15, 325, 326
Dreyfus affair, 15, 232n, 253, 325
Drieu La Rochelle, Pierre, 17, 20, 27, 69, 199, 231, 251, 259, 276, 342; anti-Semitism of, 38–9, 237; Breker exhibition and, 176, 177; épuration culturelle and, 321, 322–3, 328; in exodus from Paris, 41, 66; Malraux's friendship with, 328; NRF and, 38, 65, 67, 113, 212, 235–9, 270, 322, 328, 344; Paulhan's relationship with, 113–14, 273; suicide of, 38, 238, 322–3; in visits to Germany, 247–9
Drouin, René, 173
Drouot auctions, 62, 170, 171, 185
Druon, Maurice, 288
Dubois, André, 183
Dubois, Edmond, 41
Dubuffet, Jean, 173, 265, 346
Duchamp, Marcel, 5, 12, 35, 37, 84, 86
Dudan, Pierre, 100
Dufy, Raoul, 172, 178, 334
du Gard, Roger Martin, 10, 272
Duhamel, Georges, 114, 245, 246, 287, 328, 343
Dukas, Paul, 142
Dullin, Charles, 10, 220, 292
Dumas, Alexandre, fils, 217
Dunkirk, ix, 41, 44, 47, 76, 90
Dupeyron, Andrée, 196
Duras, Marguerite, 228, 242n, 294–6, 349
Durey, Louis, 147–8
Dutilleux, Henri, 147, 151, 283
Duvivier, Julien, 58, 188

Échec à Don Juan (Puget), 223
École de cadavres, L' (School of Corpses; Céline), 22, 252, 253
École des femmes, L', 209–10
École Libre des Sciences Politiques, 17
École Militaire, 134, 309, 312
École Nationale des Cadres de la Jeunesse (National School for Youth Leaders; École d'Uriage), 129–30
École Normale de Musique, 148, 150
École Normale Supérieure, 17, 80–1, 228, 290, 293

Écran Français, 196, 197, 202, 275
Eden, Anthony, xiii
Éditions de Minuit (Midnight Publishing), 270, 276, 278, 280, 282, 283, 291, 340, 341
Éditions Denoël, 231
Éditions du Seuil, 241
Éditions Gallimard, 36, 82, 113, 235, 236, 238, 239, 270, 273, 276, 280, 293, 294, 328, 329, 344
Éditions Grasset, 328
Éditions Stock, 242, 326
Egk, Werner, 155, 158
Ehrenburg, Ilya, 22, 23
Eichmann, Adolf, 133
Einsatzstab Reichsleiter Rosenberg (ERR), 61–2, 163–7, 169–70, 264
Eisenhower, Dwight D., 308
El Greco, 169
Éluard, Nusch, 281
Éluard, Paul, 29, 35, 122, 149–50, 177, 183, 234, 237, 270, 275, 340, 345; épuration culturelle and, 316; expelled from Communist Party, 13, 22, 279; resistance and, 279–82, 296, 311, 336, 340, 341; as Surrealist, 12, 174n
embassy, German (Paris), 51, 61, 69, 121, 133, 156, 199, 229, 320, 333, 339; Brasillach at, 233; Céline and, 251–2, 254; Gallimard's Faustian bargain with, 64–5; Gerbe and, 231; Lifar at, 160, 161; staff of, 53–4; theater and, 209
embassy, U.S. (Paris), 110
embassy, U.S. (Vichy), 88, 110n, 118, 135
Emer, Michel, 97
Emergency Rescue Committee, 72, 74, 87–8
Émile-Paul, Albert, 109–10
Émile-Paul, Robert, 109–10
Enfants du paradis, Les, 187, 203–5, 307, 333, 337, 338
England, 32, 33, 213, 215; French troops evacuated to, 41, 44, 47
Entartete Kunst (Degenerate Art), 142
Entartete Musik (Degenerate Music), 142
Epstein, Denise, 37–8, 136, 137
Epstein, Élisabeth, 37–8, 136, 137
Epstein, Henri, 175
Epstein, Michel, 37, 136, 137
Epting, Karl, 53, 54, 66, 212, 229, 243, 251, 290
épuration sauvage (savage purge), 315–37
Équinoxe de septembre, L' (Montherlant), 212
Erhart, Gregor, 169
Ernst, Max, 6, 12, 28–32, 37, 166, 171, 180; in internment camp, 29–32, 87; at Villa Air-Bel, 84, 85
Escadrille España, 23, 40
Esménard, Robert, 136
"Été à la Maurie, L' " (Summer in La Maurie; Chardonne), 237

Éternel retour, L' (The Eternal Return), 197
Étranger, L' (The Stranger; Camus), 222, 235, 242, 292–3, 294, 338, 348
Être et le néant, L' (Being and Nothingness; Sartre), 39, 243, 291
Europe, 282, 284
existentialism, 27, 39, 222, 243, 291, 345, 347, 349
exodus from Paris, 32, 41–3, 80, 81, 103, 143, 159, 292; Jews in, 41, 60, 66, 79, 87; movie industry and, 45, 58, 200; resumption of cultural life and, 50; to Vichy, 118, 119–20

Fabiani, Martin, 171, 181
Fabre-Luce, Alfred, 17, 237–8
Fargue, Leon-Paul, 291
Fascists, Fascism, 4, 16–21, 40, 133, 217, 218, 224, 228, 230–2, 234, 325, 339, 346; Drieu La Rochelle's embrace of, 235; in Italy, see Italy, Fascist; movie industry and, 59, 189; Nazi victory and, 108, 230; newspapers of, 52, 70; Vichy regime and, 119
Fath, Jacques, 104
Fauré, Gabriel, 146, 147
Fautrier, Jean, 173, 265, 346
Fauvism, 5, 173, 175, 178, 185–6
Fawcett, Charles, 75
Faÿ, Bernard, 79, 244
Ferdonnet, Paul, 34, 322
Ferenczi (later Le Livre Moderne), 241
Fernandel, 9, 188, 191
Fernandez, Ramon, 17, 120, 228, 231, 238, 295; in visit to Germany, 247–9
Feuchtwanger, Lion, 81, 193
Feuillère, Edwige, 9, 191, 207, 216, 217
Feuillets d'Hypnos (Leaves of Hypnos; Char), 286
Fidelio (Beethoven), 57, 154–5
fiestas (all-night parties), 291–2, 308
Figaro, 18, 67, 69, 122, 246, 279, 311, 324, 343
Figure humaine (Poulenc), 149–50
Fille du puisatier, La (The Well Digger's Daughter), 58
Fils de personne (Montherlant), 213
Fine Arts Committee of Inquiry, 329
Finland, 40
Finnegan's Wake (Joyce), 240
First European Writers' Congress (Oct. 1941), 247–9
First International Writers' Congress for the Defense of Culture, 22–3
Fishman, Lena, 75
Flamand, Paul, 241
Flandin, Pierre-Étienne, 40, 123
Flaubert, Gustave, 239
Fokine, Michel, 6
Folies Bergère, Les, 7–8, 93–7
Fontaine, 279, 281

Force de l'âge, La (The Prime of Life;
   Beauvoir), 25, 291, 309–10
Forces Françaises de l'Intérieur (FFI), 266,
   305, 308, 309, 312, 317, 332, 333, 343;
   collaboration avenged by, 315, 317, 318,
   329, 330
Forces occultes, 236*n,* 332
Foreign Legion, French, 30, 32
Foreign Ministry, Vichy, 71, 119
Fort Mont-Valérien, executions at, 115, 116
Fougeron, André, 173–4
Fraigneau, André, 247–50
Français Libres de France, Les (the Free
   French of France), 110
France: Allied forces in, 181, 203, 205, 266,
   267–8, 286, 292, 297, 305–8, 311; de
   Gaulle's provisional government for,
   99; economy of, 4, 14–15, 48, 121, 139,
   169, 241, 299; fall of, 44, 59, 67, 175,
   287; German efforts to break cultural
   domination of, 51–2; interwar years in,
   3–27, 157, 201, 209, 216, 339; liberation
   of, 59, 70, 87, 96, 99, 145, 152, 161, 186,
   205, 227–8, 235, 298, 306, 320–30; maps
   of, *ix,* 104*n;* war declared by, 27, 28, 29,
   33, 36, 89, 101, 132, 156, 158, 232
France, Anatole, 10
France actualités (newsreels), 192–3, 332
France-Germany Committee, 20, 53, 54,
   235
Francini, Michel, 42–3, 47, 92, 94, 157, 210,
   303, 310, 316
Franc-Maçonnerie dévoilée (Freemasonry
   Unveiled), 63–4
Franco, Francisco, 36, 37, 72, 181, 320, 326;
   art swaps and, 168–9; in civil war, 19, 23,
   24, 29, 30, 151; Hitler's talks with, 71
Franco-German Translation Committee,
   242
Franco-Prussian War, 4, 5
Francs-Tireurs et Partisans (FTP), 132–3,
   180–1, 287, 301
Free French Forces, 81, 95, 99, 115, 130,
   132, 140, 209, 215, 245, 278, 288, 301
Freemasons, 21, 29, 51, 52, 59, 65, 120*n,*
   192, 201, 230, 231, 236*n,* 302, 332; Faÿ's
   hatred of, 244; propagandistic
   exhibition about, 63–4, 244; Vichy
   regime and, 49
French National Liberation Committee,
   140
Fresnay, Pierre, 9, 191, 195, 332
Freundlich, Otto, 175, 340
Friesz, Othon, 175–6, 334
Front National de la Musique (formerly
   Comité du Front National de la
   Musique), 146–7, 148, 150, 152, 153, 157
Front National des Arts, 174, 334
Front National des Écrivains (National
   Writers' Front), 115, 274
Front National des Peintres et des
   Sculpteurs, 173–4
Front National du Théâtre, 215, 306, 335

Fry, Varian, 72–89, 179, 271
Fullerton, Hugh S., 75, 88
Fürtwangler, Wilhelm, 144, 154*n*

Gabin, Jean, 9, 35, 58–9
Galerie Braun, 128, 173, 224
Galerie Charpentier, 148, 170–1
Gallimard, Gaston, 148, 230, 237, 243*n,*
   251, 256*n,* 293, 323; collaboration and,
   64–5, 236, 238; *épuration culturelle* and,
   328; in exodus, 36, 41; Schriffin
   dismissed by, 82
Galtier-Boissière, Jean, xiii, 68–9, 71–2, 98,
   121, 123, 176, 212, 309, 313, 318; on
   Allied invasion, 306; on Bernard, 215;
   on Bonnard's homosexuality, 202*n;* on
   Drieu La Rochelle, 323; on *épuration
   culturelle,* 327; on French defeat, 132*n;*
   on jokes, 68, 69, 140; on literary
   resistance, 341–2, 343; on Paris
   insurrection, 312; on Picasso, 334*n*
Gamelin, Maurice, 46, 132
Gance, Abel, 189
Gandrey-Réty, Jean, 152
Gare de l'Est, 175, 198, 248
Garnier, Charles, 56
Gauguin, Paul, 5
Gaullists, 17, 90, 110, 115–16, 251, 252, 282,
   287, 301, 321
Gaumont, 190, 192
Gaveau, Albert, 113, 114
Gelrach, Wolrad, 199
gendarmes, French, 29, 137, 140, 165, 302
Genet, Jean, 250
George, Heinrich, 193, 211
Gerbe, 54, 55, 57, 69, 208, 212, 222, 231,
   244, 289, 326
Gerber, Eugène, 69
Germain, José, 243
German exiles, 7, 22, 28–31, 72, 76, 77–8,
   175; ban on books of, 239; Fry's aid
   to, 81
German Institute, 53, 54, 70, 154, 156, 243,
   251, 290; book translation and, 242;
   Bremer at, 212, 229, 233; receptions at,
   106, 161, 199, 339; theater and, 210–11;
   writers' trip to Germany and, 247, 249
Germans, "good," 229, 277, 278, 306
Germany, 11, 188, 325; in World War I, 15,
   26, 42, 72, 123, 139
Germany, Nazi, 3, 4, 8, 14, 16, 23–48,
   50–73, 297–316, 339; Allied bombing of,
   170, 181; army of, *see* army, German;
   artists' visit to, 175–6, 334; art
   transferred to, 167, 168, 169; Brasillach's
   views on, 232; Céline's views on, 250–2;
   cultural inferiority complex of, 51;
   defeat of, 132, 237*n,* 238, 251, 263,
   267, 299, 322; Dominican Republic's
   relations with, 197–8; economy of, 15,
   35; forced labor for, 100, 105, 127, 130,
   138–9, 153, 160, 161, 212, 285, 299–300,
   316; French classical musicians in,

144–5, 150, 156; French relations with, 4, 19, 20, 21, 26, 33, 39–43, 59; industrial, agricultural and raw material needs of, 72, 121, 130; military intelligence of, 47; movie stars' visits to, 198, 200, 201, 332; POWs in, 43–4, 48, 96–100, 105, 138–9, 147, 150, 279; resistance intelligence about, 110–11; Soviet relations with, 27, 30, 33, 40, 44, 90, 132; Soviet Union invaded by, 114, 115, 130–1, 133, 136, 160, 269, 303; Spanish civil war and, 23, 24; territorial ambitions of, *ix*, 26–7, 33, 41, 48, 149, 212; trial of prewar French leaders and, 132; unoccupied zone taken over by, *see* unoccupied zone, German takeover of; writers' trips to, 247–50, 326

Gestapo, 74, 76, 81, 177, 183, 201, 205, 217, 243, 259, 289, 315, 325, 331, 333; French (Rue Lauriston gang; Bonny-Lafont gang), 165, 302–3; Paris headquarters of, xii, 116; resistance and, 87, 113, 115, 116, 181, 237, 249, 273, 287, 288, 295, 301, 302, 341; Vichy regime and, 121

Giacometti, Alberto, 6, 37

Gide, André, 10, 21–5, 30, 65–8, 237, 239, 269–72, 290, 348; Aragon's denunciation of, 320–1; journal of, 38, 66–7, 237; *NRF* and, 237, 238–9, 270, 272; refusal to leave France, 78–9; Soviet visit of, 24, 82, 321; Vichy regime and, 120; Vildé's friendship with, 109, 112

Gide, Catherine, 78

Gide, Madeleine, 78n

Gilles (Drieu La Rochelle), 27

Gilot, Françoise, 71, 171, 173, 184–5, 186, 309

Giono, Jean, 11, 33, 68, 238, 247, 321, 326

Giraud, Henri, 139, 140

Giraudoux, Jean, 9, 33, 177, 196, 215; death of, 235; at salons, 258, 261; theater and, 207, 209, 210, 216–17, 219

Giraudoux, Jean-Pierre, 216, 261

Glanzberg, Norbert, 97

Glück, Christoph Willibald, 57, 218, 307

Goebbels, Joseph, 51–2, 54, 61, 103, 160, 242; art and, 175, 176; German music and, 141, 143; movies and, 188, 193, 194, 198, 201; writers and, 247, 248, 249

Goethe, Johann Wolfgang von, 57, 210, 211, 248

Goetz, Christine, 174

Goetz, Harry Bernard, 174

Gold, Mary Jayne, 75, 83

Goncharova, Natalia, 7

González, Julio, 184

Göring, Hermann, 46, 95n, 107, 333; art and, 60, 62, 163–4, 166, 169, 170, 171, 263–4, 308

Gorki, Maxim, 24

Gotko, Jacques, 175

Goudeket, Maurice, 261, 289–90

Gould, Florence, 118, 256–68, 273, 308, 327

Gould, Frank Jay, 256–7, 260, 263, 264–5, 267–8

Gould, Jay, 256

Gounod, Charles-François, 129, 147, 155, 336

Gowa, Hermann Henry, 30

Goyard, Paul, 174

Grand Orchestre de Radio-Paris, 143–4

Grasset, Bernard, 64, 241, 242, 328

Great Britain, 35, 41, 45, 48, 52, 146, 297–8, 305, 313; appeasement and, 26; Borotra's relations with, 126; French relations with, 33, 230, 231; intellectuals in, 23; internments in, 30; publishing in, 242; resistance and, 146; Soviet relations with, 40; Vichy regime and, 90, 110, 130; war declared by, 27; Wodehouse's broadcasts and, 80; *see also* army, British; England; London; Royal Air Force

Great Depression, 4, 14–15

Gréco, Juliette, 159

Grello, Jacques, 91

Grémillon, Jean, 196–7

Grenoble, *ix*, 37, 84, 129

Greven, Alfred, 188–95, 198, 200, 201, 203, 331–2, 333

Grimm, Friedrich, 53

Gringoire, 18, 19, 38, 70, 136, 208, 231, 261, 270, 289

Grosz, George, 5

Groth, Gerda, 87

Groupe Collaboration, 54, 144, 146, 226, 231, 245, 326

Guéhenno, Jean, 4–5, 66, 67–8, 134, 139–40, 157, 247n, 270, 273; on *NRF*, 237; on Paris insurrection, 310; resistance and, 275–6, 278, 300, 329

Guernica, 23, 182, 185

Guernica (Picasso), 23–4, 182, 345

Guggenheim, Peggy, 37, 84–5

Guitry, Lucien, 55, 216

Guitry, Sacha, 9, 34, 181, 183, 228, 230, 231, 243, 258, 329, 335, 342; collaboration and, 70, 107, 177, 186, 214, 215, 246, 317–18, 333; in Dax, 45, 55; elegant home and art collection of, 54–5, 216; movies and, 55, 194; theater and, 9, 207, 209, 214–16, 222, 226

Gurland, Henny, 78

Gurland, Joseph, 78

Gypsies, 8, 101

Haberstock, Karl, 170

Hahn, Reynaldo, 75, 145

Handel, Georg Friedrich, 141, 155

Hardy, Daphne, 30, 32

Harlan, Veit, 193

Hasenclever, Walter, 32

Haskil, Clara, 86, 87

Hauet, Paul, 110

Hauptmann, Gerhart, 211

Hautecoeur, Louis, 144, 145, 169, 208

haute couture, 103–6, 335, 339, 346–7
Hazard, Paul, 65
Heiden, Konrad, 81
Hélion, Jean, 37
Heller, Gerhard, 53–4, 66, 177, 236, 237, 238, 256, 284, 323, 334; on book burning, 240; Céline's visit to, 251; departure from Paris of, 306; French writers' visits to Germany and, 247–50; as "good German," 229; Jacob's release and, 183; memoir of, see Allemand à Paris, Un; on Picasso, 182, 185; at salons, 256–9, 261, 263, 266
Hemingway, Ernest, 7, 31
Henriot, Philippe, 303–4, 314
Héring, Pierre, 45
Hermant, Abel, 245, 329
Hérold, Jacques, 87, 175
Hérold-Paquis, Jean, 322
Herrand, Marcel, 204
Herriot, Édouard, 14, 307, 329
Herzog, Émile Salomon Wilhelm, see Maurois, André
Hess, Johnny, 102
Hessel, Franz, 35
Hessel, Stéphane, 35, 83, 89
Hewitt, Maurice, 146
Hibbelen, Gerhard, 69, 241n
Hié, Simone, 292
High Court of Justice, 318, 319
Hilaire, Georges, 169
Hildebrand, Franz von, 75
Hilferding, Rudolf, 87
Hiller, George, 272
Hirschman, Albert O. "Beamish," 75, 76, 83
Histoire générale du jazz (Coeuroy), 101–2
Hitler, Adolf, 7, 14, 16, 21, 22, 39, 71–2, 139, 227, 236, 253, 260, 297–9, 304, 313, 325; armistice and, 47–8; art and, 60–3, 163, 168, 169, 170, 176, 308; Darlan's meeting with, 123; defeat of, 238, 251; deficit financing of, 15; "final solution" and, 134, 299; French degeneracy and, 50–1, 63; French Fascists and, 119, 302; Gide's views on, 67; jokes and ridicule about, 69, 91–2, 140, 252; Jünger's views on, 229; Laval's meetings with, 71, 139; Lifar's meeting with, 160; Mein Kampf of, 224, 239; movies and, 195; music and, 142, 143, 154, 155, 156, 320; Mussolini's relationship with, 181; new Europe of, 119, 230, 339; Paris tour of, 56, 156, 160, 176; Pétain's meeting with, 71, 121, 245; racial policy and, 33–4; resistance and, 131, 341; speeches of, 242; territorial ambitions and, 26–7, 41, 212; trial of prewar French leaders and, 132
Hollywood, Calif., 8, 58, 188, 189, 209, 253, 348
Homme au mouton, L' (Man with a Lamb; Picasso), 185

homosexuality, 10, 78n, 96, 149, 202, 212, 247; of Cocteau, 177, 202, 217, 247n, 342; collaboration and, 247n; of Genet, 250; of Jouhandeau, 247, 259
Honegger, Arthur, 129, 145, 147–50, 214, 224, 234, 325
Honneur des poètes, L' (The Honor of Poets), 282
Hostages series (Fautrier), 173
Hot Club de France, 8, 101
Hôtel de Ville, 304, 312, 313
Hôtel Lutetia, xii, 45
hotels, 58, 136, 137, 265; in Marseille, 74, 82, 86; in Paris, 45–6, 229, 257, 259, 268; in Vichy, 49, 118–19, 139
Hugo, Victor, 84, 263
Hugues-Lambert, Robert, 202
Huis Clos (No Exit; Sartre), 208, 221, 291, 307, 336, 338
Humanité, 18, 311, 336, 345
Humbert, Agnès, 109–14
Humbert, Louis, 57
Huntziger, Charles, 123
Huxley, Aldous, 22, 278n

Immaculate Conception (Murillo), 168
Impressionism, 5, 164
Information Musicale, 145, 149
Institut de France, 249
Institut des Hautes Études Cinématographiques (IDHEC), 192, 348
Interior Ministry, Vichy, 183, 294, 302
internment camps, 29–32, 43, 72, 77, 80, 82, 83, 86, 127; Camp des Milles, 29, 30, 32, 77, 87, 156; Gurs, 30, 78, 87; Jews in, 60, 104, 134, 135, 138, 140n, 161n, 170, 200, 303; at Vernuche, 31, 78
interwar years, 3–27; cultural life in, 4–13, 157, 201, 209, 216, 339; politics in, 3–4, 10–27
"In the Filth of Collaboration" (article), 215
Invitée, L' (She Came to Stay; Beauvoir), 35, 235, 243
Ireland, 7, 80
Issy-l'Évêque, ix, 38, 42, 136–7
Italy, Fascist, 14, 16–17, 20, 27, 151, 298; Allied forces in, 59, 204, 298; Ethiopia invaded by, 26; France bombed by, 43; France occupied by, ix, 48, 91, 139, 140, 180, 199, 204, 298; Spanish civil war and, 23, 24; surrender of, 204; war on France declared by, 41
Ithier, Georges, 113, 114

"J'accuse . . . !" (Zola), 15
Jacob, Max, 87, 150, 182–3, 296, 340
Jamet, Claude, 222
Jansen, Jacques, 151, 153
Jardins et routes (Gardens and Highways; Jünger), 276
Jaubert, Maurice, 146

Jaujard, Jacques, 61, 164–5, 166, 169
Jazz (Matisse), 180
Jeanmaire, Renée "Zizi," 158
Jeanne au bûcher (Joan at the Stake;
    Honegger), 129, 148, 214
Jeanne avec nous (Vermorel), 214
Jeanneney, Jules, 42
Jeanson, Henri, 70
Jeramec, Colette, 39n, 323
Je suis partout, 18, 20, 70, 119, 189, 201,
    231, 232, 233, 245, 302, 310, 322, 323;
    Céline's views on, 251; last issue of,
    308–9; theater and, 209, 217, 220, 326
"Je suis seule ce soir," 100, 331
Jeu de Paume, 61, 62, 163–7, 308
Jeune France (Young France), 127–30, 173,
    213, 241, 347
Jeunesses Musicale de France, Les (Musical
    Youth of France), 144
Jeunesses Patriotes, 16
Jews, 37, 51, 58–65, 79–89, 102, 127, 198,
    237n; arrests of, 29, 30; art collections
    of, 60–3, 163–7, 308; businesses of, *see*
    businesses, Jewish-owned; classical
    music and, 142, 143, 146–50, 152, 153,
    156–7; denunciation of, 196; foreign,
    7, 8, 16, 33, 59, 60, 72, 77, 79–87, 126,
    134, 174–5, 231, 253, 259, 298–9, 303;
    French, xiii, 15, 16, 19, 29, 59–63,
    76, 134, 253, 289, 303; furniture of,
    169–70; haute couture and, 104, 105; as
    hostages, 131; in internment camps, *see*
    internment camps, Jews in; in Marseille,
    76, 81–2, 85; in movie business, *see*
    movies, Jews and; in North Africa,
    140n; protection of, 137, 138, 153, 200,
    293; resistance and, 109, 110; yellow
    stars worn by, 87, 102, 137, 159, 183,
    210, 290; *see also* anti-Semitism
Joachim, Irène, 147, 151, 152, 153
Joan of Arc, 129, 213–14, 215, 242
Jochum, Eugen, 154
jokes, 68, 69, 140
Josephine (Baker), 99
Jouhandeau, Elise, 45, 228, 259, 326
Jouhandeau, Marcel, 20, 45, 68, 120, 228,
    234, 238, 256, 266, 321; *épuration
    culturelle* and, 326–7; homosexuality of,
    247, 259; at salons, 256–62, 266, 268; in
    visit to Germany, 247–9
Jourdan, Louis, 58, 190, 200, 207
Journal (Drieu La Rochelle), 238, 239
Journal des années noires (Guéhenno),
    67–8, 237, 270–1, 273, 300
Journal littéraire (Léautaud), 45, 262
Journal sous l'occupation (Jouhandeau), 247
Jouvenel, Bertrand de, 17, 21, 242
Jouvet, Louis, 10, 209–10, 336
Joy, Geneviève, 152
Joyce, James, 7, 11, 35, 80, 240
Joyce, Lucia, 7
Jubineau, Albert, 110
Juif et la France, Le (1941), 193, 252

Juif Süss, Le, 193, 211
Jünger, Ernst, 93, 182, 193, 216, 229–30,
    256, 268, 276, 306; on Céline, 251, 254;
    at salons, 257–61, 263, 265–6
Jünger, Gretha, 259
"Justice and Charity" (Camus), 324

Kafka, Franz, 243n
Kahlo, Frida, 13
Kahn, Suzanne, 169
Kahnweiler, Daniel-Henry, 5, 62–3, 171n
Kahnweiler (now Leiris) Gallery, 62–3, 171,
    185
Kandinsky, Wassily, 7, 37, 172
Karajan, Herbert von, 155
Kempff, Wilhelm, 161, 177
Kessel, Joseph, 288
Klausz, Ernest, 157
Knappertsbusch, Hans, 154
Knochen, Helmut, 260
Kochno, Boris, 86
Koestler, Arthur, 24, 26, 30–3
Kosakiewicz, Wanda, 221
Kosma, Joseph, 195, 203
Krauss, Clemens, 154

La Bocca, 97–8, 99
labor, 74, 344–5; forced, 100, 105, 127, 130,
    138–9, 153, 160, 161, 212, 285, 299–300,
    316
labor camps, 23, 235
Labourdette, Elina, 200–1, 316–17
Lacaze, Isabelle, 256, 267
Lacaze, Victorien Maximilien, 256
Lacombe, Georges, 96, 190
L'Action Française, 15–16, 17, 21, 35, 66,
    119, 122, 233, 275, 303
Lam, Wilfredo, 84–5, 285
Lamba, Jacqueline, 36, 83, 84–5
Landowska, Wanda, 81, 169
Landowski, Paul, 175–6
Lange, Hans Joachim, 156
Langenbeck, Curt, 261
Langevin, Paul, 115
Lanvin, Jeanne, 104
Lapicque, Charles, 172, 173
La Porte du Theil, Joseph de, 126–7
Lartigue, Jacques-Henri, 58
Latin America, xi, 23, 118, 210
Laubreaux, Alain, 285, 326, 335; Marais's
    punching of, 177, 217; as theater critic,
    70, 177, 209, 211, 215, 217, 218, 220,
    225, 226
Laurencin, Marie, 258
Laval, Pierre, 40, 49, 54, 118, 119, 126, 130,
    302, 303, 305; arrest of, 307; art and,
    164, 165, 168, 176–7; consistency of,
    122–3; as foreign minister, 71, 119;
    Hitler's meetings with, 71, 139;
    labor-POW swap and, 138; as Nazis'
    favorite, 123; Pétain's dislike of, 122,
    123, 300; as prime minister, 14, 23, 123,
    124, 134, 140, 191n, 231, 238, 299, 300;

Laval, Pierre *(continued)*
  replacement of, 123; roundup of Jews
  and, 135; shooting and wounding of,
  218; trial of, 319
Leahy, William D., 88, 123, 124
Leander, Zarah, 193–4
Léautaud, Paul, 45, 185, 262–3, 266, 268,
  296, 323, 327
Lebrun, Albert, 42
Le Cannet, 178–9, 180
Le Chambon-sur-Lignon, 138, 293
Le Chanois, Jean-Paul, 190, 202–3, 331
Leclerc, Ginette, 96, 191, 195, 333
Leclerc, Philippe, 305, 312, 313
Lecomte, Georges, 274
Le Corbusier (Charles-Édouard
  Jeanneret-Gris), 119–20
Lecoutour, Noëlle, 172
Leduc, Renato, 85
Lefranc, Jean-François, 165
Left Hand of God, The (Holl), 81
Léger, Fernand, 5, 37, 166, 171, 172, 180, 346
Légion des Volontaires Français Contre le
  Bolchévisme (LVF), 133, 245
Légion Française des Combattants (French
  Legion of Veterans), 67, 130
Lehár, Franz, 154
Le Hénaff, René, 194
Leiris, Louise, 63, 185, 292, 294
Leiris, Michel, 63, 185, 275, 291, 292, 294,
  308, 312
Leiris Gallery, *see* Kahnweiler (now Leiris)
  Gallery
Lelong, Lucien, 103, 104, 347
Le Moal, Jean, 173
Lenglen, Suzanne, 257
lesbians, lesbianism, 7, 39
Lescure, Pierre, 276, 277
Le Tac, Joël, 200
"Lettre à un américain" (Fabre-Luce),
  237–8
Lettre à un otage (Letter to a Hostage;
  Saint-Exupéry), 271
Lettre aux directeurs de la résistance
  (Paulhan), 344
Lettres Françaises, 115, 147, 173, 202, 213,
  227, 246–7, 270, 274–9, 282, 291, 294,
  305, 311, 321, 336, 341, 343, 345;
  épuration culturelle and, 326, 327
Le Vernet, 30–1, 32
Le Vigan, Robert, 191, 205, 207, 307, 332–3
Lévi-Strauss, Claude, 84–5
Lévy, Lazare, 152
Lewitsky, Anatole, 109, 113, 114
Lhote, André, 186
Libération de Paris, La (documentary), 203
"Liberté" (Éluard), 149, 174, 281–2, 340,
  345
libraries, 79, 169, 240, 244, 303
Lifar, Serge, 6, 57, 158–62, 177, 186, 247*n*,
  330, 342, 347
Lifchitz, Deborah, 116
ligues (leagues), 17, 19

Lingner, Max, 30
Linz, 62, 163, 164, 170
Lipchitz, Jacques, 84, 86
List, Herbert, 184
Lohse, Bruno, 166
London, 28, 32, 99, 101, 112, 168, 200, 277,
  282, 295, 341; de Gaulle in, 47, 68, 81,
  115, 216, 261, 271, 287; Free French in,
  115, 278, 288; Gaullists in, 17, 95;
  intelligence sent to, 272–3
Lorenz, Max, 155
Lorraine, 48, 149, 307
Louis II, Prince, 267
Louis XV, King of France, 214
Louvre, 34, 45, 61, 63, 167–9, 313, 347
Lubin, Germaine, 57, 155–6, 161, 177, 330
Luchaire, Corinne, 199, 333
Luchaire, Jean, 20, 69, 107, 199, 307, 322,
  333
Luftwaffe, 41, 44, 46, 62, 154, 182, 260, 267,
  298; French mistresses of, 199, 333; jazz
  and, 101; Paris headquarters of, xiii
Luxembourg, 41, 104*n*
Luxembourg Gardens, xiii, 142, 309, 312
Lycée Camille Sée, 42, 59
Lyon, *ix*, 80, 110, 179, 266, 273, 287, 293,
  301, 302; cultural life in, 94, 128, 129,
  148, 154, 279; newspapers in, 69, 122,
  246*n*, 287, 292, 311
Lyon Opera, 129

Maar, Dora, 36, 172, 181–5, 291
Mabille, Pierre, 84
Macao, 188–9
Machine à écrire, La (The Typewriter;
  Cocteau), 217
Maeght, Aimé, 179
Maginot Line, 26, 33, 35, 41, 95, 97, 151
Magnelli, Alberto, 172
Magritte, René, 12, 13
Mahler, Gustav, 77, 141, 142
Maillol, Aristide, 5, 37, 63, 77, 176–80;
  Breker's ties to, 176, 177, 178, 334
Malraux, André, 10, 22, 79, 89, 183–4, 237,
  347; Drieu La Rochelle's friendship
  with, 228, 323; *épuration culturelle*
  and, 323; in resistance, 272, 290; on
  resistance, 112–13, 272; in Spanish
  civil war, 23, 40, 272; in World War II,
  40, 44
Malraux, Roland, 44, 272
Mamy, Jean ("Paul Riche"), 192, 236, 332
Mandel, Georges, 19, 46, 132, 304, 335
Manessier, Alfred, 173
Mann, Golo, 30, 77
Mann, Heinrich, 22, 30, 77
Mann, Thomas, 30, 74, 239
Mannheim National Theater, 154
Man Ray, 6, 37
maquis, 99, 127, 160, 161, 180, 203, 276*n*,
  285, 287, 288, 300–1, 302, 305
Marais, Jean, 177, 202, 207, 217, 317;
  movies and, 197, 201, 207, 332

Marceau, Marcel, 128
"Maréchal, nous voilà," 125–6
Margy, Lina, 100
Marion, Paul, 124, 307
Maritain, Jacques, 74, 278
Marjane, Léo, 8, 96, 99–100, 331
Markova, Alicia, 6
"Marseillaise, La," 55, 147, 154, 304
Marseille, ix, 66, 72–8, 81–8, 110, 136, 145,
    288; Baker in, 95; cultural life in, 75–6,
    86–7, 128, 129, 143, 231, 279, 285; movie
    industry in, 45, 58, 189, 192; Pétain's
    visit to, 83–4; Surrealists in, 32, 83–5;
    U.S. consulate in, 75, 85, 88
Marseille, Battle of (Jan. 1943), 138
Mascolo, Dionys, 295, 296
"Massacre of Jews in Europe, The" (Fry),
    89
Massilia, 46, 48
Massine, Léonide, 6
Masson, grandpère, 12, 84–5
Matin, 18, 69, 212, 231, 244n
Matisse, Amélie, 179–81
Matisse, Henri, 5, 7, 63, 173, 174, 178–81,
    185, 346; asylum turned down by, 36,
    79, 179; French refuge sought by, 37, 45;
    Vierny's posing for, 77, 180
Matisse, Jean, 180
Matisse, Marguerite, 180–1
Matisse, Pierre, 179–80
Matta, Roberto, 84
Maugham, Somerset, 80
Mauriac, Claude, 261, 275–6
Mauriac, François, 10, 66, 67, 114, 120, 150,
    183, 239, 243, 348; Académie Française
    and, 245, 246, 287; épuration culturelle
    and, 322, 324–5, 328, 344; NRF and,
    237, 238–9, 270; resistance and, 261, 272,
    274, 275–6, 278, 296, 341, 342, 343
Maurois, André, 10, 65, 169, 245
Maurras, Charles, 15–16, 18, 19–20, 122,
    232, 234, 244–5, 303; épuration
    culturelle and, 325–6, 329; Vichy regime
    and, 119
Ma Vie (Lifar), 161, 330
Maya (Picasso's daughter), 36, 181–2
Mea Culpa (Céline), 21
Mehring, Walter, 75, 81–2
Mein Kampf (Hitler), 224, 239
Mendès-France, Pierre, 46
Merleau-Ponty, Maurice, 290
Mermoz, Jean, 202
Merry, Georges, 92
Messiaen, Olivier, 35, 43–4, 150–1, 338,
    347
métro, 98, 114, 131, 160, 185, 200, 207, 300,
    304, 308
Metternich, Franz Wolff-, 60–1, 63, 164,
    168, 169
Meyerhof, Otto, 30, 81
Michaux, Henri, 67
Midsummer Night's Dream, A
    (Shakespeare), 86–7

Milhaud, Darius, 6, 41, 65, 142, 143, 146,
    147–8, 152, 169, 283; Poulenc's
    correspondence with, 153, 157, 161
milice, 140, 200, 205, 217, 233, 285, 288,
    302, 304, 315, 335
Militärbefehlshaber in Frankreich (MBF),
    45–6
Miller, Henry, 7
mime, mimes, 128, 203, 204
Mirbeau, Octave, 55, 216
Miró, Joan, 6, 12, 37, 166, 346
Misérables, Les (Hugo), 84
Mistinguett, 8, 45, 95–6, 99, 101
Mitterrand, François, 17, 43–4, 122, 295–6
Möbel-Aktion (Furniture Plan), 169–70
Modigliani, Amedeo, 6, 171
Molière, 9, 129, 207, 209, 211, 212, 223
Molotov-Ribbentrop Pact (1939), 27, 30,
    33, 44, 70, 269
Mona Lisa, 34, 167–8
Mon auguste grandpère (My August
    Grandfather; Guitry), 215
Mondrian, Piet, 6, 37, 180
Monet, Claude, 5, 55, 63, 216
Mon journal pendant l'occupation
    (Galtier-Boissière), 68, 132n
Montagard, André, 126
Montand, Yves, 75–6, 97
Montherlant, Henry de, 66, 68, 120, 207,
    209, 212–13, 234, 238, 243, 258;
    épuration culturelle and, 321, 327, 329,
    335; homosexuality of, 247n; trip to
    Germany declined by, 247, 248–9
Montmartre, 11, 201, 253, 265
Montparnasse, 35, 87, 93, 311
Moon Is Down, The (Nuits noires;
    Steinbeck), 278
Morand, Paul, 10, 65, 177, 230, 238, 247, 261
Morgan, Claude (Lecomte), 274, 275, 278,
    343
Morgan, Michèle, 58
Morley, Gérard, 136
Morocco, 95, 139, 140n, 272, 298
Mort à crédit (Death on the Installment
    Plan; Céline), 21, 253
Moscow, 11, 22, 24, 25, 33, 160, 345
Moscow trials, 24, 25, 26
Mouches, Les (The Flies; Sartre), 208,
    219–21, 235, 291, 293, 336
Moulin, Jean, 174, 301
Mounier, Emmanuel, 122, 129–30
Mousset, Paul, 243
movie houses, 13, 27, 33, 34, 41, 57–8, 206,
    300; German soldiers killed in, 131;
    Jews as owners of, 189
movies, 33, 50, 57–9, 96, 187–205, 227, 300,
    304, 307; censorship and, see censorship,
    movies and; collaboration and, xii, 198,
    199–200, 202, 331–4; cultural legacy of
    occupation and, 338, 340, 348; épuration
    culturelle and, 326, 331–4; French talent
    and, 8–9, 55; German, 187, 193, 339;
    Hollywood, 8, 58, 188, 348; Jews and, 8,

movies (continued)
    45, 57, 58, 59, 133, 187, 189–92, 193n,
    194–5, 200, 232, 331; music for, 153,
    197, 203; Surrealism and, 13; theater
    compared with, 207–8, 209
Mozart, Wolfgang Amadeus, 141, 142, 145,
    153, 154, 155
Munch, Charles, 147, 149
Munich, 139, 142, 175
Munich Agreement (1938), 26, 39, 212
Münzenberg, Willi, 22, 25–6, 32, 77
Mur, Le (The Wall; Sartre), 10
Muratore, Lucien, 153
Murillo, Bartolomé Esteban, 168
Murphy, Robert D., 123
Musée d'Art Moderne, 19, 27, 169, 174
Musée de l'Homme, 109, 111, 113, 116
Musée de l'Homme network, see Réseau du
    Musée de l'Homme
Museum of Modern Art, 24, 36, 85
music, musicians, 4, 6, 8, 43, 50, 54, 93–102,
    141–62, 227, 288; chansonniers, 43, 91,
    95–101, 331, 340; classical, see classical
    music; opera; épuration culturelle and,
    329–31; France as theme in, 99, 100–1;
    German songs, 93, 96; jazz, 8, 101–2,
    338; love theme in, 99–100; in Marseille,
    75, 86–7; for movies, 153, 197, 203;
    Surrealism and, 12–13; swing, 8, 102; in
    youth movements, 127, 128, 129
music halls, 8, 41, 55, 91, 92, 93, 101, 134,
    291
Musicien d'Aujourd'hui, Le, 147, 153, 275
Mussolini, Benito, 14, 16–17, 23, 151, 246;
    jokes about, 69, 140; music and, 142–3;
    ouster of, 260, 298
Mythe de Sisyphe, Le (Camus), 292–3

Napoleon I, 56, 71, 238, 242
Napoleon II (duke of Reichstadt;
    L'Aiglon), 71–2
Napoleon III, 13, 117
National Assembly, French, 132, 307, 309,
    344
National Revolution, 119, 121–4, 128, 130,
    131, 192, 230, 325
Nausée, La (Sartre), 10, 27, 290
navy, French, 46, 48, 90, 123–4, 140
navy, German, 154
N'ecoutez pas mesdames (Guitry), 214–15
Némirovsky, Irène, 37–8, 41–2, 136–7, 143,
    231, 277n, 340, 349
Netherlands, 41, 138, 252
Neveux, Georges, 194
newspapers, 17–18, 19, 21, 38, 103, 122,
    337; anti-Semitism and, 60, 69–70;
    censorship and, 33, 52, 231;
    collaboration and, see collaboration,
    newspapers and; resistance and, 111–12,
    113, 115, 116, 146, 215, 269, 303, 310–11
New York City, 12, 24, 36, 37, 72, 146, 346,
    347–8; refugees in, 80, 81, 83, 85, 86, 89,
    171, 209

Nice, ix, 67, 72, 94, 98, 151, 174, 245, 267,
    273; Carné's visit to, 203; Matisse in,
    179, 180; movie industry in, 45, 58, 189,
    192, 195, 200, 203, 204
nightclubs, 27, 34, 91, 93, 199
nightlife, 8, 41, 90–102, 197, 257; see also
    cabarets
Nijinska, Bronislava, 6
Nijinsky, Vaslav, 6
1900, 92
Nizan, Paul, 44
Noailles, Charles de, 13
Noailles, Marie-Laure de, 13, 150, 255
Nordmann, Léon Maurice, 110, 112, 114
Normandy, 36, 41, 305–6, 307
North Africa, 46, 48, 72, 74, 76, 151;
    Allied forces in, 95, 110n, 124,
    139, 140, 272, 293n, 298; Baker in,
    95; Vichy-ruled, 95, 123, 139, 140,
    272, 281, 298
Norway, 41, 297
Notre avant-guerre (Before Our War;
    Brasillach), 232
Nôtre-Dame, 304, 312, 314
Notre-Dame des Fleurs (Our Lady of the
    Flowers; Genet), 250
Nous ne sommes pas mariés (We Are Not
    Married), 222
Nouveau Ballet de Monte-Carlo, 161, 162
Nouvelle Revue Française (NRF), 10, 31,
    36, 68, 186, 248, 272, 287–8, 344; Drieu
    La Rochelle and, 38, 65, 67, 113, 212,
    235–9, 270, 322, 328, 344
"Nuit d'exil, La" (The Night of Exile;
    Aragon), 280
Nuremberg, 20, 232, 235
Nu sombre (Bonnard), 179, 180

Oberfeld, Casimir, 126
obscenity, 7, 251n
occupation: cost of, 48, 71, 121; cultural
    continuity and, 50–1, 54, 55, 107, 338;
    cultural legacy of, 338–50; degeneration
    in, 131; double entendres and, 91, 92,
    340; geography and, 138; map of, ix;
    streets and buildings as memory of,
    xii–xiii; as taboo subject, xi; Vichy's
    responsibilities in, 121; winding down
    of German presence in, 130
Occupons-Nous (Merry), 92
Oddon, Yvonne, 109, 113, 114
"Ode au Maréchal Pétain" (Claudel), 66,
    224
Oeil du serpent, L' (The Eye of the Snake;
    Chavance), 195
Oeuvre, 18, 27, 70, 119
Offenbach, Jacques, 8, 95, 142
"On Nationalism and the Jewish
    Question" (Jünger), 229
On the Marble Cliffs (Jünger), 229, 260
opera, 118, 153–7, 304; German, 153–5; in
    Paris, 41, 50, 56–7, 147, 148, 149, 151–4,
    307

Opéra-Comique, 56, 57, 144, 145, 151,
    153–4, 156, 307, 330, 331
Opéra de Vichy, 49, 117–18, 119
opera houses, 34, 56–7, 143
Operation Barbarossa, 130–1
Operation Dynamo, 41
operettas, 57, 142, 154
Ophüls, Marcel, xii
Ophüls, Max, 188, 209–10
Oradour-sur-Glane massacre, 305
Orangerie, 63, 161, 176–7, 334, 339
orchestras, 142–5, 156, 300; German, 142,
    143, 144, 154, 155, 307; youth, 153, 300
Orchestre des Cadets du Conservatoire, 153
Orchestre National de la Radiodiffusion
    Française, 87, 129, 143, 144n, 145
Orwell, George, 24
"Otto List," 64, 239–40, 245, 327
Oudeville, Claude, 276
Out of This Century (Guggenheim), 37
Ozeray, Madeleine, 210

pacifism, 4, 11–12, 19, 26, 33
Pagava, Vera, 172
Pagnol, Marcel, 9, 58, 75, 189, 234, 329
Palais de Chaillot, 154, 155, 205, 206, 211
Palais de Justice, 110
Palais Garnier, 56, 157, 158, 159, 160
Palais-Royal, 154, 173, 289
Palestrina (Pfitzner), 151
Panier, Maurice, 172
Pantagruel, 112, 146
Parade (ballet), 6
Paraf, Yvonne, 276, 278
Paray, Paul, 75, 129, 145
Parents terribles, Les (The Awful Parents;
    Cocteau), 9, 217
Paris: as cultural beacon, 4–11; fall of, 3, 10,
    45, 57, 81, 103, 167, 189n, 218, 230, 292;
    insurrection in (Aug. 25, 1944), 152n,
    203, 266, 309–13, 317; liberation of, xi,
    xiii, 79, 80, 91, 96, 104, 153, 161, 167,
    181, 226, 244, 306, 308–14; map of, ix;
    redesign of, 4
Pariser Zeitung, 92, 156, 211, 275, 311
Paris International Exhibition, 23
Paris Opera, 4, 41, 55, 56–7, 59, 142, 145,
    147, 149, 153–7, 215, 336; Dutilleux at,
    151–2; épuration culturelle and, 320,
    330; gala at (Dec. 20, 1940), 106;
    German operas at, 154–5; Wehrmacht
    at, 144, 307
Paris Opera Ballet, 6, 57, 158–61, 330, 347
Paris-Soir, 18, 60, 69, 94, 96, 98, 122, 231,
    287, 292
Paris Toujours, 98
Parti Populaire Français, 16–17, 133, 135,
    233, 235, 246
Pasteur (Guitry), 55
Pastré, Countess Lily, 86–7
Pathé-Cinéma, 189n, 190, 204
Paulhan, Jean, 31, 36, 41, 182, 183, 235–9,
    243, 248, 251, 265, 323; Académie

Française and, 268, 329; épuration
    culturelle and, 325, 326, 327, 328, 344;
    Jouhandeau's ties to, 228, 247, 258,
    259; NRF and, 65, 235, 237, 273, 344;
    Rebatet's views on, 233; in resistance,
    113–14, 115, 237, 269–70, 273–6, 278,
    296, 329, 336, 341; at salons, 258, 261,
    262, 266, 273
Paulvé, André, 194, 204
Pavillon brûle, Le, 200–1
Paxton, Robert O., xi–xii
Péguy, Charles, 17, 128, 214
Péguy, Marcel, 214
Pelléas et Mélisande (Debussy), 151, 153
Pensée Libre, 115, 269, 273–4, 276, 340
Père (Father; Bourdet), 222–3
Péret, Benjamin, 12, 33, 84, 86, 271, 340
Peretti, Serge, 158, 159, 161
Peril juif, Le (The Jewish Peril;
    Jouhandeau), 20, 247, 259
Pétain, Eugénie, 119
Pétain, Philippe, 46–9, 66, 72, 117–28,
    130–2, 138–40, 155, 161, 218, 227, 299,
    303–7; Académie Française and, 244,
    245, 329; armistice and, 46–8, 68, 151,
    233; art and, 168–9, 177; books in praise
    of, 215, 243, 246; charities of, 106,
    118; Chevalier and, 98, 101; Claudel's
    ode to, 66, 224; on French defeat,
    48, 131; Grand Chartreuse and, 65n;
    Guéhenno's views on, 67–8; Guitry's
    paean to, 215; haute couture and, 104,
    106; Hitler's meeting with, 71, 121, 245;
    Laval disliked by, 122, 123, 300; loss of
    confidence in, 131, 152, 216; Marseille
    visit of, 83–4; movies and, 189, 197;
    Mussolini's relationship with, 181;
    National Revolution of, 119, 121–4,
    128, 130, 131, 192, 325; POW problem
    and, 138–49; as savior of France, 90–1,
    108, 110, 120–1; speeches and radio
    addresses of, 46, 47, 48, 58, 67, 68, 71,
    79, 123, 128, 131, 139, 304, 307; Stein's
    admiration for, 79; theater and, 219; trial
    of, 319; and trial of prewar French
    leaders, 131–2; in World War I, 46, 131
Petit, Roland, 159, 160, 347
Petit Parisien, 18, 69, 209, 231, 233, 289, 327
Petit prince, Le (Saint-Exupéry), 243, 271
Pfitzner, Hans, 151, 155
Pharisienne, La (Mauriac), 66, 243, 270
Philipe, Gérard, 207, 216
Philippon, René, 239
photographs, 99, 106, 136, 170, 247, 253,
    287, 291, 345; at Gare de l'Est, 175, 198;
    movies and, 188, 193n, 198; in Stalag
    III-D, 97
Pia, Pascal, 292, 293, 294, 311
Piaf, Édith, 8, 35, 96–7, 118, 127, 331
Picasso, Pablo, 5, 6, 36–7, 106, 149, 177,
    178, 181–6, 224, 265, 291, 294, 309, 334,
    346; at burials and memorials, 87, 183;
    civil war and, 23–4, 181; in Communist

Picasso, Pablo (*continued*)
    Party, 186, 334, 345–6; critics of, 185–6;
        "degenerate art" of, 166, 171, 186;
        exhibitions of, 36, 172, 336; French
        nationality rejected for, 36, 181; Jünger's
        visits to, 182, 230, 334; Lifar's friendship
        with, 161; looted painting bought by,
        171; resistance and, 183–4, 186; Stein
        and, 7, 79; World War II and, 185
Pierné, Gabriel, 143*n*
Pignon, Édouard, 172, 174
Pilote de guerre (Flight to Arras;
    Saint-Exupéry), 44, 243, 271
Pleins pouvoirs (Full Powers;
    Giraudoux), 33
Ploquin, Raoul, 192
Poésie, 279, 281
Poincaré, Raymond, 14
Poland, 27, 40, 138, 175, 299
police, French, 29, 60, 62, 70–1, 77, 140,
    165, 175, 180, 205, 245*n*, 260, 274, 285,
    287, 302, 315, 332; in Marseilles, 74, 76,
    82, 83, 86–9; Paris, 13, 18, 36, 217, 300,
    308, 309, 323, 341; in roundup of Jews,
    134, 135, 137, 138
police, German, 113, 130, 134, 236, 259, 341
Polignac, Princess Marie-Blanche de,
    255–6
Politzer, Georges, 115, 273, 274
Pollock, Jackson, 346
Popesco, Elvire, 45, 188, 207
Popular Front, 19–20, 23, 46, 124, 126, 132,
    148, 224, 230, 304
Portrait of Antonio de Covarrubias (El
    Greco), 169
Portugal, 72, 74, 77, 85, 86, 95, 119, 158
Pottier, Richard, 191
Poulenc, Francis, 6, 143, 146–50, 157, 330;
    ballet and, 149, 158–9; Milhaud's
    correspondence with, 153, 157, 161
Pourrat, Henri, 246
Prade, Georges, 183
préfets, 121, 130
Préjean, Albert, 191, 198, 332
Prélude à l'après-midi d'un faune
    (Debussy), 6
Premier rendez-vous, 198
Presle, Micheline, 58, 200
Prévert, Jacques, 183, 189–90, 194, 195, 203,
    204, 291, 332
Prévost, Jean, 246, 287
Printemps, Yvonne, 99*n*
prisoners of war, xii, 43–4, 47, 48, 71,
    96–100, 105, 241, 246, 249, 300;
    Brasillach as, 43–4, 70, 232; entertaining
    of, 96–9, 331; escape of, 43, 44, 97, 110;
    labor swap and, 138–9; love songs and,
    99–100; movies and, 196; musicians as,
    143, 147, 148, 150; Piaf's dedicating of
    song to, 97; poetry of, 279, 282; release
    of, 44, 55, 70, 98, 138–9, 145, 148, 156,
    175, 178, 212, 232, 299, 330; wives of,
    125, 316, 331

Prokofiev, Sergei, 6
"Promeneur dans Paris insurgé, Un" (A
    Walker in Insurgent Paris; Sartre),
    311–12
Propaganda Abteilung (Propaganda
    Department), 52, 53, 54, 69–70, 121; on
    Brasillach, 233; *Comoedia* and, 234
Propaganda Staffel, 52–5, 57, 91–2, 144,
    192, 200, 209, 236, 340; art and, 63,
    173, 174, 175, 177; banned books and,
    64, 239, 240; German music and,
    143; Referat Film of, 188, 191, 194;
    self-censorship and, 109*n*, 239; theater
    and, 208, 210, 214, 215, 217, 220, 221,
    223, 335; writers' trip to Germany and,
    247, 248
protests, 9, 13, 18–19, 147, 154
Proust, Marcel, 10–11, 261, 287–8
Prouvost, Jean, 292
publishing, 36, 64–70, 82, 136, 137, 231–44,
    270, 307–8; *épuration culturelle* and,
    326, 327, 328; music, 145; paper for, 66,
    242, 307; in unoccupied zone, 122, 136
Pucheu, Pierre, 294–5
Puget, Claude-André, 223

Quai des Brumes, Le, 35
Quand le temps travaillait pour nous
    (Mousset), 243
Quatre Millions, 94
Quatuor pour la fin du temps (Quartet for
    the End of Time; Messiaen), 150, 338
Queneau, Raymond, 185, 292
"Que reste-t-il de nos amours?" (What Is
    Left of Our Loves?), 100
Quintette du Hot Club de France, 101

Rabaud, Henri, 152
Rabinovitch, Gregor, 58, 189
Racine, Jean Baptiste, 9, 129, 207, 210, 212,
    217
Radicals, 14, 19, 307
radio, 38, 42, 47, 48, 58, 71, 92, 123, 232,
    238; Wodehouse's broadcasts on, 80
Radiodiffusion Nationale (Radio Vichy),
    53, 75, 119, 128, 152, 291, 303
Radio Jeunesse (Radio Youth), 128
Radio Liberté, 311
Radio-Londres, 52, 99, 304, 316, 331
Radio-Paris, 52–3, 98–101, 143–4, 150, 152,
    153*n*, 231, 234, 303, 322, 332, 333
Radio Stuttgart, 34, 52, 322
rafles (roundups), 104, 134–8, 161*n*, 201,
    289; *du Vél'd'Hiv',* 135, 159–60, 233,
    275*n*, 290
Raft of the Medusa, The (Géricault), 34
Rassemblement National Populaire, 119
Ravel, Maurice, 6, 147
Ravoux, Sophie, 259, 266
Raya, Nita, 97, 99
Rebatet, Lucien, 215, 233–4, 246, 259, 307,
    325, 344; anti-Semitism of, 15, 35, 76,
    119, 189, 233, 234, 322, 328; *épuration*

culturelle and, 322, 327; *Je suis partout* and, 70, 119, 189, 209, 217, 233; theater and, 209, 214, 217, 218; Vienna visited by, 145; in World War II, 35
Reboul, Marcel, 324
réfractaires, 300
Regler, Gustav, 31
Reichsbank, 267
Reichstein, Tadeus, 30
Reine Marie-Anne d'Autriche, La (Velázquez), 168–9
Reinhardt, Django, 8, 101–2, 197
Renaud, Madeleine, 213, 224, 333
Renaud et Armide (Cocteau), 218
Renoir, Jean, 8, 55, 58, 188, 189, 194
Renoir, Pierre, 189, 205, 222, 333
Renoir, Pierre Auguste, 5
"Republic of Silence, The" (Sartre), 336
Réseau de Résistance du Cinéma Français (French Cinema's Resistance Network), 203
Réseau du Musée de l'Homme (the Museum of Man network), xii, 109–16, 237, 269, 273, 282, 340
Résistance, 111–12, 113, 115, 116
resistance, French, xii, 29, 54*n*, 65, 80, 87, 126, 130, 233, 261, 266, 299*n*, 300–6, 308, 309, 313, 334–7; art and, 166, 167, 168, 172, 173–4, 341; Baker's work for, 95; Chevalier's problems with, 99, 331; collaboration avenged by, 315; Communists in, *see* Communist Party, French, in resistance; de Gaulle and, 47, 318–19; denunciation of members of, 196; deportation and, 114, 115, 181, 284–5, 288; as idea, 108–16; legacy of, 339–44; Malraux's views on, 112–13; Merry's aid to, 92; movie, 116, 200, 202–3, 205, 341; musicians and, 146–7, 148, 150, 152, 153, 157, 341; newspapers and, *see* newspapers, resistance and; Picasso and, 183–4, 186; poetry and, 278–85, 340, 342; rightists in, 122; rural, *see* maquis; students and, 70–1, 290; theater and, 219–22, 312, 335, 336, 341; writers', 114*n*, 115, 228, 229, 230, 234, 239, 243, 245, 246, 249, 269–96, 328, 340–1
restaurants, 51, 106–7, 155, 197, 246, 276, 308; Le Catalan, 106, 184; Maxim's, 107, 161, 193, 197, 333
Retouches à mon retour de l'U.R.S.S. (Afterthoughts, Back from the USSR; Gide), 25
Retour de l'U.R.S.S. (Back from the USSR; Gide), 24–5, 321
Révolution Nationale, 233, 323
Revue nègre, La, 7
Reynaud, Paul, 14, 40–1, 42, 46, 70, 132, 232
Ribbentrop, Joachim von, 61, 169
Ricci, Nina, 104, 347
"Riche, Paul," *see* Mamy, Jean

Richelieu, Cardinal, 242, 244
Rieussec, Jean, 157
Rieux, Jean, 91–2
Rigaux, Jean, 91
riots, 6, 217, 235
Rite of Spring (Stravinsky), 6
Rivet, Paul, 113
Robbe-Grillet, Alain, 268, 300, 349
Rochas, Marcel, 104
Rochefort, Charles de, 200
Rocher, René, 335
Rodellec du Porzic, Maurice de, 88
Rodin, François Auguste René, 5, 55, 63, 177, 216
Roland-Manuel, Alexis, 147, 152
Rol-Tanguy, Henri, 308, 313
Romain Gallery, 174
Romains, Jules, 74, 271, 329
Romance, Viviane, 9, 96, 198, 332
Rome, 151, 298
Ronis, Willy, 87
Roosevelt, Eleanor, 74
Roosevelt, Franklin D., 27, 123, 298
Rosenberg, Alexandre, 167, 169
Rosenberg, Alfred, 61, 169, 251*n*
Rosenberg, Léonce, 5, 62
Rosenberg, Paul, 5, 62, 167
Rosenthal, Manuel, 87, 145, 147, 153, 283
Rossi, Tino, 8, 43, 96, 199, 331
Rostand, Edmond, 55
Roth, Joseph, 7
Rothschild family, 62, 167, 169
Rouault, Georges, 6, 174, 178, 180, 224
Rouché, Jacques, 56–7, 145, 156–8, 330
Rouff, Maggy, 104
Roy, Claude, 66
Royal Air Force (RAF), 104*n*, 277, 282, 285, 288, 341
Rubinstein, Arthur, 169
Rubinstein, Helena, 176
Rubirosa, Porfirio, 197–9
Rudier, Eugène, 177–8
Rundstedt, Gerd von, 63

Sabartés, Jaime, 184
Sadoul, Georges, 202
Sagan, Françoise, 268, 349*n*
Saint-Benoît-sur-Loire, monastery in, 183
Saint-Exupéry, Antoine, 10, 44–5, 66, 243, 271, 296
Saint-Exupéry, Consuelo, 45, 84, 130
Saint-Martin-d'Ardèche, 28–9, 31–2
Salacrou, Armand, 222, 306
Salazar, Antonio, 119
Saliège, Jules-Gérard, 135
Salle Gaveau, 101, 143, 330
Salle Pleyel, 97, 101, 143
Salon d'Automne (1940), 63
Salon d'Automne (1944), 336
salons, 255–68, 273, 308, 327
Salou, Louis, 204
"Salut à Breker" (Cocteau), 177
Samuel-Rousseau, Marcel, 160

Sang d'un poète, Le (The Blood of a Poet), 13
Sarment, Jean, 226
Sarraut, Albert, 29
Sartre, Jean-Paul, 17, 25, 148*n*, 235, 270, 290–4, 308, 345, 349, 350; *épuration culturelle* and, 316, 328, 336; fiction of, 10, 27, 290; on occupation, 65; Picasso and, 183, 185; as POW, 43–4; resistance and, 275, 290–1, 292, 309, 311–12, 335, 336, 343; theater and, 207, 208, 219–22, 235, 243, 293, 306, 307, 335, 336, 340; on World War II, 39–40
Satie, Erik, 6, 12–13
Scène Française, 215, 275, 306
Schaeffer, Karl, 267
Schaeffer, Pierre, 128–9, 152
Schellenberg, Walther Friedrich, 104
Schiaparelli, Elsa, 103, 347
Schiffrin, Jacques, 24, 81–2
Schiffrin, Simon, 189
Schiller, Friedrich von, 211, 223, 248
Schiller Theater, 211
Schleier, Rudolf, 299
Schloss, Adolphe, 165, 166*n*
Schlumberger, Jean, 65, 245
Schmidtke, Heinz, 52
Schmitt, Florent, 145, 146
Scholz, Robert, 167
Schönberg, Arnold, 7, 142, 149, 152
Schulz-Koehn, Dietrich, 101
Schwarz, Solange, 158, 159, 161, 330
Schwarzkopf, Elisabeth, 154
sculpture, 161, 172, 175, 176–8, 185
Scum of the Earth (Koestler), 30–1
Second European Writers' Congress (1942), 249–50
Second International Writers' Congress for the Defense of Culture, 23
Secours National-Entr'aide d'Hiver, 106
Seghers, Anna, 84–5
Seghers, Pierre, 279, 281, 311, 328
Segonzac, André Dunoyer de, 175–6
Segonzac, Pierre Dunoyer de, 129–30
Semprun, Jorge, 70, 220
Senate, French, xiii, 46, 49
Senegal, 90, 110
Sept couleurs, Les (Brasillach), 232
Serge, Victor, 23, 77, 81*n*, 83, 84–5
Sert, José María, 224
Service du Travail Obligatoire (STO), 299, 300, 316*n*
Shakespeare, William, 9, 207, 212, 223
Shakespeare & Company, 7
Shaw, George Bernard, 207, 214, 223
Sheridan, Richard Brinsley, 207, 223
Sicily, 204, 298
Sieburg, Friedrich, 53
Siegfried (Giraudoux), 9
Sienkiewicz, Olesia, 39
Sigmaringen, 307, 319, 329, 333
Signal, 99, 103

Silence de la mer, Le (The Silence of the Sea; Bruller), 276–8, 340, 341
Simenon, Georges, 194, 203, 242, 326
Simon, Michel, 9, 191
Six, Les, 147–50
socialism, socialists, 16–19, 25, 87
Socialisme et Liberté (Socialism and Freedom), 290
Socialist Realism, 13, 22, 173
Société des Concerts du Conservatoire, 143, 147
Society of Authors, Composers and Editors of Music (SACEM), 145
Sodome et Gomorrhe (Giraudoux), 216–17
Soehring, Hans Jürgen, 199, 333
Sohlberg Circle, 20
Solidor, Suzy, 96, 99*n*
Sologne, Madeleine, 197
Solomon, Jacques, 115, 273, 274
Solstice de juin, Le (Montherlant), 66, 212, 243, 327, 335
Sorbonne, 17, 36, 71, 293
Sorel, Cécile, 333
Sorokine, Nathalie, 291
Sorrow and the Pity, The, xii
Soulier de satin, Le (Claudel), 148, 203, 210, 223–6, 307
Souplex, Raymond, 91–2
Sous la Botte (Under the Boot), 290
Soutine, Chaïm, 6, 87, 175
Soutzo, Hélène, 261
Souvenir et solitude (Zay), 230
Soviet Union, 13, 14, 19, 21–6, 32, 133, 345; anti-Fascist "national fronts" created by, 115; Céline's visit to, 21; French relations with, 40, 41; German invasion of, 114, 115, 130–1, 133, 136, 160, 269, 303; German relations with, 27, 30, 33, 40, 44, 90, 132; Gide's visit to, 24, 82, 321; territorial ambitions of, 40; Vichy regime and, 118; in World War II, 35, 238, 245, 248, 274, 298–9, 313
Spaak, Charles, 202–3
Spain, 25, 32, 37, 88, 110, 146, 158, 183, 272, 297, 319–20, 326, 346; art swaps and, 168–9; civil war in, 19, 23–4, 27, 29, 30, 40, 81, 151, 181, 182, 284; refugees' crossing of, 72, 74, 77, 78, 81, 85, 86, 178; refugees from, 27, 29
Special Operations Executive, British (SOE), 116, 301
Speer, Albert, 51, 56, 175–6
SS, 121, 133, 285, 286
Staatskapelle, 155
Staël, Nicolas de, 172
Stalag III-D, 97
Stalag VIII-A, 150
Stalag XI-A, Altengrabow, 98–9
Stalin, Joseph, 13, 14, 24, 39, 140, 345–6
State Department, U.S., 74, 87–8
Statute on Jews: first, 59–60, 68, 94, 120, 133, 164, 192, 287; second, 133

Stavisky, Serge Alexandre, 18
Stavisky affair, 18, 209
Stein, Gertrude, 7, 79–80, 244
Steinbeck, John, 278
Storm in June (Némirovsky), 137
Storm of Steel (Jünger), 229
Strasbourg, *ix*, 111, 248
Strauss, Bruno, 81
Strauss, Johann, 154
Strauss, Richard, 4, 6, 118, 145, 150, 153, 155
Stravinsky, Igor, 6
Strobel, Heinrich, 156
Stroheim, Erich von, 188–9
students, 42, 300; university, 17, 36, 70–1, 290
Studio d'Essai, 152
Stülpnagel, Otto von, 57, 61
Suarez, Georges, 70, 243, 284, 322
Sudetenland, 26, 34, 212
Suhard, Cardinal Emmanuel, 304, 314
Suite française (Némirovsky), 41–2, 137, 143, 277*n*, 340, 349*n*
Superior War Council, 132*n*
Supreme Court of Justice, 132
Surrealism, 6, 12–13, 22, 28–9, 89, 174, 279, 284, 346; Villa Air-Bel and, 83, 84–5, 285
Surrender on Demand (Fry), 73, 76
Syndicat des Éditeurs, 64, 239
Synge, John Millington, 207

Taeuber, Sophie, 84, 86
Tailleferre, Germaine, 147–8
Tanguy, Yves, 12, 37
Tardieu, André, 14
Taslitzky, Boris, 174
Tati, Jacques, 94, 203
Tavernier, René, 279, 293
Tchérina, Ludmilla, 158
Temps, 18, 122
Temps immobile, Le (C. Mauriac), 261
theater, 9–10, 50, 134, 148, 206–26, 304, 306; censorship and, 55, 56, 208, 210, 213, 215, 217, 221, 335, 340; comedies, 222–3; cultural legacy of occupation and, 338, 347; *épuration culturelle* and, 335–6; German, 211, 339; in movies, 204; movies compared with, 207–8, 209; in unoccupied zone, 86–7; in youth movements, 128, 129
theaters, 27, 33, 34, 41, 94, 206, 226, 300; *see also* movie houses
Théâtre Antoine, 9, 226
Théâtre de la Cité (formerly Théâtre Sarah Bernhardt), 208, 220, 221
Théâtre de la Mode, 347
Théâtre de l'Odéon, 206, 208, 335
Théâtre des Champs-Élysées, 6, 7, 143, 329–30
Théâtre du Châtelet, 6, 57, 143
Théâtre Libre, 9

théâtres de boulevard, 9, 55, 207, 208, 209, 337
Thèmes et variations (Matisse), 180
Thérive, André, 249
Third Republic, 3–4, 13, 18, 19, 20, 131, 319; demise of, 49, 65; settling scores from, 122
Thiriet, Maurice, 195
Thomas, Édith, 274–5, 276, 341
Thorez, Maurice, 18, 33
Tieschowitz, Baron Bernhard von, 169
Tillion, Germaine, 110, 115
"To Die for Danzig?" (Déat), 27
Toklas, Alice B., 7, 79–80, 244
Toulon, *ix*, 124, 140, 298
Toulouse, *ix*, 99, 110, 116, 151, 174, 236, 284; cultural life in, 128, 129; resistance in, 272, 282; Saliège's sermon in, 135
Tournemire, Guillaume de, 127
Tourneur, Maurice, 191, 201
Tourneur, Michel, 331–2
Touvier, Paul, 302
Trahison des clercs, La (The Betrayal of the Learned; Benda), 17
train No. 40,044, 167
Trauner, Alexandre, 194–5, 203
Trenet, Charles, 96, 100–1, 102, 215, 331, 342
33 sonnets composés au secret (33 Sonnets Composed in Solitary Confinement; Cassou), 282–4
trials: of Debureau, 203; *épuration culturelle* and, 320–36; of Musée de l'Homme prisoners, 114; of prewar French leaders, 131–2; of Vichy regime, 319–20
Tribus du cinéma et du théâtre, Les (Rebatet), 189
Triolet, Elsa, 44, 231, 243, 273, 278, 280*n*, 328
Tristan und Isolde (Wagner), 155–6
Trotsky, Leon, 25, 81*n*
Trujillo, Rafael Leónides, 197
Tual, Denise, 148
Tulle, hangings in, 305
Tunisia, 30, 79, 239, 272, 298
Turner, Harald, 55
Tzara, Tristan, 12, 87

Ubersfeld, Annie, 184, 207, 309
Ukraine, Ukrainians, 40, 160, 175, 298
Ulysses (Joyce), 7, 11
United Resistance Movements, 287, 294
United States, 16, 23, 27, 31*n*, 96; art sent to, 84, 170; asylum in, 36, 65, 66, 72–89, 134*n*, 142, 187, 188, 189, 243, 271, 331; immigration policies of, 89; internments in, 30; publishing in, 44, 242, 243; Vichy regime and, 75, 88, 118, 123–4, 139; World War II and, 35, 90, 108, 113, 124, 139, 197, 199, 240, 263, 297–8, 305, 308, 313

Université Libre, 115, 146, 173, 249, 269, 273
Universum Film AG (UFA), 8, 188, 190
unoccupied zone, 48, 55, 60, 66–70, 76, 77, 118, 263, 290; Aryanization of Jewish-owned business in, 133; autonomy in, 122; German takeover of, 75, 87, 99, 121, 139, 140, 143, 180, 232–3, 246*n*, 287, 293*n*, 299, 325; Jewish performers in, 86, 87, 94; map of, *ix;* movie industry in, 189, 190, 194–5; publishing in, 243, 278, 325; resistance and, 113, 116, 274, 300; writers in, 66–9, 237*n,* 288*n*

Valentin, Albert, 188
Valéry, Paul, 10, 68, 114, 148*n,* 150, 269; Académie Française and, 245, 246; *épuration culturelle* and, 324, 325, 328; *NRF* and, 237, 238–9, 270
Valland, Rose, 165–7
Vallat, Xavier, 19, 133, 134
van Dongen, Kees, 5, 175–6, 186, 334
Van Eyck, Hubert, 168
Van Eyck, Jan, 168
Van Gogh, Vincent, 5
Varna, Henri, 98
Varo, Remedios, 84, 86
Vaudoyer, Jean-Louis, 210–13, 217–18, 223, 224, 226
Vaurabourg, Andrée, 150
"Veilleur du Pont-au-Change, Le" (The Watchman of the Pont-au-Change; Desnos), 284
Velázquez, Diego, 168
Ventura, Ray, 8, 26, 102
Vercel, Roger, 10, 11
Vercors, 276; *see* Bruller, Jean
Vercors maquis, 203, 276*n,* 287, 301
Verdi, Giuseppe, 155
Vermorel, Claude, 214
Vernes, Arthur, 262
Versailles, 121, 154
Versailles, Treaty of (1919), 15, 26, 123, 168
Viard, René, 243
Vichy, *ix,* 48–9, 161, 306; history of, 117–18; U.S. embassy in, 88, 110*n,* 118, 135
Vichy fait la guerre (Vichy Wages War), 110
Vichy France (Paxton), xii
Vichy regime, xi, 55, 66, 76, 117–40, 219, 224, 228, 302–7; anti-Semitism and, *see* anti-Semitism, Vichy regime and; Catholicism and, 49, 120, 124–7, 131, 192, 230; Céline's views on, 252; censorship and, 56, 75, 189, 243, 279, 281; collaboration and, 14, 54, 70, 71–2, 117, 121–4, 126, 316, 335; cultural institutions and, 50, 121, 143–4, 148, 149, 150, 152, 157, 164–5, 173, 175, 176–7, 189, 192, 197, 206, 208, 210, 217, 223; establishment of, 48–9; Freemasonry banned by, 63; French

economy and, 121, 241; French nationality and, 61*n;* Fry and, 75, 83, 86; General Commission for Jewish Questions of, 19, 133, 134, 165, 264, 320; Great Britain and, 90, 110, 130; haute couture and, 104; implosion of, 306–7; Joan of Arc and, 213, 214; *milice* of, 200, 205, 217, 302; moral values of, 49, 121, 124, 192; movies and, 189, 192, 197, 261, 348; in North Africa, 95, 123, 139, 140, 272, 281, 298; occupied-zone responsibilities of, 121, 299; POWs and, 98, 122, 138–9; sports and, 124, 126; theater and, 56, 206, 208, 210, 215, 217, 219, 223, 224; trial of, 319–20; trial of prewar French leaders and, 131–2; U.S. relations with, 75, 88, 118, 123–4, 139; youth movements in, 126–30
Victorine Studios, 189, 204
Vie à belles dents, La (Carné), 195
Vienna, 103, 141*n,* 142, 145, 148
Vierny, Dina, 77, 89, 178, 179, 180
Vilar, Jean, 129, 347
Vildé, Boris, 109–16
Villa Air-Bel, 83, 84–5, 285
Village en ruines prés du Ham, Un (Bonnard), 5
Vilmorin, Louise de, 149
Vingt Jeunes Peintres de Tradition Française (Twenty Young Painters of the French Tradition), 128, 173
Visions de l'Amen (Messiaen), 150
Visiteurs du soir, Les (The Devil's Envoys), 194–5, 334, 340
Vlaminck, Maurice de, 5, 175–6, 186, 325, 334
Vollard, Ambroise, 5
Vom Kaiserhof zur Reichskanzlei (From the Kaiserhof to the Chancellery; Goebbels), 242
Voyage au bout de la nuit (Journey to the End of the Night; Céline), 11, 21, 251, 252, 253
Voyage secret, Le (Jouhandeau), 248
Vuillermoz, Jean, 146

Waffen-SS units, 133, 299, 302
Wagner, Richard, 6, 141, 142, 154, 155–6, 218
Wagner, Winifred, 156
Wahl, Jean, 134
Wakhévitch, Georges, 195
Wall, Jean, 86
Walter, Marie-Thérèse, 36, 181–2, 184
Walter, Pierre, 113, 114
Wars I Have Seen (Stein), 80
Watteau, Jean Antoine, 169
Webern, Anton, 149
Wehrmacht, 136, 193, 237, 266, 286, 298, 311, 312–13, 315, 327; *Feldgendarmerie* of, 228; in French advance, 31, 43, 43–4, 109, 150, 159; French mistresses of, 156, 199, 333; music and, 142, 144, 154, 155;

in occupied Paris, xii, 51, 63, 93, 94,
104, 133, 154, 155, 156, 161, 182, 199,
206, 210, 229, 257, 261, 307, 314;
resistance and, 116; in unoccupied
zone, 139
Weil, Simone, 80–1
Weil-Curiel, André, 110
Weimar, writers' congresses in, 247–51,
326
Werfel, Alma Mahler-, 77
Werfel, Franz, 77
Werner, Fritz, 52
Wertheimer, Germaine, 104, 171
Wertheimer, Pierre, 104, 171
Wiener, Jean, 57, 153
Wildenstein, Georges, 62, 63, 170
Wildenstein gallery, 63, 171
Winged Victory of Samothrace, The, 34
Wodehouse, Ethel, 80
Wodehouse, P. G., 80
Wols, 30, 87, 175
women: collaboration avenged against,
315–16, 333; as forced labor, 139;
German, 103; Vichy's views on, 125
women's magazines, 102, 105, 106
World War I, 5, 33, 38, 70, 98, 253, 325;
armistice in (Nov. 11, 1918), 47, 139;
Céline and, 11, 21; deaths in, 3, 16, 17;
German reparations in, 72; literature
and, 10, 11, 229; pacifism and, 4, 11–12;
Pétain in, 46, 131; Versailles Treaty and,
15, 26, 123; veterans of, 16, 59, 130

World War II, 17, 27–49, 297–314; Battle of
France in, 44–5, 146; Battle of Stalingrad
in, 140, 298; bombing in, 43, 168,
170, 181, 253–4, 260, 304; Brasillach
in, 35, 232; D-Day landings in, 199,
292; Eastern Front in, 133, 136,
137, 138, 140, 233n, 245, 264, 298;
Franco-German armistice in (1940),
46–8, 68, 72, 119, 121, 126, 151, 233;
French declaration of war in, 27, 28,
29, 33, 36, 89, 101, 132, 156, 158, 232;
French defeat in, 48, 70, 131, 132, 216,
230, 242; Italian-Allied armistice in
(1943), 298; phony war in, 34, 37, 78,
86, 97, 102, 143, 151, 179, 216; Picasso's
work and, 185; writers' views on, 38, 39,
45, 66
writers, 18, 22, 54, 64–70, 227–54, 308, 338;
anti-Semitism and, 227–34; attracted to
Paris, 4, 7, 346; *épuration culturelle* and,
320–9; politics and, 10–12, 227; prestige
of, 4–5; resistance and, *see* resistance,
French, writers'; Surrealism and, 12; in
trips to Germany, 247–50

Yonnel, Jean, 210, 211, 213, 224

Zay, Jean, 19, 30, 231
Zehrfuss, Bernard, 130
Zimmer, Bernard, 202
Zola, Émile, 15
Zucca, André, 106

Printed in the United States
by Baker & Taylor Publisher Services